Princely Splendor

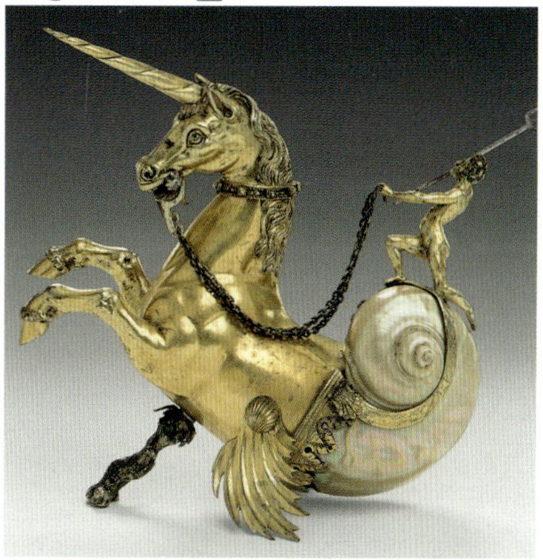

The Dresden Court 1580-1620

Princely Splendor

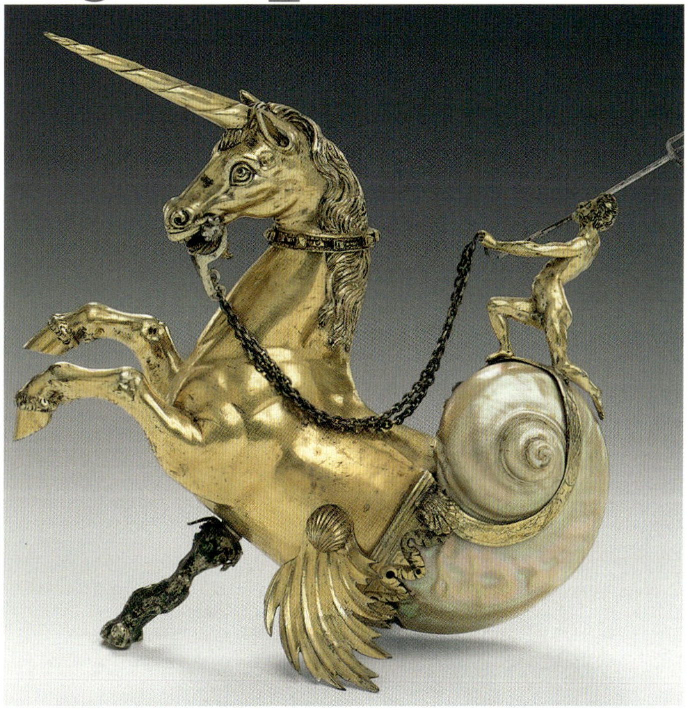

The Dresden Court 1580-1620

Edited by
Dirk Syndram and Antje Scherner

Electa

The Metropolitan Museum of Art

Staatliche Kunstsammlungen Dresden

This publication is issued in conjunction with the exhibition "Princely Splendor: The Dresden Court, 1580–1620," held at the Museum für Kunst und Gewerbe Hamburg ("Pracht und Macht: Der Dresdner Hof um 1600") from June 10 to September 26, 2004; at The Metropolitan Museum of Art, New York, from October 26, 2004, to January 30, 2005; and at the Fondazione Memmo, Palazzo Ruspoli, Rome ("Fasto Principesco: La Corte di Dresda, 1580–1620"), from March 1 to April 29, 2005.

The exhibition is made possible by Marie-Josée and Henry Kravis and the Anna-Maria and Stephen Kellen Foundation.

Additional support has been provided by ZEIT-Stiftung Ebelin und Gerd Bucerius, Hamburg, Germany, and the Laurence Levine Charitable Fund.

The exhibition was organized by the Staatliche Kunstsammlungen Dresden in collaboration with The Metropolitan Museum of Art, New York.

An indemnity has been granted by the Federal Council on the Arts and the Humanities.

Published by the Staatliche Kunstsammlungen Dresden and Mondadori Electa S.p.A., Milan

A German edition, *In fürstlichem Glanz: Der Dresdner Hof um 1600* (ISBN 88-370-2722-2) was published by the Staatliche Kunstsammlungen Dresden, 2004.

Antje Scherner and Dirk Syndram, Grünes Gewölbe, Staatliche Kunstsammlungen, Dresden, Project Directors

Antje Scherner, Scholarly Editor, with the assistance of Eva Graßhoff, Christine Nagel, and Maria Reichelt

Dario Tagliabue, Art Director

Jazz Graphic Studio, Milan, Design

Cristina Garbagna, Managing Editor

Gail Swerling, Editor with Paola Noé

Andrea Panozzo and Giancarlo Berti, Production

Daniel Kletke, Translator

The German editors thank Albero Bubach, Karin Ihlefeld, and Anne Veltrup. The English translation was reviewed at The Metropolitan Museum of Art by Wolfram Koeppe, Stuart W. Pyhrr, and Clare Vincent and John H. Leopold.

Printed by Mondadori Electa S.p.A., Martellago (Veneto)

Jacket/cover illustration (front): Detail of a Cup in the Form of a Sea Unicorn (cat. no. 109)

Jacket/cover illustration (back): Detail of an Auger for Making Bungholes (cat. no. 71)

Contents

Message of Greeting from the President of the Federal Republic of Germany Horst Köhler

When an exhibition is entitled "Princely Splendor," it immediately raises high expectations—expectations that this collection more than fulfills. Precious works of artistic mastery from the treasure chamber of the Electors of Saxony, amassed at the turn of the seventeenth century, are waiting to astound you. Above and beyond that, the exhibition introduces the Electors themselves and the Saxon Court and explains their importance at that time.

The artistic treasures on display are a testament to the Electors' passion for collecting, their taste and their knowledge of art, as well as their steady acquisition of contemporary works— something of which many museum directors today can only dream. These art collections are however also an expression of political power and proclaim the significance of the Saxon Electors' Court as one of the European cultural centers of its time.

Four hundred years on, German heads of state no longer collect works of art to underline their status. Nor has collecting remained the sole prerogative of men in power. But one truism remains valid—the importance a nation attaches to art is a reflection of how cultured it considers itself to be.

I am delighted that "Princely Splendor: The Dresden Court, 1580–1620" is now on display beyond Germany's borders.

I hope that the exhibition is a great success. I also hope that some of the people who see it are inspired to find out more about the Staatliche Kunstsammlungen Dresden and to come to our country. The Electors' collections are but one of many treasures that make Germany worth a visit.

Director's Foreword

For centuries, art pilgrims have flocked to Dresden to see Raphael's *Sistine Madonna* and the incomparable treasures of the Grünes Gewölbe (Green Vault). The wealth and scope of the rarities amassed by the former royal house of Saxony prompted the Metropolitan Museum and Washington's National Gallery to organize with the Staatliche Kunstsammlungen Dresden an exhibition, "The Splendor of Dresden: Five Centuries of Art Collecting," in 1978. Without the Raphael, but with generous selections from the Green Vault and other Dresden museums, that show offered an overview from the Middle Ages to the twentieth century. Nearly destroyed during World War II, the Residenzschloss of Dresden, which originally housed the Green Vault, is being reconstructed. This project is near completion and will once again allow a coherent view of the entire extraordinary ensemble. During the interim, most of the works of art will not be easily accessible. And once reinstalled, it is hardly likely that this vast and diverse assemblage will be available for further travel.

We did not want to miss this opportunity to single out a specific aspect of the Staatliche Kunstsammlungen, the sublime works that formed the Dresden Kunstkammer from the outset and that made it one of the major princely European collections about 1600. Mystery and symbolism surround many of the objects, from those of gold and silver incorporating exotic materials to elaborately embellished arms and armors to impeccably turned ivories with their ravishing details.

We are deeply grateful to those who made the exhibition possible, beginning with the officials who allowed the precious objects to travel, notably Dirk Syndram, Director of the Grünes Gewölbe. He mapped out this ambitious project with Wolfram Koeppe, Associate Curator in the Metropolitan's Department of European Sculpture and Decorative Arts, in collaboration with Ian Wardropper, Iris and B. Gerald Cantor Curator in Charge of that department. Dr. Syndram, Dr. Koeppe, and the Dresden curators and trusted experts in their given fields have written the remarkable catalogue. I extend hearty thanks to all staff members in Dresden, Hamburg, and Rome, as well as those in New York, who have contributed to the exhibition's éclat, its revelations of scholarly investigations, and its powerful appeal to the senses.

The Metropolitan Museum is extremely grateful to Marie-Josée and Henry Kravis and the Anna-Maria and Stephen Kellen Foundation for their generous support of the exhibition. In addition, the Metropolitan wishes to express its sincere thanks to ZEIT-Stiftung Ebelin und Gerd Bucerius, Hamburg, Germany, and the Laurence Levine Charitable Fund, which provided support for this project. Finally, the Museum is indebted to the Federal Council on the Arts and the Humanities for its kind assistance toward the realization of this exhibition.

Philippe de Montebello
Director of The Metropolitan Museum of Art

Directors' Foreword

The Staatliche Kunstsammlungen Dresden is the artistic and cultural treasury of Saxony. From the middle of the sixteenth to the twentieth century, the collection and preservation of art were among the privileges of the sovereigns. Now, in the early twenty-first century, the reopening of the Grünes Gewölbe (Green Vault) at its original location is a meaningful milestone in the almost three-hundred-year history of this Dresden museum. The losses of World War II in the Old City of Dresden are being overcome step by step. With the reconstruction of the Frauenkirche and the Residenzschloss (Residential Palace), symbols of Saxon identity are being recreated. Since January 2004 the collection of the Green Vault treasures has undergone radical changes that present a double challenge: the museum heritage left by Augustus the Strong is returning to the Residentzschloss in two phases. In September 2004 the new Green Vault on the second floor opened as a treasury displaying works from the Late Renaissance to the Late Baroque eras. In fall 2006 a Late Baroque Gesamtkunstwerk will return to the ground floor of the Residenzschloss's west wing with the inauguration of the historic Green Vault. In the interim more than two thirds of the almost four thousand objects of the Green Vault will not be on public view. This hiatus is the reason and the point of departure for this exhibition that focuses on the epoch in which the Saxon collections achieved European rank. The goal is the revelation of artistic developments during the years from 1580 to 1620. It was the time when—thanks to their Treasury, their Kunstkammer, and their impressive Rüstkammer (Armory)—the electors began to compete in this realm with Emperor Rudolf II and other European princes. The treasures preserved in the Green Vault and the Armory illuminate the princely splendor of the Saxon court as it began to evolve in the decades preceding the Thirty Years War.

In addition to the collecting and preserving of art, contemporary museums count among their many responsibilities scholarship and education. This show addresses these two tasks in a special way, combining the latest art-historical scholarship with the selection of significant and meaningful works. In presenting these objects, the structure of the Dresden collections—containing electoral treasures kept together for centuries—unfolds in all its glorious strength. Their scope enables us to paint a complete picture of an entire era from the holdings of the Staatliche Kunstsammlungen Dresden without requesting loans from other institutions. To this end the scholars of the Green Vault and the Armory have cooperated very closely. The latter preserves not only parade arms owned by many generations of rulers but also paintings, textiles, and objects from the Kunstkammer. The picture of this historic period is further enhanced by works from the Skulpturensammlung (Sculpture Collection) and the Kunstgewerbemuseum (Museum of Decorative Arts). Although the exhibition concentrates on an epoch that shaped Saxon and European history, it also offers insights into how the Dresden Residenzschloss might be used for future museum purposes and for scholarship.

It is a great pleasure and a welcome challenge for us to present these art treasures for display in Hamburg, New York, and Rome, three important venues. We are happy that the objects, as our cultural ambassadors, will be traveling advocates for the Dresdner Residenzschloss (Dresden Residential Palace Museum), which is under construction.

Our thanks go to all those in New York and Dresden who helped make this exhibition possible, notably, in The Metropolitan Museum of Art, to Ian Wardropper, Iris and B. Gerald Cantor Curator in Charge, Department of European Sculpture and Decorative Arts, to Stuart W. Pyhrr, Arthur Ochs Sulzberger Curator in Charge, Department of Arms and Armor, and to Wolfram Koeppe, Associate Curator, Department of European Sculpture and Decorative Arts, and curator of the exhibition.

We are deeply grateful to the directors of the participating museums of the Staatliche Kunstsammlungen Dresden: Heinz-Werner Lewerken (Rüstkammer), Moritz Woelk (Skulpturensammlung), André van der Goes (Kunstgewerbemuseum), as well as Tilman von Stockhausen (Head of the Communications Department) and Dirk Burghardt (Administrative Director).

We extend our sincere thanks to the conservators who prepared numerous works for this presentation. We are grateful to the authors of the essays for their scholarly contributions.

Wolfram Koeppe and Stuart W. Pyhrr generously agreed to review the English version of the catalogue, which was translated from German by Daniel Kletke.

The catalogue was expertly designed by Silvia Jazzarelli in Milan, and we trust that the book will attract a wide range of readers. The foundations for the new insights presented here were established by Jochen Vötsch in many years of diligent archival research. We are very grateful to him. Thanks go as well to Albero Bubach, who supervised the complex photographic campaign, and the photographer Jürgen Karpinski from Dresden. We gratefully acknowledge the valuable contribution of Antje Scherner, who coordinated the project's scholarly aspects and who edited the extensive catalogue with care, efficiency, and commitment.

Martin Roth
General Director of the Staatliche Kunstsammlungen Dresden

Dirk Syndram
Director of the Grünes Gewölbe

Participants in the Exhibition and the Catalogue

The Exhibition

STAATLICHE KUNSTSAMMLUNGEN DRESDEN
Dirk Syndram, Project Director
André van der Goes, Heinz-Werner Lewerken, and Moritz Woelk, Consulting Scholars

Conservation

GRÜNES GEWÖLBE
Christine Engemann-Wendt, with Eve Begov, Annika Dix, Rainer Richter, Sabine Schwab, Michael Wagner, and Katja Wolter

KUNSTGEWERBEMUSEUM
Gottfried Wachs, with Bernhard Finkbein and Frohmut Zscheckel

RÜSTKAMMER
Winfried Beckert, with Andreas Frauendorf, Uwe Böckelmann, Ramona Münzer-Scadock, Heide Hilper, and Birgit Tradler

SKULPTURENSAMMLUNG
Ursula Kral and Rainer Thiel

Exhibition in New York

THE METROPOLITAN MUSEUM OF ART

Organized by Wolfram Koeppe, Associate Curator, Department of European Sculpture and Decorative Arts, and Ian Wardropper, Iris and B. Gerald Cantor Curator in Charge, Department of European Sculpture and Decorative Arts

Michael Langley, Exhibition Designer
Sue Koch, Senior Graphic Designer
Clint Ross Coller and Rich Lichte, Lighting Designers
Nina S. Maruca, Senior Associate Registrar

Coordinated by Linda M. Sylling, Manager for Special Exhibitions, and Wolfram Koeppe

Authors of the Catalogue

Jutta Bäumel (J.B.)
Igor A. Jenzen (I.A.J.)
Jutta Kappel (J.K.)
Heinz-Werner Lewerken (H-W.L.)
Antje Scherner (A.S.)
Holger Schuckelt (H.S.)
Dirk Syndram (D.S.)
André van der Goes (A.v.d.G.)
Anne Veltrup (A.V.)
Ulrike Weinhold (U.W.)

Princely Splendor

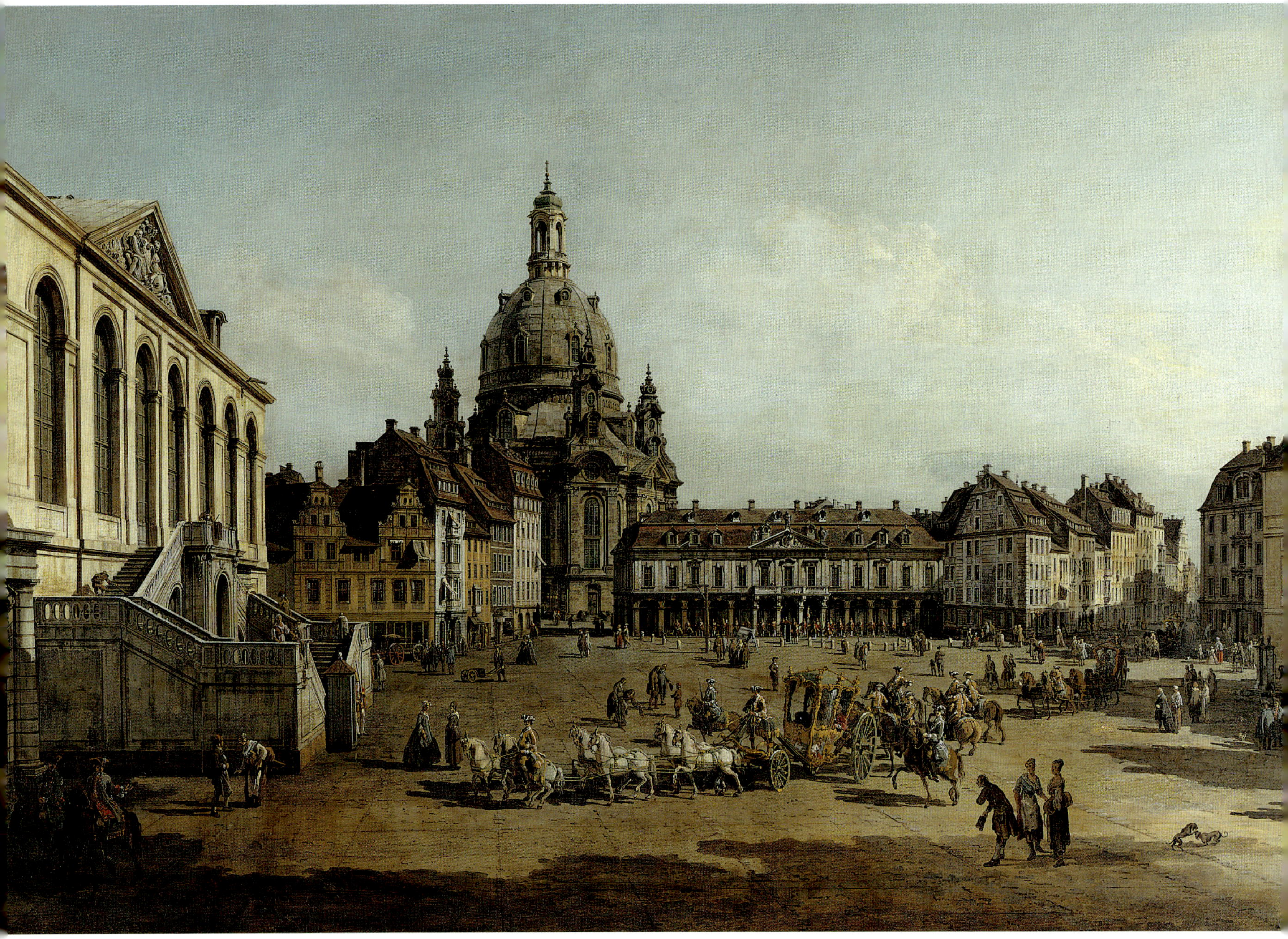

Princely Splendor: An Introduction

Dirk Syndram

Dresden's character was profoundly shaped by its history. The festive Baroque splendor under Augustus the Strong was followed in the Rococo era by the collecting passion of his son, Friedrich August II (August III of Poland). In this context, the jewels of the Green Vault (Grünes Gewölbe) come to mind as do the art treasures of the Old Masters Picture Gallery, the opulent and fantastic Zwinger, and the amalgamation of French and Italian architecture in the former Court Church (Hofkirche), today the cathedral.

In the terrible aftermath of World War II Erich Kästner wrote of his childhood memories of Dresden: "If I know not only what is terrible and ugly but also what is beautiful, this ability is due to the lucky circumstance that I grew up in Dresden. [...] I had the privilege to inhale beauty in the same way forester's children inhale the woods' clean air: the Catholic Court Church, Georg Bähr's Frauenkirche, the Zwinger, Pillnitz Castle, the Japanese Palace, the Jüdenhof and the Dinglingerhaus, the Rampische Straße with its Baroque facades, the Renaissance bay window on Schlossstraße, the Coselpalais, the Palace in the Large Garden with its little cavalier houses and, to top all of this, to take in the vista of the city silhouette with its noble, venerable towers from the Loschwitzhöhe."[1] In concluding this hymn to his native town's beauty, he states: "Dresden was a gorgeous urban area. You can believe me, and you must believe me! [...] Because the town of Dresden no longer exists. Except for a few remains, it was swept off the surface of the earth. World War II eradicated it, in a single night and with just one gesture. Centuries had created its incomparable charm. A few hours of witchcraft sufficed to exorcise it from the ground."[2]

Undiminished pain over their loss dominated the residents' collective memory for well over two generations. Since German reunification in 1990, the cityscape's groundplan—which vanished during the bombardments of February 13 and 14, 1945—is slowly beginning to reemerge. But what slowly evolved during the course of history cannot be replaced. Dresden's lost image is not that of February 12, 1945—that is, just before its destruction—but the image created by the Saxon court painter Bernardo Bellotto. Between 1747 and 1753 he created seventeen ideal city views that form our conception of Baroque Dresden. A veduta of 1749, *Dresden's Neumarkt Seen from the Jüdenhof* (ill. opposite), is a detailed depiction of the city. The mighty Royal Picture Gallery with its high windows dominates the painting at the left. King August III arrives in his carriage drawn by six horses to visit the museum, which was completed in 1747. Over the vast square rises the colossal dome of the Frauenkirche, erected between 1726 and 1743. In front of it is a group of guards who marched to the Altstädter Wache of 1715. The painterly view of town not only hon-

Dresden's Neumarkt seen from the Jüdenhof
Bernardo Bellotto, called Canaletto, 1749
Oil on canvas
53½ × 93¼ in. (136 × 237 cm)
Old Masters Picture Gallery, Staatliche Kunstsammlung Dresden, Gemäldegalerie Alter Meister, Gal. no. 610

ors the art-minded elector-king but also demonstrates the foundations from which the Baroque metropolis evolved.

In an expansion under Elector Moritz in 1548, the Neumarkt and Jüdenhof were incorporated into the city. Under Elector Christian I (ruled 1586–91) a number of stately buildings had been constructed in these areas. The Picture Gallery of August III (1696–1763) was but the remodeled New Stables, built in 1586–90 by Paul Buchner as a palatial, stately structure accommodating stables and collections. The Altes Gewandhaus, also built by Buchner in 1591–92 on Christian I's order, is opposite the Picture Gallery. This long structure with three gables, the center of civic trade, was also used as a site for festivities and gatherings. Among the multistory buildings on the east side of the square—where the Frauenkirche can be seen—are a number of gabled houses dating to the years around 1600. There are also contemporaneous bays that were later integrated into the altered structures.

Bellotto's veduta is more than just the depiction of an important Baroque city square: it also documents the careful urban planning carried out in Dresden during the last two decades of the sixteenth century. However, in the same way that the late Renaissance buildings take second place to the magnificence of the eighteenth-century architecture, the cultural achievements of the electors during the early 1600s also faded in the collective memory. It must be remembered, however, that Augustus the Strong (1670–1733) and his son, August III, were part of a tradition, begun in the mid-sixteenth century by the electoral brothers Moritz (1521–1553) and August (1526–1583). These earlier electors initiated the cultural development that propelled Saxony onto the larger European stage.

Under Moritz, the first Saxon elector of the house of Wettin's Albertine line, Saxony rose to prominence as a leading German state in terms of politics, economics, urban development, and culture. Moritz began the construction of Dresden's fortifications, taking Italian and Netherlandish defense systems as his models; as a result, the Wettins' seat was preserved from destruction and occupation, even during the Thirty Years War. Dresden had been an agrarian middle-class town (Ackerbügerstadt) before its elevation to electoral residence, but it subsequently developed into a densely populated city noted for its commerce and craft activities.

During his thirty-three-year reign, Moritz's brother August gave Dresden a new face by constructing impressive princely buildings. After the Dresden Residential Palace—begun under Moritz in 1549 as the first German Renaissance structure with four wings—was completed in 1556, he proceeded to build the Arsenal (Zeughaus, today the Albertinum) between 1559 and 1563. Its unusually large, four-wing layout with interior courtyard, intended to store war machines, was subsequently hailed by its contemporaries as a "miracle." In 1565–67, the Chancellery Building (Kanzleihaus) was erected beside the Residential Palace. Here, the elector brought Saxony's different administrative agencies together. Following a desire for order that looked forward to absolutism, he concentrated those offices in the residential city. The Chancellery Building was the electorate's oldest administrative structure and one of the first of its kind in Germany.[3] Contemporaneous with this and the Arsenal, the Kunstkammer, located in the Residential Palace, was also begun. All these structures shared efficient use as a common goal. Diverse as these three endeavors are, they were all driven by Elector August's rational spirit and his desire to reign efficiently. Within a European context, it is fair to label all three projects as innovative.

Between 1580 and 1620, the period covered by this exhibition, Dresden became a European city. This change had less to do with the physical scope of the Saxon capital and the number of its inhabitants (little more than 10,000 in 1580 and 17,000 around 1620)[4] than with the ambitions of the Wettins. Their attempts to demonstrate their rank and power and their fondness for princely display and omnipotence were grandly ambitious. The Dresden

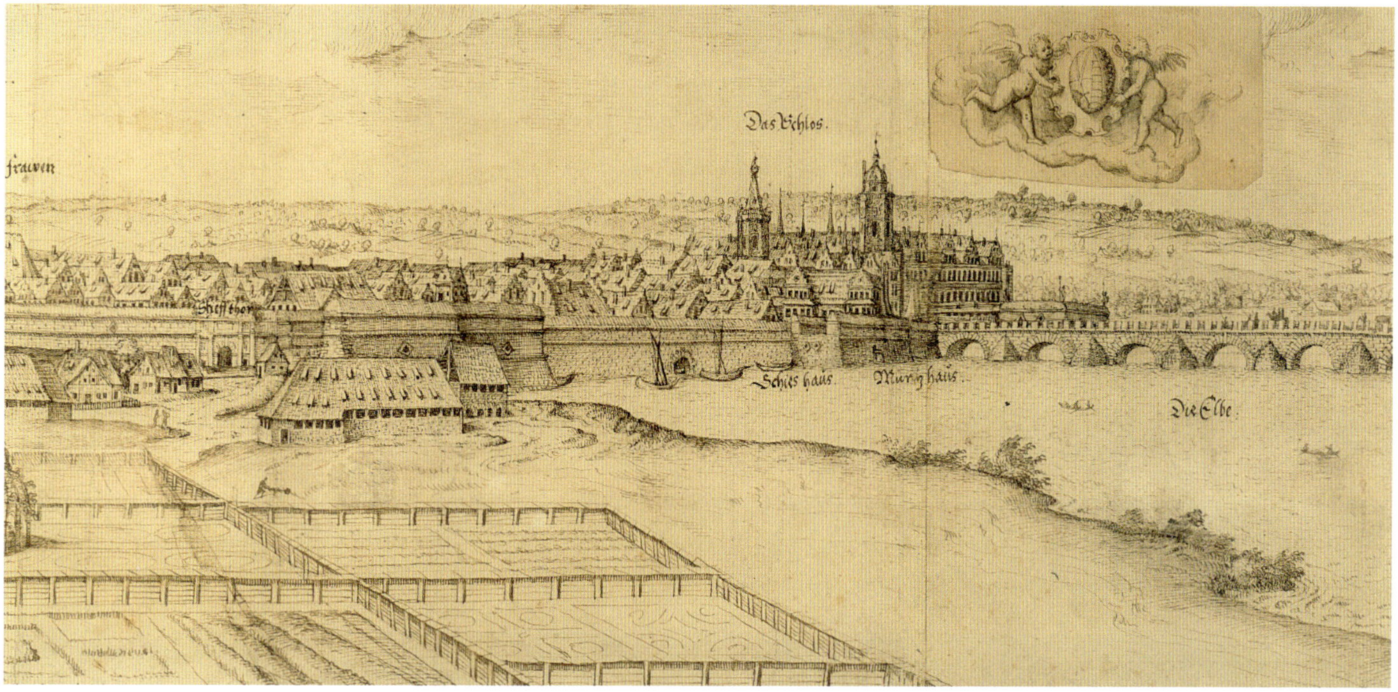

Dresden Seen from the East
Gabriel de Thola
circa 1570
Pen, sepia
9 × 75⅝ in. (23 × 192 cm)
Städtische Galerie Dresden,
Kunstsammlung,
inv. no. 1977/K201

court was a successful competitor with other electoral seats in the Holy Roman Empire of the German Nation, such as Kassel, Wolfenbüttel, Heidelberg, Berlin, Munich, Vienna, and Prague, to name only a few of the most important secular electorates. The Wettins were determined to excel in such diverse fields as architecture, collecting, and musical culture. Starting in the mid-sixteenth century Dresden and the Munich court were leaders in the German musical world. In Dresden Moritz established the Choir Command, one of whose musicians was the trombonist Antonio Scandello, a noted Italian composer of madrigals. From 1568 to his death in 1580, he was court conductor in Dresden, and under his direction Hofkapelle became renowned. Under the otherwise frugal Elector August, this orchestra consisted of forty-five well-paid members.[5] The lively musical culture was supported by ensuing electors, with the result that Heinrich Schütz, "father of German music," was called to Dresden as court music master in 1617. He stayed for almost six decades, working as conductor (Kapellmeister) and composer.[6]

The princely grandeur and the richness of Dresden's collections had their roots in Saxony's economy. At the end of the twelfth century, silver ore was discovered in the Saxon Erzgebirge mountain range. As a consequence, Saxony had become, by the Late Middle Ages, one of the wealthiest territories within the empire. In the new centuries other useful and precious ores and stones were found, among them copper, tin, iron, lead, serpentine, marble, and alabaster. Mining and metal smelting naturally stimulated the study of science and technology. Heavy industry and manufacturing enterprises were founded early on, while specialization in individual crafts became a Saxon tradition. New mining procedures, introduced in the sixteenth century, resulted in exponential rises in silver production. Within the Freiberg district alone, the sovereign's profits multiplied fivefold between 1524 and 1550, reaching their height in 1572 with the remarkable sum of 33,650 silver marks. To this day, numerous Saxon towns show this past affluence in their churches, town halls, and bourgeois houses. Another important source of revenue for the electors and the cities came from the monasteries and their estates, dissolved during the Reformation. While the towns thrived, the electors commissioned mostly four-winged palace constructions, situated in strategically and economically viable locations. Three structures were created in quick succession under August: Augustusburg near Schellenberg (1568–73), Annaburg near Torgau (1571–73), and Lichtenburg (1573–81).

All of this was based on Saxony, as the "cradle of the Reformation," becoming the center of German Protestantism. In 1547, as a result of the Schmalkalden War, Moritz obtained the electoral office (Kurwürde), and Wittenberg became part of Albertine Saxony. The Dresden-based Albertine line of Wettin rulers, from the reign of Elector August to the conversion to Catholicism of Augustus the Strong in 1697, remained strong in their role as defender of Lutheran doctrine. This shaped not only their self-image but also their political and cultural activities. As a consequence, Elector August was instrumental in negotiating the 1555 Peace of Augsburg, ending the combative phase of the Reformation within the empire.

The main focus of the exhibition are the forty years from 1580 until 1620, a "time between wars" (*Zwischenkriegszeit*). At the beginning of this phase lies the publication of the *Book of Concord* in Dresden in 1580, issued by the Saxon elector to commemorate the fiftieth anniversary of the Augsburg Confession of Faith. Claiming universal validity, this publication was the central religious writing of the German Lutheran Church. This publication was signed by the electors of Brandenburg and the Palatinate, as well as twenty additional imperial princes, more than two dozen imperial counts and barons, thirty-five imperial cities, and thousands of clergymen. This creed united two-thirds of the German Protestants, but it further separated them from the Calvinists, who were growing in strength. Although a new conflict was inevitable, the Lutheran Reformation had achieved its goal.

The year 1620, on the other hand, marks the beginning of the bloody phase of the Thirty Years War with the victory of the imperial troops over the revolutionary Bohemian estates in the Battle of White Mountain, near Prague. What began, in 1618, as a seemingly limited conflict known as the Defenestration of Prague (Prager Fenstersturz), soon spread throughout Europe and culminated in a religiously motivated war with disastrous results for the entire empire. This war about German liberty ("*teutsche Libertät*") began in Prague, chosen as royal Bohemian residence in 1583 by Emperor Rudolf II, thus becoming the center of the empire. It abruptly ended a sublime flourishing of European culture that had endured for almost forty years. Whereas Prague was ruled by a single emperor until the year 1612, the electors in Dresden changed in quick succession. In 1586 August was followed by his son Christian I; in 1591 the Ernestine Duke Friedrich Wilhelm I of Saxony-Weimar-Altenburg served as administrator for the minor Christian II until he reached his majority in 1601; Christian II was succeeded in 1611 by Johann Georg I, his younger brother. All four electors had their individual tastes, their special likes and dislikes, but there were also constants in their princely collecting that this exhibition will help make clear.

Most of the works in this exhibition come from two museums within Dresden's State Art Collections: the Green Vault (Grünes Gewölbe) and the Armory (Rüstkammer); they are generously supplemented by extraordinary pieces from the Museum of Decorative Arts (Kunstgewerbemuseum) and the Sculpture Collection (Skulpturensammlung).

The opportunity to show the Saxon Court's princely splendor and its artistic riches from the decades around the year 1600 arose thanks to the reconstruction of one of the most splendid examples of past Baroque magnificence, Augustus the Strong's Green Vault. The permanent postwar exhibition in the Albertinum closed in January 2004, and the historic Green Vault in the Dresden Residential Palace will open in fall 2006. This interval provided a unique opportunity to send an unusually large number of artworks from the Treasury Museum to New York. The Armory generously lent important objects from its permanent installation, allowing a comprehensive view of the era to be offered. It is remarkable that this survey of an era can be achieved exclusively with material from a single museum conglomerate. The art treasures united in the State Art Collections in Dresden form a compact, multifaceted portrait of Saxony's contribution to one of the most important artistic periods in European history.

The exhibition is related to and extends the major exhibitions about art and culture at the court of Rudolf II in Essen and in Vienna (1988), as well as in Prague (1997).[7] The cultural achievements of other courts in the Holy Roman Empire of the German Nation around the year 1600—namely those in Munich, Kassel, and Brunswick-Wolfenbüttel—have been examined in depth over the last twenty-five years,[8] and now the splendors of the electoral Wettin Court in Dresden take their proper place in this glorious company.

1. Translated from Kästner 1995, p. 53.
2. Translated from Kästner 1995, pp. 56f.
3. Only a few years before, in 1560, the Uffizi in Florence were begun.
4. Dresdner Geschichtsverein 2002, p. 54. Comparative numbers of inhabitants in 1575: Paris: 300,000, London 180,000, Cologne 35,000; around 1600: Rome: 110,000, Hamburg 40,000.
5. Dresdner Geschichtsverein 2002, p. 43.
6. Gross 2001, p. 95.
7. Essen 1988 and Prague 1997.
8. Munich 1980; Lemgo 1997; Brunswick 1998.

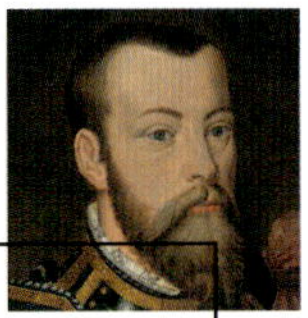

Electoral Saxony within the Empire and in Europe

Jochen Vötsch

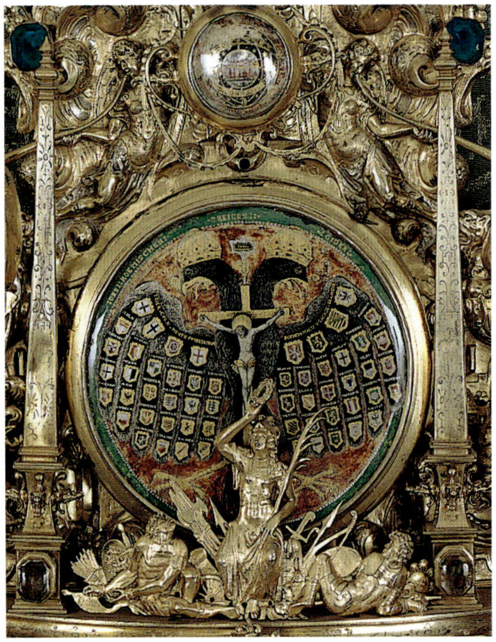

Symbolic Rendering of the Empire and Its Members
Detail from the Lüneburg Mirror
Dirich Utermarke
1587 and 1592
Silver, mostly gilt, mirror glass, glass painting
H. 45¼ in. (115 cm)
Staatliche Kunstsammlungen Dresden, Grünes Gewölbe, inv. no. IV 110

Around the year 1600, the Protestant Lutheran Electorate of Saxony—in short, electoral Saxony or Kursachsen—was not a sovereign state. Its population,[1] area, and economic development made it one of the most important territories of the Holy Roman Empire of the German Nation. Beginning in the late Middle Ages the emperors were primarily recruited from the house of Hapsburg, whose members resided in Vienna and were among the most important European dynasties. The empire, shaped by a complex body of feudal laws, was an extraordinarily complicated structure, consisting of many semiautonomous political entities—the so-called imperial states (Reichsstände)—of very different areas and populations (ill. left). The distribution of power within the empire was constantly renegotiated through ongoing mediation between the central imperial power and the interests of the princely territories. The types of government were quite diverse in the individual territories. Princely dynasties ruled over some, while in others clerics such as bishops served as elected temporal rulers. The free imperial cities were ruled as oligarchies. Smaller territories were governed by counts and imperial knights who promoted dynastic unions. It was not until its dissolution between 1803 and 1806 that the Old Empire became Germany, a modern nation-state. Until then, the empire did not have clearly defined borders; it was neither a united political entity nor a unified territory with regard to its economy or its currency. When early modern German states slowly took shape, different courses were taken in the individual territories.[2]

At the beginning of the sixteenth century, the church's medieval unity was broken by the Reformation. As a consequence, three large religious denominations were formed: the Lutheran, the Reformed or Calvinist, and—renewed by the Council of Trent (1545–63)—the Roman Catholic. Each claimed that the only true Christian teaching was manifest in their respective creeds. Competing churches were strictly opposed and stigmatized as heretic or blasphemous. Ultimately, this took hold of all aspects of life. The process—known as "confessionalism" (adherence to a particular faith)—left its mark on church, state, society, and culture throughout Europe; it also dominated the development of all German territories, independent of their religious denomination, starting in the second half of the sixteenth century.[3]

On the eve of the Thirty Years War, irreconcilable religious rifts closely linked to state rivalries and domestic power struggles had created a deeply unsettled atmosphere throughout Europe. The pervasive feeling of crisis, documented in innumerable broadsheets, was interpreted apocalyptically, giving warnings of an imminent final battle between Christ and the Antichrist (who was always the respective confessional opponent). Disputes about confessionalism and learned debates among theologians led to the formulation of a new ideal: The compulsively overbearing and quarrelsome spiritual shepherds—i.e., the German reformer Martin Luther, the Swiss John Calvin, and the pope (ill. left)—should give way to a simple trans-confessional Christian, a true good shepherd.

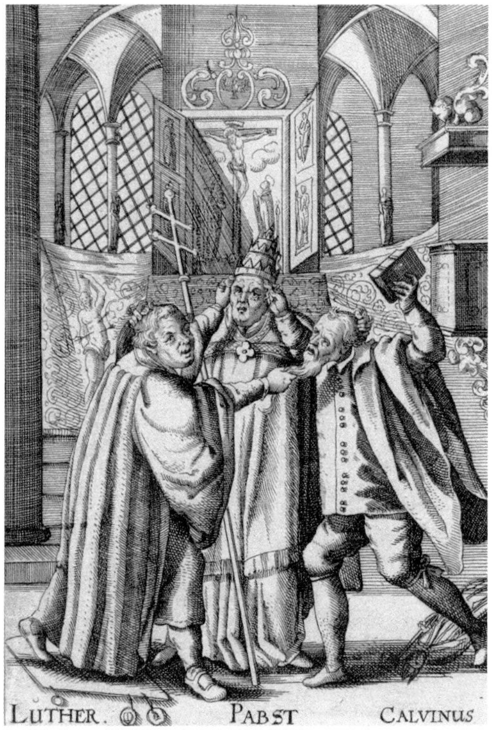

Dispute among Ecclesiastics
Detail, circa 1619
Copperplate engraving
14⅜ × 9½ in. (36.5 × 24 cm)
Westfälisches Landesmuseum
Münster, inv. no. C-8929 LM

This era of intense religious and political crisis was marked by rapid social changes. Population growth and worsening climatic conditions (Little Ice Age) resulted in diminished work and food; epidemics increased and political unrest grew. In the context of everyday problems and fear of the future, a celestial apparition, such as Halley's comet, visible in 1618, was seen as divine herald of misery and the approaching end of the world.[4]

Electoral Saxony and the Empire about 1600

In the empire's constitution and hierarchic order and among the German imperial princes, the Saxon sovereign in Dresden occupied a prominent position. As elector he belonged to the exclusive group of the seven electors of the ruler of the German-Roman elective empire along with his Catholic ecclesiastical and the Protestant secular colleagues. While the Catholic ecclesiastical electors were the archbishops of Mainz, Cologne, and Trier, the Protestant secular ones were the electors of the Palatinate and Brandenburg. This grouping was established by the Golden Bull of 1356. The highest secular rank within the electors was held by the Catholic Hapsburgs, the elected kings of Bohemia. The electors, the emperor's closest advisors, were the pillars of the empire. Holding their own gatherings, called the electors' days, they were jealous of their privileges. The electors counsel (the electors or their representatives) was a constitutional body. At the same time, they were the most eminent curia that gathered in various places on the occasion of the infrequently held imperial diets.[5] In the event that the imperial throne was vacant, the Saxon elector, together with that of the Palatinate, served as sovereign of the empire until a new emperor was elected. In addition, the Saxon elector was the imperial grand Marshal and thus performed important organizational and jurisdictional duties.

In the Upper Saxon district–Middle Germany from the Erzgebirge range in Saxony to the Baltic Sea–the Saxon elector had no rivals for the important position of regional leader. District diets or coin probation offered particularly important opportunities to take care of varied issues. They included functions of law and order such as securing public peace, the execution of imperial court judgments, collecting imperial taxes, the compilation of draft lists in the event of imminent threats by enemies of the empire (e.g., the Ottoman Empire or France), or the supervision of the mint system for the empire and the region.[6] Electoral Saxon's political power was particularly strong in Middle Germany, a historic region, roughly comprising today's federal lands of Saxony, Saxony-Anhalt, and Thuringia (see map on p. 27). Starting in the late Middle Ages, the Wettins successively established their regional dominance over the rulers of numerous smaller entities, who, bound by feudal law, owed their allegiance to them.

Just as the Electorate of Saxony–as part of the Holy Roman Empire of the German Nation–was not an independent nation, the Saxon elector did not have absolute power within his own territory. His main powers were fundamentally limited and hence diminished by the provincial estates (Landstände). The politically active members of the provincial estates were primarily representatives recruited from the landed aristocracy and the so-called knights (Ritterschaft), as well as delegates from the cities and the universities in Leipzig and Wittenberg.[7] It was the duty of the elector to summon provincial diets or smaller committee gatherings, where important topics related to the electorate were discussed. The provincial estates played an important role in passing tax laws and collecting taxes, a most important activity in early modern states which had increased needs for public funds.

In a primarily agrarian society, the execution of the basic overall manorial law together with local laws established the hegemony of the aristocracy and other elite populations. In contrast to other German regions, the rural population–despite taxes and compulsory service–lived in relatively free and secure conditions. The elector was the country's most significant landowner. His holdings, subdivided into administrative regions, together with his landed estates, were an important base of support for his reign.[8] The cities and the country's two universities retained their traditional rights, guaranteeing them a somewhat limited autonomy. The vast majority of the population was not, however, directly represented in the provincial diets, and the situation was therefore far different from today's democratically legitimized parliaments.

1. In 1550 there were approximately 550,000 residents, see Gross 2001, p. 76.
2. See overviews in Rabe 1989; Press 1991; Gebhardt 2001; summarized in Schmidt 1999.
3. See in general Schilling 1988; Schilling 1991; Schilling 1998; about Kursachsen see Smolinsky 1993, as well as Press 1990.
4. See Krusenstjern 1999, pp. 57–60.
5. Fundamentally Gotthard 1999.
6. See most recently Nicklas 2002.
7. The highest-ranking group of counts and masters held by their oaths of allegiance and intending to emancipate themselves from *Kursachsen* played a rather marginal role.
8. See Gross 2001, pp. 74–76.

Saxony and the Wettins, 1500–1550

At the beginning of the early modern period, the Saxon house of Wettin had already had an impressive history, later memorialized in Dresden's Princely Procession (Dresdner Fürstenzug), an immense nineteenth-century ceramic frieze of the Wettin rulers. In the Leipzig partition of 1485, the Wettin realms were divided between the brothers Ernst (1441/1464–1486) and Albrecht (the Brave, 1443/1464–1500) who initially coruled. This resulted in the creation of the Ernestine Electorate of Saxony with the electoral territories of Wittenberg and Thuringia, and the Albertine Duchy of Saxony with Meissen as their hereditary land and Dresden as their residence. It was in Ernestine Wittenberg in 1517 that Martin Luther attached his theses to the cathedral door, an event that initiated the Reformation. Electoral Saxony's support of the Reformation aided its triumphant progress through Germany. The division between Catholicism and Protestantism in the empire, a consequence of the Reformation, generated more intense territorial frictions and intradynastic rivalries among the Wettins. Divided since 1485, the dynasty split further into Catholic and Protestant factions. The Catholic duke Georg (the Bearded), the Albertine, resided in Dresden and supported change within the Roman church. The Protestant branch was headed by Elector Johann Friedrich of Saxony (the Magnanimous, 1503/1532–1554), the Ernestine elector. He and Landgrave Philipp of Hesse played leading roles in the 1531 formation of the League of Schmalkalden, a union of Protestant princes pledged to defend and preserve the Reformation. On Duke Georg's death his brother Heinrich (the Believer) introduced the Reformation to Albertine Saxony. The dissolution of the Catholic monasteries and the confiscation of church property were the most significant secular consequences of the Reformation. As important was the formation of a Protestant

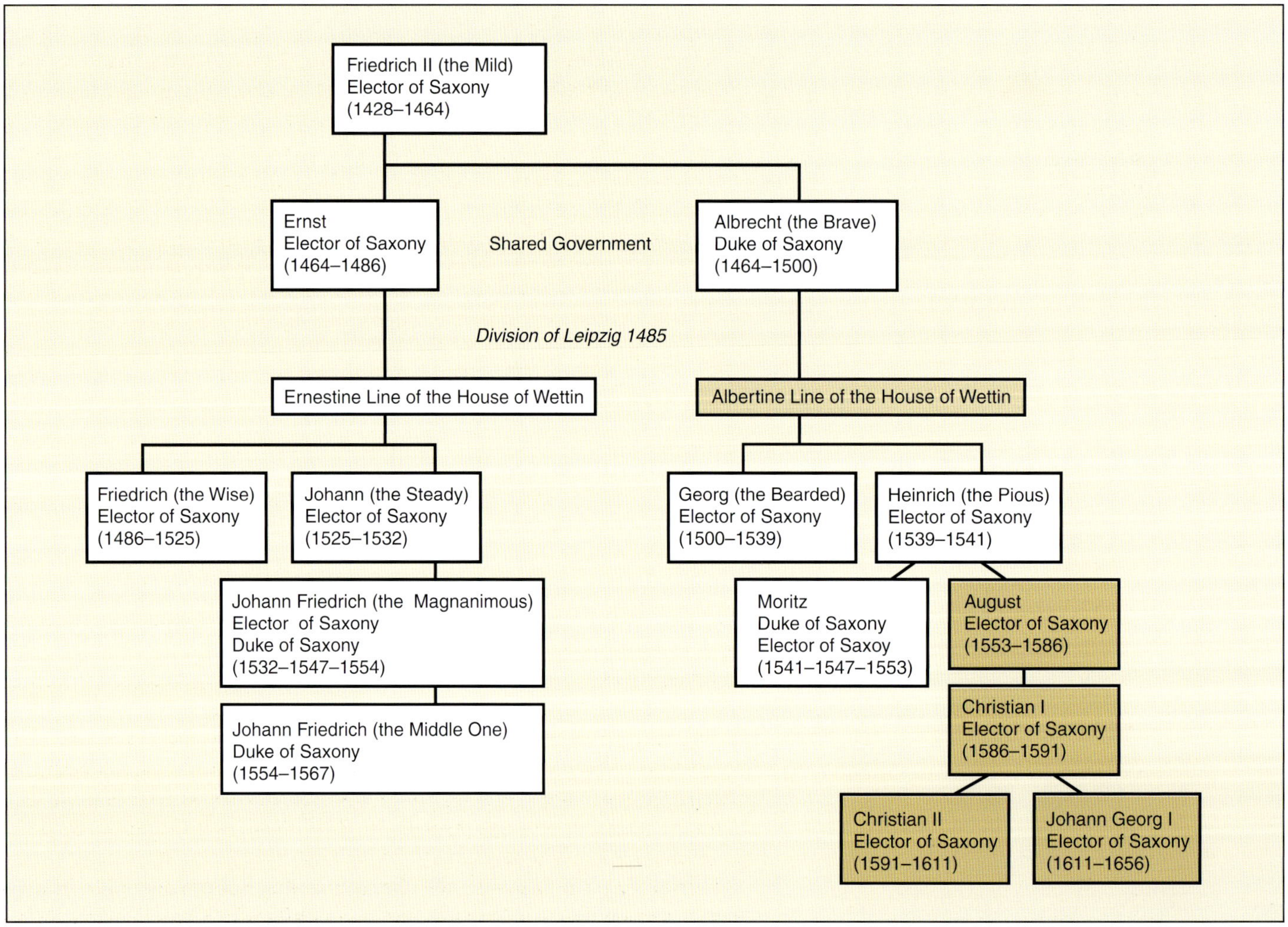

Dukes and Electors from the house of Wettin from the fifteenth until the seventeenth centuries

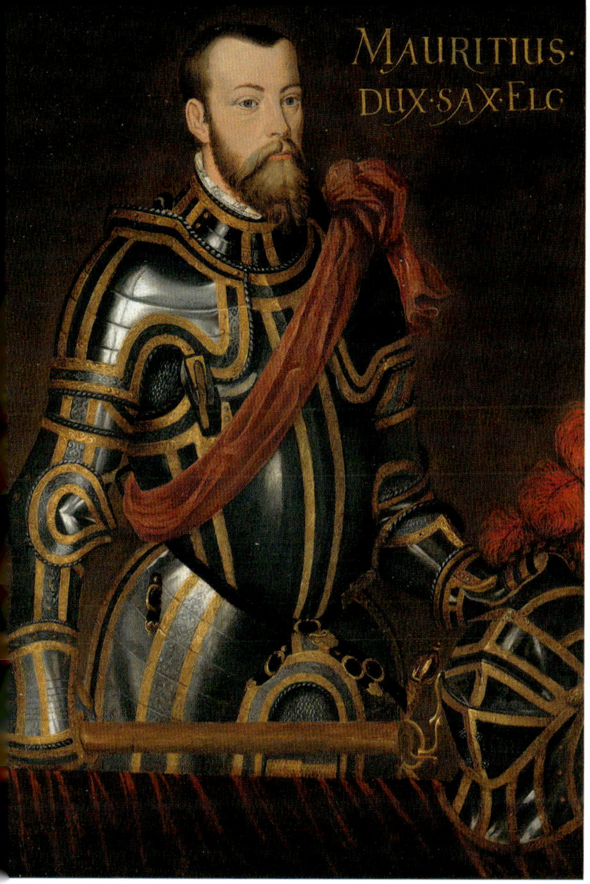

Elector Moritz of Saxony
style of Anthonis Mor
after 1555
Oil on canvas
49⅝ × 37¾ in. (126 × 96 cm)
Staatliche Kunstsammlungen
Dresden, Rüstkammer,
inv. no. H. 168

church to be headed by the political ruler rather than the pope and his bishops. This resulted in fundamental structural changes within the traditional power structure: The material (with the acquisition of church property) and the sovereign (with the assumption of church rule) foundation of the ruler's power were immensely strengthened, leading to his further domination of the early modern territorial state.

Inevitably the differences between the empire's religious parties increased. The power-seeking Lutheran duke Moritz (1521/1541–1553) unexpectedly took the side of the Catholic emperor Charles V in the Schmalkalden War. He was important in the imperial victory at Mühlberg (1547), where his father-in-law, Philipp of Hesse, and his electoral Ernestine cousin were defeated. With the consent of the other electors, the grateful emperor took the electoral office (Kurwürde) away from the vanquished Ernestine Johann Friedrich and bestowed it on Duke Moritz. This transfer of privelege to the younger Albertine line of Dresden was an epoch-making event for the Wettin dynasty and a most remarkable episode in sixteenth-century German history.

Moritz was skillful and unscrupulous in strategic politics, and some dedicated Protestants referred to him as "Judas of Meissen." In fact, he achieved a complete reversal of the territorial 1485 division. He joined the electoral lands surrounding Wittenberg with the margravate of Meissen, forcing the defeated Ernestines into Thuringia. This dynastic change had far-reaching political consequences. It forced the newly empowered Protestant (Albertine) electoral house into a long-lasting political allegiance with the Catholic emperor, with the aim of solidifying their electoral status. In the northern half of the empire, the Albertine elector acted as a junior partner to the emperor. The fear that the Ernestines might seek revenge was not unfounded and influenced the conservativism of Saxon politics regarding empire and religion. In fact, Elector Moritz did intermittently change sides: Starting in 1551, he was in the forefront of princely opposition against the further development of the Hapsburgs' imperial power which was threatening the liberty of the imperial states and the survival of German Protestantism. With the support of France, which felt constricted by Charles V's Hapsburg power in Spain, Moritz managed to defuse these threats with the 1552 Treaty of Passau. In this pact the emperor agreed to free the leaders of the Schmalkalden Alliance, Moritz's father-in-law, Philipp of Hesse, and the former Saxon elector Johann Friedrich from imperial prison. Moritz died in the Battle of Sievershausen in 1553 in which his forces defeated the bellicose Franconian margrave Albrecht Alkibiades of Brandenburg-Kulmbach. Moritz was deeply mourned in the Vienna Hofburg as one who had fought for the empire's existing territorial order. The duty of insuring the continued existence of the young electoral state fell to Moritz's younger brother and successor, August.

Elector August: Keeping the Peace

Assessments of Elector August are rather diverse. Older historical sources disdainfully include him among the "boozing and praying princes" or turn him into the simple father of the house (Father August), idealizing him as one of the people. In fact, Elector August (1526/1553–1586, cat. no. 1) had his own style and was an unusual sort, a novel imperial Lutheran ruler within his territorial state.[9] The basis was a central event of sixteenth-century German history: the Peace of Augsburg passed by the 1555 imperial diet of Augsburg. Strongly supported by electoral Saxony, this peace was a multilayered compromise: Intended to preserve the empire's unity, it also attempted to neutralize religious conflicts through political means, and to secure the property of both Catholics and Protestants based on imperial law.[10] Generally, in each territory, there was to be only one faith, determined by the particular sovereign and compulsory for his subjects. This principle was expressed by the formula "*Cuius regio, eius religio*" (he to whom the land belongs determines the religion). There were a number of exceptions, and the sometimes vague formulations had the potential to encourage future explosions, especially if political activists no longer felt bound by the compromise.

The Peace of Augsburg shaped the characters of an entire generation of princes, known as "princes of peace" (Friedensfürsten). The period after 1555 was marked by a general desire

9. Rudersdorf 1999, pp. 323–25, cf. also the overview in Bruning 2002.
10. Cf. Stievermann 1994, pp. 13–15.

for peace, supported by friendships among and gatherings of the imperial princes, many of whom were close relatives. In addition, there was a realization that a functional imperial government would be advantageous in consolidating each of the imperial realms. Elector August of Saxony promulgated a domestic and foreign policy aimed at maintaining peace: The Peace of Augsburg was his guiding principle, and he supported nondenominationalism—while opposing political Calvinism—and intense loyalty to the empire and the emperor.

However, the Saxon elector was, in fact, much more than just a peace-loving follower of the emperor. In the 1560s, Dresden was at the epicenter of imperial politics, and Elector August was the focal point of an extremely complicated system of communication among the imperial princes. (This is demonstrated by the plethora of documents in the Sächsisches Hauptstaatsarchiv in Dresden.[11]) Political and personal news was quickly exchanged; problems were discussed; artists' contracts were negotiated and gifts were exchanged. August's reach extended beyond the empire; his other partners included Italian princes, but his ties to the Lutheran kingdom of Denmark were more intense and important because of his remarkably happy marriage to the king's daughter, Anna. (This union shows the high esteem which the old European royal families had for the Wettins.)

In the 1554 Treaty of Naumburg August settled the claims of the Ernestine line to the Saxon electorate. He sacrificed a number of essential offices and made a one-time payment of one hundred thousand florins to the Ernestines. Even so, their ambitions for the electoral office, lost in 1547, remained a perpetual threat to the Albertine electorate of Saxony. Elector August renewed his friendship with Emperor Maximilian II, which dated from their youth and which led to the crucial blow against the intradynastic competition. To reinstate his dynasty, Duke Johann Friedrich der Mittlere of Saxony-Weimar entered into a dangerous game with the aristocrats' movement under the leadership of Wilhelm von Grumbach, the Franconian knight and agitator. August then persuaded the emperor to issue an imperial ban that forced August's cousin to capitulate. In 1567 the Albertine elector triumphed and Johann Friedrich der Mittlere was imprisoned for life, a term he ultimately served in Vienna's imperial prison. In addition, the Ernestines, once again humiliated, lost numerous offices as compensation for the war expenditures. Yet, even after this success, the sentiment in Dresden was one of uncertainty: As late as 1584, two years before his demise, August ordered a study to determine if he was entitled to perform the duties of electoral office and to bear in good faith the title held by the Ernestine Johann Friedrich, who had died in 1554.[12]

Beyond this, the skilled politician August achieved considerable territorial gains in a peaceful manner, including almost all of the Meissen, Merseburg, and Naumburg-Zeitz dioceses, which had become Protestant, and parts of the Vogtland region in fee from Emperor Maximilian II, as well as parts of the lands that had been held by the extinct line of the counts of Henneberg, located near the Franconian-Thuringian border.[13]

In 1560 the Palatinate's conversion from Lutheranism to Calvinism posed a strong threat to the peace promulgated in 1555. Elector August, however, prevented the Palatinate's exclusion from the Peace of Augsburg by discouraging the emperor and the Catholic church from acting as arbitrators in the intra-Protestant power struggle.[14] Given its ties to the Calvinist opposition movements in France and the Netherlands and later to the governments in Paris, The Hague, and London, the electoral Palatinate had helped broaden the increasingly international scope of imperial politics, which brought a greater awareness of the European conflicts of religion. But even a natural development, like the deaths of the 1555 generation of "princes of peace," left its imprint on the empire's political climate.

Particularly telling in this context, especially for the position of electoral Saxony, was the conflict concerning the ecclesiastical electorate of Cologne in the early 1580s.[15] The Catholic Archbishop and Elector Gebhard of Cologne decided to convert to Lutheranism and to marry, while refusing to give up his office. According to the Peace of Augsburg ecclesiastical princes of the empire had to give up their offices if they converted. While the Palatinate pursued its goal actively, trying to secure military support within the Protestant states for the archbishop and elector, Dresden quoted the Peace, thus citing existing imperial law. Elector August again feared for the empire's survival, particularly if external powers were "blowing in the fire" (*in das feuer blasen*). It was remarked that there are no more dangerous wars "than those in the name of religion" ("*als wan die Religion der praetextus sein mus*"), as the ongoing wars in

11. Bruning 2002, pp. 222f.
12. Report of the Geheimer Rat, Dr. David Pfeifer, Dresden, April 22, 1584, SächsHStA Dresden, Loc. 10053/3, fol. 7r–11v.
13. See Gross 2001, pp. 79–81.
14. Press 1994a, p. 316.
15. See Vötsch 2001.
16. Undated concept, presumably originating from close to the 1582 Imperial Diet of Augsburg, SächsHStA Dresden, Loc. 10201/5, fol. 63r–64v, the quotes fol. 64r, 64v.

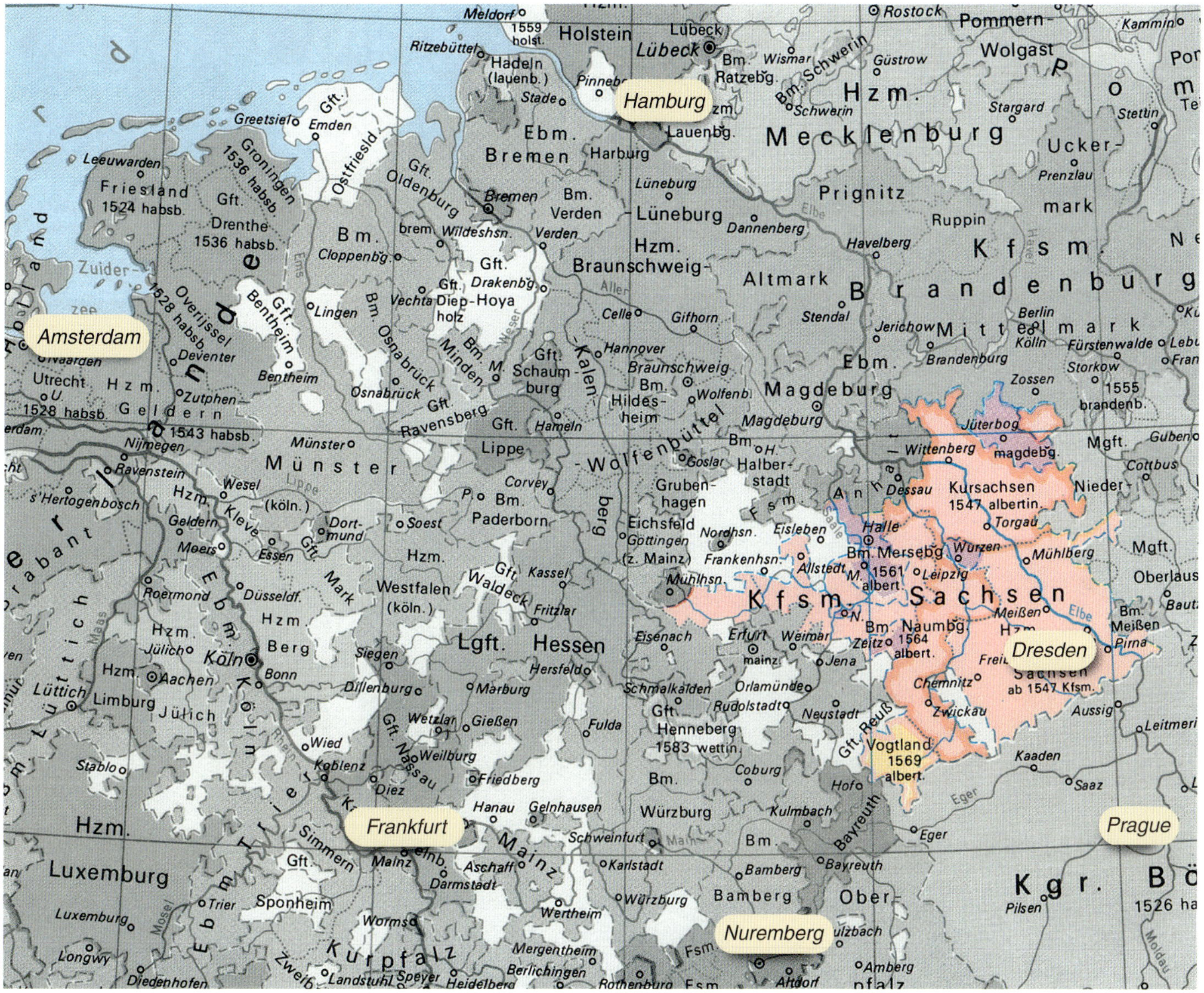

The Electorate of Saxony in the Holy Roman Empire of the German Nation after 1547

France and in the Netherlands demonstrated.[16] As the conflict evolved, a new archbishop and elector, Ernst of Bavaria—with the help of Spanish troops stationed in the nearby Netherlands—succeeded the dismissed Gebhard. The Catholics had thus defended an important bastion in the Protestant north and successfully asserted their majority in the counsel of electors.

Under the protection of the Peace of Augsburg, electoral Saxony evolved into a decidedly Lutheran state within the empire. A model of successful internal development, it was known for financial stability, support of mining, science, and technology, and reforms in the domains of justice and administration. August firmly balanced different Protestant denominations while increasingly subjecting the state's religious institutions to state control and bureaucratic organization. A moderate Lutheran theology held sway in electoral Saxony. It was grounded in the humanist ideas of Philipp Melanchthon, the great teacher from Wittenberg. Following later conflicts, it was referred to as Philippism. The slowly emerging suspicion of Crypto-Calvinism resulted in the unexpected overthrow of the Philippists in 1574 and led to the harsh repression of theologians and leading counsels. This demonstrates the elector's drastic change regarding politics and religion. The final evolution of the Lutheran faith in Saxony and in the empire took place in sharp differentiation against the Calvinists and the extremists within Lutheranism. The Formula of Concord (1577), promulgated by the electoral

Nikolaus Krell
Unknown Master
n.d.
Oil on canvas
16⅛ × 12⅝ in. (41 × 32 cm)
Städtische Galerie Dresden,
Gemäldegalerie Alte Meister,
inv. no. 1979/K 20

Saxon leadership, led to the publication of the Book of Concord in 1580, the central religious text for German Lutherans and an attempt to heal the divisiveness of the Lutheran movement since the death of Martin Luther.[17] The obstacles to theological unity were immense. One telling example is the strong reaction against the teachings of Matthias Flacius Illyricus, an extremely orthodox Lutheran, and his followers at Jena's Ernestine university. The largest cannon ball in the Dresden Kunstkammer bore the inscription: "*Ich bin ein Jungfrau wohlgestaldt, Kueß ich ein Flatianer er wird nicht Alt*" (I am a good-looking virgin, If I kiss a follower of Flacius he will soon die).[18]

Christian I and Chancellor Krell

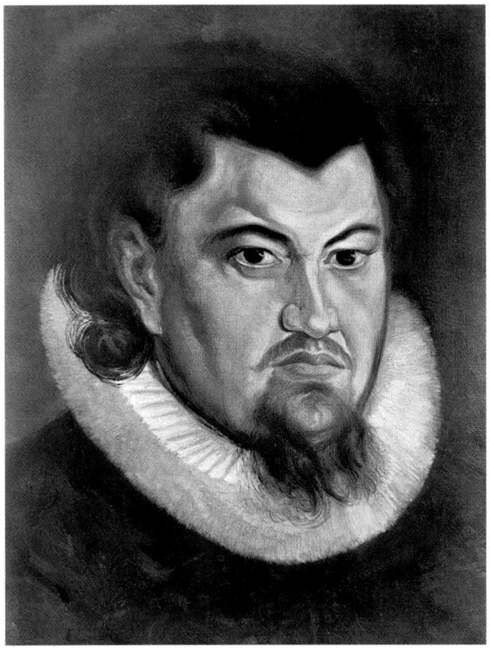

Christian (1560/1586–1591, cat. no. 2), the only one of August's nine sons to survive their father, was married to Sophie, daughter of the Elector Johann Georg of Brandenburg, in 1582. He had been carefully prepared by his father, who had written a sort of political testament to his son in 1582, concerning the moral principles a ruler should uphold and the principles he should follow in exercising power.[19] After meeting with the Secret Counsel in 1581—the electorate's highest governmental body—August assigned his son some of his own internal administration duties in 1584, which Christian handled independently.[20]

The court councillor Nikolaus Krell (ill. left)—despite his obvious Calvinist tendencies—became Christian's confidant and advisor. Originally from Leipzig, the versatile, intelligent lawyer visited the Calvinist centers of Geneva and those in France while on his grand tour and then embarked on a brilliant career. Already secret councillor in 1586, Krell was made chancellor in 1589. Christian's accession to power raised Calvinist expectations within and without Saxony: The French Protestants and Christian's Calvinist brother-in-law, Johann Casimir, the electoral administrator of the Palatinate, had high hopes for him, while the Lutheran clergy of Saxony feared religious changes in their own country.

The first efforts toward ecclesiastical reform in electoral Saxony did not occur until 1587/1588, as part of a movement known as the Second Reformation.[21] The introduction of Calvinist principles presented an immense intellectual challenge in an era of rigid Lutheran orthodoxy. After the mandate obliging the clergy to sign the Lutheran Formula of Concord was rescinded, the visitation and subsequent restructuring of the universities in the Saxon cities of Leipzig and Wittenberg began. Likewise, in new curricula for the three Saxon state schools in Grimma, Meissen, and Schulpforta, the humanistic disciplines were expanded, and the role of Lutheranism was limited. The decentralization of the highest Lutheran administrative body made it difficult for the Lutheran clerics to mount a united resistance against the electoral Saxon state church's new orientation. In addition, possible and actual opponents—primarily clergymen and professors—were dismissed, and key positions within the church, high courts, administrative offices, and universities were filled with mostly nonlocal representatives of the younger generation.

Christian I concentrated on the universities. In Wittenberg, the still-prevalent humanist heritage of Melanchthon facilitated the shift from Lutheran and Calvinist theology, and the university became popular with Calvinist students from abroad. In Leipzig, a thriving international city of publishing, trade, and fairs, religious innovation was not supported by the university but by the upper middle class. In 1591 a crucial reform of sacramental services, which were increasingly Calvinist in nature, was the abolition of exorcism during baptism. This ancient element of the baptismal liturgy was ingrained in the minds of the faithful. Such a change, visible to the public, deeply unsettled the lower orders. In the cities, in particular, there were frequent tumultuous protests. In Dresden's Kreuzkirche a butcher, cleaver in hand, insisted on the exorcism during his child's baptism. In his autobiography Urban Pierius, who had been called to teach at Wittenberg, vividly describes the religious controversies in Saxony in those days. He reported that the court guards needed to be called to protect three court preachers from physical violence following the service in the Residenzschloss church.[22] The religious politics polarized the Saxon population. If a new course was by and large accepted by the representatives of the universities and the cities, it would be opposed by the nobility

17. Koch 1989, pp. 198–212.
18. See Vötsch 2002, pp. 211f., the quote p. 212.
19. Printed in Weber 1866.
20. For the following cf. Blaschke 1986, Hoyer 1990, Koch 1989; see also the thorough investigation by Klein 1962.
21. About the characteristics see summarized in Stievermann 1997, pp. 60f.; in a more extensive overview: Schilling 1986.
22. Pierius/Klein 1970, here p. 147.
23. Hoyer 1992, Hoyer 1990.
24. See altogether Marx 2000a, esp. pp. 17–21.
25. See the brief remarks in Schindling 2001.
26. SächsHStA Dresden, Loc. 9603/7, fol. 1r–14v, 5v.
27. Cf. pointedly Gotthard 2000.
28. For Friedrich Wilhelm see Patze/Schlesinger 1982, pp. 43–55.
29. Czok 1992.

whose influence and, above all, local authority was being threatened.[23]

Because of their elevated position among the German princes, the Saxon electors had to present themselves and their court in a splendid manner. This staging of sovereigns' activities was important to the old European aristocracy as well as to vassals and subjects. Consequently, Christian I, an ardent horse lover, commissioned the New Stable (Neuer Stall, ill. p. 71), an immense structure for courtly festivities including tournaments and races. In doing so, he continued to extend Dresden's Residenzschloss, continuing construction enthusiastically begun by Elector Mortiz when he assumed the electoral office.[24] Christian initiated an order, called the Güldene Gesellschaft (Golden Fellowship), based on the model of the Order of the Golden Fleece, which was emblematic as well. The tremendous outlays for building palaces, maintaining the court, and obtaining rare works of art were essential for high-ranking princes like Christian I to affirm his ability to compete successfully with other courts.[25] A contemporary chronicle about the life of Christian I passed a favorable judgment: "*Der Ahnsehnlichen Hoffhaltung wegen mag Ihm keiner an teutschen Fürsten seyn gleich gewesen*" (Because of his admirable court, there was perhaps no other German prince quite like him).[26]

First remaining strictly neutral in its foreign policy, electoral Saxony began to alter its course around 1589. There had been important shifts within the European power structure: the Protestant English had defeated Catholic Spain's Armada in 1588 and Henry of Navarre, then a Calvinist, had become king of France in 1589. Lutheran electoral Saxony, traditionally emperor-friendly and hence pro-Catholic, now supported solidarity with the Calvinist electoral Palatinate and western European Protestantism that favored Calvinist positions. As head of the imperial Protestant Movement Party, which was willing to act independently, the Palatinate maintained connections that extended beyond the empire. In 1591 Christian I joined the electoral Palatinate Administrator Johann Casimir and other imperial princes in the Treaty of Torgau. Its goal was to help the Calvinist Huguenots (oppressed French Protestants) and to fight Catholic Spanish encroachments along the Lower Rhine. With the untimely death of Christian I, this brief period of political and religious reorientation came to an abrupt end. The news of the ruler's demise was greeted with some joy in Saxony and deemed God's just punishment for his apostasy from his ancestors' true Lutheran faith.

The year 1591 is in any event an important caesura in Saxon-German history.[27] A lasting consequences of the Calvinist intermezzo was the development of electoral Saxony into an intellectual and political bastion of Lutheran orthodoxy. With the death of Christian I, there was an end to the promising attempts toward establishing an efficient way of upholding the German Protestants' interests vis-à-vis a newly strengthened Catholicism and an emperor whose realm was structurally Catholic. A new orientation toward Western Europe as an alternative to the Hapsburg empire did not endure—but remained a promising but unfruitful episode.

The Reign of Christian II

The regent for the eight-year-old Christian II, the only son of Christian I, was officially his grandfather, Elector Johann Georg of Brandenburg. In practical terms, however, the Ernestine Duke Friedrich Wilhelm I of Saxony-Weimar-Altenburg served as electoral administrator until 1601.[28] Friedrich Wilhelm maintained a costly official court in Torgau, where he conducted his official duties. A good Lutheran by conviction and motivated by the Saxon estates, the administrator immediately changed electoral Saxon politics: Exponents of religious innovation were imprisoned, and a country-wide visitation in 1592/1593 resulted in the expulsion of recently appointed Calvinists culminating in a controversial trial of Chancellor Krell and his public beheading on Dresden's Neumarkt in 1601. Associated with the visitation of 1593, there was an uprising in Leipzig, during the course of which the houses of suspected Calvinists were broken into and plundered. As was the case with other conflicts occurring within the empire, the religious quarrels also offered a release of the long-standing political, social, and economic tensions among Leipzig's population.[29]

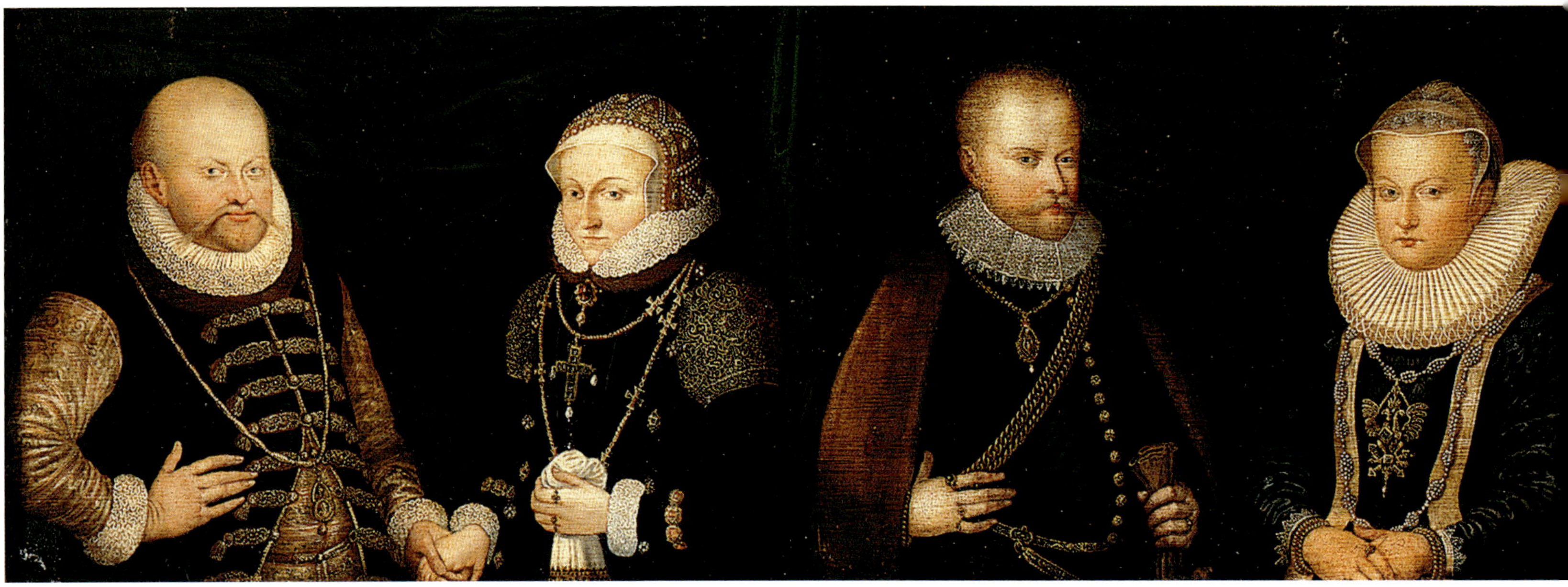

The Saxon Electors with their wifes: August and Anna of Denmark, Christian I and Sophie of Brandenburg, Christian II and Hedwig of Denmark, Johann Georg I and Magdalena Sybilla of Brandenburg
Unknown Dresden Court Painter, based on older model between 1692 and 1694
Oil on copper
7⅞ × 46 in. (20 × 117 cm)
Staatliche Kunstsammlungen Dresden, Gemäldegalerie Alte Meister, inv. no. Mo 2148

Guided by an administrator who avoided conflict, electoral Saxony's foreign and imperial politics increasingly tended to be harmonious with the emperor. Electoral Saxony reverted to the role of the emperor's junior partner in the northern empire. Unassertive as guardian and administrator, Friedrich Wilhelm could reach his objectives only in close association with the imperial court. These goals included diminishing Brandenburg's influence in Dresden and defending electoral Saxony's preeminent position in the imperial province of Upper Saxony. Again it is clear that Lutherans in general, loyal to the emperor as they were, would rather cooperate with Catholics than Calvinists within their own Protestant tradition. During the Imperial Diets of the 1590s, but also in later years, electoral Saxony supported the increasingly weakened position of Emperor Rudolf II (ill. p. 33) and refused to exploit his reverses, especially in the long Turkish Wars (1593–1606) in the East, to win concessions regarding religious reforms, especially those attempted by the Palatinate.[30] Although even in Dresden the Turkish threat was perceived as real, the wars resulted in a temporary improvement of Dresden's empty coffers through overcharging Saxon subjects for imperial war taxes.[31]

Elector Christian II (1583/1591–1611, cat. no. 3) began his reign upon attaining majority in 1601. A good-natured man, he consumed a great amount of alcohol—even given the standards of the time—and proved almost incapable of performing his duties. His way of life and the manner in which he maintained the court were so extravagant that the electoral Saxon state was threatened with bankruptcy.[32] In 1608 the ruling elector had to agree, in an accord with his brother and potential successor, Johann Georg, to make no charitable gifts, be it money or goods, for an eight-year period, in order to restore the state's financial health.[33]

Starting about 1600, the empire's religious conflicts increased dramatically. After the imperial Diet of Ratisbone in 1608, two imperial princely coalitions emerged, characterized by religious fervor and readiness for war: One was the Protestant Union, formed in 1608 under the leadership of the Calvinist Palatinate in Heidelberg, while the other was the Catholic League, founded in 1609, whose leader was Duke Maximilian I of Bavaria, the Palatinate elector's cousin from Munich. Lutheran electoral Saxony did not join the Protestant Union but tended, according to its previous political line, to form pacts with the Catholic League: "*Politice seint wir Bäpstisch*" (In politics, we are Catholic), as expressed in a 1610 self-evaluation by the electoral Saxon counsels.[34]

In this difficult environment, the deterioration of the emperor's authority was detrimental. Dresden supported Emperor Rudolf II, who eventually died in Prague's castle in 1612, in the Hapsburg family feud. At the time of his death, this lonely man, abandoned by his brother and nephew, was a largely powerless eccentric and compulsive collector. There were

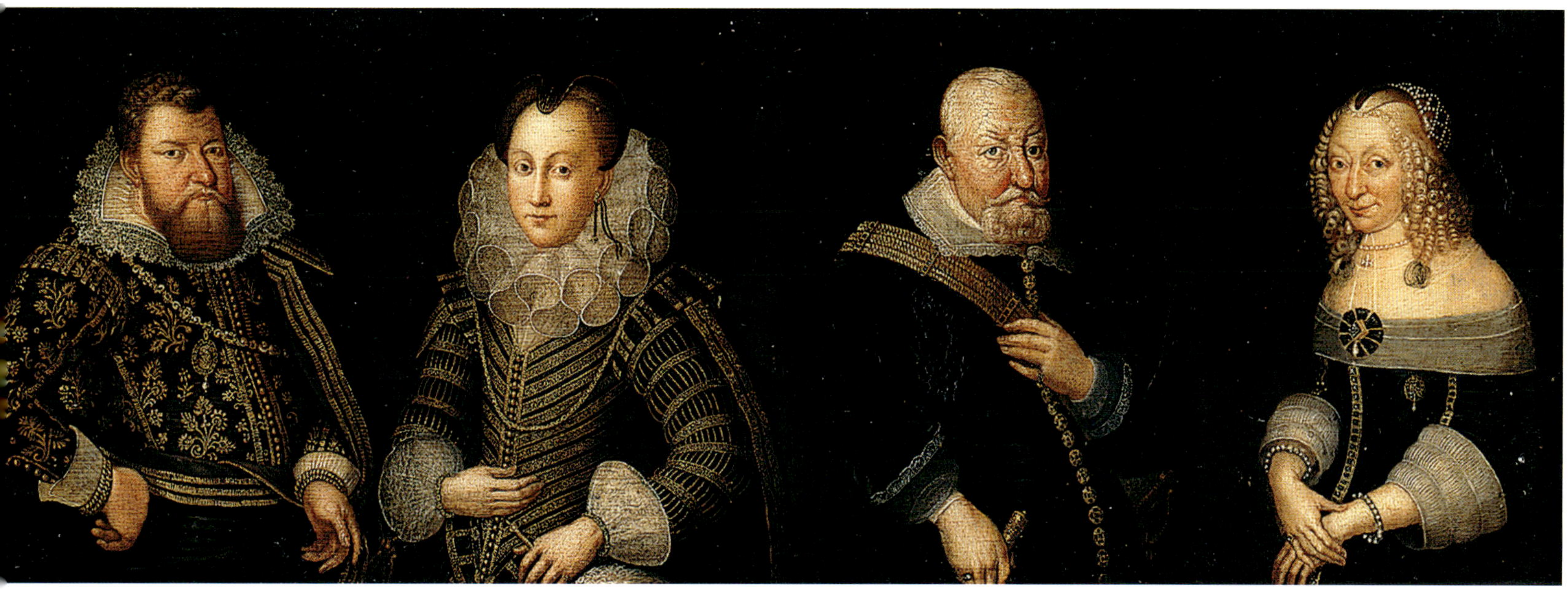

intensifying, mutually beneficial artistic exchanges between the residences of Prague and Dresden (only seventy-five miles apart), stimulated by trips Christian II took to Prague in 1607 and 1610.[35] The proximity to the emperor was profitable in another respect: In 1610, the Saxon elector received, as Rudolf II's enfeoffment, territories located in the Lower Rhine area, the heritage of the last duke of Jülich, Cleves, and Berg who had died in 1609.[36] Nonetheless, this title posed a thorny problem, as electoral Brandenburg and Palatinate-Neuburg also claimed the duchies. By placing their trust in the emperor hoping for a legal solution to the Jülicher Erbfolgestreit (War of Succession), in the end Christian II and his Ernestine cousins, also legitimate co-heirs, became passive onlookers in a game ultimately won by their two equally Lutheran challengers. The Brandenburg elector Johann Sigismund harbored Calvinist convictions and in fact converted to Calvinism, thus securing Netherlandish support, while the Neuburg Wolfgang Wilhelm converted to Catholicism and gained the support of Bavaria and Spain. A European war of religion would have brought France in against Spain, but this devastating prospect was prevented at the last minute by the 1614 Treaty of Xanten. This treaty divided the Lower Rhine heritage between electoral Brandenburg and Palatinate-Neuburg; all that remained for electoral Saxony was an impressive collection of titles as an expression of its claims, which remained in use until the end of the old empire (1806). A successful acquisition of Jülich-Cleves-Berg (a substantial part of today's North-Rhine-Westphalia) would have given a totally different future not only to Saxony but also to Germany.

Johann Georg I and the Beginning of the Thirty Years War

On the suggestion of then-electoral administrator, Friedrich Wilhelm, Johann Georg I (1585/1611–1656, cat. no. 4), Christian II's younger brother, set out on an extended visit to Catholic Italy starting in 1601, which included a lengthy stay in Verona to study Italian and Latin.[37] Apart from a sound education, the new elector, upon taking the rule in 1611, brought some practical experience to his office, since he had assumed some duties during his brother's last years as ruler.

The change in reign did not lead to shifts in Saxon imperial and religious politics. After Rudolf II's death in 1612, Johann Georg I served as imperial curate and—on the occasion of the election of Rudolf's brother, Matthias, as emperor in Frankfurt—negotiated between Catholic League and Protestant Union. Just like his grandfather August before him,

30. For Dresden's position on the 1594 Imperial Diet of Ratisbone cf. Kossol 1976, pp. 57ff.
31. Nicklas 2002, pp. 146f.
32. See, for example, the report in SächsHStA Dresden, Loc. 10053/3.
33. Dresden, January 23, 1608. SächsHStA Dresden, OU 12670.
34. In high German: "Politisch sind wir päpstisch [katholisch]," quoted after Gotthard 1993, p. 317.
35. See Dombrowski 2000, p. 71, as well as Jürgen Müller's essay in this volume.
36. See Press 1991, pp. 174–84, the electoral Saxon letter of the fiefdom, Prague, July 7, 1610, SächsHStA Dresden OU 12700.
37. Richter 1913, pp. 174f.

Johann Georg I did not have any ambitions of making the empire Protestant, regardless of much speculation about his candidacy as emperor (an eventuality that would have been acceptable to the Catholic emperor-electors).[38] The papal court also held enduring hopes for Saxony's conversion to Catholicism, but time and again Saxon loyalty to the emperor and the decidedly anti-Calvinist politics of the electors August and especially Johann Georg roiled the different denominational groups.[39]

In summer 1617 the Saxon residential city of Dresden gave the Emperor Matthias an elaborate festive welcome. Besides courtly displays and sumptuous amusements, weighty negotiations were held: Matthias was successful in his endeavor to obtain the Saxon electoral vote for the premature election of his cousin as king, in order to secure the latter's succession as future emperor. Even though the election did not materialize, his cousin, already king of Bohemia and Hungary, was elected Roman-German emperor as Ferdinand II following Matthias's death.

In 1617, some years after celebrating the anniversaries of the foundations of the Saxon universities (Leipzig 1409, Wittenberg 1502), electoral Saxony commemorated the centenary of the promulgation of Luther's Ninety-Five Theses in Wittenberg. This emphasized its position as the leading Protestant-Lutheran power in the Reformation's cradle and in the empire.[40] Such a demonstration of orthodox Lutheranism was an anomaly: there had been no remembrance of Luther's act anywhere else. "Luther, he who forcefully wrote [and] hammered the theses on the door," was the impressive personification for the memorial festivities. In Rome the pope declared a special corresponding jubilee, thereby emphasizing the schism. The theological struggles of the Reformation were fought again, most particularly in voluminous publications. In his first polemical sermon as festival preacher, Matthias Hoe von Hoenegg, the influential superior court preacher, presented the Lutherans as good subjects—to both their legitimate worldly rulers and to their Catholic emperor—contrasting them to the detestable Calvinists. The 1617 celebration was a reaction to the formation of religious factions within the empire and to the divisions within Protestantism: at the same time it was a public declaration of the electoral Saxon position.[41]

Only a year later, in an atmosphere of great religious and dynastic tension, a conflict erupted that would end only thirty years later (1618–48). The Thirty Years War was described by Burkhardt as the European war that created nations (*Staatsbildungskrieg*). It was begun by the Defenestration of Prague in which two royal officers were hurled from a window by Protestant members of the Bohemian diet. A revolt of neighboring Bohemia's Protestant majority against the Catholic Hapsburg rule ensued. After Johann Georg I refused the Bohemian crown in 1619, the Bohemian estates elected the Calvinist elector Friedrich V of the Palatinate—leader of the Protestant Union—as the king of Bohemia. Thereafter, Emperor Ferdinand II entered into an alliance with the Catholic League, led by Bavaria. These forces expelled Friedrich V at the end of 1620. Mockingly called the "winter king," he lost his electoral office and the Oberpfalz territory to his victorious Bavarian cousin. After unsuccessful attempts to negotiate in Dresden, the Bohemian upheaval was considered solely a political and certainly not a religious incident.[42] In early 1620 Johann Georg I joined with Ferdinand II and suppressed the Protestant uprisings in the countries neighboring Bohemia (Ober- and Niederlausitz, Silesia) on the order of the Catholic emperor. While initially granting Johann Georg I himself the Ober- and Niederlausitz territories as security for his war expenditures, the emperor granted them to electoral Saxony in 1635 and they became permanent Saxon property in 1648.

Dresden's political stance at the beginning of the Thirty Years War angered Protestants, and also exasperated generations of historians, because Saxony put political considerations above religious solidarity. It is certain, however, that the electoral Saxon position during the Bohemian conflict was greatly appreciated by the emperor and initially forestalled a general war of religion.[43] Following earlier policies and harking back to the 1555 Peace of Augsburg, Dresden declared an unchanged solidarity with the emperor, adhering to a nondenominational, and strictly legal course. The latter aspect has often been ignored: Vassal to the legitimate Hapsburg ruler of Bohemia[44] and tied to the Bohemian crown through an ancestral agreement, the elector of Saxony was obligated, by law, to show solidarity against "*wieder-*

38. For the Wettins see altogether Duchhardt 1977, esp. pp. 86–100.
39. See Seifert 1964, esp. pp. 79f., 83ff.
40. For the Saxon formation of traditions see Müller 2002, here pp. 5f.
41. See Robinson-Hammerstein 1992, quoted on p. 464.
42. General presentation in Müller 1997; summarized in Burkhardt 1998, pp. 4f.
43. Burkhardt 1998, p. 5.
44. Press 1994b, p. 70.
45. Quoted after Vötsch 2003, p. 182; the documents regarding the ancestral agreement p. 249, footnote 345.

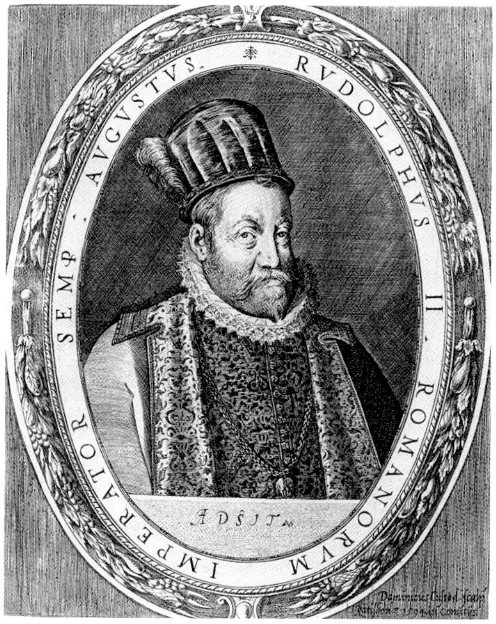

Emperor Rudolf II
Domenicus Custos, 1594
Copperplate engraving
8¾ × 7⅛ in. (22.2 × 18.2 cm)
Germanisches
Nationalmusem Nuremberg,
Graphics Collection,
inv. no. P 1802

wertige Unterthanen" (obstreperous subjects) in the Viennese phrase stipulating Dresden's obligation.[45] For Saxon history, the events of 1620/21 are indeed an epochal turning point. The economic threat resulting from the inflation of the years around 1620, the so-called Kipper- und Wipperzeit—those who changed money and either cut it (from *kippen* for cutting) or weighed it (from *wippen* for weighing)—was at least indirectly connected with current political and military events. But thanks to Dresden's politics of neutrality and its actions in Bohemia, true catastrophe did not engulf electoral Saxony until after 1635.

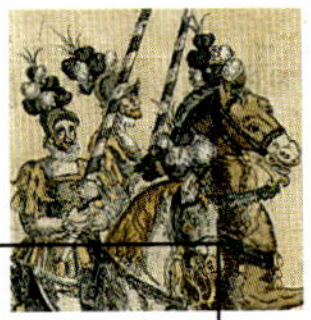

Giovanni Maria Nosseni and Art in Dresden, 1580–1620

Jürgen Müller

On January 16, 1575, Count Hans Albert von Sprinzenstein belatedly answered Elector August of Saxony's request for assistance in his search for a court artist qualified to execute somewhat delicate stonework.[1] August's query appears convincing because of the recent discovery of alabaster on electoral Saxon territory.[2] The count, writing that travel and political business prevented a timely response, proceeds to recommend his artist. While August had most likely never heard of him before, the artist's many reputed talents and abilities ought to have awakened the elector's interest. Giovanni Maria Nosseni, born in Lugano in 1544, had many things to offer: primarily his talent for sculpting in all mediums. He could make pictures, coats of arms, history paintings, doors, fireplaces, friezes, windows, and the like. He was a versatile painter who knew how to give objects their appropriate color. Sprinzenstein also praises Nosseni's art of portraiture, which he handled with great skill, fabricating portraits on canvas, in wax, glass, or other materials. Moreover, he was "an inventor of many amusing objects for masquerades, triumphs, and the like, and could be of service for carnivals and tournaments." The count goes on to say that Nosseni had agreed to fashion alabaster vessels, embellishing them with motifs. He concludes by stating that despite the artist's youth, his work is truly masterly.

There are two reasons why Count Sprinzenstein's communication is informative. It testifies to the qualities and talents of an artist who would participate in and influence life at the electoral Dresden court for more than forty years. The letter of recommendation also lists the work expected from an artist at a princely court in the late sixteenth and the early seventeenth centuries.

Court artists had to meet diverse requirements, many of which are only peripherally related to today's artistic issues.[3] The planning of festivities and triumphal ceremonies to which the court's letter refers calls for a knowledge of iconography, familiarity with court etiquette, and awareness of particular local and dynastic history. The court artist needed to have a general understanding of how to stage visually appealing material, both to please the invited guests and to meet the prince's requirements. An artist might even be involved in marriage discussions through his rendering of the prospective bride's portrait. He also gave advice in his role as counsel in art-related matters and negotiated the temporary hiring of other artists.

The terms of Nosseni's employment contract stipulate: "Most particularly, he is to perform all kinds of artwork, including sculpture, portrait painting, stone masonry, a sideboard of alabaster, supervision of building sites, invention of triumphal processions, masquerades, and the like."[4]

As events proved, Nosseni was a talented artist and art manager, who represented one of the few artistic constants within Dresden's court between 1580 and 1620 (the year of his death). Interestingly, this very time period, as well as the span of this exhibition, covers the reign of four Saxon electors: August, Christian I, Christian II, and Johann Georg I. A complicated, politically challenging era, it culminated in the Thirty Years War. Late-sixteenth- and early-seventeenth-century court art in Dresden is more difficult to characterize than that of Florence or Prague. Numerous artists active there left less distinctive marks than their colleagues in Florence, Prague, or even Munich. In this respect, Nosseni is exceptional. He is one of the best documented and studied Dresden artists of the late sixteenth and early seventeenth centuries. The elector August's search was driven by his wish to bring the splendor of the northern Italian courts to Dresden, and it has been observed that "with Giovanni Maria Nosseni, Italy's victory over Saxony was determined."[5]

And Nosseni was indeed a remarkable choice, as he had the necessary contacts to attract Italian artists, and he was familiar with the current art trends of his time.[6]

Born in the Ticino, the artist came to Dresden via Florence. It was not insignificant that Nosseni was bilingual, a fact pointed out by Count Sprinzenstein, who attested that Nosseni spoke fluent German with a heavy Austrian accent ("*der Teüttschen Sprach nach unnserer Österreichischenn artt zimblich khündig*").

Sometime in 1575 he was hired as sculptor, architect, painter, and director of decorative matters at an annual salary of 400 taler, with the additional stipulation that he explore, open, and exploit the Saxon marble and alabaster sources. For the latter project he received a special electoral privilege. During his more than forty-year-tenure he designed, among other things, furniture (see cat. no. 160) and plate; as building manager he was involved in all the important architectural projects in the residential city of Dresden; he planned weddings and processions, wrote poems and prognostic texts; and he designed and built the famous tomb for the house of Wettin in Freiberg Cathedral. That Nosseni willingly acclimated himself to the Saxon court is illuminated by the fact that within one year of his arrival, in 1576, he converted to the Lutheran faith. If conversion was not actively encouraged, it was certainly not frowned upon; Nosseni's was especially notable considering the brief period of time he had spent in Saxony.

Nosseni's Work at the Saxon Court

We do not know exactly what prompted August to employ Nosseni. Perhaps it was simply his thriftiness; although he had searched for a stone sculptor, he hired a generalist instead. Maybe it was the elector's realization that–in order to keep up with the leading courts of his time–he needed not only individual works of art but actually required an Italian court artist with managerial skills who was suited to master all tasks.

August was indeed able to put Nosseni to good use, as his son, Christian, married Princess Sophie of Brandenburg only a few years after Nosseni began to work for the court. Clearly, such a wedding needed to be celebrated appropriately and according to their station; this entailed knightly games with races and running at the ring as well as masquerades and processions. As Sprinzenstein indicated in his letter, Nosseni's artistic talents also included the organization of festivities, and it appears, that, as court artist, he accomplished these chores with particular success. Nosseni organized a four-day celebration with tournaments and masquerades for Christian's wedding. The events are documented in drawings by Friedrich Bercht and in Daniel Bretschneider's copperplate engravings.

The procession is led by Neptune (with his trident) and Andromeda (with a dragon's head) in a triumphal chariot drawn by three sea horses. Behind them rides the groom, Electoral Prince Christian, as Perseus, with a magnificent helmet and scepter. White wings are mounted on his horse's back, transforming it into Pegasus (ill. p. 36).[7] Next is the elector himself, dressed in the guise of a peasant and holding a rake in his hand, surrounded by forty peasants. He is followed by a harvest cart filled with piglets and a peasant bride who tosses eggs to the crowd. The elector, a personification of Saxon fertility and affluence, is followed by familiar examples of virtue and vice: the nude Bacchus, riding on a donkey, accompanied by the allegorical figures of Crapula (drunkenness) and Ebrietas (inebriation).

Following these allegorical figures is a boy on a pony who holds a flag painted with images of a book and a sword; they are references to the youth's need of training in the sciences and weaponry. This could possibly be interpreted as a typical Lutheran reference, implying a mandate from the sovereign that his subjects be educated.

1. I would like to thank Damian Dombrowski, Bertram Kaschek, and Andrea Kiehn for references and corrections.
2. Mackowsky 1904, p. 20.
3. About the court artist and his tasks see Warnke 1985.
4. Mackowsky 1904, p. 29.
5. Mackowsky 1904, p. 16.
6. About Italy's presence in Dresden cf. Marx 2000a.
7. Schlechte 1992, p. 83.

Procession on the Occasion of Christian I's Wedding
from: *Contrafactur des Ringkrennens undt anderer ritterspiel so uff Christiani (I) gehalten worden.*
Die fünfte Part
Daniel Bretschneider the Elder
1584
Colored copperplate engraving, gold heightening
approx. 9⅞ × 37⅝ in.
(25 × 95.5 cm)
Sächsische Landesbibliothek, Staats- und Universitätsbibliothek
Dresden, Mscr. Dresd. K. 1

Then follows Paris, accompanied by three goddesses; this is another moral lesson, since the Judgment of Paris was deemed a profound mistake that led to war and misery. The procession's impressive finale is reserved for the nude Diana and her nymphs, who stand in a basin. Actaeon rides behind them with the head of a stag;[8] the latter's fate, too, can be read as a cautionary tale for the ruler: Actaeon, as his punishment for observing the goddess bathing, was transformed into a stag and then torn apart by his own dogs. In the iconography of the time, he was considered a symbol "of a great master [...], offering an ear to those who flatter him only to be ruined by them."[9]

The procession comes to an end with the highlight and final chord of Diana, an allegory of chastity. Simultaneously, this figure expresses the great love the electoral court had for the hunt. Walter Mackowsky notes that Nosseni, when presenting his plans for the wedding to the elector, was put off with the excuse that "this is just the time to start the boar hunt."[10]

During Christian's wedding Nosseni had his first opportunity to demonstrate his expertise in organizing court festivities. In total, he was to give more than forty-four *inventionen* (projects) for Elector August and his successors, of which the costumes and carriages were

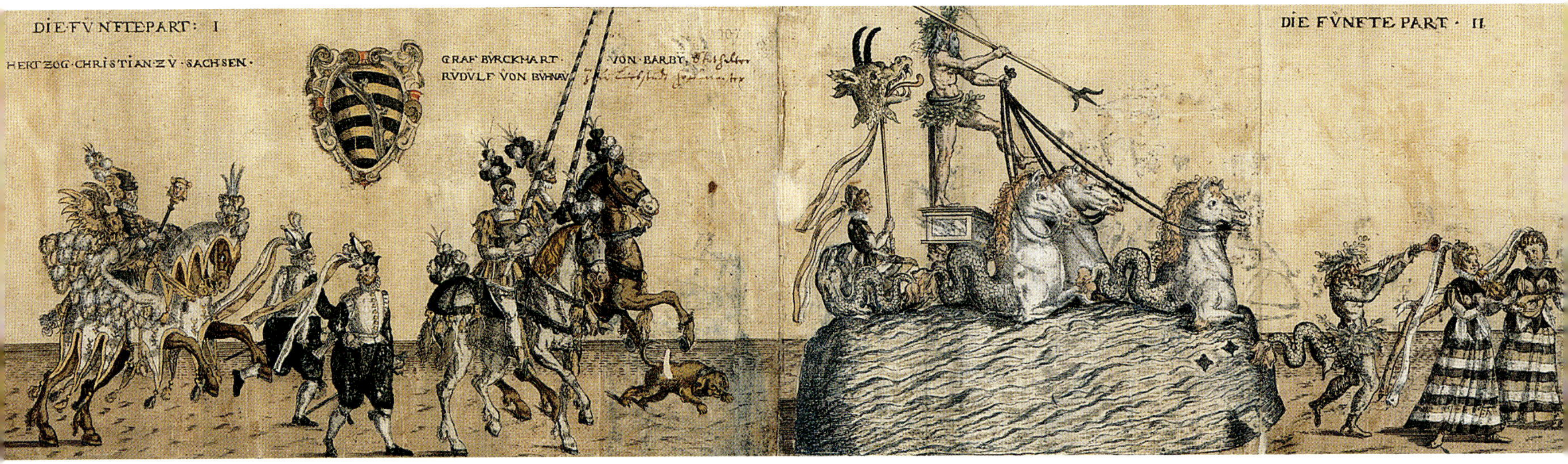

carefully preserved.[11] Nosseni can be compared to the North Italian painter Giuseppe Arcimboldo, who worked for Emperors Maximilian II and Rudolf II;[12] on every occasion, the Saxon court wanted to demonstrate its high level of artistic achievement to all, including the emperor.

Nosseni's fame regarding the inventions and the festive processions was spread beyond Saxon borders by the guests who were present. As a consequence, the artist was occasionally given leave by the Saxon court to design processions elsewhere. For example, he carried out commissions for Landgrave Ludwig V of Hesse and furnished designs for a festive procession for the coronation of Christian IV of Denmark.

Popular as Nosseni had become, based on his festival designs, it was not until later in his career that he produced works of European rank. Although the artist had offered to submit architectural designs of various types in 1581, it was only Elector Christian I who finally took him up on the offer. His architectural oeuvre is comprised of five works in which he either participated or for which he was solely responsible: the bow gallery of the Langer Gang (Long Corridor, ill. p. 72), leading from the Georgenbau to the Stallgebäude (stable building); the portal for the Residenzschloss's Kleiner Hof (Little Court); the Lusthaus (Pleasure House) in the recently erected Neue Bastei (New Bastion); the Pirnaisches Tor (Pirna Gate) furnished with an equestrian statue; and, finally, the tomb for the house of Wettin in Freiberg Cathedral.

Scholarship has documented to what degree Nosseni profited from his profound knowledge of Florence in these endeavors.[13] Almost all of his buildings take famous models as their point of reference, reflecting the aspirations of the Saxon Elector Christian I, a prince who had just come into power and who knew how to express his political ambitions in an artistic manner. Nosseni's time had come: from this point forward, he was required to demonstrate more than his engineering skills regarding mining and his ability to adapt to contemporary festival culture. Christian I wanted to compete with the most important metropolis of Renaissance art, "*quia altera Florentia visa est,*" as a Venetian visitor remarked as early as 1577.[14] The new elector's political policy was not moderate: he wanted to put the Saxon aristocracy and clergy in their places. Consequently, it was not long before the first of Christian's building projects was initiated.

In 1586, the year of Christian's accession to the throne, a vast stable building (ill. p. 71) was begun, having stalls for more than one hundred horses on its ground floor. On the luxuriously furnished upper story with marble floors were the living quarters, state rooms, and the armory, which were accessible to the riders via a ramp. The functional building, designed by Paul Buchner, cost no less than 130,000 florins.[15] Nosseni then suggested a connection, via a Long Corridor, of the stable building with the Georgentor (George's Gate) (ill. p. 72). In doing so, he resorted to Vasari's famous Medici Corridoio in Florence.[16]

The arcaded gallery also cites a quintessential Florentine idiom, such as that designed by Brunelleschi for the Ospedale degli Innocenti. Looking at the length of the arcaded portico makes the desire for elegant representation immediately apparent. This becomes increasingly evident upon considering that, along with the arcade, an interior courtyard was created that turned the connecting corridor into the tribune for the tournament field. The painted decorations, reflecting their courtly and ceremonial purpose, are not a pious Lutheran assemblage but instead a group of realistic horse portraits embodying the court's desire for representations of princely grandeur.[17]

The design for a gate leading to the so-called Kleiner Schlosshof (Small Courtyard, ill. p. 38 left) was also based on Nosseni's ideas.[18] The artist based his concept on the antique triumphal arch, in this case crowned by a tempietto on which the sculpture of Justice could be seen. The two-story edifice was built with a blind portico and terminated with a balustrade. Two trombone-playing genii to the left and right sides heralded the sovereign's glory, while additional sculptures, mounted on the architrave that was embellished with lions' heads, expressed further princely virtues such as faith and strength. This allegorical ensemble may be rightfully classified as pre-Baroque. The architrave, carried on four Doric half-columns, was itself a subtle translation into architecture of Fortitudo (Fortitude).

When one examines drawings of the original gate—it was significantly altered in 1725—the balanced harmony underlying Nosseni's design becomes evident. Apparently, the idea of moderation determined its form. One may even go so far as to state that the ruler's virtue of moderation needed no further personification because it was already expressed and contained in the architecture. Each formal peculiarity is added to and moderated by a complementary one. The rising vertical axis, leading through doorway, window, and tempietto, is counterbalanced by the stable rectangular shape of the building's form. A planar overall impression is counteracted by the protruding portico and the recessed tempietto, lending a sculptural silhouette to the entire portal.

From an iconographic perspective, the goal of the building was the regent's glorification, visualized by the keystone; it shows a pelican piercing its own chest with its beak—a symbol of Caritas (Charity), but in this context obviously also an allegory of the ruler, who, like Christ, sacrifices himself for his subjects.

The most important building project undertaken during the reign of Christian I was without doubt the Wettin tomb in Freiberg Cathedral.[19] When they converted to Protestantism, the Saxon electors moved their burial site from Meissen to Freiberg. It was here that Elector August had erected a monumental, freestanding tomb for his brother and predecessor, Moritz of Saxony, who was killed in the battle of Sievershausen in 1553. The monument, finished in 1562, shows Moritz in his armor, kneeling on a platform supported by bronze griffins.[20] With his electoral sword on his shoulder, he gazes upward beyond the crucifix, which was added sometime later in response to theological doubts vis-à-vis this innovative type of sepulcher.

8. Mackowsky 1904, pp. 87–90.
9. Translated from Schlechte 1992, p. 83.
10. Translated from Mackowsky 1904, p. 87. For references regarding Christian's exaggerated love of the hunt see Schlechte 1992, p. 82.
11. Schlechte 1992, p. 81.
12. Schnitzer 1999, pp. 118 and 308.
13. Cf. the basic essay by May 1992.
14. Dombrowski 1999, p. 110.
15. Cf. Syndram 2001, pp. 32–35.
16. This was pointed out by May 1992 in his study about courtly architecture under Christian I.
17. This important context was made accessible to scholars by Barbara Marx. Cf. Marx 2000a, pp. 17–19; about the Dresden "horse gallery" based on the model of Mantua's Palazzo Te and in connection with hippology and princely representation, see also Dombrowski 1999, pp. 119–23.
18. Cf. Syndram 2001, pp. 35–36.
19. Cf. Meine-Schawe 1992.
20. The first convincing iconographic interpretation may be found in Dombrowski 2001, esp. p. 245.

Although the initial plans and the first practical steps toward the creation of a larger burial chapel occurred during the reign of August, at this moment Christian had already been installed as coregent. In order to equip the burial place with bronze figures, the young elector sought the support of Francesco I de' Medici, through whom he hoped to secure the appropriate sculptor. The grand duke of Tuscany granted a leave to his own court artist, Carlo di Cesare, a student of Giambologna's, so that he would be available for Christian's building projects.

Nosseni was commissioned to transform the existing freestanding tomb into a burial chapel for the house of Wettin (ill. below). His initial plan foresaw the extensive remodeling of the choir that was to be extended to the length of the cathedral. This generously sized structure would have offered ample space for the tombs of future electors—"a memorial concept formulated with the future in mind," as Damian Dombrowski appropriately terms it.[21] However, this ambitious plan could not be realized: Due to Christian's untimely death, only a moderate, less expensive variant was built.

Nosseni's significantly modified plan foresaw the design of individual tombs for the electors and their wives within the choir. Together, they form a monumental burial chapel made of colored marble, alabaster, and bronze. The three-dimensional bronze effigies kneel between a pedestal level and a continuous frieze. Placed amid small pilasters and inscribed plaques, the sculptures—framed by the high markers and double marble columns crowned by Corinthian capitals—gaze toward the choir's top. There, the resurrected Christ carries his banner of victory and stands among the Virtues.[22] The stuccoed ceiling painting shows a dynamic Last Judgment. The monumental walls integrate both sculpture and surrounding architecture into a homogeneous entity. If one includes the stucco work and the painting of a powerful Judgment scene on the ceiling in this analysis, this is the first instance north of the Alps in which the boundaries between the genres of architecture, sculpture, and painting are subverted to this degree.[23]

Although there are no direct models to be found in Saxony for the Wettin funerary chapel, scholars have pointed out numerous connections with contemporary sepulchral monuments, among them: the Maximilian Tomb in Innsbruck's Court Church, Michelangelo's Medici Chapel in San Lorenzo in Florence, the royal tombs of the Valois at Saint-Denis, the graves of the dukes of Bavaria in Saint Michael in Munich, and finally the Escorial in Spain. With

Portal of the Residenzschloss leading to the Small Courtyard
erected 1592, significantly modified 1725
Engraving from the Weck Chronicle before 1680
12⅜ × 11⅝ in. (31.3 × 29.5 cm)
Sächsische Landesbibliothek, Staats- und Universitätsbibliothek Dresden

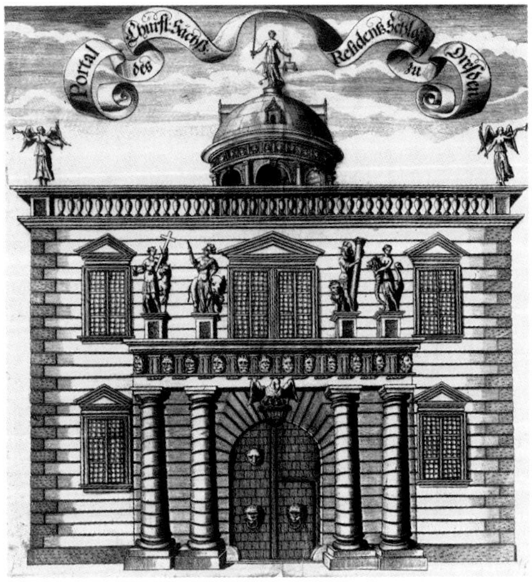

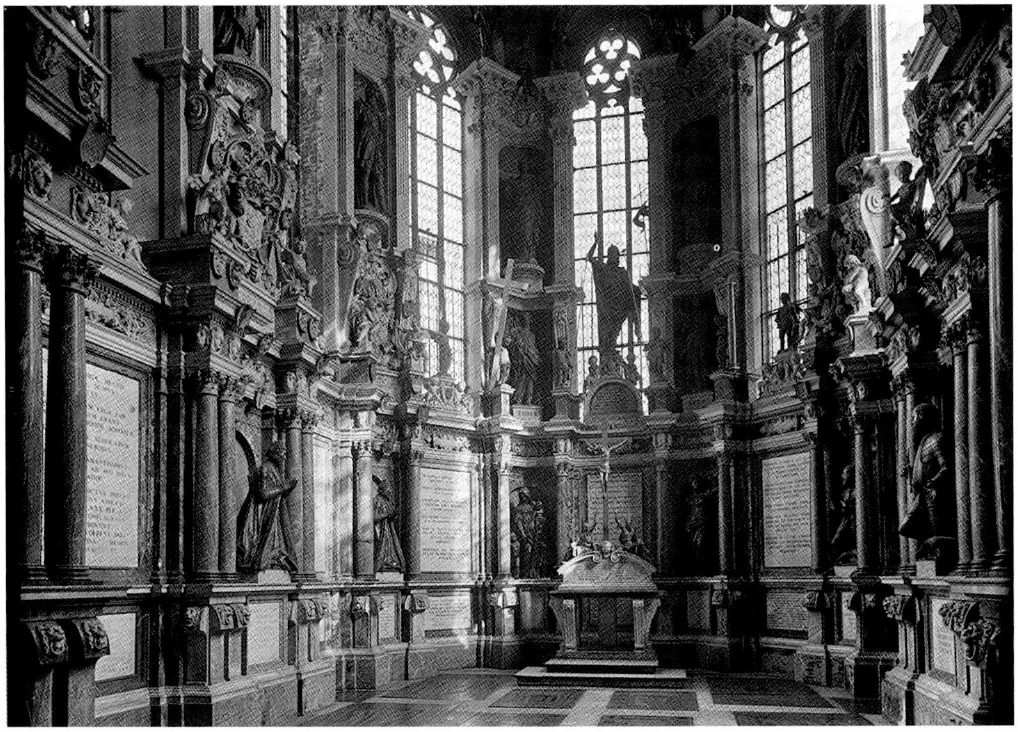

Electoral Funerary Chapel for the house of Wettin in Freiberg Cathedral

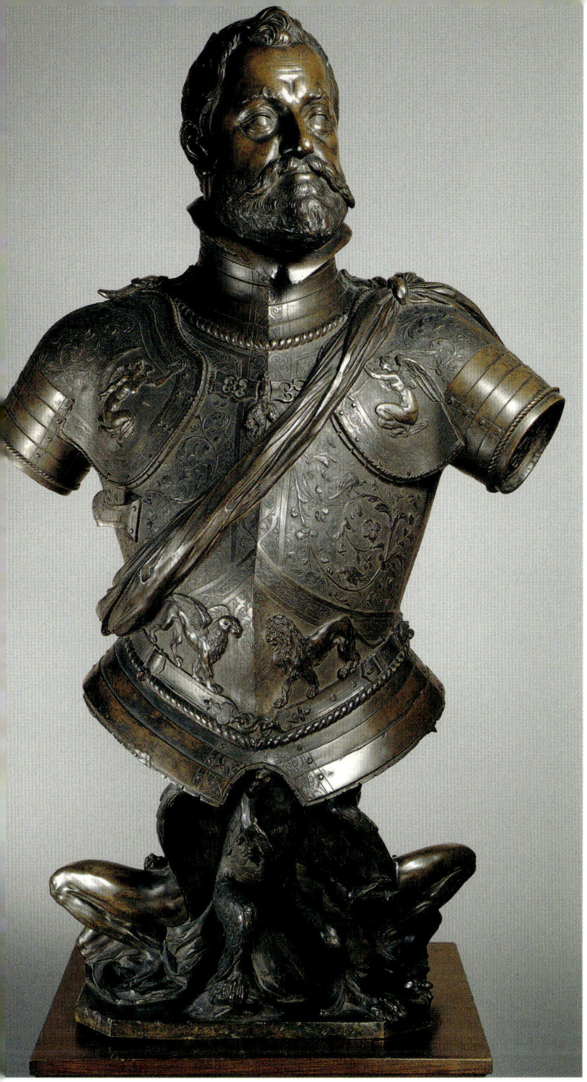

Emperor Rudolf II
Adriaen de Vries, 1603
Bronze, H. 44⅛ in. (112 cm)
Kunsthistorisches Museum
Vienna, Sammlung für
Plastik und Kunstgewerbe,
inv. no. KK 5506

his building project, Christian was obviously striving for the house of Wettin to take its proper place among the royal and imperial dynasties.[24] The exquisite memorial chapel demonstrated the superiority of the house of Wettin vis-à-vis the other six electors as a leading Protestant power. Nevertheless, the intention was not the development of an independent Protestant iconography but rather an appropriation of the royal symbolism used by the Catholic dynasties of Europe.

Although we have examined only three of the building designs that Nosseni devised for Christian I, it is apparent to what degree the representational power of art in Renaissance Dresden was recognized. Art served to create the image of the ruler that was propagated in court circles.

A bronze bust of Christian II sculpted by Adriaen de Vries (cat. no. 3) illustrates the degree to which a work of art can be an expression of political communication. During the regency of this elector (1601–1611), a clear orientation toward the Prague court is evident in numerous artworks.[25] Certainly the most obvious one is the bust of 1603, produced contemporaneously with the one of the emperor (ill. left), but given to the elector on the occasion of his visit to Prague in 1607.[26] The political context and the fact that the two objects belong together are obvious: Both sculptures follow the same design, with the figural base on a plinth supporting the bust. The use of a figural pedestal can already be found in Leone Leoni's bust of Emperor Charles V, but it is ultimately derived from classical antiquity. As is the case in the image of Rudolf II, the rendering of Christian II is also given an air of sovereignty due to the slightly extended position of his upper arms. And, like his imperial ally, the Saxon elector directs his stare far beyond the viewer into the distant regions that are inaccessible to mortals.

It is fundamental for the spectator to view the portrait both close up and from a distance. Initially, one recognizes only the aloof elector with his windblown hair, and then one notices the personifications on the pedestal and other details. The surface treatment of the Saxon sovereign's facial features is remarkable as it reflects every ray of light, thus seemingly transfiguring his head. Upon closer scrutiny, one distinguishes the personifications of Peace and Unity, from the emperor's perspective the qualities forming the basis for Christian's rule and the results of an Imperial-Saxon alliance.

Rudolf II needed a reliable ally not only in his fight against the existing Turkish threat but also against his own brother, Matthias, who had his own ambitions for the imperial throne. After the year 1600, numerous imperial gifts reached Dresden. Following an extended stay in Prague in 1607 Christian II is said to have left the city with presents amounting in value to approximately 10,000 taler.[27]

Italy as Model: Grace, *Sprezzatura,* and Wit

The art of Dresden's court was not alone in its obsession with Florence and Italy toward the end of the sixteenth century. This is particularly apparent if one looks roughly one hundred miles further to the southeast, to Prague. For the court artists of the legendary collector Emperor Rudolf II, the path to imperial service almost always led through Italy.

Painters such as Bartholomäus Spranger, Hans von Aachen, and Joseph Heintz the Elder, as well as the imperial sculptor Adriaen de Vries, were all highly conversant with the Italian art of their time. Although born in northern Europe, they completed their studies by travel or professional training in Italy. Because of their extended stays there, they were bilingual and remained connected to the current developments in Italy after their arrival in central Europe. An important source in this context is Karel van Mander's 1604 *Schilder-Boeck*, the first attempt to gather biographies of the Northern European court artists.[28] Through van Mander, we are relatively well informed about how highly regarded the Rudolfian court artists were. Sadly, he does not mention any of the masters active in Dresden at the time. According to van Mander, all the other Northern European courts remained in awe of Prague, and this was certainly because of the famous imperial collector who managed to install his legendary Kunstkammer there.

21. Ibid., p. 247; translated from the original: "ein auf Zukunft spekulierender Memorialgedanke."
22. Ibid., p. 241.
23. Ibid., pp. 256–57.
24. Ibid., pp. 265–68.
25. See Dombrowski 2000, pp. 73–76.
26. Müller/Kaschek 2001, pp. 3–16.
27. Berlin 1995, p. 442, no. 153.
28. Müller 1993.

A poem by Nosseni dedicated to the Rudolfian court artists Spranger and von Aachen has survived; written when both painters passed through Dresden, it was published in 1602. The sonnet employs customary topoi of art theory when it refers to the gilded chariot of Apollo, leader of the muses; the ancient artist Apelles; and the mountain of virtues whose summit artists are expected to reach.[29] Although some of this imagery is hardly original, the work is an important source because it shows above all the artistic self-confidence of Nosseni and his contemporaries. In addition, it testifies to the ties that existed between court artists from Prague and Dresden.[30] With Christian II's accession to the throne in 1601, the relations with the imperial court intensified. An increasing number of paintings by Prague court artists were acquired for the Dresden collection, and Spranger and von Aachen were greeted with enthusiasm when they passed through the city.[31]

Though van Mander slightly overstated the importance of Prague, his *Schilder-Boeck* clarifies the ambition of Northern European artists: While Italian prototypes were their models, it was also hoped that their efforts would equal and even surpass those of their Southern counterparts. Despite the fact that Italy was the measure and the model to be imitated, ultimately it had to be outdone.

Italian influence was not restricted to art alone. The courtly ideals of appropriate conduct in general were based on Italian culture. This is amply illustrated by the incredible success of Baldassare Castiglione's 1528 book *Il Libro del cortegiano*—a publication translated into numerous European languages and deemed exemplary more than one hundred years later.[32] In order to understand the fundamentals ruling late-sixteenth-century taste, one must look at the gifts sent from Florence to Christian I for his accession. Francesco I, grand duke of Tuscany, presented the new Saxon regent with three small bronzes by his sculptor, Giambologna: *Mercury* (cat. no. 146), *Sleeping Nymph and a Satyr* (cat. no. 148), and *Nessus and Dejanira* (cat. no. 147). The artist himself took the liberty of enlarging the series to include a Mars figure (ill. p. 270), his personal gift to the electoral collection. Together, these four works by Giambologna formed an important nucleus of Italian sculpture in the electoral collection.

This is an interesting episode, because it tells us something about the mindset prevalent at court. At the time, Giambologna was Europe's most sought-after sculptor; there was indeed hardly a single potentate who did not try to attract him to his court. Even Emperor Rudolf II was forced to make do with one of his pupils. Therefore, if the grand duke gave away three bronzes as gifts, this demonstrated his generosity as much as it underscored his own importance: He could afford to send such precious works of art.

In Florence, self-confident artists gave presents to their rulers. But this was calculated generosity because in return the artists expected equally noble gifts and remuneration.

Giambologna's *Mercury*—which won immediate renown—demonstrates the compositional problems of conceiving a floating figure. Its formal goal is to overcome the weight of the bronze, which the figure is supposed to nullify. While the divine messenger's hand points toward Mount Olympus, his right leg appears to be stepping forward quickly. Our eyes mediate between these two impulses of movement into different directions, and Mercury seems to be taking off, ever so gently, into the air. Such a design is paradoxical: it is dynamic, but it never ceases to exploit Mercury's inherent elegance.

Giambologna's bronze answers the art theoretical requirement of *difficoltà*.[33] Initially *difficoltà* (difficulty) challenged the artist to represent in art that which can only be rendered with a great deal of difficulty or skill. In the case of *Mercury* this meant a figure that—despite the bronze's heaviness—would appear to float upward. In addition, the connoisseur of 1600 was familiar with the famous High Renaissance artworks. Even if he had never set foot in Italy, the objects were still accessible to him via printed reproductions. An expert would have valued Giambologna's unexpected yet fastidious and aesthetically pleasing solutions.

The two terms *sprezzatura* (effortless ability) and *difficoltà* (difficulty) were among the most important aesthetic principles of the time. Equally fundamental was the artistic schooling of a sculptor or an architect, which would permit him to use history's successful works as his point of reference. What characterized art around the year 1600 was its goal of preserving aesthetic standards once they were achieved.[34] Consequently, the edu-

29. Johan Maria Nosseni, *Sonetti [...] fatti in laude et honore, della Serenissima casa di Sassonia*, Dresden 1602, no page numbers.
30. Cf. Dombrowski 2000, p. 84.
31. Cf. Schade 1988, p. 264.
32. Castiglione/Baumgart 1986.
33. Shearman 1988, pp. 20, 105–7.
34. For the interchange between *imitatio* and *aemulatio* see Krystof 1997, pp. 129–71.
35. For the artistic function of sixteenth-century figure fountains see Morét 2003.
36. See Marx 2000a, p. 28.
37. Henkel/Schöne 1996, columns 1829–32.

cated individual would immediately recognize, and was expected to identify, references made to works of art.

Imitatio Artis

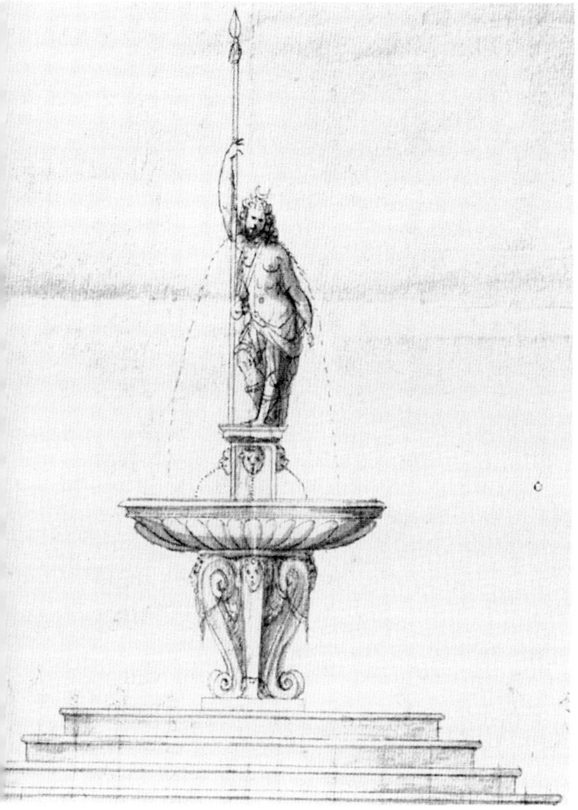

Fountain Design with the Figure of Diana
Giovanni Maria Nosseni
presumably ca. 1595
Pen and wash
Location unknown

A drawing by Giovanni Maria Nosseni of about 1595 is helpful in illuminating the process by which well-known works of art were quoted. As mentioned above, he was familiar with the greatest works of Italian sculpture thanks to his stay in Florence. His project for a fountain illustrates his supreme ability to incorporate Italian models into his work (ill. left). The fountain's basin, positioned over a stepped pedestal, is crowned with a statue of Diana. Four volutes, embellished with mascarons, support the basin. Diana is mounted on a base with water-spewing heads affixed to it. She raises her right arm and is identified as the goddess of the hunt by the spear she carries.

The composition is particularly elegant and is obviously intended to correspond to the elegance of Diana. The barely clothed goddess's posture is especially telling, as it demonstrates Nosseni's intention of synthesizing two of Giambologna's famous sculptures: the angled right leg refers to his *Venus Urania*, Diana's raised right arm is a quasi-paraphrase of his *Mercury*. Also, the design's overall format takes a Giambologna work as its model: the so-called Fountain of Venus, located in Florence's Boboli Gardens.

Nosseni's Diana statue is a *figura serpentinata*, displaying to the viewer, as one walks around her, an abstract vertical composition. The artist was clearly most interested in the sculpture's grace. Such a work always offers new, stimulating perspectives devoid of any oppressiveness for the onlooker. Nosseni certainly intended his fountain to be viewed in the round.[35]

In addition, the fountain offered an aesthetic novelty: the male spectator, at least, was identified with the ancient hunter Actaeon, who observed the bathing Diana and her nymphs. Hence, the sculptor implied that the male observer viewed the object with a certain licentious motive. The charade's irony is typical of late-sixteenth-century court art. Castiglione had a special fondness for irony, dedicating an entire passage of his *Libro del cortegiano* to the courtier's ability to make witty jokes. He went even further: the use of riddles, ready wit, lasciviousness, proper and improper jokes, true and false chastity, and mockery and innuendoes are all incorporated into his treatise. Castiglione's text draws the picture of the ideal courtier as *homo ridens* (laughing man) which does not mean that he simply knows how to tell jokes. Instead, he must prove his level of sophistication through irony.

In this context, it is appropriate to mention one of Nosseni's witty productions for the Dresden court. On the occasion of Johann Georg I's wedding to Magdalena Sibylla of Brandenburg in 1607, the guests literally devoured Italian forms: Giambologna's small bronzes were recreated in edible materials.[36]

Symbol and Conversation Game

As illustrated by a late-sixteenth-century piece from Nuremberg with Bacchus seated on a barrel (cat. no. 106), humor and drolleries were also important components of Kunstkammer objects. The god of wine had long been a popular motif, and this depiction's wittiness is grounded in the companion drunkard's corpulence. The fact that the latter sits with Bacchus, raising his vessel to his mouth, illustrates our ability to joke about ourselves and even to raise our glass to Bacchus.

The same topic can thus result in multiple interpretations: Emblematic devices proclaim that wine nourishes the spirit, and that wine has two different natures. Additionally there are warnings against the consequences of drunkenness.[37] Such varied meanings are intentional. As elements of stimulating and stimulated conversations, also known as *civile conversazione*, they go beyond the exchange of information: conversation itself becomes an art. Some Kunstkammer pieces encourage sociability. This does not prevent the goldsmith, Meinrad Bauch, from ornamenting the barrel with mother-of-pearl staves, identical to the ones a cooper would have fabricated from wood.

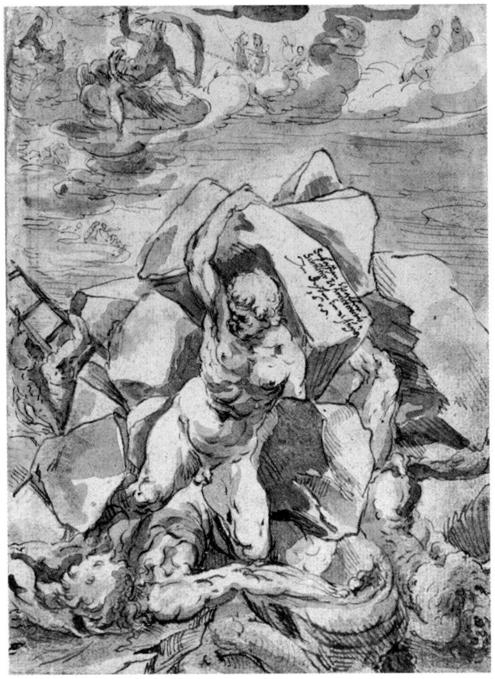

Fall of the Titans
Sebastian Walther, 1605
Pen and gray wash
10⅞ × 8¼ in. (27.5 × 20.9 cm)
Germanisches Nationalmuseum
Nuremberg, Graphics
Collection, inv. no. Hz 5137

As seen in a small Giambologna bronze from the 1580s today in the Louvre, drinking as a subject is also a typical court theme. Here, Morgante, court dwarf of Cosimo I, sits astride a barrel in a Bacchic manner. Rendered in monumental size, he can still be seen in the Boboli Gardens, providing amusement to this day.

Kunstkammer pieces were not supposed to leave people awestruck in admiration. This is revealed by three ostrich figures that could be used as drinking vessels (cat. no. 116). All three animals step forward, but only two hold a horseshoe in their beaks. The containers' bodies, worked from real ostrich eggs, were produced before 1595 by Elias Geyer of Leipzig. Their humor lies in the fact that it was almost impossible to drink from them without spilling the liquid. They are constructed in such a way that the fluid is released in a sudden gush.

Even though the ostrich receptacles were never used, their bizarre shape was certainly an entertaining topic of conversation at the table. A seventeenth-century observer concluded that the collected teachings on symbolism listed no less than five different interpretations for the ostrich carrying a horseshoe in its beak. These meanings stem from "Strength through resistance" because it was commonly believed that the ostrich, due to the high temperature of its stomach, could digest iron. Moralistic implications are at work if the ostrich is seen as an image of justice tolerating envy. Other emblematic sources cite the Lord's Compassion and the superiority of virtue.[38]

All these interpretations are possible at once and not mutually exclusive, but complement one another. It is possible that upon reaching for these goblets, people reflected upon the deeper significance of the animals. Once again, it is worth remembering how such works of art could induce a sense of community. Consequently, they were not intended to have explanation; rather they were tools to initiate stimulating conversation. Such entertaining features are incorporated into innumerable Kunstkammer works, ranging from simple drollery to sophisticated humor that would occasionally extend into carefree interpretations of the world. Regardless of whether mythological creatures or animals appear as symbols, their rendering in precious materials would not have prevented the viewer from searching for an interpretation.

The Formation of a Kunstkammer

One of the illuminating art theory documents of the time is Gabriel Kaltemarckt's 1587 text that offers suggestions for the arrangement of a Kunstkammer. Dedicated to Christian I, it outlines the ideal "picture chamber" while simultaneously making pragmatic suggestions as to how a Kunstkammer might be installed in a relatively short period of time and advising on how to inexpensively ship works of art purchased in Italy to Dresden.

While Kaltemarckt's text is of synthetic nature and resorts to Vasari's ideas concerning the fine arts, it is also instructive when quoting, in passing, anecdotes referring to artists mentioned in Pliny's thirty-fifth book of his *Natural History*. All that is known of Kaltemarckt is that he must have lived between 1579 and 1611 in Dresden, where his widow owned a house. Only a few drawings by his hand have survived, most of them based on Italian models.

His text is particularly interesting because it makes tangible the art theory discourse of the time around 1587. Joachim Menzhausen has pointed out that Kaltemarckt prefaced his reflections with a brief consideration of theological images, in which he attempts to do justice to the specific Saxon position.[39] In doing so, the author speaks as much against the iconodulic Catholics as he speaks up against the iconoclastic Calvinists, pleading for a moderate position, such as the one suggested by Lutheran theology and appropriate for the Reformation's country of origin.

Even if one has the impression that Kaltemarckt's position echoes the Lutheran one, at times applying identical terminology, the point of his thesis is different: his intention is to establish painting and sculpture as one of the "free" or liberal arts. His ideal art is thus an academic one, comparable to concepts first developed in Italy, that later ventured north into

Northern Europe. Rudolf II himself decreed, in 1595, that painting was to be elevated to the rank of a liberal art.[40] Kaltemarckt was clearly influenced by such ideas when he began to draw up a list of the most important artists, past and present, who might be included in an electoral collection.

The core of Kaltemarckt's statements envisions painting as a free art and stresses the exemplary nature of ancient art. He underscores this by reflecting on the *Laocoon*, the *Farnese Hercules*, and other great works of art, which should be used as exemplars by artists. In order to accomplish this, he suggests taking plaster casts[41] from ancient and modern works in Florence and other locations in Italy. In total, the canonical character of Kaltemarckt's text is worth emphasizing; it becomes apparent, for example, when he describes Giambologna as the greatest artist of his time.

Teaching by Exemplar

The Italian practice of *imitatio* was adopted in Dresden around the turn of the century and is evident in Nosseni's fountain design. Additionally, it is worth mentioning a drawing by Sebastian Walther, born in 1576 in Dresden, that possibly served as the frontispiece of a genealogical album (ill. p. 42). Walther, Nosseni's assistant starting in 1607, advanced to the status of "court *statuarius*" after the master's death in 1620.[42]

With its free rendering, the pen-and-wash drawing corresponds to the aesthetic standards of the time. The artist, revealing his natural talent, executed the sheet with visible spontaneity, thus following the Italian *virtuoso* ideal, also developed during the second half of the sixteenth century. The drawing's theme is the fall of the Titans, the expulsion of the primeval race of giants by the Olympian gods, as exemplified by Giulio Romano's ceiling frescos of the *Fall of the Giants* in Mantua's Palazzo Te, and, second, by the work of a contemporary of Walther associated with the Haarlem Mannerists, possibly Hendrick Goltzius or Cornelis van Haarlem. The choice of the subject alone reveals Walther's sophistication as an artist, since he makes references to certain famous images of his day. Seated on clouds, the gods can be identified: Zeus with his eagle is closest to the viewer. The artist sketched the deities furthest removed with minimal pen strokes. His main focus was the Titans in the foreground who are killed by mighty rocks. One of these unfortunates is already covered by stones, only his head and upper arm remaining visible, while another one is tumbling down under heavy rocks. The boulders, resting on the giant's shoulder, show his physical strength. It is hardly a coincidence that the artist chose this stone for the placement of his signature, which reads: "*Sebastian Walther/Schultur/Et Archettectus/Inn Dresden den 21. August/1605.*"[43]

Evidently, the ideal recipient of such a work of art was someone well versed in art theory: the central figure's posture is nothing less than a quotation of the *Laocoon* group's central figure. In doing so, Walther follows the *imitatio* teachings—of which Kaltemarckt was a representative—expecting the artist to transform generally established solutions into new compositions. However, while quotations were not to be immediately apparent, they were supposed to be recognizable upon closer inspection.

Kaltemarckt's dictum to follow established models corresponds to one of the major art principles that was followed around the year 1600. Art is not created from thin air; instead, it was considered to incorporate a corpus of significant artworks known at the time, whether they were ancient or Italian art of the High Renaissance. Starting in 1550, a greater awareness of international art may be noted in Dresden; this was the result of an increased, pan-European pressure to meet international standards. Kaltemarckt's *Unterweisung* (teaching) also relates the phenomenon in the second half of the sixteenth century of a noticeable growth of historicizing content within the arts, to which the *vitae* of Giorgio Vasari had contributed significantly.

Barbara Marx is quite correct when suggesting that Nosseni—intimately familiar with the current tendencies in art—was the catalyst behind Kaltemarckt's suggestions. At least it would be a curious coincidence for Nosseni—when he celebrated Elector Christian I, in a letter dated

38. Henkel/Schöne 1996, columns 806–8.
39. Gutfleisch/Menzhausen 1989, p. 4.
40. Nosseni also addressed Rudolf II, in July 1612, as a "Lover of the liberal arts"; see Lietzmann 1977, p. 205.
41. Here, the new availability of art, made possible by prints, is extended to the sculptural medium.
42. Schade 1969, pp. 19–21.
43. Schade 1969, p. 108, no. 130.

September 28, 1586, as the future supporter of the arts—to also mention the Medici collections and the idea of a Renaissance of the arts in Italy while emphasizing as well Michelangelo's distinguished status: These are all ideas that can be found again, one year later, in Kaltemarckt's publication.[44]

The Status of Painting

It warrants renewed mention that it was Rudolf II, who, for the first time north of the Alps, elevated painting to the rank of a liberal art. It can safely be assumed that this change did not go unnoticed by Dresden's artists. In fact, a 1592 drawing by Johann Kellerthaler (ill. p. 45),[45] *The Judgment of Paris*, is a telling example of the influence Prague Mannerism exerted on Saxon art around 1600.

After 1604, Kellerthaler was primarily active as an engraver of works by Nosseni and Kaltemarckt. However, the *Judgment of Paris* sheet reveals his independent treatment of contemporary art tendencies. In his drawing, the mythological event is staged in an ironic manner, pointing out the confusion that accompanied the pronouncement of the judgment. Paris, the Trojan prince, is seated under a tree near the right edge. He has already decided who among the three goddesses, Juno, Minerva, and Venus, is the most beautiful, as he hands the goddess of love the apple. The genius, however, approaching from heaven with the winner's laurel, is about to hand the wreath to Juno. The honor really ought to have been bestowed on her, mother of the gods and wife of Jupiter. Minerva, standing near the left edge of the picture and identified by her attributes, the lance and the Gorgon's shield, averts her eyes in anguish because of Paris' ill-fated decision. As goddess of wisdom she alone recognizes the far-reaching consequences of his judgment: when Paris is promised the unavailable Helen as his lover, the Trojan War becomes inevitable. Godfather Jupiter, presiding in heaven high above the scene, does not interfere.

Kellerthaler has staged the conflict in a manner that makes sense to the observer. His drawing not only "argues" via references inherent to the image alone; he also applies any number of quotations. His modeling of the female bodies, for example, is close to Spranger's style; likewise, Minerva's diagonally rendered eyebrows are a frequent Spranger motif. The most meaningful quotation can be seen in the composition of Paris, based on another deluded judge. His gesture is reminiscent of Federico Zuccari's depiction of a king with donkey ears entitled *Apelles' Defamation* (1572) that was widely disseminated as a copperplate engraving. Interestingly, in Zuccari's rendering too, it is Mercury and Minerva who mildly protest the king's immature judgment.

In this context, the question arises as to whether Kellerthaler also integrated a theoretical dimension into his drawing. He has used the encounter of Mercury and Minerva, characters required by the story, in order to subtly suggest that they belong together: Close inspection reveals a V-shaped composition that extends to the upper corners. It is most clearly marked by the attributes of Mercury and Minerva—i.e., the lance and the caduceus. Both deities are hereby merged, despite their spatial separation.

This connection points to the allegory of Hermathena, a combination of Hermes-Mercury and Athena-Minerva that can be seen as the ideal of European Mannerism. The divine couple may invariably be found in all important art centers during the second half of the sixteenth century—in Bologna, Caprarola, Prague, and Haarlem.

Our allegory epitomizes an academic ideal that tries to reconcile the beautiful form (Mercury as god of eloquence) with intellectual content (Minerva as goddess of wisdom). At the same time it speaks against the Reformation's devaluation of the classical Italian beauty of form.[46]

Kellerthaler's drawing testifies to the claim that the arts—symbolized by Mercury and Minerva—represent an alternative to sheer and disastrous greed—embodied by Venus—and that art, therefore, guarantees peace.

For more than forty years, Giovanni Maria Nosseni helped shape Saxon art. His eulogy states that he died on September 20, 1620. In evaluating his oeuvre, his works for Elector

44. Marx 2000b, p. 279.
45. Schade 1969, p. 64, no. 69.
46. Müller/Kaschek 2002, pp. 27–32.

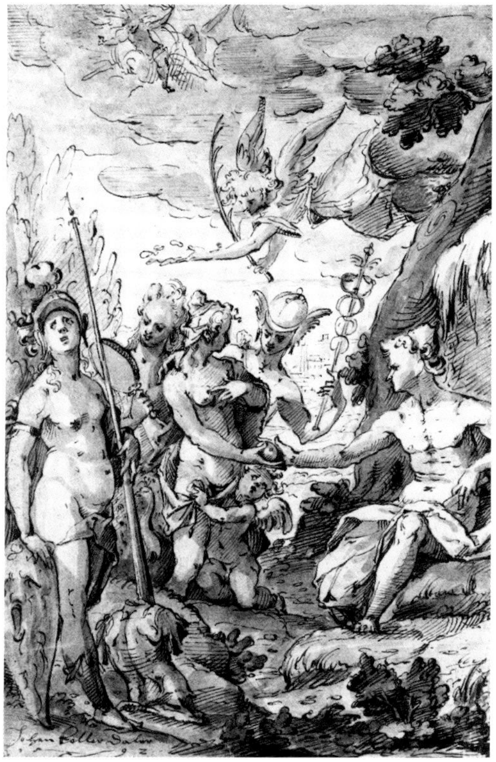

The Judgment of Paris
Johann Kellerthaler, 1592
Pen and black-brown
and brown washes
10⅜ × 7 in. (26.5 × 17.9 cm)
Wallraf-Richartz-Museum,
Cologne, inv. no. Z 242

Christian I immediately come to mind. Unfortunately, his creative standing among equals lasted only a few years. Nosseni's achievement, namely to familiarize Saxon artists with Italian art and thereby to function as catalyst for current ideas, cannot be underestimated. His influence on Kaltemarckt and the other artists of his circle has already been stated and demonstrates the thrust of modernity that accompanied his work in Dresden. Even at the electoral court, the *bella maniera* had indisputably been established. Although not a stupendous innovator himself, Nosseni is owed thanks for establishing art not simply as instructive but also as beautiful, in opposition to the latent iconoclastic ideas of his Protestant surroundings.

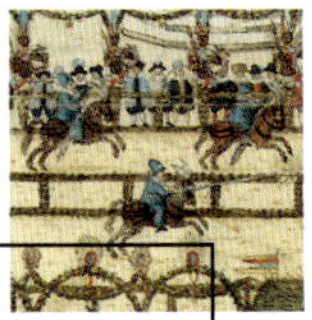

Festivities and Hunts at the Dresden Court

Jutta Bäumel

Dresden's profile as an electoral residence is based largely on the courtly festivities that were organized there by the reigning sovereigns. Wittenberg, the former residence, was soon forced into the background as a result of its utter lack of glamour. The celebrations reverberated in Torgau—once the city of the Ernestines and, thanks to the nullification in 1547 by Elector Moritz of the division of Saxony, one of the Albertine's new acquisitions—and Leipzig, Saxony's oldest and most important trade center. Because the Albertine family had only recently come to power, it attempted to legitimize its rule through a dynastic strategy centered on the cultural life of the capital, in this case the city of Dresden. The model they followed was that of the Medici family in Florence, who transformed their residence into a *Gesamtkunstwerk* reflecting their own power. The Saxons' success is reflected in the praise of Dresden as "Elb[e]-Florence"—*altera Florentia*—a term first used in 1577 (and kept alive in the ensuing centuries) by the Italian Giovanni Dolfin, bishop of Torcello, after his visit to the Saxon residence. Skillfully utilizing the political axis of Dresden–Prague–Vienna–Florence to their own advantage, the Albertines actively promoted these ties. Their efforts entailed the symbolic shaping of the residence with the participation of outstanding Italian architects (especially Rocco di Linar) and the dissemination of images of the city to a select audience.[1] While Dresden's distinguished skyline served as an easily recognizable icon, bird's-eye views and maps offered insights into military requirements and the elector's plans for displays of state authority, all of which were expressed conceptually in terms of spatial design. No less significant were the reports of the celebratory festivities held in the city itself. Events were staged and sights created for the delectation of guests who had come expressly to view them, and later to praise. The processions never followed the most direct routes. Instead, circuitous paths led, in cleverly arranged detours, to their destination. The sovereign power associated with the electoral residence is also displayed in the gala cloak obtained in 1611—the year of his accession—by Elector Georg I of Saxony as a Christmas gift from his mother (ill. p. 47). The knee-length, circular costume reveals along its edge an image of the Elbe valley executed in gold and silk embroidery. The electoral Saxon residence with its towers can be spotted, as well as all other state buildings including the Steinbrücke, the fortification with its guns, the city gates, the Residenzschloss, the stable buildings, the arsenal, and the Kreuzkirche. This is not an everyday scene but a regal and a festive one. The cloak's sea-green color can be understood as both ocean and sky. When wearing the coat, the elector was at the center of his own realm and absolute ruler of the universe.

The early Dresden court, while it created the impression of perpetual festivities, in fact made a clear distinction between the everyday and the ceremonial. Holidays were only partially tied to the church calendar, as court festivals were determined also by life in general and political events. Christian celebrations were held at court as well as in the church—in the Schlosskapelle, with Protestant services. They included performances by accomplished musicians and the court chorus and orchestra (Hofkapelle). For such events, the Netherlandish Passion tapestries were installed.[2] The festivities in the Schlosskapelle were paramount for all of Saxony and, by extension, for all Protestant territories of the Holy Roman Empire of the German Nation. In response

1. Marx 2000b, pp. 239–40, 256–57. The Dresden–Florence topic is documented extensively and discussed in Marx 2000a.
2. O'Byrn 1880, p. 24.

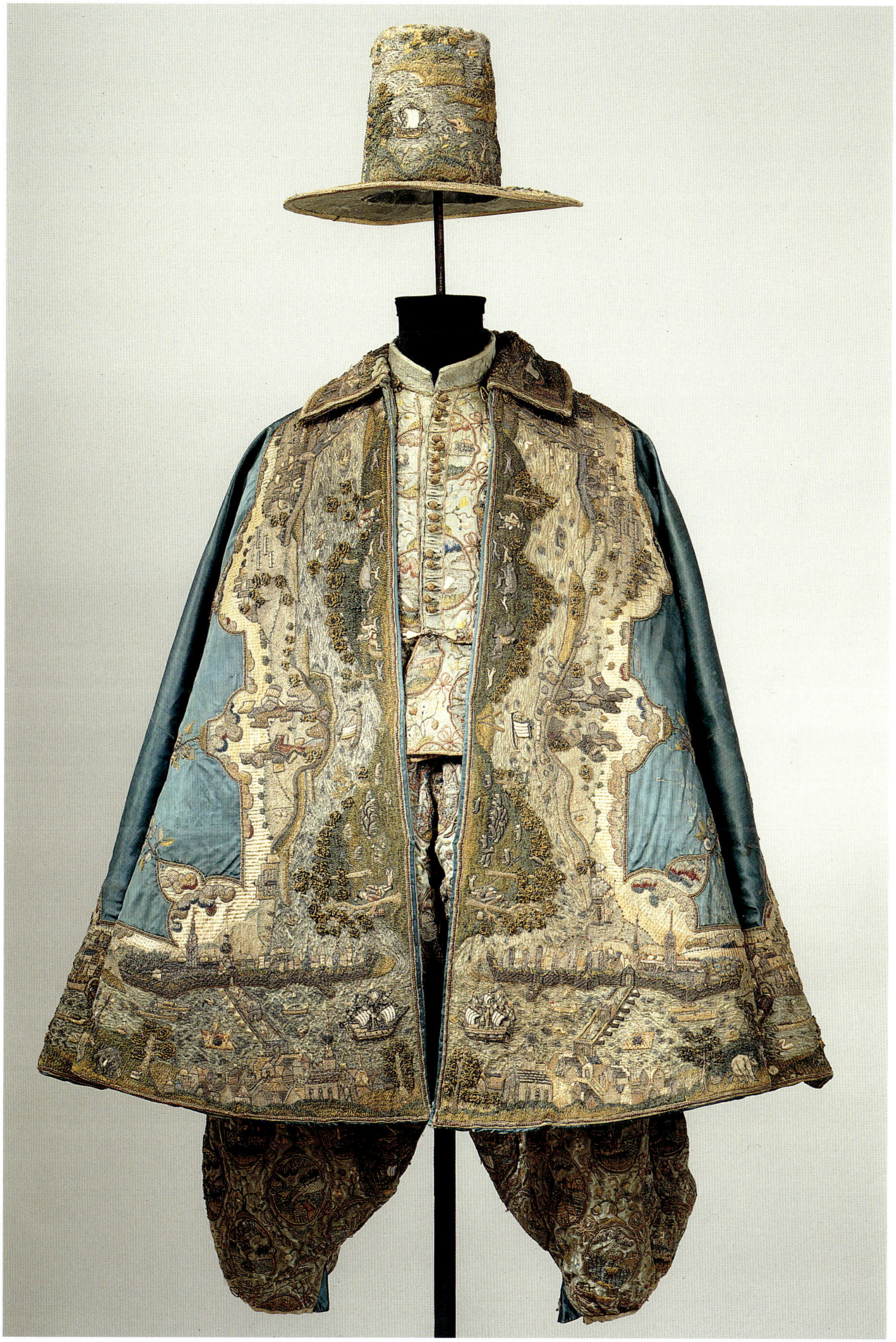

State Robe of Elector Johann Georg I of Saxony showing the Elbe landscape with views of Dresden and Meissen
Dresden, 1611
Embroidery: Hans Erich Friese: Green and blue-green silk atlas; gold and silk embroidery
Staatliche Kunstsammlungen Dresden, Rüstkammer, inv. no. I 8

to the widespread popularity of Shrove Tuesday, the Saxon electors established an annual court festival with masquerades. Nevertheless, court holidays were largely independent of church holidays as they followed secular events and hence did not have fixed dates. Two or three times each year, celebrations were held at court that extended over a week or more, and countless festivities on a smaller scale were held throughout the year.

Court Festivals as Governance

The presence of foreign imperial princes signified meetings of great import, with political ramifications and bearing on matters of state. Economic growth and the increasing pressure from the estates meant that princes had to negotiate and to jockey for their positions as leaders of society, and the religious battles that divided the Holy Roman Empire of the German Nation required that the solidarity of sovereigns be demonstrated by special alliances. In general, gatherings of foreign emissaries were called to mark dynastic events such as baptisms and weddings. The birth of princes secured the male succession and thus the continuation of territories as political and economic entities. In addition, royal births led to future marriages and chances for territorial expansion based on hereditary claims and the affirmation of treaties. Electoral baptisms and marriages were put to use accordingly, consolidating already firm associations or publicly demonstrating promises of further growth. Based on religious and political considerations, the Saxon electors, as sovereigns of the Protestant lands, repeatedly sought the union of their families with other strong Lutheran dynasties such as the royal Danish house or the electoral house of Brandenburg. The death of a ruler was always a critical event for subsequent domestic and imperial rule. With their participation in public mourning ceremonies–the wake, funeral, and obsequies–imperial princes or their representatives demonstrated official recognition of and amicable solidarity with the successor and political continuity.

Princes who were already allies also visited Dresden–even when no date had yet been set for a formal meeting–to underscore common political goals. Following the Peace of Augsburg (1555) the Albertine Saxon electors, with their representatives Moritz, August, Christian II, and Johann Georg I, advocated good relations with the imperial house of Hapsburg. To ensure internal stability and to defend against the perpetual Ottoman threat, the emperors–who were also the kings of Bohemia and Hungary (partly as dual monarchs)–sought backing from Saxony, with its solid politics and thriving economy. That a consensus had been reached was signified by mutual visits, as well as in lively exchanges of information and the presentation of gifts. Visits by the emperor, which entailed the presence of a royal entourage, were cause for Dresden's greatest festivals. The higher the rank of the visitor, the grander the festivities. To accommodate the host's desire to restrain the extravagances such gatherings involved, the visiting princes sometimes arrived incognito or agreed to private audiences. In 1575, religious issues as well as the inauguration of King Rudolf as future emperor drew the ailing Maximilian II to Dresden. Elector August did not disappoint his guest. After temporarily favoring Calvinism, which he now clearly renounced, a one-hour fireworks display was created that incorporated "*ein Bildnus herculis, wie'r die slange vmbracht*" (an image of Hercules slaying the serpent); added to it was this text: "*Wie hercules mit Feuer vnd schwert die slange vberwandt, also will der Kurfürst von Sachssen mit feuer vnd schwert alle Calvinisten ausrotten*" (like Hercules overcoming the serpent with fire and sword, the elector of Saxony will extinguish all Calvinists with fire and sword).[3] The year 1617 was the eve of the Thirty Years War in Europe. Convinced that his life would be cut short, Emperor Matthias brought King Ferdinand, his chosen successor, with him to Dresden as an expression of his determination that such a transfer of power take place.[4]

The Festival Program

The rank of participants determined the duration and expense of court celebrations. The length of a celebration depended on the arrival of the first prince and the departure of the last. Festivals under Elector August lasted approximately one week; under Johann Georg I some of them were drawn out for an entire month. The person with the highest rank determined when the main ceremony occurred. The other events thus were regarded as pre- and post-program. The *Einholung* (bringing in) of the princely visitors was followed by the events around which the ceremonies were organized—a baptism or wedding, for example, and the exchange of gifts. All this was combined with music, banqueting, dances, masquerades, processions, equestrian tournaments, fencing, shooting contests, peasant fairs, carriage and sleigh rides, fireworks, and, occasionally, performances by troupes of actors from England. The program was organized according to the preferences and abilities of the guests as well as those of the hosts, as well as events beyond state control. In 1607, for example, preparations for a wedding to take place in Dresden were all but completed when an outbreak of the plague necessitated that the entire event be moved to Torgau.[5]

Court Society and the Citizens

The majority of participants at the feasts were recruited from the electoral court. Directions were sent to the noblemen and court officials specifying how many horses and servants they should bring and the clothing they were expected to wear. This mixing of the nobility with civil servants may be considered the basis for the creation of the modern state. Apart from their military duties, aristocrats were increasingly expected to participate in cultural events. Instructions were given as to specific positions to be occupied in processions, as well as tasks to be performed in general. Clothing was uniformly black in color and more or less elaborate according to rank. While nobles were responsible for their own garments, the lower ranks received them from the elector. The sounds of a kettledrum and trumpet player signaled the beginning, middle, and end of the ceremony. Opening processions on horseback were held at the Residenzschloss and at the Schlosskapelle. The musicians were located in elevated boxes. The number of musicians assigned to any one official was designated by his rank. An elector could claim one kettledrummer and twelve trumpeters, whereas kings and emperors were accorded twice this number. At the 1602 wedding of the Saxon elector, two kettledrummers and twenty-four trumpet players were present. This presumably is related to the fact that the bride, Hedwig, was a royal Danish princess. The court bodyguards, likewise equipped with the Saxon colors and coats of arms, were in charge of the elector's personal safety. Present at all festivals, they rode on horseback or flanked the electoral entourage on foot. They also served as guards on the palace grounds. The artillery, on alert at the fortifications, would salute each of the guests in greeting. Among the visitors, local citizens formed the majority. For each court ceremony, the cities of the electorate were summoned to send citizen soldiers to the residence. For the wedding of 1602, the number of soldiers sent from Dresden was 1,600, from Leipzig 200, Freiberg 200, Pirna 150, and Oschatz 150.[6]

Entries into the Residence

The elector customarily rode about one quarter mile with his entourage to meet his visitors. The *Annahme* (reception) occurred in the open and was accompanied by a short speech, the *Oration*. The magnificence of a ceremony that was about to occur was never more clearly indicated than when the principal visitor officially entered the residence, as this was the moment when all contingents of the participatory princes were brought together. The number of entering riders was the dominant factor in determining the importance of such an event, and the number of horses was explicitly listed in the printed accounts. For the wedding of Christian II in 1602, the number was about 1,500. The order of the procession was based on social rank, beginning with the princes and proceeding, toward the end of the parade, to the lesser officials. Princes of equal rank were placed side-by-side, with three making up one rank and with their retinues interspersed. Princes of different ranks proceeded in successive order with their own retinues. Only noblemen and high court officials rode in close proximity to the prince. With the exception of baptisms, a woman, regardless of her rank, was never placed ahead of an imperial prince in a procession. If she accompanied her spouse, a princess would sit in a parade coach, following the princes. Apart from the impressive number of riders on horseback, the magnificence of a festival procession was displayed by the considerable number of horses in parade armor, the *Handpferde* (near or led horses). For this purpose, the elector selected the finest of his own horses, which were then equipped either

3. Brückner 1866, p. 240.
4. For the visit of the emperor in 1617 see also for upcoming footnotes Avenarius 1618.
5. Bäumel 1993; Bäumel 1995b.
6. For the wedding of 1602 see also for upcoming footnotes: *Kurtze vnd doch ausführliche Relation vnd warhaffte Erzehlung von gehaltenem Beylager / Des Durchlauchtigsten / Hochgebornen Fürsten vnd Herrn CHRISTIANI II. Hertzogen zu Sachsen* [...] (1602), Jena 1603.

with new parade armor or with items already present in the armory. In 1602, Christian II arranged for twelve of his horses—adorned as *Handpferde*, with blankets adorned with his coat of arms—to follow the kettledrum and trumpet players. The addition of stately coaches in processions also began in the seventeenth century. Except for the coaches for the women, the carriages were without occupants during the entrance procession. It was considered unchivalrous, and was thus exceptional for a prince to sit in a vehicle while entering in a procession. Upon his 1617 arrival in Dresden by ship, the gravely ill Emperor Matthias was briefly greeted as he stood and was then carried on a sedan chair to his coach, while King Ferdinand and Johann Georg I entered, one after the other, on horseback.[7] Surrounded by Hussars, Ferdinand wore a Hungarian outer garment; the elector, accompanied by bodyguards in black and yellow, was dressed in green and sported a high hat. Once more, the carriage display was of the greatest splendor. In his 1617 painting, Daniel Bretschneider commemorates the emperor's visit, including the parade ships and creating the impression of naval power. In 1575, Elector August sailed by ship to meet Emperor Maximilian II, and in 1617 Elector Johann Georg I himself greeted Emperor Matthias in his own ship. The emperors had sailed to the Bohemian border with many ships and each invited an elector onto his own vessel. Afterward, with their united fleets, they continued on to Pirna, where they stayed the night, and thence to Dresden. It was customary upon entering the port to give a surprise display. The bride of Christian II floated down the Elbe escorted by objects powered by mechanical engines. These took the form of a whale, Neptune with four white sea horses, and Glaucos with a trombone and four sirens. On the occasion of the emperor's arrival in 1617, five artificial *Meerwunder* (sea wonders) suddenly appeared on the river. The cannons on the fortification fired salute mortars, signaling the safe arrival of the guests. From the residence tower and from the Kreuzkirche, trumpeters added their welcome.[8]

Equestrian Games and Shooting Contests

For tournaments, the appearance of princes and the noblemen on horseback was crucial in demonstrating their claim to military leadership, which derived from their rank as knights. The only times tournaments were cancelled were during the visits of Emperor Maximilian II (who

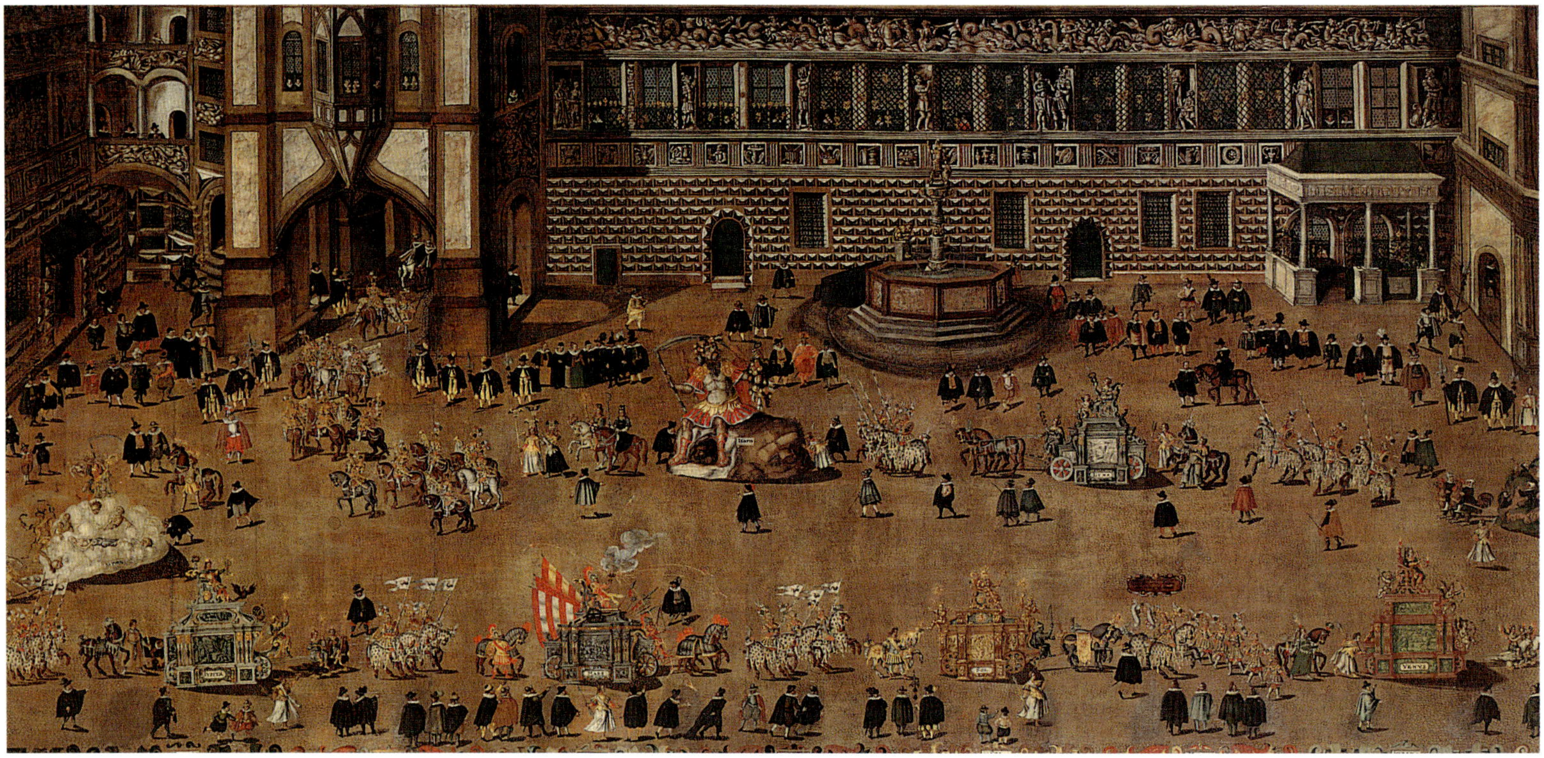

"Procession of Time and the Seven Planets" in the Dresden Residenzschloss's Grosser Schlosshof on the Occasion of Johann Georg (II's) Baptism on June 27, 1613
Daniel Bretschneider the Elder, 1613(?),
Oil on canvas
62⅝ × 100 in. (159 × 354 cm)
Staatliche Kunstsammlungen Dresden, Rüstkammer, inv. no. H 100

suffered from a severe case of gout) in 1575 and of Matthias in 1617; the guests' participation in the games would have been interpreted as a knightly offense. During tournaments, which were considered romantic equestrian diversions, riders demonstrated their ability to handle lance and sword, the knight's status symbols. The equestrian games always followed the same basic scheme: the *Mantenedoren* (the place keepers or defenders) were challenged by the *Aventuriern* (the moving equestrian warriors). The host princes usually claimed the role of the *Mantenedoren* for themselves. Published in a *Cartel*, the tournament rules were incorporated into dramatic scenes and recited by heralds in public. The dangerous encounters between cavaliers—the German joust of peace (*Deutsches Gestech*) and joust of war (*Scharfrennen*), which involved colliding with one's opponent and "*aus dem Sattel zu rennen*" (knocking him out of the saddle)—were gradually replaced by less harmful, more sporting events. In 1566, Elector August performed in the last of his fifty-five public jousts of war. He adapted the tilt (*Welsches Gestech or Pallienrennen*), an Italian joust of peace, in which the lance had to be broken on the armor of the opponent, who was from the court of the emperor (see also cat. no. 16). At approximately the same time, about 1560, he introduced the running at the ring, in which the participants no longer faced each other but raced in turn toward a ring suspended between two columns and attempted to grasp it. The ring, divided into small segments, had to be struck with the lance and then carried away (ill. p. 52 bottom). Victory was determined by the type and number of strikes, and the competitors were no longer required to wear armor. For the running at the quintain, horsemen (here, armored) also attacked goals with their lances. They aimed at a moveable wooden figure (quintain) dressed as a foreigner, most often a Turk. If the knight missed the figure and did not pass it quickly enough, the figure would be spun around and would strike him. In 1582, the foot tournament—it could be performed both indoors and outside—was incorporated into the program of equestrian games (see also cat. no. 221).[9] In this case, wreaths or silver vessels were bestowed on the victorious contestants. The number of strikes did not alone make one a winner; just as important was *Zierlichkeit* (composure and posture) while performing. Because the running at the ring was carried out without armor, there were unlimited possibilities for disguising horse and rider, and prizes were awarded for the best mask. Other disciplines not included in the traditional knightly contests were the foot tournament, and shooting contests with crossbows and firearms. Corresponding to their significance for modern warfare and the hunt, these weapons' exercises were permanently incorporated not only into festivities at court but also at those in the cities, at shooting-club matches over which the elector also presided.

Processions with Inventions

The activities of the Italian artist Giovanni Maria Nosseni for the electoral Saxon court made several innovative changes in the masquerade tournament, turning it into a veritable *Gesamtkunstwerk*. Employed by Elector August in 1575, Nosseni incorporated different art forms into the masquerade, including sculpture, painting, costume, music, dance, poetry, fireworks, and horsemanship, lending it programmatic and aesthetic coherence. Following the ancient prototype of the *trionfi*, their sole purpose was to glorify the sovereign. The wide-ranging topics of the masquerade scenes—from ancient mythology to the Old and New Testament, cosmology, history, and genre—were determined by the ruler and corresponded to his political, religious, and economic ambitions. In 1582, in a scene representing the Gospel according to John, Elector August, bearing a large cross, dragged the chained "crypto-Calvinist devil," signifying that he was the keeper of the true—Lutheran—religion. As manager of his farm at Ostra, his agricultural showcase, August dressed as a peasant and displayed his abundant harvest using a rake as his parade weapon. Wild peasant dances, performed at the same time, were staged by courtiers and intended as parodies of the courtly presentation. From these festivities developed the later peasant fairs—comprising processions, mock tournaments with straw armor and buckets, as well as women's contests—in which farmers from the elector's rural estates came to court to entertain. In 1582, Elector August filled the role of Mercury in a play, which included processions of miners, on the theme of Saxony's wealth in silver deposits. From these processions a tradition developed that is still alive today. Festivities on the theme of the planets were also held at the electoral Saxon court, with both the ancient and the modern worlds triumphantly entering Dresden. Here, the electors' roles were those of heroes, gods, and monarchs. Processions of

7. See also the painting *The 1617 Reception of Emperor Matthias in Dresden* by Daniel Bretschneider the Elder, Staatliche Kunstsammlungen Dresden, Old Masters Picture Gallery.
8. Pezold 1615.
9. For the wedding of 1582 see Dresden, SächsHStA Dresden, OHMA B, no. 1a.

"Abriß und Verzeichnis aller Inventionen und Aufzüge, welche an Fastnachten Anno 1609 [...] uff die [...] Rennbahne gebracht worden"
Daniel Bretschneider, the Elder, 1609
Gouache, 11⅜ × 20¾ in. (28.9 × 52.7 cm)
Sächsische Landesbibliothek, Staats- und Universitätsbibliothek Dresden, Mscr. J 18
above: **"Indian" or American Invention**
Triumphal chariot drawn by the elephants of a chief; with instrumentalists from the *Hofkapelle* dressed as "Moors"
below: **Elector Christian II of Saxony on horseback during a Running at the Ring in the Grosser Schlosshof**

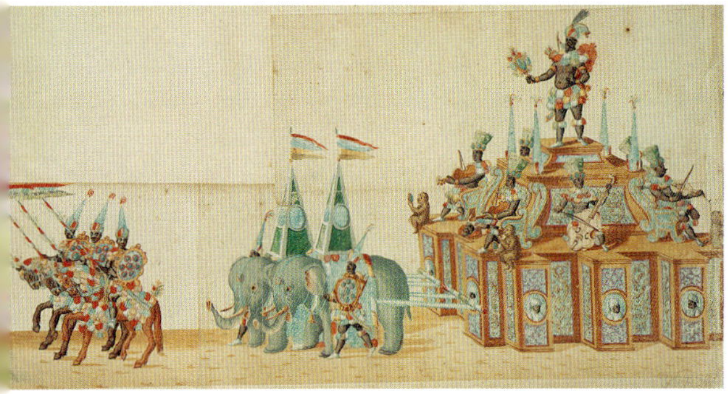

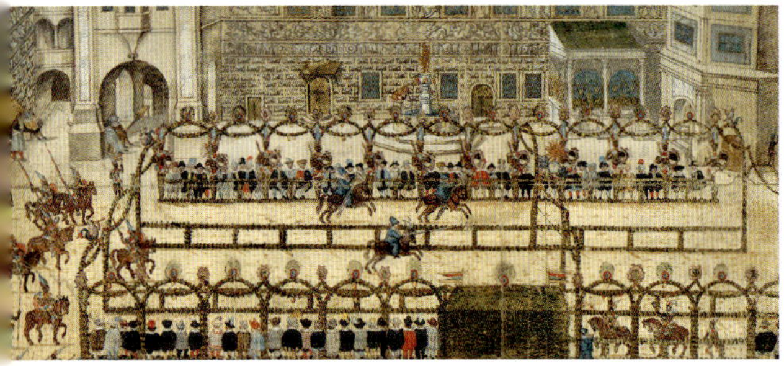

Janissars and Hussars—the military elite, respectively, of the Ottoman and the imperial armies—signified the Ottoman threat.[10] In 1607, appearing as the personification of the anticipated victory over the Ottomans, Christian II himself entered as a masked Ottoman sultan.[11] Dresden was also presented as a colonial power. In scenes with Africans and *indianischen* (American Indians), "savages" and "pagans" were presented as bizarre conflations of different ethnic types. In 1609, a triumphal chariot of indigenous Americans (*Indianer*) (ill. above left) was drawn by elephants. The "Indians," distinguished by their feathered costumes, are shown as dark-skinned Africans. The stout clan chief, positioned on the chariot's top pedestal, typifies the African ideal of beauty. Intended as a parody of the "world-upside-down" and as a reflection of cultural arrogance, the Native Americans, impersonated by court musicians, played fine instruments while monkeys with mirrors cavorted at their sides. In 1614, Johann Georg I, to present himself as a conquering hero, adopted the role of an African prince. Before Nosseni, most processions were composed of unintelligibly strung together stagings by different courtiers. But in 1613, Nosseni introduced a new thematic and aesthetic cohesiveness in the "Procession of Time and the Seven Planets," staged for the baptism of Johann Georg I's first-born son. In the procession, the assembly of gods, magnificently attired, were presented in ancient Roman chariots as they entered the courtyard of the Residenzschloss (ill. p. 50). It was not until the reign of Johann Georg II that similar aesthetic changes were made. The electoral sleighing excursions were often specifically tied to the Shrove Tuesday festivities and offered another welcome opportunity for invention. The masquerade sleighs followed the themes of the tournament processions (ill. p. 53). When a new snow had fallen, eight to twelve parade sleighs might be fetched from the armory to accommodate the members of the court who would sleigh ride through the towns and surrounding countryside, the bridle bells of the horses ringing brightly.

Pleasure Hunts

In general, it is fair to state that the electors attached great importance to the hunt, which they also considered a source of income, for while they cared for forests and fields, nurtured their stock of game, and enjoyed their personal outings, there was also a central administration that had to be managed. The hunts that took place during court festivals reflected these countrywide activities and used them as a thematic focus. At the same time, festival hunts were very different, as they were carefully staged. For example, hunting scenes that appear on the cloak worn by Johann Georg I show golden stags and lions (ill. p. 47), mirroring the exclusive hunt held during court festivities. The electoral hunting processions of the seventeenth century, which depict servants of the electoral hunters' office uniformly dressed in green, with hunting accoutrements, and accompanied by hunting dogs and the entire spectrum of Saxon game—boar, lynx, and wolf—took as their point of departure tournament parades of the sixteenth century. For the wedding of Christian I in 1582, hunters were incorporated into a spectacle for a running at the ring. They were "*grün und weiß angethan, haben hunde, Dachssen, Füchsse vnd Hasen bei sich gehabt, vnnd auff der Bahne eine Jagt gehalten*" (dressed in green and white, had dogs, badgers, foxes, and hares, and performed a hunt on the course). The year 1591 marks the date when—on the occasion of his daughter Dorothea's baptism—Christian I, together with Prince Christian of Anhalt, during a running at the ring, presented a demonstration of an electoral hunt, with hunting aids dressed in gray. Based on the "world-upside-down," courtiers appeared disguised as hares, abducting hunters and trying them at court. The "hares" pinned their enemies' heads on lances. During the course of the seventeenth century, the hunt pageants were separate from the tournaments and were held at the commencement of the court hunts. The latter were inevitably great successes for the visiting prince and the host alike, whether on the grounds or in the residence. Bears, stags, boars, and wolves were in enclosures and brought at the "appropriate" moment in front of the prince, who would be positioned under a hunting umbrella. In this manner, "they kill one animal after the other," notes an eyewitness at the stalk hunts held in 1617 by the emperor, the Bohemian king, and the archdukes on their way to Dresden. These hunts still had an element of excitement. In 1575, when the bear brought to Maximilian II by the elector of Brandenburg went out of control, the Elbe was a natural site for the water hunt. Large groups of people gathered on the fortifications to see the exciting spectacle on the opposite bank of the river near the Jägerhof. The water hunt that was undertaken for the electoral baptism of 1614 was painted by Daniel Bretschneider in a large picture for Johann Georg I with the Residenzschloss in the background.[12] When Emperor Matthias visited in 1617, the elector organized various water hunts—on the Elbe, on the way to Dresden, in the Residenzschloss itself, and near and in the Ottendorfer Teich. Hunts were also held in enclosed areas within the city—in the residential courtyard and on the Altmarkt (ill. bottom left). The game was chased through a corridor onto a square where trees and shrubs had been planted for the event and where cooling basins had been installed. Hunters ready to strike were gathered with their spears and dogs. The princes and the princesses followed the action from the loggias of the Residenzschloss or from tribunes erected in front of City Hall. From there, the elector himself would take aim at the game with his crossbow, as illustrated in a series of pictures illustrating a chase hunt on the Altmarkt in 1609. An account of the visit of Emperor Matthias, written in 1617, gives a description of how such an event was organized. The spectacle on the Altmarkt had numerous rounds. Cruelty to animals was a popular feature. In a sport called bruising, foxes and badgers were chased across ropes with the result that their bones would be broken. It was also customary to pit animals—bears, oxen, and wolves—against one another. As the culmination, the elector himself would proceed to the arena to kill a bear with his hunting spear. The hunt was then declared at an end (*abgeblasen*; literally, blown off or out). Confrontations with wild animals, sometimes integrated into chase hunts, were occasionally also staged as single encounters. In 1582, Elector August, who had built a bear pit and a lion's cage in Dresden, initiated a contest between a lion and a bull during the wedding festivities. The laconic note in the festival report states "*Der Lew hat gesiegt*" (the lion won).

Sleigh with "Astronomer"
from: "*Ein Buch von allerley Inventionen zu Schlittenfahrten*"
Daniel Bretschneider the Elder, 1602
Gouache, gold heightening
5⅞ × 15 in. (15 × 38 cm)
Sächsische Landesbibliothek,
Staats- und Universitätsbibliothek
Dresden, Mscr. Dresd. B 104

Animal Chase on Dresden's Altmarkt under Elector Christian II
Daniel Bretschneider, the Elder, 1609
Gouache, 18⅛ × 48¼ in. (46 × 122.5 cm)
Sächsische Landesbibliothek,
Staats- und Universitätsbibliothek
Dresden, Mscr. R 31

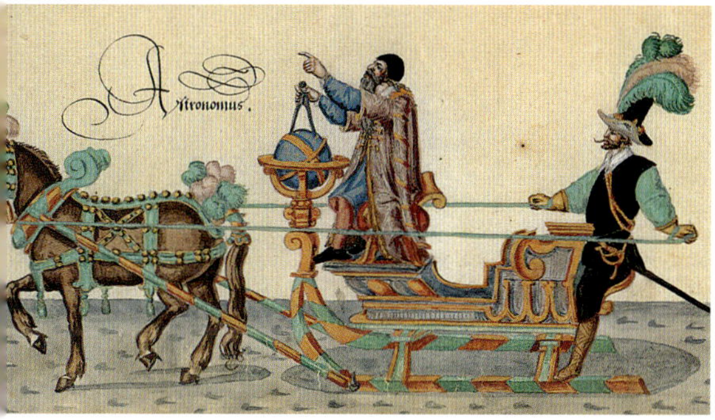

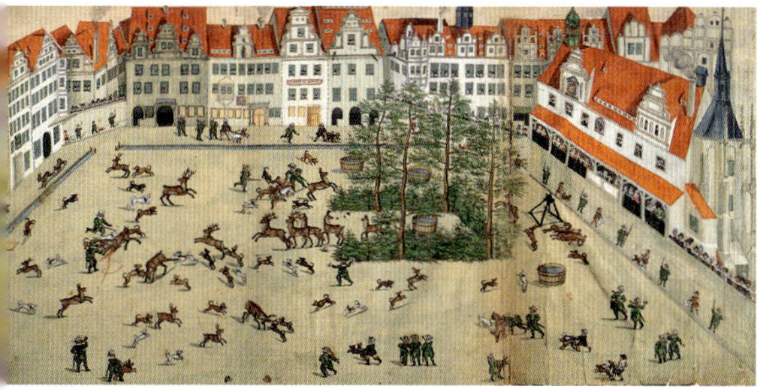

10. The topic is extensively discussed in Dresden 1995.
11. For Shrove Tuesday 1607 see Daniel Bretschneider the Elder, "*Eigengliche abkondrafagttur des Ringkrennen Welches* [...] *Christian the Ander Hertzog zu Sachssen* [...] *auff den Nauen stal renbanen an itzo vorgangen fastnacht Anno 1607, den 24. 25. vnd 26. Febrvarivs*," Dresden, Sächsische Landesbibliothek Staats- and Universitätsbibliothek, Mscr. Dresd. J 10.
12. Old Masters Picture Gallery, Staatliche Kunstsammlungen Dresden.

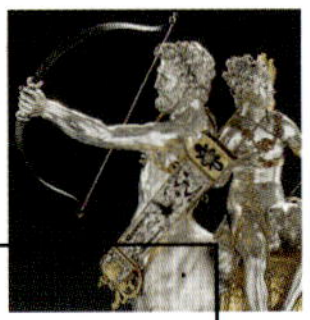

Princely Diversion and Courtly Display: The Kunstkammer and Dresden's Renaissance Collections

Dirk Syndram

In his first printed description of the Dresden Kunstkammer in 1671, Tobias Beutel was completely certain about the origin and age of this universal collection. The art chamberlain stated that the "*grosse und herrliche Werck der Chur-Fürstlichen Kunst-Kammer*" (great and magnificent creation, the prince-electoral art-chamber) had been founded in 1560 by Elector August.[1] Therewith, one of the most important attractions of the electoral Saxon residential city was assigned a birth date that is still commonly accepted today. The history of Dresden's Kunstkammer has never before been written. Nevertheless, an analysis of the archival sources and a detailed examination of the four inventories dated between 1587 and 1619 facilitates a portrayal of its inception and its development.

Inspired by French and Italian precursors, the Kunstkammer developed in the Holy Roman Empire of the German Nation in the second half of the sixteenth century. In the beginning it extended to only a few collections primarily belonging to a prince's domain. Within a few decades, until about 1600, the Kunstkammer came to represent the sovereigns' world view. The Dresden Kunstkammer was one of the first to bear this name. It was predated by the Kunstkammer of Emperor Ferdinand I in Vienna's Hofburg, first mentioned in archival documents in 1550. In 1558 the emperor commissioned an independent art building (Kunsthaus), Germany's first museum.[2] Almost contemporaneous with the space created for the collections in the top story of the Dresden Residenzschloss, Duke Albrecht V of Bavaria erected a Kunstkammer and royal stables building (Marstallgebäude) near Munich's Residenz between the Alter Hof and in the Neuveste (1563–67). The exhibition floor was largely completed about 1578.[3] Also initiated in the 1560s was the famous collection of Archduke Ferdinand II of the Tyrol, temporarily housed in the Kunstkammer of Schloss Ambras from 1576 to 1580.

"What Belongs in a Kunstkammer"

Few sixteenth-century sources deal with the Kunstkammer as a collection type. One title written in Dresden was "*Bedenken wie eine Kunst-Cammer aufzurichten seyn möchte*" (Thoughts on how to establish a Kunstkammer). This theoretical treatise and guide to collecting relates how Late Renaissance artists and collectors defined a Kunstkammer. The pamphlet's author, the largely unknown draftsman Gabriel Kaltemarckt, was likely close to Christian I when the duke was still an adolescent. Kaltemarckt's publication shows that he had a sound background in art history and knew Vasari's writings. Following his return from Italy in 1586, he presented his "*Bedenken*" to Christian I, who had just inherited the title. It appears that the artist intended to contribute to the most current discourse. He postulates that a well-equipped Kunstkammer ought to specialize in objects derived from three categories: sculpture and painting, domestic and foreign specimens originating from all areas of natural life, and everything made from the latter that could be transformed into drinking utensils or other objects "through nature and art."[4] The classifications used by

Kaltemarckt are still applied when trying to establish a systematic order in the confusing overabundance characteristic of these collections.

Princely Kunstkammers of about 1600 all contained objects originating from all areas of the known world and all realms of experience. The ideal of the Kunstkammer was the portrayal—as far as possible—of the cosmic order of the universe as created by God, i.e., to reproduce the macrocosm in the microcosm of the Kunstkammer. The part of the collection reserved for *naturalia*—i.e., the rare, noble, or unusual and thus "*curiose*" products of nature that arouse the observer's curiosity—represented the diversity, wonder, and abounding fantasy of divine creation. Coral and mother-of-pearl were exhibited beside minerals and crystals and taxidermized animals and their teeth, horns, and antlers. One of the important intents was to illustrate the expanse of the collector's territories and their economic potential. In the Dresden Kunstkammer this was primarily achieved through the inclusion of rarely encountered silver ore steps and sumptuous precious gems, as well as other stones such as serpentine and alabaster.

Kaltemarckt's publication separated painting and sculpture from the applied arts, but most Renaissance collectors treated them as one category since they were convinced that these were all products of human creativity or artistic dexterity (Kunstfertigkeit). Artists' dexterity and artists' products, known as *artificialia,* were the constituents that gave this type of collection its name: Kunstkammer. Today Kunstkammer pieces are considered those works created by human fantasy and virtuosity that are made of extraordinary natural products and are distinguished by great aesthetic and technical achievement as well as by impractical and unusable shapes. These objects without practical application served solely for contemplative pleasure and for the entertainment of the collectors and their guests. They embody the playful and intellectual qualities inherent in a Kunstkammer. Such vessels, pouring devices, drinking and board games, small boxes, and pieces of furniture were distinguished by the rarity and sumptuousness of the natural products employed, the degree of difficulty in working with the material, the plausibility of form, and the secret powers attributed to them. The masterful technical skill, inventive design, and subtle artistic rendering of these objects, rather attributable to the term art object than applied art, remains impressive. The creation of *artificialia* reached an intellectual zenith especially with regard to automatons, objects that combined the arts of the engineer and the goldsmith in an attempt to give life to a human creation. Connected with the exotic component of *artificialia* are *ethnographica*, not specifically treated by Kaltemarckt. Like the untreated or unembellished objects made of exotic materials, as well as "Indian," "Turkish," or "Moorish" objects—including Chinese porcelain and Turkish weapons—they speak of European exploration and conflicts with the Islamic world.

Only in the context of the foundation of Dresden's Kunstkammer does Kaltemarckt's emphatic segregation of instruments concerning music, astronomy, and geometry, as well as artistically embellished tools and machines, make sense. The artist does not see in them the work, i.e., the product of a creative process, but much more the means.[5] The means entailed *instrumenta* (instruments) required for the practice of the liberal arts or akin to them. Comprised in the *scientifica* were time-measuring machines as well as astronomical clocks, models, globes, and other scientific tools. Artistically designed implements such as crafting tools or even functional machines were more scarce in the holdings of Mannerist Kunstkammer toward the end of the sixteenth century.

A Collection of Sophisticated Technology

In the generation of princes to which August belonged, collectors were indeed interested in inventive and carefully designed crafting tools. His enthusiasm was shared by the landgrave of Hesse, the duke of Brunswick, the elector of Brandenburg, the king of Denmark, the duke of Savoy, and the archduke of the Tyrol.[6] Archduke Ferdinand II dedicated an extra *kasten* (showcase) to his iron tools, the seventh case in his Ambras Kunstkammer.[7]

The Saxon Kunstkammer, characterized more than any other through the highest achievements in the fields of craft and engineering represented by crafting tools, machines, and instruments, may even be said to owe its existence to this collection. The first Kunstkammer

1. Beutel 1672, [p. 42].
2. Kugler 2003, p. 210.
3. Seelig 1989, pp. 102f.
4. Gutfleisch/Menzhausen 1989, p. 11.
5. Ibid., p. 31. Kaltemarckt suggests keeping them closer to the library.
6. Moran 1981, pp. 260f.
7. Scheicher 1979, pp. 105ff.

inventory listed more than seven thousand tools and in excess of four hundred scientific instruments and watches, together constituting approximately 80 percent of the entire inventory.[8]

The collection's founder, Elector August, was a capable organizer, expanding and consolidating his territories from 1553 until 1586 and introducing an efficient administration. His practical inclination, his financial concerns, and his Protestant faith also shaped his collecting activities. Shortly after his accession he began collecting instruments for measuring time and distance, as well as technologically advanced instruments and machines. His first contact with Nuremberg-based Leonhard Danner in 1554, maker of cabinets and screws, appears to be related to these activities.[9] Danner, a renowned inventor of tools, was a key figure in the Dresden Kunstkammer, supplying functional, modern, and artistically ennobled articles over more than three decades; his contributions ranged from breaching tools to open doors, window grills, and walls to multipart toolboxes and an innovative wire-drawing bench (ill. p. 57).

The economy-minded August was eager to keep definitive specialists at his court. In this way, Danner's cousin, the cabinet- and screw-maker Paul Buchner, was appointed official Dresden court servant in 1558; he pursued a career there for decades, first as head toolmaker then as vigorous building master. In 1576 Balthasar Hacker, a student of Danner's, came to Dresden as screw-maker and toolsmith.

From early on, August tried to find a suitable watchmaker. In the same year that he negotiated about a master with the elector of the Palatinate, Hans Geber of Innsbruck was hired as his first watchmaker. Another of the elector's desires, namely to secure a capable art turner, remained unsatisfied for nearly twenty years, despite numerous negotiations.[10] The skilled craftspeople employed by the court were expected not only to produce display objects for the collection and to keep them functional but also to instruct the elector in the execution of their arts.

Even before the year of the Kunstkammer's inception, 1560, as mentioned by Beutel, an exceptional collection was being formed in Dresden. This is proven by a letter dated April 1558 and sent from the Saxon elector to Landgrave Wilhelm IV of Hesse thanking him for a clock with a torquetum, a sophisticated instrument for the measurement and observation of stars.[11] The landgrave harbored a passion for astronomy similar to that August had for supreme technological achievements. In 1560, August turned to Johann Humelius, a professor of mathematics from Leipzig whom he had put in charge of the first land surveys in Saxony. Now he asked him to obtain adequate bussols (compass dials) and compasses.[12] August's keen and tangible interest for land surveys is an important indicator for the fact that the so-called Reißgemach (literally, drawing room) on the fourth floor of the Dresden Residenzschloss's west wing was furnished around 1560; thus the foundation for the future Kunstkammer was laid. The Reißgemach served as August's study cabinet, for the creation of maps, and later formed the center of the Kunstkammer. In 1564, the elector commissioned Humelius's successor, Valentin Thau, to make odometers for carriages, and in 1565 he acquired, thanks to Danner's negotiations, an extensive set of tools from the famous goldsmith Wenzel Jamnitzer.[13] The technical collection grew after 1560, after Danner's inventions were procured: included were a set of turner's tools (1561), various scales (1562), and, as mentioned above, the famous wire-drawing bench (1565).[14] In the 1560s, the holdings were further supplemented by cabinet-making tools and other masters' astronomical clocks as well as numerous art and reference books.

The First Art Chamberlain

In 1572 Elector August employed the young David Uslaub as art chamberlain and the sole keeper of the Kunstkammer. He was supported by an electoral stipend and apprenticed to a cabinet- and screw-maker and thus had the same rare combination of crafts as did Danner and Buchner. His employment contract, dated March 19, 1572, outlined his duties:[15] in addition to practicing his learned trades for the benefit of his employer, he was put in charge of the keys and the Kunstkammer inventory including its astronomical, geometric, and other instruments, as well as the turner's tools, the maps, and the paintings. He was ordered to

8. Menzhausen 1985, p. 26.
9. Thieme-Becker, vol. 8, pp. 373f, keyword "Leonhard Danner" (Th. Hampe).
10. As early as 1556, he was looking for an "artistic turner/kunstreichen Drechsler"; see SächsHStA Dresden, Copial 277, fol. 36r.
11. SächsHstA Dresden, Copial 345, fol. 147r.
12. SächsHstA Dresden, Copial 300, fol. 261r–262r.
13. Wunderlich 1977, p. 56 and Engelmann 1914, p. 46.
14. SächsHStA Dresden, Copial 300, fol. 343r, Haenel 1914, pp. 39f.
15. SächsHStA Dresden, Rep. LII Gen. 1918b, Loc. 32961 (Bestallungen 1570–75), fol. 13r–14r; see Spitzer 1987.
16. SächsHStA Dresden, Loc. 7303/1 fol. 182r–183r.
17. See also the essay by Jürgen Müller in this volume.
18. See also the essay by Jutta Kappel on "The Art of Ivory Turning" in this volume.
19. The offer of the imperial antiquarian Jacopo Strada—who claimed that he had "assembled, up to twenty years ago, a kunstkammer including a library, that remains unsurpassed to this day within Germany, except for F. G. in Pairn" (*vor etlich vnnd zwanzich Jarn ein khunstkhamer, mit samt einer Liberey, zw samen gebracht, vnnd was gewiss, the heindtigs dags, khain Herr, the gleichen hatt im Deizlandt ausgenomen, Ihr F. G. in Pairn*)—was declined by August, despite rigorous efforts on the part of Strada; see among others SächsHStA Dresden, Loc.8523/2, fol. 181r–182r.
20. SächsHStA Dresden, Copial 440, fol. 112v–113r.
21. SächsHStA Dresden, Loc.8523/2, fol. 335r.
22. Menzhausen 1985, p. 69.
23. Regarding the reconstruction of Elector August's *Kunstkammer* see: Watanabe-O'Kelly 2002, pp. 74–84.

Wire Drawing Bench
Leonhard Danner
Nuremberg, before 1565
Walnut inlaid with various woods, etched metal and painted iron
L. 174 in. (442 cm),
H. 31⅛ in. (79 cm)
Musée de la Renaissance, Écouen, inv. no. 88CE5129

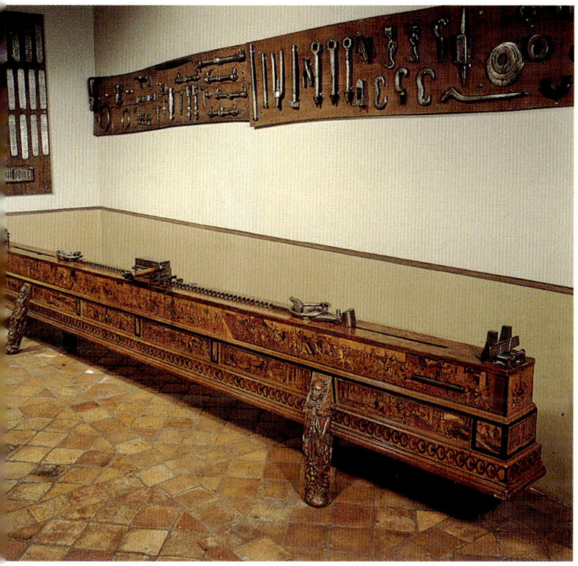

keep a list and record acquisitions and deaccessions, and to take proper care of the objects. Starting in 1572 Uslaub appears regularly in the court books, initially as attendant (Aufwärter), but soon thereafter as "commander" of the Kunstkammer. He was apparently justified in claiming in a letter dated 1595 that he set the Kunstkammer on its way ("*zu werck gerichttet*").[16] He continued in this position until 1615, working for forty-three years in the elector's service.

The years after 1572 were of pivotal importance for the further development of the Saxon Kunstkammer. The alabaster veins, discovered in 1574, along with the other decorative stone, serpentine, utilized since the mid-fifteenth century, led to the artistic turning of stone. Subsequently, various alabaster vessels were transferred to the Kunstkammer. Almost at the same time, Count von Sprinzenstein, envoy of the grand duke of Tuscany, helped negotiate a contract for Giovanni Maria Nosseni to be brought to Dresden.[17] Elector August hired the versatile artist in the summer of 1575. In 1576, with the generous approval of the duke of Bavaria, along with a powerful lathe, Georg Wecker, son of the Bavarian court turner, arrived in Saxony from Munich. This helped lay the foundation for the substantial collection of turned artworks, a feature that distinguished the prestigious electoral collection for all time.[18] Located above the Kunstkammer and connected to it by a spiral staircase, an ultramodern turning workshop was established, where August himself worked with his court turners.

First mentioned in 1572, the Kunstkammer appears with increased frequency in the electoral Saxon files. It was not comparable to the ones in Vienna, Munich, and Ambras.[19] August was familiar with these encyclopedic Kunstkammer collections: Their founders all knew each other, be it from meetings during Imperial Diets (Reichstage) or on electors days (Kurfürstentage), on the occasion of visiting each other in their respective residences, or through contacts between their courts. August was on most amicable terms with Emperor Maximilian II, his friend from youth, and with the Bavarian Duke Albrecht V and his son Wilhelm V, despite religious differences. He called Archduke Ferdinand II of the Tyrol his "*gutten freunde*" (good friend), supporting the passionate collector.[20] Saxon silver ore handstones were sent to Maximilian II and Rudolf II as well as the Bavarian dukes. The processing of serpentine, supported by Nosseni, resulted in many Saxon objects that were acquired by friendly or related dynasties that placed them in their Kunstkammers.

Within the empire, August functioned as the leader of Lutheran Protestantism, loyal supporter of the empire, militant enemy of a strengthening Calvinism, and diplomatic mediator in imperial political disputes. Beginning in the 1570s, this all led to increased contacts with Italian princes, especially the grand duke of Tuscany and the duke of Savoy. Initially this left the electoral Saxon Kunstkammer largely unaffected; it remained the elector's personal collection of technological objects: a place for the sovereign to retreat to—in good Lutheran tradition—to work actively as land surveyor, turner, cabinetmaker, or wire-drawer. But then the Kunstkammer began to become more of a Lustkammer (pleasure chamber), as the Leipzig professor of medicine Simone Simoni calls it in a letter dated 1577.[21]

Elector August's Kunstkammer

Uslaub's 1587 inventory, the first that survives, describes the organization and contents of the Kunstkammer or "Kunst stuben" (art room), another name given to it. Compiled for Christian I approximately eighteen months after its founder's death, it relates that the Kunstkammer was then made up of seven rooms in the top story of the Dresden Residenzschloss's west wing. The objects and groups of objects ascertained by Uslaub numbered 9,586. If one subtracts from this all items not in the Kunstkammer prior to Christian's reign, one comes very close to the original holdings.[22] Upon first sight it appears that the material was dispersed throughout all rooms without discernible logic, an impression confirmed by Uslaub himself. However, closer inspection of the first inventory in conjunction with the second one of 1595 reveals that the electoral patron did indeed intend a structured order.[23]

The Kunstkammer was reached by a stairway in the southwest turret, which went past the electoral rooms on the second and the state rooms on the third floors. On the top floor an unimpressive door opened onto a small shadowy antechamber (außwendigen Vorsaal)

250 square feet in area. In the beginning, this space did not serve as foyer but held display cases for clocks and measuring instruments. Pictures and a geneaological tree of the house of Wettin covered the walls. Beyond this area, entered through a latticed door, was a chamber more than 650 square feet in area whose usefulness was limited by poor light and slanted ceilings. This room's dominant theme was natural minerals, the exploitable *naturalia*. A table was covered with Saxon and Italian stone samples. Examples of south European woods were kept here as were maps of Saxon forests. Paintings of wild game, some showing bizarre anomalies, and numerous painted and prepared antlers gave this space its atmosphere. Hunting implements were kept in a green cabinet. There were also three functioning printing presses. In an account dated to 1587, the instruments and crafting tools already kept there were characterized as older and partly unusable. The model of a labyrinthine garden, as well as multiple plans for mills, sluices, war bridges, and fortifications, were also stored in these rooms.

Palace Model with Removable Floor Segments
View of the Electoral Kunstkammer,
Located in the West Wing's Attic (back center)
Paul Buchner, before 1590 (destroyed)

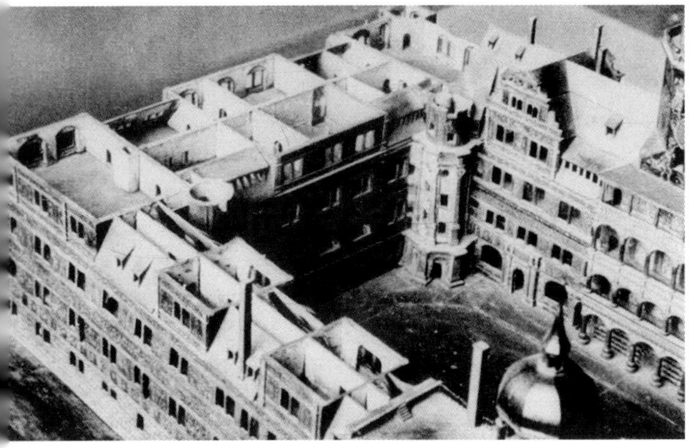

The next four rooms contained the collection's main spaces and were arranged in pairs facing the court or the fortification; two of the rooms measured approximately 450 square feet each, while the other two galleries were each more than 1,000 square feet. The theme of the first small chamber, located in front of the large room beside the ladies' room facing the palace's court ("*vor der großen Stube neben dem Frauenzimmer gegen den Schlosshof*") was the continuation of the courtly hunt. More than three hundred hunting tools were stored in two armoires. Another cabinet was filled with printed and drawn maps, city views, depictions of animals, and portraits of members of the house of Wettin. Placed on a round table were five models of Netherlandish fortresses. In addition, this small room also contained worn-out watchmakers' and cabinet-makers' tools.

Then followed the gallery "beside the ladies' room," accommodating the elector's cabinetmaker's shop, containing, apart from a carpenter's bench with apparatus, a vise, tools for fretwork, and a large tool counter, as well as more than one hundred smaller instruments for carpentry. In addition, August could turn agate and coin medals there. For the pursuit of the latter activity, a long table with special tools was supplied, in whose drawers minting stamps were preserved. The gallery was dominated, however, by the twelve-foot-long wire-drawing bench (ill. p. 57), today in the Musée de la Renaissance in Écouen, also outfitted with innumerable special gadgets and a tool armoire.

In two large cabinets were more than five hundred medical and surgical instruments, most assembled by Professor Simoni. Among all those finely executed and artfully embellished devices, two automatons—one in the shape of a ship, the other a gilt elephant—were the only objects with a true Kunstkammer character. They stood, along with three weight-driven clocks, on a long table. Further *artificialia* included a Netherlandish portrait with eyes that moved automatically and a satyr who could blow warm and cold water out of his mouth. Apart from various framed maps and antlers, two paintings hung on the wall with human faces made of flowers and animals. The furniture of this workspace, procured according to the elector's needs, consisted of a desk, two benches, an armchair, and a swivel stool with moveable desktop.

The "large back room" was the gallery facing the fortification, on whose walls innumerable tools were hung. In addition to technological masterpieces such as highly specialized breaching tools, these were primarily devices for cabinetmakers, locksmiths, and rifle makers, as well as large angle rules for land and mine surveys. This decorative bounty was supplemented by a workbench as well as nine large boxes containing hundreds of special tools for carpenters, locksmiths, and goldsmiths. Additional cabinets and boxes accommodated rifle makers' tools and devices required for the fabrication of fireworks. Extensive letter cases for book printing, an armoire with the elector's fishing rods, and four other pieces of furniture containing objects pertaining to horticulture revealed some of the collector's further fields of interest. In addition, the large back room contained the reference library with the numerous scholarly publications and art books that August kept within reach of his collection.

The *artificialia* appropriate for a Kunstkammer were presented on a table. They included almost three hundred pieces of tableware made of alabaster and serpentine. Two paintings presented the elector's Protestant principles, which were the basis of his Kunstkammer: they

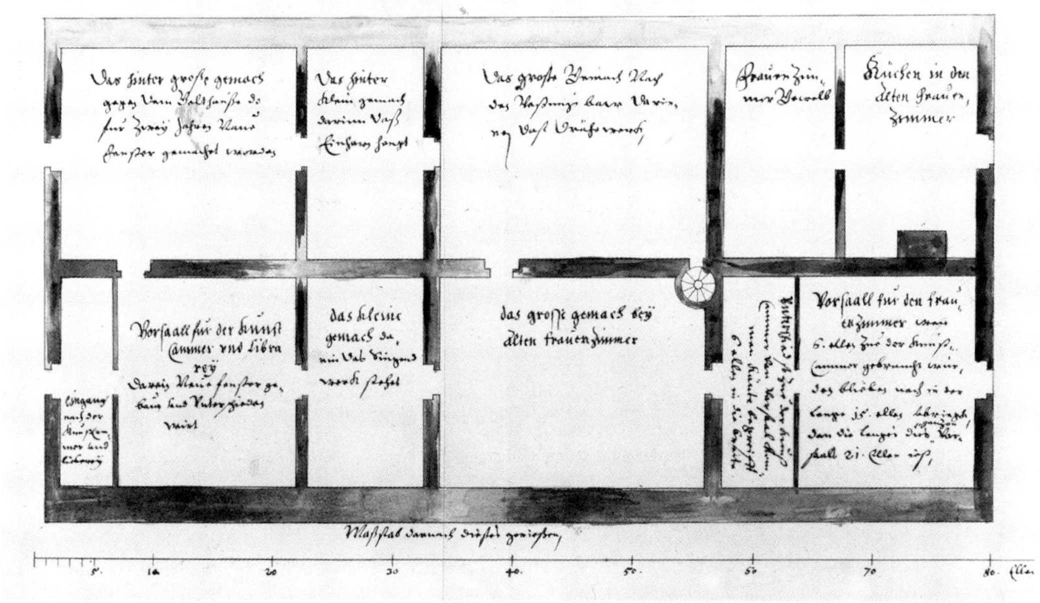

Ground Plan of the Kunstkammer, 1615 commissioned by David Uslaub
Pen and red and black wash
9½ x 17⅛ in. (24 x 43.5 cm)
SächsHStA, Dresden, 10024 Geheimer Rat (Geheimes Archiv), Loc. 7324/1, fol. 258

were *Adam and Eve* by Lucas Cranach the Younger and a depiction of Christ as Savior. A spiral staircase connected the large back room to the turning workshop located in the attic. The 1587 inventory relates that a tiny room, situated in front of the lathe studio, belonged to the Kunstkammer. A type of storeroom, it contained mostly old cases and tools.

The intellectual center of the Kunstkammer, however, was the relatively small Reißgemach next door. At a writing desk near the window, August produced maps of his territories. A dozen of them were framed and hung on the walls. Five additional desks offered space for drawing and surveying tools, horological devices, astronomical parade clocks, and astronomical instruments for observation and illustration, as well as a number of automatons. While the Reißgemach contained the tools that allowed August to measure his realm through the help of mathematics and geometry, it also housed astronomical instruments permitting the elector to speculate about the planets' orbits. In the Reißgemach, August's study, he kept, in addition to functional and used instruments, contemplative works of art such as the statues of the Times of Day after Michelangelo. A gift of Grand Duke Cosimo I of Tuscany, they presumably entered the collection before 1574, as may be deduced from a pencil postscript in the 1640 inventory.[24] The Reißgemach, a place of active contemplation, is thus comparable to the studiolo Francesco I de' Medici had constructed between 1573 and 1586 in his Palazzo Vecchio. The study also expressed through a worldly atmosphere such items as rock crystal works, presented by the duke of Savoy, and portraits of European rulers. Especially prominent was a silver-gilt writing table decorated with enamel, a gift to Electress Anna from Emperor Maximilian II when he visited Dresden in 1575.[25]

The 1587 inventory does not present a visitor's walk through the Kunstkammer; instead it begins with the Reißgemach, the Kunstkammer's center, going from there to the exit. This demonstrates that, under Elector August, the Dresden Kunstkammer's purpose was not to present decorative objects or to represent the ruler: its sole purpose was to serve the needs of its founder.

August, Humanist and Knight

Elector August did not limit his collecting activities to his Kunstkammer. He also added to other collections, some of which he inherited, adapting them to his own changing requirements. Among these were numismatic collections, presumably begun by Duke Georg (the Bearded) at the beginning of the sixteenth century. August added to them with foreign support, and thanks to the medal cabinet furnished by David Uslaub in 1573, he established an independent systematic order. Following contemporary humanist concepts, the Dresden coin collection united *historia* and *antiquitas,* i.e., a spirit of historic research and a love of antiquity. In addition, it contained contemporary rulers' portraits and coins from Saxon mints. The numismatic cabinet, together with the electoral library, may have originally been kept in Annaburg near Torgau, the elector's favorite seat.[26] In 1586, Christian I transferred the library to the Dresden Residenzschloss, installing it in the large southern hall in the west wing's attic. There, in direct proximity to the Kunstkammer, the elector ordered the new medal cabinet to be installed, containing at least a portion of the collection.[27]

The Kunstkammer, distinguished by its emphasis on technology, and the coin collection,

24. I owe thanks to Antje Scherner for this reference; see also the essay by Scherner in this volume, esp. footnote 6 with reference to the source.
25. Brückner 1866, p. 240.
26. For information about Elector August's library, see Watanabe-O'Kelly 2002, pp. 84–88.
27. Arnold 1995, p. 139.

as well as the library—extensive by the standards of the day—were culturally and historically significant but not essential to the elector's prestige. The Armory (Rüstkammer), on the other hand, with its splendid weapons and armorers' works, was integral to the electoral *repraesentatio*. In the beginning, the armor chamber (Harnischkammer) occupied space on the ground floor of the Residenzschloss's main tower, a functional installation along with the Large Palace Court (Großer Schlosshof), that was well suited for tournaments. An ambitious horseman himself who completed fifty-five jousts, August enlarged the collection of parade weapons, called the Rüst- und Harnischkammer since 1567, to such an extent that, at the end of his life, it had to be dispersed throughout the Residenzschloss.[28] On his succession in February 1586, Christian I used the considerably enlarged holdings of parade weapons while recognizing the opportunity presented by the collection for princely self-representation.[29]

Christian I's New Stable (Neuer Stall)

The twenty-six-year-old Elector Christian I was highly qualified for his duties, power-conscious, and independent, and he was willing and able to put princely splendor to good use for his political goals. The plan of adding a large, almost palatial stable building to the existing Residenzschloss appears to have predated Elector August's death; it would contain, along with the Armory (Rüst- und Harnischkammer), the Saxon elector's horses. This is confirmed by an inscription on the most important entry gate to the New Stable.[30] In only a few years, between 1586 and 1590, an impressive structure was erected, connected to the Residenzschloss by a corridor about 350 feet long. It served as an ancestral gallery for the house of Wettin, as a screen for the area used for knightly contests, and as a barrier between the Stable Court (Stallhof) and the city; it could also be used as visitors' gallery. The New Stable's ground floor had sumptuous stables for up to 128 horses. Located on the upper floor were museumlike spaces including the Sleigh Chamber (Schlittenkammer) and the Room for Tilting Armor (Pallienkammer) that served as a type of dressing chamber during tournaments. Numerous systematically arranged spaces were located in the attic: They included two Saddle Chambers (Sattelkammern), the Sword Chamber (Schwertkammer), the Electoral Chamber (Kurkammer) with the insignia of electoral power, the Feather Chamber (Federkammer) with sumptuous feather plumes, the Room for Mule Equipment (Maultiergegatter), the Turkish Chamber (Türkenkammer) with weapons, parts of tents, clothing, and armor of the Ottoman enemy, numerous Rifle Chambers (Büchsenkammern), and the Hunter's Chamber (Jägerkammer) with hunting apparatus. A suite of rooms located on the first floor, the Electoral Chambers (Kurfürstliche Gemächer), formed the ceremonial centerpiece. These spaces were arranged as double enfilades separated by a small room and then joined by a longer corridor. Their primary purpose was the display of two artificial mountains made of silver ore on which state silver goblets were exhibited in abundance, demonstrating Saxony's affluence (ill. p. 207). Twelve magnificent chairs (cat. no. 160) arranged around exquisite stone tables of Saxon rock had been located in the turret rooms. This furniture, produced by Nosseni for August, found a new home in the stable building. The Electoral Chambers' character was thus reminiscent of a Kunstkammer in that they demonstrated Saxony's riches. Christian I also seems to have intended for the spaces to be used for princely events and festivities. The Dresden stable complex was similar to such edifices in Munich and Prague, also taking Florentine architecture as a model. Christian demonstrated the same vigor, enthusiasm, and energy in planning this structure as he did in displaying property in the Treasury and the Kunstkammer.

Silver Chamber (Silberkammer) and Treasury (Schatzkammer)

A month after Elector August's death in March 1586, a silver plate inventory was compiled,[31] but it has been lost since 1945. An extant partial inventory of the Silver Chamber from the same year shows that the habit of keeping objects in the Silberkammer that really befitted a Kunstkammer—a tradition initiated under Elector Moritz—was practiced until Christian I's reign. According to this partial inventory, these lavish objects were stored in the back vault of the Silver Chamber, located in the Residenzschloss's Schössereiturm. Besides small works

28. Bäumel 1995, pp. 5f.
29. See also the essay by Heinz-Werner Lewerken in this volume.
30. The German translation of the inscription after Weck 1682, pp. 54f: "*Nachdem der Durchleuchtigste Churfürst Herr Augustus Todes verfahren / hat Herr Christian Hertzog zu Sachsen / etc. als ein Erbe der Chur: und anderer Fürstl. Dignitäten / auch als ein Liebhaber der Tugenden / dieses ansehnliche Hauß zur Stallung der Roße aufbauen / und darbey einen geraumen Platz zu Ritterlichen Übungen verferttigen und anrichten lassen: die jenigen welche so wohl ietzo / als auch künfftig leben / sollen Ihrer Churfürstl. Durchl. viel Glückseligkeit und Friede / so wohl alle Prosperität dero hohen Hauses / und langwierige Gesundheit wünschen / iedoch darbey gedencken dass iegliches Wolfarth mehr auf Gottes als der Menschen Beystand beruhe.*" (After the death of Elector August, Duke Christian of Saxony, as his heir and lover of virtues, mandated that this edifice as horse stable be erected. By doing so, a generous space for equine games and exercises was created. All people alive are to wish to the electoral majesty and his high house all happiness, peace, and prosperity, as well as health. But they ought to bear in mind as well that our well being is determined by God alone.)
31. O'Byrn 1880, pp. 30ff.
32. SächsHStA Dresden, Loc.235 Abt. XVI. No.1024. *Inventarivm Registratur vnd vorzeichnus aller Originall vorschreibungen vnd briefen, sambt anderer Fharnus so In the Churfurstlichen Sachsischen Silber Cammer zu Dreßden Im Ihare nach Christi vnsers Hern vnd Sehligmachers geburtt Ein Tausent Funf Hundert vnd Sechß vndt Achtzigk die Wochen Egidy befunden worden vnd Gregor Vnwirdt the zeitt Cammermeyster In seinen Empfangk angenommen*, fol. 42r–49r.
33. SächsHStA Dresden, Loc 894, Inventar über Schmuck und Silbergeschirr. Anno 1541 bis 1662, fol. 62–91. By citing the Emerald Cluster, the inventory mentions an object also listed in the Kunstkammer inventory of 1587.
34. Walther 2003, p. 50.
35. SächsHStA Dresden, Loc. 8696/12, fol. 374r–378r.
36. Gutfleisch/Menzhausen 1989, p. 10.
37. Dombrowski 2000, p. 76, footnote 78: Dresden SLUB, Mscr. Dresd. D. 68: *Beschreibung der Churfürstlichen Sächsischen Weitberühmbten Haubt Vhestung und löblichen Uhralten Residents Stadt Dreßden... Durch M. David Outtho Schürern Itziger Zeitt Gerichts-Notar daselbst Anno 1627*, fol. 63r.

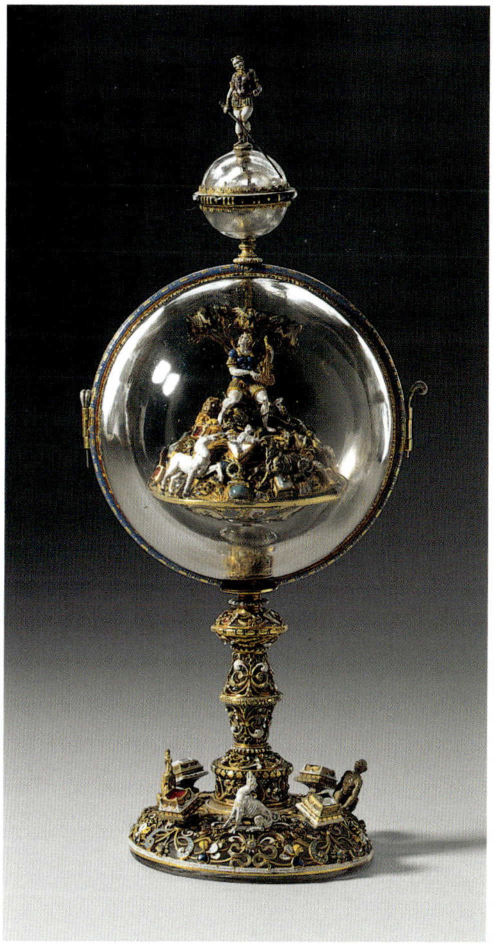

Sphere with Orpheus Making Music and Small Clock Work, so-called Orpheus Sphere
Stone cut and mounted South Germany, presumably Augsburg, before 1580
Glass, rock crystal, gold, enamel, precious stones
H. 8½ in. (21.5 cm)
Staatliche Kunstsammlungen Dresden, Grünes Gewölbe, inv. no. VI 19

of art made of precious materials and dynastic souvenirs, numerous rare *naturalia* are listed. They include mandrake, tortoise shell, "viper tongues," rock crystal, and coral branches, but most importantly the artistically ennobled silver steps made of concentrated ore.[32] Some of these handstones must have been transferred to the Treasury shortly thereafter, as they appear among the 1,144 entries of a Treasury list requisitioned by Christian I and apparently compiled before the early autumn of 1587.[33]

The compilation of this inventory may be connected to Christian I's conversion of the enfilade rooms in the west wing's ground floor. These had been used by August as dining quarters, garden hall, and banquet chamber but now became the State Vault (Geheime Verwahrung).[34] In April 1586 the new elector ordered that the coins of different currencies that originally belonged to his deceased father should be stored in the new treasure chamber (neue Schatz Cammer). The colloquial term for this treasury, Green Vault (Grünes Gewölbe/ Grunnen Gewelb), was first mentioned in the archives in November 1586.[35] The inventory, put together shortly thereafter, mentions the content of six cabinets; most of the material kept in them could have entered a Mannerist Kunstkammer as *artificialia*. The first cabinet contained mostly ore matrices; in total there were fifty-five matrices containing locally found semiprecious stones embedded in ore, among them a round, elongated artificial matrix that can only be the famous Emerald Cluster (cat. no. 162). Kept in the second cabinet were "little boxes made of silver and gold, also coral branches and other beautiful things" (*silbern and goldenen Kästchen auch die Corallenzinken und andere schöne Sachen*), and in the third "crystal glasses along with other lovely golden and silver items" (*Cristallen Gläser, samt andern schönen gulden und silbern Sachen*). The latter included—apart from the Orpheus sphere (ill. left), given in 1576 to the elector of Saxony by the duke of Bavaria—a large rock crystal sphere and a rock crystal flask, both from the Saracchi workshop. Altogether, there were 194 objects in the third cabinet; thirty-three of them were larger rock crystal containers. The fourth cabinet was reserved for turned agate objects, 350 in total. Cabinet five contained "silver-gilt plate" (*volgulden silbergeschirr*); it must have been a large piece of furniture, as 310 objects are mentioned, among them 140 vessels, many of them depicting drinking games, as well as coconut and ostrich-egg cups. It appears that this was also where the serpentine goblets that Nosseni designed were housed (cat. nos. 92, 93); they are early examples of purpose-free design. The sixth, and last, cabinet accommodated the much-venerated silver plate, a gift of the duke of Savoy. It is significant to note that the system at work here—taking the Kunstkammer of Archduke Ferdinand of the Tyrol on Schloss Ambras as its model—had no bearings on the new order of the Kunstkammer.

Acquisitions for the Kunstkammer

It did not go long unnoticed outside the court that Christian I intended to alter his Kunstkammer. Gabriel Kaltemarckt made a note to this effect in his text dedicated to the new ruler. He stated that the text was only written because he learned that Christian "intended to furnish a Kunstkammer (that still has gaps) ... to the best of his abilities" (*eine KunstCammer Welche noch mangelt*) [...] (*uffs beste anrichten zu lassen vorhaben*).[36] However, the changes Christian I undertook did not result in the radical effects suggested by the artist. But in his Dresden description of 1627—preserved as a manuscript—David Otto Schürner remarks: "The first Kunstkammer was initiated by Elector Christian in 1587" (*Solche KunstCammer hatt Anfangs Churfürst Christiann die erste Anno 1587 angerichte*).[37]

In principle, the young elector kept his inherited technological and mechanical masterpieces intact as a collection. He even added instruments and tools soon after his accession. The clock (ill. left), acquired from Johannes Reinhold and Georg Roll in 1586, came to the Reißgemach in the same year. While the 1587 inventory lists thirty-four instruments and tools as Christian I's new acquisitions, the 1595 inventory mentions—in additon to fifteen new specialized books—363 individual pieces, as well as a barber's cabinet (Barbierlade) and a work desk by Balthasar Hacker as recent additions. The insistence on maintaining the traditional Saxon Kunstkammer may be explained by Christian's view of it as dynastic testimonial. For him, the collection served as a memorial to Elector August: Due to its existence alone, but also through the paintings, the memory of the deceased elector was kept alive.

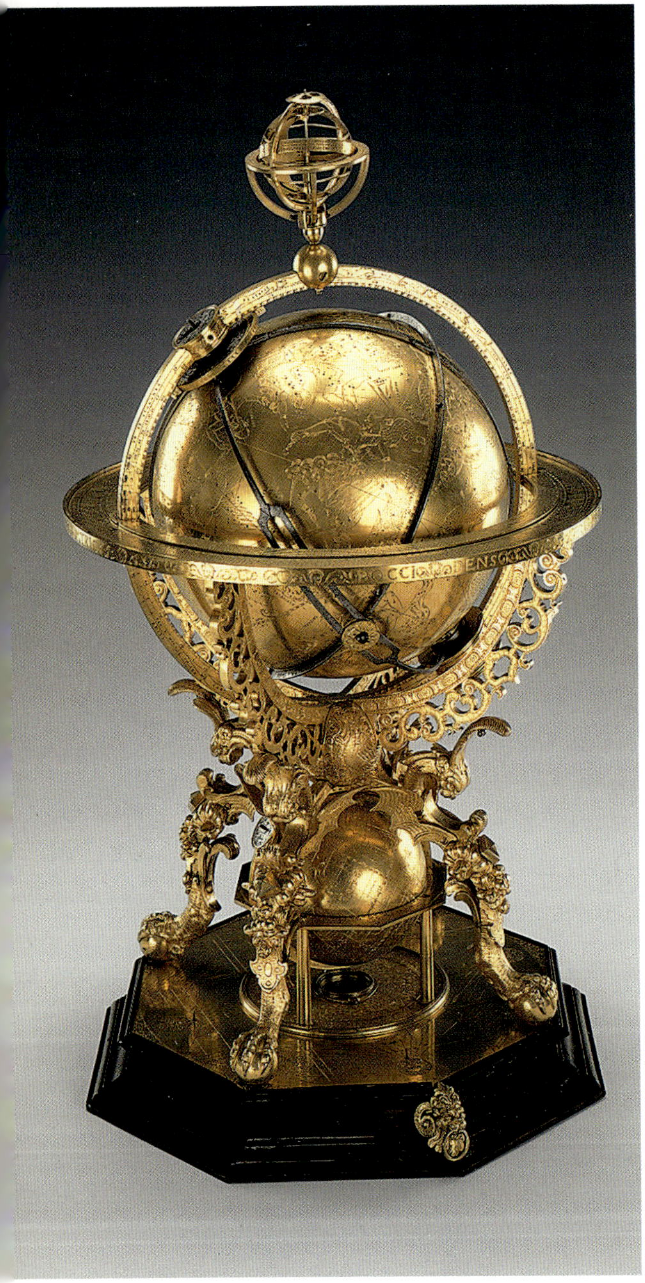

Mechanical Globe Clock
Augsburg 1586
Brass gilt
H. 22⅞ in. (58 cm)
Staatliche Kunstsammlungen Dresden, Mathematisch-Physkalischer Salon, inv. no. E II. 2

Whereas there were already five portraits of the elector and his wife kept in the Kunstkammer spaces in 1587, another ten were added by 1595. In addition, on October 12, 1586, Christian I moved the 134 turned ivories that his father had made to the Kunstkammer, where they were exhibited in the "large back chamber" (*hindternn grossen Gemach*) in an impressive pyramidal presentation, on an octagonal table with colored mounts.[38]

Initially, the "modernization" was concentrated on the small Reißgemach, the collection's heart. This is also where, in April 1587, Giambologna's bronze statuettes (cat. nos. 146–148)—a gift from Francesco I de' Medici commemorating the new elector's accession—found a worthy place.[39] They constitute a sumptuous princely present and are an impressive token of friendship between the houses of the Medici and Wettin, but they also fulfilled the dreams of Kaltemarckt and Nosseni for new Italian works in the collection.[40] Christian ordered the Emerald Cluster—since 1581 declared a national treasure (i.e., it could not be sold from the dynastic collection)—to be placed on his father's drawing table in the Reißgemach. Spectacular as *naturalia,* the "unicorn" was given a gold-enamel mount and suspended from the Reißgemach's ceiling by a golden chain—Urban Schneeweiß's invoice for his work, dating to the spring of 1587, survives.[41] Thereby the room received another Kunstkammer piece of programmatic relevance. Through the integration of both rarities—they also distinguished the emperor's Kunstkammer—Christian I attempted to nobilitate his Kunstkammer and to lend it a royal rank. This ambition may also be observed in Christians I's contemporaneous building projects.[42]

In his now-lost diary, begun in late December 1587, the art chamberlain Uslaub recorded the increasing number of holdings at length. At this time, the transformation of the Dresden Kunstkammer was underway,[43] a process in which Nosseni himself had participated in different ways. In a communication to the elector from the late summer of 1586, he suggested that contemporary Italian art, as well as horses, should be bought for the New Stable.[44] In early April 1587, Nosseni gave portraits of Rome's first twelve emperors to Christian's Kunstkammer. The elector also collected much more art. In 1588, he purchased a suite of sixteen paintings by Hans Bol, whom he greatly admired.[45] In his book *Bedenken,* Kaltemarckt lists him among the famous living Netherlandish painters, praising him as an exquisite landscape painter.[46] In the following years, ten more canvases and sixteen watercolors by Bol, as well as a painting by his stepson Frants Boels, were added. Until 1591, vast portions of Lucas Cranach the Younger's estate, as well as 113 woodcuts and sixty-nine copperplate engravings by Albrecht Dürer came to the Kunstkammer.[47] With the latter acquisitions, Christian I followed the fashion for Dürer developed at the Prague court of Emperor Rudolf II; the elector purchased three paintings between 1588 and 1590 from the emperor's court painter for his own Kunstkammer. Christian also had Arcimboldo's *Four Seasons,* given by Maximilian II to his father, transferred to the Kunstkammer.[48] With regard to painting, the recommendations set forth in Kaltemarckt's book *Bedenken* thus brought good results. In addition, Nikolaus Schwabe, the young medalist and wax embosser from Nuremberg, fabricated so many wax figures with electoral portraits, fantastic animals, and Christian and mythological themes for the elector, that two new cabinets containing them were placed in the rear gallery.[49]

Princely Portraits

The 1595 inventory documents the Kunstkammer's rapid development between 1586 and 1591, a time when its workshop character gave way to its role as an embodiment of princely power and splendor. While Christian I's decision was probably inspired by the Kunstkammers in Munich and Ambras, he also saw his collection as competing with Rudolf II's Kunstkammer, then being assembled in Prague's castle. Apart from the Reißgemach, the other spaces were also changed in the years before Christian's death. Two precious caskets were exhibited together on a newly purchased round table in the large rear chamber. The first was a 1588 New Year's gift from the elector to his wife, Sophie of Brandenburg (ill. p. 285); the second arrived in 1590 as a present from his Brandenburg mother-in-law (cat. no. 155).[50] Numerous automatons by the famous artist-engineer Hans Schlottheim were added to this chamber. Among them was a ship automaton, similar to that purchased by elector August, as well as a golden peacock and two crawling crabs. Presumably another automaton—intended to complement an ivory by the Saxon court turner Egidius Lobenigk—is also by Schlottheim. It decorated another table in the same space, along with seven other large format "pyramids" and a sculptural work. By employing both Georg Wecker and Egidius Lobenigk, electors August and Christian I had two court turners simultaneously, artist-engineers who managed to combine highly developed artistic ambitions, mathematical principles, and mechanical arts, resulting in unique works. In 1577 Georg Wecker moved from Munich to Dresden—a transfer approved by his patron, Duke Albrecht V of Bavaria—where the technically accomplished turner assistant worked first for August and later for Christian, serving them in their lathe work. His first independent works are documented in 1581. Lobenigk was made court turner in 1584. Each proceeded to support Christian I not so much in his personal production but to further the Dresden Kunstkammer's stock. In 1591 thirty additional objects had been added to the forty exhibited works Lobenigk had already created through 1586. In Wecker's case, the thirty-one older pieces were supplemented between 1588 and 1591 by an impressive fifty-five further objects worked on the lathe. Most items were signed and were often dated, and demonstrate Christian I's ambitions as collector. The Dresden Kunstkammer's comprehensive collection of lathe-turned ivories also made it superior in this area to other contemporaneous collections.

Gathered on a table in the Kunstkammer's second large chamber, the room beside the ladies' room, were seven large, partly artistically ennobled steps of silver ore. The wealth of silver belonging to the Saxon electoral territories was attested to by multiple ore samples and maps of the silver mines and tunnels that were kept in three armoires with drawers. The first hall of the Kunstkammer, the so-called dark chamber (finsteres Gemach) was now also used to represent the state; exhibits included the elector's new acquisitions, among them a collection of rare Chinese porcelain given in May 1590 by Ferdinando I de' Medici and further *ethnographica.*[51]

Under Christian I the outer antechamber (außwendiger Vorsaal), connecting the Kunstkammer and the library, was a densely hung picture gallery. Apart from works from the Cranach estate that depicted members of the Wettin family and mythological themes, it also contained portraits of important men. The Kunstkammer's entrance became grander: visitors were now expected.

Mirabilia and *Curiosa*

Apart from acquiring paintings, sculptural works, and sumptuous instruments for his Kunstkammer, Christian I also added new *mirabilia* and *curiosa,* thereby making his collection quite comparable to other large contemporary Kunstkammers. Apart from the "unicorn," the Emerald Cluster, and a large rhinoceros horn, the skeleton of a dwarf and the plaster cast of a giant's hand were added to the collection. Thanks to the famous cherry pit "with 186 faces," one of the very few Seychelle nuts extant in Europe at the time, and the seven ostrich-egg drinking vessels (cat. no. 116), the Kunstkammer began to fulfill the expectations of its name. Under Christian I, it gained more public attention. During his father's lifetime the Kunstkammer was considered totally private—neither Emperor Maximilian II, his friend and fellow collector, nor Duke Albrecht of Bavaria were permitted to enter during their respective visits in 1575 and 1576—but princely callers were admitted during Christian I's brief reign. One of the guests was the administrator of the electoral palatinate Johann Casimir, leader of the empire's Calvinist faction, who upon his official state visit in November 1590 went to the electoral Kunstkammer.[52]

Many of the important new acquisitions under Christian I entered the Kunstkammer as gifts. The elector's accounts list expenditures for the Kunstkammer: the year 1588 specifies 3,840 taler, 1589 only 1,000 taler, and in 1590 the amount increased again to about 3,100 taler. Compared to the court's expenses for entertainment and the upkeep of the household, these are moderate sums. But it should be noted that a painting by the imperial court painter Spranger cost sixty taler, while instruments such as the table clock by the Nuremberg master Paul Schuster could cost seven hundred taler. Family Christmas gifts later transferred to the Kunstkammer were purchased using other funds.[53]

38. SächsHStA Dresden, Loc. 9835/15 fol. 7r (1r).
39. For the same occasion, Duke Guglielmo Gonzaga of Mantua sent Filarete's unique equestrian statue of Marcus Aurelius to Dresden, it was also presented in the *Reißgemach*.
40. Marx 2000b, pp. 253, 255, 263.
41. Gurlitt/Nerling 1888, p. 205.
42. See Dombrowski 1999 and the same 2001.
43. Archive of the Generaldirektion X a, 19, lost today. The document continues in different hands until the year 1620; see Hantzsch 1902, p. 235.
44. SächsHStA Dresden, Loc. 8517/5, fol. 256r–v; see Marx 2000b, p. 262.
45. Hantzsch 1902, pp. 235ff.
46. Gutfleisch/Menzhausen 1989, p. 26.
47. Hantzsch 1902, pp. 236f.
48. *Kunstkammer* inventory of 1595, fol. 250v.
49. *Kunstkammer* inventory of 1595, fol. 92r, 251r–253r; SächsHStA Dresden, Copial no. 558, fol. 181r.
50. *Kunstkammer* inventory of 1595, fol. 167v–169r.
51. Marx 2000b, p. 272.
52. SächsHStA Dresden, Copial no. 573, fol. 87v–89r.
53. Hantzsch 1902, p. 238, Staatliche Kunstsammlungen Dresden, Mathematisch-Physikalischer Salon, inv. no. D V 8.

The Administrator and the Widow

In September 1591 the politically independent and ambitious Elector Christian I died a sudden and presumably not altogether natural death. For the next ten years, Friedrich Wilhelm I of Saxony-Weimar-Altenburg served as guardian and administrator of the electorate. During this time, the Kunstkammer's role as a prince's stately collection became secondary, although it emerged as a destination for foreign travelers. Jost Bürgi, the Hessian mathematician and instrument maker, is the first documented nonaristocrat to visit (he was on his way to the emperor's court in Prague). Possibly in connection with this summer sojourn of 1592, a planetary clock (ill. p. 283)—fabricated in 1568 for Elector August according to the specifications of Landgrave Wilhelm of Hesse—was installed in the Kunstkammer.[54] In the winter of 1592, the young Count von Leiningen was permitted to visit.[55] By 1596, the number of guests had increased to such an extent that the administrator mandated that people could enter the collection only with his or Christian's widow's consent.[56]

Although Friedrich Wilhelm continued to take care of the collection, no further acquisitions were made. The Kunstkammer's accounts for 1596–97 list expenses only in the amount of nineteen taler, the sum for 1598–99 amounted to forty-six taler. During this time, Sophie of Brandenburg, Christians I's widow, started to influence the further development of the electoral Kunstkammer. At the age of nineteen, she had begun to collect Kunstkammer objects. In 1587 her husband gave her seven ore steps with electoral provenance that she had installed in her bedroom's antechamber "in the new cabinets that contain any number of secret and bizarre items" (*in die neuen Schränkchen, darinnen allerlei geheime und seltsame Sachen verwahrt wurden*).[57] An inventory of 1588, no longer extant, was dedicated to the content of these cabinets.[58] Invoices also mention expenditures starting at the end of 1589 "for the electress of Saxony M: G: F: Kunstkammer and little art chamber" (*Vor die Churfurstin zu Sachßen M: G: F: Kunst Cammer vnd Kunststublein*).[59] A little later, the electress's collection was installed directly beneath the balcony on the Georgenbau's third floor,[60] a space that remained the repository of the collector's spouse for many years. Sophie thus founded a tradition that was continued by the electresses in the seventeenth century. For the duration of the guardianship, Sophie repeatedly utilized her influence to preserve the Kunstkammer holdings for her two sons: She insisted that the clockmaker Hans Kurzrock continue as an electoral employee—"because of the clocks' movements in the Kunstkammer" (*von wegen der Vhrwergk inn der Kunstcammer*).[61]

The Kunstkammer's Renovation

Starting in 1600, the Kunstkammer is mentioned more frequently in documentary sources. During the course of this year, repairs were made to Elector August's embossing machine (Prägewerk)—damaged due to "long use" (*langk wierigen gebrauch*).[62] While still a minor, Duke Christian (later Elector Christian II) emerged as art patron, increasing the Kunstkammer holdings by procuring, among others, turned ivories from Georg Wecker. He thus continued his father's collecting tradition. Duke Christian and his brother Johann Georg took a vital interest in their inherited Kunstkammer and its technical instruments, a fact used by the aged art chamberlain David Uslaub in the spring of 1601 to convince the administrator that Peter Probsthain ought to be hired as Uslaub's assistant. Probsthain had already helped Uslaub to compile the inventory and would assist him in looking after larger groups of visitors.[63]

Interestingly, the close relationship between Christian II and Emperor Rudolf II was initiated via Kunstkammer objects.[64] On January 10, 1600, Rudolf wrote to the sixteen-year-old Duke Christian that he had heard of his enthusiasm for paintings and other works of art and that he wished, therefore, to send him "numerous pieces I have presently at my disposal" (*etliche stuck, so ich hic bei der handgehabt*). This shipment of presents was accompanied by the hope that the intimate and honest relations between the two houses of Austria and Saxony would henceforth remain intact.[65]

Two artworks in the Dresden Kunstkammer prove that the emperor's expectations were not disappointed: the first is the sumptuous Lüneburg Mirror, whose iconography focuses on

54. *Kunstkammer* inventory of 1595, fol. 297r, Staatliche Kunstsammlungen Dresden, Mathematisch-Physikalischer Salon, inv. no. D IV d 4.
55. SächsHStA Dresden, Special-Rescripte 1592 vol. II., fol. 59r–v and fol. 265r; see also Hantzsch 1902, p. 239.
56. SächsHStA Dresden, Loc. 7305/1, fol. 178r–v.
57. Sponsel 1929, p. 105.
58. "*Vber die Schräncke, vnd was an Bechern Erzstuffen, vnd anderm in des Churfursten Gemach zu Dreßden, befundn worden, Anno 1588 aufgerichtet.*," see SächsHStA Dresden, Loc. 7207/12, fol. 7v.
59. SächsHStA Dresden, Loc. 7344/1, fol. 160r–164v.
60. SächsHStA Dresden, Loc. 10935, Haupt-Rechnung ... 1596., fol. 11v–12v.
61. SächsHStA Dresden, Special-Rescripte 1592 vol. I., fol. 85v.
62. SächsHStA Dresden, *Rentkammer-Rechnungen* no. 184 (=Crucis 1600–Crucis 1601), fol. 125r.
63. SächsHStA Dresden, Special-Rescripte 1601 vol. I., fol. 197r–198r.
64. DaCosta Kaufmann 1998, p. 16.
65. DaCosta Kaufmann 1978, p. 111.
66. Staatliche Kunstsammlungen Dresden, Grünes Gewölbe, inv. no. IV 110; see SächsHStA Dresden *Rentkammer-Rechnungen* no. 184 (=Crucis 1600–Crucis 1601), fol. 227r.
67. SächsHStA Dresden, *Rentkammer-Rechnungen* no. 184 (=Crucis 1600–Crucis 1601), fol. 333r and SächsHStA Dresden, Loc. 7339/1, fol. 532r.
68. DaCosta Kaufmann 1978/1979, p. 22.
69. Ibid., p. 22.
70. Staatliche Kunstsammlungen Dresden, Grünes Gewölbe, inv. no. II 434; Kappel 1990; Kappel 1995b, pp. 124, 132; Dresden 1995, p. 139 cat. no. 130.

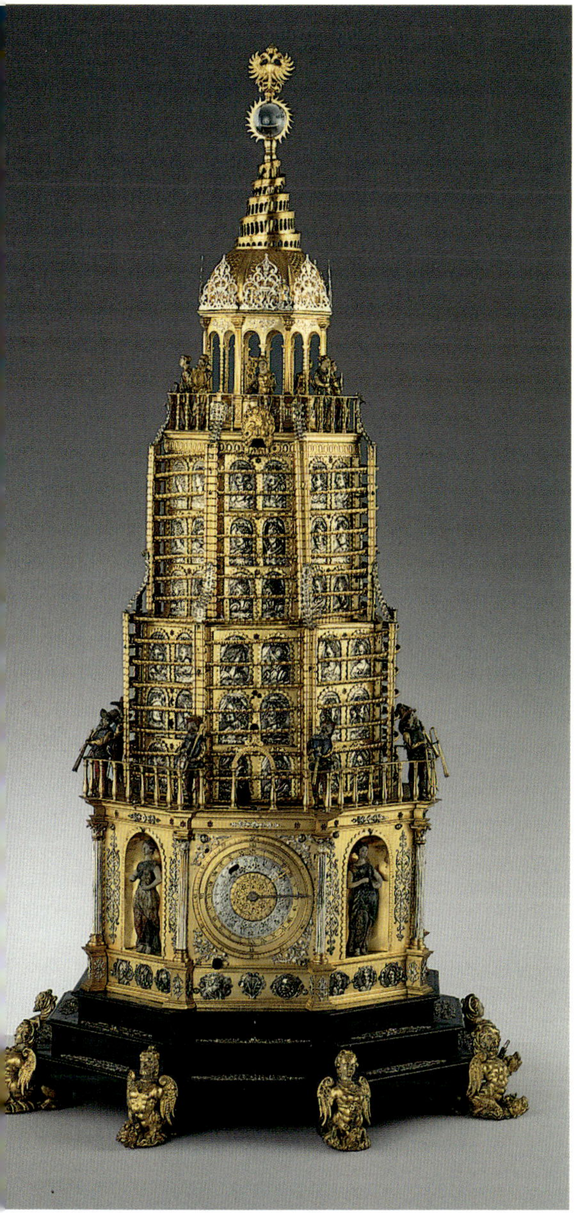

Rolling-Ball Clock
Hans Schlottheim
Augsburg, ca. 1600,
Brass gilt, silver, partly gilded, steel, wood, rock crystal
H. 44 in. (111.8 cm)
Staatliche Kunstsammlungen Dresden, Grünes Gewölbe, inv. no. V 140

imperial aspects of the Holy Roman Empire of the German Nation (ill. p. 22). The ceremonial object was finished in 1592 and was acquired by Sophie in May of 1601 for 1,657 taler and "transferred into her beloved sons' Kunstkammer" (*in dero geliebter Söhne Kunst cammer*).[66] In the same year, the elector's widow commissioned Hans Schlottheim to manufacture a rolling-ball clock in the shape of a tower for her son Christian. The price was 2,400 taler, and the piece was equipped with the most advanced technical features and an organ movement. Its iconography symbolized the continuity of imperial majesty from antiquity to Rudolf II. This masterpiece of artistic and technological accomplishment served as a replacement for an automaton, dated shortly before 1600, that was removed from the electoral Kunstkammer and presumably sent as a gift to the emperor in Prague.[67] In the coming decade, Rudolf II repeatedly returned this kindness with imperial magnanimity.

The ties between Dresden and Prague grew more intense because of the exchange of sumptuous gifts, but there was also a lively exchange of artists and engineers traveling between the new imperial residence in Bohemia and Dresden. In 1599 Georg Wecker installed a lathe for Rudolf II on the Hradshin; two years later—presumably on the occasion of his accession—Christian II presented thirteen artworks by his court turner Wecker to the emperor, and that same year Rudolf II hired Wecker's son, Johann, as chamber turner.

The Elector and His Emperor

Christian II's attitude toward the emperor was quite different from that of his father, Christian I. The latter had a politically calculating, competitive relationship with the emperor, while Christian II felt attached to the emperor and, moved by intense personal sentiment, was eager to emulate him. This led Christian II to invest significant sums in his Kunstkammer during his decade-long reign. In doing so, the Saxon elector followed the emperor's model, as well as that of numerous other imperial princes.

Rudolf II owned one of the largest and finest princely collections of his time: Europe's foremost ruler, he wanted to be Europe's foremost collector. The artworks created for the emperor by goldsmiths, lapidaries, and clockmakers are among the best produced in Europe at the time. As ruler by the grace of God and as God's representative on earth, the emperor believed he was elevated above the world—like God above the universe. For Rudolf II, the Kunstkammer was an elitist power tool. Tied to the idea of the Kunstkammer was an anthropomorphic interpretation of the world. This view, based on Macrobius, held that each human being is a small, self-contained world. Everything was subsumed in the Creator-God, since he was himself present in nature as well as in humans, revealing himself through nature's wonders. In creating humans, God had formed his own perishable likeness. Rudolf II's religious exaltation of the Kunstkammer was certainly at odds with the doctrines of the Roman Catholic Church. But around 1600, this religious element became the subject of humanist discourse and princely competition alike.

An invitation to the imperial Kunstkammer on Prague's Hradshin was considered a notable privilege, granted primarily to important ambassadors or ruling princes.[68] The emperor granted Christian II a special favor when he received him for a private audience in his Kunstkammer during Christian's first visit to Prague in June of 1607 (the two then viewed the collection together).[69] Just as meaningful as this gesture were the two gifts Rudolf II presented to the Saxon elector at this time: a bronze bust by Adriaen de Vries (cat. no. 3) and an allegory dedicated to Christian II, painted on stone by Hans von Aachen, whose obverse has a *commesso di pietre dure* (Florentine mosaic) showing the electoral Saxon coat of arms.[70] Both presents commemorate the harmonious relationship between the Catholic emperor and the leader of the empire's Lutheran states.

Christian II as a Collector

Christian II's love of splendor was evident even while he was still a minor and later became a significant burden to the state finances. In May 1601 he purchased a variety of objects for the impressive sum of 932 taler from the Leipzig dealer Veit Böttiger, consisting of mother-of-pearl and coconut drinking containers, as well as twenty-eight additional silver gilt

following page
Diana on a Centaur's Back
Hans Jacob I Bachmann
Augsburg between 1600 and 1610
Silver, partly gilded, basse-taille,
precious stones, ebony
H. 19½ in. (49.6 cm)
Staatliche Kunstsammlungen Dresden,
Grünes Gewölbe, inv. no. IV 150

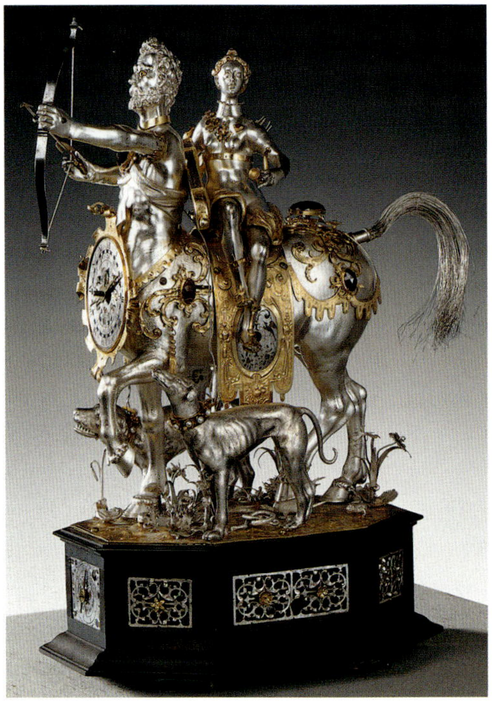

Diana on a Centaur's Back
Hans Jacob I Bachmann
Augsburg, ca. 1605
Silver, partly gilded, enamel, precious stones,
wood, H. 15½ in. (39.5 cm)
Kunsthistorisches Museum Vienna,
inv. no. KK 1166

vessels.[71] The young elector harbored a special love for the fine shimmer of mother-of-pearl. At Leipzig's Easter Fair of 1602 he purchased objects worth 8,500 taler from the same dealer; they included furniture, display caskets, pouring garnitures (cat. no. 100), and drinking game vessels made of mother-of-pearl and nautilus and sea snail shells (cat. nos. 108, 109) and numerous works by the Leipzig goldsmith Elias Geyer.[72] These sumptuous objects were placed in the electoral Kunstkammer and are listed in its 1610 inventory.

During his second visit to Prague in 1610, Christian II bought the extraordinary table clock with automaton depicting Diana and a centaur by the Augsburg goldsmith Hans Jacob I Bachmann (ill. right).[73] The counterpart to this key work of contemporary goldsmiths' art was kept in Rudolf II's Kunstkammer (ill. left and opposite).[74] Following family tradition, the Saxon elector was obviously fascinated by automatons.

By 1610 the Dresden Kunstkammer had become quite crowded, thanks to the purchase of "many elegant and important pieces" (*viel vornehmer vnnd wichtiger Stucken*). Apart from acquisitions and gifts, the entire output of Dresden court painters was incorporated as well, and a new inventory was badly needed. At the end of 1609, following the recommendation of the art chamberlain Uslaub, Balthasar Zimmermann was commissioned to compile it.[75]

The Silver Chamber, consisting mostly of table and state silver plate, also grew rapidly during the first decade of the seventeenth century. The elector and his brother shared a passion for the princely hunt, which Christian I took part in to an unusual degree. The hunts, which led the elector deep into the Saxon woods, developed into social events, celebrated by the elector with extraordinary hunting garnitures (see cat. no. 27) commissioned from Saxon goldsmiths. Christian II was also an eager participant in tournaments. Parade armor and weapons were produced for these occasions. While riding at the rings (a type of joust), the twenty-eight-year-old elector died on June 23, 1611, not on horseback but from apoplexy after "a heavy drink of the much-loved Merseburger [beer]" (*starken Trunk des vielgeliebten Merseburgers*).[76] He was succeeded by his brother, Johann Georg I.

The Dresden Kunstkammers after 1600

At the beginning of the seventeenth century, the electoral Kunstkammer was not the only collection of its kind in Dresden. The elector's mother Sophie had continued her own Kunstkammer. In September 1602, one year after her son's marriage to Hedwig, princess of Denmark, she moved to the widow's estate, Burg Colditz, taking her Kunstkammer with her.[77] In July 1612 her collection was inventoried there by David Uslaub and his son Kaspar.[78] Her daughter-in-law Hedwig followed the Saxon electress's example of collecting. Objects were often transferred to her Kunstkammer from the electoral Kunstkammer. For example, the new rolling-ball clock by Hans Schlottheim (ill. p. 65) reached Dresden in February 1603 and was appropriated by Hedwig on New Year's Eve of the same year. The new electress kept her Kunstkammer in the traditional location, i.e., in the four spaces on the Georgenbau's third floor. In 1603 numerous paintings by Hans Bol and Frans Boels were moved there, followed in 1605 by turned works—subsequently lost—made by the elector himself.[79]

It is not known if Duke Johann Georg also owned a collection. In 1609, however, Christian II, extremely generous with presents for his family, gave him three figural drinking vessels (*trinckgeschirr*), possibly works by Elias Geyer from Leipzig, as Christmas and New Year's gifts.[80] The Kunstkammer of Giovanni Maria Nosseni, established over some decades, was guided by the ideals described in Gabriel Kaltemarck's 1587 publication. Thus, in the decade following the year 1600, there were at least four Kunstkammers in Saxony.

Florence and Dresden after 1600

During his first decade as elector, Christian II moved away from the Florentine culture that had captivated his father. Around 1600, Italian influences came to Dresden only through the cultural center of Prague. Yet Italy's cultural currents continued to be of major importance for the Saxon rulers. Although the contacts with the princely houses of Italy had become

71. SächsHStA Dresden, Ausgaben der Churfürstlichen Sächsischen Renth Cammer 1600–1601, fol. 248.
72 SächsHStA Dresden, Ausgaben der Churfürstlichen Sächsischen Renth Cammer 1600–1601, fol. 322.—after Holzhausen 1935, pp. 238f.
73. Staatliche Kunstsammlungen Dresden, Grünes Gewölbe, inv. no. IV 150, Kunstkammer inventory of 1610, fol. 94.
74. Kunstkammer of the Kunsthistorisches Museum, Vienna, inv. no. 1166.
75. SächsHStA Dresden Loc. 7319/3 fol. 334r–v: "Postscripta."
76. Posse 1897, plate 29; Gross 2001, p. 92.
77. The Inventory *Vber die Kunst Cammer so Ao. 1603. Aufgerichtet* is unlocated; see SächsHStA Dresden, Loc. 7207/12, fol. 9r.
78. SächsHStA Dresden, Loc.10551/20, fol. 36–40r.
79. Hantzsch 1902, p. 246, p. 257; SächsHStA Dresden, Loc. 7207/9 Gemälde, pp. 1612–15, fol. 31v.
80. SächsHStA Dresden, Loc. 8680/3, fol. 2v–3v.

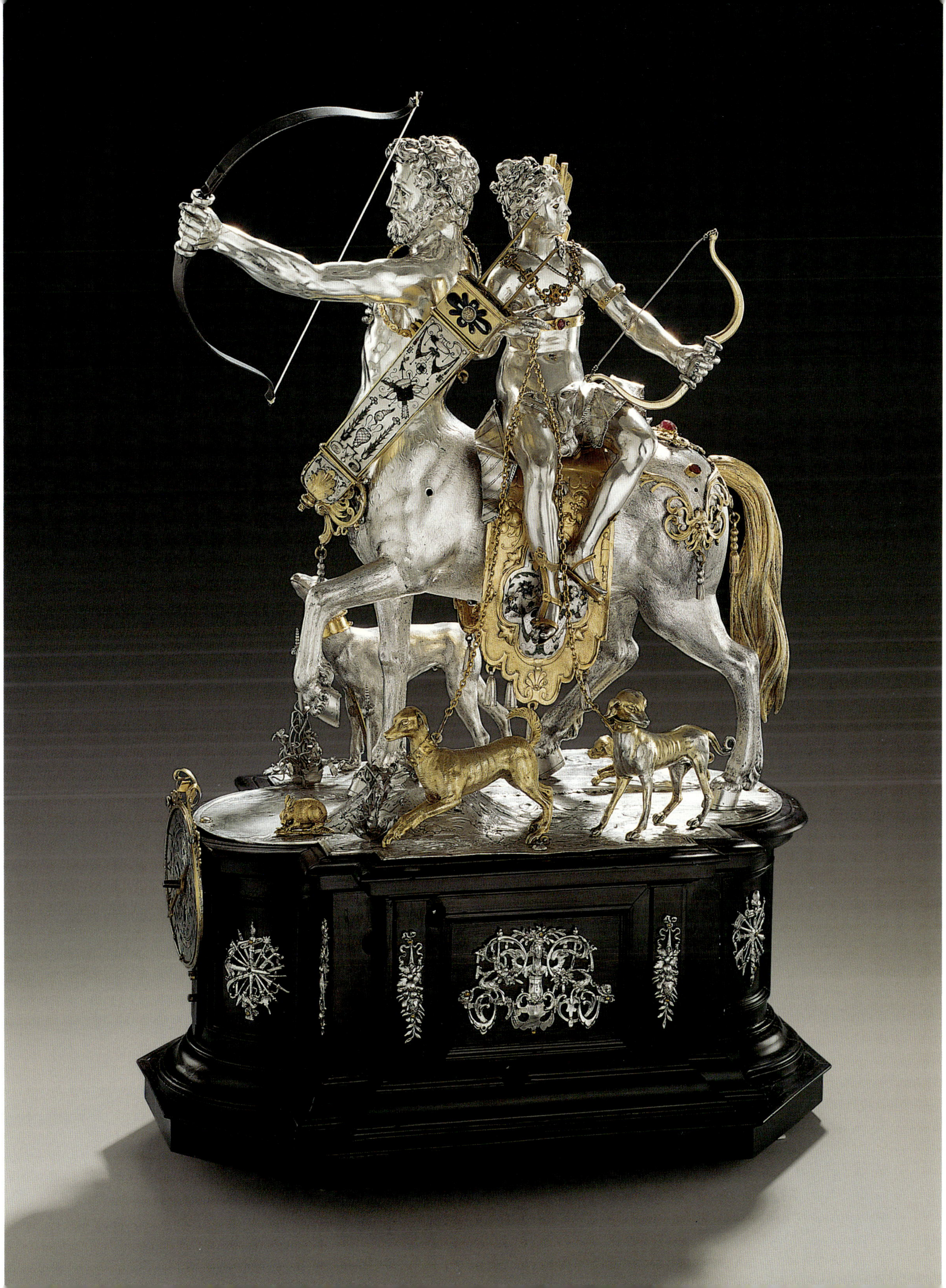

less warm, Duke Johann Georg became the first member of the Saxon dynasty to travel to Italy. On his grand tour, from January 1601 until February 1602, the duke visited Verona, Ferrara, Venice, Rome, and Naples, returning via Milan to the empire.[81] He learned Italian during his sojourn. These efforts notwithstanding, the duke made a poor impression on Fabrizio Colloredo, envoy of the grand duke of Tuscany to the Prague court. In the summer of 1609, Colloredo came to Dresden himself to see the by-now famous Kunstkammer.[82] In a letter, sent from Prague to Florence, the ambassador relates his impression of the electoral brothers to the grand duke: "I found Duke Christian, elector of Saxony to be quite subservient to the person of the emperor, and a very partisan servant of his majesty, quite addicted to wine, leaving him perpetually nebulous and rendering him rather monosyllabic [...] He takes great pleasure in the hunt [...] Duke Johann Georg, his brother, is a chivalrous and stern prince, but quite choleric, he also loves the hunt and does nothing but go to the countryside."[83]

Johann Georg and the Kunstkammer

For forty-five years Elector Johann Georg I determined the fate of Saxony and of Dresden's Kunstkammer. Although restricted by the Thirty Years War, he made some strategic acquisitions and had crucial influence on its future development. The overwhelming force of Rudolfian court art as a model had dissipated by the time of the emperor's demise in 1612. In Dresden a new generation of artists, among them Hans and Daniel Kellerthaler and the sculptor Sebastian Walther, were capable of continuing the Prague art tradition, especially in the realms of sculpture and decorative objects. The ivory artist Jakob Zeller, who arrived in Dresden in the summer of 1610 to replace the aged Wecker, created masterworks of turned and sculpted ivory. His ivory frigate of 1620, the epitome of all Kunstkammer pieces, was purchased for the unheard of price of 3,000 taler.[84] This monument (*Denkmal*) to the Wettin dynasty and warning (*Mahnmal*) about the precariousness to the changing luck of rulers' fortunes dates from the opening of the Thirty Years War, which was to bring misery to many.

During the first years of his rule, Johann Georg continued to procure foreign goldsmiths' works for considerable sums. But with the dawning of the economic crisis, the accessions were increasingly limited to Saxon artists. When it was almost impossible to enlarge his holdings, the elector had them reorganized to highlight their didactic content. In February 1612, shortly after his accession, he decreed that plate required for the court ceremonies was to be separated from artfully rendered figural and drinking game vessels. The Antiquitäten (antiquities) and Curiositäten (curiosities) were hence entrusted to the electoral art chamberlain and thus stored safely in the Green Vault.[85] In 1616 the elector established the Anatomy Chamber above the Kunstkammer, presumably located in the former den beside the old Turners' Chamber, where until then boxes and similar items were stored.

From 1615 to 1619 the Kunstkammer itself was remodeled, enhancing its stately atmosphere. In July 1615 the art chamberlain David Uslaub suggested that windows be installed in the attic to provide better light to the dark rooms; he also proposed the addition of one room to the fourth floor enfilade for storage space.[86] In 1619 the renowned mathematician Lukas Brunn—famous beyond the country's borders and much valued as scholar—started his work as new art chamberlain.[87] He began his work by creating a meticulous inventory[88] and before long presented his suggestions for a new Kunstkammer organization to Johann Georg I, which included the addition of an eighth room.[89] This plan was still under consideration in October 1619 when the former court architect, Johann Maria Nosseni, offered the elector parts of his collection of "artworks and bizarre natural objects" (*Kunstsachen und Naturmerkwürdigkeiten*) for 6,632 florin, an offer initially ignored by Johann Georg I. In February 1621, after Nosseni's death, the elector appointed a commission to discuss the acquisition. The committee voted in favor of purchasing works of art in the amount of 6,931 florins, 9 pennies, 6 Pfennige.[90] The purchase of most of Nosseni's collection in 1622, combined with the state furniture and objects that were bequeathed in March 1623 by the elector's widow, Sophie, resulted in the most significant increase in the Kunstkammer in decades. This also made the extension and the restructuring of the electoral collection inevitable. Starting in the summer

81. Vehse 1854, p. 51.
82. SächsHStA Dresden, Loc.7319/3, fol. 296r.
83. Florence, Archivio di Stato, Archivio Mediceo del Principato, Filza 6377, quoted in Marx 2004 (at press), footnote 48, translated from Antje Scherner's German version of the quote.
84. SächsHStA Dresden, *Rentkammer-Rechnungen* no. 187 (=Crucis 1620-Crucis 1621), fol. 485v.
85. O'Byrn 1880, pp. 49f.
86. SächsHStA Dresden, Loc.7324/1 fol. 173r–176r and SächsHStA Dresden, *Rentkammer-Rechnungen* no. 187 (= Crucis 1620-Crucis 1621), fol. 241r–385r.
87. Wunderlich 1977, p. 20.
88. Hantzsch 1902, pp. 247f.
89. SächsHStA Dresden, Loc. 9835/15, fol. 42r–45v.
90. Hantzsch 1902, p. 250.
91. Dombrowski 2000, p. 85.

of 1623, the plans were executed in an Early Baroque style. Jakob Böhme, who did not come to Dresden until 1624, could thus still witness the splendor prevailing at the electoral Saxon court during the beginning of the Thirty Years War: "Dresden is a jubilant town, like Prague was in the past" (*Dresden ist eine Jubel-Stadt, wie es vor der Zeit Prag war*).[91] This statement also applied to Dresden's Kunstkammer.

Four successive Saxon electors added to the Dresden Kunstkammer. Despite tendencies toward modernization, it kept its original character as a display collection of predominantly technical objects. The commemorative function associated with the memory of its founder, Elector August, remained a constant factor in its history. The idea of the Protestant ruler as *artifex* (creative craftsman) shaped the self-awareness of the Saxon rulers and is epitomized by the Kunstkammer. The collection in Dresden, unlike those in Munich, Ambras, or Prague, was not tied to a single sovereign's personal ambition but was a princely family project, pursued, developed, and maintained by every generation until the late eighteenth century.

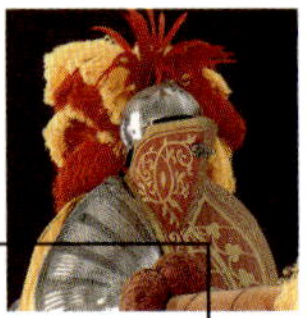

The Dresden Armory in the New Stable

Heinz-Werner Lewerken

During the late sixteenth and early seventeenth centuries, armories were among a court's most precious possessions. Princes often favored them over their picture collections and Kunstkammers, and Dresden's Armory follows this trend, although like most collections of its type, the exact year of its inception remains opaque. Since 1423, when the electoral office (Kurwürde) was bestowed upon the Saxon Wettin family, a considerable collection of weapons had accumulated, dispersed in numerous castles and palaces all over Saxony. It was not until after the Leipzig partition of 1485—when Duke Albrecht named Dresden as the seat of the new Albertine Duchy of Saxony—and the accession of his son Georg (the Bearded), that an armory (Rüst- und Harnischkammer) was established in the Dresden palace. Since that time, the armory grew continuously, above all through the acquisition and gifts of parade armor. Shortly before his death in 1539, Duke Georg hired the first administrator of his armory, Hans von Dehn-Rothfelser, who was also master of public works and forestry. By that time the armory, located on the ground floor of the palace's central tower (Hausmannsturm), was already held in high esteem as evidenced by a visit to the collection by King Ferdinand I on May 19, 1538.

When Duke Moritz gained the electoral office for the Albertine line in 1547, the old castle was transformed into a noble princely residence. In 1549, Moritz decreed that the existing edifice was to be partly demolished and replaced by a new structure twice the size of its predecessor.[1] Thus evolved a spacious, four-winged structure based on French and Italian models, with a stately interior courtyard designed for equestrian tournaments and other festivities. After the participants in the tournaments were equipped in the armory, they could directly access the palace's courtyard. In 1553, Elector Moritz led the Saxons in the battle of Sievershausen, where he was mortally wounded.

Whereas Moritz is primarily remembered as a commander-in-chief with outstanding abilities as a statesman,[2] his successor and brother, August, is considered the most significant economist among the Saxon electors. In his thirty-three-year reign, the country underwent—supported by Saxony's abundant ore deposits—an enormous economic boom. Until the time of the Thirty Years War (1618–48), electoral Saxony was one of the most advanced German territories with regard to technical and economic standards. Under August, a splendid culture of festivities emerged at the Dresden palace, in which equestrian tournaments and hunts played a key role. The holdings of the armory increased so much that the number of objects multiplied tenfold. Most of the additions were objects related to tournaments, experiencing an unprecedented burst of growth under August.[3] Apart from armor for different types of tournaments, the additions to the collection included helmets, shields, precious rapiers and swords, excellent firearms, powder flasks, crossbows, and riding equipment, as well as hunting gear and utensils. It appears that abundant holdings of the imperial armory in Vienna during the reign of the Hapsburg emperor Maximilian II, the elector's friend, served as the model for Dresden, as did the systematically arranged Armory of Heroes belonging to the emperor's brother, Archduke Ferdinand of Tyrol, in Schloss Ambras near Innsbruck.

1. See Delang 1992.
2. Most of the arms and armor from his reign preserved in the Armory document important historic events. Among them are his electoral sword (Kurschwert) of 1547 and the field armor he wore during the siege of Magdeburg in 1550–51.
3. For the history of the Dresden Armory see Haenel 1923, pp. III–VII.
4. The most detailed description of the entire building complex was undertaken by Anton Weck in his 1680 City Chronicle (pp. 53–61). His statements regarding the building history are essentially still valid today.
5. Weck 1680, p. 53.
6. Gurlitt 1901, p. 405.
7. Weck 1680, p. 53.
8. Apart from the 1606 main inventory, important information concerning the setting of the New Stable may be derived from the travel account of the envoy Philipp Hainhofer, who visited Johann Georg I in 1629 and stayed at the Dresden court (published by Doering 1901), and from Anton Weck's City Chronicle. Tobias Beutel published *Cedern-Wald* (1671), which also contains relevant information.
9. The two columns are based on designs of Nosseni that were executed by Gottschalk Specht and Benedix Bachstädt. Martin II Hilliger cast the columns. The columns and the Rosschwemme (i.e., a trough used for bathing horses)—originally filled with running water and remodeled in 1745—as well as eighteen bronze balusters are still extant today. See also Löffler 1987, p. 43.
10. Sponsel 1924, p. 20.

In 1567, an inventory of the entire holdings dispersed over many different chambers within the palace was first drawn up by Heinrich von Schönberg and Valerius Cracus; further inventories followed in 1568 and 1576.

The Armory in the New Stable

After his death on February 11, 1586, Elector August was succeeded by his son, Christian. In June of the same year, the new elector, only twenty-six years old at the time, laid the foundation stone for the Neuer Stall (New Stable), an independent building to house the electoral horses and the armory (ill. below).[4] In doing so, he followed the ambitions of his much admired uncle Moritz, who intended to transform Dresden into a refined princely residence. The Prague court of Emperor Rudolf II—under whose patronage collections were founded that were among the most comprehensive and richest in Europe—may have served as another source of inspiration for Christian I's activities.

In order to secure the necessary land to build on, Christian procured and demolished citizens' houses bordering the eastern grounds of the palace's Georgenbau.[5] The architect of the new stable edifice is thought to have been Paul Buchner from Nuremberg, an accomplished precision toolmaker by trade, whose rise at the Saxon court was stellar.[6] Numerous artists, among them Giovanni Maria Nosseni, and about two thousand craftsmen participated in the creation of the mighty structure that was already largely complete in 1588.[7]

The multipart building complex consisted of the stable itself, an interior courtyard for tournaments, and the northern boundary with the so-called Long Corridor (Langer Gang), a roughly three-hundred-foot-long arched gallery connecting the palace with the stables.[8] To the south, the chancellery and the old outer city wall enclose an inner courtyard, which consequently, to this day, takes an initial rectangular course and then widens to a square toward the stable building. Situated in the court's elongated portion, the tiltyard is defined by chains connected through low bronze balusters. Stretched between two richly adorned bronze columns was the rope from which the ring for the Running at the Ring was suspended.[9] In order to get dressed for the tournament the participants could ride directly from the courtyard via a stone ramp to the tilting chamber (Pallienkammer) located on the second floor of the New Stable. The loggia for the tournament judges was located in the chancellery area that faced the courtyard. In 1589, the first Running at the Ring took place at the stable building's new tiltyard.[10]

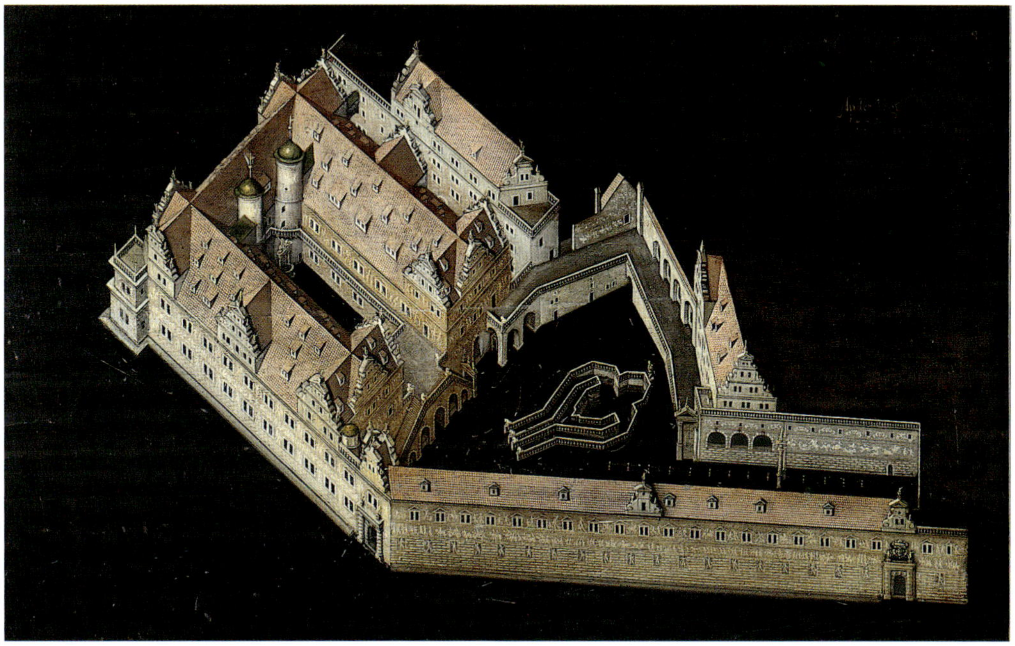

The New Stable at Dresden
with Stables (left) and
the Long Corridor (foreground)
Andreas Vogel, 1623
Oil on wood
12⅝ × 19½ in. (32 × 49.5 cm)
Staatliche Kunstsammlungen Dresden,
Rüstkammer, inv. no. H 235

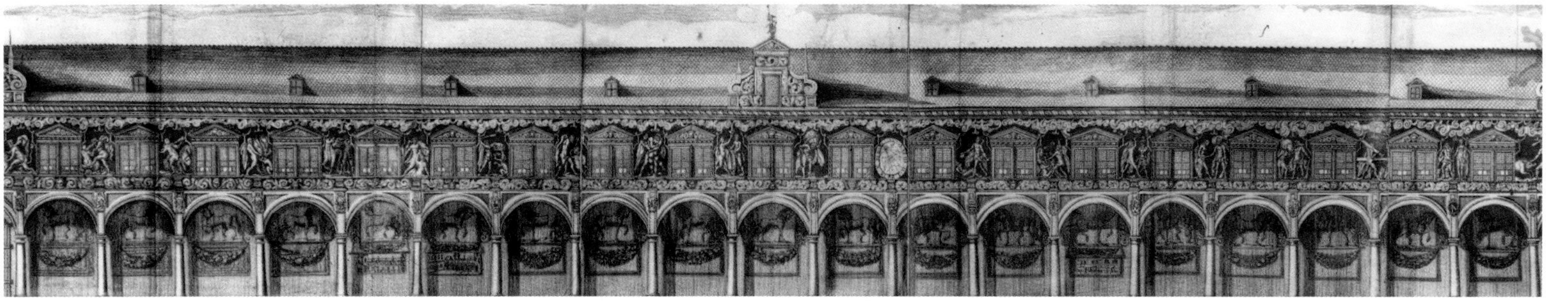

Long Corridor
Engraving from the Weck Chronicle, before 1680
9⅝ × 43¾ in. (24.6 x 111 cm)
Sächsische Landesbibliothek, Staats- und Universitätsbibliothek Dresden

The Long Corridor

As mentioned before, the Long Corridor (Langer Gang) connects the palace's Georgenbau with the stable building. It extends over two gates, of which the gate (Jagdtor) located beside the Georgentor warrants special attention. Andreas III Walther created its figural and heraldic decoration, as well as the sculptures of the stable.[11] Above the entablature, two lions flanked by warriors in classical armor display the electoral Saxon coat of arms. A plaque, mounted directly above and framed by scrollwork, contains an inscription to the effect that after his father's death, Christian erected this building to hold equestrian exercises in its courtyard.[12]

The Italianate structure of the Long Corridor (ill. above), open to the courtyard and displaying an arcaded walkway of twenty Tuscan-order columns, is today ascribed to Giovanni Maria Nosseni.[13] Although we have no documentary evidence of his active involvement in the execution, it can be surmised that the versatile Italian artist—he held the post of supervising director of arts (Kunstintendant) at the electoral Saxon court—was the true source of inspiration for the Long Corridor.

The facade of the Long Corridor facing the tiltyard was richly decorated. Located on the rear wall of the arcades below the arches were framed depictions of tournaments and festive processions. Painted by the Saxon court artist Heinrich Göding,[14] the pictures referred directly to the festival activities in the Stable Court. Frescoes of exquisite horses were placed above. As late as the eighteenth century, a visitor reported: "[*Es sind*] *viele fremde Pferde von berühmten Maitres verfertiget, zu sehen, sind allein wegen ihrer Schönheit und Annehmlichkeit nicht genugsam zu verwundern*" ([There are] many foreign horses by famous masters to be seen, because of the appeal and their beauty one can never sufficiently admire them).[15] In those days, noble horses were considered an indispensable part of any princely household. In October 1586, Christian I thus sent a special envoy to Italian princely courts to purchase expensive horses.[16]

The images between the windows of the top floor showed a series of nineteen depictions of the labors of Hercules. The roughly three-hundred-foot-long middle frieze of the rear facade—today, the side facing Augustusstraße, which can be seen in Vogel's painting (ill. p. 71)—was adorned by the depiction of a triumphal procession in ancient style with infantry, cavalry, and the victorious ruler shown in his triumphal chariot. The triumphal motifs and the Hercules cycle were perfect tools with which to illustrate ideals of rule. Associated with the ancient hero Hercules were such virtues as courage, strength, and personal integrity. As the prototype of the victorious hero and one who overcomes the greatest menace, he is predestined to be any prince's ideal.

The Ancestral Gallery of the Wettins

Christian I decreed that the interior of the Long Corridor's top floor be the Ancestral Gallery of the house of Wettin: "*hiesiger Albertischen Linien hochlöbl. uhralten Anherren und Vor Elten in gerader aufsteigender Männlichen Linie*" (the local Albertine line's much venerated ancestors mentioned in a direct male line).[17] A total of twenty-nine tournament pictures hung below the twenty-one rectangular double windows, depicting the jousts of war and peace in which Elector August participated during the years 1543 to 1566. Painted in oil on wood, the images—ten of which have survived—were created in 1589–90 for Christian I by the court

11. Löffler 1987, p. 43.
12. "Augusto electore pie defuncto Christianus Saxoniae dux dignitatis haeres virtutis imitator domum hanc equorum statiori extruendam, areamque adiunctam militarium exercitationum causa complanandam exornandamque curavit." This inscription is also included in Weck 1680, p. 54 (see also p. 60, footnote 30).
13. May 1992, pp. 65f.
14. For the life and work of Heinrich Göding the Elder see Berling 1887.
15. Iccander 1726, p. 41.
16. See also Marx 2000a, pp. 19f.
17. Weck 1680, p. 56.
18. Berling 1887, p. 327.
19. Beutel 1671, fol. J4r.
20. In 1629, Hainhofer reported that he first visited the gallery from where he entered into the stable building's sleigh chamber. See Doering 1901, p. 187.
21. Such as the "Sächsisches Stammbuch," a codex of pictures probably begun around 1500 under Friedrich the Wiseby by an unidentified artist. Sächsische Landesbibliothek, Staats- und Universitätsbiliothek, Mscr. Dresden R. 3.
22. In his 1541 *Chronica und Herkomen der Churfürsten und Fürsten des löblichen Hauses zu Sachssen*, published in Wittenberg, Georg Spalatin draws a direct line from the Wettins to Widukind.
23. See the unpublished master's thesis by Adrian Lewerken (Lewerken 2002).

painter Heinrich Göding.[18] The paintings are based on depictions in a tournament book, painted in 1584 for Elector August. Since the Scharfrennen, the German joust of war, had largely gone out of fashion by the late sixteenth century, its depiction, accordingly, was largely of a memorial character: The scenes were reminders of Elector August as a model of chivalry. In his 1671 publication *Cedern-Wald*, Beutel refers to the tournament paintings in the same vein: "Dabey auch abgemahlt seyn alle Chur=Fürst Augusti (höchstseeligsten Andenckens) gehaltene Scharf=Rennen so Er mit unterschiedlichen Fürstlichen Personen [...] gethan" (Among them are also paintings of the German joust of war in which the blessed Elector August participated [...] with different princely persons).[19]

The lunettes over the windows as well as the remaining wall space were ornamented with grotesques. The focal point of the program was the series of large, full-figure portraits of princes executed by Göding and his workshop. Mounted on the walls between the windows, they formed an integral part of the wall composition from the very beginning. Below the over-lifesize portraits of the princes, ovoid, strapwork-embellished cartouches contained historical scenes. They included important episodes from the sovereigns' lives, mostly famous battles, or special achievements of the respective princes. Plates with inscriptions below the historical scenes reported about the lives and deeds of the portrayed individuals and listed their mottoes.

Primarily created between 1588 and 1590, the ancestral gallery originally comprised forty-six paintings, some of which were portrayals of legendary Saxon rulers, others historically documented Wettins up to and including its commissioning patron, Christian I. As a dynastic monument, this gallery was held in such esteem by the Saxon court that all of Christian's successors until the early eighteenth century were added.

An offical visit through the stable building complex usually began in the Stable Court Gallery (Stallhofgalerie),[20] affording access to the armory's *bel étage*. Coming from the Georgenbau, the guest would walk through the room along its northern long wall. He would encounter the row of pagan Saxon rulers in successive order, strictly adhering to the paternal line, from Harderich, said to have lived around 90 B.C., up to Wernike. Placed above the entrance to the armory was the portrait of Widukind, the war-duke who led the Saxons in their battle against Charlemagne (778–85). The long wall facing the stable courtyard continued the series of the legendary Saxon rulers with images of Margrave Konrad and Otto the Rich (ill. left), leading to the historically documented Wettin line of ancestors and terminating with the image of Christian I. The portraits, particularly the ones of the legendary Saxon sovereigns, followed the idealistic iconography of warriors and heroes. The sitters, accordingly, are shown in armor and are armed with swords, stressing each sovereign's military capabilities. This iconographic pattern was abandoned only if the person in question had been endowed with the electoral office.

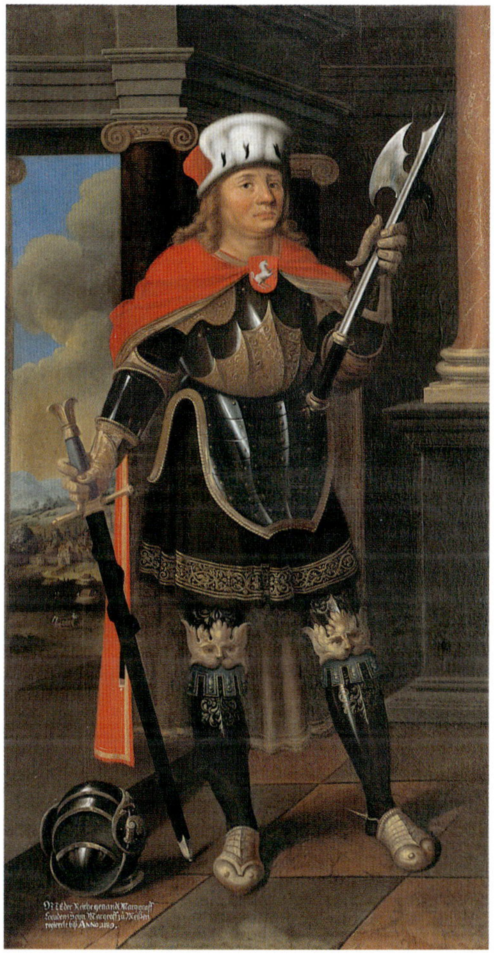

Otto the Rich
Heinrich Göding the Elder (?)
1588–89
Oil on canvas
96 × 55⅛ in. (244 × 140 cm)
Staatliche Kunstsammlungen
Dresden, Rüstkammer, inv. no. H 276

Christian I claimed the famous Saxon war hero Widukind as an ancestor of his family and thus linked his line with older Saxon history. The impetus for this claim can be traced back to 1423, when the formerly Askanian Duchy of Saxony, and with it the electoral office, had been bestowed upon the Wettins as a fief. The program of Dresden's ancestral gallery was based on earlier Wettin family chronicles[21] and historiographic writings,[22] in which an attempt had already been made to establish a direct family link between the Wettins, Widukind, and the Saxon dukes.

Thus, a continuity was created—indeed only partially based on historic documents—that placed Christian I in line with illustrious rulers. This not only contributed to the glorification of his house but also underscored his claim that the electoral office was legitimately bestowed upon his family.[23] As recently as the times of Christian's father, August of Saxony, the electoral office had to be defended by force against the assaults of his Ernestine relatives.

During the sixteenth century, an interest in their family's history inspired numerous royal houses to establish noble ancestral galleries in their residences. In this context, the endeavors of Maximilian I are of particular importance: By the early sixteenth century, he had seriously begun to research his own forefathers and their representation in works of art. His historiographic and artistic undertakings—such as the project for his tomb in Innsbruck's Court Church and the series of woodcuts for the Ehrenpforte and the Triumphal Procession—served to glorify his person and the house of Hapsburg. The emperor's great-grandson Ferdinand II,

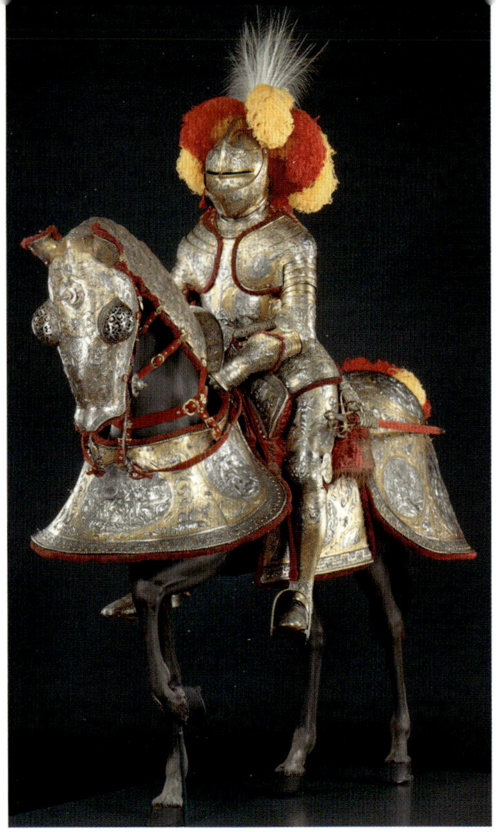

Parade Armor for Man and Horse
Eliseus Libaerts, Antwerp, 1563–64
Made for King Erik XIV of Sweden, captured by Denmark, and purchased by Elector Christian II of Saxony in 1606
Iron, embossed, chased, etched, and gilt
Weight man's armor: 61 lbs (27.7 kg), horse armor: 71½ lbs (32.5 kg)
Staatliche Kunstsammlungen Dresden, Rüstkammer, inv. no. M 100

archduke of Tyrol, decorated the Spanish Hall of Schloss Ambras, built in 1569–71, with a series of twenty-seven portraits of Tyrolese sovereigns, the monumentality of which is comparable to those in Dresden.[24]

The concept of an ancestral gallery was by no means new. Among its predecessors are the wall cycles with the partly legendary forebears of Charles IV, erected in the third quarter of the fourteenth century in Prague Castle's main hall and in the pallas of Castle Karlstein. Dynastic series such as the Dresden ancestral gallery are also related to the Italian Renaissance cycles of *uomini famosi* or the so-called Nine Heroes series, which originated in part from the secular art of the later Middle Ages and focused on ideas of chivalry and leadership.

While the ancestral gallery did have a public dimension, the privileged world of a princely court in those days comprised a very different audience from today. A select few were given access to the stable gallery and the neighboring armory. Envoys, such as the group led by Philipp Hainhofer of Augsburg in 1629, and important guests from foreign courts as well as domestic nobility were permitted entry. The ancestral gallery's central message—the noble descent of the Albertine Wettins from the glorious lineage of Saxon rulers—was geared to a small and exclusive audience.

The Stable Building and Its Collection

In its original structure, the New Stable was a building of horseshoe shape with three wings, each having two floors as well as two gable and three attic floors. Its central courtyard opened toward the tiltyard. In each corner a spiral staircase made each floor accessible and thus led into the building's interior.[25] A single-story balcony (Altan), from whence a corridor encircled the courtyard, connected the two side wings of the edifice.

The main facade toward the so-called Jüdenhof was dominated by two rusticated and column-framed portals and two-storied corner bastions—erected for defensive purposes—giving it a monumental appearance. The strongly sloped roof was crowned by two stepped gables on the main facade and by three stepped gables on each side wing.

Corresponding to the building's purpose as a ducal armory, the facade was decorated with numerous images of a predominantly war-related nature.[26] Visually, the paintings of the facades were in keeping with the palace's *sgraffiti.* A broad and long frieze depicting an impressive equestrian battle scene decorated the side facing the Jüdenhof, now promoted to the principal facade. Indeed, all available wall space was covered with frescoes.

The vaults of the ground floor rested on columns and served as the stables for the ducal horses, as well as for those of the mounted retainers (reißige Knechte), offering space for 128 horses. Twenty-four columns of the elegant stable were fitted with shell-shaped stone fountains filled with water running from bronze spouts in the shape of horse heads. Due to the stalls for the horses, the windows were placed relatively high. The ground was covered with sandstone slabs from the quarries at Pirna. The walls were probably covered with frescoes depicting horses. Symmetry and axial direction determined the stable building's architectural structure. As a princely stable (Marstall) containing comprehensive collections on its upper floors, this edifice was an early example of a new building type.[27]

To this day, the basis of Dresden's Armory comprises both the arms and armor transferred from the palace to the new stable building and the precious examples that Christian added during his brief reign. This transferral was completed no later than 1591. By 1593, the crossbows from the so-called electoral Shooting House (Schießhaus) were added. Only some of the elector's personal arms remained in the palace's Rüststüblein (little armory). In 1605–6, during the reign of Christian II, the holdings were inventoried in their entirety: The 1,602 handwritten pages of the single-volume inventory, completed in 1606, offer a comprehensive impression, covering a dazzling assortment of armor, weapons, accessories, riding equipment, garments, sleighs, and carriages.[28] As can be deduced from the inventory, the extraordinarily rich collections were accommodated on the upper floors, reaching all the way up to the attic of the stable building, distributed into thirty-two chambers, rooms, and spaces. Mostly arranged by thematic groups, they contained everything required for tournaments, processions, festivals, and the hunt, including armors, weapons, and other objects considered

24. For a comprehensive survey of the building history and the painted decoration see Scheicher 1975.
25. Based on plans by Maximilian von Fürstenhof, the building was transformed into a paintings gallery between 1722 and 1731. After remodeling in 1872-76, it was called the Johanneum in honor of King Johann. Today, it houses Dresden's Traffic Museum (Verkehsmuseum).
26. For a comprehensive analysis of the stable building's facade see Heckner 1995, pp. 144ff.
27. Heckner 1995, pp. 144. Other court stables were created in Vienna, Munich, Heidelberg (from 1590), and Kassel (1591-93). There are strong similarities between Dresden's stable building and the "Spanish Stables," begun in 1585 under Rudolf II at Prague's Castle; see Dombrowski 2000, footnote 83.
28. *Inventarium über die Rüst- und Inventionskammern auf dem* [...] *Neuen Stall. Anno 1606 revidieret.*

worthy of being kept and preserved. The most important storage areas, often incorporating more than one room, were the elector's apartments, the Black Horseman's or Sleigh Chamber (Schwarze Reiter- or Schlittenkammer), the Chamber for Tilting Armor (Pallienkammer), the Armor Chamber (Harnischkammer), the Electoral Chamber (Kurkammer), the Long Arms and Hungarian Chamber, numerous gun chambers (Büchsenkammern), the Indian Chamber, and the New and the Long Invention Chamber (Neue and Lange Inventionskammer).[29]

The Elector's Apartments

The electoral apartments were located in the building's main portion facing the Jüdenhof. A narrow, centrally placed corridor divided them into two units, each consisting of a bedroom and a living room. The ambitious design of the suite of spaces was modeled on Italian prototypes. The elaborately decorated wall coverings of soft, gilt cordovan leather were restricted to the state rooms. The ceilings were also influenced by Italian models, with paintings showing scenes from classical mythology, ancient battle scenes, and triumphal processions. The floors in all four spaces were covered with Saxon marble according to Nosseni's specifications.[30]

The most remarkable furnishings of the electoral apartments were two display buffets more than ten feet tall in the shape of mountain steps (ill. p. 207). The tiered and abundantly adorned pieces of furniture were fitted with matrixes fashioned from different types of ore. They served as tabletops and for the display of goblets, carved wooden figures, and animal sculptures.[31] In the oriels of the outer apartments, two sets of twelve serpentine and jasper-embellished chairs were placed around a marble table, also produced by Giovanni Maria Nosseni for Elector August (cat. no. 160).

The elector's apartments, equipped like a Kunstkammer, were not just a dwelling place for the ruler and his family; important guests were also invited to stay there. While the windows extended the vista to the city life outside, the viewer was also able to study the works of art preserved in these rooms.

The Black Horseman's or Sleigh Chamber

The ducal apartments were bordered by the Black Horseman's or Sleigh Chamber (Schwarze Reiter- or Schlittenkammer) in the east wing and by the Chamber for Tilting Armor (Pallienkammer) in the west wing. According to the inventory, the administration of the objects kept in these chambers was entrusted to the armory official (Rüstknecht) Hans Werner. The Sleigh Chamber and Chamber for Tilting Armor were not rooms in the strict sense of the word but rather spacious halls supported by columns. The 1606 inventory, which also includes additions and deletions until 1612, makes extensive mention of the fifty-two precious sleighs on exhibit together with related blankets, bells, and feather plumes for the horses. The mostly gilt, silver-plated, or painted sleighs were decorated in the most imaginative manner, with motifs including ancient deities, biblical scenes, Turks' heads, wild beasts, birds, heads of donkeys, stags, lions, dragons, fruit, flowers, and garlands.[32]

Many more items were stored here, including suits of field, tournament, and parade armor, horse caparisons, gorgets, gloves, saddles, bridles, stirrups, rapiers, sabers, daggers, pikes, cuirasses, helmets, burgonets, hunting and target guns, pistols, muskets, musket rests, powder flasks, cartridge belts, clothing, waistbands, boots, and even stockings. Most of the cuirasses, helmets, and weapons were part of the equipment for the ducal bodyguard. While some of the armors were displayed on stands, fifteen were displayed on carved wooden horses. Among the outstanding pieces preserved here was the blackened infantry field armor of Duke August of Saxony, which he had worn during the battle of Mühlberg on April 25, 1547. Also kept here was the simple blackened infantry armor used by him during the siege of Magdeburg in 1567.[33] Further displays included three parade armors of gilt copper with matching chanfrons made in Dresden in 1590. The richly engraved half armors had been worn by Elector Christian I, Duke Christian I of Anhalt-Bernburg, and Prince Johann Georg of Anhalt-Dessau during a festival in Dresden.

29. The second floor housed the Schwarze Reiter- or Schlittenkammer (in later inventories referred to only as Schlittenkammer, or Sleigh Chamber), the Rüststüblein and the Pallienkammer (Chamber for Tilting Armor), as well as four preciously embellished ducal rooms. The spaces above were reserved exclusively for the armory.

30. For Nosseni's work in Saxony see Meine-Schawe 1989/1990, pp. 285f. It took more than the Saxon artists to work the domestic marble, alabaster, and serpentine. Therefore Christian I sent Nosseni to Italy in 1588, where he hired good stonecutters and sculptors; the latter also laid down the approximately 3,000 marble floor slabs in the ducal chambers.

31. Vermisste Kunstwerke 1990, p. 96, cat. no. 275f.; see also the essay by Ulrike Weinhold in this volume.

32. Apart from the sleighs and the display buffets, all other works mentioned in this essay are still preserved in the armory.

33. Haenel 1923, p. 6, plate 3 a/b. The field armor worn at the battle of Mühlberg, made by the Annaberg armorer Peter von Speyer the Elder, is embellished with bands of etched decoration showing floral motifs. The breastplate bears the quartered ducal Saxon coat of arms, and the left side shows a kneeling knight praying in front of a Crucifixion. The other field armor created by Wolf von Speyer also displays—on the side of the heart—a knight kneeling in front of a crucifix.

Parade Armor
France, before 1588
Gift of the Duke of Savoy
to Elector Christian I
Iron, embossed, chased, and gilt
Staatliche Kunstsammlungen
Dresden, Rüstkammer,
inv. no. M 62 (see cat. no. 15)

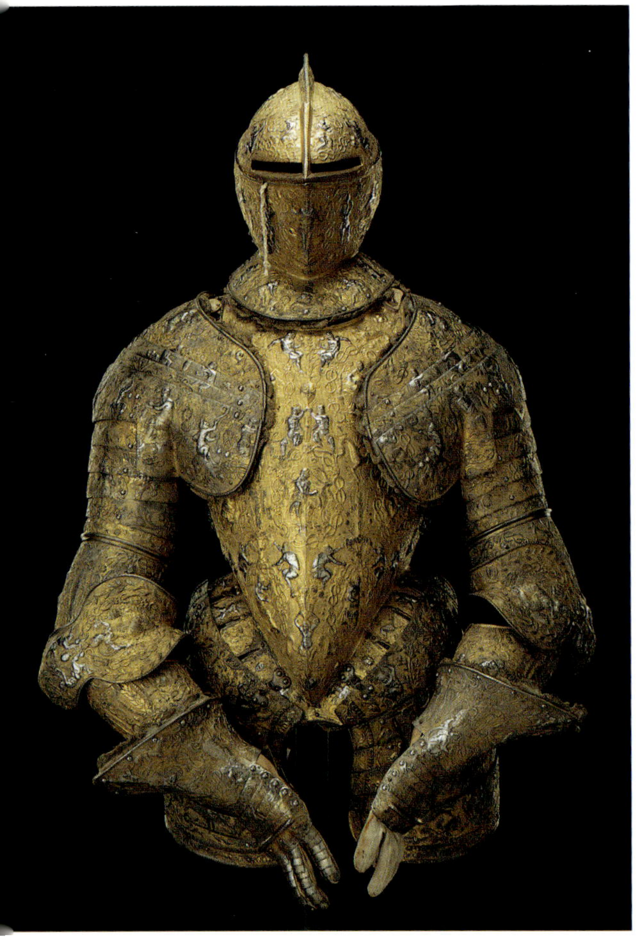

The Chamber for Tilting Armor (Pallienkammer)

Georg Schauer and the armorer Peter von Speyer were responsible for the Chamber for Tilting Armor, a repository primarily of armor for different types of tournaments, precious riding gear, helmets, shields, and edged weapons. The 1606 inventory describes the armor extensively, generally noting the name either of its owner or of someone who wore the armor during a tournament or campaign. The Pallienkammer offered visitors the impressive sight of twenty-five wooden horses presenting armor for man and horse, as well as numerous other armors and cuirasses exhibited on stands. Out of the plethora of objects, some warrant special mention: the field armor for man and horse worn by Duke Heinrich "the Pious" in 1499–1500 when assuming his responsibilities as temporary governor of Frisia on behalf of his father, Duke Albrecht of Saxony; the half armor with etched and gilt decoration that was worn by Elector Moritz during the 1550–51 siege of Magdeburg; and the field armor that Elector August of Saxony received in 1588 as a gift from Archduke Ferdinand of Tyrol.

Noteworthy among the numerous tournament armors are an armor for the joust made in 1550 by the Dresden armorer Hans Rosenberger (ill. p. 77) and the one produced in 1553 by the Wittenberg armorer Sigmund Rockenberger for Elector August, weighing close to 190 pounds each. Of the fifty-five official German jousts in which Elector August participated between 1543 and 1566, thirty-three took place in Dresden on the Altmarkt, the courtyard of the palace, and on an area behind the palace where the stable building was later erected. In 1584 Elector August had these jousts recorded in watercolor on parchment.[34]

A complete armor can theoretically be compared to a sculpture that may be perceived as a three-dimensional image of its former wearer, often a historically documented individual. Thus armors may also serve a memorial purpose. Not only were they displayed in courtly armories, but full-length figurines or portrait-like heads were often added, endowing the armor with the alleged character and personality of the person who wore it—as, for example, in the Heroes Armory (Heldenrüstkammer) in Schloss Ambras. Armor thus not only memorialized specific persons but, like an image, could keep the memory of historic events alive.

To some extent, the Dresden Chamber for Tilting Armor is comparable to the Heldenrüstkammer in Schloss Ambras established by Archduke Ferdinand II, one of the house of Hapsburg's most significant patrons. The so-called Unterschloss, which he began building in Ambras in 1571, housed five thematically arranged rooms for his precious collection of arms and armor. The most important part of this collection was the Heldenrüstkammer, containing armor, weapons, and portraits of those men who distinguished themselves on the battlefield by virtue of their singular courage, chivalry, and "manliness" (Mannhaftigkeit).[35] Archduke Ferdinand vigorously pursued the acquisition of armor from allied dynastic families in order to integrate them into his "[honorable] company" ("ehrlichen [ehrenwerte] Gesellschaft"). In a letter dated April 26, 1576, Ferdinand thus requested that Elector August bequeath him the personal armor that the latter had worn during the siege of Gotha, as well as the personal armor of his deceased brother Moritz of Saxony.[36]

As at Ambras, a comparable "honorable company" was formed in the Pallienkammer at Dresden with a number of armors formerly belonging to Wettin rulers of both lines, Saxon noblemen, and other allied princes. This is supported by Sigmund von Birken in his 1677 publication entitled *Chur- und Fürstlicher Sächsischer Helden-Saal*, a combined history of Saxony and genealogy of the Wettins. The frontispiece is adorned with an Ehrenmantel, or series of portraitsß of Saxon princes with a background of parade armor displayed on wooden horses and figures, forming a heroic panoply of the house of Wettin. The purpose of this armory containing parade armor of the Saxon electors was thus primarily of a dynastic nature.

The Hungarian Chamber

Of the approximately nineteen chambers located on the third floor, the stately Hungarian Chamber (Ungarische Kammer), referred to since 1674 as the Turkish Chamber (Türckische Kammer), is of notable importance. In the inventory of 1606, its holdings are listed on more than 130 pages, as comprising weapons and accessories predominantly of oriental origin, but also including Hungarian and Italian examples. The entries list sabers, daggers, maces, battle-axes, Turkish bows, quivers, arrows and folding leather cups, firearms and combination weapons, powder flasks, helmets, shields, saddles, horse accoutrements, and riding garments.[37]

Centuries of military encounters, diplomatic relations, and steady trade with the Ottoman Empire kept the interest of European princes and wealthy patricians in oriental art and customs alive, ultimately giving rise to an actual Turkish fashion. Items that came to the Dresden Türkenkammer—as princely gifts, purchases, or war booty—included luxurious Ottoman weapons and riding equipment, lavishly embellished with precious stones; exotic garments; and elaborately decorated Ottoman tents. Numerous trips by Saxon envoys on diplomatic missions to Italy are recorded, including visits to the courts in Turin, Mantua, Florence, and Ferrara. In 1587, the electoral Saxon Hofmarschall Heinrich von Hagen brought back presents for Christian I from the duke of Mantua, the grand duke of Tuscany, and the duke of Savoy, including more than thirty mostly eastern weapons, as well as parrying daggers with spring-loaded blades, double rapiers, battle-axes with retractable thrusting blades, walking sticks containing hidden blades, and a number of parade shields of Italian provenance.

Emperor Rudolf II also offered presents on numerous occasions as tokens of gratitude for military support given to him during the so-called Long Turkish War (1593–1606). In 1602, Christian II thus received three horses with horse equipment, as well as weapons and Turkish

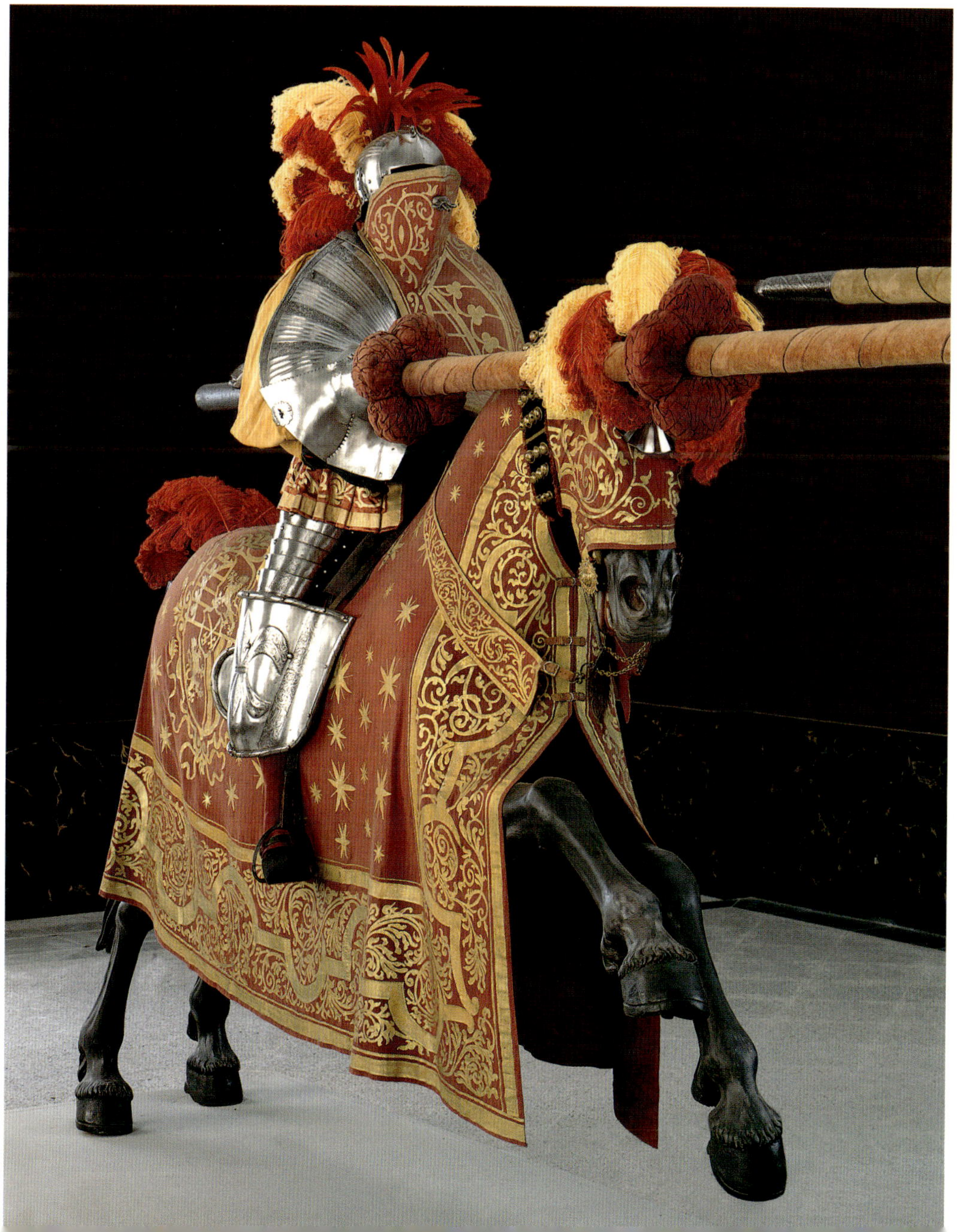

Armor for the Joust
Hans Rosenberger
Dresden, circa 1550
Armor: iron, partly etched and filled in with lead
Targe (shield): wood, covered with canvas, painted
Weight (without targe and tilting sockets)
187½ lbs (85 kg)
Staatliche Kunstsammlungen Dresden, Rüstkammer, inv. no. M 14

34. Berling 1887, pp. 319f.

35. See Gamber 1981, p. 28.

36. *Nachdeme wir ain sondere naigung vnnd begierde tragen vnnd vnns befleissigen vnnserer hochloblichen voreltern vnnd anderer vnnsers Hauß Österreichs verwanndten, vnnd guetten freundt, Leibharnisch wie Sy dieselben zu Kriegs zeiten vnnd Veldtzugen gefuert von guetter vnnd ewiger gedechinus wegen in vnnser Rust Camer zusamen zubringen vnnd zubehalten* (since we feel a special desire and wish in us to honor our forebears and other relatives of our house of Austria, and good friends, we will be gathering, for eternal memory, their personal armor, as carried during wars and campaigns, in our armory where it will be kept). SächsHStA Dresden, Loc. 8503/1 (Österreich, Ertzherzog Ferdinand Schreiben an Churfurst Augustum zu Sachßen ao. 1550. 1585), fol. 142r.

37. *Inventarium über die Rüst- und Inventionskammern auf dem* [...] *Neuen Stall. Anno 1606 revidieret.* The holdings are meticulously listed, mentioning even "*eine alte Tigerhaut mit roter Leinwand gefüttert*" (an old tiger's skin lined with red linen) (p. 1005) and "*zwei moscowiterische wohlriechende Katzenfelle mit einem Schwanz*" (two fragrant cats' skins with tails from Moscow) (p. 1007).

facing page
Rapier and Dagger
Pere Juan Poch, Vienna, 1575
Rapier blade: Forgas Foo Lopes
Diamond-section blade, hilts: gold, enamel
Weight of rapier 2 lbs 9 oz (1,300 grams)
Staatliche Kunstsammlungen Dresden,
Rüstkammer, inv. no. VI 413/p 213

Pallasch
Johann Michael, Prague, 1612
Straight, double-edged blade, hilt: silver gilt, enamel, precious stones, scabbard: wood covered with silver gilt, precious stones, L. 40½ in. (103 cm), L. of scabbard 33⅞ in. (86 cm), weight 4 lbs 4 oz (2,000 g)
Staatliche Kunstsammlungen Dresden,
Rüstkammer, inv. no. Y 353 a

below
August of Saxony's Electoral Sword
Nuremberg, 1566, blade Passau (?)
Blade double-edged, hilt and sheath: silver gilt, enamel
L. 52½ in. (133.5 cm), Weight of sword: 6 lbs 2 oz (2,800 grams), weight of sheath: 5 lbs 3 oz (2,400 grams)
Staatliche Kunstsammlungen Dresden,
Rüstkammer, inv. no. VI 362

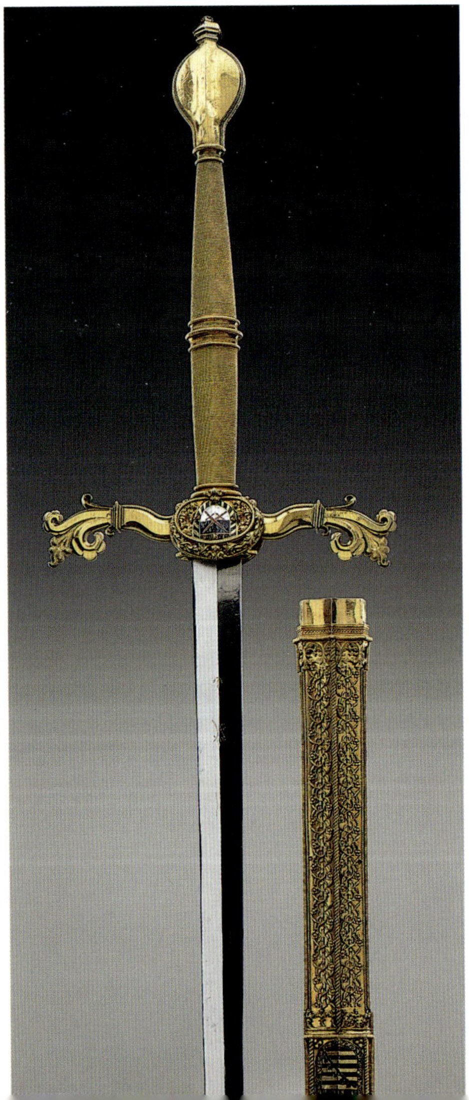

captives. When Christian II received the duchies of Jülich, Cleves, and Berg during a ceremony in Prague on June 7, 1610, the emperor presented the duke with a rich garniture of turquoise-studded weapons made by the Viennese goldsmith Gross.[38]

The Electoral Chamber

The Electoral Chamber (Kurkammer) was of singular importance for the ruling house of Wettin's princely self-awareness. Also located on the third floor of the stable building, it contained the most elaborate swords, rapiers, and daggers with matching sword belts and sword carriers. The electoral swords, which could be seen here, were—from a dynastic and an imperial point of view—among the most precious weapons of the entire armory.

The 1606 inventory, on page 465, lists the electoral sword of Friedrich "the Belligerent," which he received from Emperor Sigismund at the 1425 ceremony in (Ofen) Budapest that celebrated Friedrich's electoral enfeoffment of 1423. It ranks among the most magnificent medieval ceremonial swords belonging to European rulers that survive today. An elaborately silver-mounted ceremonial sword, made by the Nuremberg goldsmith Lorenz Trunk and dated 1547, commemorates the year in which Emperor Charles V bestowed upon Moritz the Electorate of Saxony and the office of the imperial grand marshal (Reichserzmarschall). Although it was not until the 1548 imperial diet in Augsburg that Moritz officially received the sword as a present from the emperor, the 1567 inventory already refers to it as his electoral sword.[39] After his brother's death in 1553, Duke August of Saxony succeeded legitimately to the Saxon electoral office. In 1566, he ordered a new electoral sword in Nuremberg (ill. left). The silver-gilt hilt on the obverse shell guard displays the coat of arms of the Electorate, while the reverse shell guard is adorned with the ducal arms. August carried this electoral sword in April 1566 during a ceremony at the imperial diet in Augsburg when Emperor Maximilian II bestowed upon him the electoral office and the imperial grand marshal's office.

Multiple precious edged weapons came to the Electoral Chamber as princely presents. They testify to the far-reaching diplomatic ties the Albertines had with the leading European royal houses, especially the house of Hapsburg. Among the numerous masterpieces contained in the Kurkammer, special mention must be made of the ceremonial sword garnitures by the Spanish goldsmith Pere Juan Poch of Barcelona. When Emperor Maximilian II stayed in Dresden in 1575, he presented both Elector August and his son Prince Christian I with an enameled gold parade garniture, each consisting of rapier and dagger (ill. p. 79, above). In 1562 the future emperor, King Maximilian II, had presented the loyal elector August with a similarly extravagant rapier garniture with enameled gold hilts, also made by the Spanish goldsmith Poch, at the occasion of Maximilian's election as king during the imperial diet in Frankfurt.

Despite religious differences, relations between the Saxon court and the Hapsburgs during the reign of Elector August were very close. In 1542–43, August spent one year at the courts of Vienna and Prague, where he came to admire the elegant Hapsburg tournaments. August was close friends with Emperor Maximilian II and his younger brother, Archduke Ferdinand of Tyrol. In addition to its political significance, the Hapsburg court—which modeled itself on Italian court culture as well as Burgundian chivalric and courtly traditions—had a major cultural impact on the young Albertine Wettin dynasty throughout the sixteenth century.

The Armory in the Time of Christian II

The administrator Duke Friedrich Wilhelm of Saxony-Weimar-Altenburg—who, after the untimely death of Christian I in 1591, ruled on behalf of, and served as guardian for, the latter's underage son—restricted art-related expenditures to a minimum. Thus, it was only after Christian II came to power in 1601 that a renewed increase in the armory's acquisitions of precious weapons and goldsmith's works is noticeable.

Christian II primarily acquired parade armor, as well as weapons and riding equipment made from precious materials and richly adorned with precious stones. In September 1602, he bought a splendid armor for man and horse from an Augsburg master, which, according to the 1603 inventory, was placed on a horse in the Pallienkammer.[40] This armor, embossed and chased and perhaps made in Augsburg, is entirely decorated with bunches of fruit, birds,

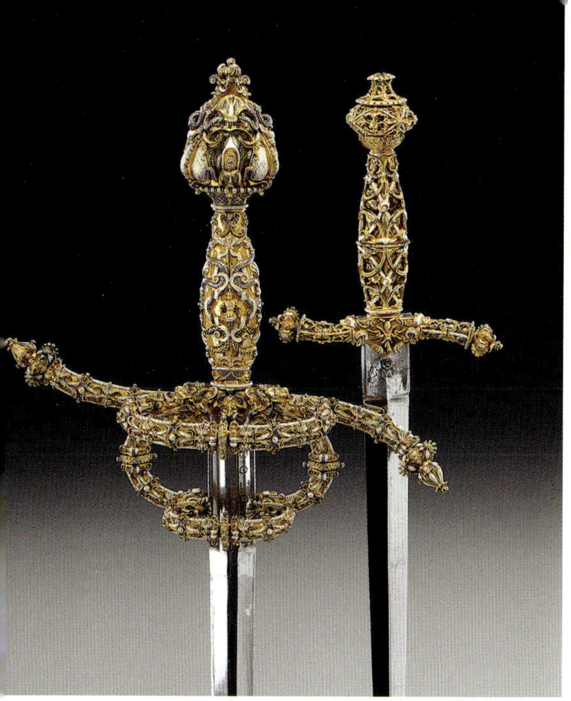

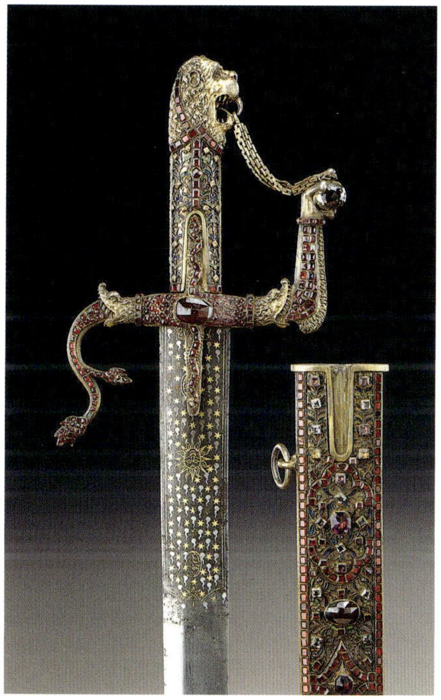

trophies, and scrollwork. Mounts of gilt copper, showing equestrian and battle scenes, add an effective contrast to the gray steel surface. Dated 1599 in the decoration on the sole of the left sabaton, this armor is a remarkable example of Mannerist art.[41]

Formerly kept in the Chamber for Tilting Armor, the parade armor for man and horse (ill. p. 74) by the Antwerp goldsmith Eliseus Libaerts is to this day considered the most significant work of art owned by the Dresden Armory.[42] Documented to 1563–64, it was purchased in 1606 by the ostentatious elector Christian II for the immense sum of 8,800 guilders (Gulden), which was paid in installments until 1609. The acquisition had been negotiated by the Nuremberg goldsmith Heinrich Knopf.[43] This garniture, embossed, chased, etched, and partly gilt, is one of the most outstanding examples of the armorer's art in existence. It was originally made as a commission for the Swedish king Erik XIV. However, this sovereign of the house of Vasa, suitor to the English queen Elizabeth I, never came into possession of this set: The Danish king Frederick II, at war with Sweden, captured it as war booty in 1564. The garniture is decorated with repoussé tendrils, flowers, fruit, butterflies, snakes, dolphins, masks, and putti, as well as medallions with scenes from ancient mythology. While the armor for man primarily depicts events from the Trojan War and the legend of the Argonauts, the horse armor is embellished with fourteen medallions showing the Labors of Hercules. In 1611, a so-called Freudenritter (literally, "joyful knight"), the squire Hans von Drandorf, wore this suit at the elector's funeral *in effigie* (i.e., as an image of the deceased).[44]

An extraordinary example of oriental influence on Central European art is Christian II's garniture of parade arms, which he apparently ordered from Johann Michael in 1610 during a visit to Prague.[45] It was not delivered until 1612, after Christian II had died. The garniture consists of pallasch, mace, saber, spurs, riding gear, saddle, and saddle blanket, the last having the name of the elector inlaid in rubies. The silver-gilt hilts of the weapons, as well as the mounts, are embellished with garnets, topazes, amethysts, and crystals, as well as filigree ornaments of enameled wire. Christian's brother and successor, Johann Georg I, honored the outstanding payment to the Prague goldsmith, who also worked for the courts in Prague, Vienna, and Munich.

After the early death of Christian II, the collection retained its late-sixteenth-century structure, although some changes are noticeable: Chambers were remodeled or divided because the old needed to make room for the new. Under Electors Christian I and Christian II, acquisitions and additions to the armory had reached a climax. Although their successors, Electors Johann Georg I and Johann Georg II, added a number of extraordinary pieces of armor and riding equipment, their activities as collectors were primarily focused on weapons and accessories for the hunt. The tournament as a courtly pastime had lost much of its importance, whereas elegant hunts increasingly emerged as a princely focus of attention.[46] Until the beginning of the eighteenth century, the armory—along with the Kunstkammer and the Riesensaal (Hall of the Giants)—remained one of the Dresden palace's greatest attractions. When visiting Johann Georg I in September 1629, the Augsburg envoy Hainhofer aptly remarked about the Dresden court: "*Vnd ist in disen Rüstkammern so vil dings zu sehen, das ainer nicht augen, nicht zeit, vnd nicht hirns genug hat, alles zu observieren vnd in acht zu nemmen*" (there is so much material kept in these armories that one has neither the eyes, the time, nor brains enough to observe and take it all in).[47]

38. Schuckelt 1998/1999, p. 42.
39. *Inventarium über des [...] Fürsten und Herrn [...] Augusten, [...] Rüstkammer und Wehren, November 1567*, fol. 76.
40. Complete inventory of 1606, p. 175; Armory inv. no. M 101.
41. Haenel 1923, p. 30.
42. *Rustkammer*, inv. no. M 100.
43. Bäumel 1995c, p. 64.
44. Further acquisitions and additions worth mentioning include a muli-part, turquoise-embellished hunting garniture fabricated in 1606 as a commission from Christian II by the Dresden goldsmith Gabriel Gipfel, as well as a hunting garniture by the same master adorned with 193 emeralds and comprising hanger, trousse, horn with suspension gear, hunting bag, and dog's collar. In 1608, Christian II gave this garniture to his brother Johann Georg (I) as a Christmas gift (cat. no. 27).
45. Haenel 1923, p. 122.
46. Both electors were passionate hunters and, like their predecessors, held the office of Erzjägemeister (Master of the Hunt) of the Holy Roman Empire.
47. Doering 1901, p. 194.

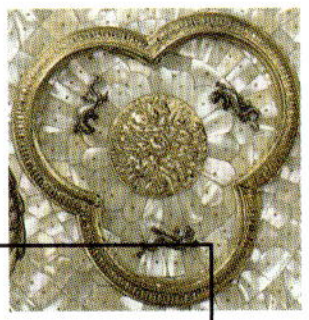

Exotica and the Kunstkammer: "Snake Stones, Iridescent Sea Snails, and Eggs of the Giant Iron-Devouring Bird"*

Wolfram Koeppe

"It had embossed on its surface the entire history of the world and mankind. Its wondrousness derived from the cumulative effect of diverse subjects and details and from the bringing together in one space apparently dissimilar things."[1] Homer's description of the shield of Achilles, legendary hero of the Trojan War, could also serve as a definition of a sixteenth-century princely Kunstkammer. Such a wondrous object exemplifies the theoretical underpinning of these kinds of curiosity rooms. The extravagant and the mysterious were in demand, regardless of whether they were created by an artist or by nature in a capricious mood. Domestic or exotic monstrosities and platonic theories concerning shape and beauty were part of the same idea, inseparably united like the two faces of a Janus head or like the obverse and reverse sides of an ancient coin or a Renaissance medal. However, none of this was a sixteenth-century invention: the admiration of beauty of all kinds and a thirst for knowledge appear to have been always part of the human character. Suetonius reports that the Roman emperor Augustus "decorated his villas not only with statues and pictures but also with *curiosa* of considerable age or great rarity, such as the gigantic remains of deformed creatures, called the 'giants' bones,' as well as heroes' weapons."[2]

The World in the Kunstkammer

The Renaissance was the era of discovery, especially of the New World, and an epoch in which one constantly attempted to achieve the supposedly impossible. Since the middle of the sixteenth century, detailed information about newly discovered territories was gathered. The growth of the long-distance trade with foreign countries brought ever new, curious natural products and ethnological objects to the amazed Europeans.[3]

The Kunstkammer played an important role in this period of change, characterized by fundamental political tension and religious conflicts on the eve of the Thirty Years War. The Kunstkammer united and exhibited, in an encyclopedic manner, dissimilar works of art as universal reflections of the world. The objects were mostly produced from diverse materials and artistically embellished by adding exotic materials (*exotica*).

The three most important areas of interest were artworks created by human hands (*arteficialia* and *artefacta*), extravagant natural products (*naturalia*) such as the Emerald Cluster (cat. no. 162), and scientific instruments (*scientifica*), in those times regarded as a mirror measuring and influencing the change of the world.

Compared to other European collections, the Dresden had a strikingly large number of *scientifica*. In the words of Philipp de Mornay, "sure the sky is as the great wheel of a clock."[4] The exact functioning of a clock symbolized the rational, centrally guided order of the world in a tangible way. The fabrication and function of a complicated clock or an automaton work were considered artistic metaphors for the creator of the universe, for "God as clock maker," as the center of a cosmic miracle and the almighty ruler of the universe, his own "Kunstkammer."

*Dedicated to Professor Willibald Sauerländer, Munich. My special thanks go to Ulrike Weinhold, who gave me access to all inventory files and information regarding the Dresden Kunstkammer objects. For references I would like to thank the following individuals: Dirk Syndram, Jutta Kappel, Antje Scherner, Eva Graßhoff, Dresden; Bernhard Heitmann, Hamburg; Ian Wardropper, Clare Vincent, Marina Nudel, Ruth Stanton and especially Richard E. Stone and Joern Lohmann, New York; as well as Michelangelo Lupo, Trento and Yvonne Fritz, Heidelberg.

1. *The Iliad*, 18.478–613. See also Koeppe, "Collecting for the Kunstkammer," at http://www.metmuseum.org, keyword "Timeline."
2. G. Suetonius Tranquillus, *De Vita Caesarum: Divus Augustus*, chapter 72. For the reproduction of similar settings in modern times see Mauriès 2002.
3. Brunswick 2000, pp. 16–17 (with further bibliography).
4. Patry 1933, p. 9, see also the essays by Dirk Syndram in this volume, as well as cat. no. 154.
5. The title page was decorated with allegories and served as the model for a silver "mirror frame" preserved in The Metropolitan Museum of Art (inv. no 17.190.620), created by Wenzel I Jamnitzer around 1568. The ovoid mirror with faceted edge, is distinguished by a crowning lion mascaron in silver repoussé: a clear reference to the maker's mark of Jamnitzer, the letter "W" over a lion's head. This leads to the assumption that a portrait of the artist or of a princely first owner was formerly mounted in the oval below. While this image might have been painted on copper, parchment, or carved out of exotic mother-of-pearl, or any other delicate material (like Limoges enamel), it was later lost. The central part of the once larger cover of a precious silver book binding of Jamnitzer's treaty was subsequently readopted as a mirror. For more information about this see Koeppe (like footnote 1), keyword "Timeline" and "Jamnitzer."
6. Guide Green Vault 1997, p. 9.
7. Quoted after Distelberger 2000, p. 19.
8. "gantz dunkelgrün, mit dergleichen aber schwärtzern Flecken, wie auff den [exotischen] Schlangenhäuten zu sehen, davon ihm auch der Name gegeben worden." Hoyer 1995, p. 1.
9. Comprehensively in: Berlin 2003, pp. 188–93.
10. See the so-called Natterbaum, circa 1500, Green Vault, inv. no. IV 108, Guide Green Vault 1997, p. 61, no. 9; Schiedlausky 1989.

Works of ancient mythology, science, and philosophy also formed an important section. The most popular Renaissance manifestos were mandatory readings for the exclusive circle of those who owned them and were trained in humanist teachings. The *Perspectiva corporum regularium* written by Wenzel Jamnitzer in 1568 was such a standard work.[5]

Natural products and curiosities could also be found in a Kunstkammer if they furthered knowledge or if they could be admired and researched in a scientific fashion. All items of the collection had in common was to represent a most exquisite finish as well as the most recent technical and artistical developments. This distinctive characteristic of the Saxon Kunstkammer descends from the centuries-old local industrial tradition which remained in force up until the eighteenth century.[6]

Montefeltro Madonna
Piero della Francesca
1472–74
Oil on wood
97⅝ × 66⅞ in. (248 × 170 cm)
Pinacoteca di Brera, Milan

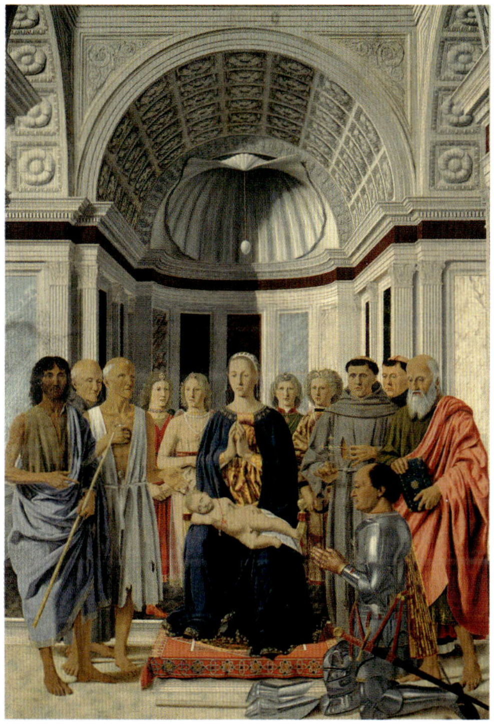

Order and the Grotesque

Objects were stored in wall cabinets and on shelves and particularly in precious cabinet furniture of miscellaneous sizes, which also functioned as independent display pieces. Included in this exhibition are a small cabinet from Augsburg (cat. no. 157) and the Kunstkammer hunting and work desk of Elector Johann Georg I of Saxony (cat. no. 161). The polished black surface of exotic ebony, a valuable material then traded by the pound, was adorned with minutely engraved, contrasting silver inlays. Thus, such furniture, extraordinary artistic achievements, were raised to the sphere of multifunctional, courtly works of art. Their refined design and technical brilliance, *ars* and *natura* amalgamated, further intensify the aura of these objects' almost unbelievable virtuosity. Numerous drawers offered space for the storage of medicine, precious objects, and foreign *curiosa nova*. The larger cabinets in Dresden contained small collections symbolizing, as microcosmic "collections within the collection," the world in its entirety within the Kunstkammer. A richly decorated case with heterogeneous content united scientific observation and humanist discourse. Eccentric objects with multilayered meanings, often entailing sexual overtones, gave rise to entertaining and amusing discussions.

If a natural product was grotesque, rare, wondrous, different, and of indeterminable age or of striking beauty—either before or after embellishment by human hands—it was frequently given multiple symbolic meanings. If *naturalia* were of exotic origin or if they were procured with much effort and danger, possibly unearthed from domestic soil, their material value was equal to that of the most lavish luxury items made of precious metal. Rudolf Distelberger, the eminent Kunstkammer scholar, defined three subcategories for natural products: *mineralia* (the subterranean realm), *vegetabilia* (the terrestrial realm), and *animalia* (the superterrestrial realm). The Augsburg collector and art agent Philipp Hainhofer, who provided objects for the most renowned of the courtly European collector's cabinets, stated in 1605: "If someone gives something exotic, be it a natural product or a work of art, to my small Kunstkammer, the pleasure I derive from it is larger than that I take from any gift of cash." ("Wenn mir ainer etwas solches frembdes es sei jezt von rebus naturalibus or artificialibus in mein Kunstkammerlein schencket, so geschüht mir mehrers wohlgefallen daran, als wenn er mir baargeld gibt.") Emperor Maximilian II took a pragmatic approach and without hesitation stated his motto regarding collecting: *Quanta rariora tanta meliora* (The rarer, the better).[7]

"Snake Stone"

Serpentine played a substantial role in Saxony. A contemporary source described it as "entirely dark green, with the same but black spots, like those seen on [exotic] snake-skins, this is also from whence the name is derived."[8] Since ancient times, serpentine was considered a magical substance with apotropaic powers, especially protection from poison. The material was thus predestined for transformation into precious tableware, vessels (cat. nos. 92–96), as well as other Kunstkammer objects (cat. no. 160) for the Saxon court. According to the princely users' views, natural healing powers and divine mercy formed a symbiosis in serpentine. The constant fear of poisoning gave rise to strict ceremonial rules for courtly banquets.[9] The cup-bearer or the court official precutting the meat touched the food with a piece of unicorn horn (narwhal tusk), viper's tongue (petrified sharks' teeth),[10] or serpentine to as-

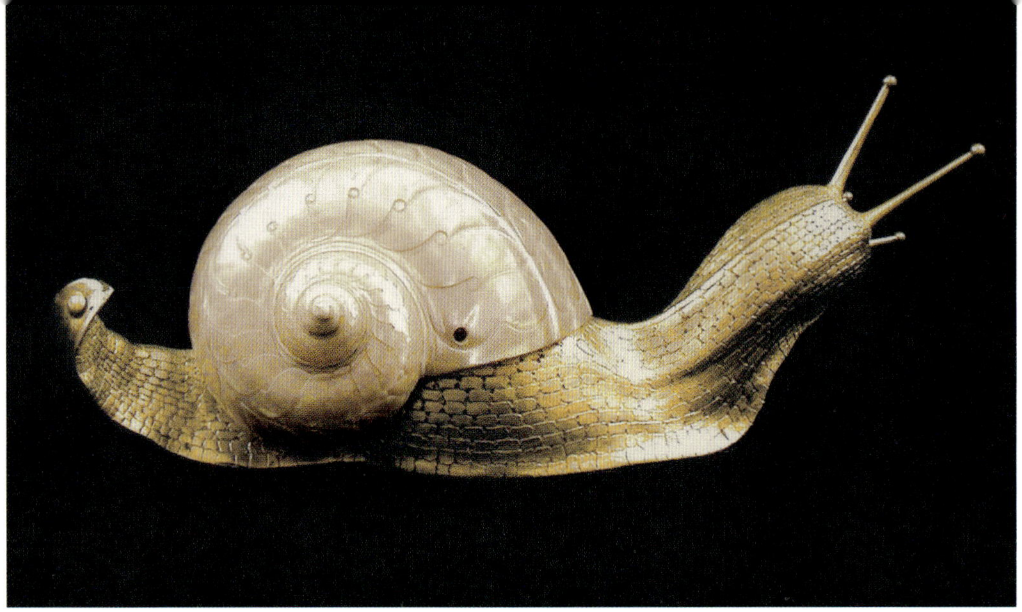

Giant Snail as Versatoio
Florence, circa 1608
Turban snail
(*Turbo marmoratus*)
with European decoration,
silver-gilt
H. 3⅞ in. (10 cm)
W. 12⅞ in. (32.8 cm)
Museo degli Argenti, Florence,
inv. no. Bg. 1917 (V), no. 18

certain that the food was innocuous. Ambroise Paré, personal physician to King Charles IX of France, noted that unicorn horn was ten times more expensive than gold. Before the vast Saxon serpentine deposits began to be exploited during the course of the sixteenth century, the price for "snake stone" was almost equal to that of unicorn horn; consequently the sovereign's administration enforced strict regulation of the mining industry. The Saxon esteem for serpentine and its ability to prevent poisoning and evil grew to almost absurd superstitious levels.

In 1524 Georg the Bearded, the last Catholic duke of the Wettin Albertine line, commissioned a portal in the fashionable style of the Augsburg Renaissance. Made of light-colored limestone, this entrance to his funerary chapel in the cathedral of Meissen was embellished with serpentine columns. At the same time, the duke ordered a new superstructure, in the same "Italian [Renaissance] taste" and adorned with serpentine and having a comparable color scheme, for Saint Benno's tomb in the cathedral (destroyed in 1539, during the Reformation after Georg's death). The duke thus appears to have appointed himself as the saint's successor and "faithful servant of the old [Catholic] faith," as the ruler is called on a contemporary medal. Interestingly in a 1518 letter addressed to Duke Georg Martin Luther used the term "Reformation" for the first time. The question remains whether the abundant use of serpentine only served the princely urge for *repraesentatio* or whether Duke Georg wanted, based on his conviction, to prevent the "poisonous" and "new reformed faith" from contaminating his tomb and the relics, i.e., the "quasi-sacred, wondrous Kunstkammer pieces of his favorite Saint Benno."[11]

Coral

Following Ovid and Pliny the Elder, many Renaissance collectors believed that noble red coral was a flexible plant that turned into stone upon being removed from its marine surroundings.[12] Stone or petrification, the mythological origins of coral were undisputed at the time: The blood-red coral was believed to have come into being when Perseus, flying over the seas on Pegasus, held up the decapitated Medusa's head, which dripped blood into the water with hissing sounds, causing the coral to grow. According to Paracelsus, coral protected against fits, sorcery, charms, and poison and healed ailments of the blood. With its bizarrely ramified shape, this hard shiny material gave a domestic stag's antlers an exotic character and an air of strength, while it also commanded apotropaic powers (cat. no. 117). Decorated with coral, a drinking vessel in the shape of Actaeon (cat. no. 118) or two drinking vessels in the shape of a courtly couple in contemporary Renaissance costumes (cat. no. 119) were characterized as mythological creatures.

A special combination of two natural materials is revealed in the cup and cover incorporating a turban snail with feet of Venus shells (cat. no. 107). The piece of coral that serves as the lid's finial could be turned upside down and immersed in the liquid in the turban snail

11. Koeppe 2002. In addition to the magical meaning attributed to serpentine, increasing emphasis was placed on its practical characteristics; see the essay of Jutta Kappel in this volume.
12. Scheicher 1995; Philippovich 1966, pp. 121–38.
13. Stahl 2003, p. 61.
14. Scheicher 1995; Fritz 1983; Rasmussen 1983; Mette 1995; Tax 1995; Stark 2003/2004.
15. Koeppe 1989, ill. 1; Syndram 1991a, p. 40, color plate 8; Gabbi 2000, p. 54; in general: Emerson/Feininger 1972, p. 239, no. 3-22a.
16. Quoted and translated after: Brunswick 2000, pp. 52–53.

Gatshina Cup and Cover
Joerg I (Georg) Ruel
Nuremberg, circa 1610–20
Turban snail
(*Turbo marmoratus*), silver-gilt
H. 14⅝ in. (37.1 cm)
From the Collection of Gregory
Orlov, Gatshina Palace near
St. Petersburg, after 1917
in the Moscow Armory, today
Lemmers-Danforth-Sammlung,
Wetzlar, inv. no. G04

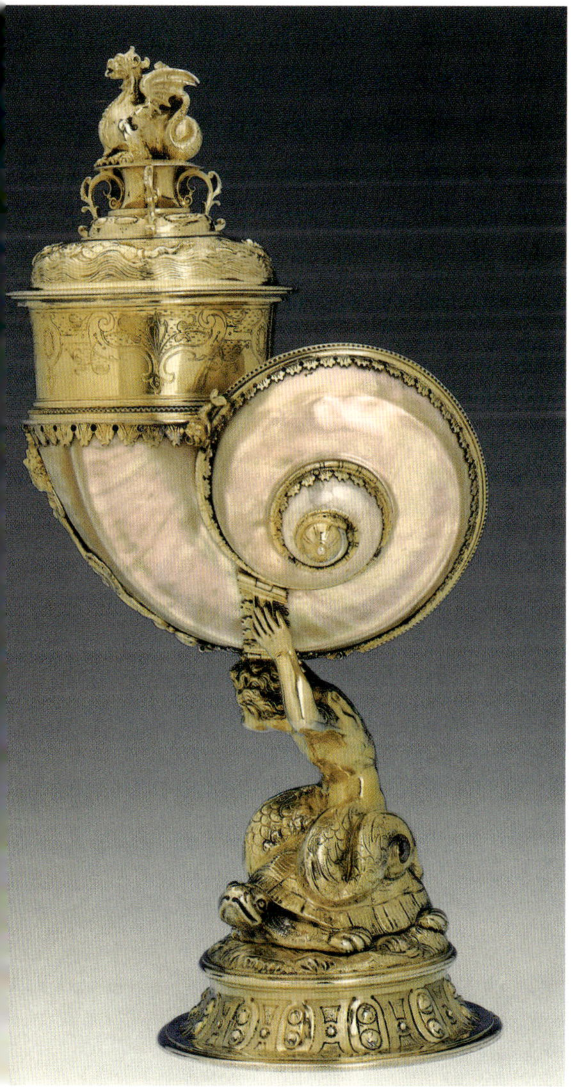

cup. The pharmaceutical and aphrodisiacal effects of the applied coral and snail would complement each other. The gesticulating creatures on the shaft give tribute to Venus as goddess of love. She is also present through the shells (presumably formed after *Chlamys rubida/varia*) that symbolize her and give the object stability.

Turban Snail

The 1612 coronation diaries of Emperor Matthias give a vivid account of the festival banquet. Between the electoral tables stood three-tiered, velvet-covered presentation buffets that displayed the electoral gold and silver—ewers and basins, wine coolers, chain-bottles, as well as diverse cups with buckles, cups with mounted coconuts, ostrich eggs, or nautilus shells—which were "all very precious and heroic to look at" ("*alles gantz prechtig und Heroisch* [an] *zusehen*"). The preciousness of the exhibits and the buffet's number of tiers indicated that those present were of the highest social ranks. The imperial buffet surpassed all others.[13] This description reveals the importance of the vessels made of natural products—such as coconut cups (cat. nos. 121, 122) and nautilus cups (cat. nos. 113, 114)—in court ceremonies as well as those festivities that proclaimed the princely *magnificenza*.

There have been recent monographs dedicated to numerous exotica, including coconut and nautilus cups and bezoar stones. Two exotica abundantly represented in the Dresden collections merit further attention: the ostrich egg and the turban snail, which in particular epitomize humanist thought during Renaissance and Early Baroque periods.

The turban snail is found in the Indian and the Pacific Oceans. For the inhabitants of those coastlines, the exotic sea, with its mostly constant warm temperatures, was the source of fertility and the origin of the vast diversity of all living creatures. The *Turbo marmoratus* (or *Turbo olearius*), the largest representative of the family of spiral-formed snails (*turbinides*) in the species of snails (*gastropoda*) is the shell creature most often confused—in the art historical context—with the *Nautilus pompilius*. In contrast to that of the nautilus, the shell of the much rarer turban snail has a one-sided spiral, visible on the exterior. Added to the exotic appeal of the iridescent mother-of-pearl layer (*hypostracum*), revealed when the outer surface is cut away,[15] was the complex symbolic meaning of the snail itself as an allegory of Vanity. Klaus Minges wrote: "On the one hand, the fascinating 'wonder' is that a mollusk is capable of creating, from nothing but water, a hard shell, later transformed into shell lime [washed ashore onto beaches before the waves grind the fragments that are ultimately completely dissolved]. Conchs were considered examples of Aristotle's doctrine of transformation which held that every element can be transformed into another one. With the roaring heard from the large snail shells, suggesting waves and wind, even the element air gained access. The shell itself is distinguished, [...] in the case of snails, through its lucid luster, comparable to the one admired in Chinese porcelain. Apart from its beauty, the shell's spiral construction also shows theoretical perfection, as it proved in detail through the Fibonacci sequence [in *Practica geometriae*, circa 1220], and thus drawing a line between the *artes liberales* and nature. In addition to that, there is a similarity between the shell's opening and the female genitalia. This gave rise to multitudes of symbolic references concerning fertility and erotic connotations later projected onto the [snails]. The mythical birth of Venus from a shell describes a pagan symbolism of fertility and love later adapted by the Christians. Apparently out of nothing, the pearl emerges inside the shell and thus transforms it, symbolizing the immaculate conception of the Virgin"[16] (ill. p. 81). Embodying its cathartic and aphrodisiac powers was the shell's bizarre shape: here, the element of growth and therefore the dimension of time are connected to the spiral construction of the conical snail shell. In the sense of *sic transit gloria mundi* (thus vanishes the world's glory), the shell signified the mortal frame that an individual could not take to the beyond—a reference to the transitory nature of all earthly things.

The symbolism was also extended to the special living conditions of the snail: the animal is forced to carry its shell for the duration of its life. Thus, the notion of Vanity entered into an interplay with the emblematic interpretation of nature, emphasizing human enslavement to enduring burdens and worldly goods. In his 1567 *Science of Hieroglyphs*, Pierio Valeriano interprets the snails as follows: "Snail means the soul captured in this passion and animalistic lust. Hesiod explained this secular slavery as something from which the soul cannot free itself in the same way the snail is insolubly connected with the house it carries on its back"[17] (ill. p. 82).

The English term for the turban, "the great green turban snail," emphasizes the marbled green layer covering the mother-of-pearl. The shell's spiral shape is reminiscent of that of a turban. In England and on the European continent, the turban stood for the pagan, Islamic world. The alien headgear aroused—like the turban snail—curiosity about the exotic East. At the same time, the "turban" symbolized the Muslim rulers, the sultans, and hence represented power and wealth. Queen Elizabeth I of England stated: "Better the turban than the tiara" (the latter referring to the triple papal crown) and thereby intimated the changing alliances with the Ottoman Empire in the fight against Catholicism.[18] Arnold von Harff, a fifteenth-century traveler to the Near East, reported that in Cairo "the Christians wore a blue turban, the Turks a white turban, and the Jews a yellow."[19] A "green turban was an indication of a direct lineage from the prophet," whose color is green.[20] It is likely that before the Dutch East India Company was founded in 1601—when such exotic items first began to be imported in large numbers—the rarity and preciousness of the green turban snail popularized such associations. In every collection of *conchils*, the turban shell was the owner's pride. This was evident in the gesture of the collector Jan Govertz, who presents a large turban shell to the viewer in his 1603 portrait by Hendrick Goltzius.[21]

Sea Snails and Goldsmithing

Turban snails first came to Europe via the traditional trade route, that is, by the Silk Road to Cairo or Constantinople and then to Venice and other European ports. Portuguese maritime trade with Muslims grew rapidly during the early modern period.[22] Early gold-mounted snail shells are known in Russia, where even imported shells with Chinese inscriptions are documented. Previously used as cups for ceremonial purposes in the Middle Kingdom, they were adapted as boxes.[23]

A turban snail with a simple, gilded mount forms an integral part of the *teatro delle cose naturali* in a small travel box in Dresden,[24] where it served as a tumbler. The use of turban shells for the cups of artistically rendered cups was a solution that presented itself quite naturally. A multitude of different variations in Dresden's Kunstkammer (cat. no. 107) testifies to their popularity.[25]

Another Kunstkammer piece demonstrating extraordinary German (more particularly Nuremberg) skill was the so-called Gatshina Cup and cover, made by Joerg (Georg) Ruel around 1610–20 (ill. p. 83).[26] Its iconographic program emphasizes the liquid element, the water of the distant, exotic ocean, where the snail originated before it became an integral part of this Nuremberg piece. The master was a specialist in such challenging tasks resulting in inventively conceived artworks of which numerous examples have survived in Dresden and other princely collections (cat. no. 101).[27]

The basin, inlaid with mother-of-pearl tessarae, belonged to a lavabo garniture in Dresden (ill. p. 86), which comes from the Gujarat region in India (see also cat. no. 100). The decoration and gilding of the light-reflecting silver-gilt mount with turban snail cabochons between three-dimensional reclining figures on the basin's border transform the exotic iridescent materials into an artificial display garniture that could only be found in a princely Kunstkammer. There is an obvious connection between the small basilisk on the Gatshina Cup and lid and the magnificent basilisk ewer with its three integrated turban snails. The latter functions as a monumental rose-water ewer, and the symbolism of the first elevates the same model to the rank of a much admired small-scale sculpture embellishing the finial of a *figura serpentinata*-like turban cup, as it would be the large ewer's *cousin en miniature*. Both intricate objects display the mythological creature with its muscled leg and claws poised to strike. Through the location on a high pedestal, the grotesquely animated physical demeanor of both individuals is raised to an astonishing Mannerist artistic level. Recent research and detailed scrutiny reveal that the small volutes at the back of the head and the incised

17. Koeppe 1992, p. 458; see also Piero Valeriano, *Hieroglyphica*, 1567, p. 203 and Zurich 1985, pp. 5ff.
18. Matar 1996, p. 42.
19. Harff/Letts 1946, p.113.
20. Matar (like footnote 18), p. 45.
21. Amsterdam 1992, p. 200; Amsterdam 2003, cat. no. 104, p. 287.
22. Comprehensively: Vienna 2000; Risso 1995.
23. Koeppe 1997.
24. Menzhausen 1977, ill. 10, inv. no. III 247.
25. Additional pieces in the Guide Green Vault 1997, p. 43, no. 25, pp. 46–47, no. 43, 48 and presently in the reserves of the Green Vault.
26. The cup (most recently published in Heidelberg, cat. no. 271) reveals numerous technical details that reappear in Ruel's *Kettenflasche* (Drinking Flask with Chain), such as the elevated 'wave or comb line' that underscores the mount's straps (cat. no. 101 and Koeppe 1989, ill. 18/19); only done in this way by this master (examination of the *Kettenflasche* with Ulrike Weinhold and Dirk Syndram on January 20, 2003 in Dresden). For other works by Ruel in Dresden see: Guide Green Vault 1997, p. 40, no. 8. Two members of the "*Forschungsprojekt zur Nürnberger Goldschmiedekunst*," Germanisches Nationalmuseum Nuremberg, have called into discussion the Nuremberg provenance of this cup (Karin Tebbe, letter dated May 23, 2002 and Ralf Schürer, email dated June 5, 2002 to the author): The base without ornamental volute bands is "not only atypical for Rühl, but also atypical for other Nuremberg works." Without further comment, it suffices to point to Dresden inv. no. III 200, III 156/193, IV 261, and III 163. The "atypically profiled lip reveals an engraving not typical of the 17th century." (K. Tebbe) The "type of lip, normally with outwards curving [...], but never [occurs] with such a pronounced profile" (R. Schürer), and "Decorated edges of this type did not belong to the customary Nuremberg embellishment of such vessels [...] mostly, the motifs are [...] of maritime nature [... [and]...] the border decoration observed in Nuremberg is barely engraved but mostly planar etching (before 1600)... or later line etching." The Turban Cup by Ruel, preserved in Amsterdam and many other Nuremberg works reveal a lip with engraved and not etched lip decoration. Among them the Turban Cup in Skokloster, cat. no. 112 in this exhibition, as well as other Nuremberg cups in Dresden and the Ostrich Egg Cup by Ruel in the Germanisches Nationalmuseum Nuremberg (inv. no. HG 11771). K. Tebbe remarks: "the figure of a basilisk is placed on the lid, for which there is no comparison in Nuremberg" (for this see ill. p. 86 and this text). "The lid," states R. Schürer "we do indeed not encounter in Nuremberg in this shape; especially the two-part 'lid-on-the-lid' is really not customary." The *Kettenflasche* (cat. no. 101) and the Amsterdam Turban Cup by Ruel (Amsterdam 1992, cat. no. 100) reveal an even more pronounced form of 'lid-on-the-lid,' that may be encountered in a still more exaggerated manner in the Turban Cup in Skokloster (*Quasi Centrum Europae. Europa kauft in Nürnberg ein, 1400–1800*, exhibition catalogue, Nuremberg 2002, cat. no. 71, p. 227) and in those by Petzolt in Stuttgart/Budapest. The Wetzlar Cup was examined, among others, by W. Scheffler, K. Pechstein, H. Tait (Waddesdon Bequest, vol. III, cat. no. 33, p. 286), G. Schiedlausky, B. Heitmann, G. Markova, Helmut Seling (the latter after detailed photos) and most recently by Clare Vincent, and Richard E. Stone, The Metropolitan Museum of Art, in the laboratory in New York (for example, aside from the material, R. Stone investigated the screws that did not correspond to the "metric system," that was not introduced until the late eighteenth century). The cup was called "original" by all mentioned above.
27. In addition, the drinking vessel from the collection of Gregory Orlov (ill. p. 83) in Gatshina Palace incorporates typological details of similar works in this exhibition: the Triton as shaft figure testifies to the influence of Italian small bronzes, that can also be grasped in the Hercules figure on a cup by Friedrich Hillebrandt (cat. no. 112; see also cat. no. 129). The efficient Nuremberg goldsmiths were indeed intimately familiar with such small bronzes. The Praunsche Kunstkabinet, as well as the collections of other Nuremberg patricians contained a rich variety of Italian bronze sculpture. Further models belonged to the formal canon of local masters, or they could be obtained as casts and collected as prints during the obligatory journeymen's travel period [*Wanderjahre*]. As a goldsmith, Christoph Jamnitzer, the grandson of Wenzel I Jamnitzer, was understandably proud of his familiarity with Italian sculpture. Conscious of his own social status as he was, he had himself portrayed with a *bozzetto*—based on an original either from the circle of Michelangelo or Jacopo Sansovino—made of red wax and created by himself. See also Seelig 2002, cat. no. 58.

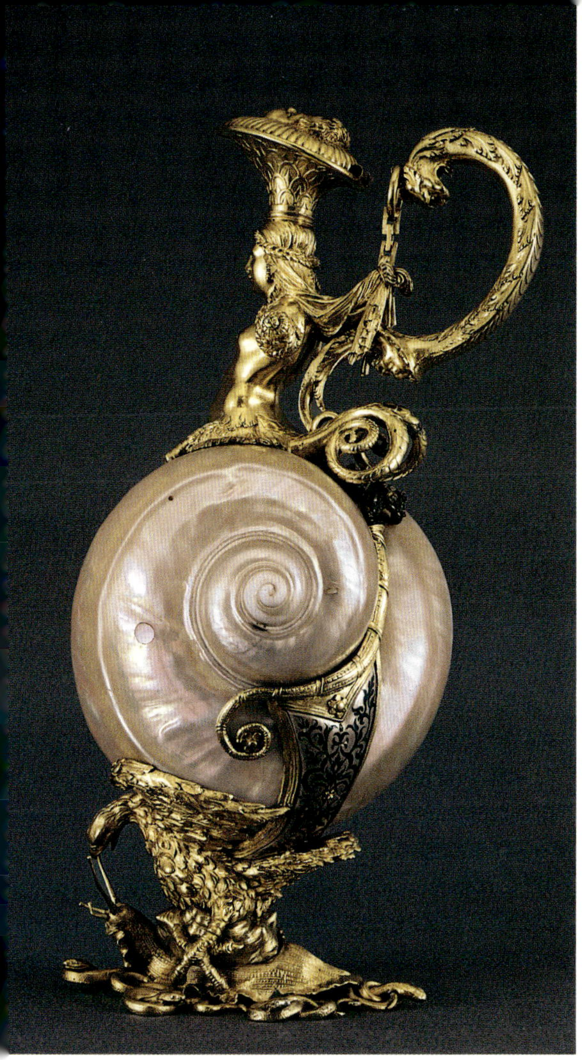

Parade Ewer
Wenzel Jamnitzer
Nuremberg, circa 1570
Two turban snail shells
(*Turbo marmoratus*)
Silver, partly gilt, enamel
H. 12¾ in. (32.5 cm)
Residenz Munich, Treasury,
inv. no. Res.Mü.Sch. 567

teardrop-shape breast decoration of both pieces are unmistakably inspired by a series of engravings by Hans Collaert the Elder, published in Antwerp in 1582.[28]

Wenzel I Jamnitzer was likely the first to integrate more than one exotic snail shell into a precious ewer. He had produced his masterwork, possibly the most elaborate Kunstkammer object with turban snails ever produced, a parade ewer preserved in Munich's Treasury (ill. left) a generation earlier. Its base is formed of a tangle of serpents cast from nature, as was the snail, both of which were given detailed finishing touches by the goldsmith. The eagle, serving as the heraldic base, displaying its wing-spreads and physical power evident to each beholder, was created by human hands. Despite its miniaturization the bird is shown in a forceful attack and contributes to the monumentality of the whole composition. The combination of *ars* and *natura*, essential to the Kunstkammer concept, could only be realized with such perfection by a great artist.

Elias Geyer, active since 1589 as a goldsmith in Leipzig, the prosperous city of fairs, apparently specialized in mounting exotica and in creating outstanding silverware, as did Joerg Ruel and Friedrich Hillebrand in Nuremberg. The Dresden collection unites no fewer than fifteen of Geyer's marked works. Regarded as infinite, the oceans' depths were the mythical realm of Neptune and his entourage, the Nereids, Tritons, and sea horses, as well as other wondrous marine creatures. Geyer created multiple, highly imaginative interpretations of these aquatic creatures for the Saxon electors who often exchanged them as personal gifts. Made of silver-gilt, these sculptures were full of fantasy and often integrated turban snails (cat. nos. 108–110). In her catalogue entries, Ulrike Weinhold refers to the respective Kunstkammer inventories mentioning the cups as "*Meermänlein, Meerweibsbild*" (little man from the sea, mermaid) and "*Meer Rosse mit Perlmutter Schnecken*" (sea horses with mother-of-pearl snails). Their appearance is so distinctive that even without his maker's mark the objects can unmistakably be attributed to Elias Geyer.[29]

The use of turban snails with their shiny color spectrum and the dynamic motion of the circular spiral pyramid in conjunction with the intricate silver work lend the figures a seemingly unsurpassable position as sparkling Kunstkammer pieces *par excellence*. A comparable visual effect can in my opinion be seen only in some of the Dresden collection's turned ivories (see cat. nos. 87, 88).

Another extraordinary piece by Elias Geyer is his mother-of-pearl ewer (cat. no. 100). What look to be ovoid mother-of-pearl pieces in cabochon form mounted into the vessel's wall are in fact calottes of turban shells. This is proved by the knotty striations on the spiral's surface. Based on this observation, Geyer must have had a very efficient supplier for such costly items. It seems that long-distance dealers specializing in exotica fulfilled a portion of the demand during Leipzig's trade fairs.[30] The mother-of-pearl cabochons might originate from damaged turban shells that could thus be used in first-class artworks without incurring a large depreciation of this commodity. They might likewise be parts of exotic semi-finished products such as *Laffen*, that could be transformed into bowls or spoons.[31] The turban cabochons are not an individual case, as they can also be seen in the basin of the Lavabo (ill. p. 86). The painted still life of some Kunstkammer vessels of the English Paston family shows a drinking flask with chain, made with such turban snail calottes and embellished with delicate hinged silver-gilt straps (this object is in a private collection in New York). Another similar flask without mounts from the Gujarat region is in the Kunsthistorisches Museum Kunstkammer, Vienna.[32]

From time to time, the goldsmiths attempted to achieve even more illusionistic effects by creating the most extreme type of naturalism feasible. In such instances, they even reproduced the details of the snails' fleshy parts. This is documented in a cup in the Musée de la Renaissance in Écouen, in a snail with nautilus shell in the Wadsworth Atheneum in Hartford, and in the giant snail in the Museo degli Argenti in Florence (ill. p. 82).[33]

Small silver-cast snails (*Gibbula magnus* ?) with knotty striations on their mother-of-pearl shells gaze curiously at the beholder from the corners of a lid for a display casket that once belonged to Elector Christian I (cat. no. 155) and have a realism similar to that of nature casts. Thanks to its strongly exotic overtones and total adornment, this casket with its diverse applications of naturalistic objects echoes *stile rustique*.

28. Koeppe 1989, ill. 16, footnote 20; in general: Cherry 1997.
29. In this context, the jewelry designs of Hans Collaert the Elder were stimulating. The silver and gilt portions of a Basilisk with Turban Snail in Dresden (inv. no. IV 158) go directly back to a model by Collaert (M. De Jong/I. De Groot 1988). A few related objects by Geyer have also survived outside the Green Vault. They include one in the French collections of the Rothschild family, as well as one in the Hans Cohn Collection in the Los Angeles County Museum of Art. For more pertinent information regarding other *Meerweibsbilder* see also: Hackenbroch 1979, pp. 236–38, footnote 16, ill. 638ff.; Cohn 1991, p. 254 and frontispiece.
30. Investigations concerning the relations between merchants of exotica and goldsmiths are a desirable research project that would certainly stimulate further explorations.
31. Vienna 2000, pp. 168ff., cat. nos. 73–82 (Sigrid Sangl).
32. Hayward 1976, ill. 690; Vienna 2000, cat. no. 68 (Sigrid Sangl).
33. Koeppe 1992, p. 458; Hanover/NH 1991, p. 256, cat. no. 30; The Hague 2003, cat. no. 25.

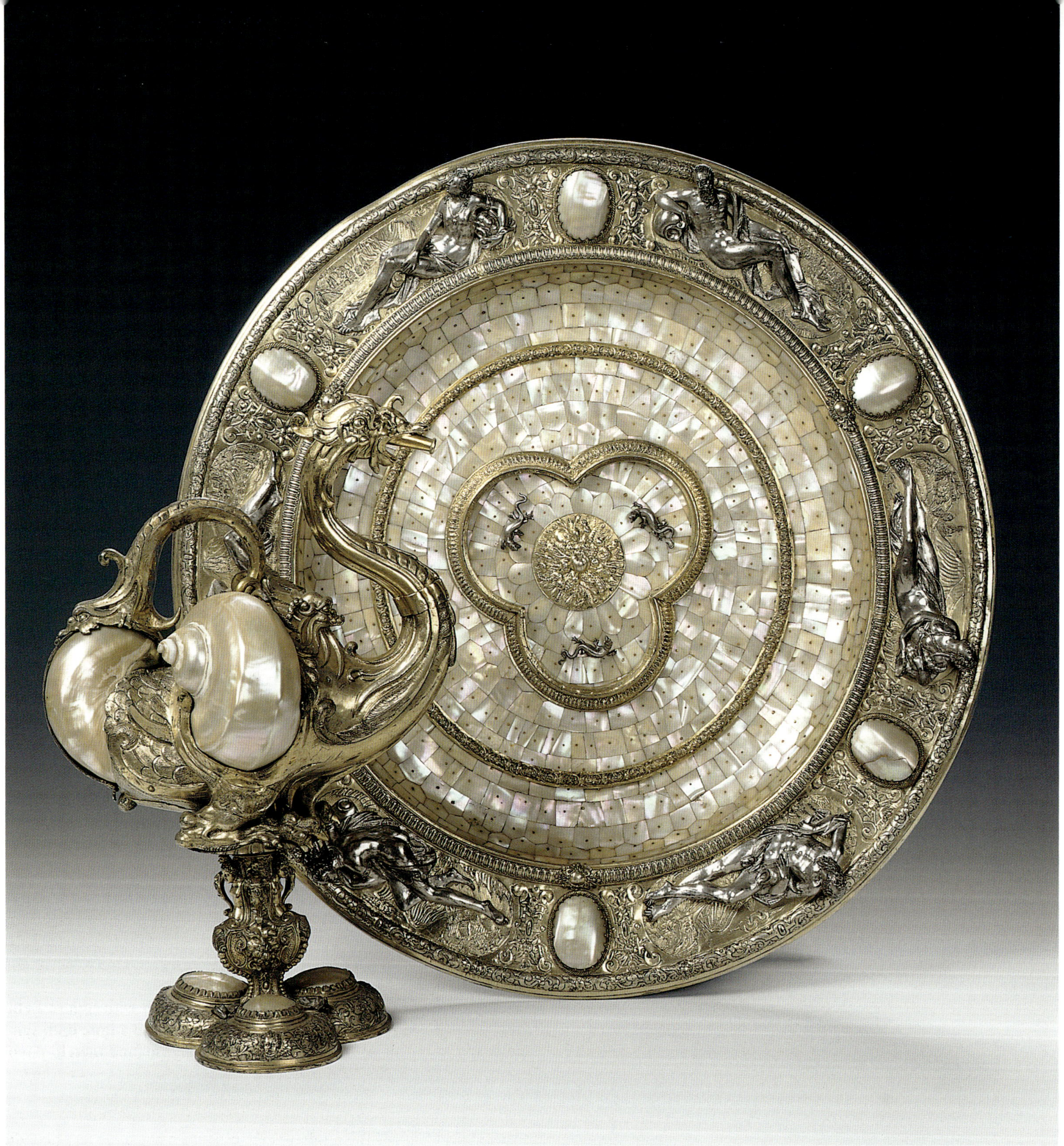

Lavabo Garniture
Mother-of-pearl work
of the basin: Gujarat, India
end of the sixteenth century
Mount and ewer by
Nikolaus Schmidt,
Nuremberg, circa 1600
Three turban snail shells
(*Turbo marmoratus*)
Silver-gilt
Ewer H. 16⅛ in. (41 cm)
Basin D. 22 in. (56 cm)
Staatliche Kunstsammlungen
Dresden, Grünes Gewölbe,
inv. nos. IV 248 and IV 157

Ostrich Eggs

Few natural products have been given as many multilayered, symbolic meanings as the egg of the giant ostrich (*Struthio camelus*, its name referring to to its hooflike, two-toed "camel feet"). The bird, too heavy to fly, grows almost ten feet tall and weighs up to two hundred pounds. Its energy as a fast runner is remarkable. An ostrich egg can weigh more than three pounds, and it must be incubated for forty-two days before the chicks can crack the hard shell. Their present habitat is largely restricted to Africa, but in antiquity ostriches were found throughout Asia Minor and southern Russia (overhunting caused a great decline in their numbers).

Ostrich eggs were prized in ancient Egypt. In Pharaonic times the royal household used ostrich plumes for ceremonial fans, a tradition that was adapted to Christian rituals and was continued in the flabella, the liturgical papal fans, in use until the pontificate of John XXIII (r. 1958–1963). Since antiquity the bird's eggs were used as containers for sacred oils and perfume or as drinking vessels.[34] They were valued for their symmetrical form, sturdy shell, and legendary origin, and ancient authors in particular attributed magical and therapeutic powers to them regarding indigestion. The eggs signify the realm of fertility and the new (still) hidden life for whose coming into being the shell must be broken. In Christian iconography, the ostrich egg was seen as a symbol of the Virgin Birth (ill. p. 81). The ostrich was said to hide its eggs in the sand and have the sun incubate them. In Christian iconography the egg—filled with life while still intact—was noted as a sign of Christ's Resurrection from an early period on. In this sense, the ostrich egg was interpreted as a symbol of eternal life.[35]

In medieval cathedrals the ostrich egg, a symbol of the Resurrection, was displayed on Easter, the climax of the ecclesiastical year, by the highest-ranking clergyman, who took the egg from its place of concealment in the crypt or a treasury vault. Carried in a festive procession, it was revealed to the congregation. The egg was presented to the enthroned bishop, representing the successor of Christ on earth, with the words "*Christus resurrexit*" (Christ has risen). Ultimately, the egg was exhibited for veneration on the high altar during Eastertime. Apparently, this practice survived in France until the French Revolution.[36] The Ostrich Egg Vessel in Munich's Treasury might have had such a hitherto unknown function (ill. p. 88). The precious mounts on a high stand allow a safe and widely visible exposition of the piece. The form of the pilgrim's flask refers to the pilgrimage to the distant Holy Land and to Jerusalem, surrounded by walls and towers. In addition, the spout is reminiscent of a pinnacled tower, a sacred architectural reference reinforced by two praying angels. On the occasion of Easter, when the bishop, the clergy, and the commoners celebrated Mass, the ostrich egg and its mount revealed to all believers that the New Jerusalem, God's heavenly city promised in the Bible, was symbolically present. Another example of an ostrich egg in a liturgical object is described in an inventory of the treasury of Emperor Maximilian I as "*ein Monstranzen unten und oben vergult, in der Mitte ein Gross Straussenei*" (a monstrance silver-gilt at top and bottom, in its center a large ostrich egg).[37]

According to a legend, one of the Three Wise Men brought an ostrich with him to Bethlehem, where it is said to have laid two eggs from which sprang a lamb and a lion, both symbols of the newborn Savior (the lamb is also the Lamb of the Apocalypse [and therefore represents the New Testament]; the lion is the Lion of Judah [and therefore represents the Old Testament]).[38] The exhibition presents three subtly shaped cups in form of the giant bird by Elias Geyer (cat. no. 116). In one, between the bird's long legs there is a little lion that could be a direct reference to the biblical legend. The miniaturized beast does not serve any heraldic purpose here (cat. no. 130) but it appears to have only recently hatched from the ostrich egg above, taking its first hesitant steps into an unknown world. This notion may be deduced from its tail, which is between its legs, a clear sign of insecurity.[39] Numerous medieval church treasuries mention ostrich eggs. Examples from the Gothic era can be found depicted on paintings with collections of relics and are preserved for instance in the church treasuries of Halberstadt, Vallendar, Saint Servatius in Maastricht, and in Zurich's Landesmuseum.[40] Enamel plaques with renderings of ostriches holding a horseshoe in their beaks, can be identified on the frames of three Marian paintings that King Louis the Great of Hungary donated to the treasury of Aachen's Cathedral in 1367.[41]

34. Houlihan 1996, p. 42, p. 167, ill. 120.
35. *Lexikon des Mittelalters*, vol. III (1997), columns 230–31 and columns 1663–64; about the symbolism of the Virgin, see Meiss 1976, footnote 14.
36. "*Das Ei und der mohammedanische Glaube,*" in: "http:/www.historisches-Franken.de/osterbrunnen/osterei/straussenei.htm.
37. Thanks to Bernhard Heitmann, who reminded me of the Munich ostrich egg bottle; for the inventory, see *Jahrbuch Wien* 1887, p. 26.
38. About the legend of the Three Magi, see Wagner 1985, p. 37.
39 The elongated, octagonal profile plinth of the cup is unusual and dependent on Italian base shapes, see Koeppe 1989, ill. 7.
40 Fritz 1982, ill. 18/176/368; Wagner 1985, ill. 3.
41. Lepie / Minkenberg 1995, pp. 83–85.

Ostrich Egg Vessel
presumably French or German
circa 1410–20,
Ostrich egg (*Ovum strutionis*)
silver-gilt, H. 11⅜ in. (29 cm)
from the former Benedictine Monastery
Herrieden near Ansbach, in 1803
transferred to the Munich Treasury,
Residenz Munich, Treasury,
inv. no. Res.Mü.Sch. 18

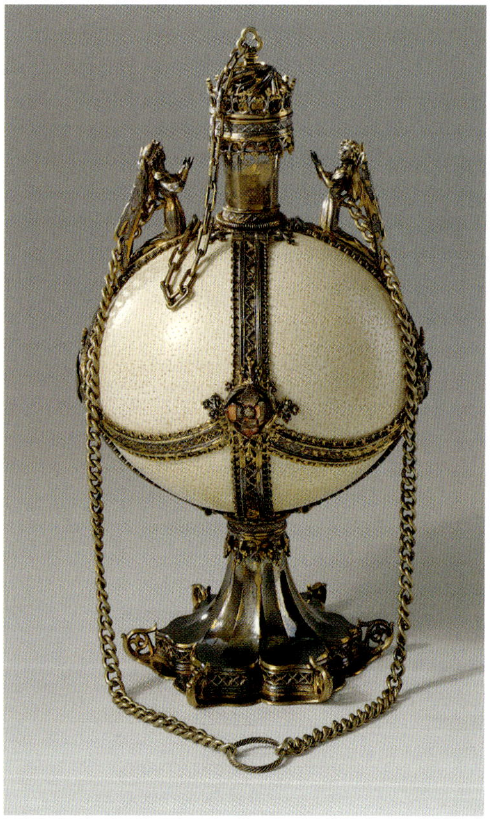

Ostrich eggs seem to have been first brought to central Europe by pilgrims who had visited Jerusalem. The 1440 receipt of eggs in Rio de Oro by Portuguese merchants proves the ongoing trade of such exotic commodities during the Middle Ages. A late-fifteenth-century woodcut, made in Saragossa from the *Defensorium inviolatae virginitatis,* shows a standing ostrich and a nest with chicks in the process of hatching. The stylized "mask of the sun" above breathes life into the entire scene and thus establishes the connection between the hatching of the eggs through the sun with God as the "true sun."[42]

The 1410 inventory of the bishop of Trent, Georg von Lichtenstein, lists—in his private residence, today the Castello del Buonconsiglio and not in the treasury of the cathedral—a special rarity: "*quatuor ouastrucj decorata cum auro et argento*" (four ostrich eggs embellished with silver and gold). A comparable mount from 1562 decorates an ostrich egg in Stuttgart (ill. p. 89 top) that could be suspended.[43]

The treasury inventory of Emperor Maximilian I attests to an impressive spectrum of feudal and secular luxury objects. Apart from dozens of display items, it also mentions "*ain silbern ubergolten han, allain die fügl, haubt und fuesz; in der mitt ain straussenai*" (a rooster with silver-gilt wings, head, and feet, and in the middle an ostrich egg). The earliest rooster goblet may be the example preserved in Moscow's Armory, formerly incorporating an ostrich egg. Dated by an inscription that establishes its manufacture no later than the end of the fifteenth century, the original ostrich egg was at some point replaced with a silver imitation. Apparently, no ostrich egg could be found that fit into such a custom-tailored haute couture mount. The same phenomenon can be seen in another Dresden ostrich cup (cat. no. 116) where the mounts do not fit tightly around the egg. This underscores the fact that although ostrich eggs do indeed resemble one another upon first sight, each one of them, following the laws of nature, reveals individual—often only minimal—deviations in proportion, weight, and size. Surprisingly, the only known surviving cockerel cup with a body made from an ostrich egg is the one kept today in the Lemmers-Danforth Collection in Wetzlar.[44]

It seems that in the Mediterranean area, farmers attempted early on to grow ostriches to gain independence from costly imported feathers and eggs: After a visit to Rhodes in 1521, Ottheinrich, Count Palatinate *bei Rhein* (at-the-Rhine), reports about the technical precursor of modern incubating devices: "*do wart ich geführt zu einem ofen, dirinnen honer unndt straussen ayer* [...] *ausgebrütet werden*"[45] (there I was led to an oven wherein chicken and ostrich eggs [...] were being incubated).

The interpretation of ostrich eggs as the *sol verus* (true sun) and the belief that the ostrich turns its gaze toward heaven at night, and thus the firmament of God, was interpreted as admonition to the faithful to pray regularly. Interestingly, all three major world religions in the Near East explicated this similarly: Ostrich eggs were and are suspended—mostly from chains and with iron and lead mounts—as a reminder to pray in synagogues, mosques, and Christian churches of varying faiths (ill. p. 89 bottom). In addition, the vast number of votive gifts with ostrich eggs is tied to the egg as symbol of fertility and the desire to be blessed with many children. It needs to be stressed that until modern times, the wild ostrich could be found in the regions of the Near East. In late 2002, archaeologists from the University of Southampton (UK) unearthed an ostrich egg: They found it in a mausoleum of a wealthy young man near the harbor of Quesir on the Red Sea, bearing a fifteenth-century Arabic inscription (ill. p. 89 center). The text includes poems and quotations from the Koran describing the soul's journey from death to life. During the fifteenth century, Quesir was a trading center of considerable importance between the Middle East and India, as well as an important stop for pilgrimages from North Africa to Mecca.[46]

Different symbolic layers of the oyster shell—seemingly, the pearl is created from nothing—and the ostrich egg—as metaphor for the Virgin Birth—are united in Piero della Francesca's *Montrefeltro Madonna* (ill. p. 81). Suspended on a delicate golden chain from the shell-shaped calotte, reminiscent of a halo, is an ostrich egg that hovers over the Virgin's head.[47] During the Renaissance, most interpretations of the ostrich were based on the writings of ancient authors and the bestiaries. Pliny the Younger's text *Naturalis historia* (10, I–II) was of pivotal importance. According to this reference, the ostrich not only devoured iron and stones but could also digest them, which was taken as a token of its (mental) strength. Hence, the "iron-devouring giant bird" was frequently depicted with a horseshoe in its beak (cat. no. 116, left and center).[48] Other sources report that the ostrich could eat shards of glass. One ostrich is supposed to have swallowed a rough, olive-sized gold nugget that emerged polished and shiny when excreted.[49]

42. Fritz 1983, p. 11, footnote 24; about the woodcut see: Marienlexikon 1994, p. 313, keyword: "Strauß."
43. Koeppe/Lupo 1991, p. 243, Fig. 94, the quote on p. 250.
44. Koeppe 1992, cat. no. G03, pp. 455–57.
45. Röhricht/Weissner 1880, p. 387.
46. For the ostrich egg as votive gift, see Butler 1884, pp. 77–79; S. John Whitfield, *Fifteenth-century ostrich egg found,* in: www.nature.com/nsu/021125/021125-11.htm1.
47. Meiss 1976; about the association of halo and shell, see Koeppe 2002, ills. 24–27.
48. Lexikon des Mittelalters, vol. VIII (1997), column 230–31; McCullough 1960.
49. Jewish Encyclopedia, XI (1905), p. 442.
50. Nicolas Reusner, "Sic Nutriuntur Forte" in: *Emblemata / Et Physica*, Frankfurt 1581, vol. II; Juan de Boria, *Empresas Morales*, Prague 1581, quoted and translated after: Henkel/Schöne 1996, column 806.

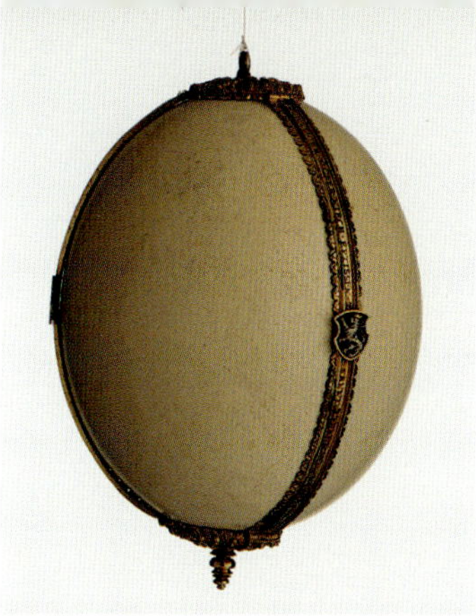

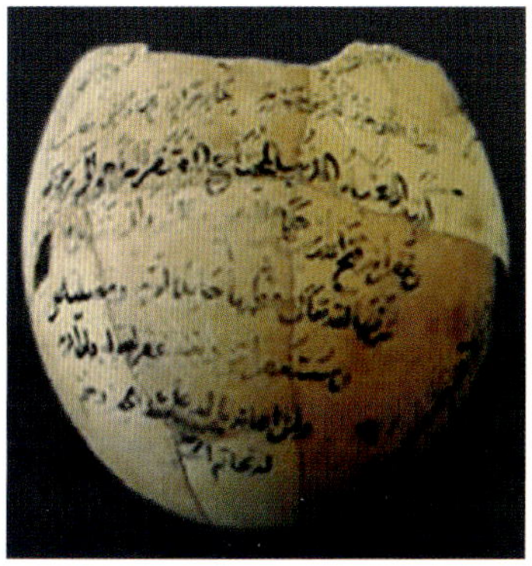

above
Ostrich Egg with Band Mounts and Fastening for Suspension
Bartell Birtsch, Strasbourg 1562
Ostrich egg (*Ovum strutionis*)
silver-gilt, enamel, H. 6¾ in. (17 cm)
Württembergisches Landesmuseum Stuttgart, inv. no. KK 129
center
Fragments of an Ostrich Egg with Arabic Inscription
restored condition, fifteenth century
excavated in Qusir / Red Sea, Egypt
Egyptian Administration for Antiquities
below
Three Ostrich Eggs as Votive Offerings
fifteenth to eighteenth centuries, Egypt, Monastery of Saint Antonius, Cathedral

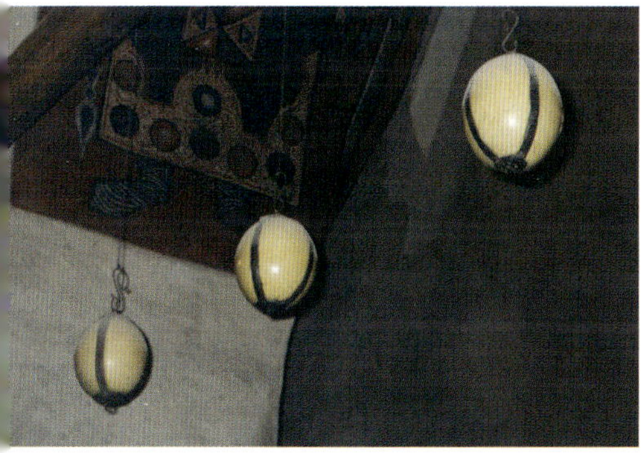

As an emblem, the motif of the bird with its self-assured stride, horseshoe in beak, also refers to the virtue of strength. This is how the ostrich is rendered in the 1581 *Emblemata* of Nicolas Reusner and in the *Ornithologiae* of Ulysses Aldrovandus, published in 1599. In the *Empresas Morales,* written by Juan de Boria in 1581, it is said: "*Tapffere und strenge Leuthe wissen nicht allein im Glücke ihrer Tugend zu gebrauchen / sondern auch aus den größten Widerwärtigkeiten und Unglücke / sonderbahren Nutzen zu ziehen* [...] *Wie dieser Vogel mit einer solchen Wärme des Magens und Hefftigkeit der Geister begabet / dass er Stein und Eisen verzehren und sich damit nehren kan*"[50] (Courageous and strong people know not only to use their virtues in times of happiness / but also during the greatest hardship and misery / they are able to derive advantages [...] such as this bird, blessed with such warmth of stomach and endurance of spirit / that it can devour iron and stone and feed itself on it).

The early modern interpretation of the ostrich egg and the animal itself are in many respects surprisingly positive. This is in clear contrast to the mention in the Old Testament (Job 39.13–18): "Gavest thou the goodly wings unto the peacocks? Or wings and feathers unto the ostrich? Which leaveth her eggs in the earth, and warmeth them in the dust, and forgetteth that the foot may crush them or that the wild beast may break them. She is hardened against her young ones, as though they were not hers: her labour is in vain without fear; because God hath deprived her of wisdom, neither hath he imparted to her understanding. What time she lifteth up herself on high, she scorneth the horse and his rider." Interestingly, the wings of the three Geyer cups are mounted on moveable hinges. When the drinker removes the head and lifts the cup up, the bird will "lifteth" itself up and its wings will flap, scorning and surprising the drinker in his enjoyment of delicious libation. The passage from Job and especially the hatching of the eggs by the sun, i.e., with the help of God, is what Guillelmus Durandus stressed in his *Rationale divinorvm officiorvm* as analogous with the human search for God.

The Green Vault's 1725 Pretiosen inventory describes a goblet as "*ein silbern vergoldeter Pelican, das Corpus von einem Straussen Ey*" (a silver-gilt pelican, the body of an ostrich) (cat. no. 115). At least from a thematic point of view, this is a highly refined and distinguished key item in the Kunstkammer of the most influential Protestant electors in the German-speaking world. According to Lutheran teachings, Christ is at the center of human salvation: Consequently, this object, now believed to be the creation of an unidentified seventeenth-century goldsmith from the Saxon city of Torgau, combines the Virgin Birth (ostrich egg) with Christ's sacrificial death by using the popular image of the pelican sacrificing itself for the benefit of its young. This means that the goblet—one individual work of art—unites and merges the beginning and the end of the Savior's terrestrial existence. This metaphor is strongly connected with the idea of the Protestant sovereign as protector of church and people.

The 1595 Dresden Kunstkammer inventory recorded "*ahn Straussen Eiern oder Trinkgeschirren in silber eingefast vnd Vorgolt*" (for ostrich eggs or drinking vessels mounted in silver-gilt, no fewer than fourteen goblets). This mention was repeated until the 1725 Pretiosen inventory reported: "*diejenigen Straussen Eyer und Pocale so den 20. September 1724. aus der Kunst Camer zum Grünen Gewölbe seind abegegeben worden*" (the ostrich eggs or goblets transferred to the Green Vault on September 20, 1724, from the Kunstkammer). The 1733 inventory of the Pretiosensaal mentions "*10 Strausseneipokale*" (ten ostrich-egg goblets) and "*Einundzwanzig Stück glatte ungestochene* [*undekorierte*] *Straussenеier*" (twenty-one pieces with smooth, untouched surfaces [undecorated] ostrich eggs). The Green Vault collection owns an unusually large quantity of ostrich eggs, variously mounted (e.g., inv. no. III 9) and unmounted, often adorned with Far Eastern carving, engraving, or punchwork (inv. no. III 229) or embellished in Europe (inv. no. III 108). Many of them postdate the year 1620 and can therefore not be considered in this exhibition. The group of later ostrich eggs certainly merits an article of its own.

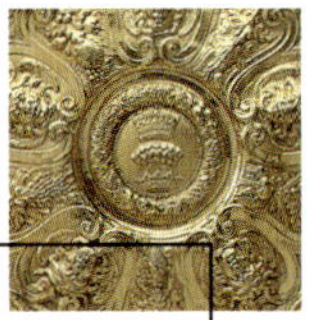

Serving the Prince: Forms and Display of Courtly Parade Silver

Bernhard Heitmann

Owing to its thematic and stylistic diversity, as well as its great quantity, the Green Vault's group of goldworks (predominantly dated from 1580 to 1630) does not constitute a coherent ensemble. However, in the late sixteenth and early seventeenth centuries, a number of these objects were gathered together and splendidly presented on a tiered pedestal constituting the Saxon court's presentation buffet. Such decorative arrangements were customary backdrops for princely celebrations,[1] functioning as eye-catching embellishments and including goldwork of all types, stones mounted in valuable settings, and natural curiosities, as well as ostentatious utensils designed exclusively for show.

There is a record suggesting that the Dresden golden buffet (güldenen Büffet) was exhibited alongside this heterogeneous group of works until the end of the seventeenth century: When elected king of Poland in Warsaw (as August II), Frederick August I of Saxony set about preparing the coronation festivities in Krakow. His orders to Dresden included not only that the gilt table silver had to be shipped but also that an express envoy be sent to Krakow with the instruction to include the gilt buffet in the shipment as well.[2] The goal was to furnish the coronation festivities as magnificently and nobly as they were at the court in Dresden.

At first, it is surprising to find, as late as 1697, the inclusion of vessels and utensils that could then have been deemed old-fashioned. Apparently, Frederick August chose to ignore the dictum that all courtly display was to be in accordance with the latest fashion and that interior design as well as clothing adhere to current standards. It is this decision, among other factors, that accounts for the survival of secular Late Renaissance goldwork. While dining services were by necessity modified according to changing customs, the more elaborately worked plate neither fell victim to such changes, nor was subjugated to fashion. Indeed, its artistic value was acknowledged and appreciated. It was understood that melting down display pieces fabricated from precious metals and exotic materials, such as shells or coral from the Pacific Ocean, diminished the value of their gold and silver content, while also destroying a work of art. In the event that a piece's metal weight was significant, its having been in the dynasty's possession for generations apparently kept it unharmed for the simple reason that it was considered an "antique" with an honored status.

It was not until the eighteenth century that people were prepared to melt down and refashion old, out-of-style pieces in order to create new silver objects in the latest fashion. Although wars and economic crises took their tolls, the surviving German state silver provides us with an accurate impression of the quality and the diversity of the applied arts before that time. Conversely, in southern Europe, only an infinitesimal percentage of Renaissance and Baroque silver has survived.

In 1697, the Saxon court's gilt buffet still held its firmly established inventory, which was known to the Dresden court officials. Therefore, the command to send it to Krakow needed no further specification of the works desired.[3] These utterly diverse objects were assembled into a multitiered display that adorned the Krakow banquet hall, while, at almost the same time, a magnificent set of ceremonial silver was created in Augsburg for the Rittersaal (Knights

Hall) in Berlin's Palace. The shape and decoration of the latter ensemble were integrated, resulting in a balanced design in which each item could be identified as belonging to the group.[4] Whereas the Saxon elector celebrated his coronation with recourse to the tradition of his own lineage, thereby implying dynastic continuity, the first Prussian to wear the royal crown prepared for his, in 1701, by indulging in the most fashionable style. In contrast to the Saxon buffet, whose arrangement could be varied, the objects in Berlin were incorporated into the Knights Hall according to a preconceived plan.

It would be impossible to introduce seventeenth-century animal-shaped pieces into such a rigidly arranged grouping as that in the Knights Hall. This was one of the reasons why eighteenth-century artists proceeded to render animals–be they conceived as menageries or as game for the hunt with packs of hounds–primarily in porcelain and no longer in gilded silver. The animals on the Saxon buffet are represented as individuals or as pairs, such as rooster and hen (cat. no. 113). Although these earlier works form a harmonious whole when displayed together, they also work when seen alone or as subgroups, retaining their integrity independent of the ensemble's arrangement.

Despite their age, and notwithstanding the vicissitudes of many hurried transports, the goldworks surviving today are for the most part perfectly preserved. Except for two broken bowls on the ostrich-egg goblets (cat. no. 116), this also holds true for the mounted natural and exotic products, which survived either intact or with negligible damage. We therefore have relatively accurate impressions of the courtly festivities and dining parties. The treasures, surely used as table decorations before they found their final destination within the buffet's ensemble, were appreciated at the time of their manufacture and by later generations as highly accomplished works that epitomized artistic versatility and masterly skill. Recognition of their value, the high standards underlying the granting of commissions, and the investment of considerable means in their execution prevented any careless handling.[5] It can be assumed that, although the mechanical automatons and joke vessels provided much amusement, these works of art were also employed according to their intended function. At the same time, it is fair to suggest that only select guests were ever invited to touch or to use such priceless objects. In this context, mention should be made of the *Willkomm-Trunk* (Welcome Drink) ceremony, a ritual during which guest and host celebrated an arrival or a special reception by toasting with vessels expressly fabricated for such events.

Gold and silver objects were not the only items used to beautify a table. The forms of the objects decorating the buffet or kept elsewhere within the courtly collections were sometimes imitated by pastry makers,[6] who charmed the guests by duplicating an object which simultaneously adorned the table. Since the ceremonial nature of festive banquets prohibited frequent or careless handling of the much-admired artworks, their splendor must have been predominantly displayed as table and buffet decoration.

Some of the works in this exhibition will be selected and analyzed by illuminating various aspects of their appearance or use. This will inevitably entail comparisons with works preserved in other collections, including juxtapositions with depictions in a contemporary collection of drawings created in or around 1600. This portfolio of works on paper may have been created by Jacob Mores, a Hamburg goldsmith and art dealer; it is possible that the collection was assembled by his sons.[7] The sheets illustrate works in the style prevalent around the year 1600 and are thus connected to the Dresden objects. Neither designs nor models, they represent copies of existing objects, executed in actual size. Some of them bear marks indicating the weight of the object, along with the owner's or patron's name. Since they are rendered in color, these drawings offer a vivid record of the works of art. To date, only one illustrated object, the so-called Schlüsselfelder Silberschiff,[8] now in Nuremberg's Germanisches Nationalmuseum, has been identified.

The Mores portfolio contains three sheets with lions comparable to the crowned lion in this exhibition (cat. no. 130). Presenting the orb and electoral coat of arms, this animal shows all the physical characteristics of the feline, although its posture and striding movement are human. In this context, it is not merely a naturalistic, exotic animal but also an allegory of strength and power, and therefore a worthy representation of the prince. The proud pose on hind legs alone distinguishes the beast as a heraldic animal. This Saxon-Palatine lion forms part of a larger group of similar heraldic images that continued to be widely used well into

1. Stahl 2003, p. 61, with ill., as an example, the banquet of Matthias I in the Frankfurt Römer, in 1612. The buffet of the elector had three steps, whereas the emperor's was designed with five steps.
2. Bäumel 1997, pp. 68–76.
3. Since the buffet's inventory is no longer complete, and since the exhibition "Princely Splendor" includes but a portion of the pieces preserved in Dresden, only the following objects formerly belonging to the buffet can be cited: The lavabo basin with the depiction of the times of day (cat. no. 99), the grape goblets (cat. nos. 125, 126), double goblets, the lion carrying the coat of arms (cat. no. 130), a *Saint George*, one of the two pelicans (cat. no. 114 or 115), and the owl (cat. no. 127), see Bäumel 1997, pp. 70–73.
4. Keisch 1997, ill. 16, 17, 118. On the occasion of Elector Frederick August II's wedding to the Austrian Archduchess Maria Josepha in Dresden in 1719, a buffet was obtained as well. A service was formally arranged on it; see Arnold 1994, p. 27.
5. Two documents, dated 1562 and 1575, and published in 1888 by Julius Lessing, describe the variety and the somewhat convoluted concepts of vessel types at the time. Although the documents mention the forms, they neglect to account for the materials the services were made from. Therefore, we cannot conclude that the precious goldworks were indeed regularly used at the table or for drinking ceremonies. For Lessing's quotes see Koeppe 1992, pp. 455f.
6. Marx 2000a, pp. 28f. The reference is a Dresden banquet of 1607; during the feast, reproductions of small bronzes were used as table decorations.
7. Winkler 1890.
8. Germanisches Nationalmuseum Nuremberg, inv. no. H.G. 2146. Cf. Kohlhaussen 1968, pp. 266–77, cat. no. 338.

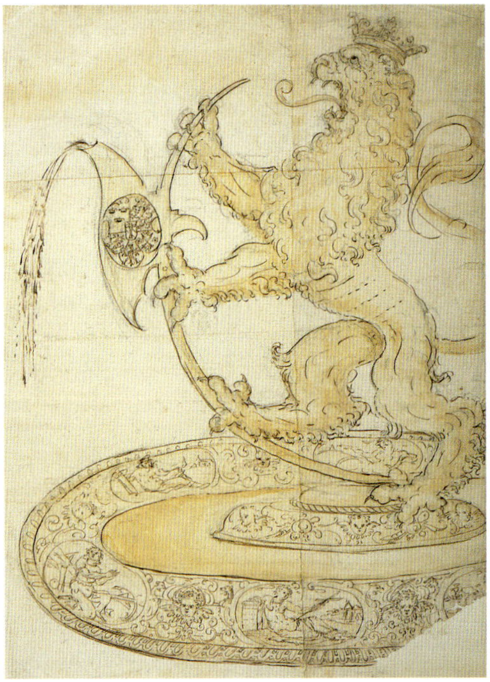

Norwegian Lion
(Pouring Vessel)
from the portfolio
of Jacob Mores
Hamburg, circa or shortly
after 1600
Pen with yellow wash,
24¾ × 17¾ in. (63 × 45 cm),
Staatliche Museen zu Berlin,
Preußischer Kulturbesitz,
Kunstbibliothek,
inv. no. Hdz 1488

the mid-nineteenth century. The lions in the Mores portfolio rise up like the Dresden lion but are shown holding halberds instead. One of them, functioning as a pouring vessel in a lavabo garniture (ill. left), represents the faithful rendering of the lion on the Norwegian coat of arms as a utilitarian object.

A mid-sixteenth-century owl (cat. no. 127) is the largest and one of the earliest examples of its kind. A small group of approximately ten surviving faience owls (ill. p. 93), created about 1540, could conceivably be connected with this piece because they share many identical features. Since the ceramic owls invariably predate the examples made of precious metal, it is likely that they served as prototypes for the goldsmiths.[9] The natural shapes of the silver owl have been combined with the distinguishing marks left in the clay by a potter's wheel. The feathers, meticulously and schematically arranged, are reminiscent of a bouquet of laurel leaves. The bird's fixed gaze and the feet, looking like casts from nature, count among the vessel's realistic details. It is difficult to attribute a specific meaning to this bird, distinguished by its naive expression and complex iconography. This owl does not appear to be an attribute of Minerva, goddess of wisdom; it also lacks a menacing demeanor and the expression that appeals to merry drunks. It is most likely the bird's ambiguous layers of meaning that attracted the owners and their contemporaries. Its later crowning with the coat of arms mount further attests to the values placed on the owl, because such changes document the deliberate appropriation by its new owner. The crowning is so similar to that on conventionally conceived goblets that contemporaries undoubtedly grasped the figure's double character as both the image of an owl and a drinking vessel.

The leaping stag with coral antlers (cat. no. 117), on the other hand, is much more straightforward. The quintessential game piece, it was the prized trophy of a courtly hunting event. In this case, the coral embellishment lends the dramatic escape of the animal a particularly exotic charm. The shape of the coral was appropriate for antlers. A playful fantasy easily transformed the bizarre prongs into attributes of a creature belonging to the familiar world of patron and goldsmith. In Mores's drawing of a doe (Hdz. 1483), the animal wears a jeweled necklace. Naturally graceful, the forest animal listens attentively. The priceless jewels have been bestowed as an honor in preparation for its placement on the princely table. Mounted on wheels and adorned with figures and arabesques, the pedestal elevates the beast into the courtly sphere. Although the Dresden stag, ennobled by its coral antlers, is also splendidly mounted on a base, it is the hunted animal's dramatic expression that first strikes the viewer.

Not all motifs of animal vessels originated from the court's everyday activities such as the hunt. In fact, they were primarily derived from Christian iconography and ancient mythology. Drawn from the world of myths, in this case Ovid's *Metamorphoses,* is Actaeon (cat. no. 118), also displaying coral antlers that signal his imminent transformation into a stag. Despite the delightfully realistic dogs that Actaeon keeps leashed, the figure is squarely placed within the context of classical antiquity: Its posture and the armor's design are obviously adapted from the armor of Roman emperors.

In another reference to myths, the celestial globe from Nuremberg is carried by a Hercules figure (cat. no. 129) whose hands are disproportionally large in order to emphasize their grip on the sphere. In contrast to Atlas, who supports the heavens, Hercules has been given the Nemean lion's skin for a loincloth. This drinking vessel is distinguished by the high quality of the sphere's engravings. Seemingly awakened as living creatures, the zodiacal signs populating the dense surface demonstrate a horror vacui. In its design, this goblet (Globenpokal) refers to earlier globes fabricated for scientific studies, such as those created by Gerhard Mercator in the Dutch town of Louvain, and, later, by Jodocus Hondius in Amsterdam. Mercator's globe of the earth dates to 1541, and his celestial globe was made in 1551. During the second half of the sixteenth century, they were among the most frequently used models. These prototypes were adopted, for example, by Jost Bürgi and Antonius Eisenhoit, who fabricated celestial globes with mechanical clockworks for the landgrave of Kassel.[10] The Nuremberg goldsmith transformed his globe into a cup and cover and created a decorative work of art by employing the supporting figure. However, the sphere with the zodiac is not designed for scientific purposes; its use is limited to that of a drinking vessel.

9. See König-Baudouin-Stiftung 2003, pp. 28f., for examples and illustrations of additional ceramic owls.
10. Paderborn 2003, cat. nos. 62–66.
11. Schönberger 2001, p. 10. For the pelican's significance see also Wolfram Koeppe's essay in this catalogue.
12. Lexikon der Kunst, vol. 5 (1978), pp. 10f., entry: Tageszeiten.

The legend of Saint George and the Dragon is of Christian origin. As a military saint, George had been patron of the Order of the Garter since 1348 and became patron saint of the house of Wittelsbach's Order of Saint George in 1729. Works of art depicting his fight with the dragon are therefore legion. Each of the Dresden groups is differently conceived. The Augsburg work introduces the figures in a summary manner, citing rider, horse, dragon, and princess as elements of the legend without incorporating them as a group with dramatic power (cat. no. 132). The Nuremberg object was designed as a somewhat autonomous piece of sculpture with intricate interdependencies (cat. no. 131). Here, the saint's triumph in battle is the theme, portrayed with more dynamism than the piece from Augsburg or the contemporaneous group from Basel, which resembles a miniaturized equestrian monument celebrating a ruler's apotheosis.

Equally Christian in content is the figure of the pelican (cat. nos. 114, 115), which certainly can not be envisioned as the centerpiece of a high-spirited banqueting party. As the masters and the defenders of the Lutheran church, the Saxon electors awarded the motif of the self-sacrificing bird nearly the status of a coat of arms. A symbol of Christ himself, giving up his own life for the salvation of humankind, the pelican is also an allusion to the Last Supper.[11] Among the diverse and fabulous creatures in the Dresden collections, the pelican is almost always included; it even appears on a snaffle bit in the Saxon Armory (cat. no. 23).

Electoral Owl
South Germany, circa 1540,
Faience, H. 10⅞ in. (27 cm)
Museum für Kunst und Gewerbe,
Hamburg, inv. no. 1921.163

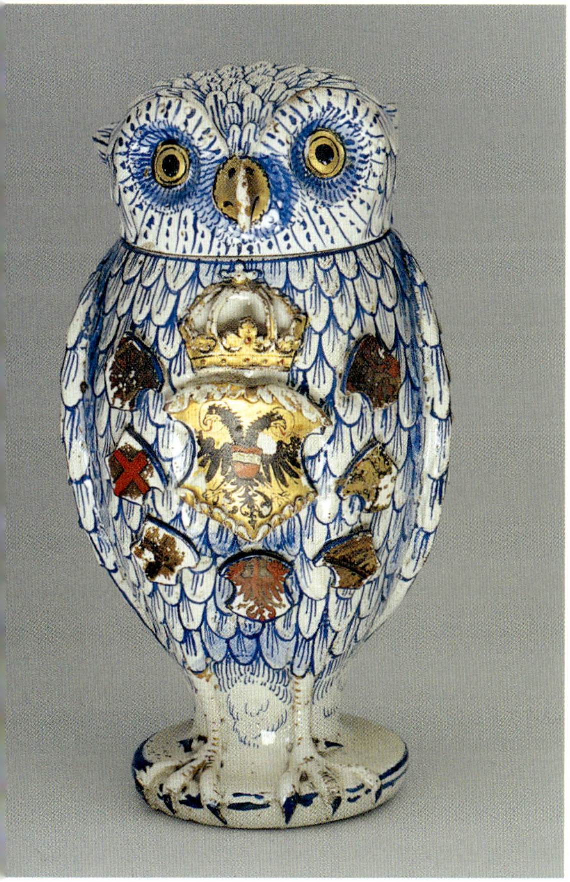

When standing on the electoral buffet, the rooster and hen might be viewed with little interest, as they are the quintessential farm animals. But the use of a nautilus bowl to fashion their bodies transforms their appearance into something sublime and precious (cat. no. 113). Much more surprising are five grotesque creatures–Triton and Nereid, unicorn, and two sea horses, all adorned with the gleaming shells of turban snails (cat. nos. 108–110), whose ancestors may be found in ancient wall paintings. Reclaimed by Raphael in his Vatican loggias, the grotesques were widely disseminated in engravings and emerged as fantasies placed on walls, columns, pilasters, or silver services. The works of the Leipzig-based Elias Geyer are notable early transformations of the grotesques into three-dimensional creatures. A naturalism emanates from his three animals, which display a timeless beauty. Triton and Nereid, on the other hand, are cheerfully depicted creatures derived from ancient prototypes. At the same time, they seem to epitomize the old German burghers, as if one looked at classical antiquity through a distorting lens.

It is natural that the artistic ambition involved in the creation of three-dimensional figural goldwork was different from that applied to the fabrication of utilitarian objects, even deluxe editions. Frequently, the monumental dimensions of familiar tool and vessel types impressed contemporaries. This was certainly true of Hans IV Pfleger's large lavabo basin (cat. no. 99), with its typical decoration of "gnarled" ornaments and four cartouches with figural images. Not executed as a deep bowl to contain water, the domed body has instead the taut flatness of the plafond of an oval hall. The four fields with reliefs do in fact correspond to those reserved for painting in domed ceilings. There is no stringent allegorical program for the decoration but rather a carefree arrangement of the times of day. The figures and their movements are presented in formal harmony: Morning (top) is personified as a young man with a rooster at his side, greeting dawn with its crowing; Day (left) is shown as a Sol figure, crowned with rays of sunlight and emerging from the clouds, with putti in the background busily studying spheres and other scientific instruments; Evening (right) is represented by Aeolus, master of the winds, who has gathered them together and rolls them into his cave as the day comes to an end; Night is personified by Nyx, who reclines on a bed of clouds with her attribute, the owl.[12] The vertical arrangement of the four allegories confirms that the basin was intended to be displayed in an upright position and thus was made solely as a presentation object.

Two of the ewers belonging to such basins may be seen in the exhibition. The one by Balthasar I Grill (cat. no. 97) of Augsburg is so surprisingly close to Italian types that a South German origin is not necessarily assumed. This can be explained because the shapes of traditional objects were much more easily influenced than those of more regionally diverse object types such as those in animal form. So little Italian Renaissance silver has survived–often, it can be traced only in paintings–that the opportunity for comparison with the object from the Schroder Collection (ill. above right) is particularly fortuitous. However, the Augsburg

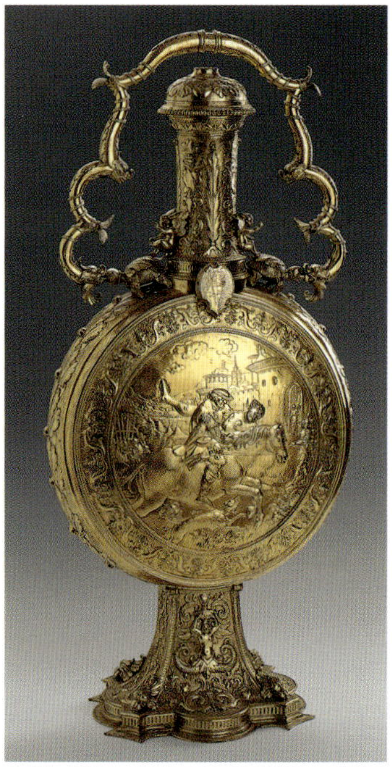

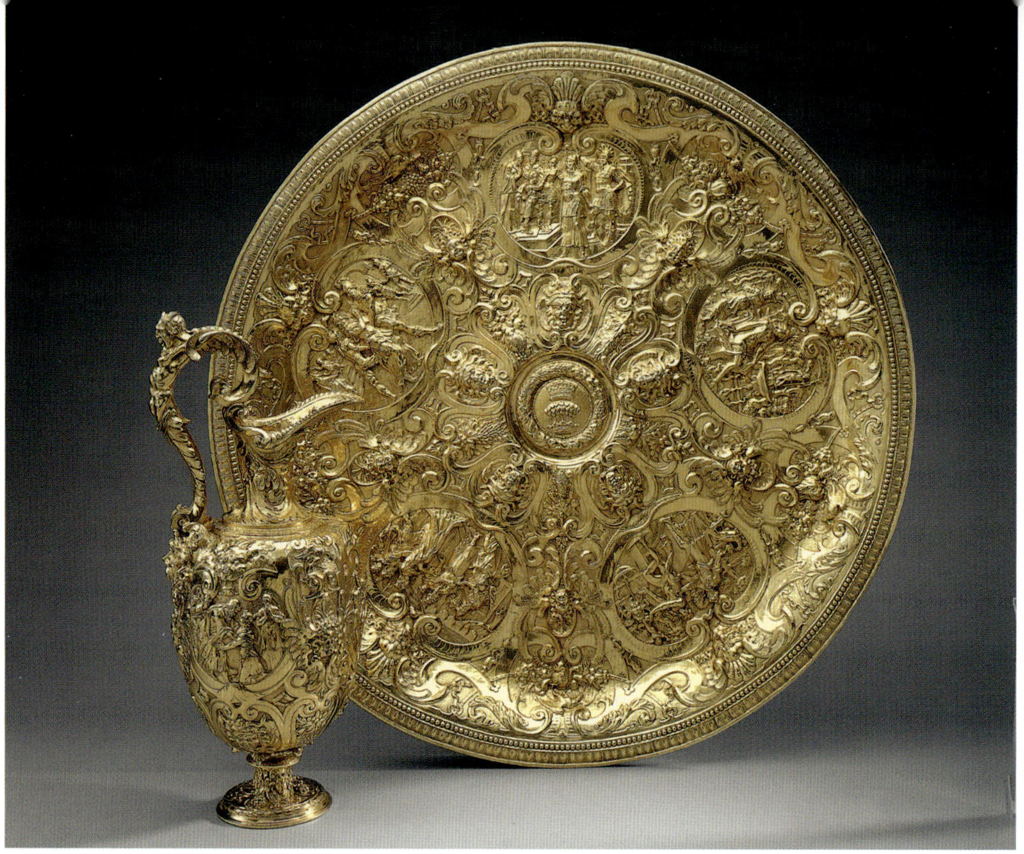

left
Handled Bottle with Scenes of a Siege
presumably Austria/Hungary
mid-16th century
Silver-gilt
H. 31⅞ in. (81 cm)
Staatliche Kunstsammlungen Dresden, Grünes Gewölbe, inv. no. IV 253

right
Ewer and Basin
North Italy, early 17th century
Silver-gilt
H. 15½ in. (39.4 cm)
Ewer, diam. 23⅛ in. (58.9 cm),
The Schroder Collection, London

guild was not the only one to derive inspiration from southern models; comparable ewers were also manufactured in Paris, Antwerp, and Amsterdam.

The goblets represented in the exhibition demonstrate in only a few examples the endless variety of form, decoration, and size of such works (cat. nos. 123–126). These exuberant drinking vessels, whether commissioned or received as gifts, formed the basis of any silver collection and filled the buffet.[13] Thanks to the myriad protruding surfaces and facets on its foot, body, and lid, it was the grape goblet's task to reflect, diffuse, and enhance the light emanating from torchlights, candles, and fireplaces.

In order to cool their contents, wine bottles were made of tin and copper and then placed into basins of water. Those made from silver and gold, on the other hand, were created as presentation pieces (see cat. no. 101), as was the mid-sixteenth-century bottle from Dresden (ill. above left), shown here as an exemplary Renaissance silver object. The body of the bottle is plain and round and meant to be seen frontally; its facadelike structure is enhanced by the folding handle's profile arch. Despite the large size and decorative composition of the vessel, its function as a bottle remains evident. One generation later, in Mores's drawing of a state bottle (ill. p. 95), the function is less apparent. The body has a richly decorated front and a tower mounted on its top, and its profile is reminiscent of those of Baroque epitaphs; the exaggerated elevation of the tower-shaped neck is softened by the lattice ornament on the handle. A noteworthy combination of features may be observed here: architectural components for the construction, sculptural components for the figural decoration, and painterly elements for the colorfully enameled low reliefs. In this instance, rather than competing, the arts cooperate.

A direct architectural replica can be found in the goblet whose foot and shaft are rendered as rock formations and which represents the small pleasure castle (cat. no. 128) situated about 1604–5 on the Sonnenstein Fortifications in Pirna. The graceful edifice, with a jagged design characterized as typically Old German, is, paradoxically, a truly monumental miniature. Its height of approximately two feet adds greatly to the striking effect of the goblet, which was intended to contain the ceremonial welcome drink. The realistic rendering of nature and buildings is attested to by the fortunate survival of numerous contemporaneous examples. Mention must be made in this context of Dirich Utermarke from Hamburg. His so-called Räucherberge (ill. p. 95)—centerpieces created during the first quarter of the seventeenth century to hold confectioneries—were equipped with smoking devices for burning incense. Although made for the Danish court, they have been kept since 1628 as part of the czars' treasures in the Kremlin, Moscow.[14] Whereas Utermarke's works are dominated by massive rocks, with the palatial

13. The vast quantity of goblets, commissioned as honorary gifts by one early-seventeenth-century Hamburg goldsmith, can be traced only archivally; see Dirich Utermarke in Heitmann/Scholz 1985, II, pp. 60–65.
14. Cf. Hamburg, 1986, p. 93, ill. pp. 7, 9.

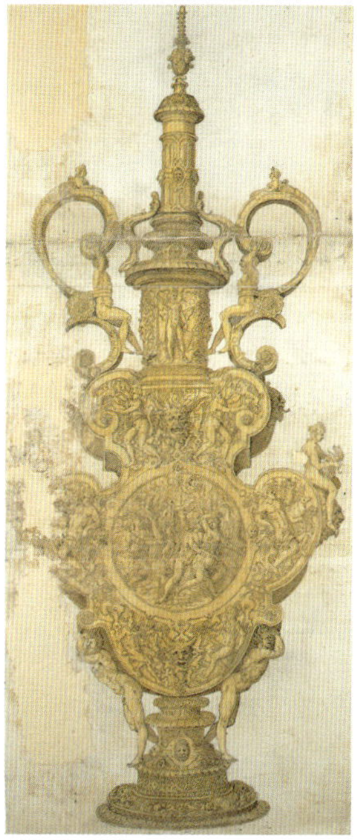

State Bottle
from the portfolio of Jacob Mores,
Hamburg, circa or shortly after 1600
Pen with yellow wash,
48⅜ × 21⅝ in. (123 × 55 cm)
Staatliche Museen zu Berlin, Preußischer Kulturbesitz, Kunstbibliothek, inv. no. Hdz 1464

Incense Burner
Dirich Utermarke, Hamburg, 1599–1628
Silver-gilt
H. 21¼ in. (54 cm)
Armory, Kremlin, Moscow, inv. no. MZ-422/1-5

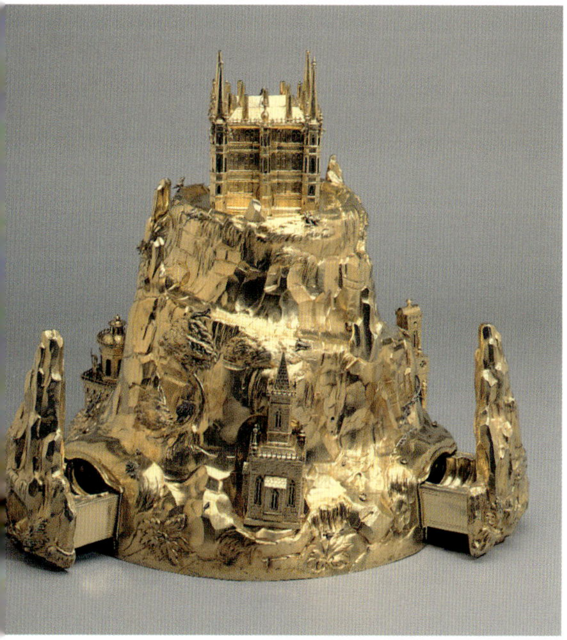

architecture decoratively crowning the top, the tiny Dresden pleasure castle is a unique invention. The cup's basic shape was not sacrificed, but it was still possible to execute a realistic imitation of the building. What the goldsmith did was respect his princely patron's request for a work of architecture as a golden sculpture. This process is analogous to the rendering of animals and mythical beasts in precious materials for Renaissance drinking games. Given life as works of art, these creatures attained an elevated mode of existence. Like most of the goldwork exhibited here, the goblet in the shape of a small castle also addresses the five senses, primarily that of sight.

The function of these works of wonder was invariably secondary to their artistic mastery and precious materials. In sum, they were meant as colorful reflections of life to be admired by viewers. These pieces were not devoid of all function, however. Their presence and presentation were not merely intended to keep their princely owner delighted and entertained; they were also part of the court's artistic atmosphere, which aspired to portray and to celebrate the ruler's higher level of existence. Their diversity, in which the various different levels coexisted, was seen as fitting. Represented in this mélange were animals and fabulous beasts, humans and mythological creatures, the spheres of the sacred and the bucolic, as well as priceless natural curiosities and tools crafted into elaborate gold and silver showpieces. There was a fundamental understanding of the nature of a ruler and how to show it within the courtly context—first, in contemporary society, as represented by the artists and the craftspeople; and, second, as defined by the sovereign himself. Naturally, the art of the goldsmith, once termed the queen of the arts, entered into this agreement, and it, too, was at the elector's service.

Catalogue

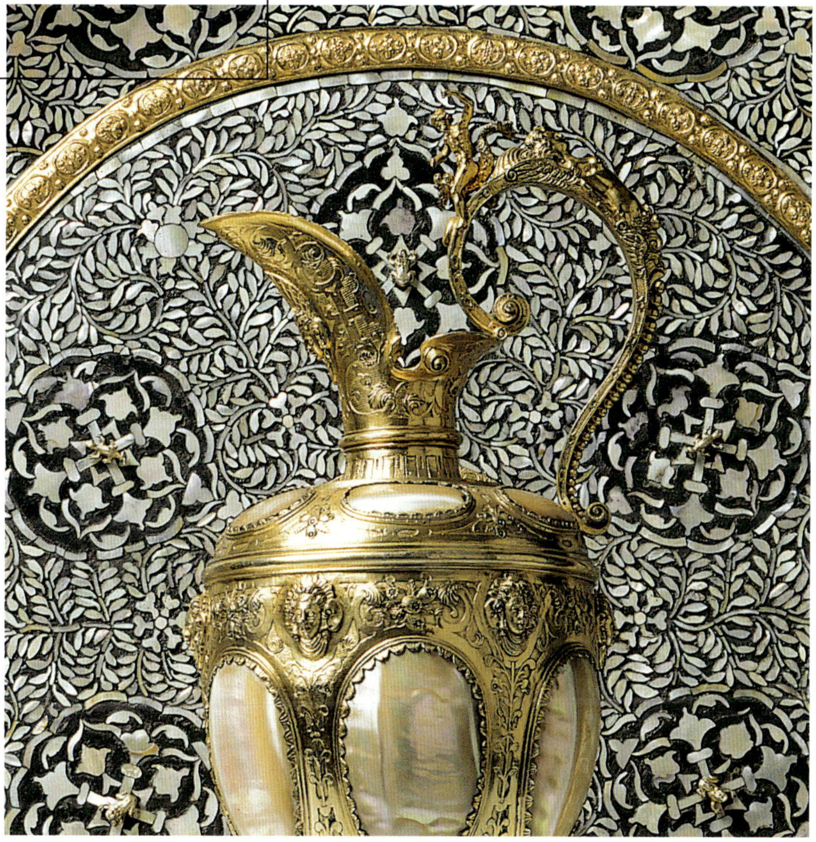

Princely Collections

Courtly Life

Kunstkammer and Treasury

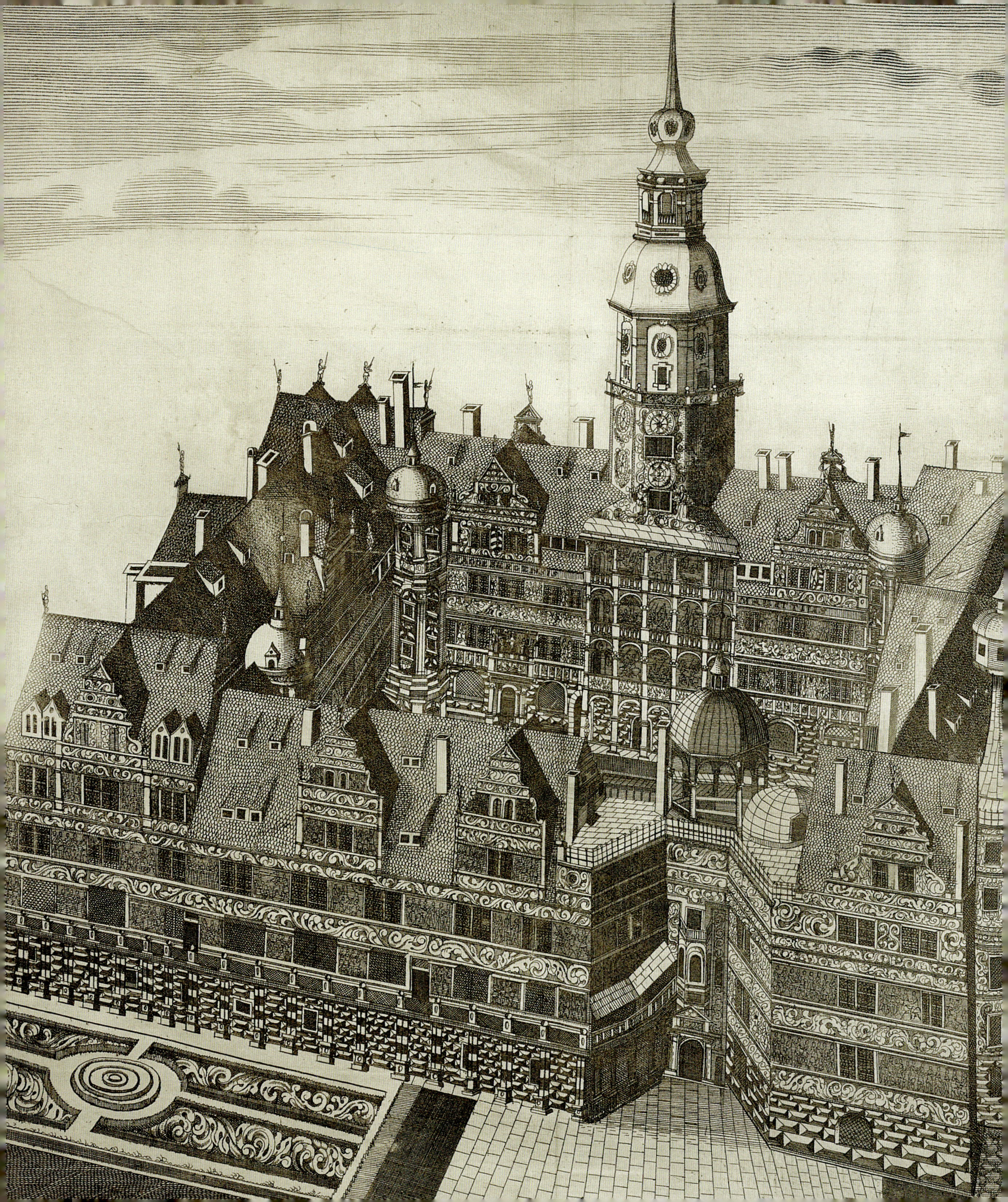

Princely Collections

Portraits

Other Representations

Costumes

Elector August of Saxony (1526–1586)

On July 11, 1553, Duke August inherited the reign and the office of elector from his brother Moritz, who had been mortally wounded in the Battle of Sievershausen. His marriage to Anna, sixteen-year-old daughter of King Christian III of Denmark, had been celebrated five years before (in 1548), and this combined with the elevation of the Albertine line of the house of Wettin to the electoral rank brought a new level of importance. With the Naumburg Treaty (1554) and the military victory over the Ernestine Johann Friedrich II in 1567, August permanently secured the electoral office for his family. At the same time, he also inherited aristocratic estates (Henneberg) and secularized ecclesiastical properties and monastic structures, thereby peacefully expanding the Saxon territories (included were the Vogtland area and the monasteries of Quedlinburg and Naumburg). His good relationship with the emperors, especially Maximilian II, who visited Dresden in 1575, strengthened these policies.

Opposed to Calvinism, August was an important champion of Lutheranism, contributing to the Peace of Augsburg in 1555 and gaining support for the *Book of Concord* in 1580, codifying Protestantism in the empire. Since 1574 he had battled all forms of Calvinism in Saxony. As sovereign, he vigilantly strengthened Saxony's economic power, he restructured the administration in an exemplary manner, and in 1574 he founded the Secret Council, the electorate's highest government authority. In 1572 Saxony received the empire's first legal code, followed by a church and school code in 1580. Elector August is remembered as the strict, albeit fair, "Father August."
D.S.

1 Full-Length Portrait

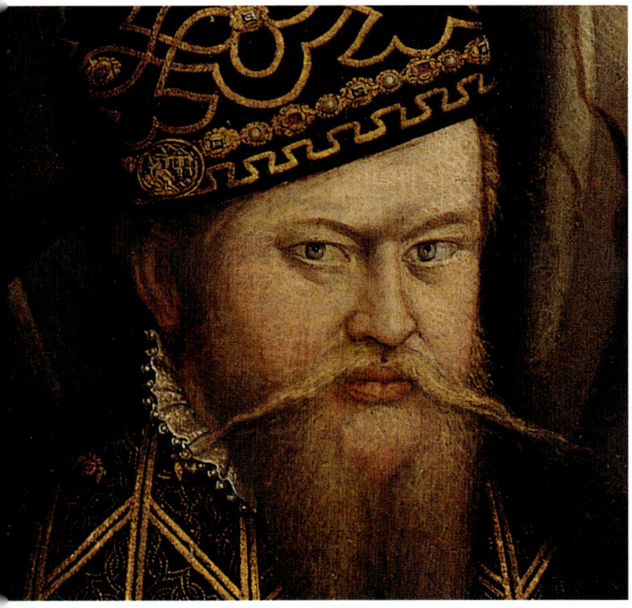

The state portrait depicts August as a self-confident sovereign and a resolute character. The elector appears full length, dressed in a Spanish outfit (*"spanisches habit"*). His apparent corpulence is due to his elaborate black-and-gold garment; although not preserved, it is described in detail in the elector's 1564 Garment Inventory.

The cloak and the short-sleeved jacket of black velvet beneath it are lined in sable. The doublet, visible at the arm, shows squares outlined in gold. The full trunk hose consist of slashed (*mit schniten*) black velvet and gold colored breeches. The garment is richly embellished with trimmings of "well-drawn Hungarian gold threads" (*"vonn vngerischen guten getzogenen goldt"*). Initially, a coat belonged to the outfit, but it was not included in the portrait. Eighteen gold buttons bear August's enameled monogram "A," as well as a diamond and a ruby each. The 255 "gilt flying hearts with crowns" (*"güldenen fliegenden hertzen mit kronen"*), also decorated with diamonds and rubies, are symbols of friendship, possibly directed at Ferdinand II of Tyrol. Along with this "garment of hearts," Elector August wears the present from this long-time friend, who, when he visited Dresden in 1556, gave August a gold rapier and matching dagger garniture with colorful enameled serpents, a work created for the imperial house by the Spanish goldsmith Pere Juan Poch, active in Vienna.

The painting, hung in the "first room or the antechamber" (*"Erst zimmer oder Vorgemach"*) in Dresden's Kunstkammer and was not included in the 1587 inventory.
J.B.

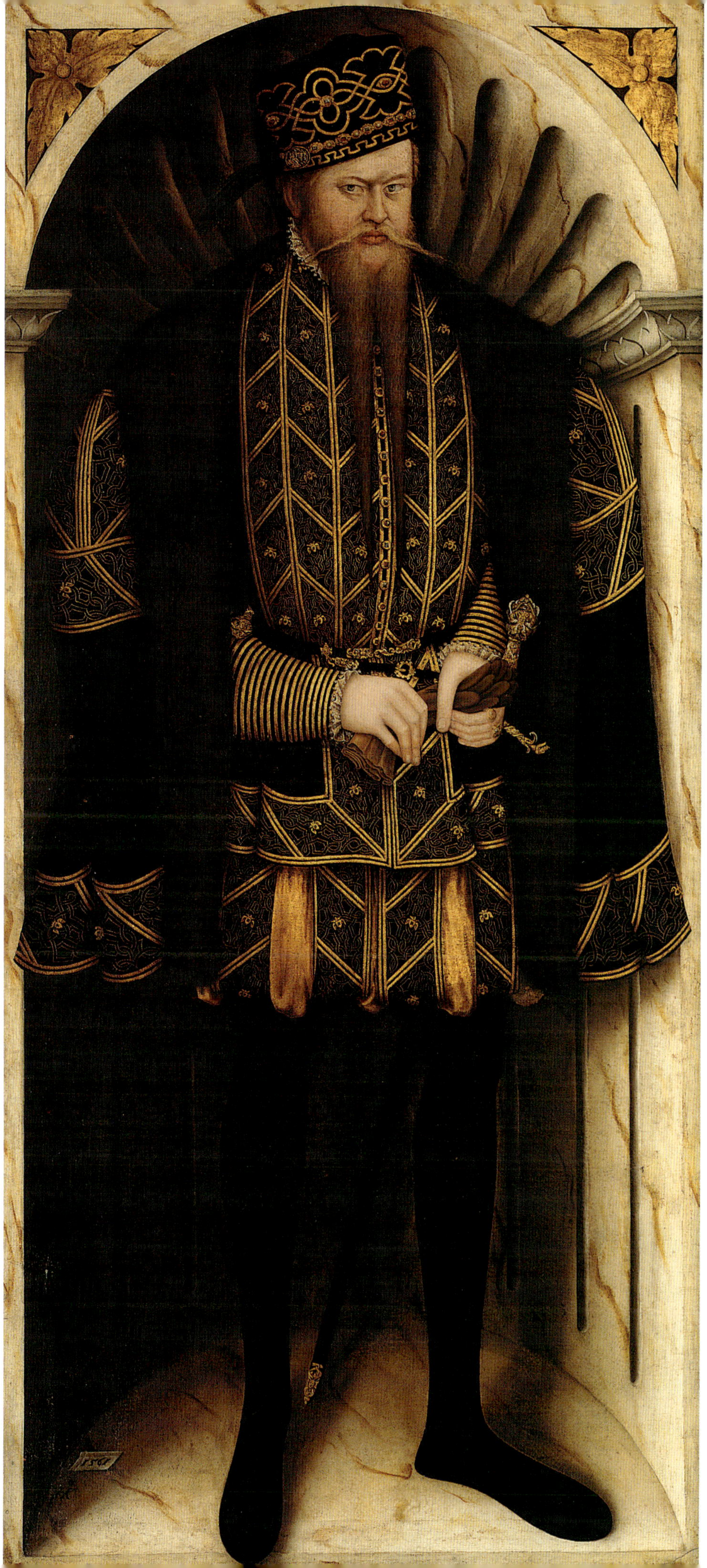

Hans Krell, Leipzig (?), 1561
Oil on canvas
81⅛ × 37⅝ in.
(206 × 95.5 cm)
Signed in lower left "HK"
dated "1561"
First mentioned in the 1610
Kunstkammer inventory
fol. 6, 1832 transferred
from the Kunstkammer
to the Armory.
Staatliche Kunstsammlungen
Dresden, Rüstkammer,
inv. no. H 93
Lit.: Sponsel 1906, p. 37,
text image no. 30, plate
no. 75; Schaal 1991, pp. 12f.,
cat. no. 7; Bäumel 2003

Elector Christian I of Saxony (1560–1591)

Christian I was the only one of August's nine sons to survive. In 1582 he married Sophie, daughter of the elector of Brandenburg. His father had him begin government work in 1580, making him head of the Secret Council in 1581 and appointing him head of the *kleinen Regierung* (small government) in 1584. Christian was thus well prepared when he assumed the office of elector in 1586. In close cooperation with his confidant, Nikolaus Krell, who was promoted to secret counselor in 1586 and made chancellor in 1589, Christian opened Saxony to Calvinism and thereby established the basis for alliances with the elector of the Palatinate. Christian maintained political relationships with German and other European princes who sought independence from the empire, and he supported Henry of Navarre in his struggles for the French crown. Through the initiation of the order *Goldene Gesellschaft* (Golden Fellowship) and the fortification of Königstein in 1589, Christian I emphasized his autonomy. In his domestic policies, he slashed the power of the orthodox Lutherans and diminished the influence of the estates, especially the aristocracy. In February 1591, Christian instigated the Alliance of Torgau between Calvinist and Lutheran rulers. A short-lived attempt to unify politically the different religious groups, it failed because of Christian's unexpected death in October of that year. The Saxon aristocracy and clergy then adopted the rigorous anti-Calvinist policies of Christian I's successors. Ever since then he has been unjustifiably considered a weak sovereign, guided by Krell, and lacking any political goals, one who ultimately fell victim to dissolute habits, most especially overindulgence in alcohol.
D.S.

Carlo di Cesare del Palagio
1591–93
Bronze, H. 37⅝ in. (95.5 cm)
(with base)
Inscribed on the front of the pedestal:
CHRISTIAN. D. / G. DVX. S. EL.
First mentioned in the 1595 Kunstkammer inventory, fol. 318r
Staatliche Kunstsammlungen Dresden, Skulpturesammlung, inv. no. H^4 1/3
Lit.: Holzhausen 1933, pp. 73–75, 87; Dresden 2001, pp. 62f., cat. no. 4 (with additional bibliography)

2 Bronze Bust

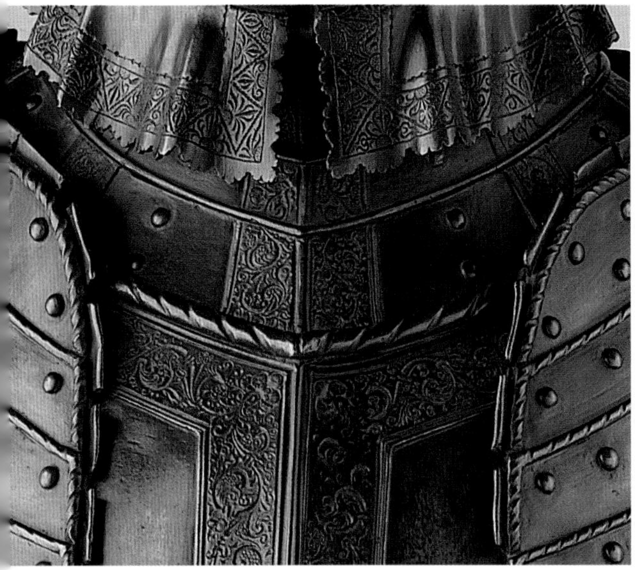

Carlo di Cesare produced this bust as a commission from the widowed electress Sophie, presumably between 1591, the year of Christian I's death, and 1593, the year the artist left Dresden. It is contemporary with a kneeling figure of the deceased elector for the funeral monument of the house of Wettin in Freiberg Cathedral; the bust portion of that figure is nearly identical to this bronze portrait. In 1594, the Dresden medalist Heinrich von Rhenen was paid for the chasing and the addition of a base to the bust, which was transferred to the Kunstkammer. The first mention of the work in the Kunstkammer inventory, with a misattribution to Nosseni, appears in 1595.

With the arrival of di Cesare in 1590 Saxony had a sculptor from the school of Giambologna. Di Cesare had worked for such patrons as the Fuggers, the duke of Bavaria, the emperor, and the grand duke of Tuscany. The bust of Christian I thus combines northern and Florentine elements. Although the head's frontality, its self-controlled expression, and its almost introverted air are reminiscent of Giambologna's bronze bust of Cosimo I de' Medici (1550s), Christian I's portrait reveals a more pronounced stylization uncharacteristic of work by Giambologna. This is most clearly apparent in this sculpture's hair and beard, which have an ornamental flavor. This trait recurs in the Freiberg tomb figure of Christian I, and thus it may be inferred that the stylization was introduced by di Cesare and not in the chasing by von Rhenen.
A.S.

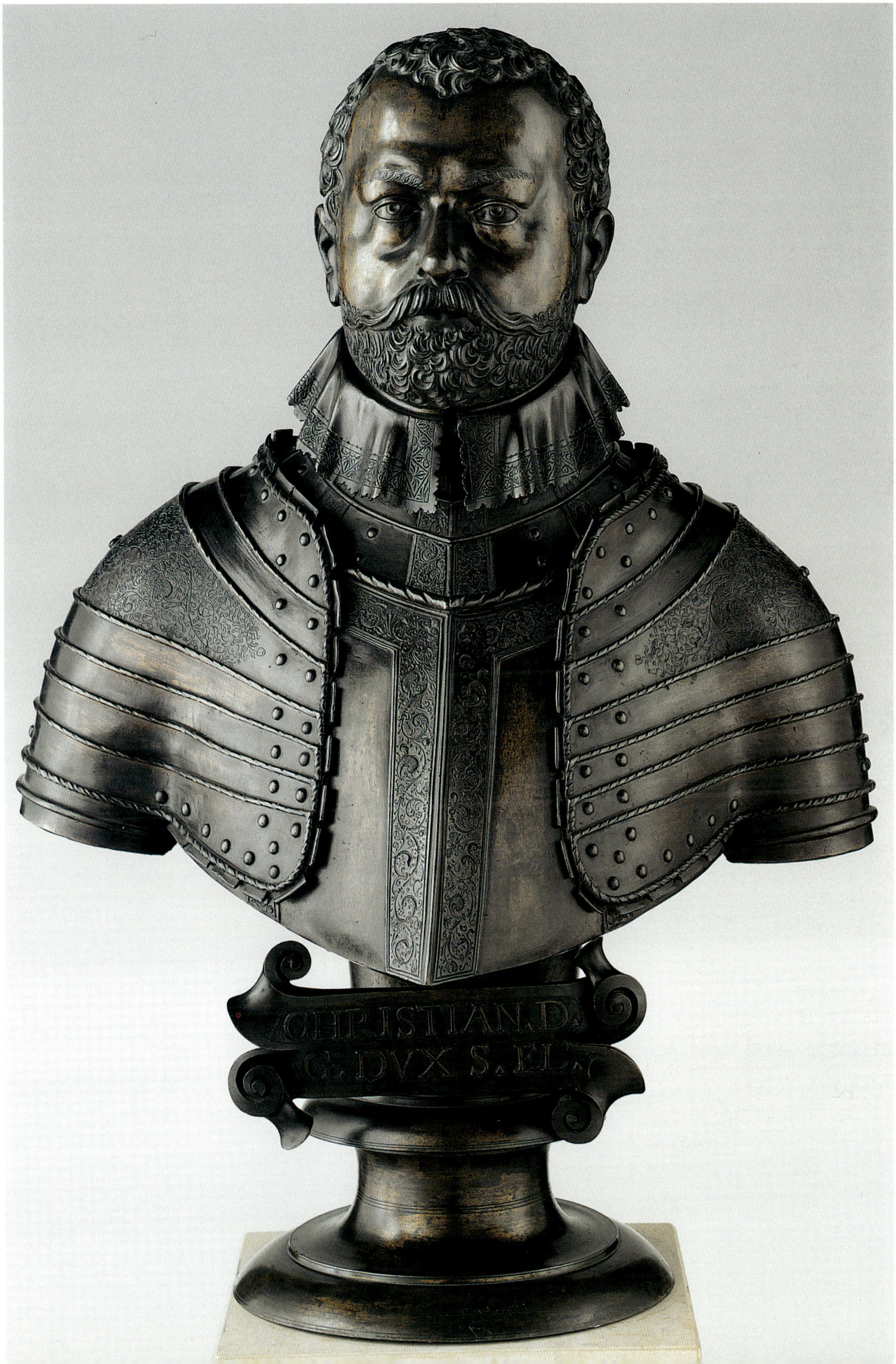
CHRISTIAN. D.
G. DVX S. EL.

Elector Christian II of Saxony (1583–1611)

Christian II was the eldest of Christian I's three sons. His father's untimely death left the eight-year-old a ward of his grandfather, Johann Georg of Brandenburg and the Ernestine Duke Friedrich Wilhelm I of Saxony-Weimar-Altenburg, a strict Lutheran who served as the Saxon administrator. Shortly after the death of Christian I, there was a severe reaction to his Calvinist politics, which came to an end just days after Christian II's accession in 1601: former Chancellor Krell was executed, a measure much debated in the empire and at the emperor's court. As elector, Christian II was loyal to Emperor Rudolf II, whom he visited in Prague in 1607 and 1610, and whom he supported in his struggle to retain power. In the War of Succession of 1609, the emperor endorsed Saxony's position and gave to Saxony the duchies of Jülich, Cleves, and Berg, and the county of Ravensberg. It turned out to be impossible for Saxony to enforce its legal title to these lands. In the increasingly aggressive position taken by the Protestant estates vis-à-vis the Catholic majority, Christian II tended to sympathize with the emperor. The Saxon sovereign's maintenance of an ostentatious court combined with the lavish presents he gave in his attempt to secure prominence resulted in the near bankruptcy of Saxony's state finances. Christian II, obese and alcoholic, died childless at the age of twenty-eight in 1611.
D.S.

Adriaen de Vries (model/chasework),
Martin III Hilliger (cast), 1603
Bronze, H. 37⅛ in. (94.2 cm)
Signed and dated on the back of the plinth:
ADRIANUS FRIES HAGENSIS / FECIT 1603
Inscription on the emperor's medallion:
RVD·II·ROM·IMP·CÆE·AUG·
Gift of Emperor Rudolf II to Elector Christian II during his visit to Prague in 1607
First mentioned in 1610 Kunstkammer inventory, fol. 115
Staatliche Kunstsammlungen Dresden, Skulpturesammlung, inv. no. H 4 1/4
Lit.: Holzhausen 1933, pp. 79f.; Larsson 1967, pp. 38f.; Essen 1988, pp. 135f.; Dresden 1992, p. 47, cat. no. 29; Berlin 1995, pp. 442f., cat. no. 153; Scholten 2000, p. 30; Dresden 2001, pp. 64f., cat. no. 5; Basset 2002; see also Müller/Kaschek 2001

3 Bronze Bust

In 1607, Christian II returned home from his visit to the emperor's court in Prague with gifts amounting to a value of 10,000 taler, among them this bronze bust. Adriaen de Vries produced it in 1603, shortly after becoming Imperial Court Sculptor. It is probably based on relief portraits of the elector.

The armored bust of the unbearded ruler, who gazes into the distance, rests on the shoulders of two female allegorical figures who display the Saxon electoral coat of arms and join hands as a sign of harmony.

The imperial patron honored Christian both with this portrait and with the type of depiction. This bust is nearly the equal of Rudolf's bust (Vienna, Kunsthistorisches Museum, ill. p. 39), except for its smaller size and portions of the armor shown. The bust of Christian II similarly follows the prominent model of Leone Leoni's 1555 bust of Emperor Charles V.

The differences between de Vries's bronze portraits are just as telling. Whereas the emperor's armor is covered with scrolling vines and embellished with heraldic and allegorical elements, including personifications of Victory and Fame, and the Order of the Golden Fleece on the breast, the equally vine-covered armor of Christian II is adorned with only three figural motifs: the heads of a gorgon and a lion (on the back) and the Hapsburg double-eagle suspended from a broad cloth band, presenting a medallion with a likeness of Emperor Rudolf II. The diminution of allegorical and heraldic decoration emphasizes the portrait of the emperor, thereby almost making the medallion an emblem of an order. This was clearly specified by Rudolf II, who surely wanted to visualize Christian II as politically faithful and trustworthy. With the women reaching for each other's hands and the bundled arrows at the foot of the pedestal representing peace, this bust stresses emphatically the regents' *concordia*, for which Rudolf II, who maintained close ties with Saxony, was striving resolutely.

As demonstrated by documentation and by recent technological examinations, the bust was cast in one piece by Martin III Hilliger, using the lost-wax process. The cast's irregular thickness shows that de Vries continued to alter the form at the core by adding wax in some places. The sculptural details—such as the Medusa and feline heads and the emperor medallion—were precisely planned and thus needed little refinishing after casting. A.S.

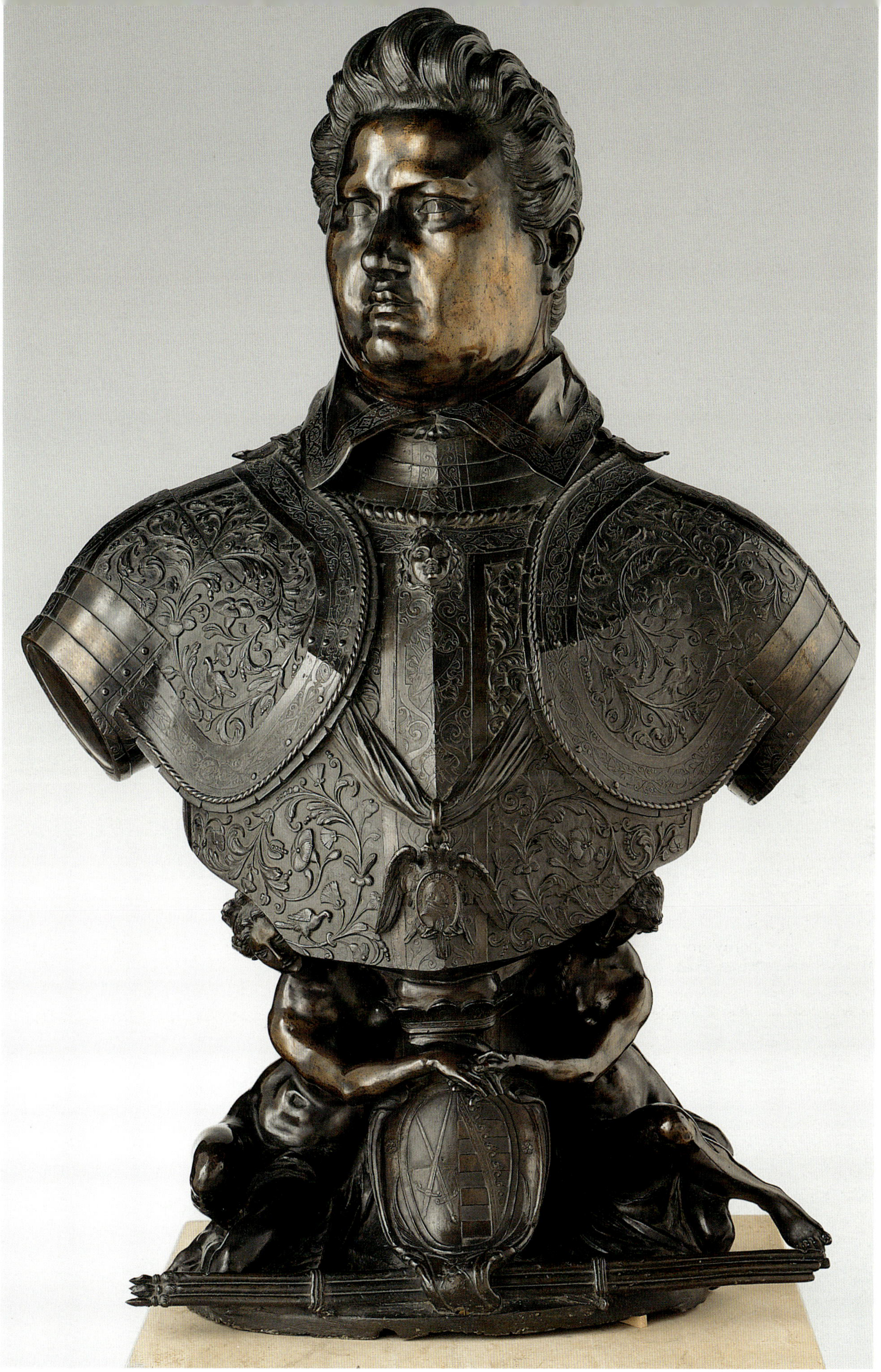

Elector Johann Georg I of Saxony (1585–1656)

It was impossible to know that Johann Georg I's reign would continue for forty-five years when he succeeded his brother Christian II, his elder by two years, as elector in 1611. He became the longest-ruling elector in Saxon history. A decade before, in 1601, he went on a year-long Grand Tour to Italy, which led him via Venice and Rome to Naples. As early as 1607, the year he married Magdalena Sibylla of Brandenburg, his brother invited his participation in ruling the country, leading, in the ensuing years, to repeated confrontations between the brothers, mostly about the elector's financial affairs. When Johann Georg I assumed power, he adopted Lutheran standpoints. In the complicated political atmosphere that existed just before the outbreak of the Thirty Years War, he played an important diplomatic role, serving as Imperial Curate (*Reichsvikar*) in 1612. He also successfully negotiated in favor of Matthias between the Protestant Union and the Catholic League on the occasion of the emperor's election. In 1617 he received the emperor and his future successor Ferdinand II in Dresden; afterward, he hosted the electors of Brandenburg and the Palatinate; and, finally, he organized a jubilant celebration on the one-hundredth anniversary of the beginning of the Reformation. The landed Bohemian estates offered him the royal crown of Bohemia in 1618, which he did not accept; in 1620 he stepped in as representative of the Bohemian crown for Ferdinand II and took on the role of appeasing the rebellious Silesia and the two Lausitz territories. He was granted the latter territories as security for incurred expenditures and subsequently integrated them permanently into his lands. Despite considerable effort, he was unable to keep Saxony out of the disastrous war.
D.S.

Dresden Court Painter
Dresden, circa 1620–25
Oil on canvas
88⅛ × 49⅝ in. (224 × 126 cm)
To the Historisches Museum (Armory) in 1911 by exchange from the Royal Arsenal Collection (Zugangsverzeichnis Historisches Museum, no. 530/7)
Staatliche Kunstsammlungen Dresden, Rüstkammer, inv. no. H 167
Lit.: Dresden 1990, p. 108, cat. no. 154; Schaal 1991, pp. 30f., cat. no. 45

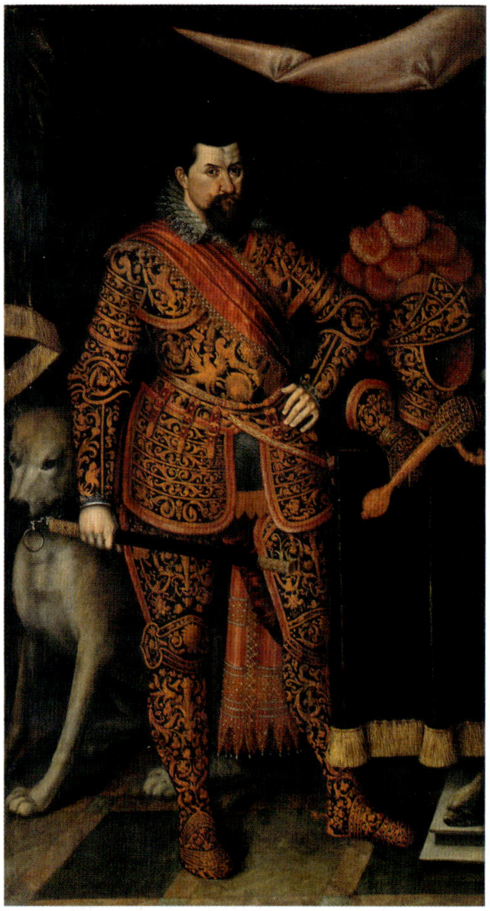

4 Full-Length Portrait

Johann Georg I is depicted full length, wearing his personal armor. He has his rapier, command staff, sash, the nearby electoral sword, and—as in most of his portraits—his dog. The parade armor was made about 1562 by the Antwerp goldsmith Eliseus Libaerts for King Erik XIV of Sweden. Acquired third-hand in 1603 by Christian II for Johann Georg, the armor (cat. no. 13) is faithfully rendered, showing its reddish decoration in great detail. The helmet, with its lavish plumes, and the gauntlets are placed on the table near the electoral sword. The lower leg pieces with spurs are additions by the painter to the half armor. In 1566, on the occasion of the imperial enfeoffment in Augsburg, Elector August of Saxony had the electoral sword carried for him. It was thenceforth considered the valid insignia of Saxon electors.

Johann Georg's pose as a determined commander-in-chief may be read as a response to the military challenges posed by the Thirty Years War. The Wettin dynasty successfully participated in numerous battles in this war.

While the composition of this painting confers on it the status of a state portrait, its artistic merit is lacking. Since the picture is not signed, it may be unfinished. The mass-produced characteristics of the frame indicates that it hung in a princely gallery. The dating of this work is based on comparisons with other likenesses of Johann Georg I. J.B.

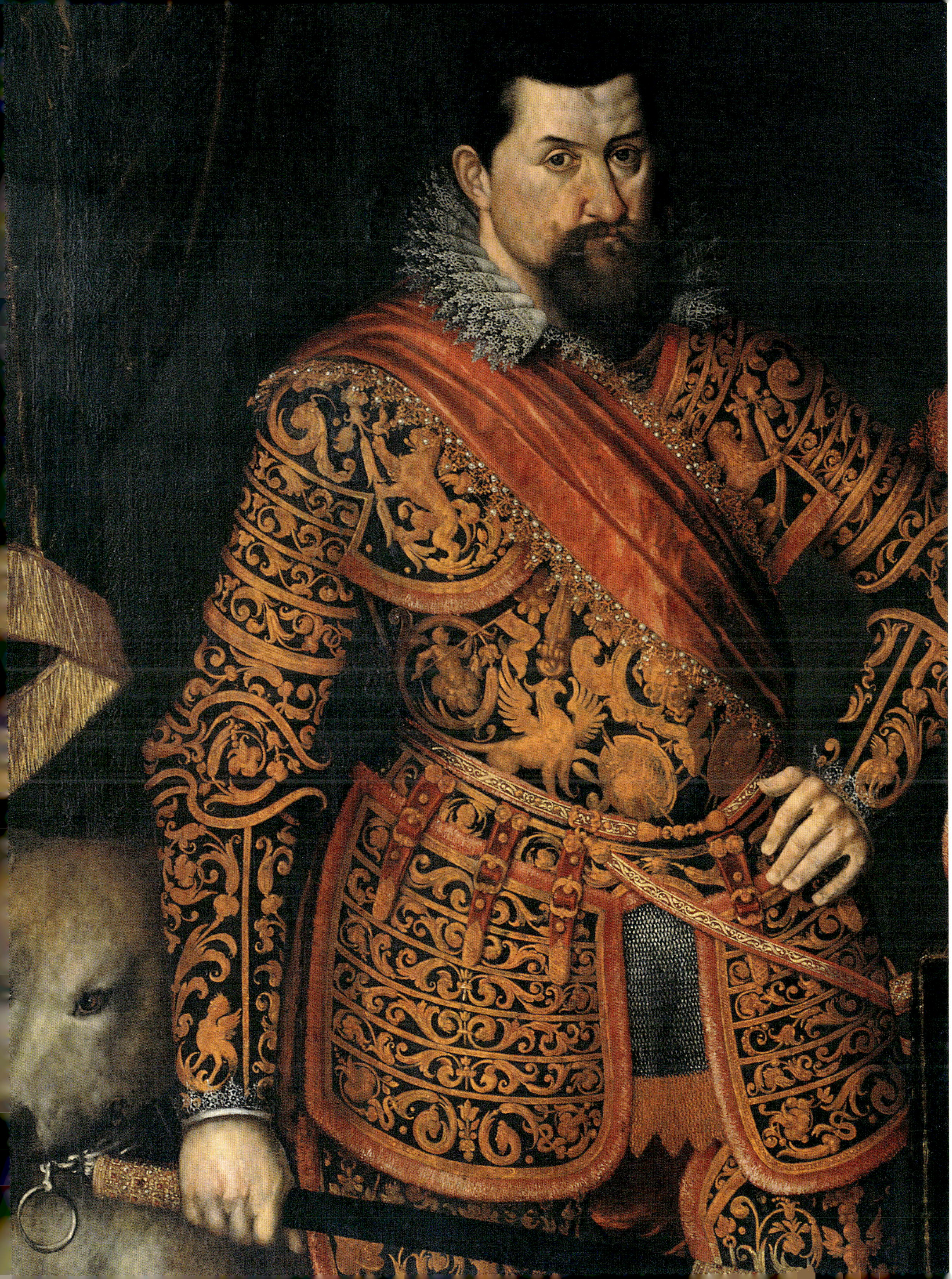

5 Elector's Tankard (left)

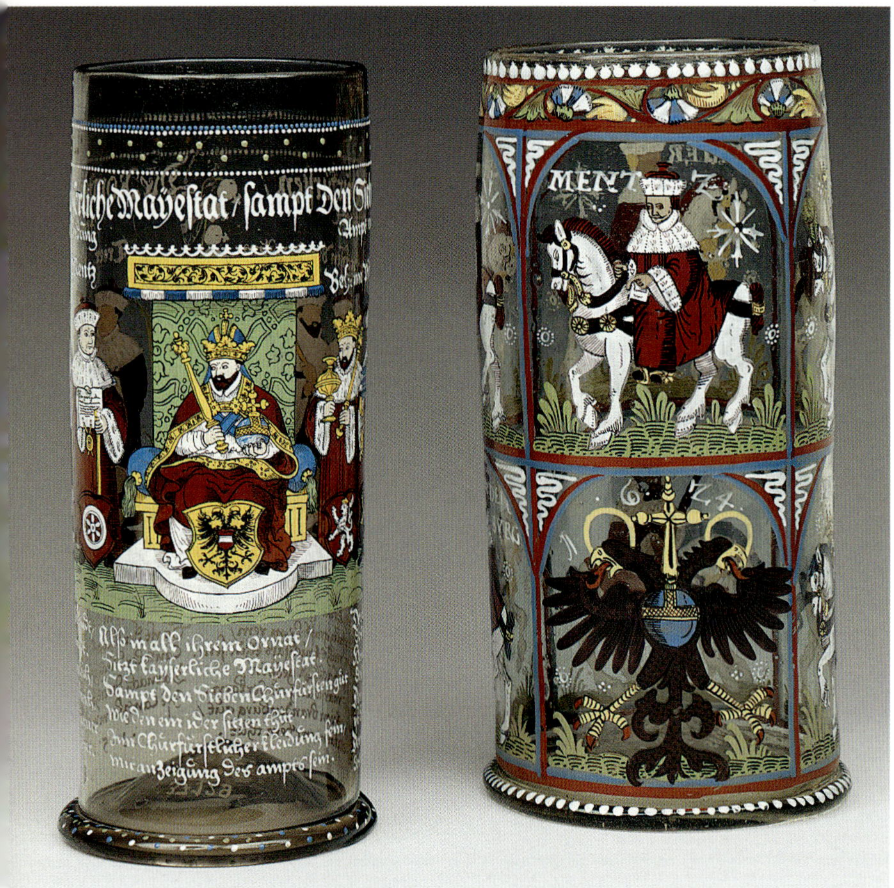

The theme of the tankards that depict the imperial eagle and the electors is the political order of the Holy Roman Empire of the German Nation. Based on a woodcut from Schedel's *Weltchronik* of 1493 and its successors—in this case a sixteenth-century woodcut by Hans Vogel—the tankard depicts, both in word and image, the emperor and the seven electors with the insignia of their imperial offices. The three ecclesiastical electors and chancellors are shown to the right of the emperor according to their rank: Mainz (Mayence), Cologne, Trier (Treves). The four secular electors are the king of Bohemia as Erzschenk (it was his privilege to pour libation for the emperor), the count Palatine of Rhein as Erztruchsess (the empire's honorary head of the court household), the duke of Saxony as Erzmarschall (imperial grand marshal), and the margrave of Brandenburg as Erzkämmerer (imperial treasurer) of the Holy Roman Empire of the German Nation. The so-called "glasses with the imperial eagle" were masterpieces of the Bohemian glass painters in Kreibitz. Guild rules stipulated that these vessels had to be produced within a day and a half, which led to their popularity. The equally extensively produced elector's tankards share the same story, although the guild documents for those have not yet come to light. This glass from 1588 with its electoral Saxon provenance is the earliest of its type; an example dated 1630 is owned by the Los Angeles County Museum of Art. I.A.J.

Bohemia, dated 1588
Colorless glass with enamel painting and gilding, H. 10¼ in. (26.1 cm)
Depiction of enthroned emperor, surrounded by electors.
So-called Schlossbergung Moritzburg, purchased 1999 from the house of Wettin
Staatliche Kunstsammlungen Dresden, Kunstgewerbenmuseum, inv. no. 37 129 (left and on p. 107)
Lit.: Dresden 1981, p. 76, cat. no. 63; Saldern 1965, p. 55, fig. 39, p. 70, fig. 59, 60 (graphics) and pp. 69ff.

6 Elector's Tankard (right)

Bohemia, dated 1624
Slightly green glass with colored enamel painting
H. 14½ in. (36.8 cm)
Inscribed: *"Pfaltz, Sachsen, Brandenburg, Mentz, Behem, Trier, Cöln"* (Palatinate, Saxony, Brandenburg, Mainz, Bohemia, Trier, Cologne)
Bergungsgut (salvaged item) 1963
Staatliche Kunstsammlungen Dresden, Kunstgewerbenmuseum, inv. no. 37 085 (right)
Lit.: Dresden 1981, p. 77, cat. no. 64; Saldern 1965, pp. 75ff.; Haase 1988

The large group of glasses that show electors on horseback in varying designs is slightly later than the type of the Kurfürstenhumpen with standing princes. This type can be found both with, as here, and without an arcade. The arches or arcades are symbols of the electors' dignity, and they epitomize the notion of order. The use of columns and arches as symbols of creation and evidence of divine wisdom may be seen on medieval Easter panels depicting the order of the ecclesiastical year. During the Renaissance—a period in which interests turned increasingly to the divine order of the world and investigation of how it operates—the motif of the arcade was indispensable for illustrating different systems. In its form, the secular order shown here, namely the order of the Holy Roman Empire of the German Nation, corresponds with renderings of the celestial order of the apostles or the evangelists depicted on ceramic or tin jugs or glass tankards. On this tankard, the order of time is depicted by the stages of life, each under a separate arch of the arcade.

A third variant of the Kurfürstenhumpen is represented by sets of tankards or glasses, each of which illustrates a single elector or the emperor. The Museum of Decorative Arts, Dresden, owns glasses produced in Saxony that come from two sets, which differ in height (Haase 1988, p. 295, cat. nos. 8 and 9).
I.A.J.

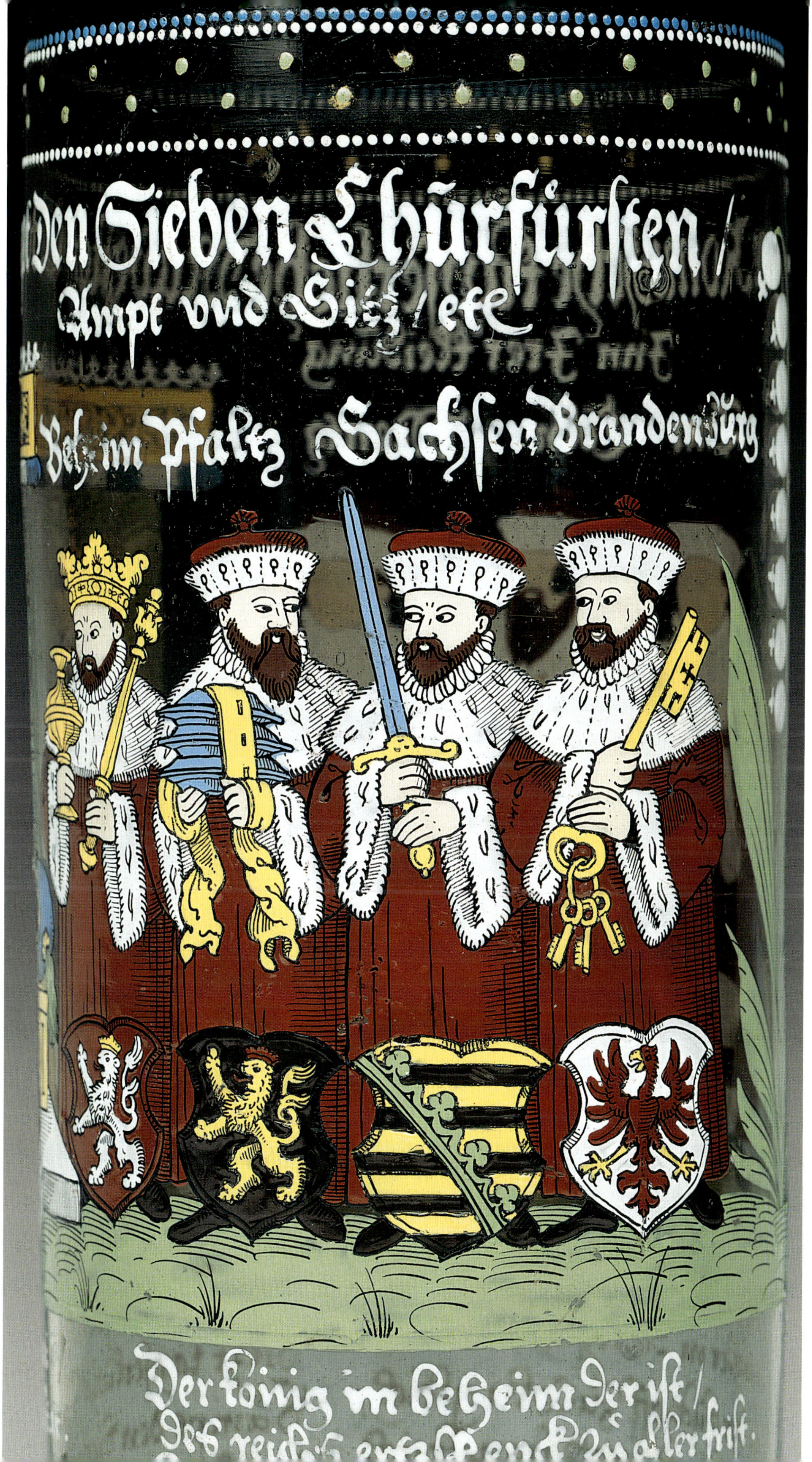

The tankard (cat. no. 5) has the following inscription:
"Die Römische kayserliche Mayestät,
sampt Den Sieben Churfürsten:
Inn Irer Kleidung Ampt und Sitz etc."
(The Roman Imperial Majesty,
with the Seven Electors:
In their garment, office, and seat.)

Below:

Der ertzbischoff zu mentz bekande,
ist Cantzler im Deutschen lande.
Sonst der bischoff zu Cöln gleich /
Cantzler durch gantz franckreich.
Darnach der ertzbischoff zu trier,
Ist Cantzler in welscher refier.

1588

Also in all ihrem Ornat /
Sitzt kayserliche Mayestat,
Sampt den sieben Churfürsten gut
wie den ein ider sitzen thut.
Inn Churfürstlicher kleidung fein /
Mit an Zeigung des ampts sein.

Der König in Beheim der ist /
Des reichs ertzschenck zu aller frist.
Hernach der pfaltzgraff beim rein
Des heiligen reichs truchsäss thut sein.
Der Hertzog zu Sachsen geborn
Ist des reichsmarschalch auserkorn.
Der Marggraff von brandenburg gut /
Des reichs ertzkämmerer sein thut."

The archbishop of Mainz
Is the chancellor of the German Lands
Equal to him the bishop of Cologne
Who is the chancellor for all of France
He is followed by the archbishop
of Trier
Who is chancellor in the Italian territories

1588

Thus in the robes
Is seated the imperial majesty
With the seven electors
All of whom are seated
Wearing their elegant electoral vestments
That indicate their office

He who is the king of Bohemia
Is at all times the empire's arch tapster
Followed by the Count Palatine near
the Rhine
Who is the empire's honorary head
of the courtly household
The duke born in Saxony
Is selected to perform the office
of imperial grand marshal
The margrave of Brandenburg
Does good work as the empire's treasurer

7 Tankard, so-called Willkomm (Welcome) of the Ölbing Brothers

For a Willkomm, this tankard is relatively small. On one side it shows St. George on horseback. The rest of the surface is taken up with texts and a scene of courtiers, who can be identified by inscriptions and their national costumes. A Spaniard, a Frenchman, and a German surround a woman, who makes fun of them by *"Füs tretten"* (kicking them with the feet), *"Hand drücken"* (pinching their hands), and *"lachen"* (laughing at them). The meaning of the scene can be deduced from inscriptions, not included here but contained in the model, a 1590 woodcut by an artist with the monogram BKGF. In the print, three verses of four lines each correspond to the men and describe the subtle signs of love with the idiosyncrasies of the three nationalities: The Spaniard can *"zu ihr machen"* (approach her) if she *"thut an lachen"* (laughs at) him. The Frenchman goes to her *"zur Nacht"* (for the night) as soon as the maid pinches his hand. The *"teutsche Hoffmann"* (German courtier) only knows that he *"haben muß"* (must have) her when she steps on his foot. In this rendering, the theme of national characteristics, variously depicted in the sixteenth and seventeenth centuries, is mixed with that of female domination. As a Willkomm into a fraternity, there was a ceremony in which every new member had to empty this humorous glass in one go. Nothing is known about the Ölbing Brothers. Material and theme of this Willkomm suggest that this group was not a professional or a spiritual one, but likely an assembly of noblemen who gathered for drinking. They might have been members of the Order of the Teutonic Knights, since the Hanseatic League city, Elbing, located east of Gdansk, belonged to the territory of the Teutonic Order.

There are two additional glasses with variations of this scene, one in the Museum für angewandte Kunst in Vienna, dated 1599, (No. F 153), and one formerly in the Blumka Collection, dated 1621 (Saldern 1965).
I.A.J.

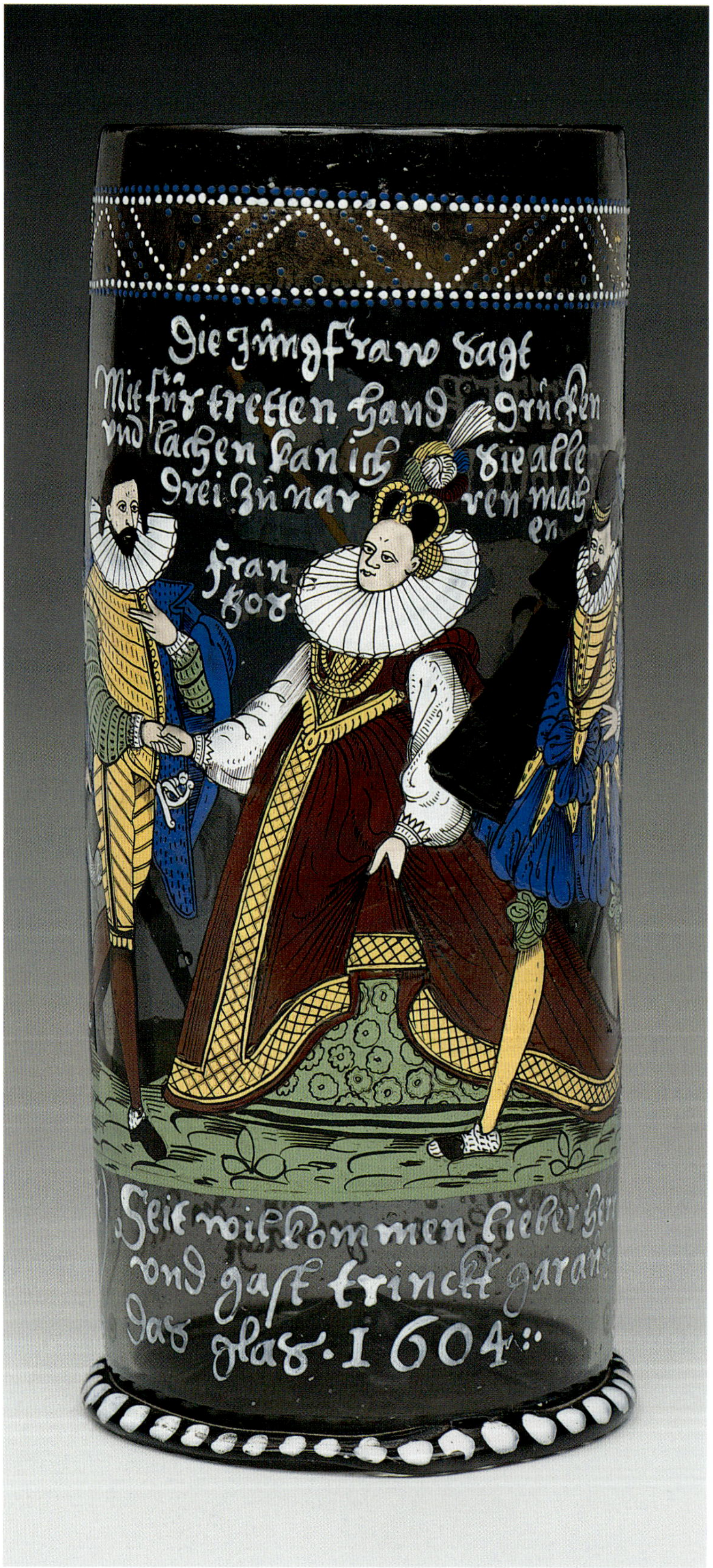

Bohemia, 1604
Smoky glass with enamel painting
H. 9¾ in. (24.8 cm)
Inscribed above the depiction of St. George on horseback: "RITTER S. GEORGIUS," below: *"Dieser wilkommen ist gantz wool geacht / den Brüdern zu ölbing zu allen / ehren gemacht"* (Take note that this Welcome is made to honor the Ölbing Brothers). Opposite three courtiers, entitled as: *"Frantzos, spaniger, teutscher"* (Frenchman, Spaniard, German) with a lady: *"Die Jungfraw sagt / mit füs tretten Hand drücken / und lachen kan ich sie alle drei zu narren machen"* (The young Lady says: If I kick them with my feet, pinch their hands, and laugh at them, I can fool all three of them)
Below: *"Seit wilkommen lieber Herr / und gast trinckt garaus das Glas 1604"* (Be welcome dear Lord and Guest and empty this glass 1604)
Bergungsgut (salvaged item) 1963
Staatliche Kunstsammlungen Dresden, Kunstgewerbenmuseum, inv. no. 37 088
Lit.: Dresden 1981, no. 60;
Saldern 1965, p. 106,
fig. 152–54

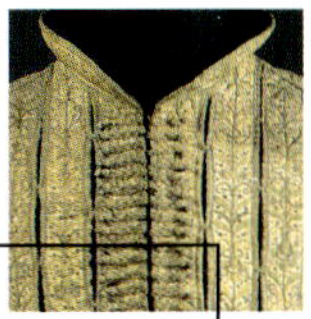

Costumes

Jutta Bäumel

Dresden's collection of electoral garments dates back to Elector August of Saxony. The death of his brother, Elector Moritz, in 1553 prompted him to inventory the latter's clothing. August then proceeded to keep his own outfits and to have them inventoried during his lifetime. Successive generations of electors followed his example. The necessity of having the princely clothing systematically documented and administered was based on its phenomenal dynastic and material value. The stress on the dynastic principle is revealed by the fact that—with the exception of Johann Georg I's family—only the male garments were earmarked for permanent preservation. Special connections to such dynastic festivities as weddings were distinctively emphasized.

The point of departure for the initial systematic approach was based on official sixteenth-century clothing regulations issued by the authorities, which determined a hierarchy regarding the value of materials and garments. Among the fabrics, the most esteemed were patterned silks woven in gold and silver; the favorite furs were ermine and sable; and the coat was the preferred article of clothing. The increasing number, differentiation, and layering of items of dress is a result of the sixteenth century's economic progress, resulting in multifaceted types and styles of clothing, multiple cuts, colors, fabrics, and embroideries, as well as the growing prestige of ensembles. Specific garments for certain occasions, opportunities, or events in one's life were introduced. They entailed ceremonial garments (electoral outfits), clothes for festivities, weddings, the military, the hunt; national costumes and those for tournament, house, sleeping, and bathing; as well as winter and rain clothes and clothes for children, the elderly, those in mourning, and burial of the dead.

Even the otherwise frugal Elector August is documented as having extremely luxurious garments. The growing quantity and costliness of his clothing was augmented by thousands of precious jewels sewn on as buttons, pegs, decorative figures, clasps, and buckles. These were made of gold, enamel, precious stones, and crystal, and there could be hundreds attached to a single garment. Expressive motifs such as hearts and initials addressed specific persons.

During the seventeenth century, there was a remarkable increase in the number and variations of accessories. New outfits were furnished with matching hats and hatbands, sashes, belts, sword belts, gloves, stockings, knee roses, garters, shoes, and shoe roses—frequently in numerous variations. This development was accompanied by an eruption of color as well as the exaggerated application of laces, trimmings, and ribbons. Fashionable cuts were further enhanced by gold trim along the edges and padded stitching. From the hundreds of items produced during the years between Elector Moritz and Johann Georg I, the Dresden collections still contain twenty-three men's outfits, four ladies' dresses, and numerous accessories. These holdings are a unique manifestation of the High and Late Renaissance European princely fashion with its Spanish and Italian dominance.

8 Man's Doublet and Breeches

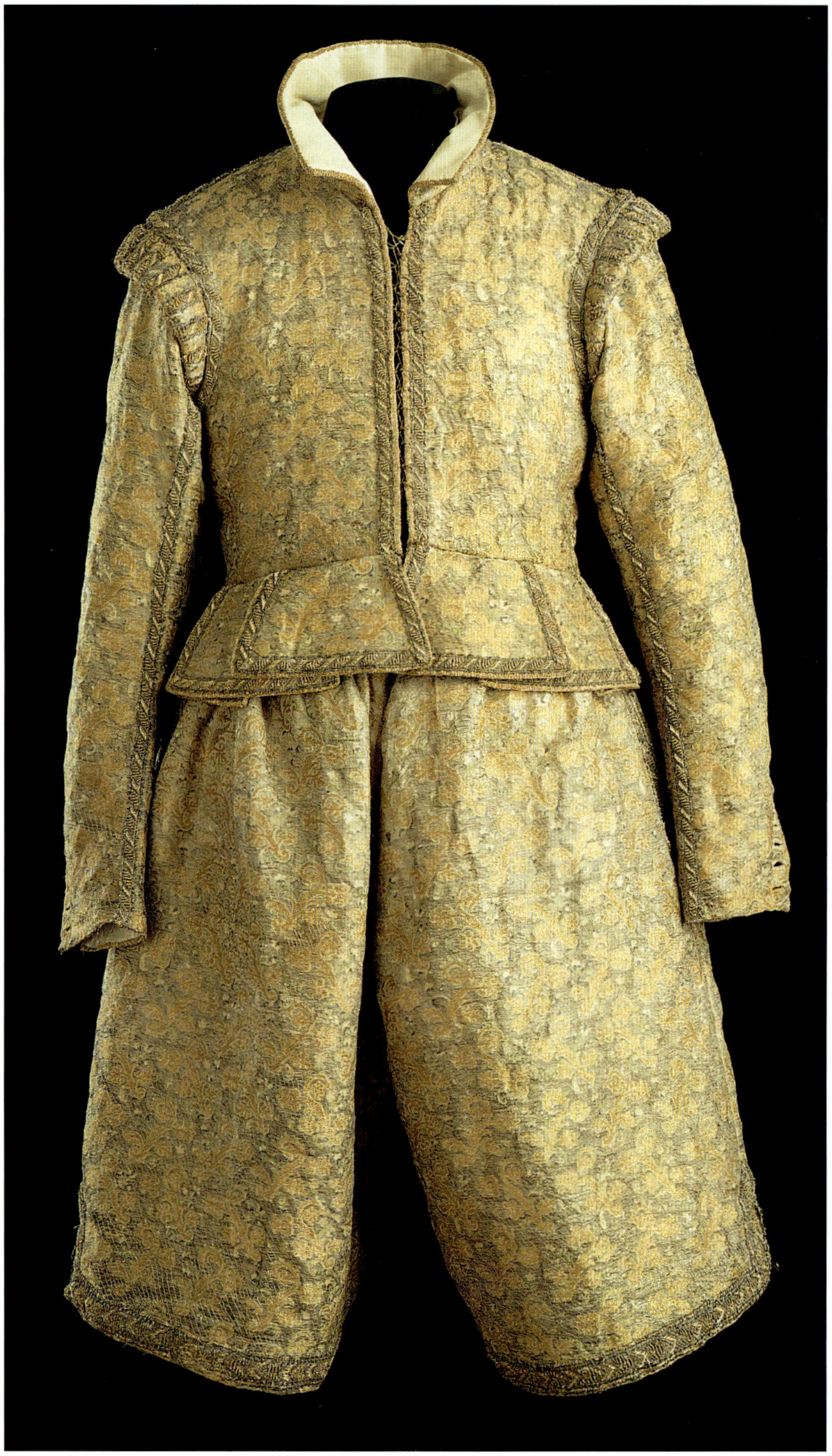

Johann Georg I of Saxony wore these garments in Dresden, when he married his first wife, Sibylla Elisabeth of Württemberg, *"den ersten Tagk"* (on the first day), meaning for the wedding and the ensuing nuptials, on Sunday, September 16, 1604, in Dresden. Overall the white-silver lampas with gold flowers, decorated with salmon red, ivory, and blue-violet petals and green foliage, gives the impression of being wedding white. The tradition of white as the bridegroom's color was initiated at the electoral Saxon court at Duke August's wedding in 1548. Regarding its material, this costume is among the most precious of all of Johann Georg I's clothes. It follows the latest Italian fashion and takes its shape from the padded lining and the application of elaborately woven gold and silver trim. The tightly fitting doublet is slightly shortened at the front. It has a small stand-up collar, shoulder wings, tiny protruding and overlapping double skirt panels, and a distinctive fastening of gold lace. The knee breeches are wide and free-falling; they have similarly trimmed pockets at the sides. The outfit was well-suited to Johann Georg, who wore a gold-embroidered black cloak over it (cat. no. 9).
J.B.

1604
Upper fabric: Italian tailoring presumably Dresden, Electoral Tailor Shop
Trim work: presumably Saxon
Upper fabric: white-silver lampas, gold-brocaded, patterned with colored silk
Lining: quilt lining, padded, light off-white linen, white taffeta, white silk satin
Trim spun gold and silver yarn, woven, in part napped; lace-up fastening spun gold yarn
Doublet: L., front center 11¾ in. (30 cm), back center 15 in. (38 cm, each without doublet skirts)
Circumference of the waist 35 in. (89 cm)
Doublet skirts: W. 4¾/7⅛ in. (12/18 cm), H. 4⅜ in. (11 cm)
Breeches: L. 23⅝ in. (60 cm)
Circumference of the waist 35⅞ in. (91 cm)
Buttocks inseam 13¾ in. (35 cm)
W. legs 31 ½ in. (80 cm)
Inventory Electoral Tailor Shop 1660, no. 19
Staatliche Kunstsammlungen Dresden, Rüstkammer, inv. no. I 15
Lit.: Haenel 1911, pp. 50–52; Bäumel 1993; Bäumel 1995b; Bäumel 2002

9 Man's Cloak

1604, reworked 1607
Tailoring and embroidery: presumably Dresden Electoral Tailor Shop
with the initials "ISMG" (Johann Georg and Magdalena Sibylla) repeated 27 times
Upper fabric: black silk velvet, chiseled
Cord: embroidery spun gold and silver yarn, cantils silver-gilt
Lining: yellow taffeta, off-white linen
L., back center 35 in. (89 cm)
Collar: H. 6⅞ in. (17.5 cm), L. upper edge 19 in. (48.3 cm)
Bridegroom's Dress of Duke Johann Georg I of Saxony 1604
Inventory Electoral Tailor Shop 1612
Inventory Electoral Tailor Shop 1660, no. 19
Staatliche Kunstsammlungen Dresden, Rüstkammer, inv. no. I 14
Lit.: Sponsel 1906, plate 40; Haenel 1911, pp. 50–52, ill. p. 43; Nicht 1960, ill. 18 and 19; Bäumel 1993; Bäumel 1995b

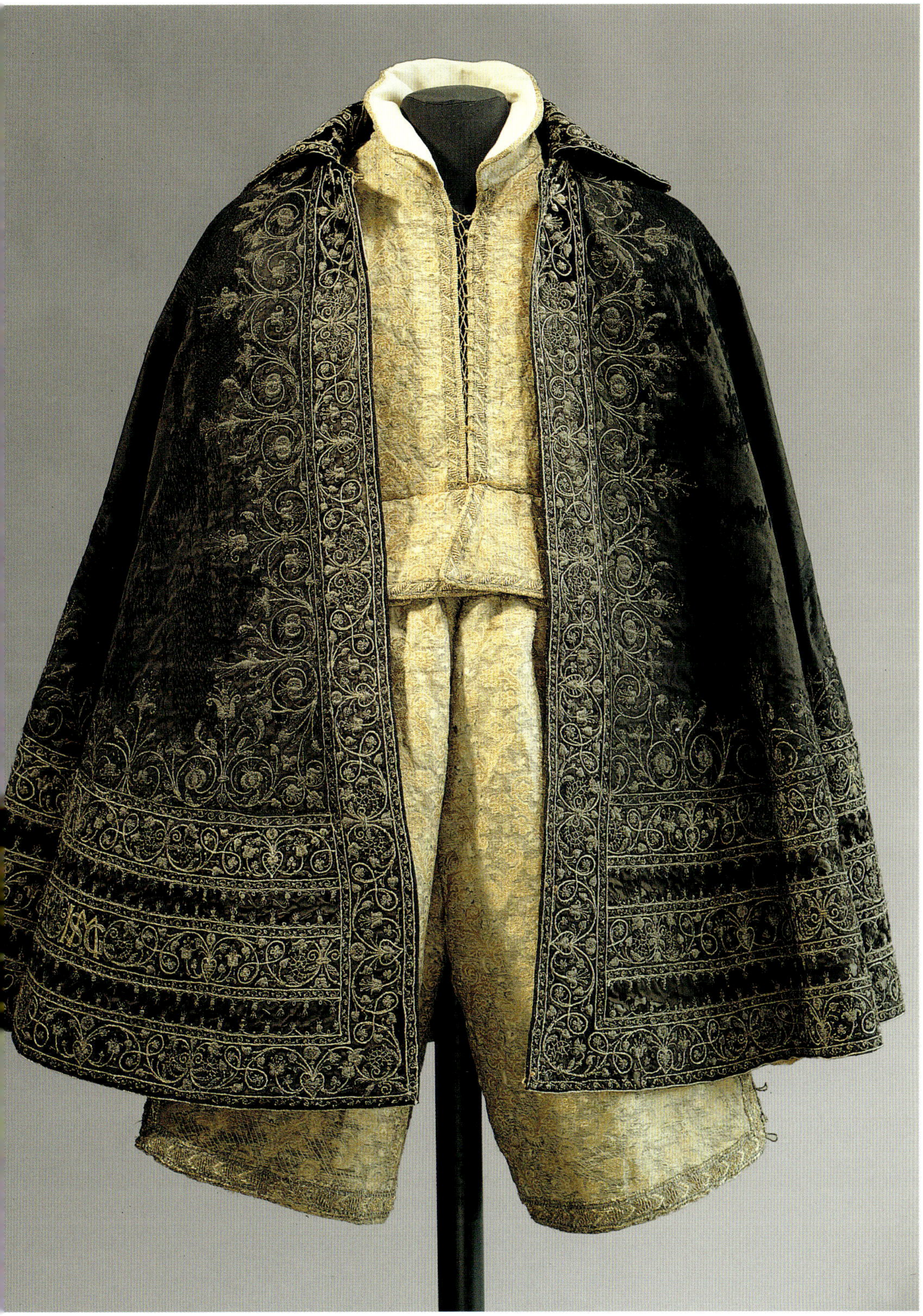

The black cloak has three bands around it of tendrils, hearts, and palmetto flowers in gold and silver—"*hochgebrehme von Vntzengoldt streichweis gestigkt*" (thick golden reliefs embroidered in stripes). It was the bridegroom's cloak of Johann Georg I, who wore it for two weddings: in 1604 in Dresden, when he married Sibylla Elisabeth of Württemberg, who died from childbed fever in 1606, and in 1607 in Torgau, when he married Magdalena Sibylla of Brandenburg. In 1604, he wore the cloak *"den ersten tagk"* (the first day), together with the aforementioned ensemble (cat. no. 8). In 1607, he put on the cloak "*den andern tagk*" (the other day), September 17, to receive the so-called Morgengabe during the ceremony that followed the next morning. For that event, the gold and silver embroidered initials "ISEG," for Johann Georg and Sibylla Elisabeth, were changed to "ISMG," for Johann Georg and Magdalena Sibylla. The lining of the cloak was a silver fabric with a white pattern and gold stripes; it was even more precious than the outside fabric. A portrait of Elector Johann Georg I, dated 1617 and lost since 1945, shows how the knee-length circular cloak was supposed to be worn. Draped over the left shoulder, it was pulled under the right shoulder and the ends were tied together at the front. The lining, which was later replaced, was intentionally exposed. The collar, embroidered on both sides, could be worn either up or down. The cloak is depicted in the mural of the Princely Procession (Fürstenzug) on Augustusstraße, near the Dresden Residenzschloss, where it is erroneously worn by Elector August.
J.B.

10 Man's Doublet and Trunk Hose

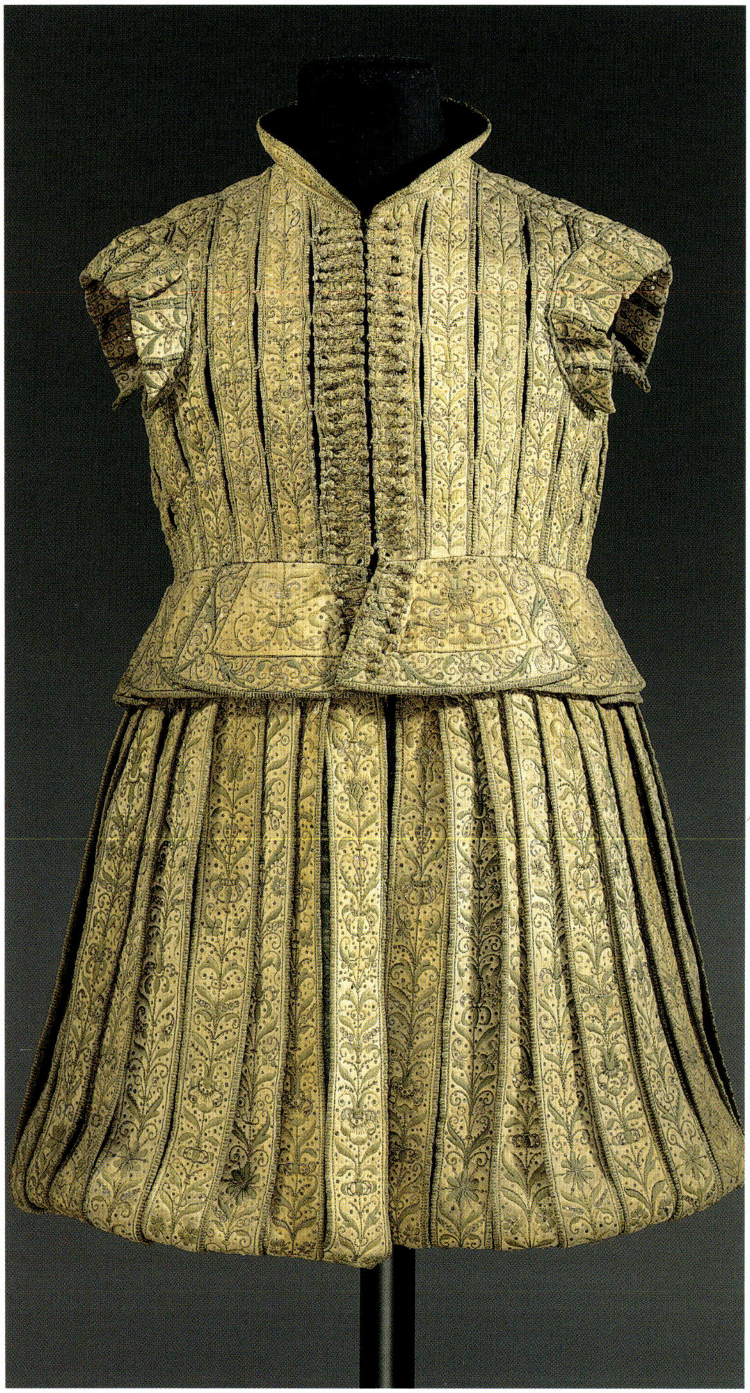

The "white" leather garments with green and silver embroidery were entered into the list of additions (Zugangsverzeichnis) in the Electoral Tailor Shop on May 19, 1615, as a new creation for Elector Johann Georg I of Saxony. At the time, the ensemble with this doublet and breeches included two additional green and white/silver doublets, a pair of leather stockings, two pairs of silk stockings, a pair of leather gloves, and a leather sword belt. The various combinations of the individual elements provided options for their different uses. Another source mentions green cloaks and coats. The color and the materials indicate that the costume was intended for various kinds of hunting events. The striped trunk hose are shown here, as they are in contemporary princely portraits, in their last incarnation: wide and with a distinct edge that makes them look as though a hoop was inserted. This impression is created by turning under the overlapping leather stripes and sewing them tightly. The underhose, visible through the leather trunk hose, consist of a particularly elegant silk satin with green and silver horiontal stripes.
J.B.

Saxon, 1615
Upper fabrics: Italian
Tailoring: presumably Dresden, Electoral Tailor Shop
Embroidery: presumably Dresden
Trim: presumably Saxon
Upper fabric: off-white chamois leather
Embroidery: green silk, silver spun yarn, silver sequins
Satin liseré green silk and white, flattened silver wire; trim, cords, green silk buttons, silver spun yarn, wood.
lining: green taffeta, off-white linen
Doublet: back center, L. 15 in. (38 cm), front center, L. 11¾ in. (30 cm, each without doublet skirts),
L. shaped pad 4⅜–4¾ in. (11–12 cm), circumference of the waist 40⅛ in. (102 cm), W. stripes 1⅝–2 in. (4–5 cm)
Breeches: L. circa 18⅞ in. (48 cm)
Circumference of the waist 40⅛ in. (102 cm), inseam 20⅞ in (53 cm),
L. stripes 23¼–24 in. (59–61 cm), W. stripes 2–2⅛ in. (5–5.5 cm)
Electoral Tailor Shop, list of additions (*Zugangsverzeichnis*) 1612 ff.
Staatliche Kunstsammlungen Dresden, Rüstkammer, inv. no. I 16
Lit.: Haenel 1911, pp. 50–52, ill. p. 45; Thiel 1980, p. 195, ill. 342; Antwerp 1977, cat. no. 102, ill. 41 and 43; Bäumel 1995a

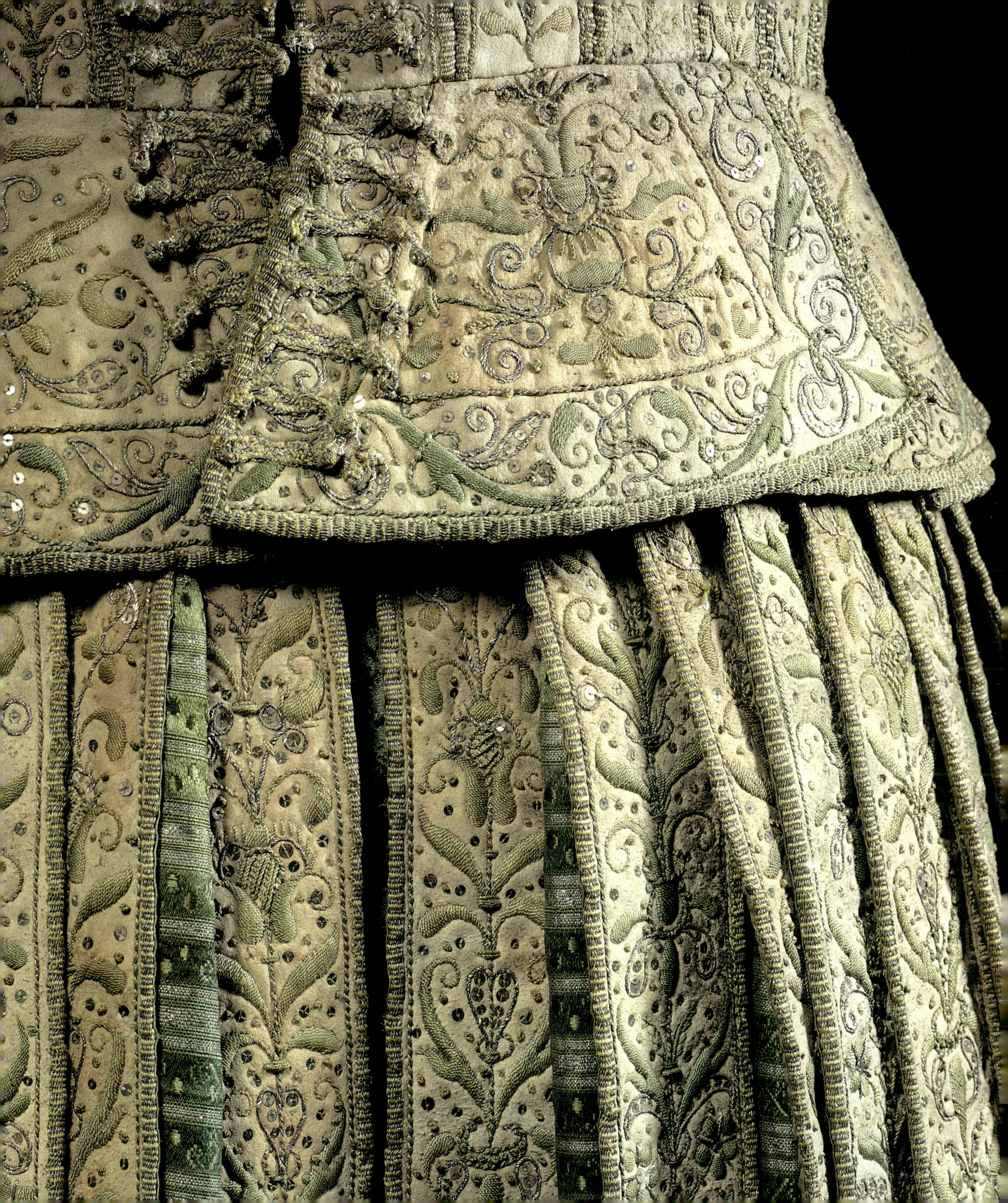

11 Man's Parade Costume

This parade costume was among the personal belongings of Elector Johann Georg I of Saxony. Based on its style, it may be dated to about 1625–30. In the electoral garment inventory, it is listed as "*golden stück Kniehosen und zerschnitten wambs mit gülden und grün seidenen schnüren gebrehmet*" (gold breeches and slashed doublet with gold and green silk cords applied in relief). Baggy breeches were introduced into princely European fashion in the late sixteenth century. The doublet—"*zerschnitten*" (slashed) along the upper chest, the back, and the arms—became popular during the second quarter of the seventeenth century; this fashion began in Western Europe. The holes in the tiny stand-up collar were used to fasten a protruding, capelike cloak. The tailor created a visual accent by applying gold and colored silk crowns and palmettes over a green ground. The new fashion is further emphasized by the green-gold trim along the edges and the inseams, as well as by the rows of tightly spaced, gold-covered buttons and knots of various types. Johann Georg I had another outfit of the same fabric in a slightly different style (inv. no. I 10). The quality of the present costume, its principal color (green), and the loops to fasten hunting weapons and equipment place it in the context of festive hunting events, such as a banquet or processions, or contests in the Dresden Residenzschloss's court.
J.B.

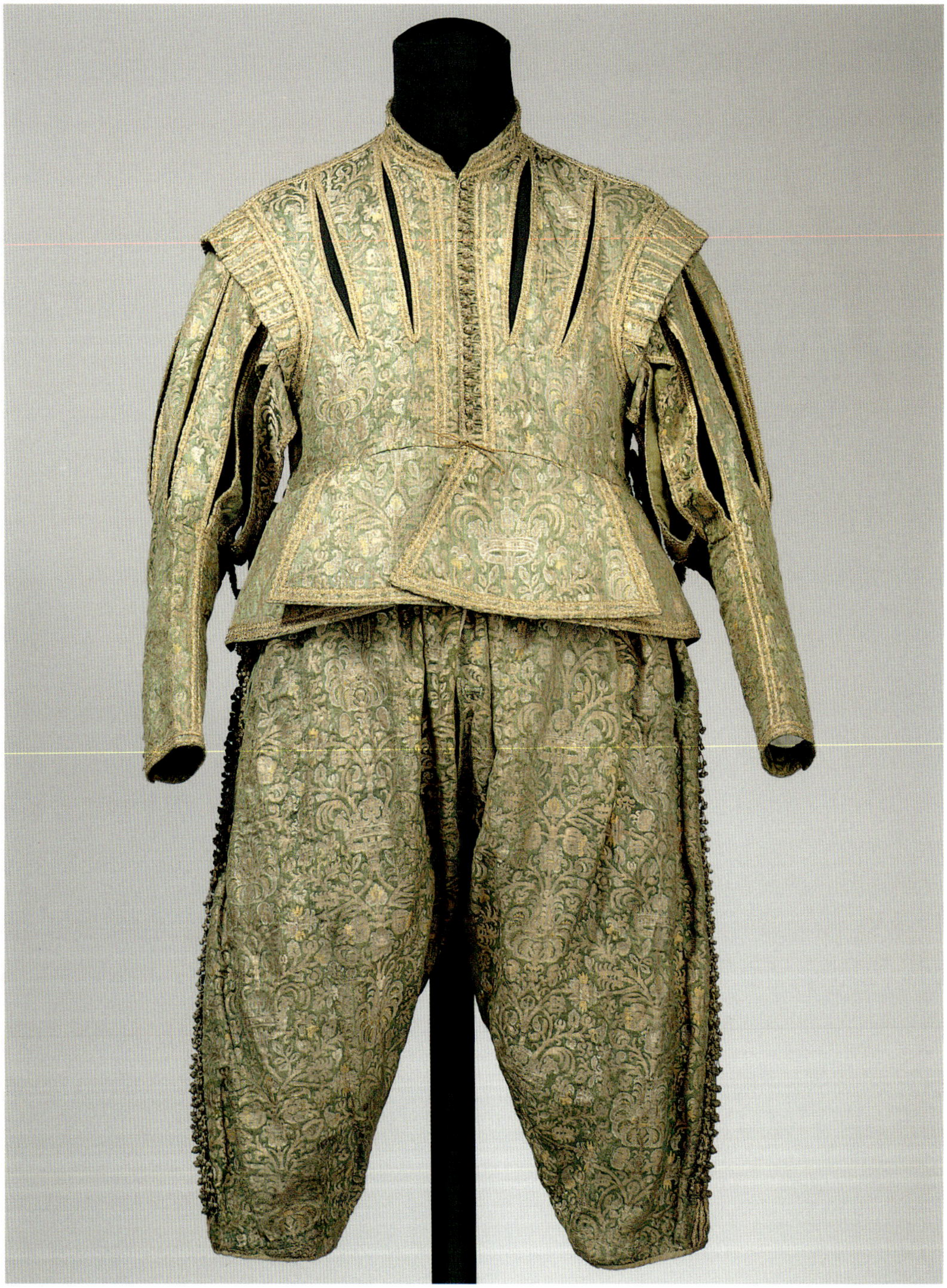

Exhibited in Rome only

Saxon, circa 1625–30
Upper fabrics: Italian
Tailoring: presumably Dresden, Electoral Tailor Shop
Trim work: presumably Saxon
Upper fabrics: lampas, patterned; ground green silk, green in satin weave, figures in gold wire (silver-gilt) as well as gold brown silk, blue white, salmon red, and yellow in twill; lining green silk satin, green taffeta, linen off-white in tabby, brown-black starched linen in tabby, waxed, leather (goat or sheep) bright, tanned chamois leather (goat or sheep)
Trim: spun gold yarn, green silk; buttons trim work, wood, covered with braided spun gold yarn and green silk, hooks and loops: brass
Doublet: L., back center 22⅜ in. (57 cm), front center 18¼ in. (46.5 cm), circumference of the waist 41¾ in. (106 cm)
Breeches: L. 29⅜ in. (74.5 cm), W. waist 43⅛ in. (109.5 cm)
Inventory Electoral Tailor Shop 1660, no. 71
Staatliche Kunstsammlungen Dresden, Rüstkammer, inv. no. I 11
Lit.: Haenel 1911, p. 51; Nienhold 1961, pp. 58f., plate III; Thiel 1980, p. 223, ill. 395; Zittau 2002, p. 358, cat. no. B 79

12 Sword Belt

The sword belt is abundantly embroidered with flowers and birds, among them peacocks, parrots, and pelicans. It was part of a present sent by the Leipzig City Council to Elector Johann Georg I, which also contained a parade rapier and a dagger dated 1620, as well as a cartridge pouch with writing tools, a gun with a balsam stock, an ivory powder flask with a silver plaque depicting the electors in front of a Dresden cityscape, and a silver spanner. The sword belt and the cartridge pouch complemented a gift from the Leipzig City Council in 1618: a violet colored parade saddle with embroidered relief depictions of animals and plants in the same manner. The council procured the saddle from the silk embroiderer Hans Erich Friese, who worked extensively for the elector.
J.B.

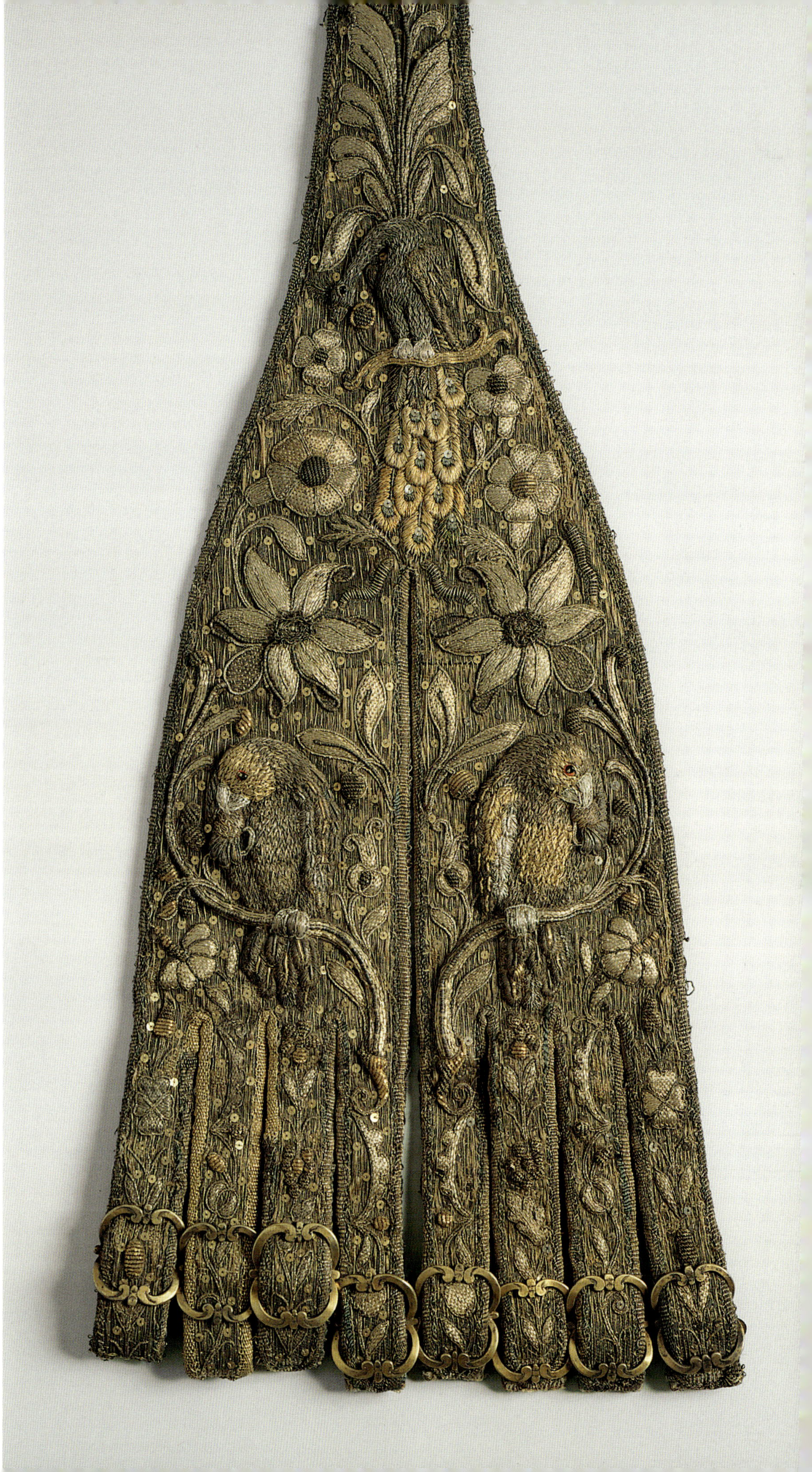

Hans Erich Friese
Dresden, 1620 (?)
Leather, silk, relief embroidery: spun gold and silver yarn, colored silk, sequins and cantils silver-gilt, black glass pearls, gold braid
Lining: violet silk velvet; mounts: silver and brass, in part engraved gilt
L. 69⅝ in. (177 cm), B. 9½ in. (24 cm),
B. belt 1⅜–2⅛ in. (4–5.5 cm)
Gift of the Leipzig City Council, presumably 1620,
Complete Armory Inventory (Gesamtinventar Rüstkammer) 1719, fol. 284f., no. 186
Staatliche Kunstsammlungen Dresden, Rüstkammer, inv. no. I 355
Lit.: Meisterwerk 1992, pp. 86f., plate 31

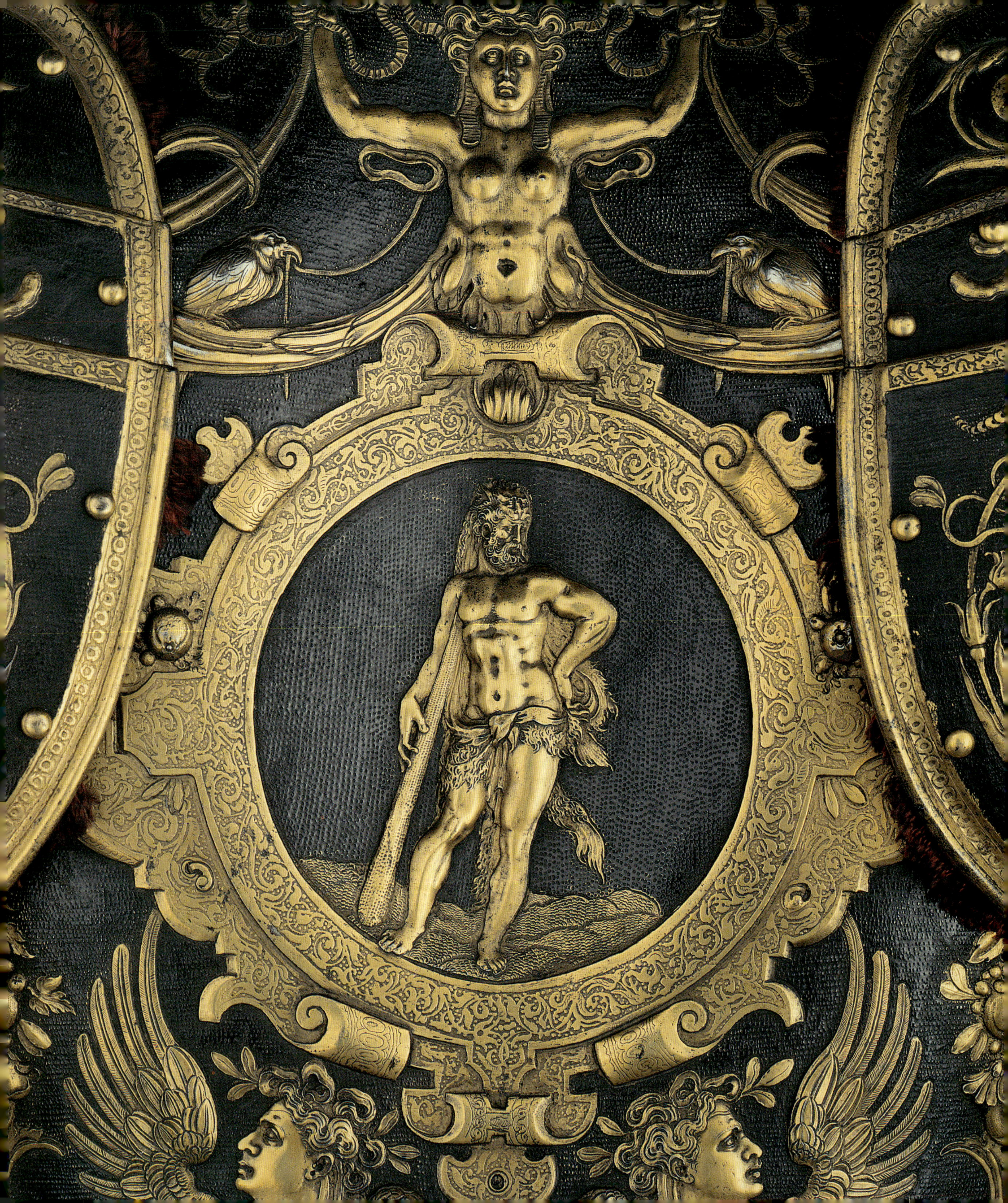

Court Festivities

Armor

Weapons

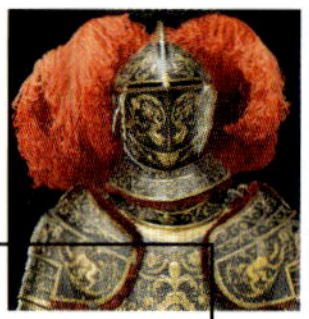

Tournament and Parade Armor

Holger Schuckelt

The striving for the knights' best protection led to the perfection of plate armor during the course of the fourteenth and fifteenth centuries. Shirts of mail were increasingly reinforced with iron plates, until more or less the entire body was totally covered with individually connected, moveable plates. At the same time, the variety of armor shapes increased as well. Local taste and fashion played as much a role as did military concerns regarding combat techniques and weaponry. Since the high-ranking aristocracy began to withdraw from the battlefield, increasingly leaving the troops' command to the lower nobility, a more distinct separation between field, tournament, and parade armor emerged.

Initially, the tournament served as practice for the handling of arms and armor in the event of war. The same equipment was at first used for both events. It was only as time went by and tournaments were no longer the exercise grounds for battles that they began to be featured as part of the courtly entertainment. Special types of armor were developed for the tournament that eventually had very little in common with field armor. The relatively short duration of a tournament enabled the use of more massive and therefore safer armor. The optimal protection of the wearer was more important than his personal comfort. Different types of tournaments left their marks on the armorers' works. Armors for jousts of war (Rennzeuge) and jousts of peace (Stechzeuge) were created, as were armors for foot tournaments and the baston course (Kolbenturnier). Elements could be exchanged among armors, and it was thus possible to adapt them to various subcategories of the joust. Thus, it was always the left side that was reinforced with different plates in the overall asymmetrical jousting gear. The armor for the Italian joust made in 1588 by the Augsburg-based Anton Peffenhauser for Elector Christian I of Saxony (cat. no. 16) is equipped with a jousting shield, a grand guard, and a pasguard. Depending on the requirements, these items could be screwed onto the armor. The complete garniture also included a saddle with steels, a half chanfron, and a vamplate for the lance.

Toward the end of the fifteenth but primarily in the sixteenth century, preciously embellished parade armor based on ancient models began to be developed. In their form, they corresponded to field and tournament armor. Initially, the center of this development was Italy, where numerous renowned masters worked in Milan. Made from iron and decorated with repoussé, preciously engraved and abundantly damascened with gold and silver, these armorers' works reached the peak of their artistic potential (see cat. no. 14). Another independent and highly sophisticated school developed in Paris (see cat. no. 15). Italian and French parade armor, as well as sets comprising a matching helmet and shield, had a great influence on other centers of production. While local craftsmen followed these models, they usually failed to achieve the same high quality.

Parade armor in the style of such masters as Negroli, Piccinino, and Libaerts (cat. no. 13) was often completely covered with decorative reliefs. Less richly decorated armor was also created that was still far superior to simple everyday armor. In this context, mention should be made of works in the Dresden Armory by the Augsburg armorer Anton Peffenhauser (cat. nos. 16, 19) and by the Dresden court armorer Christian Müller (cat. no. 21). Based on the unusual materials used, two richly decorated armors fashioned entirely in silver (cat. no. 17) and three of gilt copper, their surfaces densely etched overall with Renaissance ornament, warrant special mention. Finished in 1590 for the electoral baptism in Dresden, they represent a unique type of parade armor.

Parade armor was frequently furnished with saddles fitted with matching steel plates. The most elaborate armor garniture kept in the Dresden Armory, a suit of parade armor for man and horse embossed by Anton Peffenhauser in Augsburg for Elector Christian I of Saxony, is equipped with numerous saddles with plates of different sizes and shapes. Richly decorated, individual parade saddles were also produced; of this category, numerous examples are preserved in the Dresden Armory. They were often gifts of high-ranking personalities. The so-called Nosseni saddle (cat. no. 22), intended as a Christmas gift of Giovanni Maria Nosseni for Elector Christian I of Saxony, is one of the most impressive examples of its kind.

Most of the armor kept in the Dresden Armory was stored in rooms expressly made for this purpose, primarily the Harnischkammer and the Pallienkammer (the Armor Chamber and the Chamber for Tilting Armor); certain armor was also kept in other rooms. There never existed a strict division among the storerooms of the Armory between field, tournament, and parade armor. Hence, various tournament armors could be found in the Armor Chamber, and the Chamber for Tilting Armor contained tournament and tilting armor as well as parade armor. The matching saddles were not always stored in the same room. For most of the saddles, there was a specific Saddle Chamber (Sattelkammer), where riding equipment, stirrups, and other equestrian gear were kept. Italian helmets and shields were stored in the Turkish Chamber (Türkenkammer) for reasons that remain unclear.

Firearms

Heinz-Werner Lewerken

By the middle of the sixteenth century, the development of firearms was advanced to the point that—due to their greater efficiency—they began to replace other competing projectile weapons such as bows and crossbows. The invention of lock constructions with firing mechanisms revolutionized the development of firearms. Late-fifteenth-century matchlocks already contained essential elements of the firing mechanism that—modified and perfected—were used until the nineteenth century. Until the middle of the seventeenth century, matchlock muskets, relatively simple to operate, were customary weapons used by regular foot soldiers. The obvious disadvantages of this type of lock mechanism included the constantly burning match whose odor scared away the game, the highly inflammable powder, and the extinction of the match by wind and rain. This inevitably led to the construction of new lock types.[1]

The invention of the wheel lock in the early sixteenth century was an important advance in the development of firearms. While it counts among the most important technical innovations of that century, its function—comparable to the flintlock that was developed later—was based on the ignition of the powder by sparks. Similar in principle to the modern cigarette lighter, the spark in the wheel lock is generated by a flint (actually iron or sulphur pyrites) through the friction caused by a rotating rough-edged wheel of steel. The loaded weapon could be carried along primed and ready to fire and therefore was far superior to the match lock. By the mid-sixteenth century, the development of the wheel lock was so advanced that it could be produced by the leading gunmakers throughout Europe. Despite high production costs, the superiority of the wheel lock was attractive for both military and civil purposes. Since the acquisition of wheel-lock pistols and carbines was expensive, they were initially mostly employed as riders' weapons. It became much easier to shoot from the saddle thanks

1. Nickel 1974, pp. 242f.

Parade Armor by Eliseus Libaerts (cat. no. 13) seen in the foreground of the portrait of Elector Johann Georg I of Saxony (cat. no. 4), who is shown wearing it.

to the wheel-lock mechanism. Pistols were carried in pairs and kept in holsters to the left and the right of the saddle's front bow.

The introduction of the wheel-lock pistol as a weapon for the cavalry by the middle of the sixteenth century caused a tremendous change in military tactics and led to decisive changes within the army. German "horse pistols" are characterized by a large-bore barrel and an obtuse-angled stock with a large, spherical pommel. These pistols were suitable for firing at short distances. From a distance of fifteen to eighteen meters (forty-five to sixty feet), the projectile could pierce a light breastplate.[2]

While in the Renaissance the traditional hunters continued to use the crossbow—because of its almost inaudible shot—as well as a prodd, or pellet crossbow (Kugelschnepper), to shoot bullets for hunting birds and small game, with the introduction of the wheel lock the firearm became increasingly popular and was ultimately accepted as the weapon of choice for the hunt. For a long time, the wheel lock was also the preferred lock mechanism used in precision target shooting by the nobility and city dwellers. The courts' and the wealthy citizens' high demand for artistically embellished and technically sophisticated weapons advanced the gunmaking trade, resulting in a significant burst of growth.

The hunt formed an integral part of the important sixteenth- and seventeenth-century court festivities with their precious costumes, coaches, noble horses, dogs, and hunting equipment of all types. The elaborate hunts—often stretched out over days or even weeks—required weapons and hunting tools not only for the host's personal needs but also for his numerous guests. Therefore, most courts employed gunmakers, stockmakers, gold- and silversmiths, iron cutters, and etchers, whose responsibilities entailed the production of new weapons and the maintenance of the existing ones. Large numbers of exquisite wheel-lock rifles and pistols fabricated by gunmakers working at Dresden's court in the sixteenth and early seventeenth centuries have survived. The creators include Lorenz Dreßler, Balthasar and Steffan Schickradt, Christian Drechsler, Zacharias Herold, Georg Geßler, Hans Stockmann, Simon Helbig, and Balthasar Herold.[3]

The gunmakers were always striving to devise technical improvements and thus to perfect the firearms. This is why many princely collections of firearms contain not only abundantly decorated and artistically compelling weapons but also innumerable ones that are technically brilliant and interesting for their construction. Apart from the aforementioned wheel lock—whose complicated lock mechanism often led to sophisticated modifications and refinements—multibarreled weapons, breech loaders, and revolver systems began to be produced to increase firing speed. All these special constructions are expressions of continued searching and experimentation.

Another possibility to increase a weapon's efficiency was the creation of combination weapons whose manufacture required inventiveness, innovative construction, and the highest technical and mechanical aptitude, as well as artistic skills. Combination weapons customarily unite two or three different weapon types into one. These also include walking staffs with blades hidden inside, as well as combinations of a weapon and a utilitarian object. Barely a single weapon type was excluded. Thus, swords, rapiers, hunting knives, daggers, halberds, boar spears, battle-axes, maces, crossbows, and shields were combined with firearms. Richly adorned by artisans, the technically challenging combination weapons were often princely commissions that ordinarily came to Kunstkammers or armories as sought-after collector's items, diplomatic gifts, or presents from family members.[4] The works preserved in the Dresden Armory testify to the Saxon electors' lively interest in such distinctive constructions.

2. Müller 1979, p 74. The Dresden Armory preserves more than 300 heavy horse pistols (also marked as the Puffer type, i.e., with large, spherical pommels by the Saxon electors' civil guards).
3. Haenel 1923, p. VI, and Schaal 1979. In addition, the Armory owns numerous works by renowned European continental riflemakers, as well as Ottoman hand firearms.
4. See Lewerken 1989.

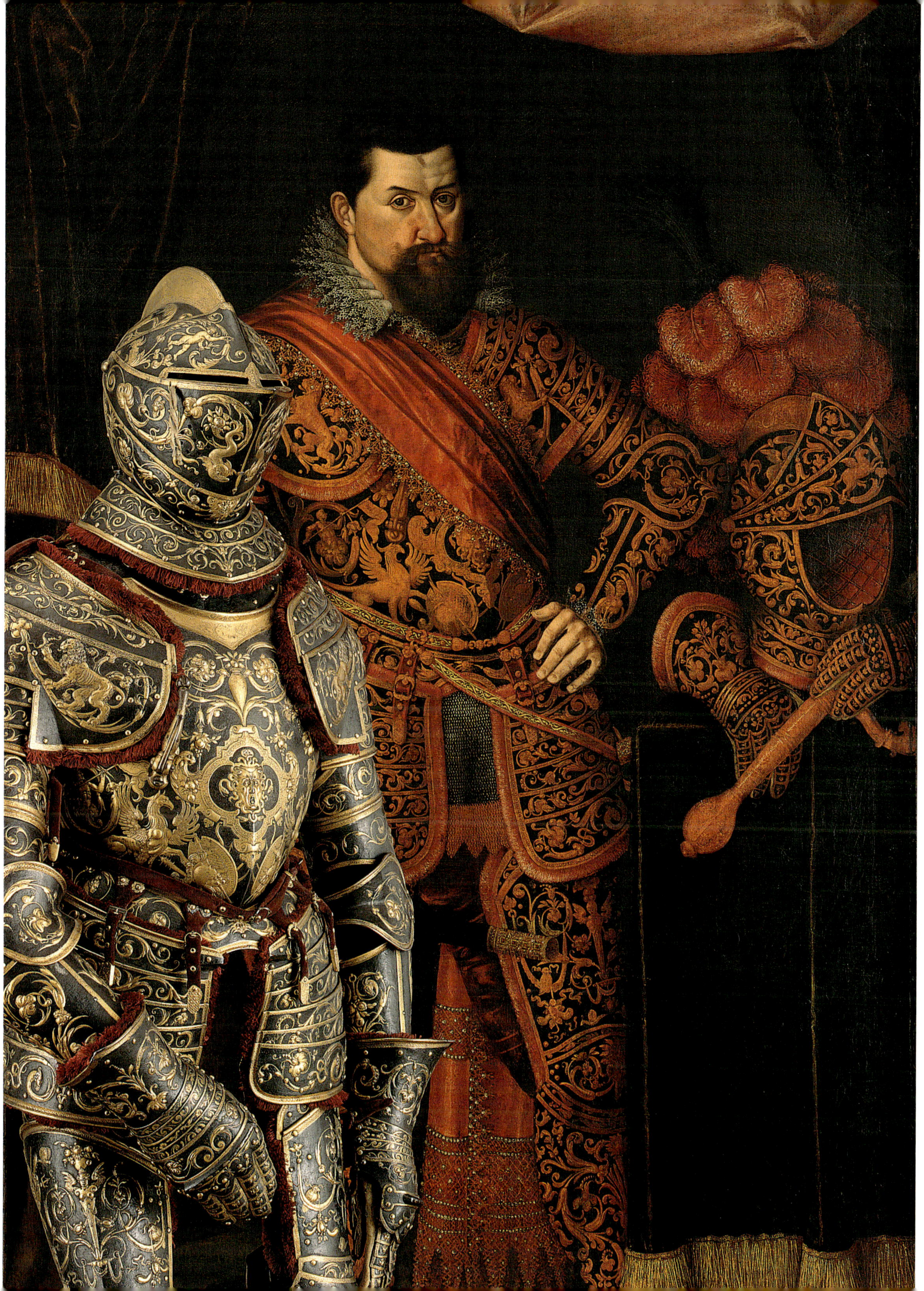

13 Parade Armor

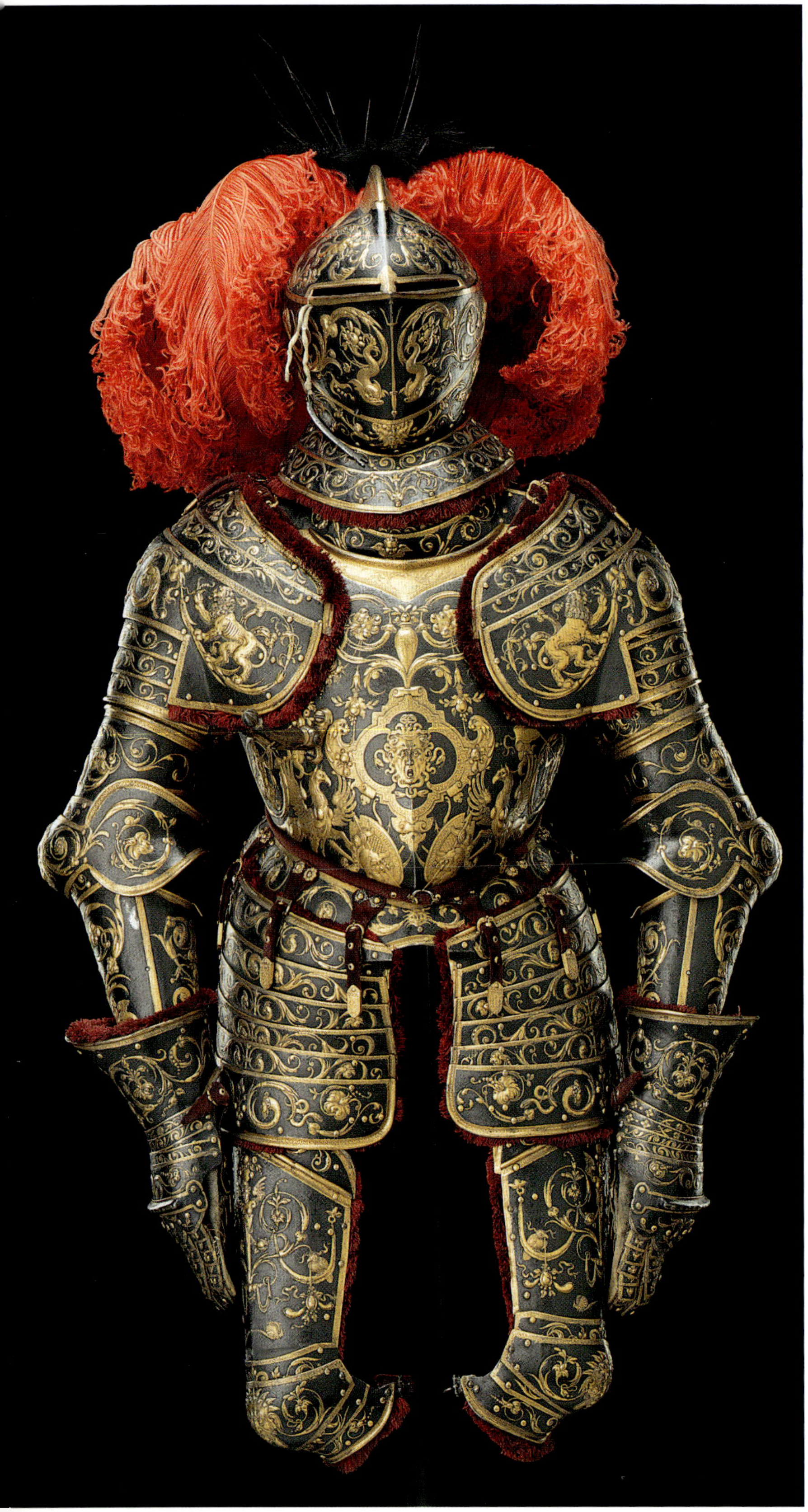

Eliseus Libaerts
Antwerp, circa 1563–64
Iron embossed, blackened, partly etched, and gilt
Weight 55¼ lbs (25.5 kg)
Made for King Erik XIV of Sweden when he intended to ask for the hand of Queen Elizabeth I of England
Armory inventory of Duke Johann Georg I of 1608, p. 169
Staatliche Kunstsammlungen Dresden, Rüstkammer, inv. no. M 106
Lit.: Ehrenthal 1899, p. 58, E 12; Haenel 1923, p. 34, plate 17; Schöbel 1973, p. 29, no. 11

Shortly after his coronation as king of Sweden in 1560, Erik XIV asked for the hand of the English queen Elizabeth I. As evidence of his serious intentions as a suitor, he commissioned a number of parade armors from the Antwerp goldsmith Libaerts, which were probably forged in Sweden before being sent to Antwerp for decoration. Libaerts himself intended to bring two of them personally to Stockholm by ship. However, they were seized by Danish troops and taken to Copenhagen. It was not until 1604 and 1606 that Elector Christian II of Saxony purchased both armors for a total price of 9,525 guilders. He kept the more elaborate armor for man and horse, the so-called Hercules armor, for himself and gave the black and gold one to his younger brother Johann Georg I. The latter armor, exhibited here, is constructed as a conventional field armor and consists of close-helmet, gorget, breastplate with lance-rest and tassets (upper thigh defenses), backplate, complete arm defenses and fingered gauntlets, cuisses with poleyns (thigh and knee defenses), and saddle with matching steels. The armor is adorned with lions, griffins, dolphins, and other motifs. The two main decorative features are a Gorgon's head on the breastplate and Hercules leaning on his staff, represented on the backplate. Libaerts's model for the latter image was the so-called Hercules Farnese (today preserved in Naples), a Roman copy after a Greek original by the sculptor Lysippus, unearthed in 1546 in Rome's Baths of Caracalla.
H.S.

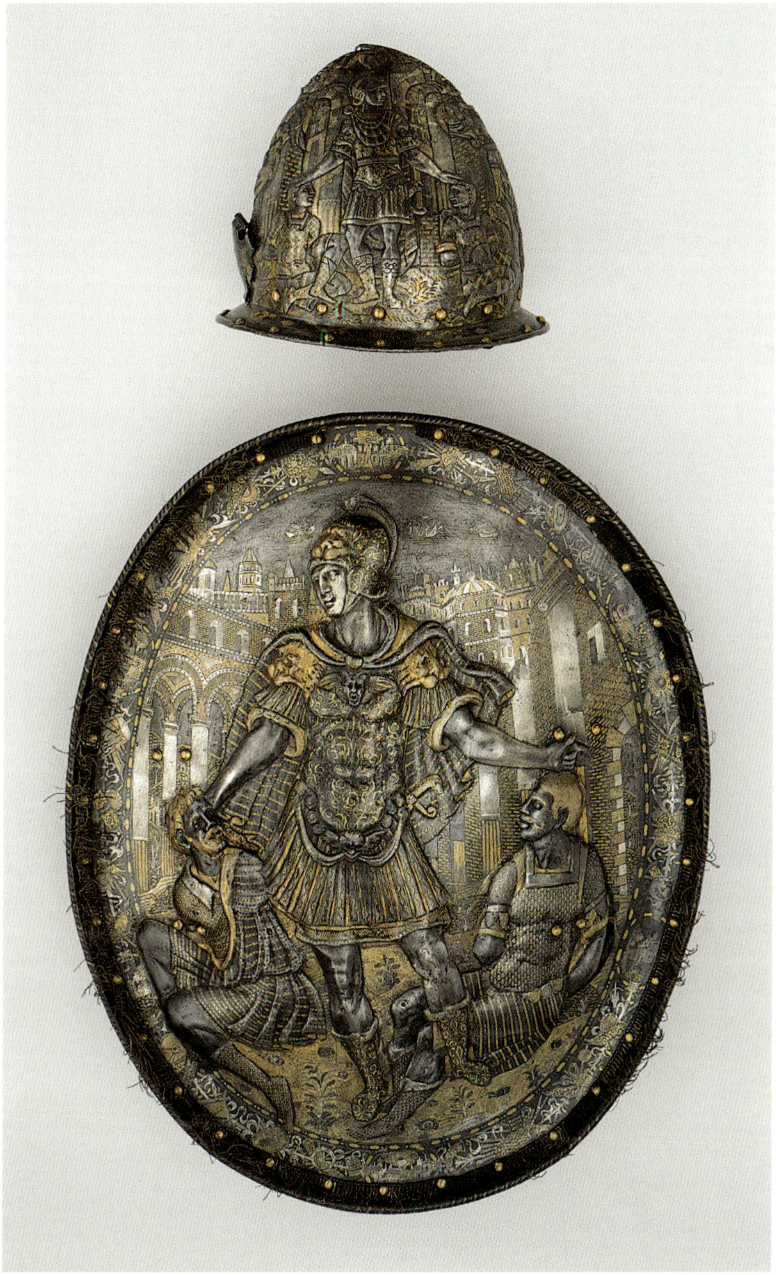

14 Pointed Morion and Shield

Milan was one of the most important European centers for the production of armor. Although simple, unadorned pieces were a more important economic factor, the city attained fame through its abundantly decorated parade armor for European rulers. Names such as Negroli, Pompeo della Cesa, and Lucio Piccinino are inseparably tied to Milan's celebrity. The pointed morion and shield originate from a long tradition of high-quality work by Milanese armorers, whose demise could be clearly sensed in the second half of the sixteenth century. Essentially, the two pieces share the same decoration, deviating only in details or in the quality of execution. In the center stands a warrior holding his defeated opponents by their hair. The warrior sports a Roman muscled cuirass. The shoulders and the front of the burgonet are decorated with lions' heads, typical of a style that can frequently be encountered in different sixteenth-century Milanese workshops. On the breastplate the winged Gorgon's head may be seen. In the background an ancient city is depicted with high arcades, towers, and partly domed roofs. In 1588, the garniture was brought to Dresden from Italy by Carel Dettau.
H.S.

Milan, circa 1570
Iron embossed, blued,
silver and gold damascened,
shield surrounded with fringed braid
made of silver and gilt wire around silk
core; shield's lining black silk velvet
with applied cord embroidery
of silver and gilt wire around silk core,
upholstery (made of hair?), arm loops
leather, with black silk velvet
and covered with cord embroidery,
buckles and mounts iron gilt
Helmet: H. 8⅞ in. (22.5 cm),
weight 3½ lbs (1.5 kg)
Shield: H. 24⅛ in. (61.3 cm),
weight 9¼ lbs (4.22 kg)
Brought to Dresden from Italy in 1588
by Carel Dettau; inventory of the Turkish
Chamber of 1674, p. 6, no. 9
Staatliche Kunstsammlungen Dresden,
Rüstkammer, inv. no. N 140 (cabasset)
and N 139 (shield)
Lit.: Ehrenthal 1899, p. 86, E 360 a, b;
Schöbel 1972, p. 50, nos. 10, 11;
Geneva 2003, p. 466, cat. no. 63

15 Breastplate from a Parade Armor

As an exchange piece, this breastplate belongs to a complete parade armor presented to Elector Christian I of Saxony in 1588 as a gift from Duke Carl Emanuel I of Savoy (ill. p. 76). In the previous year, he had presented a number of weapons to the Saxon elector through Heinrich von Hagen.

The breastplate has an elongated peascod belly, hooks at the sides, and, instead of tassets, "lobes" that protrude almost at a right angle. It is embossed, chased, and gilt with a matte ground. The decoration covers the entire surface, and it consists of tendrils, flowers, vases, animals, putti, and muses. Only the raised, figural parts are of bright iron and worked in repoussé. The muses, surrounded by wreaths made of intertwined knots–symbol of the Savoy Order of the Annunciation–are seated on or among the tendrils with their attributes. The order was originally founded as the Order of the Collar in 1355 (or 1362) by Count Amadeus VI of Savoy on the occasion of the oath he uttered during a crusade. In 1518, Charles III of Savoy renewed it as a clerical knightly order and dedicated it to the Holy Virgin.
H.S.

French, before 1588
Iron embossed, chased, gilt
Weight 3 lbs 8 oz (1,720 g)
Gift of Grand Duke Carl Emanuel I of Savoy to Elector Christian I of Saxony in 1588; Kunstkammer inventory of 1595, fol. 530
Staatliche Kunstsammlungen Dresden, Rüstkammer, inv. no. M 62
Lit.: Ehrenthal 1899, p. 45, D 1; Haenel 1923, p. 22, plate 11; Theumert 1963, p. 59, no. 16, ill. 18; Schöbel 1973, p. 31, ill. 17

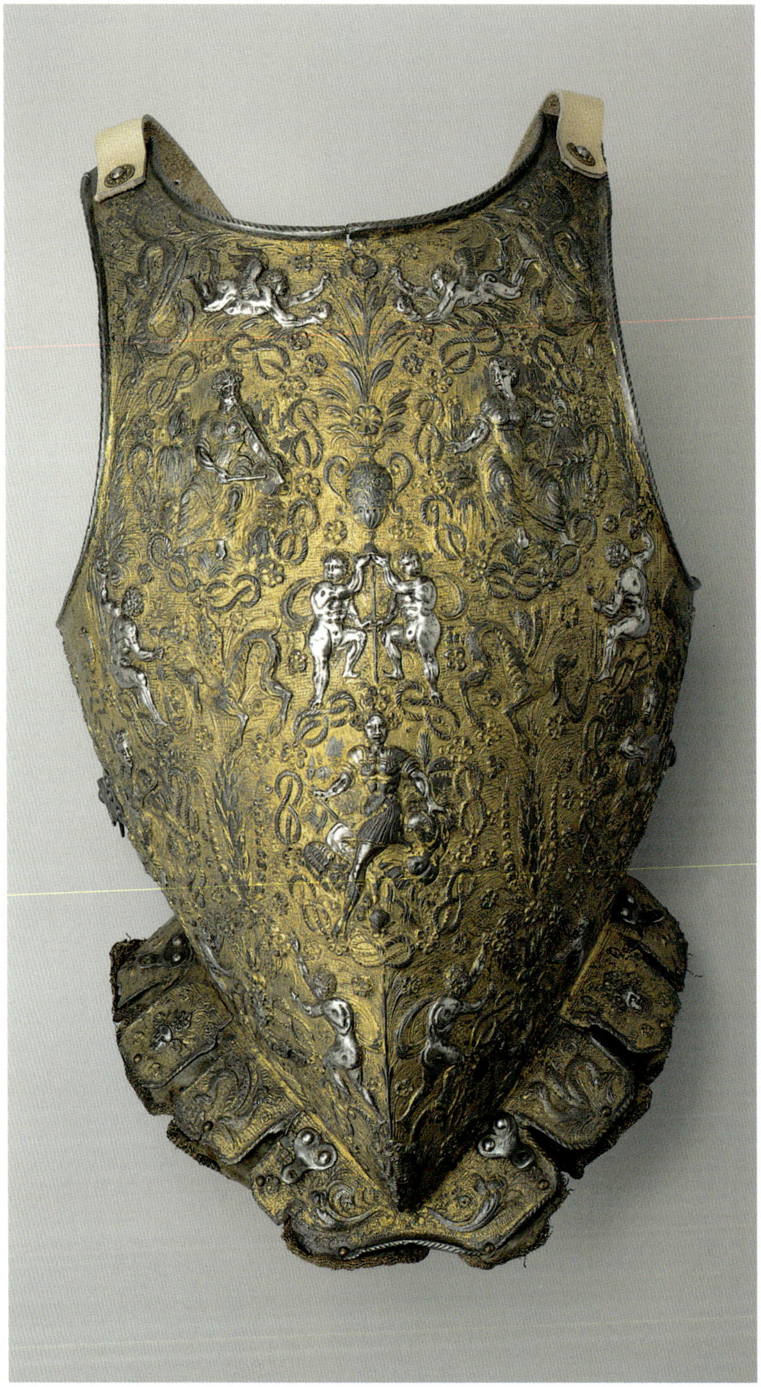

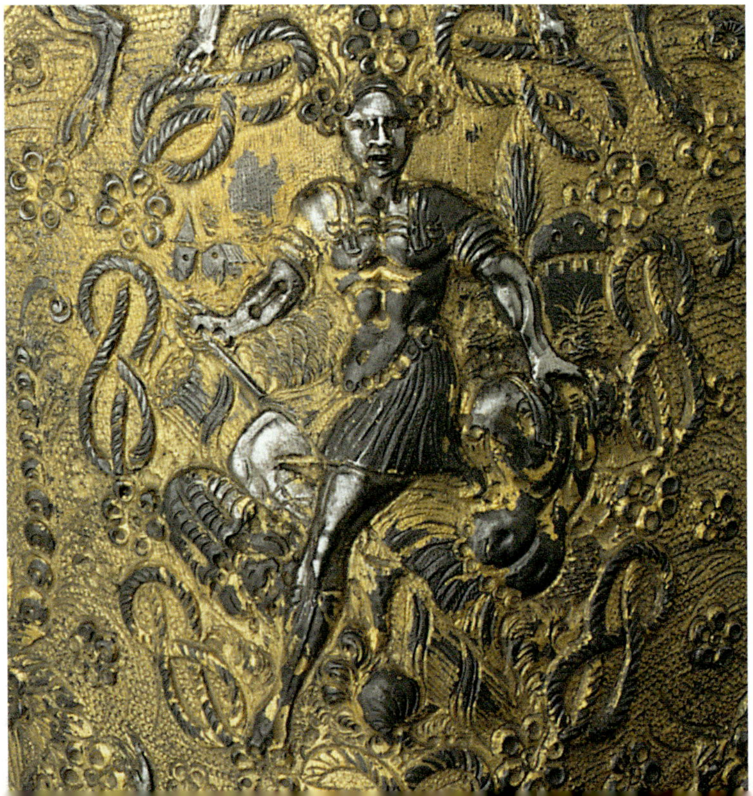

16 Armor for the Italian Joust of Elector Christian I

Anton Peffenhauser is one of the most celebrated European armorers. Among his patrons were Emperors Maximilian II and Rudolf II, King Don Sebastian of Portugal, and the Spanish high aristocracy. While relations with the Saxon court are documented as early as 1576, the armorer's extensive work for the Saxon electors did not begin until 1582 and lasted until the end of his life (1603). The Dresden inventories list a total of thirty-six armors by the Augsburg master, of which fourteen more or less elaborate garnitures have survived to this day. Thus the Dresden Armory owns the world's largest collection of works by Anton Peffenhauser.

Made for Elector Christian I, the armor consists of a helmet with deep bevor, the two bolting rigidly to the breast and backplate. The right edge of the bevor at face level has a hinged and pierced door for ventilation, and lower down it has a raised flange, or "haute piece," as a defense for the right shoulder. The breastplate with its deep "peascod" profile is fitted with a lance-rest and tassets of three lames each, complete arms and fingered gauntlets, and complete leg defenses. The left side of the armor is reinforced with a large shield, or "targe," bolted to the buffe and a large pasguard reinforcing the elbow. There is also a half chanfron. The etched and gilt ornament, highlighted with black lines, is arranged in vertical bands emanating foliate tendrils and is typical of "Peffenhauser decoration." There are depictions of a maiden with the victor's wreath surrounded by foliated tendrils on the targe and on the chanfron. The armor, one of the most elegant of its kind, was used in the Italian joust. This was a type of courtly tournament in which the two combatants, who were separated by a wooden barrier, broke lances on the racetrack. This made the Italian joust far less dangerous than the older German jousts, run without a separating barrier.
H.S.

Anton Peffenhauser
Augsburg, 1588
Iron worked in repoussé and polished,
partly etched and gilt
Weight 83¾ lbs (38 kg)
Multiple marks with the Augsburg hallmark (pinecone)
Made 1588 together with two other armors
for Elector Christian I of Saxony;
Inventory of the Armory of 1606, p. 190
Staatliche Kunstsammlungen Dresden, Rüstkammer,
inv. no. M 27
Lit.: Ehrenthal 1899, p. 40, C 15 a; Schöbel 1973, p. 34, no. 36, ill. p. 71; Wozel 1979, p. 85, no. 32; Meisterwerke 1992, p. 82, plate 27; Schuckelt 2002

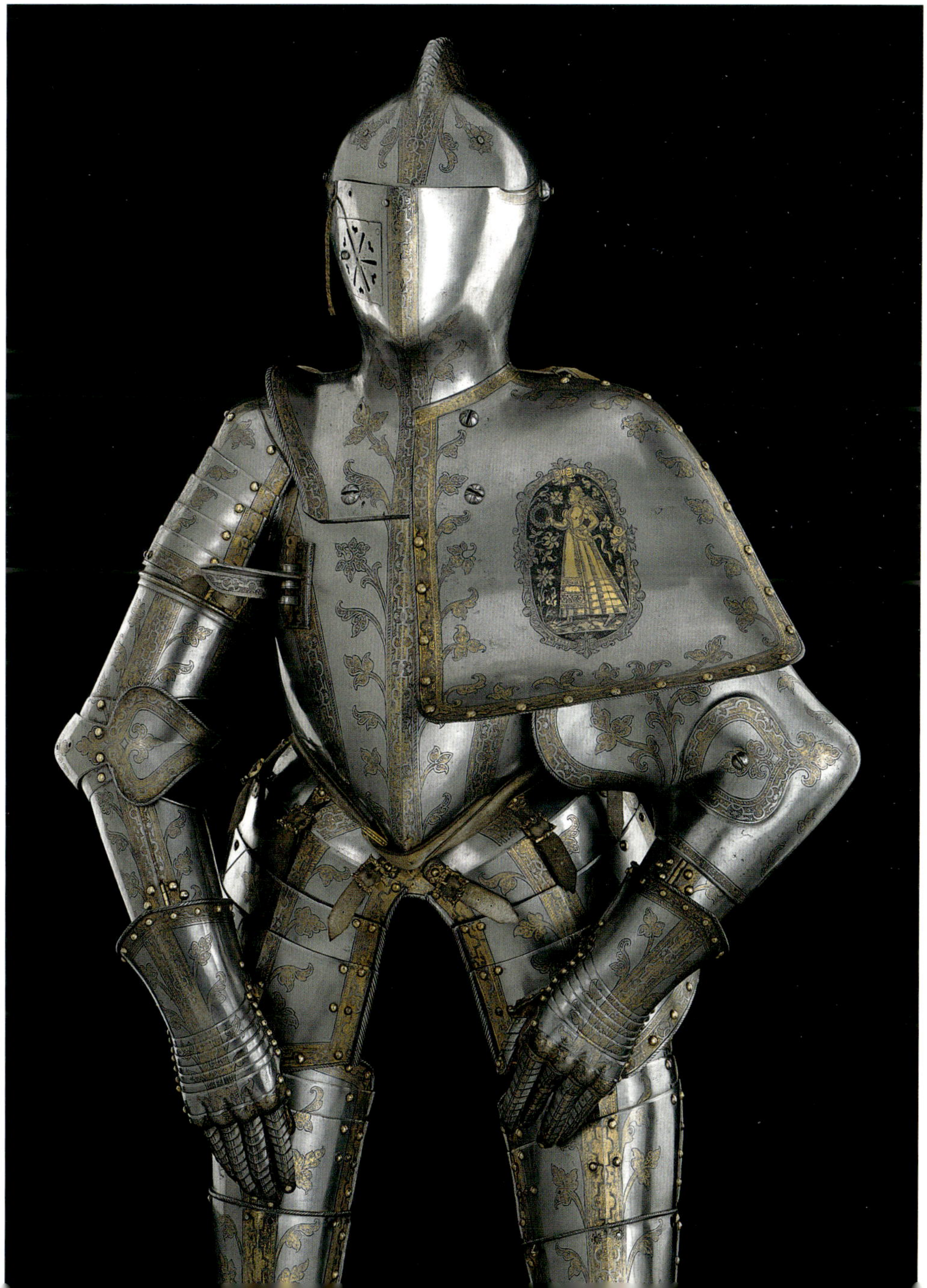

17 Parade Armor and Chanfron of Elector Christian I

This armor is one of a group of two silver and three copper gilt parade armors that were made in 1590 for Elector Christian I of Saxony and his special guests of honor. The occasion was the festivities planned to accompany the imminent electoral baptism. On January 7, 1591, Dorothea was born. Later abbess of Quedlinburg, she was to be the last child of Christian and his wife, daughter of Elector Johann Georg of Brandenburg. Part of the baptism festivities were a running at the ring and a boar hunt on January 29, 1591. Both silver armors, intended for the elector himself and for Duke Christian of Anhalt-Bernburg, count among the extraordinary monumental works in silver of the time. The main decoration of the armor consists of numerous oval medallions with depictions of war scenes (partly in classical, partly in contemporary costume) and trophies of arms. The space between the medallions is filled with tendrils, flowers in the style of the Near East, and war trophies.

The armor consists of a close-helmet that turns on the gorget and has a plume-holder in the shape of a lion's head, a gorget of four lames, a breastplate of deep "peascod" form without a lance-rest, a backplate, complete arm defenses including asymmetrical pauldrons, and fingered gauntlets. The matching half chanfron, like the helmet comb, bears the electoral Saxon coat of arms.
H.S.

Dresden, 1590
Silver, richly etched
Armor 27½ lbs (12.5 kg); Chanfron 2 lbs (0.86 kg)
On the comb of the helmet and on the chanfron the electoral Saxon coat of arms
Made for Elector Christian I of Saxony for the occasion of the 1591 electoral baptism in Dresden
Inventory of the Armory of 1606, p. 459
Staatliche Kunstsammlungen Dresden, Rüstkammer, inv. no. M 63
Lit.: Ehrenthal 1899, p. 46, D 2; Haenel 1923, p. 28, plate 14; Schöbel 1973, p. 29, no. 9, ill. p. 44; Washington 1978, no. 142; Wozel 1979, p. 87, nos. 47 and 48; Meisterwerke 1992, p. 57, plate 17

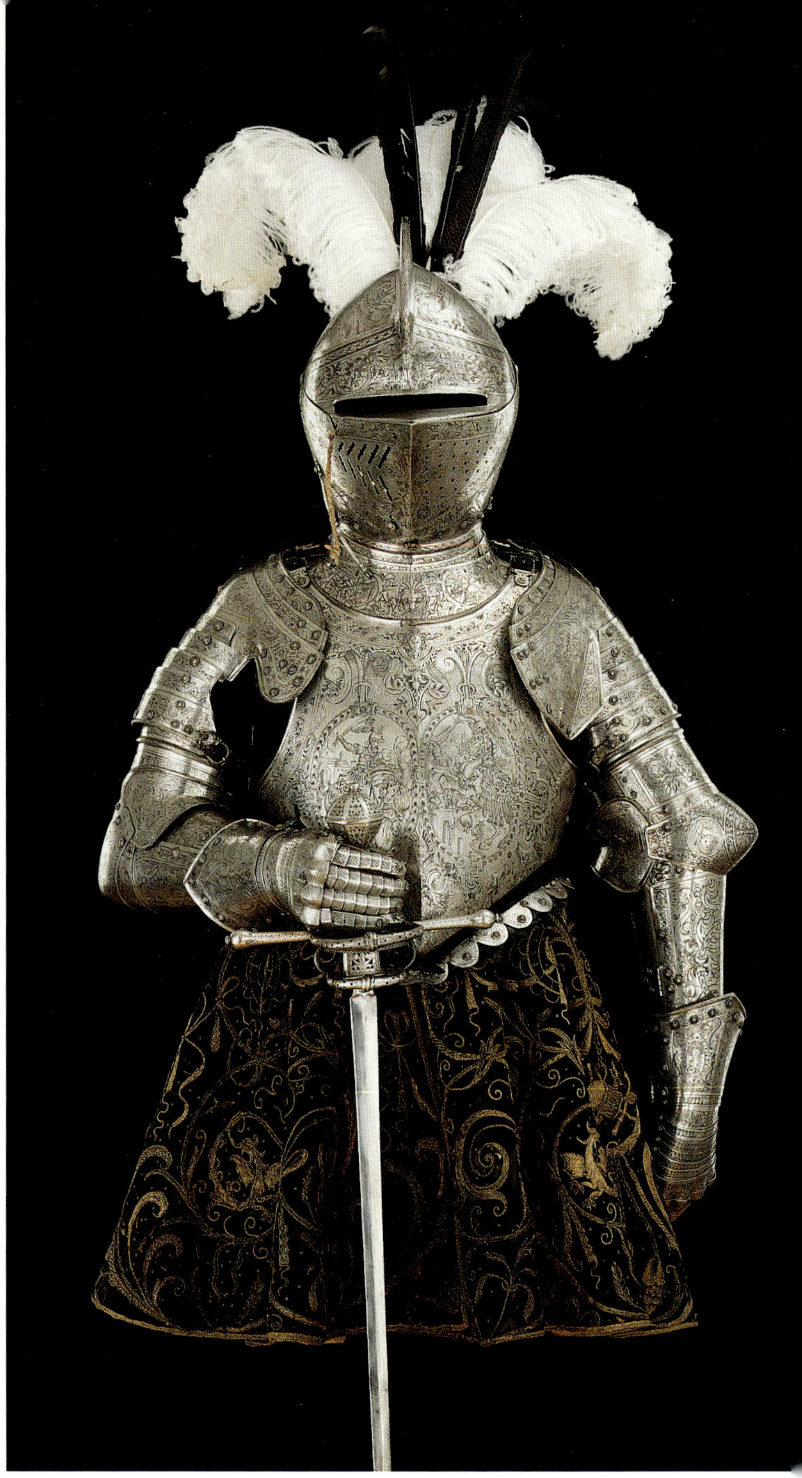

18 Rapier

Rapiers of this type, accompanied by a matching dagger, served members of the electoral Saxon court who accompanied the elector when he entered his residence, traveled, or participated in processions for tournaments. The rank of the court member was reflected in how the weapon was equipped, the degree of silver embellishments, or other distinguishing features. This led to a number of different variations on the same basic design of these courtly weapons. Rapiers and daggers whose hilts were completely covered with silver were reserved for the princes, nobility, and knights. The goldsmith's work in the majority of these weapons may be attributed to Wendel unter der Linden; some of the garnitures reveal on the mouth piece of the scabbard the master's mark and the Dresden view mark and repeat the main motif of the ornamental double lily.
J.B.

Dresden, end of the 16th to beginning of the 17th century
Diamond-section blade, flattened, hollow cut, hit mark; hilt iron, completely covered with silver; silver mounts partly pierced, etched, blackened in the ground; grip wrapped with silver wire
Total length 45¼ in. (115 cm), blade length 39⅜ in. (100 cm), weight 4 lbs (1,860 g)
Staatliche Kunstsammlungen Dresden, Rüstkammer, inv. no. VI 344
Lit.: Haenel 1923, p. 116, plate 58; Holzhausen/Kesting 1966, p. LI, cat. no. 20; Bäumel 1995c, pp. 62f.

19 Boy's Armor for a Duke of Saxony

The Dresden Armory owns numerous boys' armors that were produced for the dukes of Saxony. The use of weapons and armor formed part of their required education and princely display. Based on the requirements, a number of the armors are lavishly decorated. Especially appealing is the boy's armor made by Anton Peffenhauser for Duke Johann Georg I of Saxony or his elder brother Christian II. On its blued ground, it bears abundant etched and gilt decoration in the form of scrolls and flowers. The armor consists of close-helmet with a high comb, gorget consisting of four overlapping lames, breastplate of deep "peascod" shape, tassets of four overlapping lames, complete arm defenses, and fingered gauntlets; the leg defenses consist of cuisses with poleyns, greaves, and sabatons. The Augsburg view mark may be found on breast and back, as well as on the gorget, both tassets, both gauntlets, and the pauldrons.

According to the inventory, the armor was made for Duke Johann Georg I. This was possibly erroneously entered into the inventory by the writer, as the person meant was presumably Christian II, who succeeded his father in 1591 as an eight-year-old boy. Both in its overall build and in some of its etched decorative details, this armor is similar to a foot tournament armor ordered in 1591 by Elector Christian I of Saxony. The two could thus be contemporaneous. Also, the armor's size would correspond to the boy's size at this date.
H.S.

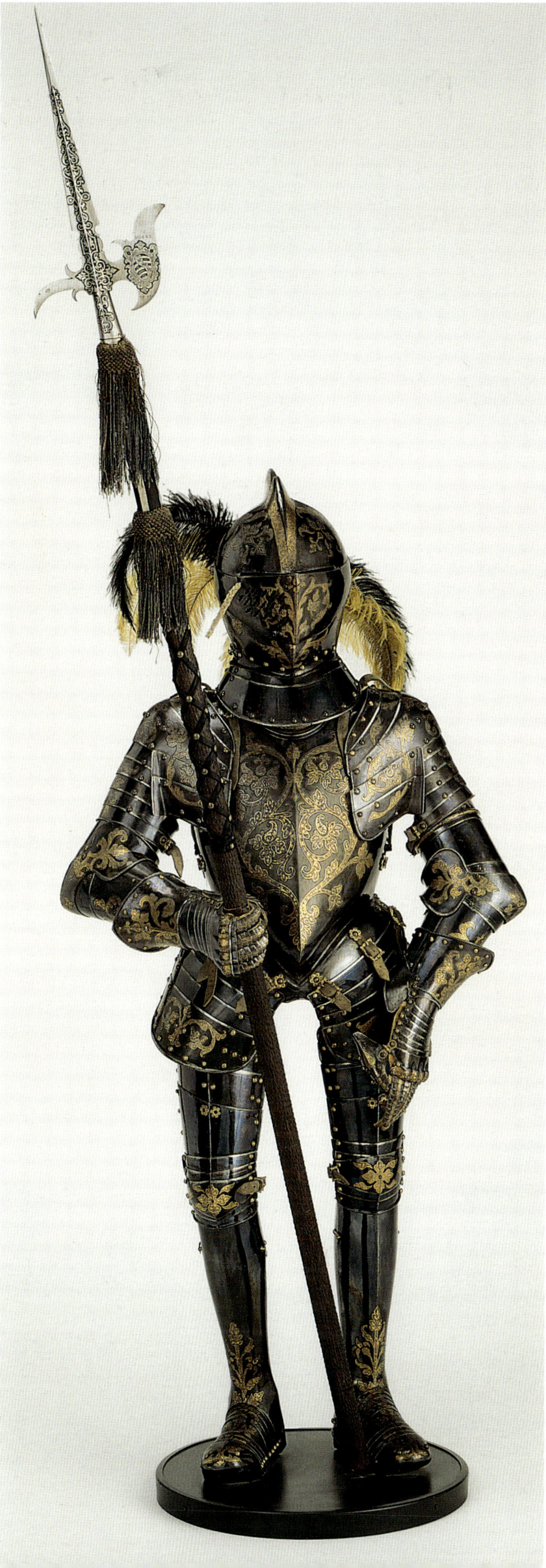

Anton Peffenhauser
Augsburg, circa 1592
Iron, blued, partly etched and gilt
Weight 27½ lbs (12.5 kg)
Multiple strikes of the Augsburg view mark (pinecone)
Derived from a group of armors for foot combat owned by Elector Christian I of Saxony and made for one of his sons, Christian II or Johann Georg I
Inventory of the Armory of 1606, p. 235
Staatliche Kunstsammlungen Dresden, Rüstkammer, inv. no. M 85
Lit.: Washington 1978, no. 140; Meisterwerke 1992, p. 63, plate 21; Schuckelt 2002

20 Halberd

This halberd was made for the seven-year-old electoral prince Johann Georg I as part of the equipment for his new armor. The figure of the allegorical woman with a child likely refers to the early loss of the prince's father. His brothers, Christian II and August, received similar halberds.
J.B.

German
Blade dated: 1592
Blade iron, etched, blackened on the ground; shaft wood, leather wrap (renewed); fringes of blue silk and gilt silver wire around silk core
Total length 73¼ in. (186 cm), blade length with Dille 15¾ in. (40 cm)
On the blade the ducal Saxon coat of arms and the initials "HIGZS" [Herzog Johann Georg zu Sachsen]
Inventory of the Armor Chamber of 1688, fol. 40 , no. 124
Staatliche Kunstsammlungen Dresden, Rüstkammer, inv. no. S 60
Lit.: Meisterwerke 1992, p. 63, plate 21

21 Armor for Foot Combat

This armor belongs to a group of foot tournament armors made in 1612 as Electress Magdalena Sibylla's Christmas gift to her husband, Elector Johann Georg I of Saxony. Six of them—of which one is now in the Philadelphia Museum of Art—are only etched, whereas one is also gilt. In their outer appearance, they are almost identical and differ from one another only in the details of their etched decoration (vertical bands with foliate scrolls, trophies, and battle scenes of cavalry and pikemen). Characteristic of these armors are the helmets with openings for eyes, nose, and mouth, of so-called Savoyard type. The rest of the armor consists of gorget, breastplate of short "peascod" form, backplate with a four-lame culet (rump defense), deep symmetrical pauldrons and complete arm defenses, fingered gauntlets, and long two-part cuisses ending at the knees that comprise twenty overlapping lames.

On May 31, 1613, Johann Georg II was born, the eldest son of Johann Georg I and future elector of Saxony. The festivities in honor of his baptism also entailed a running at the ring with a procession of the planets (June 28; see ill. pp. 50, 52), a boar hunt on Dresden's Altmarkt (July 1), an animal combat in the Löwenhaus (July 3), and a foot tournament (July 4), during which Elector Johann Georg I of Saxony wore the gilt armor from this set.
H.S.

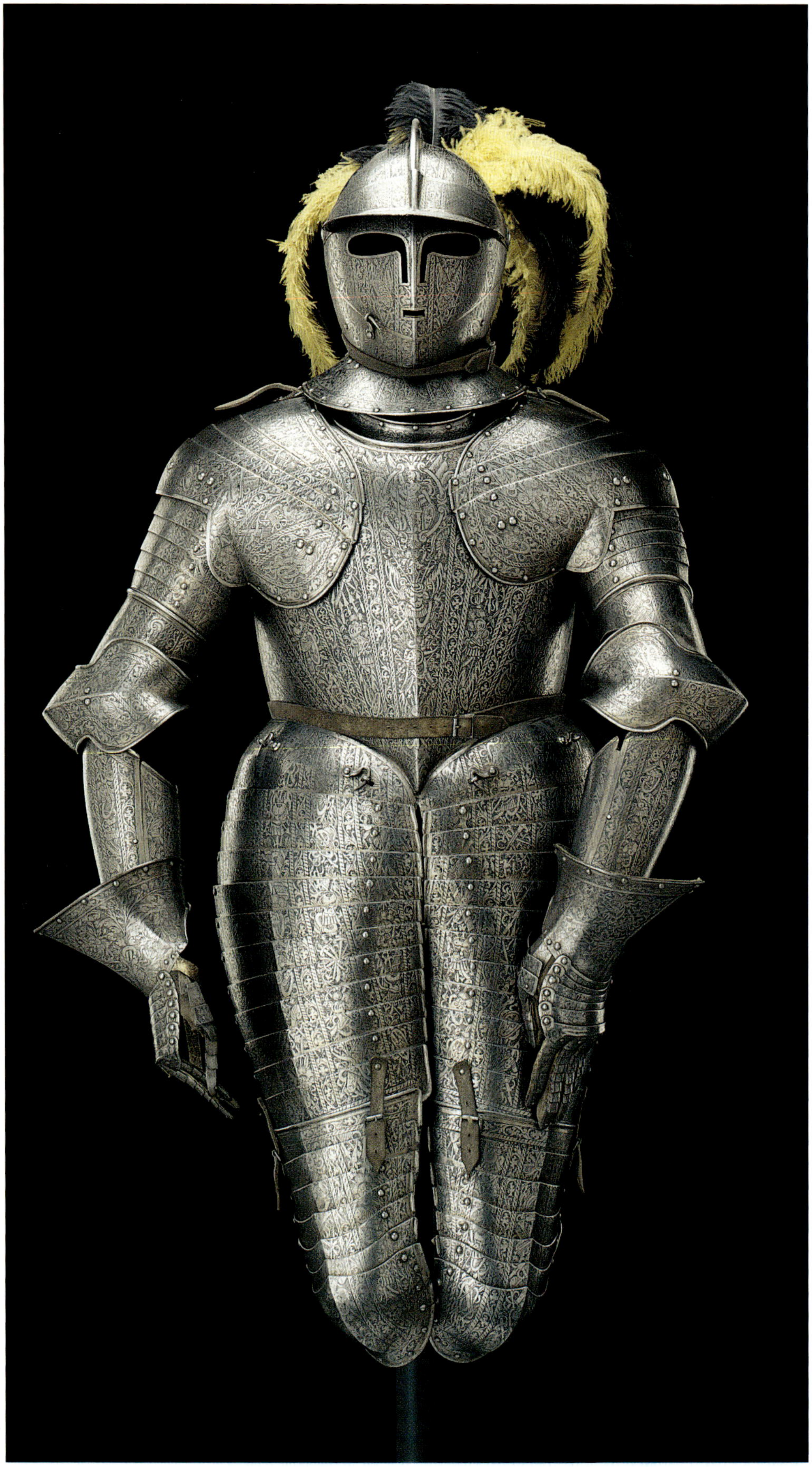

Christian Müller
Dresden, 1612
Iron, etched
Weight 61½ lbs (28 kg)
1612 Christmas gift of Electress Magdalena Sibylla to Elector Johann Georg I of Saxony
Inventory of the Armory of 1606, p. 181
Staatliche Kunstsammlungen Dresden, Rüstkammer, inv. no. M 66
Lit.: Ehrenthal 1899, p. 46, D 4–10; see also Wozel 1979, p. 88, no. 52; Geneva 2002, p. 85

22 Saddle with Steels

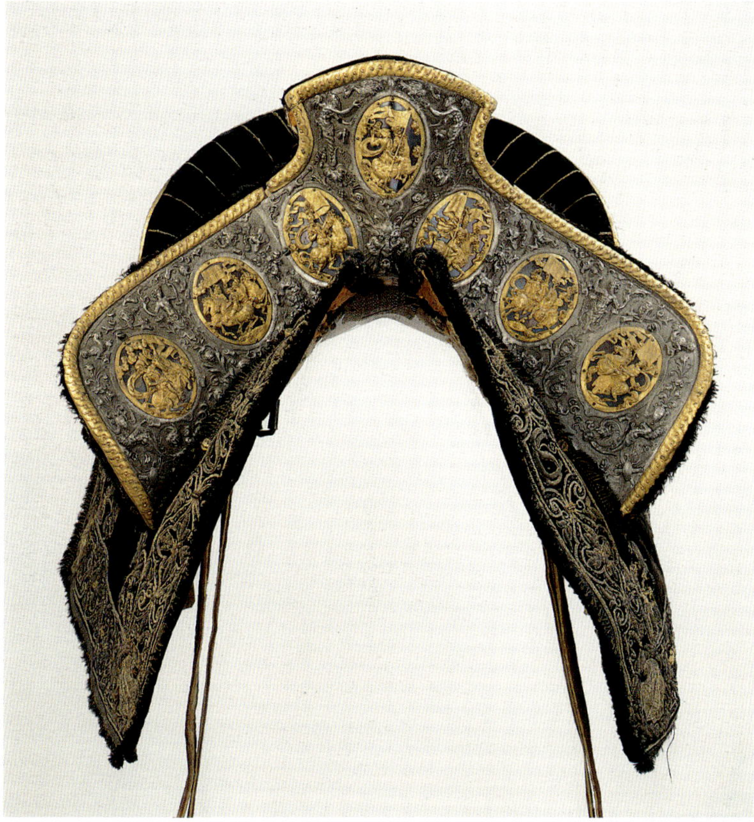

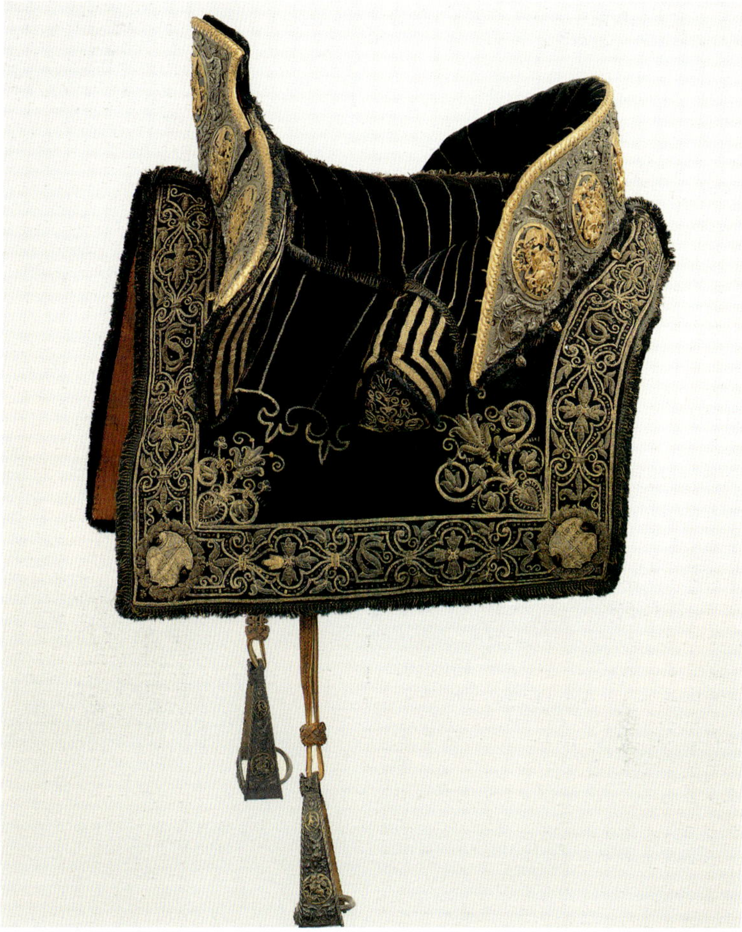

Mounts South German (Augsburg?), 1587; saddle and embroidery presumably Saxon
Saddle covered with velvet, relief and cord embroidery of silver and gilt silver wire; fringes of black silk and gold; mounts iron embossed, chiseled, punched, and chased; medallions blued, brass gilt and pierced
L. circa 26 in. (66 cm), W. circa 24 in. (61 cm), H. circa 25¼ in. (64 cm)
1587 Christmas gift of Giovanni Maria Nosseni to Elector Christian I of Saxony
Inventory of the Armory of 1606, p. 1048, no. 39
Staatliche Kunstsammlungen Dresden, Rüstkammer, inv. no. L 372
Lit.: Ehrenthal 1899, p. 196, Schrank V; Münzberg 1999

This saddle was a 1587 Christmas gift from Giovanni Maria Nosseni, an Italian sculptor and master builder at Dresden's court, to his lord Elector Christian I of Saxony. The gray iron saddle plates, presumably fabricated in Augsburg, are embellished with vases of flowers, fruit, grotesques, trophies, and diverse animals, among them snails and insects, griffins and dolphins. There is an obvious stylistic similarity to the so-called Hercules armor by Eliseus Libaerts (see cat. no. 13). Copperplate engravings with generally similar ornament may have served as sources for the designs, among them those by the French painter and copperplate engraver Marc Duval, the Augsburg master Hans Friedrich Schrorer, and Johann Sibmacher, active in Nuremberg. The plates on the front and back of the saddle each contain seven blued oval medallions with riveted, gilt brass plates, whose pierced decoration shows various riders. The riders, some shown individually, some in groups, carry banners with different symbols (crosses, sun, harp, lily, crown, lion, etc.) On one of the rider's flags the SPQR may be seen, an abbreviation of the Latin term *Senatus Populusque Romanus* ("the Roman senate and the Roman people") that was frequently encountered in antiquity on banners, coins, and buildings. The stirrups belonging to the saddle reveal a design comparable to that of the saddle plates and are partly gilt.

Saddle steels and stirrups were customarily commissioned from an armorer, whose name is unknown in this case. It is likely that the saddle itself was later fabricated and decorated in Saxony. It is entirely covered with black silk velvet and richly embroidered with gold and silver. The saddle plates' lower corners and the inside of the saddle's pommel contain the electoral Saxon coat of arms. The trimmings surrounding the outer side of the saddle plates contain stylized flower tendrils and numerous pointed medallions with the intertwined letters "CS" (Christian of Saxony).
H.S.

23 Snaffle Bit

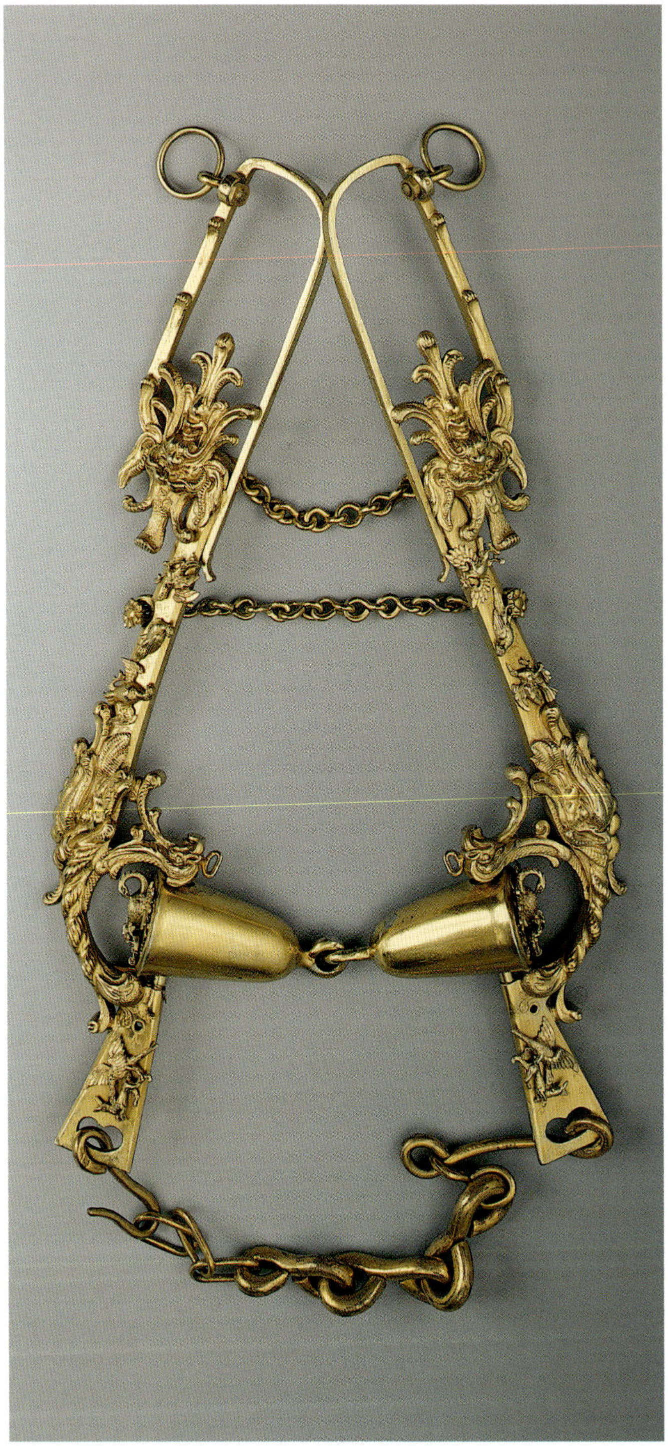

Daniel Kellerthaler
Dresden, circa 1615–19
Gilt iron, silver, cast, chased, and gilt
L. of the lever pole 15½ in. (39.5 cm), weight 4 lbs 3 oz (1,960 g)
Gift of the Leipzig City Council to Elector Johann Georg I of Saxony
Inventory Gute Sattelkammer of 1674, fol. 42, no. 147
Staatliche Kunstsammlungen Dresden, Rüstkammer, inv. no. L 241
Lit.: Holzhausen/Kesting 1966, p. LVI, plate 54

24 Stirrups

The snaffle bit and the pair of stirrups were made as a set. The major decorative elements consist of an eagle and a pelican feeding its young with its own blood, symbol of Christ's sacrifice. The eagle may be seen at the apex of the stirrup; the pelican is shown on the outside of the bit on the boss. In heraldic terms, the eagle is the German royal eagle and could thus refer to Johann Georg I's Imperial Curate of 1619. This would also tie the motif of the pelican into a program of government. To attribute political meaning to motifs placed on horse equipment is in keeping with their status as knightly trappings. Hunting motifs—birds of different species, among them falcons, swans, peacocks, herons, a pheasant, and a bustard, as well as a hare caught by a falcon during hawking and grotesque masks—speak for the elector's passion for the hunt. The stirrups are decorated with a series of round medallions enclosing the various birds. Almost all of the figures are rendered three-dimensionally and are set into the medallions of the stirrups and onto the functional parts of the bit. The set, indebted to the formal language of the Baroque, illustrates the diversity of the work of Daniel Kellerthaler and his pioneering role in the art of the goldsmith in contemporary Dresden. It can be assumed that the gift of the Leipzig City Council was a commission. In its decoration with birds, this work recalls the elaborate riding equipment, including a saddle and cartridge pouch, given by the Leipzig City Council to Johann Georg I in 1618, which was procured from the Dresden silk embroiderer Hans Erich Friese. While these items were stored together, recent research reveals that the sword belt (cat. no. 12) may also be part of the same ensemble.
J.B.

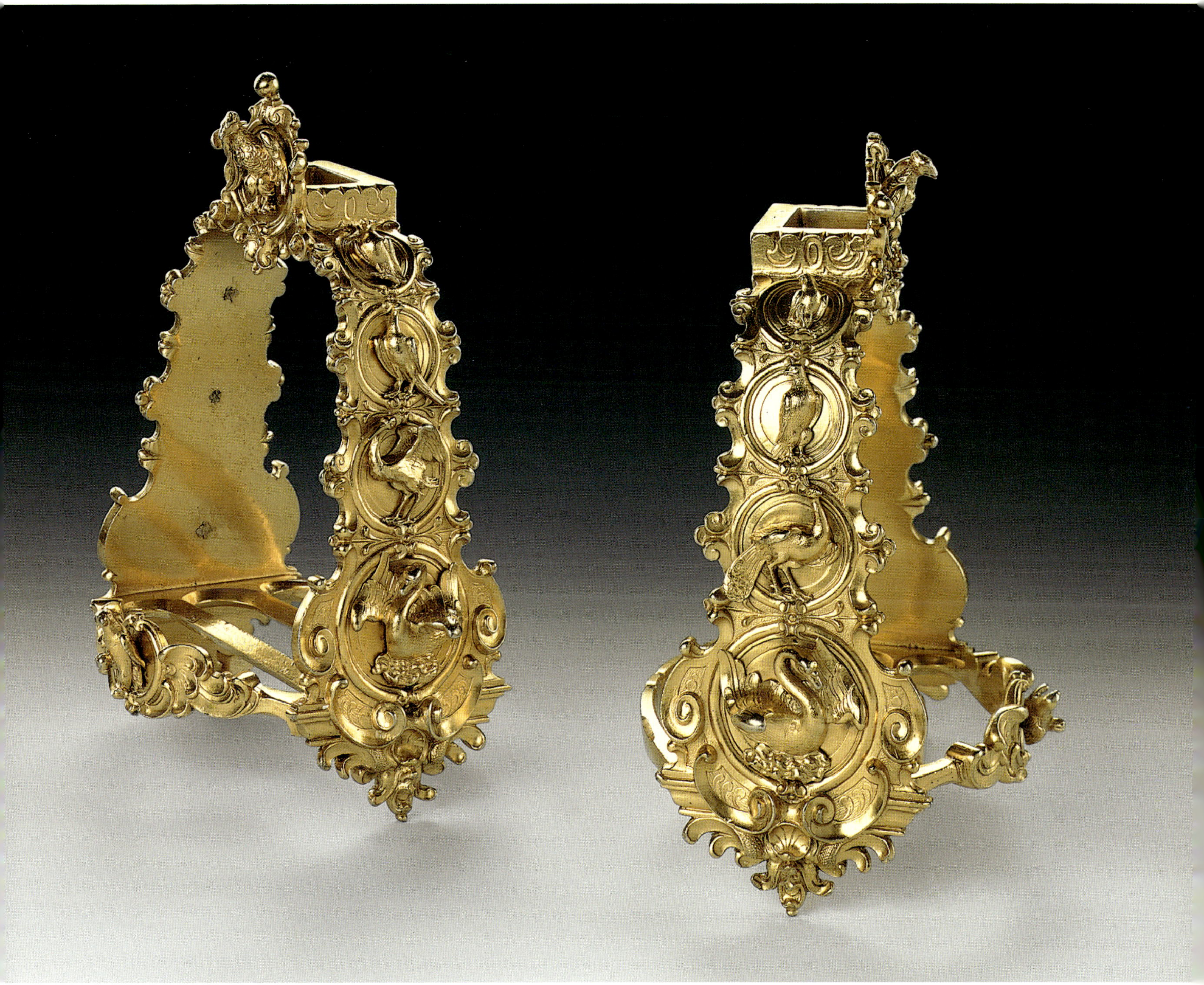

Daniel Kellerthaler
Dresden, circa 1615–19
Silver, cast, chased, and gilt
H. 7⅛ in. (18 cm), W. 5½ in. (14 cm),
weight 5 lbs (2,275 g)

View mark D [Dresden] and maker's mark "DK"
Gift of the Leipzig City Council to
Elector Johann Georg I of Saxony
Inventory of the Good Saddle Chamber of 1674,
fol. 36, no. XIV

Staatliche Kunstsammlungen Dresden, Rüstkammer,
inv. no. L 294
Lit.: Holzhausen/Kesting 1966, p. LVI, plate 55; Meisterwerke
1992, pp. 88f., plate 31 (with further literature)

25 Hunter's Trumpet

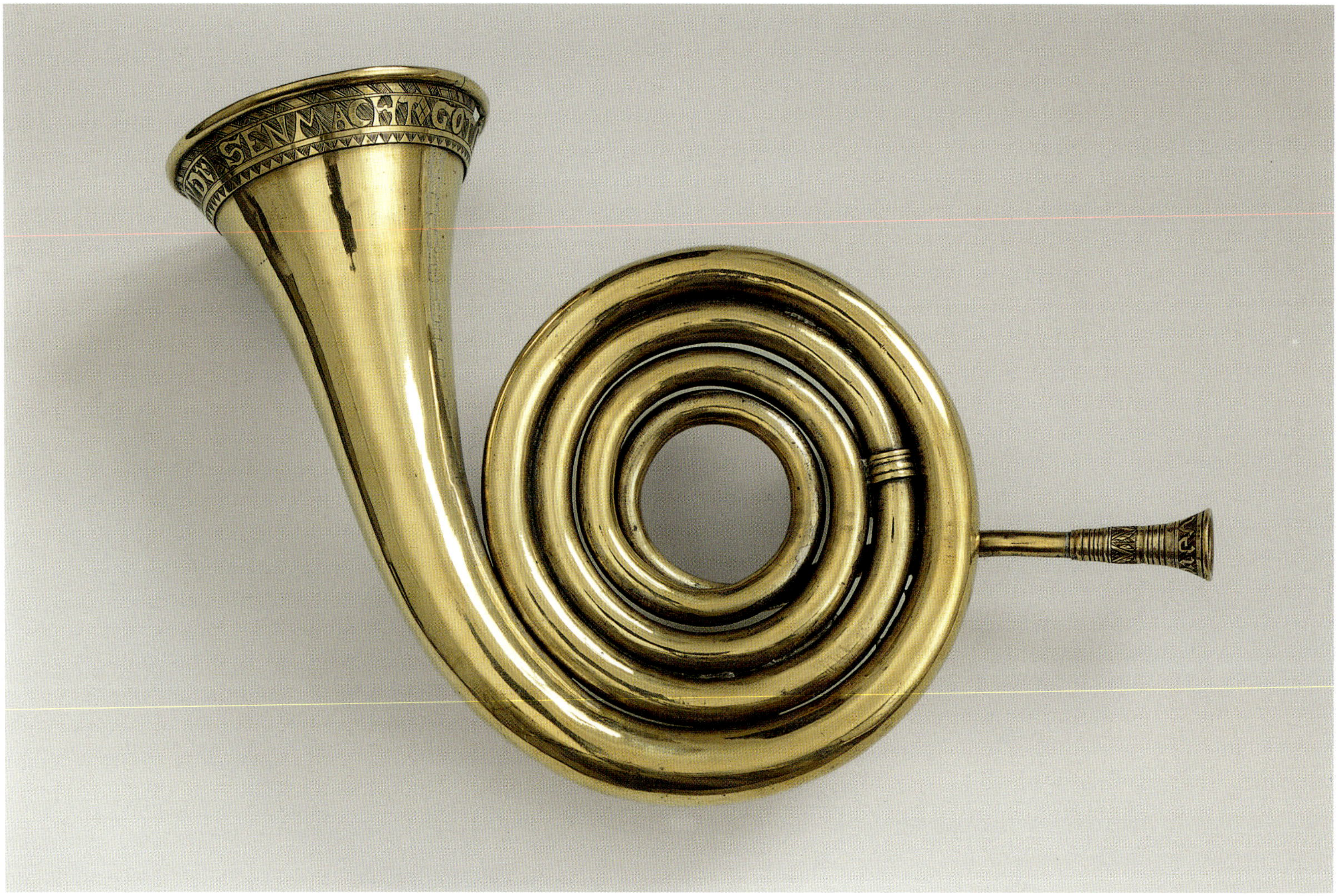

Valentin Springer I
Dresden, circa 1575–80
Brass, hammered and engraved, toothed joint consists of two equally long pipe segments
Mouth pipe: L. 27¾–28 in. (70.5–71.2 cm), Diam. 3–5¼ in. (7.6–13.2 cm)
Sound piece: L. 28 in. (71 cm)
Total length of pipe 55¾–56 in. (141.5–142.2 cm)
Mouth piece: L. 1⅜ in. (4.1 cm)
Signed and inscribed on the mouth piece: "*zv dresen*" and on the sound projector: "GOT IST MEIN HELFER V. S. ZV DRESEN MACHT"
Four turns in G alto (high tune), according to today's diapason G sharp, with original funnel mouth piece
Inventory of the Jägerkammer of 1688, fol. 126v
Staatliche Kunstsammlungen Dresden, Rüstkammer, inv. no. X 476
Lit.: Heyde 1986, p. 199, no. 86; Bäumel/Blaut 1998; Hofmann 1970

This hunter's trumpet is an early example of its type and a precious document of music history. In his 1620 publication entitled *Theatrum instrumentorum*, Michael Praetorius counted hunting horns among the regular musical instruments. He included an illustration of this piece, which he had seen with other hunting horns in the Armory. The caption beside the illustration reads *Jäger-Trommet* (hunter's trumpet). While this trumpet had approximately the same tonal range as its contemporary the long trumpet, its resonance was not equal to the latter's. In his *Fourth Intermedium of the Christmas Story*, Heinrich Schütz also featured horns among the participating instruments, presumably a type comparable to this hunter's trumpet, a precursor of the parforce horn that later evolved into the French horn.
J.B.

26 Prodd (Pellet Crossbow)

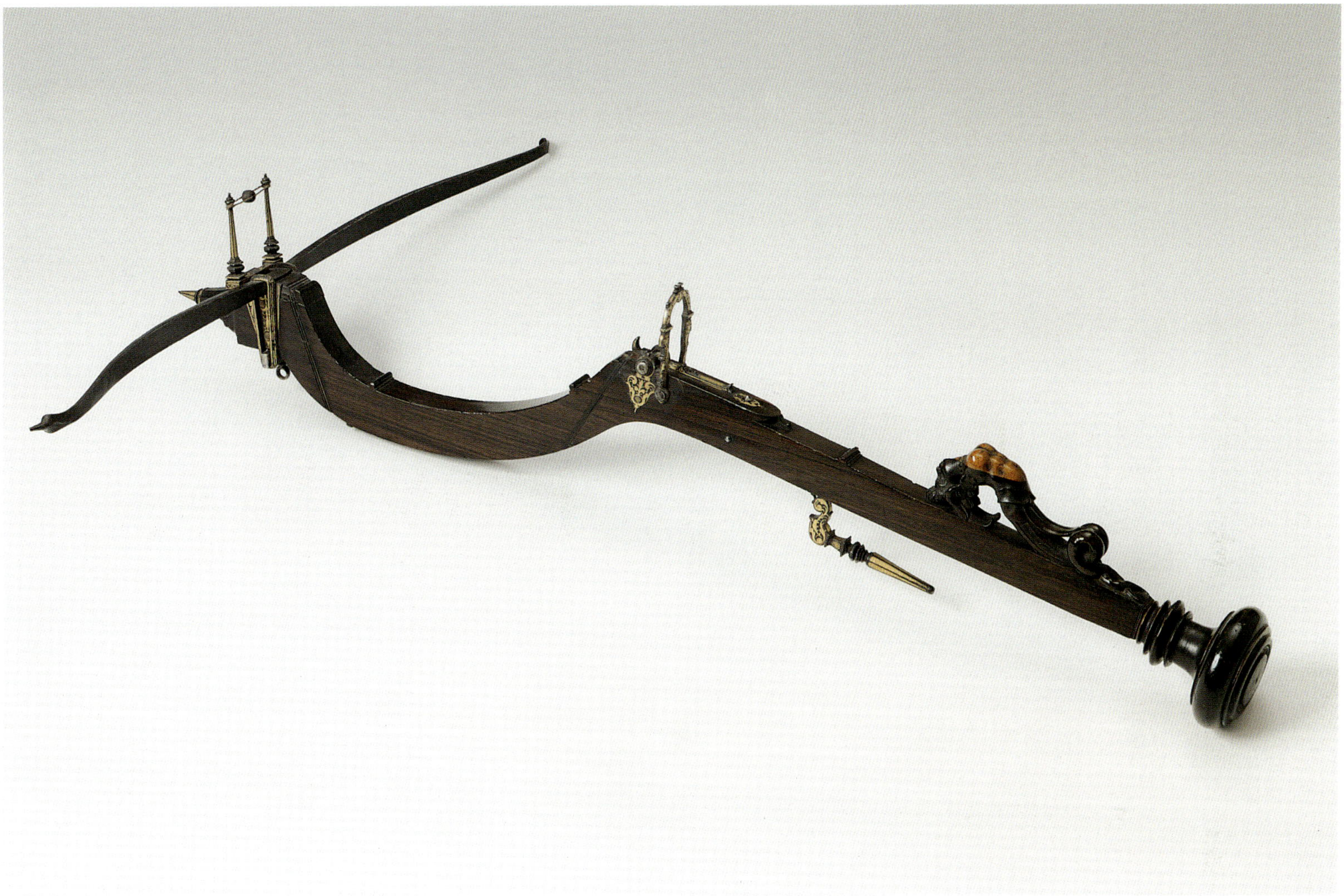

Italian, beginning of the 17th century
Ebony, partly turned and carved,
iron, partly blued, partly etched, gold damascened, partly gilt
L. 30¼ in. (77 cm), W. 23⅝ in. (60 cm),
weight 2 lbs 9 oz (1,300 g)
Staatliche Kunstsammlungen Dresden,
Rüstkammer, inv. no. U 168
Lit.: Schöbel 1976, ill. p. 48, p. 85, cat. no. 19

The prodd, a sporting crossbow used to shoot bullets in the hunt for birds and other small game, is of highly unusual design despite its practical use. At the back of the elegantly fluted column of black and light ebony (wood from the core and sapwood) a large balancing pommel may be seen. At the front a spike emerges from a lion's mouth. For the sirene—attached to the back of the column—a carved wood piece was applied in such a way that the rising body is light in color, whereas the remainder of the body is black. The iron sight device and lever trigger show a decoration of gold-damascened mauresques.
J.B.

27 Garniture of Hunting Weapons

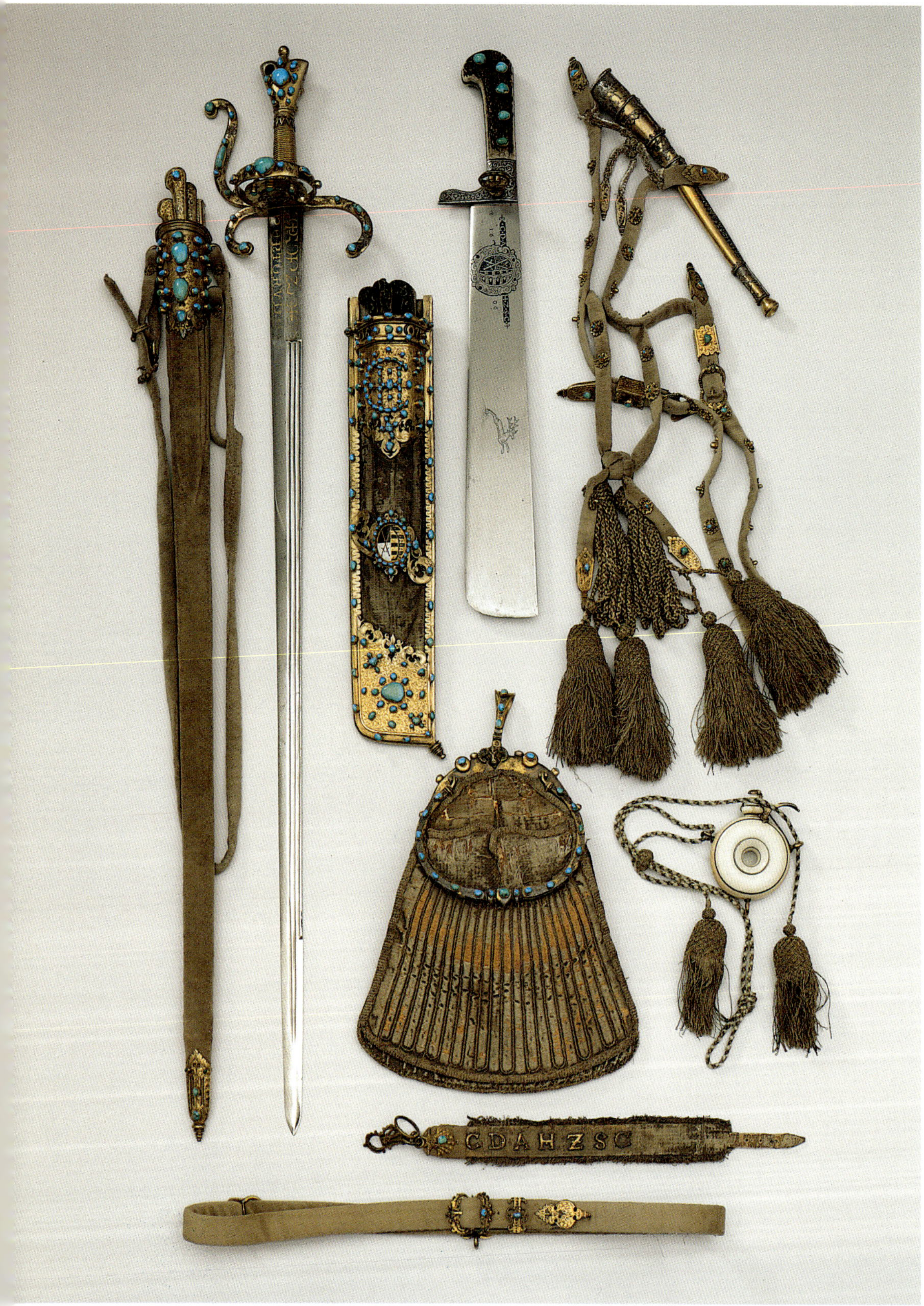

Gabriel Gipfel
Dresden, 1606–7

Hunting Sword with Sheath, One Knife, and One Bodkin (left)

Back-edged blade, double-edged tip, hollow ground, punched mark, blued, gold damascened; hilt: brass, chased, gilt, silver, gilt; turquoise trimmings; grip wrapping brass wire, gilt; sheath: wood, leather, cover originally silk velvet, black-and-white checkered, newly covered, mounts silver, chased, gilt, turquoise trimmings; cutlery: facings of staghorn, turquoise trimmings (partly lost)
Total length 39⅛ in. (99.5 cm), blade length 33⅛ in. (84 cm), weight 2 lbs 3 oz (1,050 grams); sheath: L. 33⅝ in. (85.5 cm)
Blade inscribed: "HORTUNO RVDO / AGVERVI TOL" [near it a half moon; imitation of a Toledo blade]

Trousse, Comprising Cleaver, Sheath, Two Knives, One Rasp (center)

Broad, strong back-edged blade, etched; hilt brass, chased, gilt, facings of staghorn; turquoise trimmings (partly lost); sheath wood, leather, cover silk velvet, black-and-white checkered, mounts brass, chased, gilt, partly color enameled, turquoise trimmings
Cleaver: L. 20½ in. (52 cm), blade length 15 in. (38 cm); blade width 2⅝ in. (6.8 cm); sheath: L. 16⅛ in. (41 cm)
Blade inscribed: "CDAHZSC" [Christian der Andere Herzog zu Sachsen, Churfürst; i.e., Christian the other Duke of Saxony, Elector] and dated: "1606" as well as the electoral Saxon coat of arms
At the mouth piece of the sheath dated: "1607" as well as the initials "CH" [Christian and Hedwig], on the middle band the electoral Saxon coat of arms

Hunting Horn (right)

Brass, worked in relief, gilt; mounts silver, engraved; horn strap leather, cover originally silk velvet, black-and-white/silver checkered, newly covered: turquoise trimmings (thirty-six stones), tassels black-and-white silk, gilt silver wire around silk core
L. 10¼ in. (26 cm)

Hunting Bag (bottom center)

Silk velvet, black-and-white checkered, border gilt silver wire around silk core; mounts silver, gilt, turquoise trimmings (partly lost)
H. 14⅛ in. (36 cm); W. 10¼ in. (26 cm)

Powder Flask (bottom right)

Ivory, turned, partly blackened; mounts brass, gilt; cord with tassels black-and-white silk, silver and gilt wire around silk core
H. 3⅛ in. (8 cm)

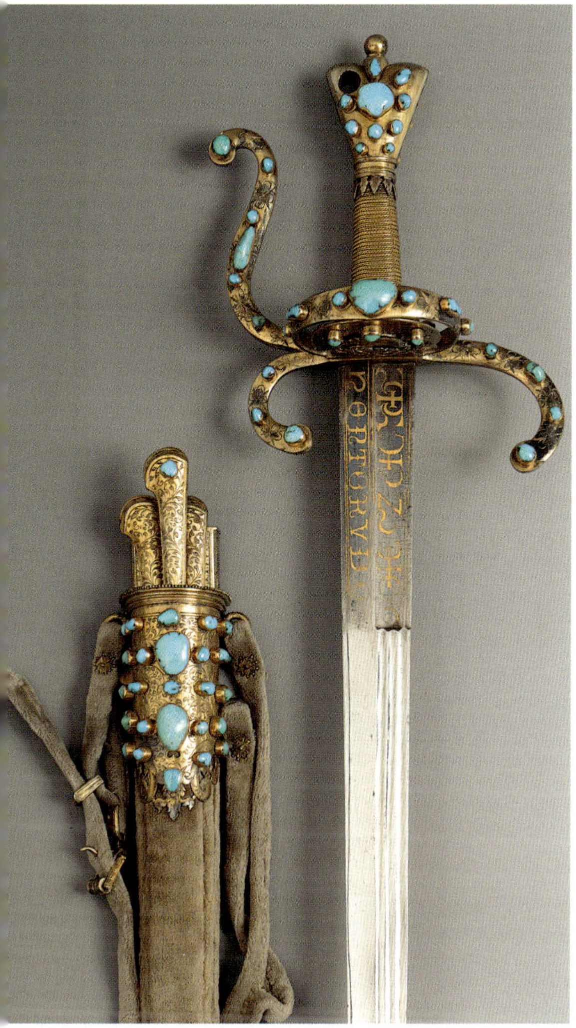

Dog Collar (bottom)
Leather, silk velvet, black-and-white checkered, fringed braid, silver and gilt wire around silk core; Inscribed: "CDAHZSC"
mounts brass, gilt, turquoise trimmings
L. 11¼ in. (28.5 cm); W. 1⅜ in. (3.5 cm)

Belt (bottom)
Leather, silk velvet, black-and-white checkered, mounts silver-gilt, turquoise trimmings
L. 44½ in. (113 cm)

Jägerkammer inventory of 1620, Bl. 89, no. 18, Bl. 98, no. 11, Bl. 101, no. 60
Staatliche Kunstsammlungen Dresden, Rüstkammer, inv. no. X 144: hunting sword (X 144e), trousse (X 144d), hunting horn (X 144a), hunting bag (X 144c), powder flask (X 144f), dog collar (X 144b), belt (X 144g)
Lit.: Ehrenthal 1899, p. 222, M 265 a–f; Watzdorf 1935/1936; Schöbel/Schaal 1981, p. 74, cat. no. 40; Bäumel 1995c, pp. 95–97

This garniture of hunting weapons, embellished with more than three hundred turquoises, belonged to Christian II of Saxony. The matching hat cord is lost. Rendered in densely placed turquoises, the monogram "CH" can be seen from afar and refers to the elector and his wife, Hedwig. The coat of arms and Christian's initials also appear on other elements of the uniformly designed garniture. The cloth-covered parts were originally made from "diced," i.e., checkered, silk velvet, a fashionable material at the time. The silver-gilt mounts show depictions of duck hunts and birds. Gabriel Gipfel's invoice for the turquoise garniture was made out to Christian II; amounting to 2,000 guilders, it specified the number of 351 turquoises. This illustrates the working method of the goldsmith, who gave subcontracts based on his own specifications to other craftsmen—including a bladesmith, gunmaker, ringmaker, strap and bag maker, and hat embellisher—and then finished the prefabricated pieces himself. In 1608, Christian II gave a similar garniture by Gipfel (with emerald decoration) to his brother Johann Georg I. The precious character reflects the use of such objects during festive court hunting events, for instance a procession of hunters. These garnitures exemplify the equipment carried by a noble huntsman. The first prerequisite was his ability to defend himself; thus the most important piece in this garniture was the sword, a status symbol long associated with knighthood. The captured game was stabbed to death (it was given the so-called Fangstoß) with the sword, while the cleaver served to cut away branches and shrubs, to cut off the antlers of a killed stag, and to cut the game into pieces. Communication during a hunt occurred via the hunter's horn, an obligatory element of all hunting equipment. The large hunting bag, attached to the belt, was called a Schwedler. The presence of a powder flask makes clear that the equipment of a hunter was complete only with the inclusion of pistols or a hunting rifle. The huntsman's personal dogs wore dog collars with the master's coat of arms.
J.B.

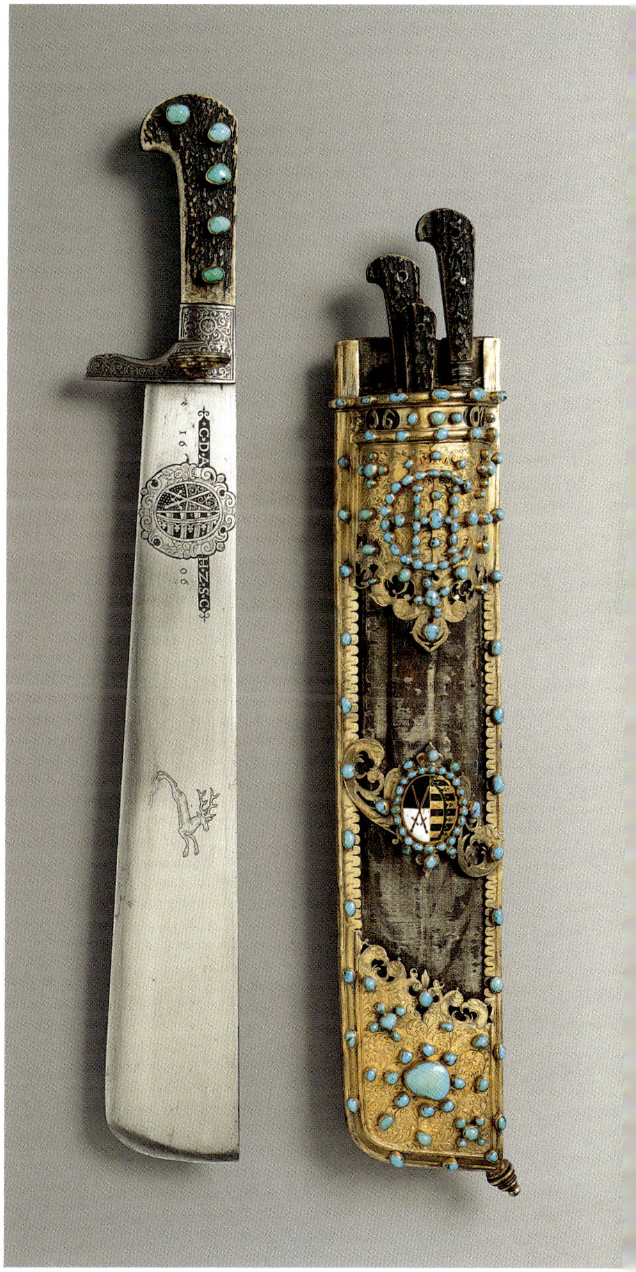

28 Rapier and Dagger

The pierced plate inserted into the guard of this particularly noble garniture of parade weapons shows the coat of arms and the initials of Wolf Ernst von Wolfframsdorf, electoral Saxon chief stable master and court marshal between 1588 and 1611. The massive silver hilts and the mounts of rapier and dagger are adorned with a distinctive wave design and large and small shells, as well as satyr heads and masks. Possible makers of this set, an impressive example of the goldsmith's art, include such Dresden goldsmiths as Wendel unter der Linden, Urban Schneeweiß, and Valentin Geitner, who were all familiar with these types of objects. The blade is a high-quality imitation of a work by the renowned master Sebastian Hernandez of Toledo. Bladesmiths, especially from Solingen, took a certain delight in imitating the much sought-after Spanish blades to increase their own sales. A belt and a sword hanger of yellow velvet with gold and silver trimmings, as well as silver mounts with wave design, also originally belonged to this garniture.
J.B.

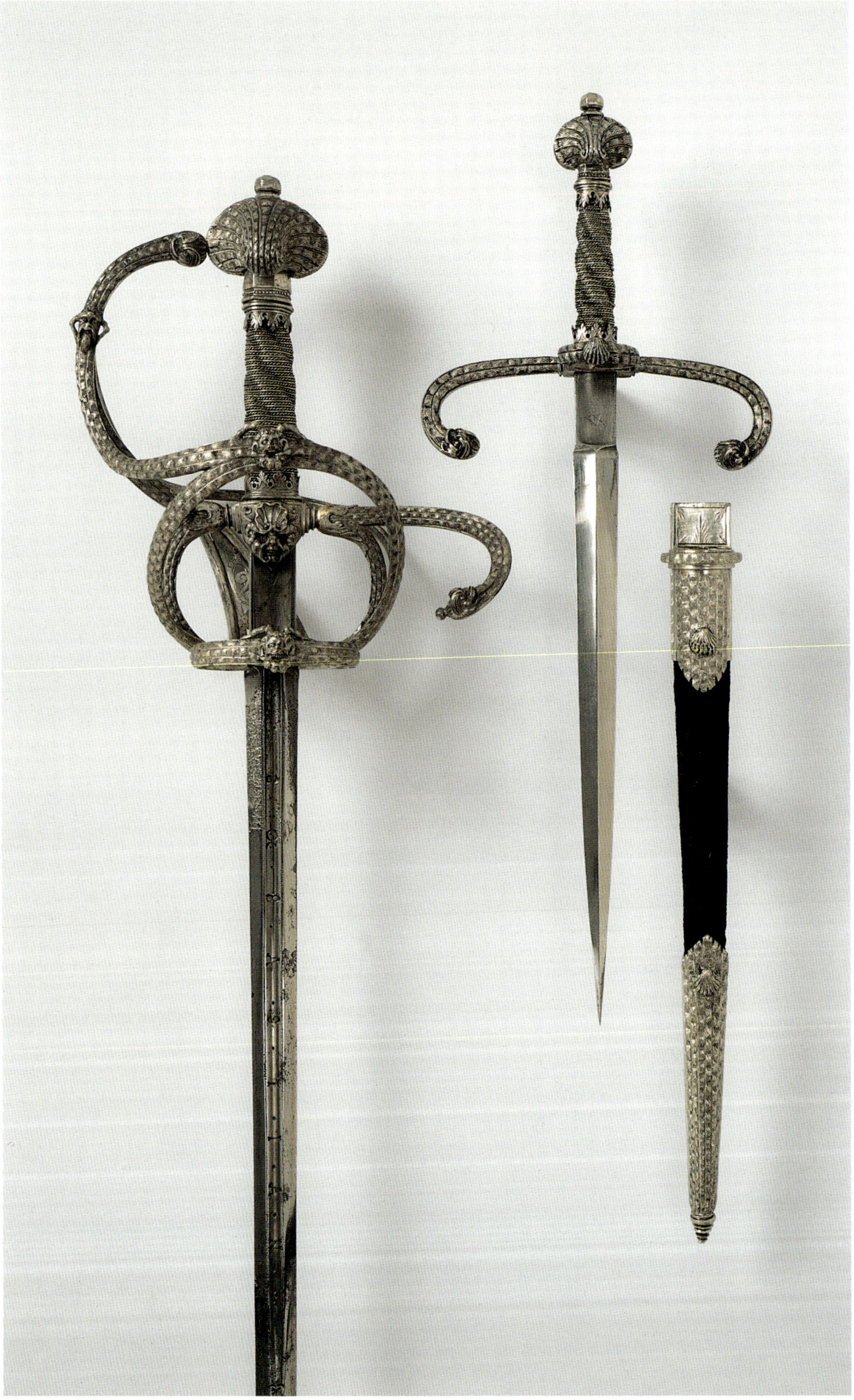

Presumably Dresden, beginning of the 17th century
Blade: presumably Solingen, imitation of a Toledo blade
Rapier: diamond-section blade, flattened, hollow cut, punched mark and mark inscription; hilt silver, cast, chased, partly pierced; grip wrapping silver wire
Total length 46½ in. (118 cm), blade length 41⅛ in. (104.5 cm), weight 3 lbs (1,400 g)
Blade inscribed: "SEBASTIAN HENANTEZ," marked: fish on the hilt: coat of arms and initials "WE.V. W." of Wolf Ernst von Wolfframsdorf
Dagger: diamond-section blade; hilt and sheath mounts silver, cast, chased, partly pierced: grip wrapping, silver wire
Total length 14¾ in. (37.5 cm), blade length 10⅜ in. (26.3 cm), weight 11 oz (320 g, without sheath)
Inventory of the Spießpagenkammer of 1677, fol. 55–56, no. 262
Staatliche Kunstsammlungen Dresden, Rüstkammer, inv. no. VI 370 (rapier), p. 201 (dagger), XI 4 (dagger sheath)
Lit.: Ehrenthal 1899, p. 79, E 249; Haenel 1923, p. 144, plate 57 a

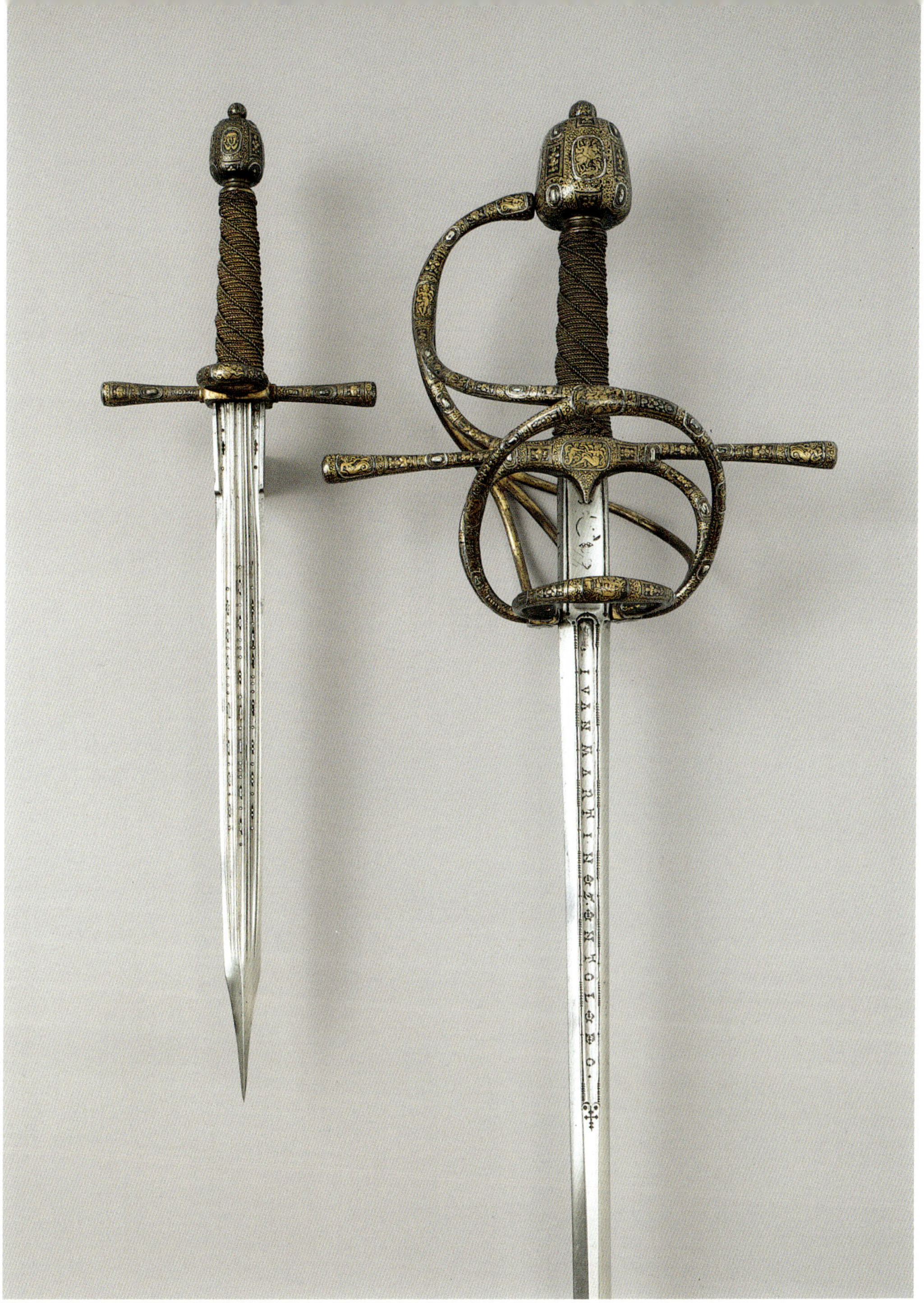

29 Rapier and Dagger

This garniture of parade weapons marks the zenith in the development of rapiers around 1600. The rapier was developed as a special weapon for fencing and was indispensable as a noble's sidearm. It has a long and narrow blade, primarily intended for the thrust, as well as a number of guards to protect the hand. In order to effectively parry, it was customarily accompanied by a left-handed dagger. This garniture is distinguished by its high-quality Spanish blades and its damascened decoration. Among the bladesmiths from Toledo, the leading European center of bladesmiths, Juan Martinez the Elder was the most famous at the time. The art of damascening was adapted from the Near East. Its use in combination with classical motifs was characteristic of arms and armor ornament of this period, particularly in Milan. The medallions, set in arabesque tendrils, depict—in a slightly sketchy manner—St. George, Marcus Curtius, Venus and Cupid, and Mars as well as Diana. Silver-damascened "pearls" provide further decorative accents.
J.B.

Hilts Milan, circa 1600, blades Spanish
Rapier blade: Juan Martinez the Elder, Toledo
Rapier: diamond-section blade, flattened, hollow cut, punched marks and marks inscription; hilt iron, gold and silver damascened, blackened ground, partly gilt
Total length 50 in. (127 cm), blade length 44⅛ in. (112 cm), weight 3 lbs 2 oz (1,440 g)
Rapier blade inscribed: "IVAN MARTINEZ EN TOLEDO / IN TE DOMINE SPERAVI / ESPADERO DEL REI" and marked: half moon (maker's mark), crowned lily (mark of the royal blade smith), "TO" crowned (Toledo view mark)
Dagger: diamond-section blade, flattened, hollow cut, pierced; hilt iron, gold and silver damascened, blackened ground, partly gilt
Total length 16 in. (40.5 cm), blade length 11 in. (28 cm), weight 11¼ oz (320 g)
Gift of Elector Christian II to his brother Johann Georg I in 1602
Armory inventory of Prince Johann Georg I of 1608, p. 108
Staatliche Kunstsammlungen Dresden, Rüstkammer, inv. no. VI 190 (rapier), p. 36 (dagger)
Lit.: Ehrenthal 1899, p. 75, E 198; Schöbel 1973, p. 91, cat. no. 74b

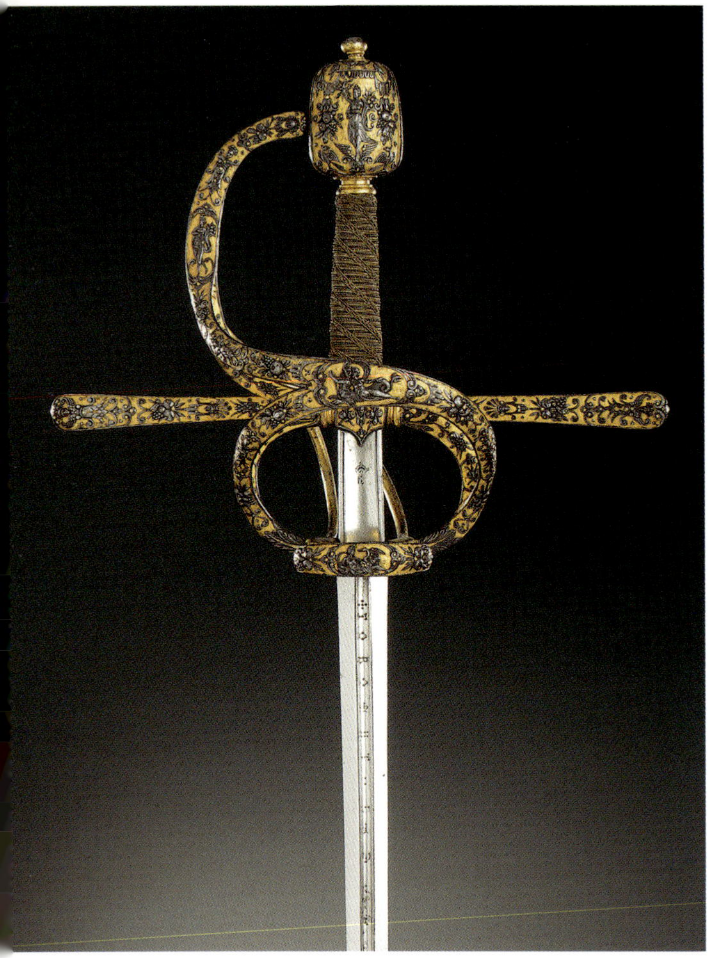

30 Rapier

Daniel Sadeler, Prague or Munich, early 17th century
Diamond-section blade, flattened, hollow cut, punched marks and inscription
Hilt iron, chiseled, ground gilt
Total length 46½ in. (118 cm), blade length 40⅛ in. (102 cm); weight 2 lbs 6 oz (1,200 g)
Blade: Pedro de Toro, Toledo, imitation (?)
Signed: "PETRO DE TORO EN TOLEDO"
Marked: "S" crowned, "PO" crowned
Gift of Emperor Rudolf II to Elector Christian II in 1610
Armory inventory 1614–20, fol. 42–43, no. 59
Staatliche Kunstsammlungen Dresden, Rüstkammer, inv. no. VI 421
Lit.: Ehrenthal 1899, p. 107, E 688; Haenel 1923, p. 120, plate 60; Stöcklein 1922, pp. 52f., plate XI; Schöbel 1973, p. 87, cat. no. 55

In 1610, this rapier was given by Rudolf II to Elector Christian II of Saxony in Prague. With it came a belt and a sword hanger "*von gulden Tuch*" (of golden cloth) with pearl embroidery. All parts of the rapier's hilt by Daniel Sadeler are adorned with fruit garlands as well as figures of female grotesques and masks. Fortune appears on the pommel like a goddess of victory. The guards are embellished with a Nereid with Triton and Leda with the swan. The exquisitely rendered motifs are based on engravings by Etienne Delaune (Fortune) and Egidius Sadeler (Leda). The hiltmaker Daniel Sadeler, originating from a Munich family of artists, is particularly renowned for his masterly command of the iron chiseling. Between 1602 and 1607, he worked as gilder at the emperor's court. In 1610, he returned to Munich, where he worked for Duke Albrecht VI of Bavaria. The latter also presented Elector Johann Georg I with a garniture of hunting weapons by Sadeler.
J.B.

31 Rapier

The rapier belongs to a group of Dresden-made hilts of about 1610 (see cat. nos. 32, 33). The pommel is decorated with a vase surrounded by delightful flower tendrils. The quillons and other branches of the guard terminate in dragon heads, their undulating form reminiscent of winding dragons' necks. On the diagonal branch at the front of the guard a female face is flanked by dragons. The branch rising up from the base of the hilt is made to look like a prisoner menaced by a hissing dragon's head.
J.B.

Dresden, circa 1610
Diamond-section blade, flattened, hollow cut, gilt on the ricasso; hit inscription
Hilt brass, cast, chased, partly etched and chiseled, gilt; grip wrapping brass wire, gilt
Total length 44⅝ in. (113.5 cm), blade length 38⅜ in. (97.5 cm), weight 2 lbs 6 oz (1,200 g)
Inventory of the Electoral Chamber 1671, p. 48, no. 315
Staatliche Kunstsammlungen Dresden, Rüstkammer, inv. no. VI 450
Lit.: Washington 1978, no. 164

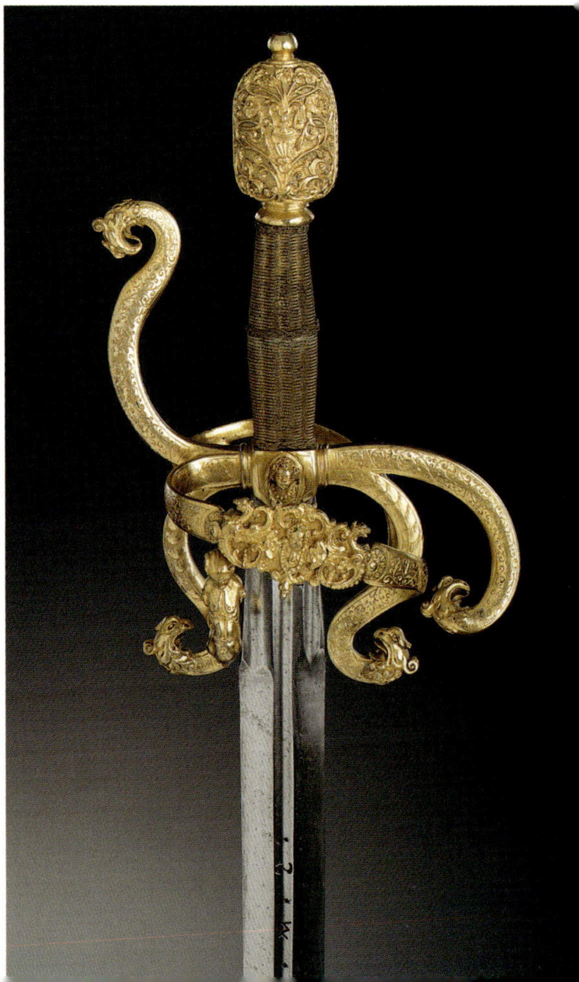

32 Rapier and Dagger

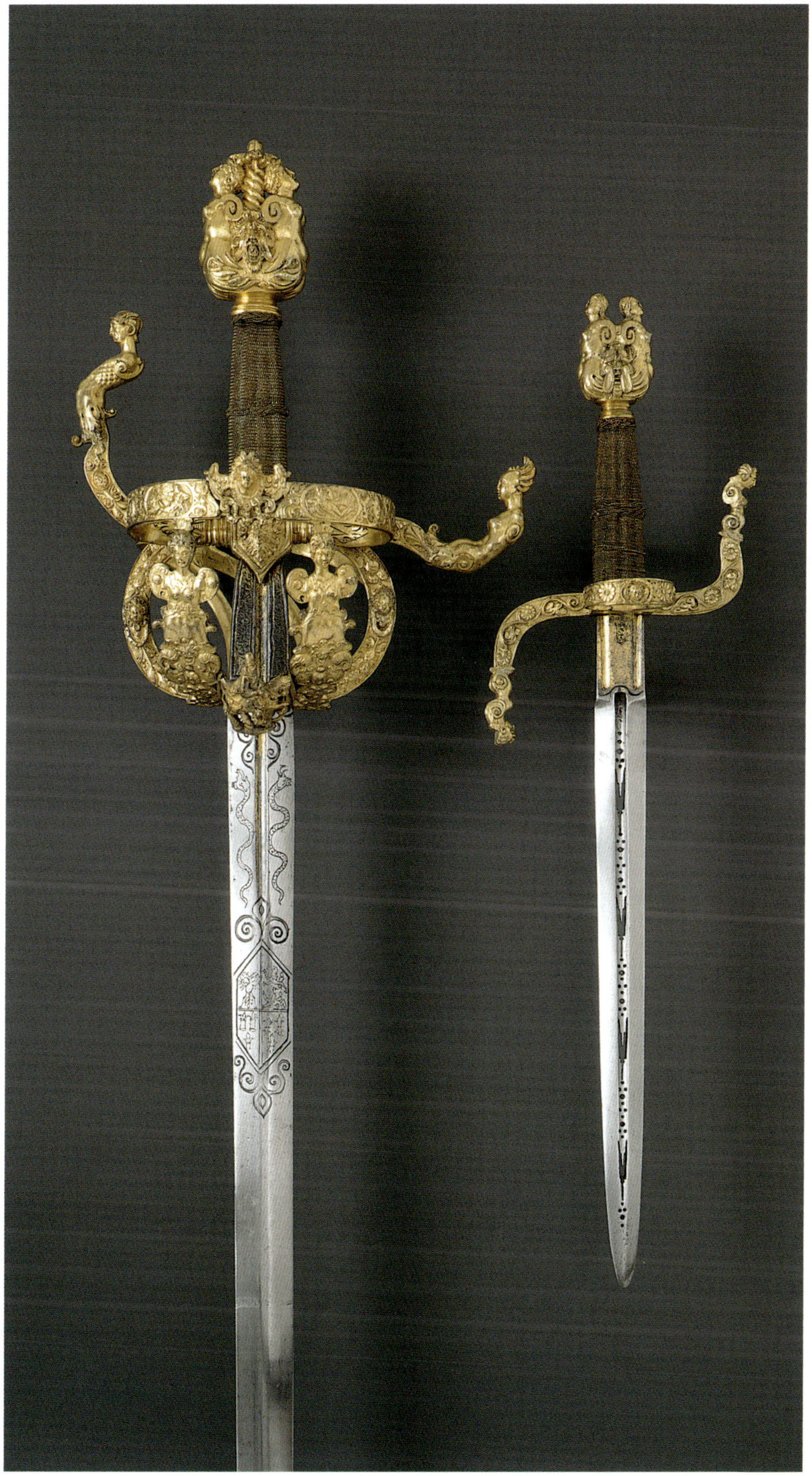

The pommels of this rapier and dagger are fashioned as two herms with *"Engel köpffen"* (angels' heads) that are arranged opposite one another and gaze out the sides. The quillons terminate in the figures of a Roman warrior and a woman. On the rapier, two herms appear as upstanding branches rising from the base of the guard. In the inventory, this garniture may be identified not only based on the description of the gilt hilts but also because of the rapier's blade—*"mit Schlangen und Wappen"* (with serpents and coat of arms). The small, three-dimensional figure of a rider at the base of the rapier's guard shows the elector on horseback dressed in court costume. If one considers the context of its usage, this parade weapon assumes a symbolic meaning: one of a group of rapiers made in Dresden around 1610, this example might thus be associated with the trip Elector Christian II took to Prague, where he received from the emperor the much disputed enfeoffment of Jülich, Cleves, and Berg. The elector could conceivably have carried this weapon on that occasion. The color and the material of the matching belt and sword hanger of *"donnetbraunen [braunviolettem] Atlaß"* (brown-violet silk satin) appear likewise in the parade costume Christian wore—according to a note included in the electoral garment inventory of 1610—in Prague. This costume is also preserved in the Armory.
J.B.

Dresden, presumably 1610
Rapier: diamond-section blade, flattened, hollow cut, gilt on the ricasso; inscription etched; hilt brass, cast, chased, and gilt, formerly partly color enameled; handle wrapping brass wire, gilt
Total length 46⅞ in. (119 cm), blade length 40⅛ in. (102 cm), weight 3 lbs 2 oz (1,460 g)
Four-part coat of arms on the blade with eagle, two lions, and lily motifs (unidentified)
Dagger: diamond-section blade, flattened, hollow cut, pierced; hit mark; hilt brass, cast, chiseled, chased, and gilt; grip wrapping brass wire, gilt
Total length 16 in. (40.5 cm), blade length 10⅞ in. (27.5 cm), weight 14 oz (400 g)
Inventory of the Electoral Chamber 1671, pp. 145f., no. 310
Staatliche Kunstsammlungen Dresden, Rüstkammer, inv. no. VI 232 (rapier), p. 112 (dagger)
Lit.: Ehrenthal 1899, p. 103, E 652

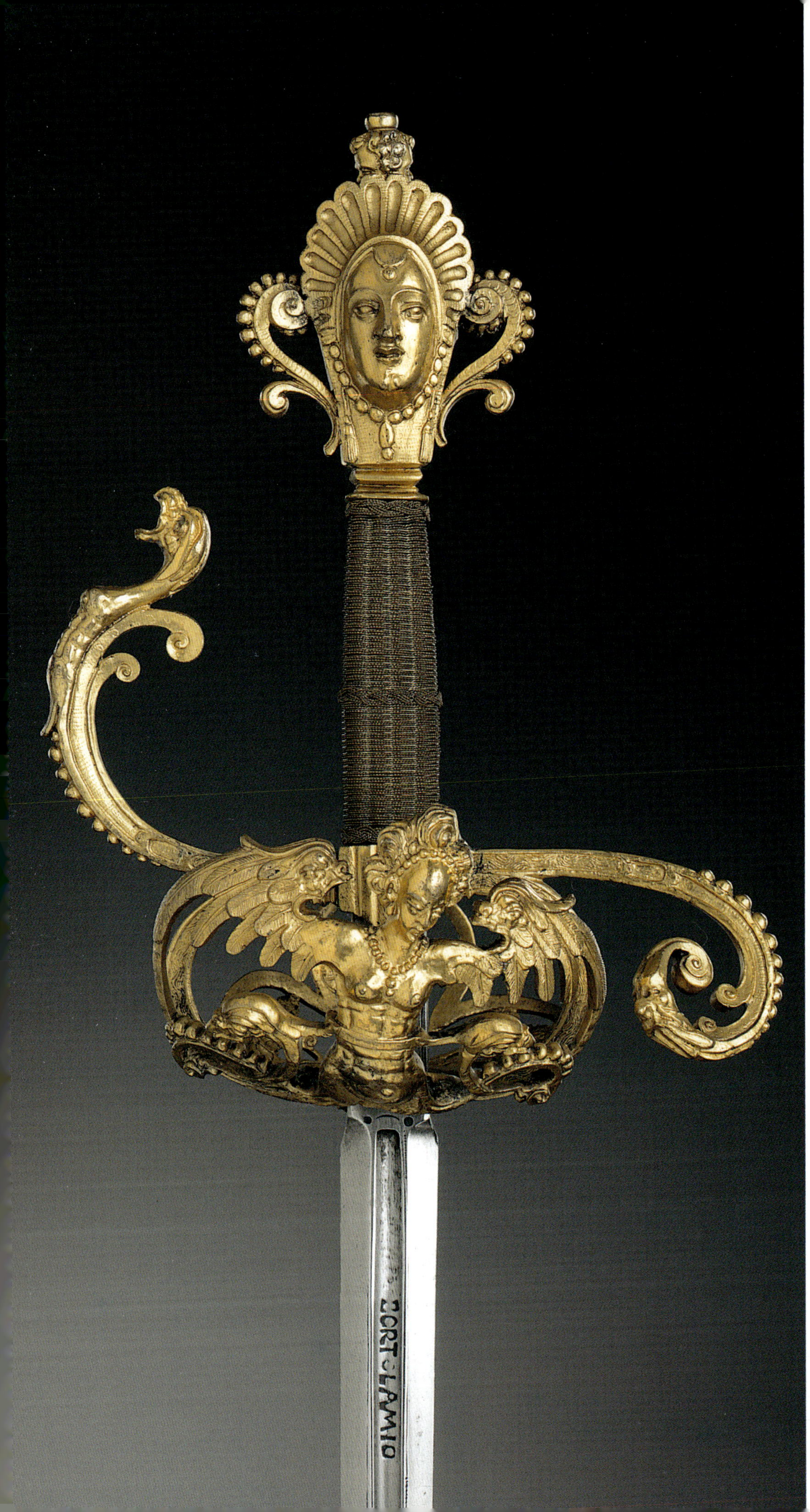

33 Rapier

The rapier belongs to the same group produced in Dresden around 1610 that includes cat. nos. 31 and 32. The rapier and the daggers of this set are distinguished by their sculptural abundance, similarity of motifs, and homogenous artistic idiom. The hilts are mostly made from cast and gilt brass. They were produced by a hiltmaker with the professional training of a goldsmith. A parade rapier, closely related to this group, is in the Metropolitan Museum in New York and bears the signature of the Dresden hiltmaker Israel Schuch. The pommel of this rapier is decorated *"mit zwey schönen vergüldten angesichtern"* (with two beautiful gilt faces), a shell guard with a siren—a *"vergüldt brustbildt, mit einem schönen angesicht vnndt Engelsflügeln"* (a gilt half-length figure with a beautiful face and the wings of an angel)—and quillons in the guise of a dragon. Both of the diadem-wearing women look like classical deities; while one looks ahead, the other one is turned to the back. On the reverse of the pommel is a Gorgon's head. Originally, a belt and a sword hanger made of black silk atlas, gold embroidery, and gilt mounts also accompanied the rapier. In 1610, Electress Sophie gave a similar garniture of rapier and dagger with angels, sirens, and Moor's head to her husband as a Christmas gift.
J.B.

Dresden, presumably 1610
Diamond-section blade, flattened, hollow cut, punched mark and inscription; hilt brass, cast, chased, and gilt, formerly partly color enameled; grip wrapping brass wire, gilt
Total length 46⅞ in. (119 cm), blade length 39¾ in. (101 cm), weight 3 lbs 1 oz (1,430 g)
Blade inscribed: "BORTOLAMIO CIVIDAL"
Gift of the electoral Saxon court marshal Christoph von Loß to Elector Christian II for Christmas 1610
Armory inventory of 1614–20, p. 33
Inventory of the Electoral Chamber of 1671, p. 144, no. 308
Staatliche Kunstsammlungen Dresden, Rüstkammer, inv. no. VI 419
Lit.: Ehrenthal 1899, p. 99, E 609; Thomas/Gamber/Schedelmann 1963, no. 66; Schöbel 1973, p. 88, ill. 62a; Washington 1978, no. 163

34 Pair of Wheel-lock Pistols

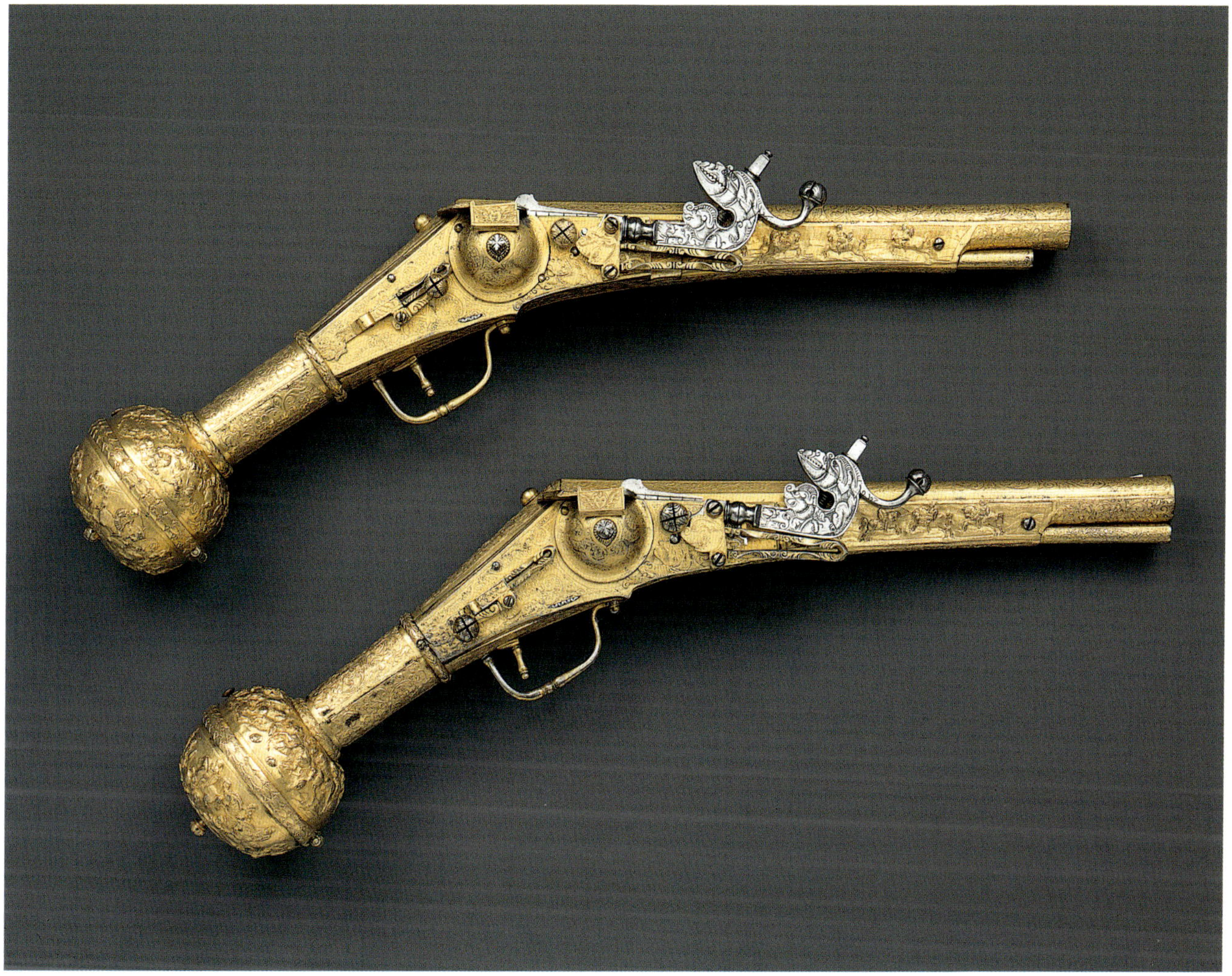

Augsburg, end of the 16th century
Barrels and locks iron, etched and gilt; stock copper, worked in repoussé and gilt
Total length 20½ in. (52 cm), length of barrel 12¼ in. (31 cm), length of bore ⅝ in. (15 mm), weight 4 lbs 8 oz (2,200 g)
Barrel marked: Augsburg view mark, initial "KT"
Inventory of the Pistol Chamber of 1683, p. 262, no. 49
Staatliche Kunstsammlungen Dresden, Rüstkammer, inv. no. J59/J1435
Lit.: Ehrenthal 1899, p. 118, F 58; Haenel 1923, p. 148d, plate V; Schöbel 1973, p. 161, ill. 128; Washington 1978, cat. 184 (J59)

Since the middle of the sixteenth century, hand firearms with metal stocks were produced in South Germany, especially in Augsburg and Nuremberg, but also in Brunswick. In contrast to weapons with wooden stocks, they were almost indestructible. Besides firearms whose stocks were worked in iron or copper repoussé, until the beginning of the seventeenth century the most sought-after stocks were embellished with cast brass or silver plates. These generally richly decorated, luxurious rifles and pistols chiefly entered princely armories.

Except for the cocks and the pan-covers, the barrels and locks of these pistols are richly etched and gilt. Their barrels—in the back third octagonal, then round and toward the muzzle slightly wider—are decorated with fine tendril work. The eight-sided barrel section of each pistol bears the Augsburg view mark and a crowned male head in a medallion, as well as the initials "KT." Erich Haenel interpreted these letters not as the etcher's mark but as belonging to the depiction: possibly "King Theodorich."

The lock with exterior wheel, strongly domed wheel-cover, sliding pan-cover, press button, and polished iron cock also possesses a safety catch with a spherical knob. The iron, round-profiled trigger guard and the trigger are also gilt. Etched and engraved fabulous beasts decorate the cock and pan-cover. The stock and globular pommel are entirely made from copper and adorned with figures and tendrils worked in relief. In the front portion of the stock, on the lock and its counterside, dynamically animated classical equestrian battle scenes can be observed.

Consisting of two halves, the hollow pommel can be opened through the pressure of a spring. One of the halves contains cleaning tools for the barrel that can be screwed onto an iron fitting on the front end of each wooden ramrock. The pommels are equally divided into two zones and also bear ancient battle scenes with riders and tendril work.
H-W.L.

35 Powder Flask

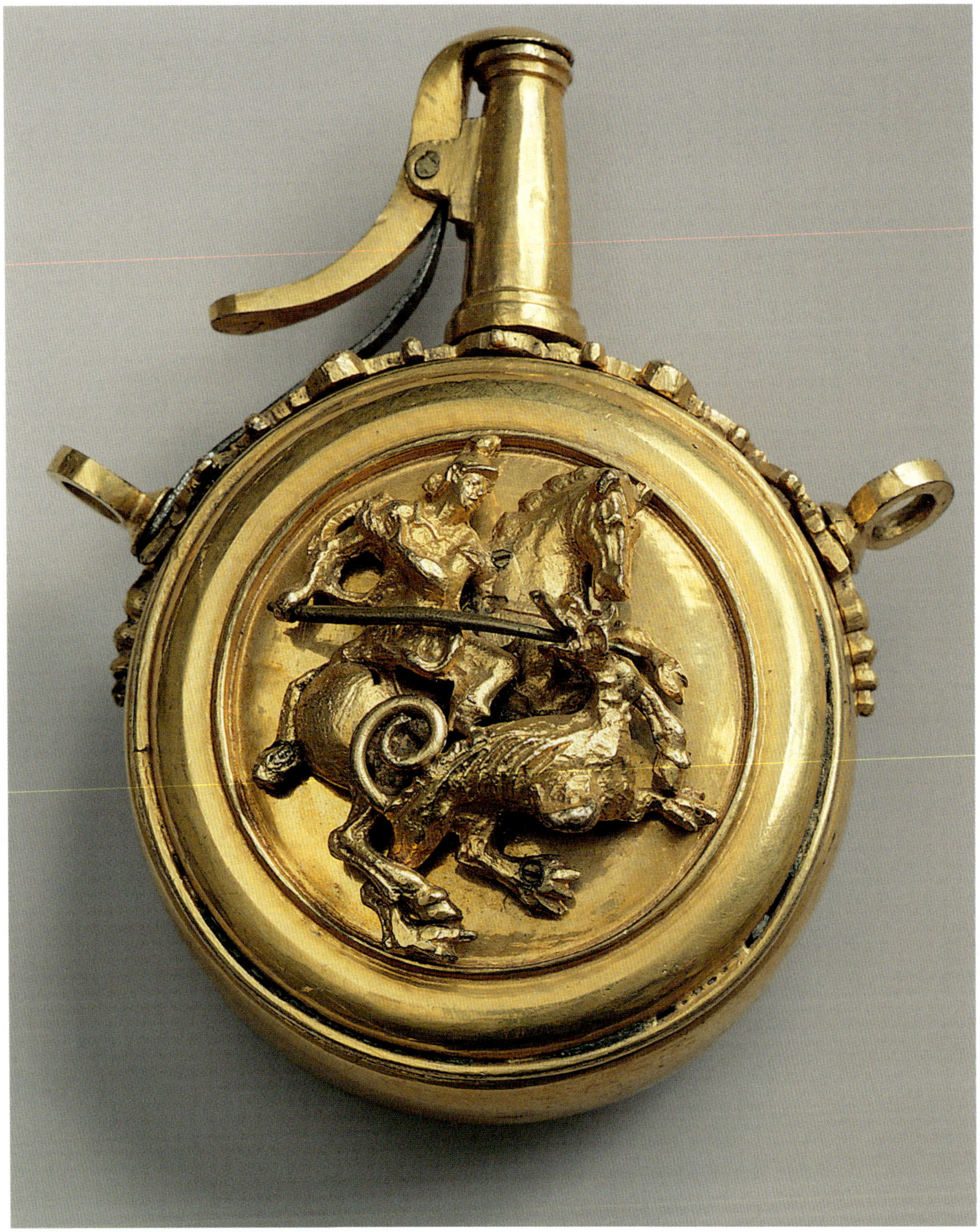

In addition to gunpowder and bullets, the use of hand firearms required a number of different tools and instruments. In order to wind the wheel lock, an appropriate spanning device was needed, as were powder measures and powder knives to test powder quality and bullet shape. Bullet tongs were required to cast the bullets. Further indispensable items included powder flasks and bullet bags. Gunpowder was a compound of saltpeter, sulfur, and charcoal added in differing proportions and grain sizes. In order to expedite the loading process, musketeers began to carry bandoleers by the beginning of the sixteenth century. Attached to the bandoleer were bottle-shaped containers, each filled with the powder required for one shot. A further innovation to accelerate the loading process occurred toward the end of the sixteenth century: the introduction of the paper-cartridge that contained powder and bullet. Powder flasks, powder horns, and cartridge boxes for the princely huntsman, marksman, or traveler were mostly fabricated from costly materials and displayed rich artistic embellishments employing diverse decorating techniques.

The round brass corpus of the powder flask shows on its front the raised figure of St. George and the dragon cast in brass. The conical spout possesses a spring lock. Attached to the powder flask's top narrow side are two carrier loops of pierced brass. The Armory preserves another, identical powder flask.
H-W.L.

South German, early 17th century
Brass, partly cast, chased, and gilt
H. 3⅞ in. (9.8 cm), Diam. 2½ in. (6.5 cm), weight 6½ oz (190 g)
Staatliche Kunstsammlungen Dresden, Rüstkammer, inv. no. X 748
Lit.: Ehrenthal 1899, p. 124, F 107/108; Historisches Museum 1985, p. 18

36 Wheel-lock Revolver with Four Shots

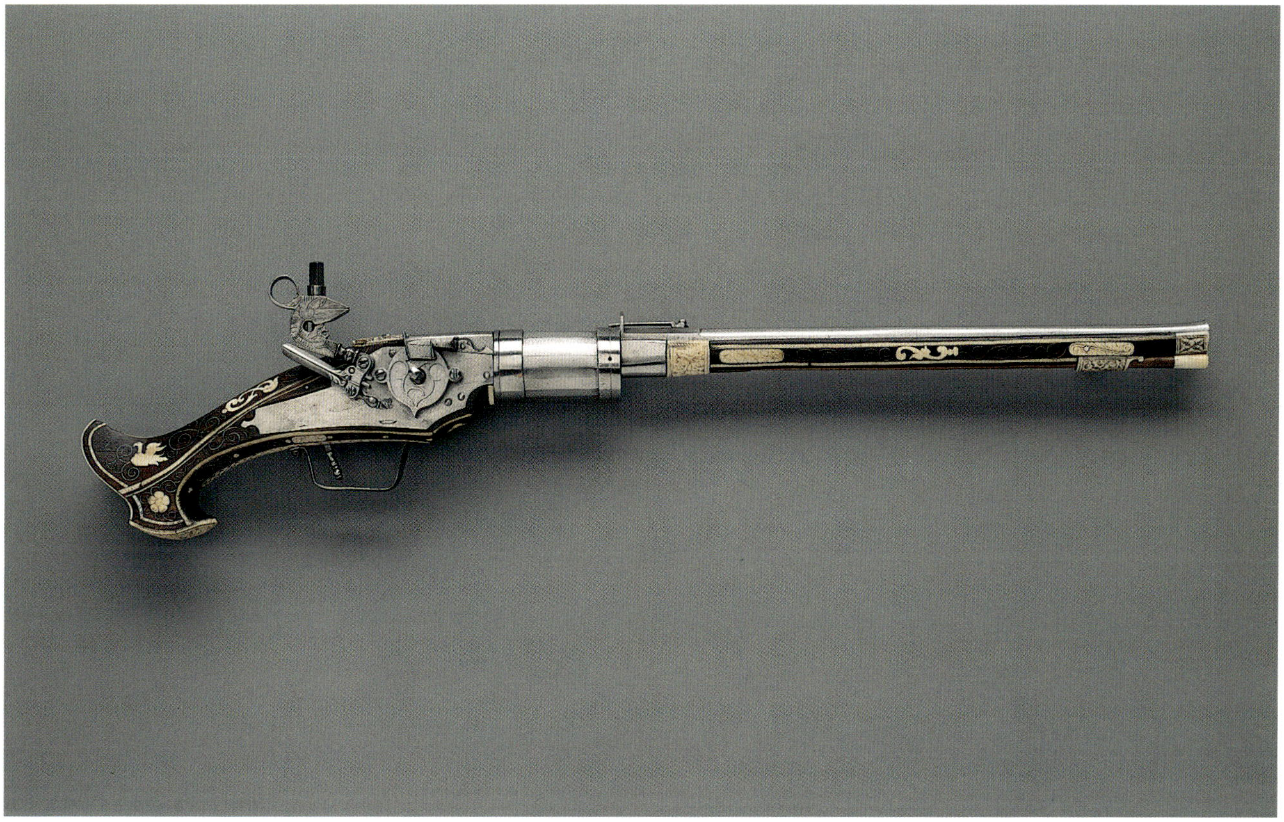

Master "HR"
Nuremberg, circa 1600
Iron; stock walnut, bone inlays
Total length 26⅜ in. (67 cm), barrel length with cylinder 16½ in. (42 cm), length of cylinder 2¾ in. (7 cm), length of bore ½ in. (9 mm), weight 3 lbs 3 oz (1,500 g)
Lock signed: "HR" over sun
Staatliche Kunstsammlungen Dresden, Rüstkammer, inv. no. J 489
Lit.: Schedelmann 1972, p. 50, ill. 93; Heer 1979, p. 1089

Since firearms began to emerge in the early fourteenth century, inventive gunmakers kept striving for technical perfection. With the creation of hand firearms with two, three, and four barrels for match-, wheel-, and flintlock firearms, the gunmakers fulfilled their patrons' desire for arms with multiple shots. Breechloaders, revolvers, and repeating weapons were further future developments. Toward the end of the sixteenth century, the first revolver systems for match-lock and wheel-lock firearms had already begun to appear.

In a certain way, the illustrated pistol represents the prototype of the modern cylinder revolver, though the mechanism still had to be worked by hand.

The cylinder, revolving around an axle attached to the underside of the barrel, is equipped with four chambers. A circular iron plate, firmly screwed to the axle, makes the chambers tight. The cylinder is engaged by a spring attached to the end of the barrel. While the spring's beak-shaped front end reaches into the bore located over the chambers, it is also positioned by the spring. Although four consecutive shots could be fired in relatively quick succession, the wheel spring needed to be spanned after every single shot, and the powder had to be placed onto the priming pan; this process delayed the firing speed. The stock of the pistol, which fits comfortably in the hand, is decorated with engraved bone inlays and shows birds, fabulous beasts, and flowers between tendril work. The Dresden Armory owns another wheel-lock revolver with six shots that follows the same construction. Another very decorative six-shot wheel-lock revolver, dated circa 1610 and originally owned by Emperor Matthias, is preserved in the Kunsthistorisches Museum in Vienna.
H-W.L.

37 Wheel-lock Pistol with Two Shots

Georg Geßler, the son of the gunsmith Elias Geßler, was born in Strasbourg in 1569 and came to Dresden in 1603. By 1606, he was already admitted to the Dresden guild of gunmakers—without producing a masterpiece and pursuant to the recommendation of Elector Christian II. In the same year, he was hired to be the master of the electoral firearms cabinet. His honorable court office required him to maintain and to conserve the guns and pistols kept in the various armory rooms located in the Stable Building.

The weapons Geßler made were primarily commissions of Electors Christian II and Johann Georg I or their family members. Preserved in the Dresden Armory, they are distinguished by their technical quality and their handsome artistic embellishment. The pistol is equipped with a pear-shaped pommel, characteristic of Dresden-made wheel-lock pistols. It is decorated with engraved bone inlays and gilt brass mounts. Although the pistol possesses only one barrel, two shots can be fired in quick succession. The barrel is equipped with two firing channels that permit the intake of two loads. In order to prevent an unwanted double explosion in the barrel, with terrible consequences, it was essential that for the initial shot only the front load be ignited. The touch hole at the front is therefore connected with the powder pan through a square and narrow firing channel mounted laterally on the barrel. The firing channel at the back can be closed with a sliding lid and terminates directly in the powder pan. To release the second shot, the sliding lid needed to be opened and the wheel cocked again.

H-W.L.

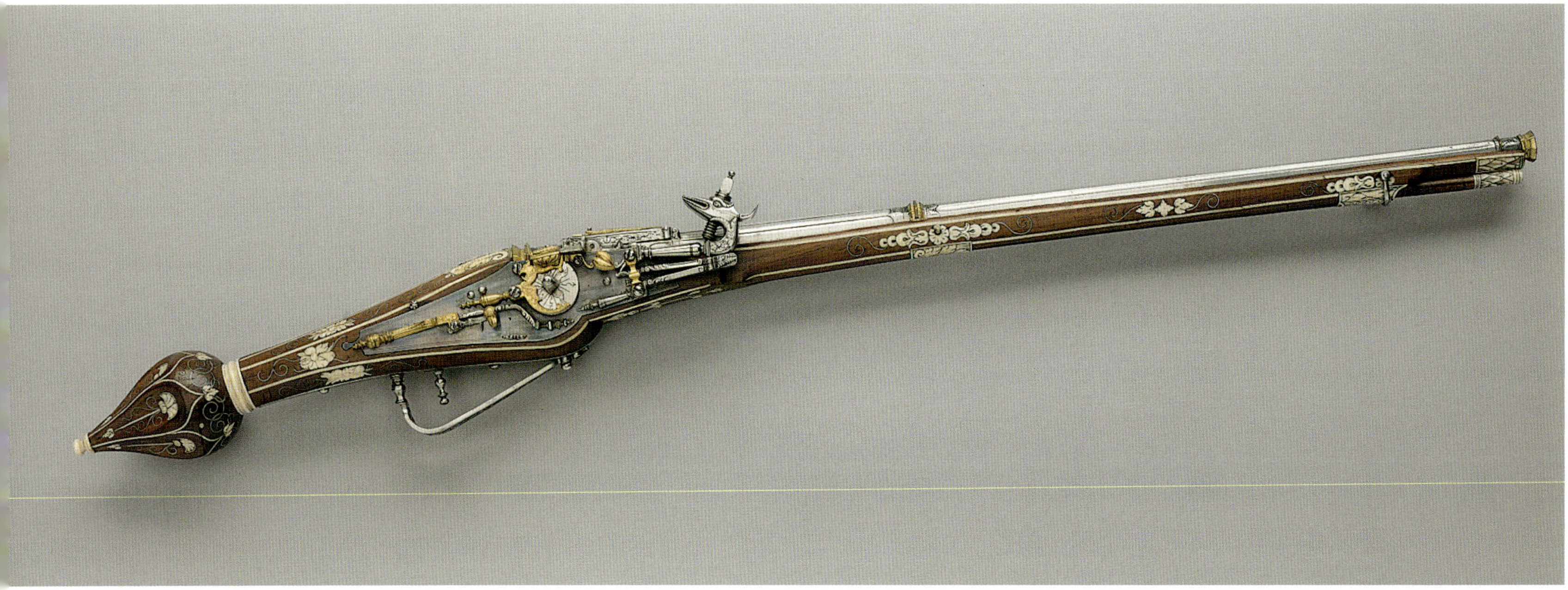

Georg Geßler
Dresden, circa 1610
Iron, engraved, partly pierced;
lock plate blued, brass, engraved, and gilt;
stock pear wood, bone inlays partly engraved
Total length 32¼ in. (82 cm), length of barrel 22 in. (56 cm), bore ½ in. (9 mm), weight 3 lbs 2 oz (1,450)
Barrel signed: "GG"
Inventory of the Rifle Chamber of 1667, p. 114
Staatliche Kunstsammlungen Dresden, Rüstkammer, inv. no. J 363
Lit.: Schaal 1975, p. 40, cat. no. 119

38 Pair of Pistols

Hans Stockmann
Dresden, circa 1610
Iron, partly blued, etched, and engraved; plates in brass, gilt, partly cast, pierced, and engraved; stock walnut, bone inlays, partly engraved
Total length 30¾ in. (78 cm), length of barrel 20½ in. (52 cm), bore ⅝ in. (12 mm), weight 4 lbs (1,800 g)
Barrel signed: "H.S."
Inventory of the Rifle Chamber of 1667, p. 114
Staatliche Kunstsammlungen Dresden, Rüstkammer, inv. no. J283/J284
Lit.: Ehrenthal 1899, p. 134, F 349; Schaal 1975, p. 46, p. 50, cat. no. 145/146; Heer 1979, p. 1225

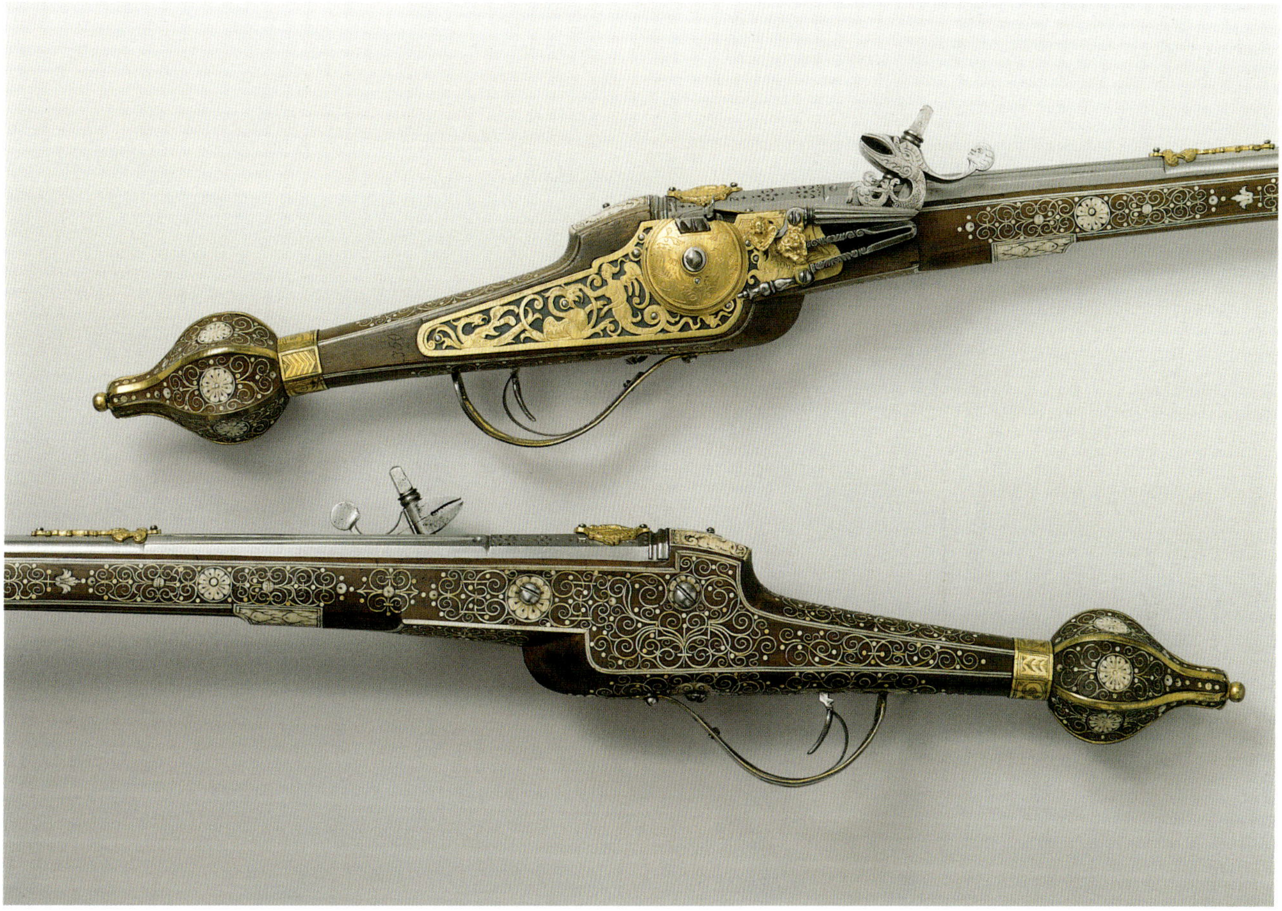

In 1590, Hans Stockmann, whose oeuvre is the most comprehensive of all Dresden gunmakers, delivered the first *Schrotflinte* (shotgun) in the Rifle Chamber. From the year 1600, he was working as gunmaker in the arsenal. Without fabricating a masterpiece and at the command of Elector Christian, he was admitted to the Dresden gunmakers' guild as guild master in 1603. It was not until 1605 that he became a Dresden citizen and purchased a house on the Große Frauengasse. The 1667 inventory of the Rifle Chamber lists 197 hand firearms by Stockmann, of which the Armory presently preserves eleven rifles and 111 pistols. Based on the large number of weapons produced in series—the so-called pear-pommel pistols produced expressly for the electoral civil guards—Hans Stockmann became relatively wealthy. Apart from weapons for the civil guards, he also fabricated exquisite guns and pistols (*Radschlosspistolen*) such as this pair. The barrels with multiple flutings are made of brightly polished iron; their front halves are circular, the rear halves octagonal. Their muzzle rings are of gilt brass. Mounts of relief-cast gilt brass are set onto the center of the barrels and over the chambers, the latter representing an ancient warrior. The locks with their flat, blued lock plate are also decorated with pierced, gilt brass mounts engraved with tendrils and fabulous beasts. Further elements of the locks include the external wheel with a gilt brass pan cover, an engraved cock made of bright iron, and the little head of an angel in gilt brass that serves as press button release for the pan cover. The flat iron trigger guard is pierced; a spring is located behind the trigger. Spiraling inlays, dots, engraved rosettes, and narrow stripes in bone decorate the stock with its faceted pear-shaped pommel. The pommels are further accentuated by an engraved brass sleeve at the end of the stock as well as by strips of brass outlining its facets. H-W.L.

39 Pair of Wheel-lock Pistols

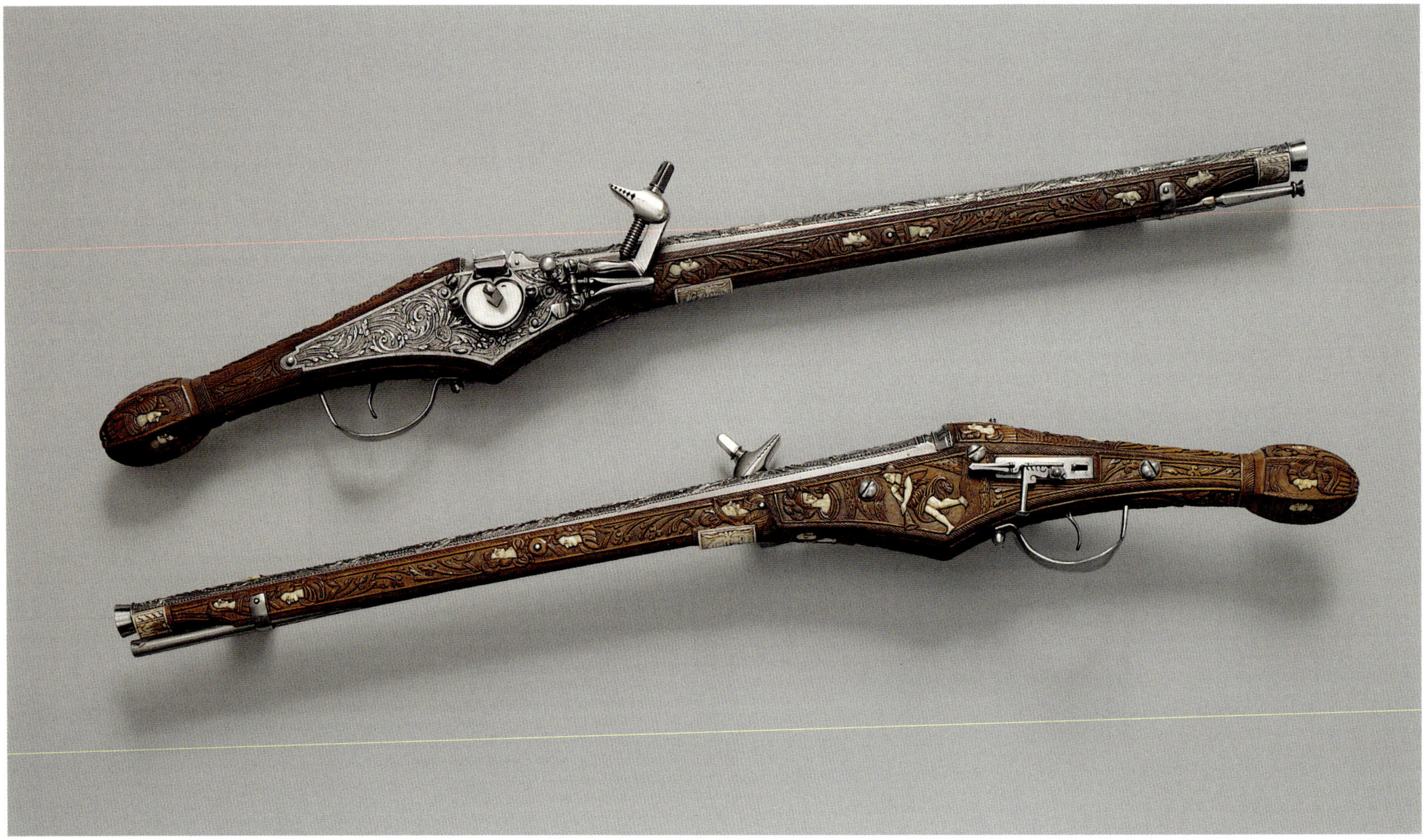

The city of Suhl, located on the southern slopes of the Thuringian Forest, was for centuries the center of German weapons production. This was where vast quantities of hand firearms were fabricated, predominantly for military usage but also for civilian purposes. Thanks to their superior artistic and technical qualities, numerous Suhl rifles and pistols were acquired by princely and other noble armories.

This slender long-barreled pair of pistols belongs to the outstanding seventeenth-century Suhl production. They are distinguished by the refinement of their barrels and locks as well as the masterful execution of their carved stocks. The richly decorated barrels show raised birds and figural representations on punched ground between the foliated tendrils. Full figures of Jesus, St. Peter, Jacob, and a bishop, displaying their attributes and their richly draped garments, are framed by a decorative border. Inscribed bands at their feet reveal their names: IEHSVS, S. PETRVS, and S. IACOBVS. The bishop is distinguished by his miter and crosier.

The bright steel locks with their external wheel—kept in place by a circular bridel—sliding pan cover, press button, and slightly rounded cock are worked with the greatest precision. A safety catch is attached to the lock's counterside. The lockplates are chiseled in relief with foliated tendrils on a punched ground. The deeply carved stocks, accentuated by profiled edges, are populated by groups of full figures and heads of men and women, and they are framed by foliated tendrils. The faces and the body parts are worked in ivory. The slightly flat, ovoid pommels, faceted into six segments, are likewise adorned with male and female faces in profile.
H-W.L.

Maker "WH"
Suhl, circa 1615
Iron, chiseled; stock from wood of an apple tree, richly carved, ivory and bone inlays engraved
Total length 29½ in. (75 cm), barrel 20⅛ in. (51 cm), bore ⅝ in. (12 mm), weight 3 lbs 9 oz (1,770 g)
Barrel and lock plate signed: "WH" over a star
Inventory of the Rifle Chamber of 1617, p. 28
Staatliche Kunstsammlungen Dresden, Rüstkammer, inv. no. J 274, J 275
Lit.: Ehrenthal 1899, p. 122, F 97; Schaal 1979, p. 27, cat. nos. 9, 10; Schaal 1981, p. 83, cat. no. 18

40 Wheel-lock Rifle

In the year 1611, Georg Geßler made this rifle as a commission of the electress's mother, Sophie, who presented it to Elector Christian II as a gift. The most striking feature of this intricately decorated rifle is the decorative mounts of pierced brass, characteristic of Dresden products in those days.

The blued-iron dark background forms an effective contrast with the mounts. The rifle's barrel, divided into numerous differently designed segments, is of phenomenal quality. The cannon-shaped muzzle protrudes from a dragon's head. Then follows a scale-patterned section with decorative rings. The posterior half of the barrel is decorated with sturdy flutings, which are alternately blued and gilt. A gilt dragon's flappable wings serve as a rearsight. The lock, with exterior wheel, sliding pan cover, and engraved iron cock, is embellished with gilt and partly pierced brass mounts. The square shank (a wind-up device) is located not in the wheel's center, as is customarily the case, but off to the side. Due to their transmission ratio, the two differently sized cog-wheels on the inside of the lock cause a quarter of a turn of the square shank to result in one complete turn of the wheel. This feature shortened the cocking process considerably. The rifle has a trigger-guard shaped to the fingers and a hair trigger.

The stock with profiled edges in bone shows hares, foxes, stags, and an elephant between tendrils. On the butt cheek, a medallion encloses a hunter in contemporary dress who leads a strong hunting dog on a long leash that reaches all the way to the butt's neck.
H-W.L.

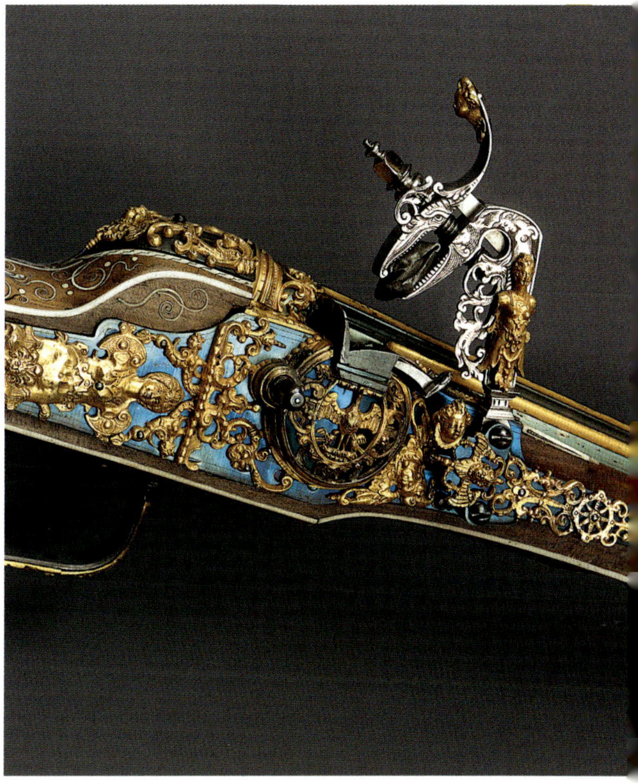

Georg Geßler
Dresden, 1611
Iron, blued, gilt, partly engraved; mounts brass cast, partly pierced, chased, and gilt; stock wood, bone inlays, engraved, blackened at the ground

Total length 44¼ in. (112.5 cm), barrel 33⅝ in. (85.5 cm), bore ½ in. (11 mm), weight 7 lbs 2 oz (3,290 g)
Barrel signed: "GG" and dated: 1611
Inventory of the Rifle Chamber of 1667, p. 66

Staatliche Kunstsammlungen Dresden, Rüstkammer, inv. no. G 237
Lit.: Ehrenthal 1900, p. 23, no. 237; Schöbel 1973, p. 163, ill. 139; Schaal 1975, p. 40, cat. no. 120

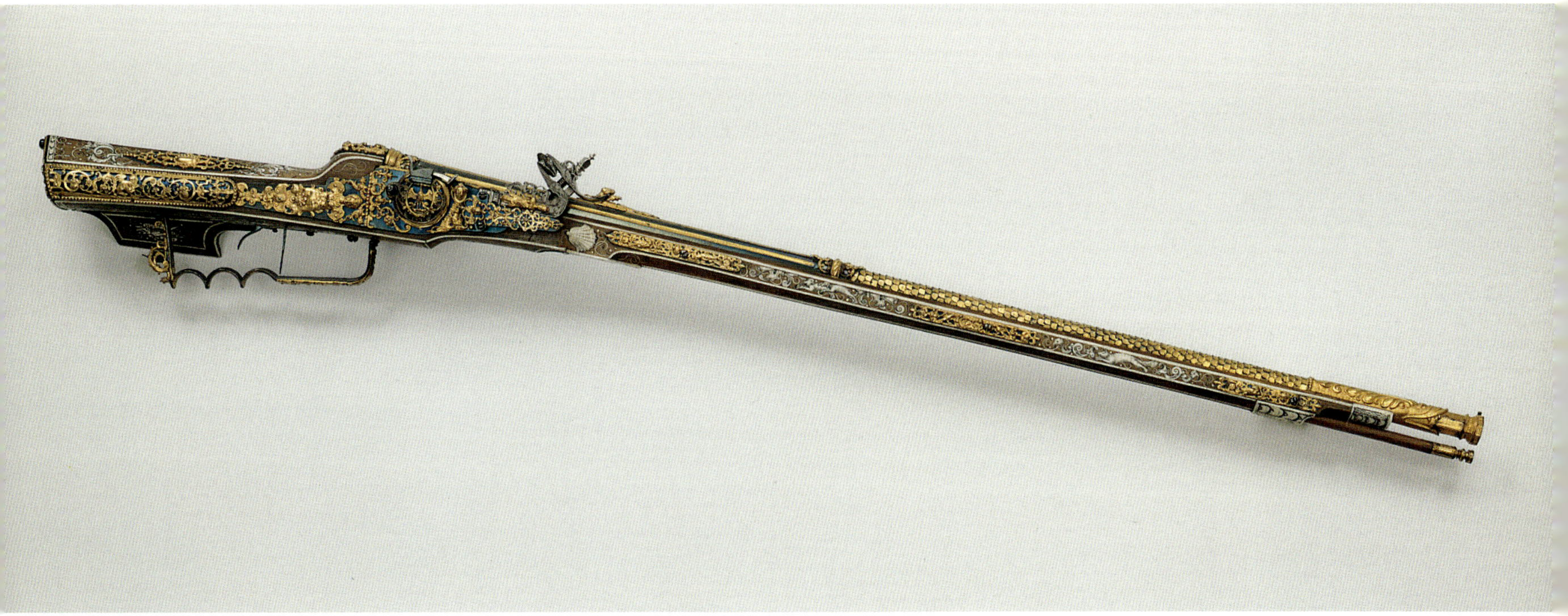

41 Wheel-lock Rifle

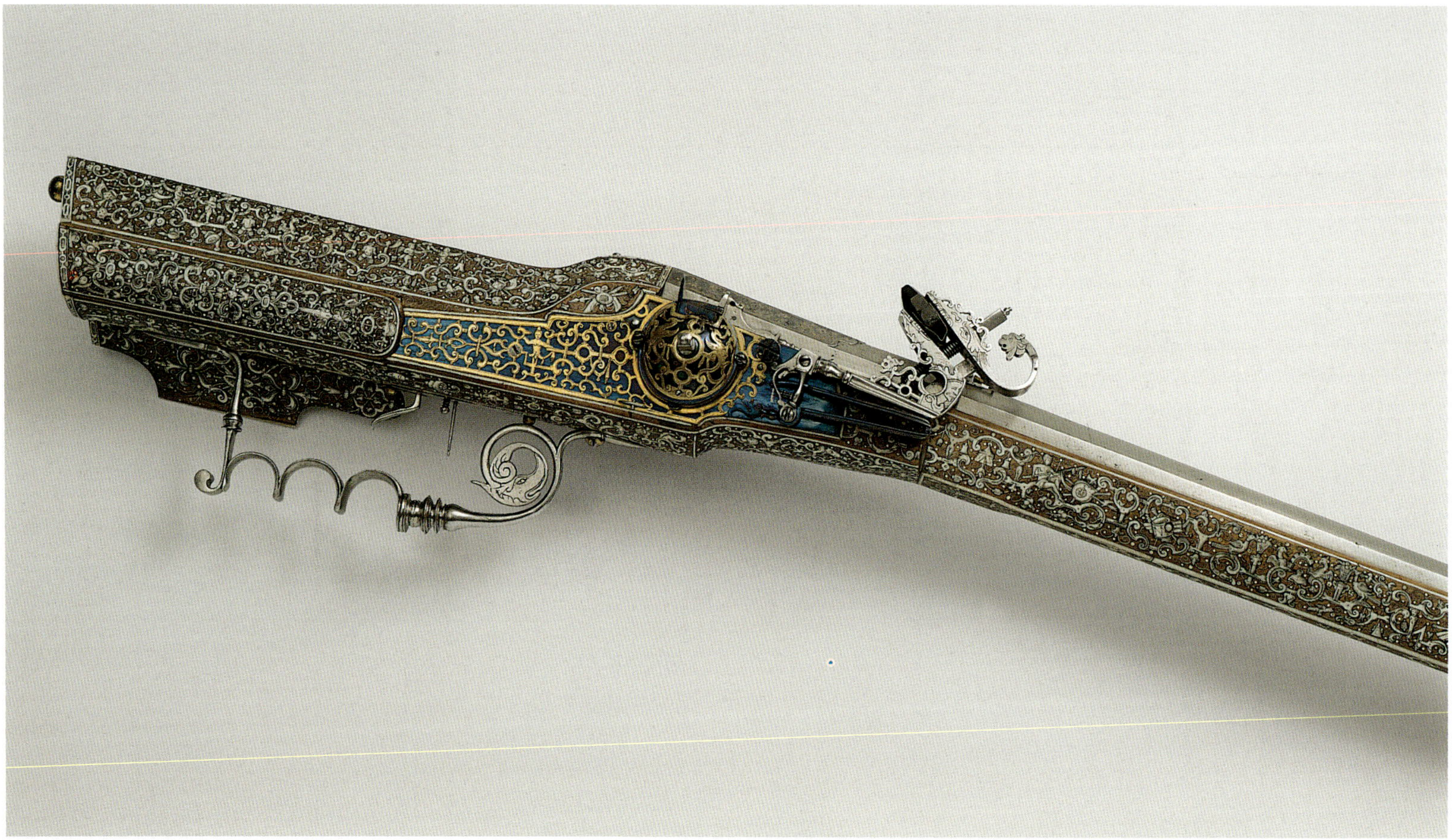

Marx Götersdorfer
Linz, 1601
Stock: Elias Leckner
Bright and partly blued iron,
gilt and gold-damascened;
brass plaques pierced, gilt;
stock walnut, bone inlays, engraved
Total length 45⅝ in. (116 cm),
barrel 34¼ in. (87 cm), bore ¾ in.
(16 mm), weight 10 lbs 2 oz (4,640 g)
Barrel signed: "MARX
GÖTERSDORFER LINNZ 1601,"
stock signed: "EL"
Inventory of the Rifle Chamber
of 1667, p. 59, no. 135
Staatliche Kunstsammlungen Dresden,
Rüstkammer, inv. no. G 228
Lit.: Ehrenthal 1900, p. 23, no. 228;
Hayward 1968, p. 222, no. 58;
Schöbel 1973, p. 160, no. 117

It is not documented whether the young elector Christian II purchased this rifle in 1601, the year he ascended to the throne, or whether he received it as the gift of Emperor Rudolf II, who resided in Prague. According to an undated inventory list of the Imperial Kunstkammer that also entailed the holdings of the Prague Armory, there were fifty-seven hunting and target rifles by German and Austrian gunmakers, whose stocks were decorated with luxurious ivory and bone inlays. Because of the amicable relationship between the courts of the emperor and electoral Saxony, it can be surmised that this rifle, fabricated by the Linz-based gunmaker Marx Götersdorfer, came to Dresden as a present of the emperor. Its shiny octagonal barrel reveals gold-damascened tendrils and flowers in the areas of the breech, the center of the barrel, and the muzzle. All lock parts are blued except for the bright engraved cock and the pan cover. The lock plate and wheel-cover bear decoratively pierced, gilt brass mounts. The rifle is equipped with an adjustable rear sight, a foresight, and a hair-trigger. The trigger-guard is shaped to the fingers and scrolls at the front where it is engraved with an animal head. The stock, made by Elias Leckner and entirely covered by a delicate network of engraved bone inlays, is distinguished by the outstanding quality of its decoration. Located between the finely grained scrollwork are occasional masks, grotesques, fabulous beasts, trophies of arms, birds, snails, and butterflies, as well as fruit baskets and figural representations. The butt cheek displays a cartouche with the electoral Saxon coat of arms and the inscription VIRTVTIS SAXON: DECVS ET ASYLVM.
H-W.L.

42 Battle-ax with Wheel-lock Firearm

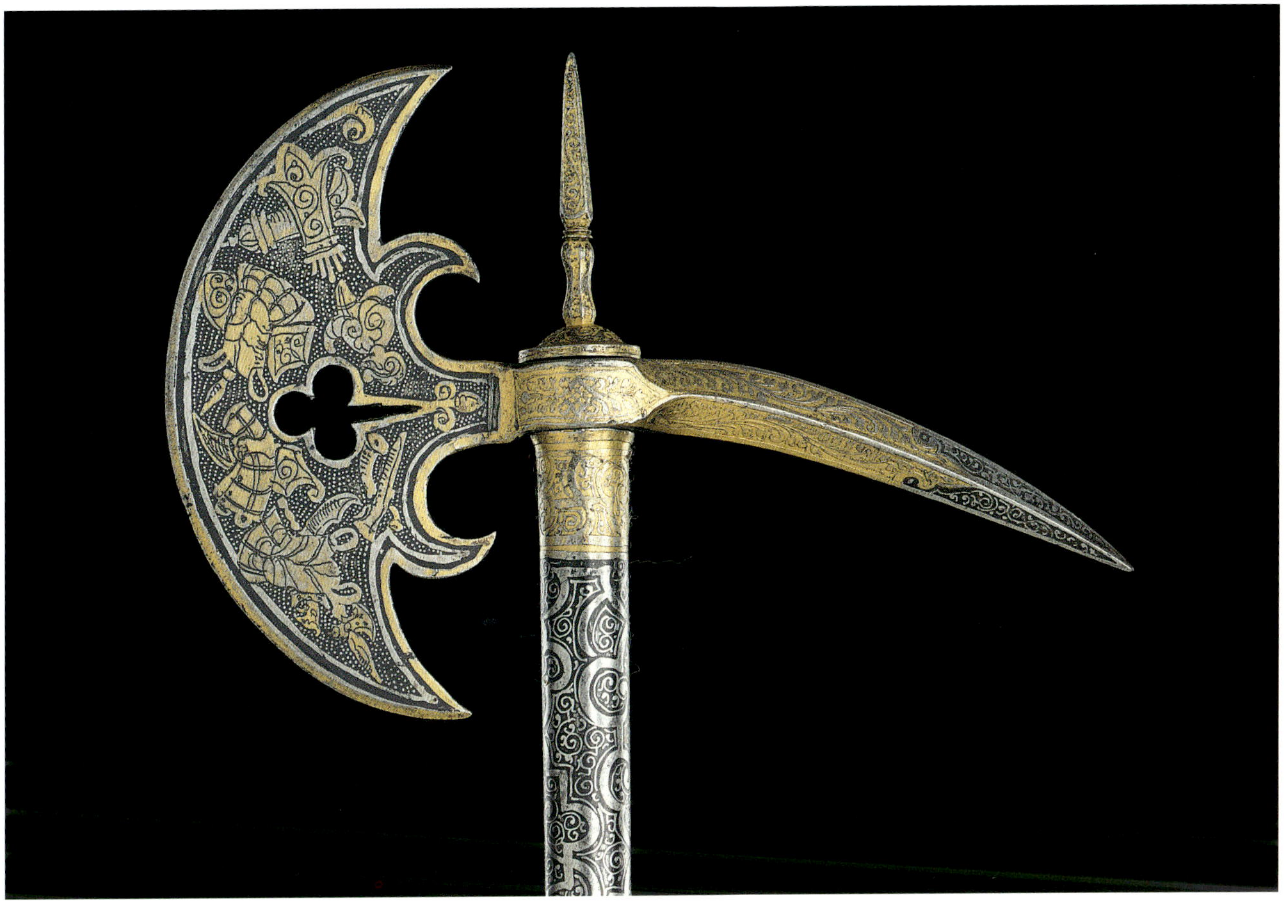

Augsburg, circa 1580
Iron, etched, blackened, and partly gilt; handle wrapped with twisted iron and brass wire
L. 24 in. (61 cm), barrel 16⅛ in. (41 cm), bore 4¾ in. (12 cm), weight 2 lbs 7 oz (1,210 g)
Barrel marked: pinecone (Augsburg view mark)
Inventory of the Turkish Chamber of 1674, no. 100
Staatliche Kunstsammlungen Dresden, Rüstkammer, inv. no. T 78
Lit.: Ehrenthal 1899, p. 101, E 627 u. E 635; Müller/Kölling 1981, no. 312, ill. p. 276; Lewerken 1989, p. 211, cat. no. 9

At the end of the fourteenth century, the first combination weapons began to be produced. Their purpose is to combine the advantages associated with the various different arms types into one hand weapon in order to increase efficiency. With the introduction of the wheel lock in the early sixteenth century, it was primarily the firearm that was combined with other weapon types such as the mace, battle-ax, and edged weapons such as swords, daggers, and long-staff weapons. The artistically decorated, often technically interesting combination weapons were frequently princely commissions that came to aristocratic Kunstkammers or armories as much-desired collector's items.

All the parts of this battle-ax, entirely made from iron, are richly decorated. Its hollow stock also serves as barrel. The ax blade with a trefoil-shaped opening is etched and partly gilt on both sides with arms and trophies on black dotted ground.

The square-sectioned fluke (spike) curves toward the handle and is etched with tendrils on the black ground at its tip and tendrils in gold etching the rest of its length. The barrel muzzle is closed by a cover that bears a pyramidal spike. The grip, fitted with a domed guard, is wrapped with twisted iron and brass wire. The spherical pommel consists of two halves and opens under pressure induced by the spring. The hollow handle accommodates a four-part iron ramrod. The wheel lock, decorated with arabesques in black etching technique, is attached laterally to the shaft. Its exterior wheel has a blued wheel-cover with applied gilt copper ornament. The cock bridle, safety catch, trigger-guard, and belt hook, attached to the opposite side, are gilt.
H-W.L.

43 Battle-ax with Wheel-lock Firearm

All parts of this heavy weapon—except for the polished ax edge and tips of the hammer—are lavishly decorated with delicate scrollwork in gold and silver damascening. The ax is fitted to a tapering columnar shaft and is balanced by a four-pronged hammer. The complicated wheel-lock mechanism is accommodated in an almost ideal way in the compact cylindrical box in front of the grip. The sturdy, hollow shaft forms the barrel, so that the combination of two weapon types is not immediately apparent. The mechanism for cocking and releasing is fundamentally different from the basic type of wheel lock. The functional parts were carefully put together with great precision and based on a well-thought-out principle. Particularly interesting is the lock mechanism with a main spiral spring. Even if in simplified form, this same principle had already been used by Leonardo da Vinci, who, among other pursuits, occupied himself with issues of warfare and fortification. Leonardo was also the author of the earliest images of wheel-lock mechanisms. Among the sketches and designs of technical gadgets and tools of war contained in the Codex Atlanticus (Biblioteca Ambrosiana, Milan) are two drawings dating between 1500 and 1505 depicting wheel-lock mechanisms. Since they are not connected with weapons, they likely served to produce sparks and were hence part of a lighter Leonardo had conceived.
H-W.L.

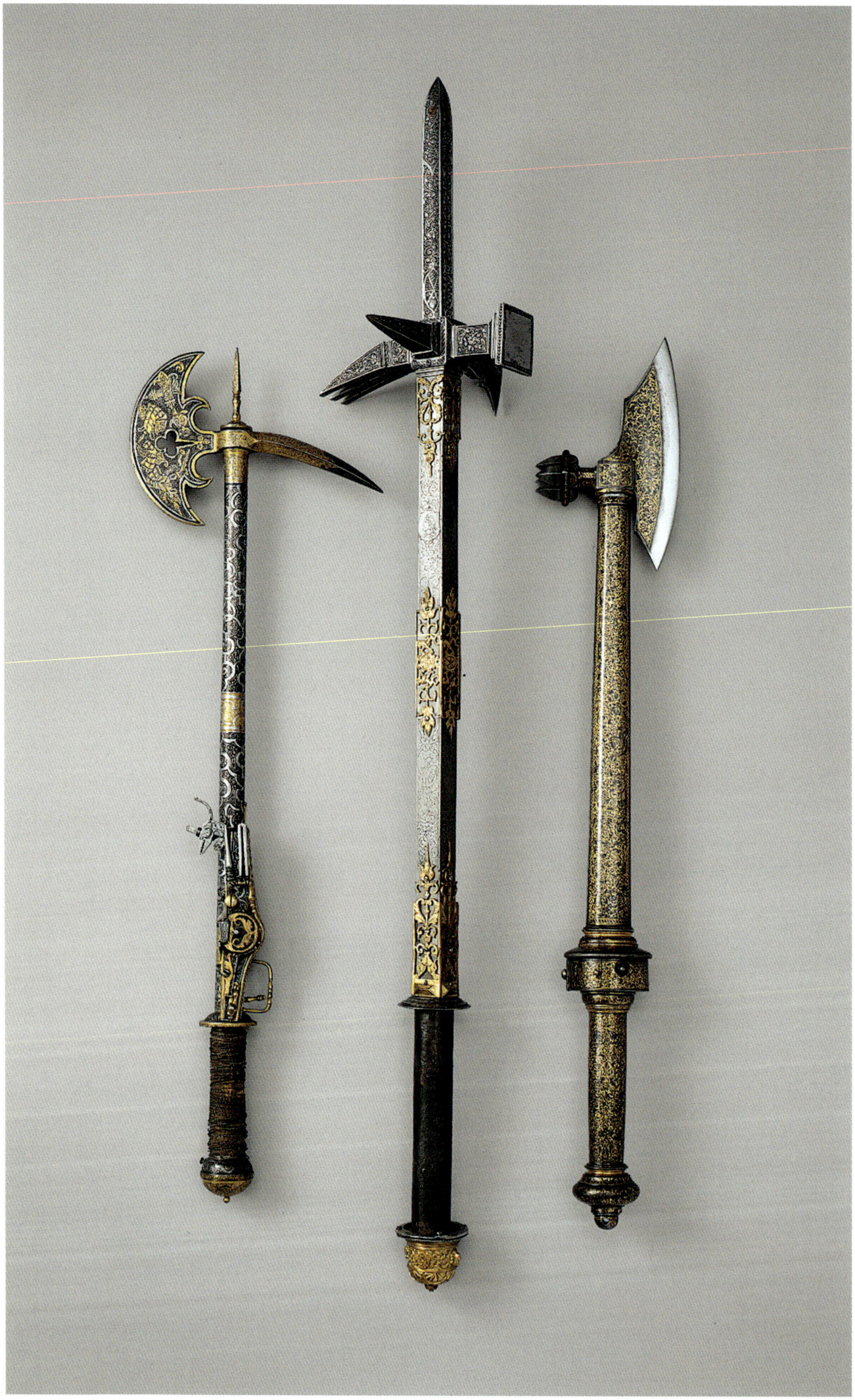

Presumably French, mid-16th century
Iron, blued, gold and silver damascened
L. 25¼ in. (64 cm), barrel 15 in. (38 cm),
bore 4½ in. (11.5 cm), weight 5 lbs 1 oz (2,320 g)
Inventory of the Armory of 1606, p. 974
Staatliche Kunstsammlungen Dresden, Rüstkammer, inv. no. T 75
Lit.: Ehrenthal 1899, p. 101, E 622; Koetschau 1905, p. 117; Haenel 1923, p. 146, plate 72 c; Schöbel 1973, p. 164, no. 145a; Lewerken 1989, pp. 208f., cat. no. 4

44 War Hammer with Thrusting Blade

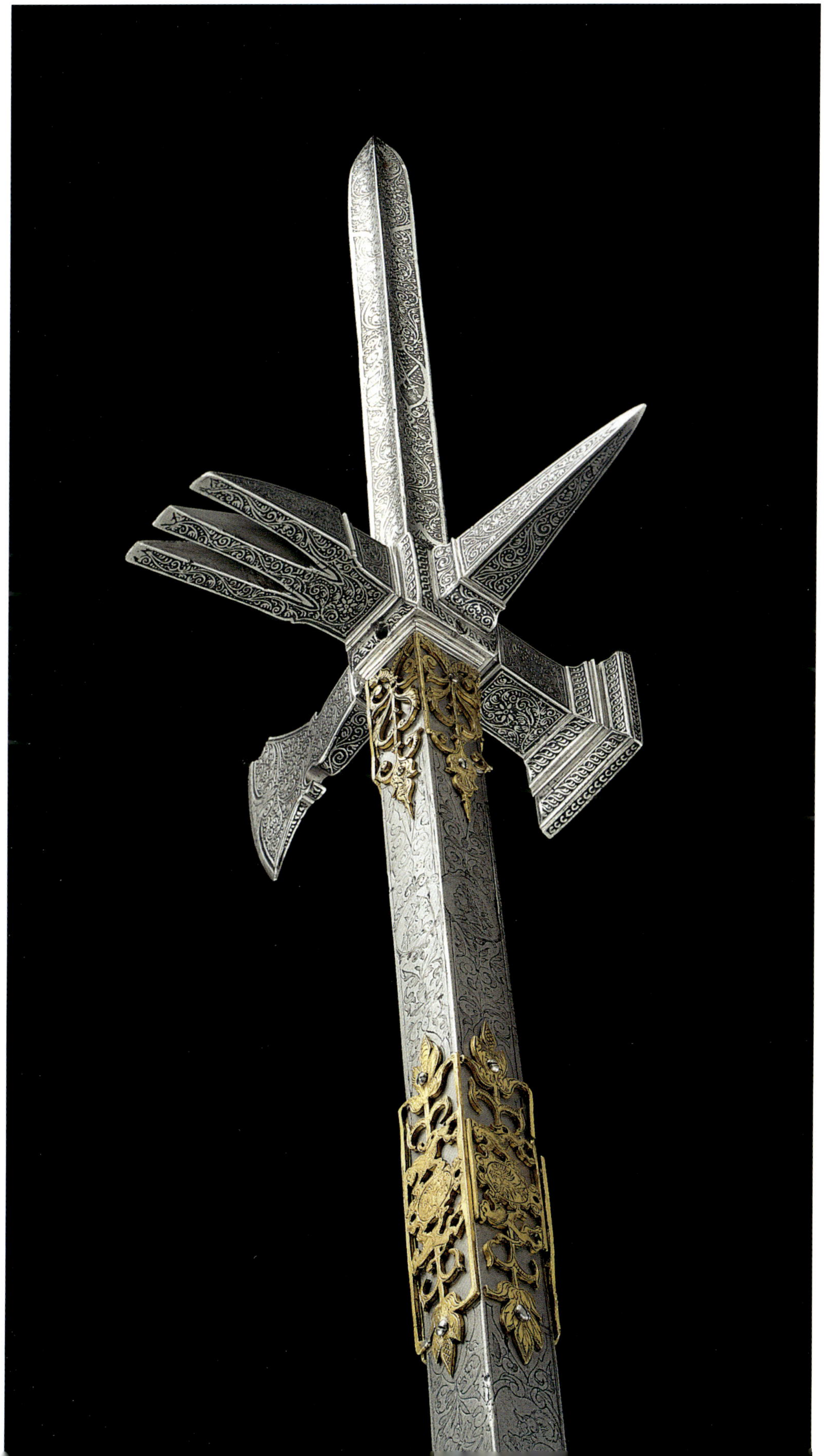

Although hardly suited for practical usage, the war hammer with retractable thrusting blade is an interesting combination of weapon and tool. The heavy object, entirely worked in iron, possesses a robust, four-sided hammer head, consisting of an ax, a pyramidal spike, a nail iron, and a hammer. A stout four-sided thrusting blade is located in the hollow shaft. It can be retracted by turning the pommel, so that the weapon can also be utilized as a tool. The hammer head and the thrusting blade are exquisitely decorated with finely etched foliate scrolls on black ground. In its hollow cut, the thrusting blade bears the electoral as well as the ducal Saxon coats of arms. The shaft is adorned with engraved scrolls and foliage, trophies, and warriors' heads, as well as pierced mounts in cast and gilt brass. The latter include, in the center of the shaft, the coats of arms of the duchy of Saxony and of electoral Saxony supported by lions. The detailed description of the weapon in the inventory of the Armory of 1606, mentioning the master's name and the purchase price of thirty taler, as well as noting the day this object was transferred to the Hungarian Chamber by the stable master Nicol von Miltitz (July 1, 1593), permit us to conclude that even when it was procured, this unique weapon was already considered a cabinet piece.
H-W.L.

Balthasar Hacker
Dresden, 1593
Iron, etched and engraved
Mounts cast brass, gilt
Total length 37⅜ in. (95 cm), L. with sunken blade 27⅛ in. (69 cm), weight 5 lbs 5 oz (2,460 g)
Inventory of the Armory of 1606, p. 975
Staatliche Kunstsammlungen Dresden, Rüstkammer, inv. no. T 66
Lit.: Ehrenthal 1899, p. 164, G 156;
Haenel 1923, p. 144, plate 71c;
Lewerken 1989, p. 286, cat. no. 181

45 Rapier with Spring-Loaded Blade and Concealed Dagger

This unusual weapon fascinates because of its rich artistic embellishment and its complex mechanism. The rapier, in whose hollow grip a dagger is housed, possesses a moveable blade. While it can be moved back into the hollow handle, on its narrow sides the ricasso takes the shape of a rack. Two spring boxes, mounted between quillons and a lower side ring, are each equipped with a cog that reaches into the bore of the ricasso. When the blade is pushed back into the handle, the springs are wound around the core of the rotating cog-wheel; they are thus cocked. An engaging device, screwed to the back side of the spring boxes and equipped with a trigger, fixes the cocked blade. When the trigger is being used, the blade suddenly thrusts forward an additional seven inches (18 cm).

The dagger housed in the rapier's hilt has a diamond-section blade. It has a small shell guard with short folding quillons that expand when it is removed. The grip consists of a sturdy spiral spring that gets cocked when moved into the rapier's hilt. When the engaging device is released, the dagger emerges about one inch out of the rapier's handle, when it can be pulled out by hand.

The Armory owns a second elaborately decorated mechanical rapier of this type. Because of its considerable weight, these rapiers were not really suitable for single combat. However, they offered the advantage that due to the unexpected release of the blade, the distance to the opponent was suddenly considerably shorter; this could be beneficial from a tactical point of view. Despite the possibility of a practical application, this is primarily an expensive display weapon, in keeping with other fascinating Kunstkammer pieces.
H-W.L.

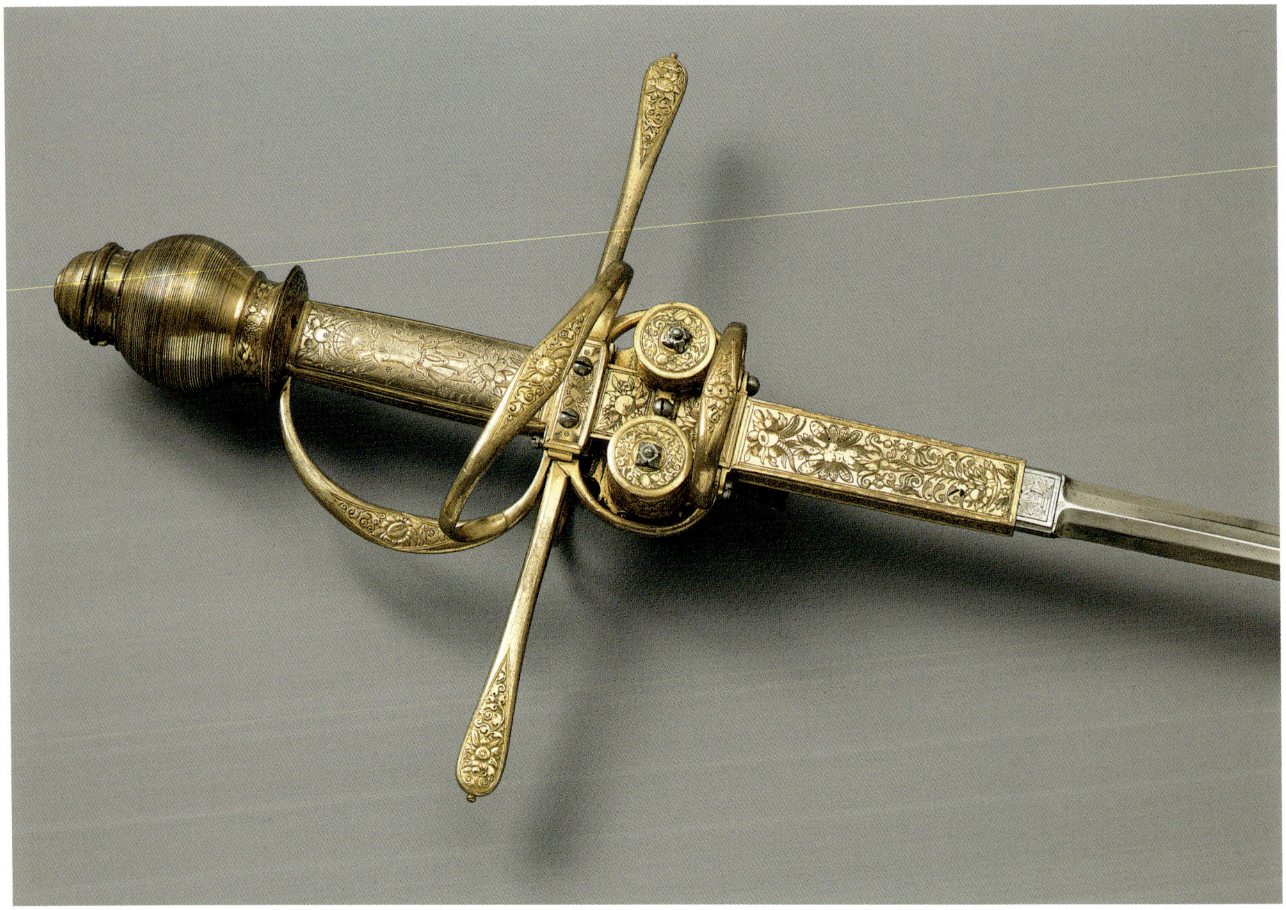

South German, circa 1570
Blade, polished iron, partly engraved
Hilt, brass, cast, chiseled, engraved and gilt
Blade, brass, cast, engraved, and gilt
Rapier: total length 63¾ in. (162 cm), blade 52 in. (132 cm), total weight with dagger 5 lbs 3 oz (2,400 g)
Dagger: total length 13¾ in. (35 cm), blade 10⅝ in. (27 cm)
Ricasso of the blade with unclear mark
Inventory of the Electoral Chamber of 1671, p. 138, no. 298
Armory, inv. no. VI 410
Lit.: Ehrenthal 1899, p. 164, G 158; Schöbel 1973, p. 95, ill. 91; Lewerken 1989, p. 266f., cat. no. 138; Washington 1978

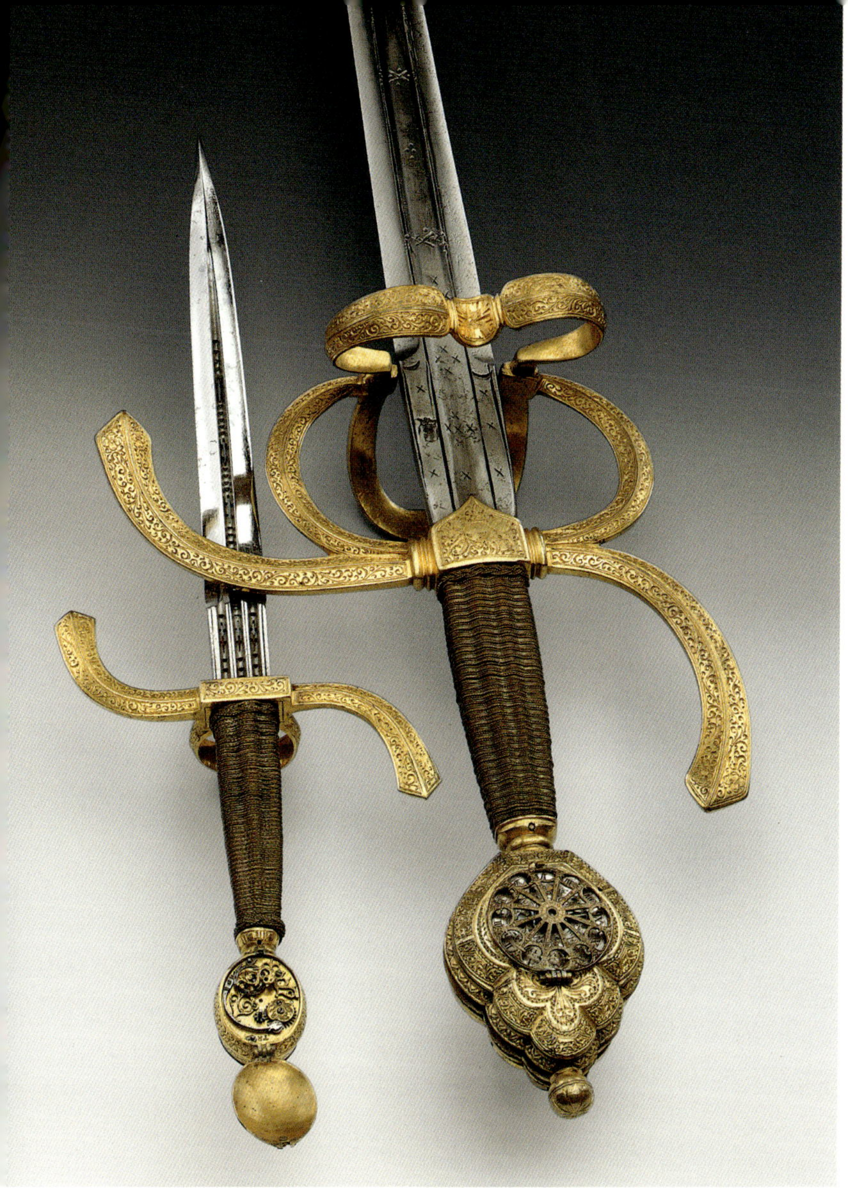

46 Rapier with Watch in the Pommel

Dresden, 1610
Watch: Tobias Reichel, Dresden
Blade, iron, hilt, brass, cast, engraved, and gilt; handle, wood, wrapped with gilt copper wire
L. 43¾ in. (111 cm)
Blade 37 in. (94 cm), Weight 2 lbs 2 oz (1,020 g)
Watch marked: TR (mark of Tobias Reichel)
Inventory of the Electoral Chamber of 1671, p. 141f.
Armory, inv. no. VI 434
Lit.: Ehrenthal 1899, p. 108, E 690; Haenel 1923, p. 108, plate 59; Lewerken 1989, p. 286f., cat. no. 182a/b; Meisterwerke 1992, p. 84f., plate 29; Washington 1978, p. 120, no. 157

In 1610, Elector Christian II of Saxony received this rapier and a dagger (cat. no. 47) as a Christmas gift from his brother Duke Johann Georg (I). The pommel of this precious and extraordinary rapier is furnished with a watch. It has a robust blade, in whose upper third so-called *Weihekreuze* (consecration crosses) are struck on both sides. All parts of the cast and gilt-brass hilt are engraved with fine scrollwork. The guard consists of S-shaped quillons with arms of the hilt and a side-loop below. On the inner side is a small loop counterguard. The vertically profiled wooden grip is wrapped with gilt-copper wire, with braided "Turks" heads at each end. The hour-striking watch with a blued-steel hand is encased in the pinecone-shaped pommel. The full hour is indicated by the striking of a small dolphin-shaped hammer on a flat bell. The silver dial has two chapter rings protected by a hinged lid with pierced decoration, with Roman and Arabic numerals from I to XII and 13 to 24. The placement of the openings in the cover over the numerals on the dial is such that when the cover is closed the hand can be seen only at the full hour. On the back plate of the movement is struck the mark of the Dresden court clockmaker Tobias Reichel. The rear lid is pierced with tendril decoration and thus offers an opening for the sound to emanate.
H-W.L.

47 Dagger with Watch in the Pommel

Dresden, 1610
Watch: Tobias Reichel, Dresden
Blade, iron, partly pierced; hilt, brass, cast, engraved, and gilt; handle, wood, wrapped with gilt copper wire; sheath, wood, covered with black leather; gilt-brass mounts engraved
L. 12⅜ in. (31.5 cm), blade 7⅞ in. (20 cm), weight 7 oz (200 grams)
Watch marked: "TR" (mark of Tobias Reichel), blade signed on the narrow sides of the ricasso: WB
Inventory of the Electoral Chamber of 1671, p. 141f.
Armory, inv. no. p 222
Lit.: Ehrenthal 1899, p. 108, E 690; Haenel 1923, p. 108, plate 59; Lewerken 1989, p. 286f., cat. no. 182a/b; Meisterwerk 1992, p. 84 f., plate 29; Washington 1978

Forming a set with the rapier (cat. no. 46), this dagger has a blade with a rhombic cross section. Its central gutter, reaching almost to the tip, and similar channels in the ricasso are decoratively pierced. The watch, with its brass-gilt dial, is marked with the Roman numerals I to XII and has a blued-steel hour hand. The oval watch forms the pommel. The spring of the watch is regulated by a stackfreed. The punch mark TR of Tobias Reichel is struck on the watch's back plate. Back and front of the watch are each protected by a domed, hinged lid, decorated with engraved tendrils and birds.

Rapier and dagger, commissions of Duke Johann Georg (I), document the close cooperation between different crafts that was elsewhere sometimes obstructed because of guild rules. Such "state commissions" offered the craftsmen multiple opportunities to show their artistic abilities. This is how, thanks to the cooperation of clockmaker, blade and goldsmith, engraver, and hiltmaker, exclusive and unique weapons were created. There is no doubt that the union of weapons and watches belongs to the most extravagant variation within the field of combination arms. These pieces underscore the lively interest Elector Christian II took in combined weapons, clocks and watches, automata, and measuring devices. Tobias Reichel produced numerous precious clocks, watches, and automata for him.
H-W.L.

48 Powder Flask with Sundial and Magnetic Compass

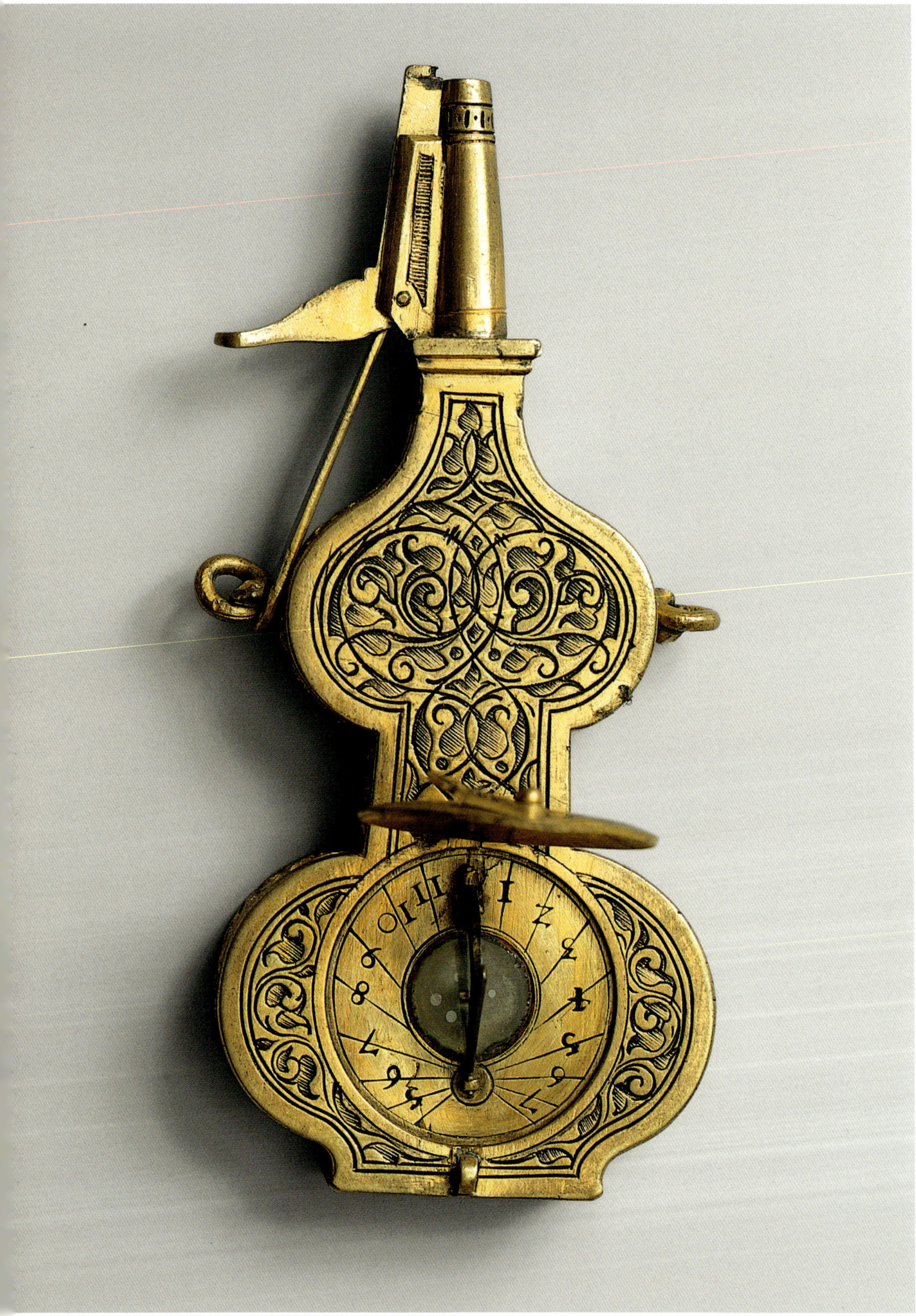

In the sixteenth and seventeenth centuries, the centers for the production of precious and complicated clocks and watches, scientific instruments, and automata were Nuremberg, Munich, and especially Augsburg. The clock, watch, and instrument makers of these cities delivered their innovative and costly products to princely courts in Central Europe as well as to affluent bourgeois patrons. Made in South Germany for a princely huntsman, this combination instrument of powder flask and sundial can be utilized in multiple ways. Its gilt-brass case with conic nozzle and two suspension loops is engraved on both sides with fine scrolls and arabesques. The front side is decorated with the head of a warrior with helmet, the back with a half length portrait of a woman within a medallion. The little circular horizontal sundial with folding style is protected by a hinged lid with a catch hook. In its center, a small compass enables its owner to orient the sundial. The sundial is calibrated for the hours from 5 A.M. to 8 P.M. identified in Arabic numerals.
H-W.L.

South German, circa 1550
Brass, fire gilded
H. 4⅜ in. (11 cm), W. 2 in.
(5 cm), weight 4 oz (110 g).
Armory, inv. no. X 1258
Lit.: Lewerken 1989, p. 140,
p. 288, cat. no. 183

49 Powder Flask with Watch

Back and front of this particularly precious ivory powder flask with built-in watch are adorned with hunting scenes full of Baroque pathos. The front shows a hunter on horseback who shoots a lion with his gun. Another hunter accompanied by his dogs attacks the lion with a pike. A boar hunt is depicted on the back. The sides of the powder flask are overlaid with a brass band with pierced tendril work, to which four suspension loops are attached to receive the braided strap. The conical nozzle on a square spout is furnished with a snap closure with blued-steel spring.

The oval watch can be opened; it strikes of the hour on a bell. Its dial is protected by a hinged lid with an engraved hunting scene. The front of the hinged lid shows the scene of a stag hunt, the reverse side of the watch reveals a boar hunt. The applied silver chapter ring is marked with the Roman numerals I to XII for the hours and there is an arrow-shaped brass hand. The watch is furnished with a stackfreed to equalize the force of the spring as it unwinds. There are circular holes in the side of the watch case to let out the sound of the bell. The pierced back of the case is decorated with a wolf hunt. A similar powder flask with a built-in watch by the Augsburg clockmaker Andreas Stahl is preserved in the Green Vault.
H-W.L.

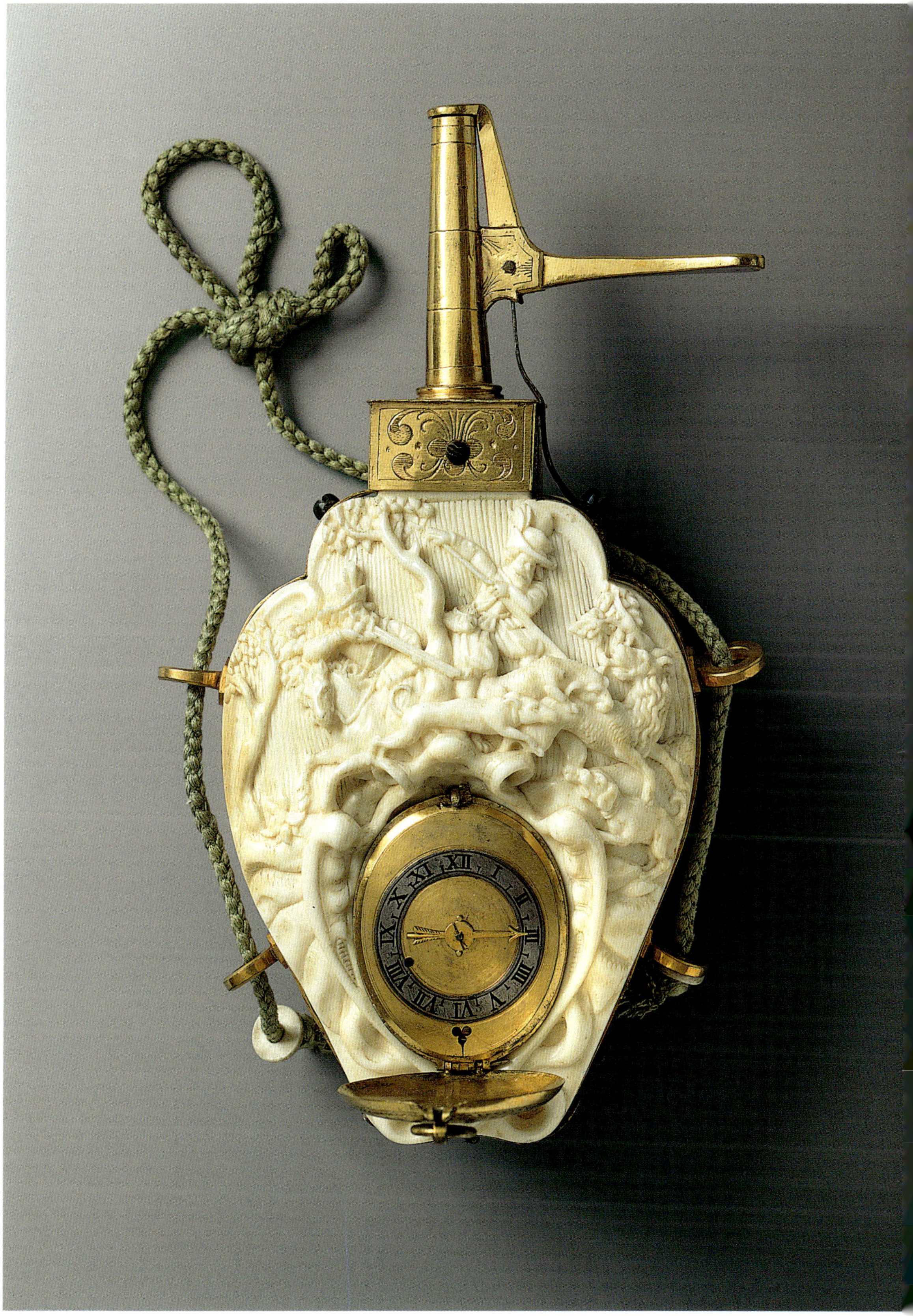

Augsburg, circa 1620
Powder flask, ivory, carved;
mount, brass, fire gilded;
snap closure with blued-steel spring;
plaited strap; watch, brass, fire gilded
H. 8⅞ in. (22.5 cm), W. 4⅜ in.
(11 cm), weight 1 lb 8 oz (800 g)
Armory, inv. no. X 1255
Lit.: Schöbel 1973, p. 177, ill. 116;
Lewerken 1989, p. 288, cat. no. 184

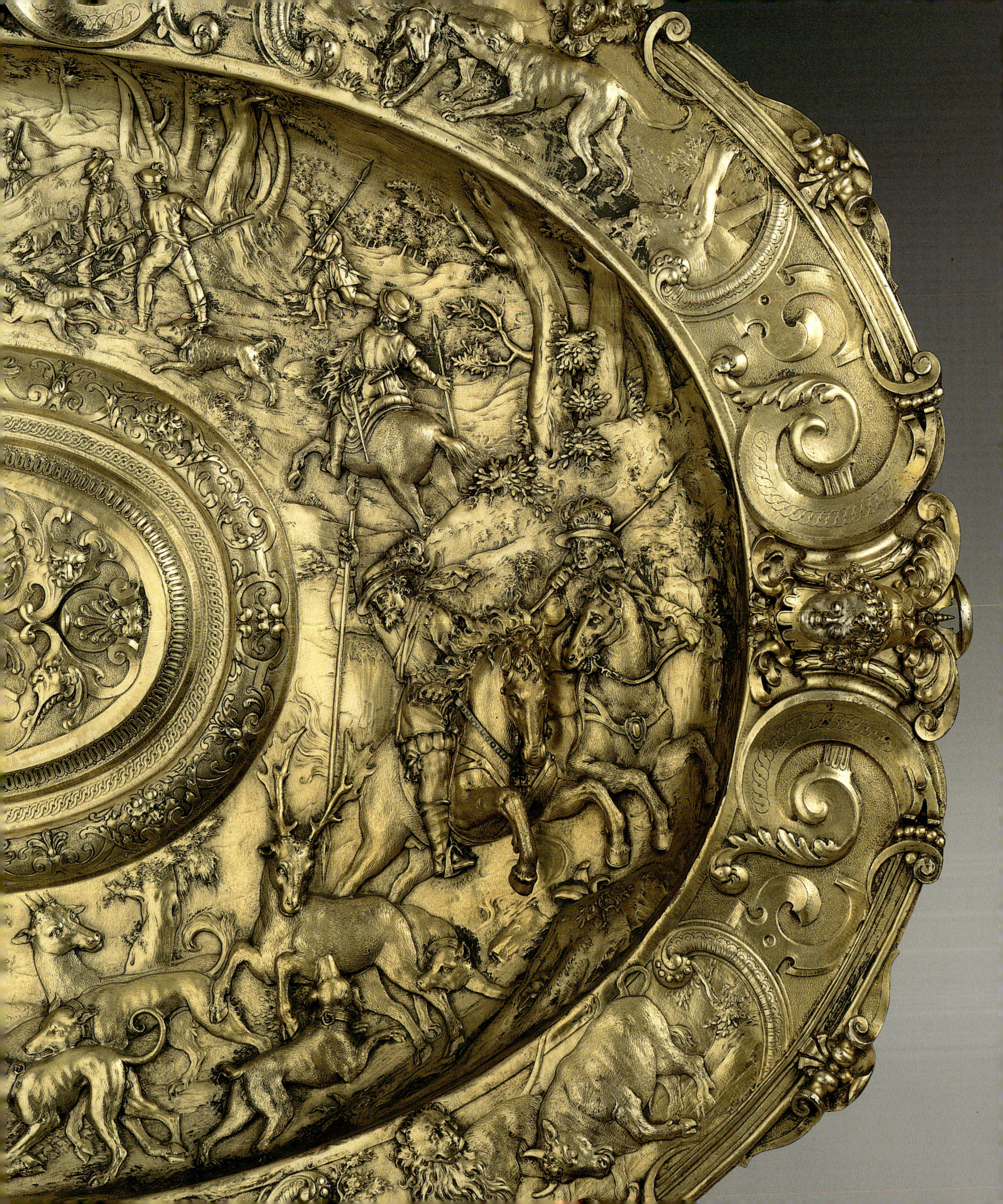

Kunstkammer and Treasury

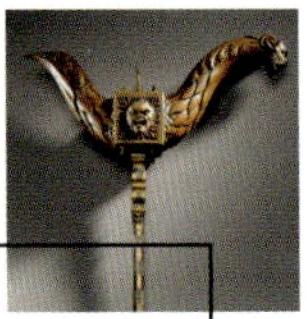

Electoral Tools and Gardening Implements

Jutta Bäumel

The exhibited tools for various trades and gardening implements originate from the personal collection of Elector August. While this concise selection is a symbolic representation of the initial holdings, amounting to hundreds of similar items, it also documents how practical the orientation of the Dresden Kunstkammer was during its early years. Thanks to its highly professional, specialized workshops for processing wood and metal, it enabled the elector to explore and further develop horticultural interests. Whereas some of Elector August's interest in exploration and exploitation of domestic resources were motivated by his desire to stimulate growth and administrative efficiency, the sovereign's curiosity was also fired by his extraordinary personal commitment and his Protestant work ethic. The 1587 Kunstkammer inventory reveals August's interest in iron breaching tools (Mauerbrechzeug) related primarily to military needs. The consequences of the progress artillery made during the sixteenth century included the need for ever stronger fortifications of cities and castles. The lifting tools and breaching screws served to destroy iron lattices and supposedly invincible fortification walls. The latter posed the greatest challenge to the craftsmen specializing in wrought iron. As inventions that ultimately served economic ends, breaching tools, winches to construct mines and wells, printing presses, and tools for minting were manufactured. The success of Leonhard Danner's workshop in Nuremberg was the result of the requirements of the time. Elector August was an extraordinary customer who knew how to stimulate Danner's talents and put them to work. The elector assured the continuity of this mutually beneficial connection after the death of Danner by appointing numerous craftsmen originating from the Danner workshop to his court, among them Paul Buchner and Balthasar Hacker. Buchner was a specialist in fortification work, artillery, and tools, as well as ironsmith's work. Leonhard Danner's key work is the wire-drawing bench he made for Elector August (today in the Musée de la Renaissance, Écouen, ill. p. 57), listed in the 1587 Kunstkammer inventory as "draw bench with all the respective pulls for silver and gold wire" (*ziehebanck sambt derselben zugehörunge zum silbern vnd güldenen Drathziehenn*). Gold and silver wire were potential material for export as a product of silver mining. As decorative wire, they were applied to weapons, furniture, and containers. In spun thread, used in weaving, embroidery, and trimmings, it grew into a profitable trade in Saxony.

The practical value of tools was acknowledged by decorating them in an aesthetically pleasing manner. Embellishments included etched and figural depictions in metal (ill. p. 161), which sometimes were partly gilt. Bone inlay and artful lathe ornaments and carvings, partly in exotic woods and ivory, were used as well. The impressive harmony between utilitarian shape and artistic form inherent in these tools is owed not to the highly praised love for decoration but to the electoral commission. The direct relationship with the elector is underscored by the initials, the coat of arms, and inscriptions on the objects (see, for example, cat. no. 50). Elector August's distinct interest in craftsmanship and his own talents as a craftsman are further illustrated by surviving objects, such as vessels and figures that he turned himself (see ill. p. 178).[1] Of economic relevance were his activities addressing the improvement of mining and ironworks, as well as the application of mechanical arts. When he ordered the construction of a foundry near the Dresden Residential Palace, August himself drew the design for a smelting furnace. Iron was a much desired commodity and was always in short supply. The electoral iron reserves were stored in the Iron Chamber (Eisenkammer) and were therefore kept under special surveillance. Consequently, the value of the innumerable steel tools kept in the Kunstkammer is comparable to that of the silver vessels. The elector recorded some of his alchemical experiments in his Probierkünste; he was as interested in creating gold as he was concerned with the purity of other metals. Expenditures for the foundries led to exploration for more effective fuel, such as hard coal. Ultimately, Elector August put his own abilities as a craftsman and his knowledge of mechanics to use in surveying. With the help of a newly invented measuring vehicle, he took notes and drew maps of his personal travels within the electorate and beyond. The postal and the trading routes were extended. It is fair to say that with his activities as a craftsman and his research Elector August not only pursued a personal passion but an entire economic agenda.

Saw Blade
Matthias Schwerdtfeger
Nuremberg 1564
detail from cat. no. 60
Armory, inv. no. P 244

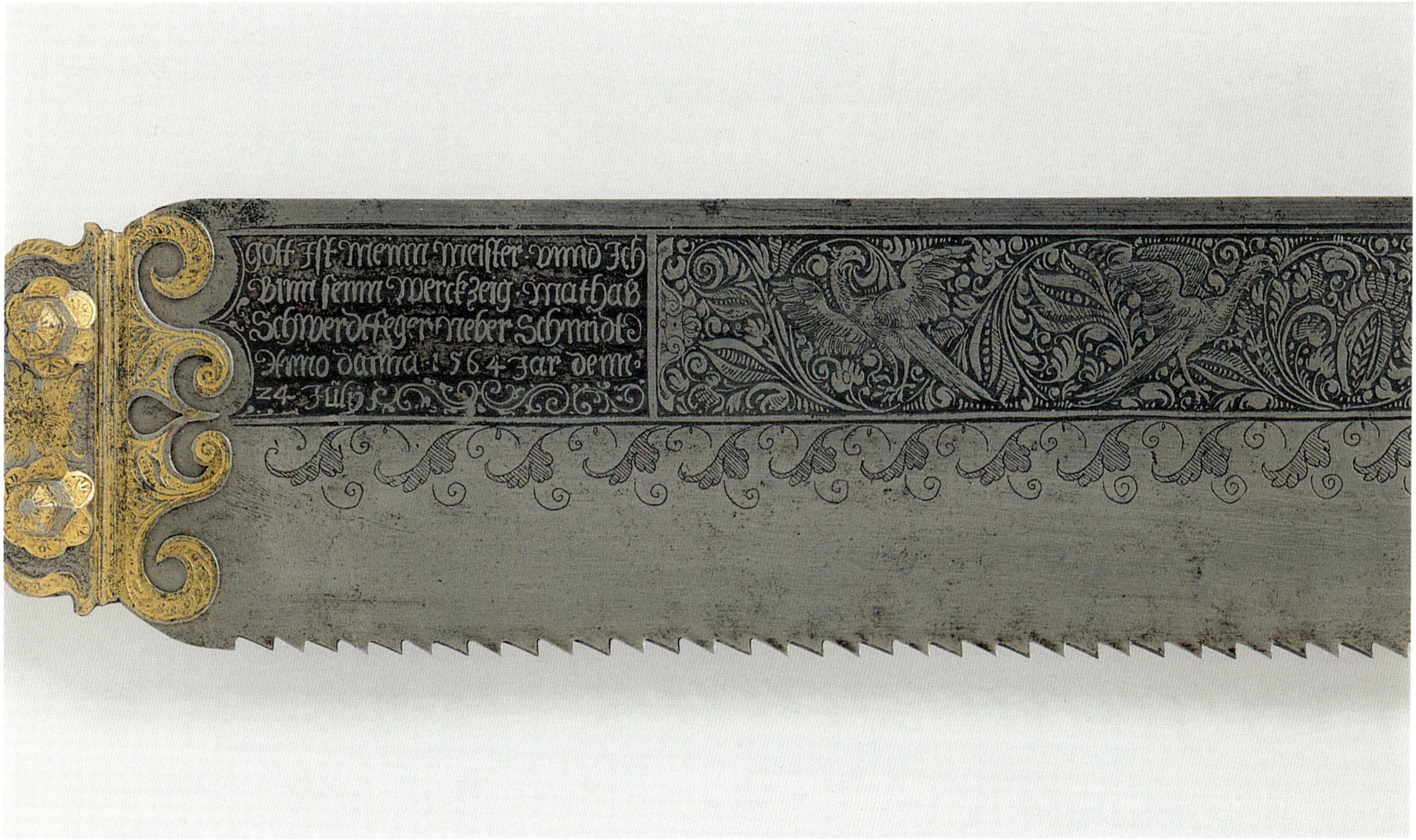

The documented nicknames "Father August" and "Mother Anna," for the electoral couple August and Anna, relate to their personal activities, such as farming, gardening, and medicinal arts, and are expressions of their general care for their country. A fundamental domestic motivation for progress did not originate from feudalist decrees, as they could be enforced in mining and forestry law where people were subjected to forced labor. Instead, the good example provided by the cultivation encouraged on the electoral landed estates (Kammergüter) resulted in improvements in the electorate's farm production. The activities included

1. See also the essay by Jutta Kappel on "The Art of Ivory Turning" in this volume.

intensive agriculture, cultivation of gardens, dairies, sheep farming, wine and hop agronomy, as well as fishing. On his estates, August responded harshly to "folly," "disloyalty," and "indolence" among the servants. In order to realize his goals, the elector used himself as a model, relied on the electress' support and his own comprehensive knowledge, practiced strict surveillance, and demanded high levels of discipline. The purchase of more farms—their number rose from forty-five in 1558 to seventy-two in 1578—meant not only an increase in personal revenue, but also had lasting effects on the way other estates were cultivated. At the time, the electoral library in Dresden owned all the important works about agriculture and horticulture published during the sixteenth century. The books contained instructions for the creation of utilitarian, pleasure, and herb gardens, which were indeed being laid out in numerous palaces in Saxony. For each month, the required chores are specified, and reference is made to the proper handling of gardening tools. August and Anna actively exchanged information with other princely courts in order to obtain or to pass along new plants, seeds, or dairy cattle. Among other results, new plants were cultivated, some after several attempts. Certain species initially came for ornamental purposes and eventually turned out to be important practical plants; the potato, for example, arrived in Saxony in 1591.

Title Page of the "Kreutterbuch"
Johannes Kenntmann, 1563
Pen and gouache
circa 18⅞ × 11⅜ in. (48 × 34 cm)
Sächsische Landesbibliothek,
Staats- und Universitätsbibliothek
Dresden, Mscr. Dresd. B 71

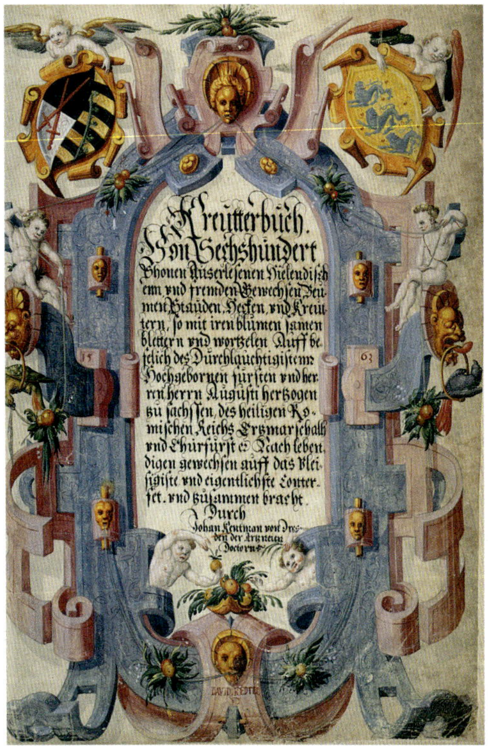

The gardening implements kept in the Kunstkammer were especially strong in the domain of fruit cultivation. Two tubular seeders preserved in the Armory sport the double monogram of the electoral couple, "AA," and have symbolic value. According to the entry in the Kunstkammer inventory, August used them himself to set seeds (cat. no. 59). Elector August recognized and supported the importance of grafting and exporting fruit trees as a potential source of revenue for the entire country. He was able to graft trees himself, ensuring the introduction of new and more plentiful species that would be more resistant to pests. The majority of young fruit trees were grown on model farms in Ostra near Dresden and in Stolpen; thousands of seedlings were either sold or passed on to the other electoral farms. In order to develop fruit cultivation on a large scale, August traded grain for the seeds from wild fruits, which would be the basis of fresh grafting attempts. The pits from the fruit born of the newly grafted fruit trees were stored as if they were art treasures, in a special vault. In 1563 Johannes Kenntmann, city physician (Stadtphysikus) in Torgau and one of the most important Saxon scholars, dedicated an herbal (Kreutterbuch) with six hundred color illustrations of trees, shrubs, bushes, and domestic and wild plants to Elector August (ill. left). In 1571 Andre Langer of Magdeburg wrote a garden manual (Gartten Ordtnung) along with an appendix about meadows and forests (von Wiesen undt Wäldern) for the elector. Finally, August himself wrote his own booklet based on his personal experiences with fruit cultivation, entitled *Künstliches Obst- und Gartenbüchlein*. Published in 1571, the book was reprinted several times. These publications offer insight into the diversity of fruit that was available—apple, pear, cherry, quince, fig, mirabelle, peach; and for the flower garden also almond, orange, and lemon. Instructions include how to spice fruit, how to make it smell good and how to make it red or even form faces in it.

When on the farms, Electress Anna was preoccupied with dairy products, made commercially viable in Saxony for export to her native Denmark. In addition she also initiated the creation of a court pharmacy. For her own experiments, she started her own herb garden and an herbarium, and she pursued the arts of healing and cooking. In 1563, Katharina Werner dedicated an herbal to her, with advice concerning pestilence, hepatitis, insomnia, cough, sore throat, and gynecological ailments. In later years, Anna wrote a book on gynecology herself. Her extensive correspondence demonstrates that her medical and also her cosmological counsel were sought by many princesses and princes, even by Emperor Maximilian II, who demanded the recipe for a poison antidote. The fact that the gardening tools of August and Anna—rare surviving examples from the sixteenth century—are preserved to this day is due to the special aura of the electoral couple and the lasting effect of their activities.[2]

2. About the electoral couple August and Anna's economic policy, see especially Falke 1868.

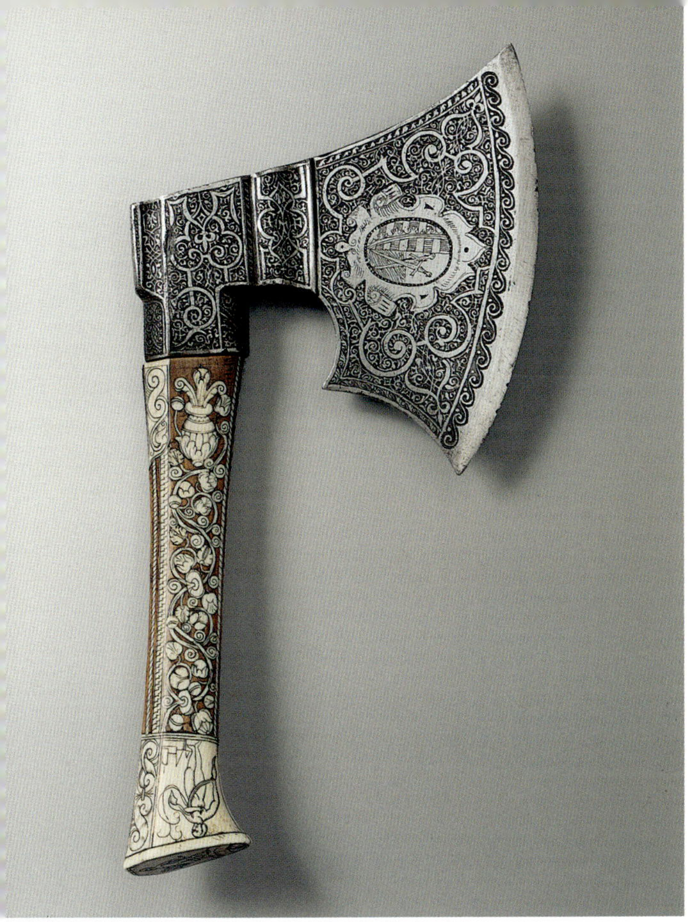

50 Ax

German, circa 1570–80
Blade: iron, etched, with blackened ground
Shaft: wood inlaid with bone, engraved, partly blackened
L. 11 in. (28 cm)
First mentioned in the Kunstkammer inventory, 1587, fol. 105 or 206.
Armory, inv. no. P 7
Lit.: Hager 1916, no. III 29; Bernt 1939, p. 138f., no. 139a/b

The blade of this ax displays the royal Danish and the electoral Saxon coats of arms of Anna and August. The entire surface is decorated, reminiscent of a parade weapon. On the engraved bone foot of the shaft the figure of Fortune can be seen. Hand axes are listed in the 1587 inventory of the Kunstkammer, where they appear with the tools belonging to the desk (see cat. no. 69): "*1 Geetzt klein Hundbeil mit einem beinernen Helm*" (one little hand hatchet with a "helmet" made of bone), as well as the gardening tools (see cat. no. 52). Hand axes are indispensable for grafting fruit trees, something Elector August did extensively. J.B.

51 Miner's Ax

Silver mining underwent a new boom in Saxony thanks to the modern technology Elector August introduced. As part of his campaign to promote economic growth, he led a masquerade procession in 1574. In the tournament, he appeared in the role of the god Mercury along with miners with their tools and mountain steps. This was the beginning of the great tradition of miners' processions in Saxony. Connected with this process was the elevation of the miner's ax to parade ax.
J.B.

German, circa 1570–80
Blade: iron, with punched marks
Shaft: wood, inlaid with bone, engraved, partly blackened
L. 37 in. (94 cm)
Marked: crossed hammer and mallet, different miners' marks
Armory, inv. no. P 14
(group ill. left)
Lit.: Unpublished

52 Ax

The ax's decoratively shaped, perforated and etched blade is covered with tendrils and birds. It is particularly useful for carpentry and gardening tasks. The royal Danish coat of arms on the blade refers to Electress Anna. The 1587 Kunstkammer inventory mentions long and short axes for gardening, setting, and grafting: "*10 Hacken und Beil mit kurtz vnd langen hundleen, geezt vnd vngeezt, vorbeint vnd vnverbeint*" (ten hoes and axes with long and short handles, etched and not etched, bone and not bone). The velvet cover on the shaft indicates that this was a parade item. J.B.

German, circa 1570–80
Blade: iron, perforated, etched, ground blackened
Shaft: wood; fragments of a black-brown silk velvet cover
L. 21¼ in. (54 cm)
First mentioned in the Kunstkammer inventory, 1587, fol. 206
Armory, inv. no. P 10 (group ill. right)
Lit.: Hager 1916, no. III 31, plate 163; Bernt 1939 , p. 140f., ill. 141/142

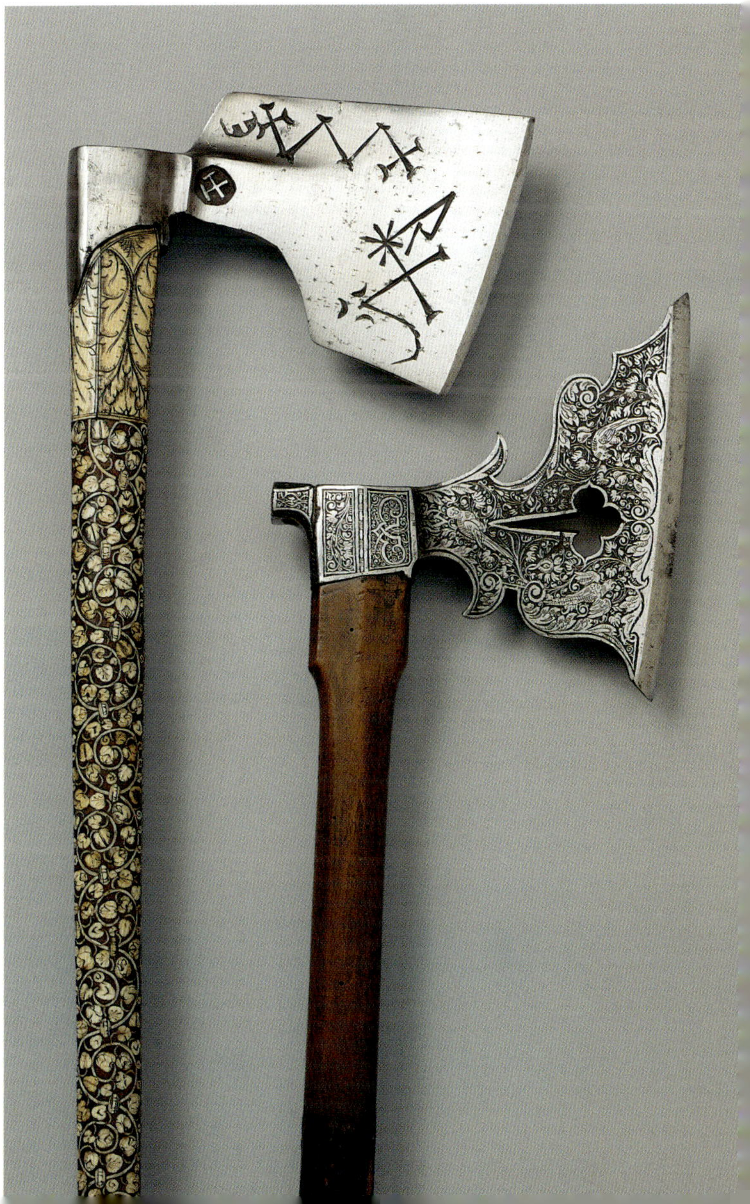

53 Spade

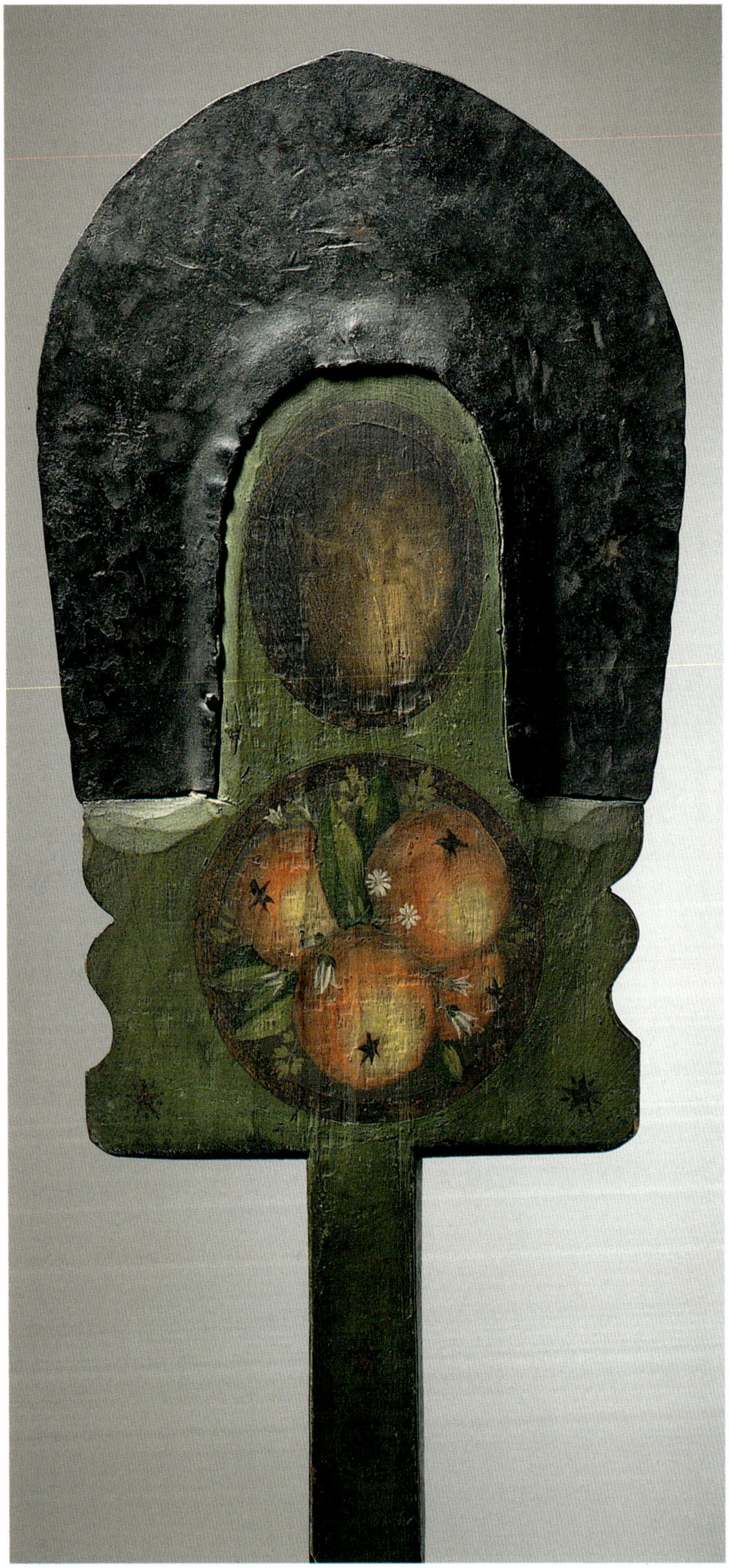

There are two spades preserved in the Armory that are painted with fruit and flowers on their wooden mounts. This specialty was also mentioned in the 1587 Kunstkammer inventory: "*2 Grün gemahlete beschlagene Spaten*" (two spades painted green with mounts). The decoration of these display pieces is a symbolic reference to a good harvest.
J.B.

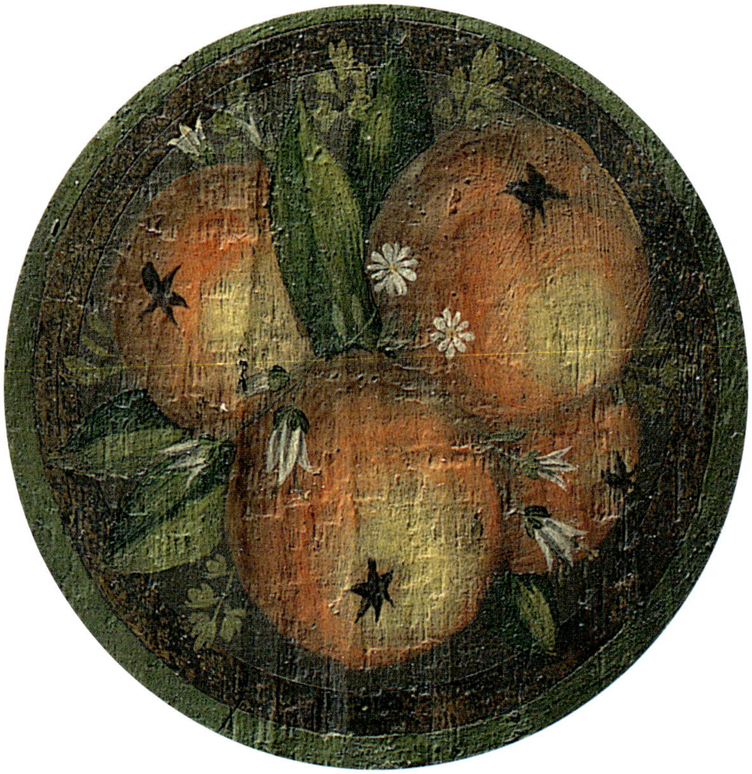

German, presumably Dresden, circa 1560–80
Iron, blackened
Handle: pear wood, painted
L. 49⅝ in. (126 cm)
First mentioned in the Kunstkammer inventory, 1597, fol. 207
Armory, inv. no. P 70
Lit.: Hager 1916, no. III 93 or III 94

54 Spade, Improved Dibble, Adz, Rake, and Common Dibble

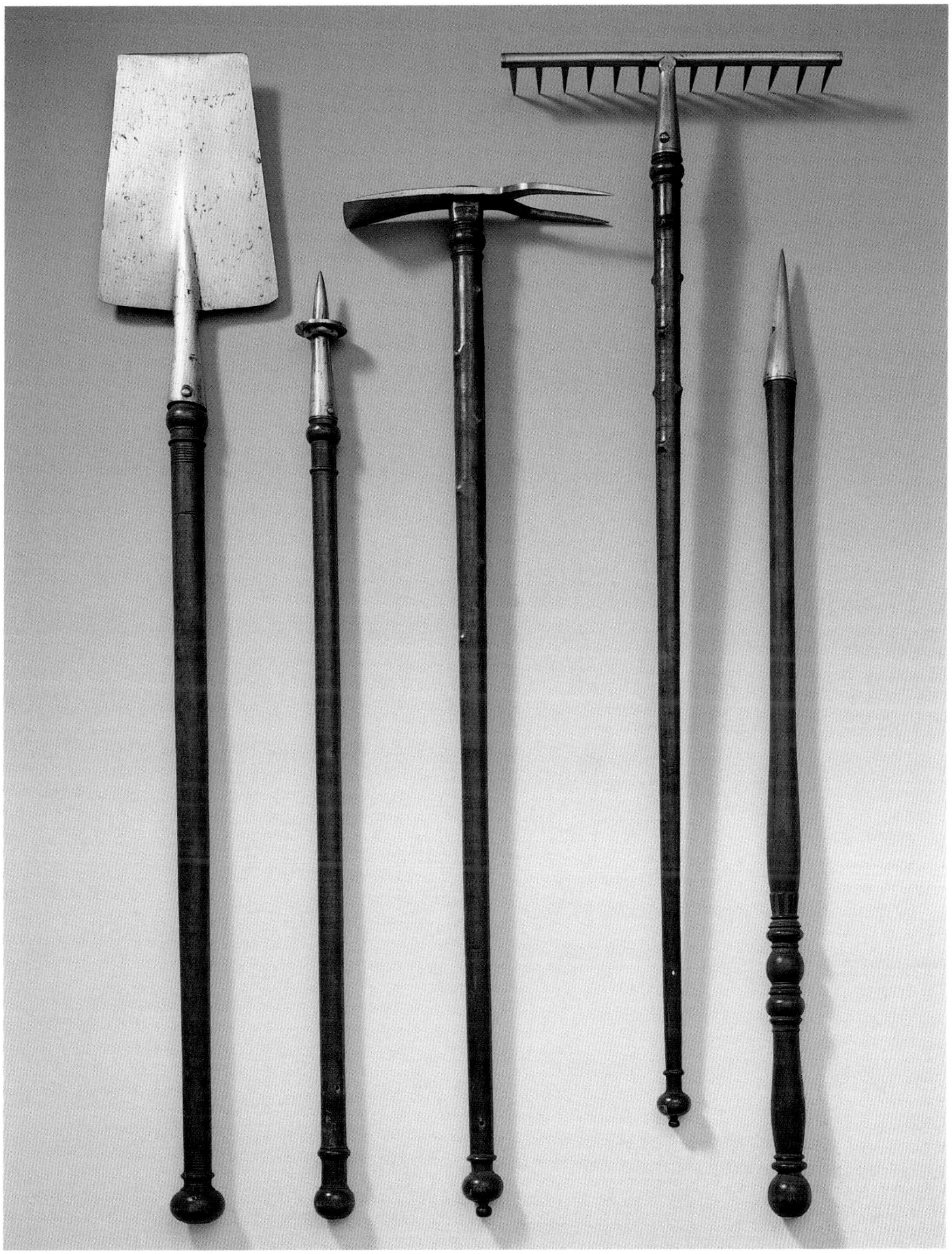

Numerous garden implements procured by Elector August are listed in the 1587 inventory of the Kunstkammer among the gardening, seeding, and grafting tools. Among them are four spades: "*4 Eiserne Polirte Spaten mit gedrehten hundleen*" (four shiny iron spades with turned handles"; three improved dibbles: "*3 Eisern stichel mit runden eißen Scheibleinn vnd gedröheten hefften zum Kernsezen*" (three iron dibbles with round iron disks and turned handles to plant seeds); ten hoes: "*10 Polirte Wein, kraut vnd Hoppe Hackenn mit gedröheten hundleen*" (ten polished adzes to work the vineyard, cabbage, and hops, with turned handles); four rakes: "*4 Eiserne Harcken mit roth gedröheten hundleen*" (four iron rakes with red, turned handles); and five dibbles: "*5 Eisern glette stichel mit gedröheten hundleen zum Kernsezen*" (five smooth iron dibbles with turned handles to plant seeds).

The spade's blade has a straight, sharp edge to work in hard soil with plenty of roots; it is also useful for cutting the edges of flower beds and paths. The improved dibble and the dibble are used to prepare holes for pits and seeds. The disk on the improved dibble determines how deeply the tool is inserted into the ground and assures a consistent depth for the holes. For the rake, it is relevant that the inventory mentions wine. Beginning with the rule of Elector August, the Saxon electors started to grow wine grapes in Dresden's Elbe Valley. There were numerous tools pertaining to wine cultivation in the Kunstkammer.

Since they were intended for princely use, the handles, as well as those of most of the other gardening tools, are artistically embellished fruit woods turned on the lathe.
J.B.

German, circa 1560–70
Iron polished, with hands of pear wood, turned on the lathe, partly carved; rake with thirteen riveted teeth
Spade: L. 49⅜ in. (125.5 cm)
Improved dibble: L. 40⅜ in. (102.5 cm)
Weeding hoe: L. 43¾ in. (111 cm)
Rake: L. 114 cm, B. 14⅝ in. (37.2 cm)
L. prongs 2⅜ in. (6 cm)
Dibble: L. 41 in. (104 cm)
First mentioned in the Kunstkammer inventory, 1587, fol. 207, 208
Armory, inv. no. P 71, P 104, P 82, P 86, P 102 (from left to right)
Lit.: Hager 1916, no. III 11, III 46, III 19, III 23, III 44

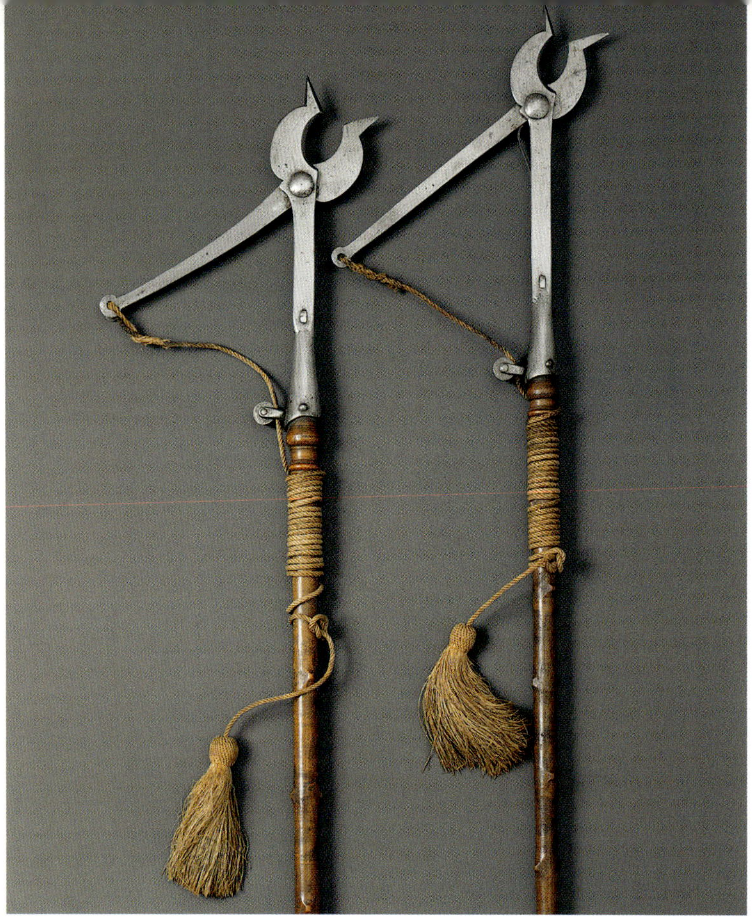

55 Two Long-Handled Clippers

The long-handled clippers serve to trim trees and shrubs. Thanks to this tool, plants can be kept at a certain height, and infested branches trimmed. The long handle enables the user to reach high up. The clippers are used by pulling the cord that is attached to the end of one of the handles. Depending on the plant's shape, different *Raupeisen*, literally "caterpillar scissors," are applied. The 1587 inventory of the Kunstkammer lists different gardening, planting, and grafting gadgets acquired by Elector August, among them: "*10 Raupenscherer dreyerley art mit roten hundleen vnd weißen schnüren*" (ten clippers of three different types with red handles and white cords).
J.B.

German, circa 1560–70
Clippers: bright iron
Handle: pear wood, turned on the lathe
Cord and tassel: hemp
L. each 44½ in. (113 cm)
Clippers: L. each 11⅜ in. (29 cm)
First mentioned in the Kunstkammer inventory, 1587, fol. 207
Armory, inv. no. P 92 (left) and P 93 (right)
Lit.: Hager 1916, no. III 7 and III 8

56 Two Gardening Compasses

The compass illustrated among the gardening, planting, and grafting instruments purchased by Elector August and listed in the 1587 Kunstkammer inventory is called: "*1 Holtzern browner Circkel mit einer Schrauben, runden Bogen vnd Spitzen zum Böthen außteilen*" (one brass wooden compass with one screw, round arch, and tips to insert into the ground). Also a second compass, not illustrated here, is mentioned with another one of this type in the 1587 Kunstkammer inventory: "*2 Undere holtzern Circkell mit halbrunden Bögen zum Beume setzen*" (two wooden compasses with semicircular arches to plant trees). If the compass is opened to its maximum width, it measures two Dresden *Ellen* (1 *Elle* equals roughly 1 yard). The outside of one of the legs is incised with measuring units in *Zoll* (1 *Zoll* equals roughly 1 inch) so that it could be used as a measuring staff. In order to assure the legs' parallel position, a tiny peg is inserted to secure them when the compass is folded up.
J.B.

German, circa 1560–70
Cherry wood, ebony, brass, iron
L. 45¼ in. (115 cm), L. regulator screw 15½ in. (39.5 cm) (P 108, ill. right)
Pear wood, ebony, red wax, brass
L. without arch 6½ in. (16.5 cm)
Inscribed: "*Vom A biss B. seindt zwo Dreßnische Elen*" (From A to B is two Dresden yards).
On the joint a large red "A"
The end piece with the letter "B" was broken off and lost (P 107)
First mentioned in the Kunstkammer inventory, 1587, fol. 206
Armory, inv. no. P 108 (ill. right) and P 107 (not illustrated)
Lit.: Hager 1916, no. III 50 and III 48

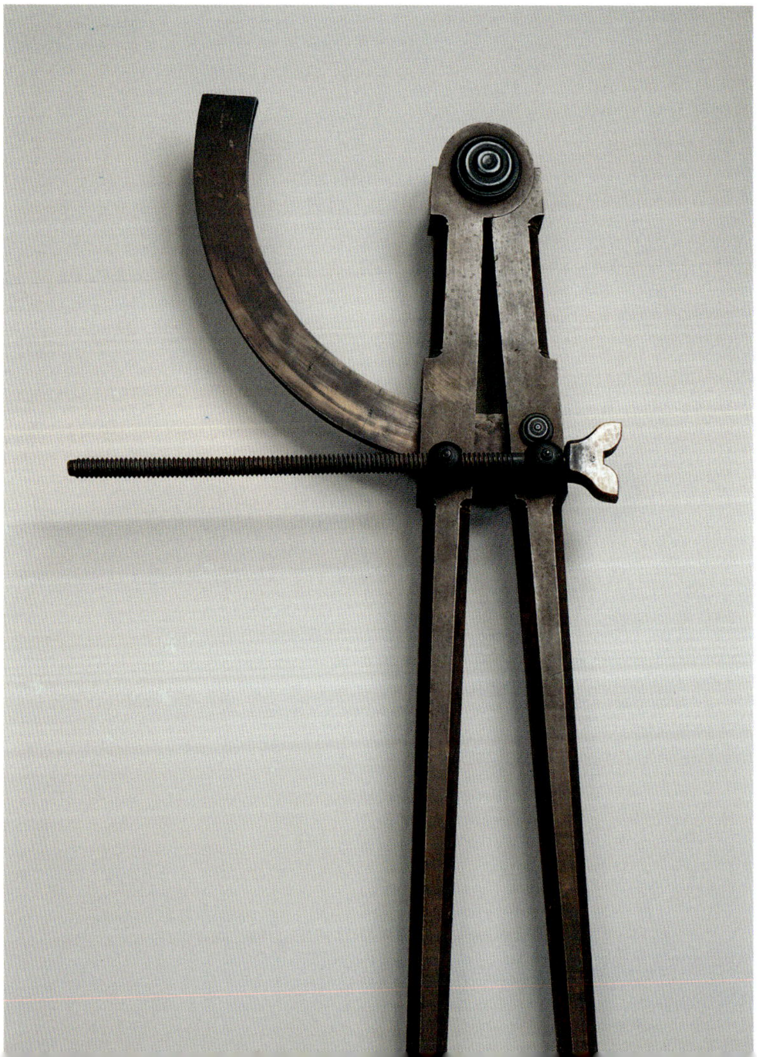

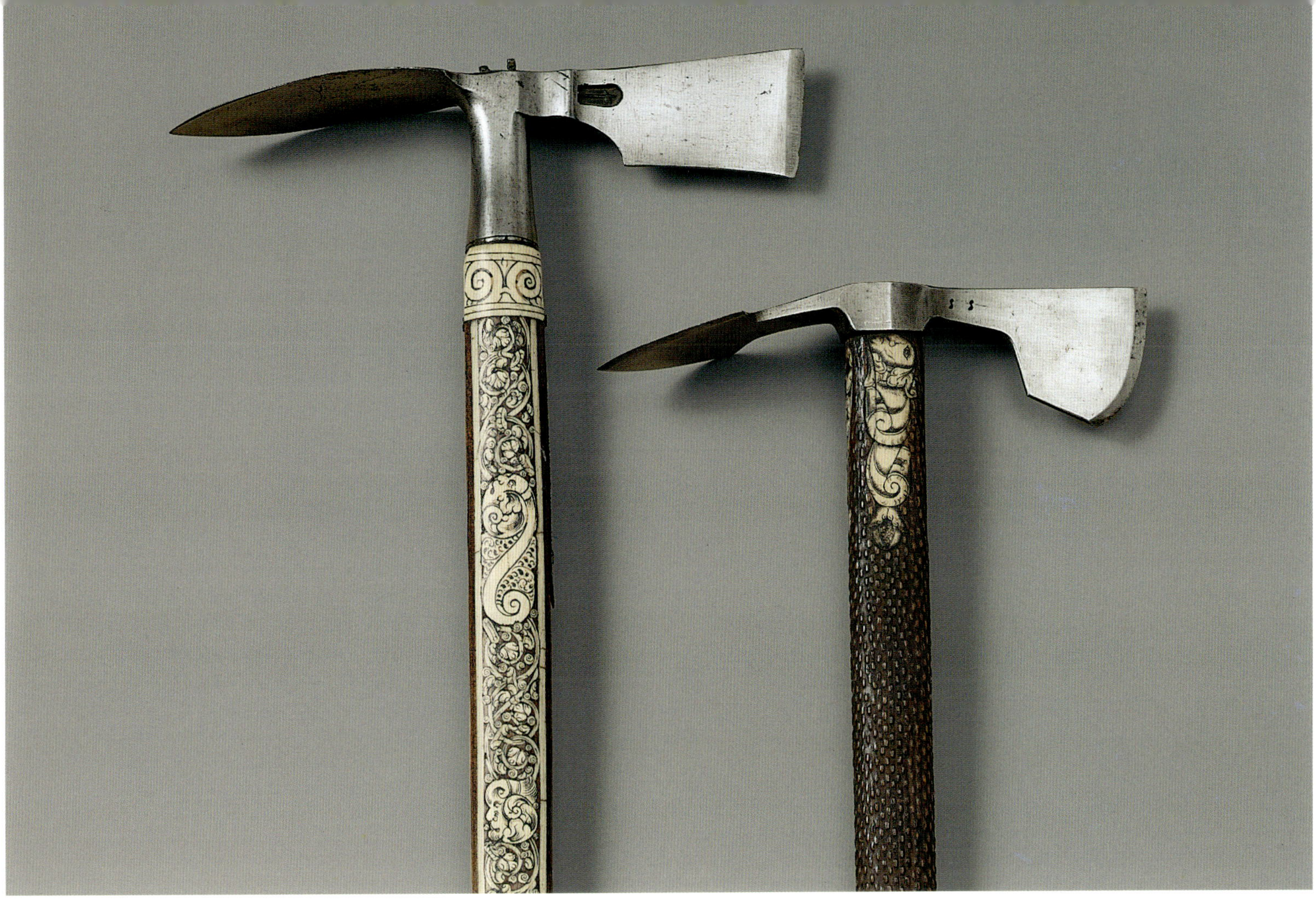

57 Adz

This adz for weeding is combined with a little ax; it can thus be utilized also to cut out roots and tree shoots. Such adzes were used to clear and to cultivate soil for gardening and agriculture. The importance of this activity is underscored by virtue of the object's artistic embellishment, comparable to a parade weapon. The entire length of the shaft is covered with floral bands of bone inlay. The 1587 inventory of the Kunstkammer lists various types and qualities of adzes among the tools for gardening, planting, and grafting Elector August purchased: "*10 Hacken und Beil mit kurtz vnd langen hundleen, geezt vnd vngeezt, vorbeint vnd vnverbeint*" (ten adzes and axes with short and long handles, etched and not etched, with and without bone inlay).
J.B.

German, circa 1570–80
Head: iron; shaft: wood with inlay of bone, engraved and partly blackened
L. 40⅛ in. (102 cm)
First mentioned in the Kunstkammer inventory, 1587, fol. 206
Armory, inv. no. P 77
Lit.: Hager 1916, no. III 35; Bernt 1939, p. 138f., ill. 140

58 Adz

This adz formerly belonging to August may also be used to lean on. In the portrait by Cyriakus Reder, Elector August leans on a war hammer. The grooves along the shaft lend the instrument a better grip when working with it.
J.B.

German, dated 1571
Head: iron, punched marks; shaft: wood, inlaid with bone, engraved and partly blackened, iron
L. 37⅝ in. (95.5 cm)
Blade marked: S-loop
First mentioned in the Kunstkammer inventory, 1587, fol. 206
Armory, inv. no. P 75
Lit.: Hager 1916, no. III 33

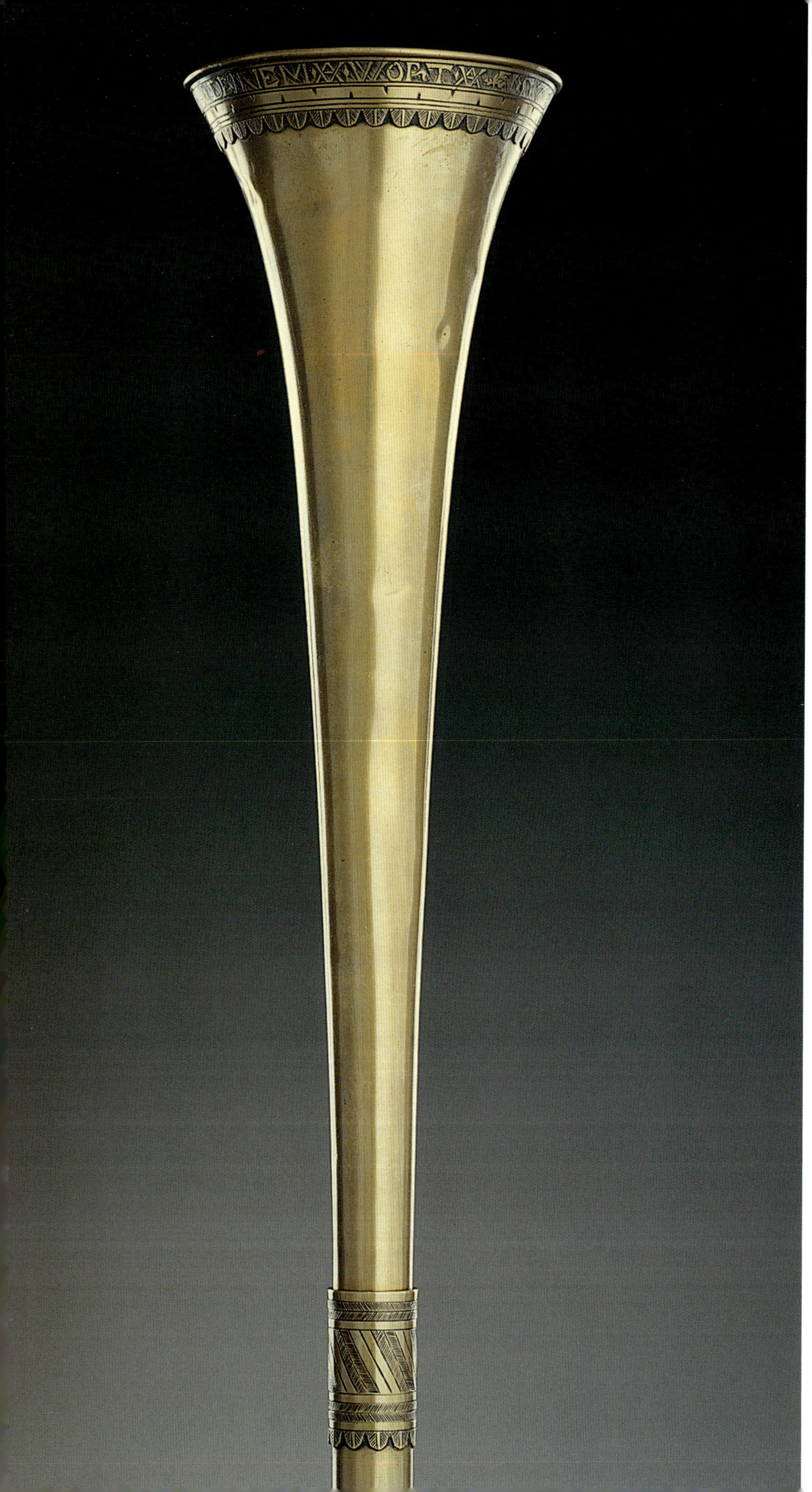

59 Seeder

According to the Kunstkammer inventory of 1587, this and another similar surviving seeder were used by Elector August himself: "*2 Mößene Rohr in einem schwarz liedern Sacke, haben S. Churf. G: zum kernsezen gebrauchet*" (Two brass pipes in a black leather bag which His Highness the Prince Elector used to set pits). This tool enabled the quick planting of seeds in the prepared holes without having to bend over. It was purchased as one of a pair, possibly indicating that Electress Anna, who shared her husband's passion for gardening, also used one. Both seeders–different, simpler variants are mentioned–were possibly invented by the elector himself, who then had them produced by a maker of musical instruments. There is a striking similarity to the brass hunter's trumpet by Valentin Springer from Dresden (cat. no. 25).
J.B.

German, presumably Dresden, 1572
Brass, partly repousséd and engraved
L. 43¾ in. (111 cm)
Inscribed and dated on the funnel with the double monogram "AA" (August and Anna) and inscribed "ERHALT VNS HERR BEI DEINEM WORT. 1572"
(Let us remain faithful to your word, Lord)
First mentioned in the Kunstkammer inventory, 1587, fol. 205
Armory, inv. no. P 96
Lit.: Bäumel 1995c , p. 22

60 Frame Saw Blade

The saw blade with tendril decoration is signed by the Nuremberg Neberschmied (drill maker and smith) Matthias Schwerdtfeger and fulfills the requirements postulated by the Nuremberg trade for a masterpiece in the craft of the Neberschmied: "*Ein Klobseegen, sampt der Schrauben, damit man solche Seegen anzeucht*" (one saw blade together with the screws that tighten the blade). The blade is adorned with the coats of arms of Saxony and Denmark, referring to the electoral couple August and Anna. The saw appears in the 1587 inventory of the Dresden Kunstkammer, where it is listed among the cabinetmaker's tools: "*1 Geetzt Cloben segen blatt mit zweien geezten vorguldten Cloben vnd zugehorigen schlüßell*" (one etched wood saw blade with two etched, gilt frames and the matching key). Neither the key nor the frame into which the saw blade was mounted has survived. The saw for use by two men served to saw wooden planks and veneer.
J.B.

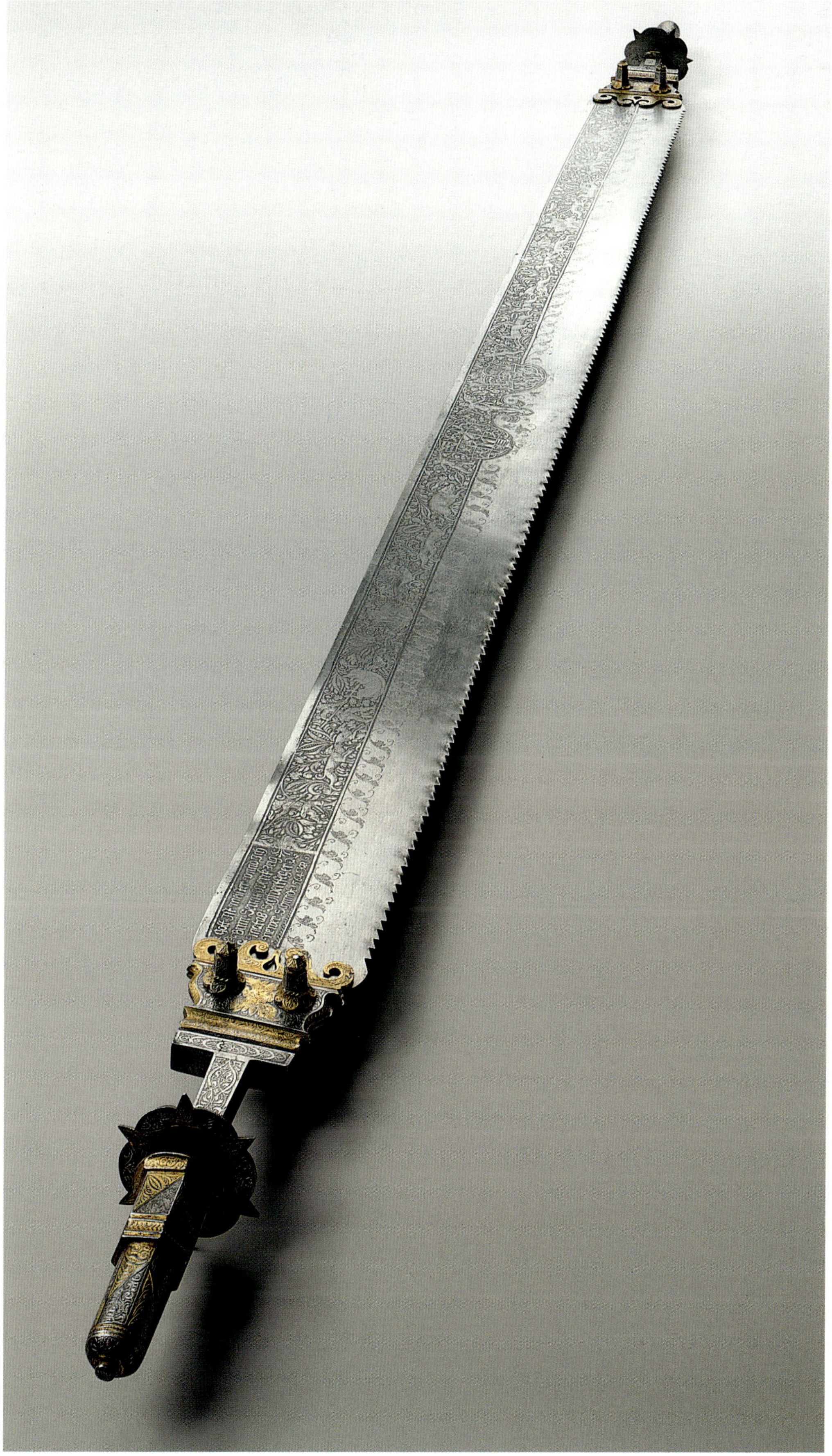

Matthias Schwerdtfeger
Nuremberg 1564
Iron, etched, blackened ground, partly gilt
Total L. 63¾ in. (162 cm), blade L. 50¼ in. (127.5 cm), blade width 3½ in. (9 cm)
Marked: toothed wreath and rosette
Inscribed: "*Gott Ist Meinn Meister vnnd Ich Binn seinn Werckzeug . Mathaß Schwerdtfeger Neber Schmidt Anno danna 1564 Jar denn 24. July*"
(The Lord is my Master and I am his tool. Mathaß Schwerdtfeger, smith in Nuremberg, in the year 1564, on July 24)
First mentioned in the Kunstkammer inventory, 1587, fol. 228
Armory, inv. no. P 244
Lit.: Hager 1916, no. II 85, plate 114; Bernt 1939, pp. 106–09, ill. 109a/b; Menzhausen 1985, p. 26f.; Welker 2002 , p. 125f. and p. 468, cat. no. 37

61 Folding Multipurpose Tool

The iron case is embellished with the figure of Fortune. The case has a sliding lid containing an inserted pivot for fourteen small tools; on the one side are three rasps, a pointed drill, one ruff saw, a knife, and a cutter; on the other side are a key, four files, a pointed drill with a square base, and a rough drill. This tool is a forerunner of today's pocketknife.
J.B.

Nuremberg, circa 1560–70
Iron
Case etched, partly blackened
L. 11 in. (28 cm), W. 1½ in. (3.7 cm),
H. 1⅜ in. (3.6 cm)
Armory, inv. no. P 260
Lit.: Hager 1916, no. II b 5, plate 149;
Bernt 1939, p. 194f., ill. 211;
Washington 1978, cat. no. 86

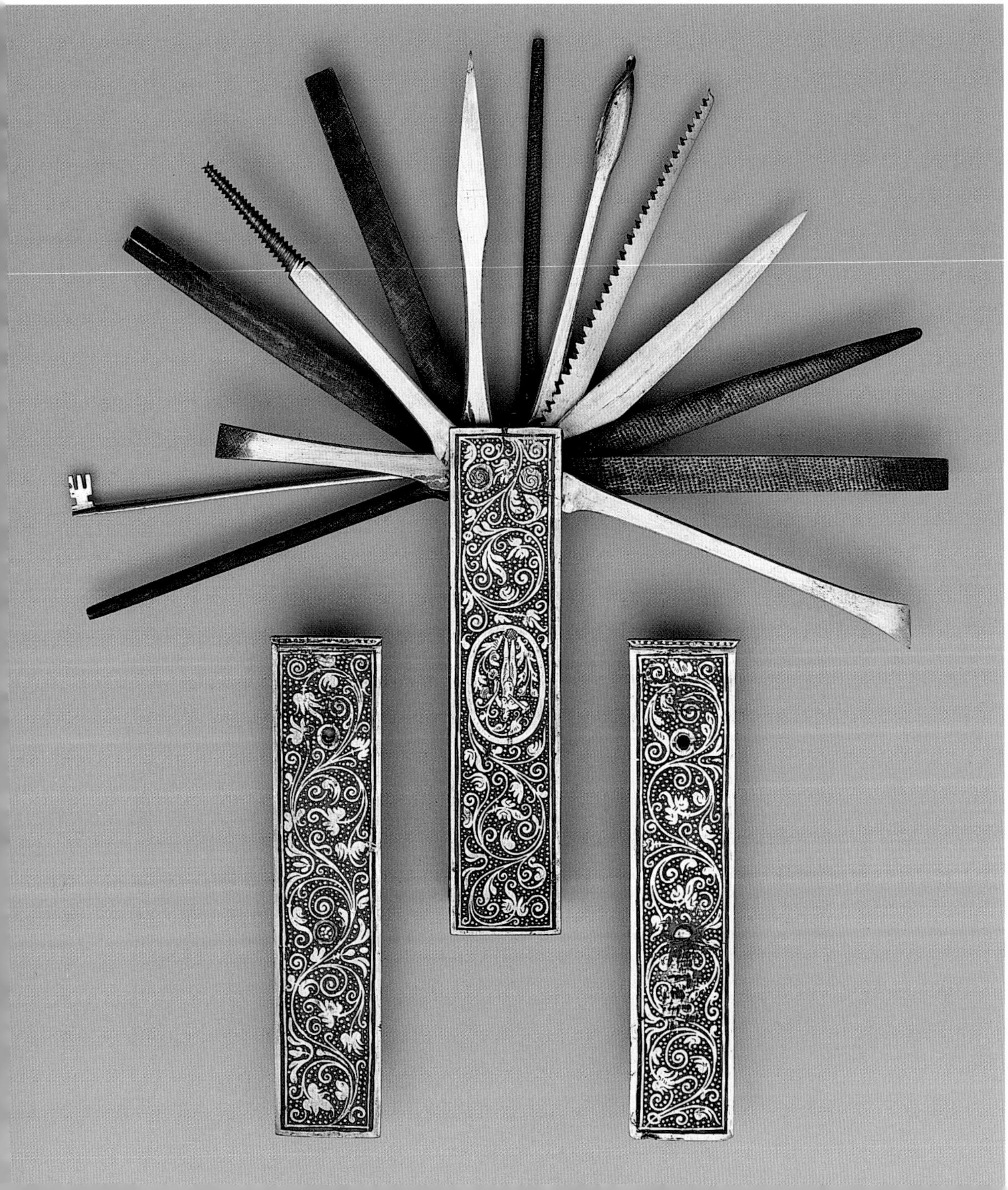

62 Grappling Hook

Balthasar Hacker (?)
Nuremberg or Dresden,
circa 1575–80
Iron, etched, blackened
ground; spring bolt,
H. 5¾ in. (14.7 cm)
First mentioned in the
Kunstkammer inventory,
1587, fol. 91
Armory, inv. no. P 227
(without illustration)
Lit.: Hager 1916,
no. VI 2, plate 191;
Bernt 1939, p. 188f.,
ill. 204

This grappling hook appears among the breaching, climbing, and lowering tools in the 1587 Kunstkammer inventory: "*1 Gelb seiden steigseill mitt einem sechszänckigten eisern Hackenn*" (one yellow silk rope with a six-pronged iron hook). The rope has not survived. In the inventory of tools of 1828–29 (Mathematisch-Physikalischer Salon) this object, also practical for mining, is termed "*Brunnensucher*" (well searcher). Elector August distinguished himself in the realm of silver mining in the Saxon Erzgebirge region as well as in the construction of wells. According to Bernt, the grappling hook could also be used to make a six-strand rope if combined with a winch.
J.B.

63 Fret Saw, Embossing Hammer, Measuring Staff, Hammer, and File

In the Kunstkammer inventory of 1587, the fret saw with its turned ivory handle is listed among the cabinetmaker's tools: "*4 Lobsäglein, eines geetzt mit einem helffen beinen Hefft*" (four small fret saws, one etched, with an ivory handle). This appears to be the oldest and possibly the most beautiful fret saw (a German invention) preserved in Germany. A similar example was depicted on the tomb of the Nuremberg drill maker and smith Voytt, dated 1566.

The high quality of the gilt embossing hammer with its turned ivory handle reveals that it was for princely use. Embossing hammers, goldsmith's files, and other specialty tools for the work of the goldsmith are frequently listed in the Kunstkammer inventory of 1587 among the tools procured from Leonhard Danner. This speaks for Elector August's intense involvement in the trade and the art of the supreme metal-related crafts. This object cannot be identified as one of those specified in the 1587 inventory.

The measuring staff with indication of *Zoll* (1 *Zoll* = about 1 inch) is of unusual shape and enables the quick measurements of diameters and the depth of openings.

The hammer, with its ivory handle, could be used in the workshop as well as for garden work, especially for grafting.

The file has an ivory handle and is fitted with a thumbpiece. It is particularly good for goldsmith's work. In the Kunstkammer inventory of 1587, it is not possible to identify this one among the numerous other files.

The especially high quality of these tools, with their turned ivory grips and gilding, indicates that they were intended for princely use.
J.B.

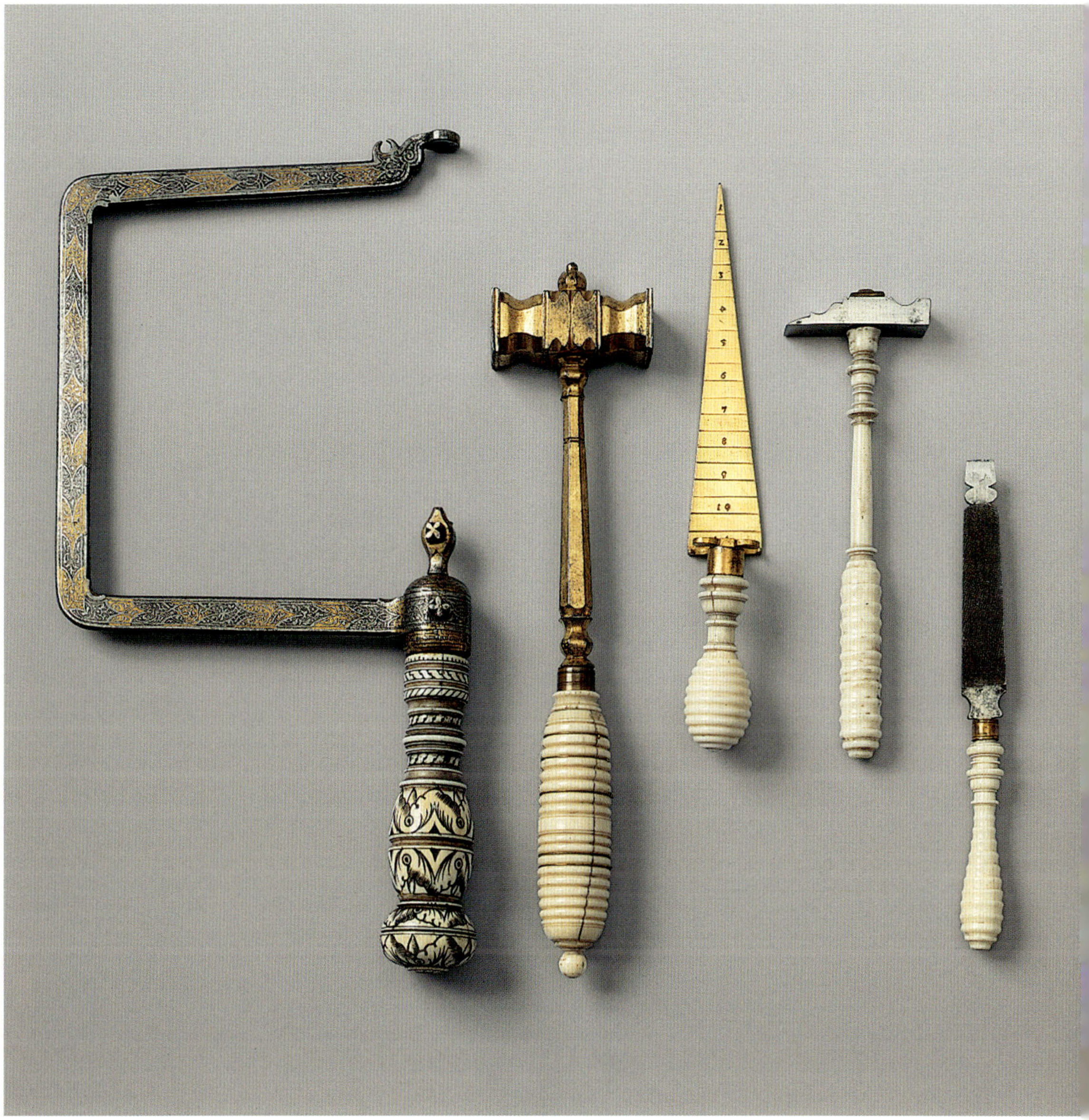

Nuremberg, circa 1565
Fret saw, iron, partly etched, partly gilt
Haft: ivory, turned on the lathe, engraved, partly blackened
Fret saw, L. 10½ in. (26.8 cm)
Embossing hammer, L. 9 in. (23 cm)
Measuring staff, L. 7¼ in. (18.5 cm)
Hammer, L. 5⅞ in. (15 cm)
File, L. 6¼ in. (15.8 cm)
First mentioned in the Kunstkammer inventory, 1587, fol. 228 (fret saw)
Armory, inv. nos. P 245, P, 254, P 230, P 255, P 256 (v.l.n.r.)
Lit.: Hager 1916, no. II 87, plate 105 (fret saw), no. V202, plate 183 (embossing hammer); Bernt 1939, p. 104f., ill. 105 (fret saw)

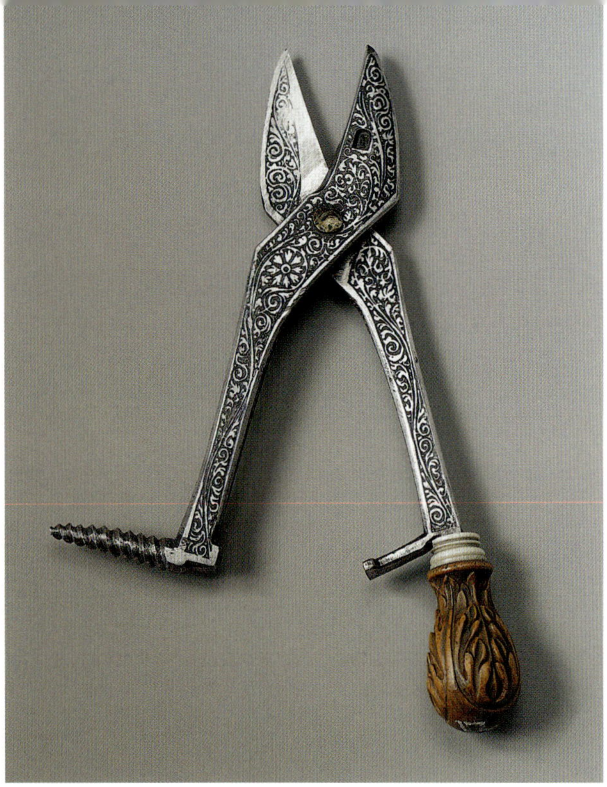

64 Bench Shears

This pair of shears comes from the Kunstkammer and was contained in the same desk (cat. no. 69) as the tools for screwing and cutting: "*1 Geetzte Stockschere mit einem Buxbaumen hefft*" (one etched pair of bench shears with a boxwood handle). The shears, intended for cutting tin, were attached to the workbench. Such shears were used, among other things, for making armor and for cutting printing plates.
J.B.

Nuremberg, circa 1570
Iron, etched, blackened ground; boxwood, carved, L.8⅜ in. (21.3 cm)
Mark: illegible
First mentioned in the Kunstkammer inventory, 1587, fol. 105
Armory, inv. no. P 261
Lit.: Hager 1916, no. VII 72, plate 216; Bernt 1939 , p. 86f., ill. 79

65 Hacksaw

The iron hacksaw, subtly decorated with tendrils and foliage, is intended for metalworking. The saw blade nut is secured with a winged nut in one of four positions. The blade can be fitted either in a parallel or a rectangular manner to the frame. In the Kunstkammer inventory of 1587, numerous hacksaws made of iron are mentioned among the tools acquired from Leonhard Danner, among which: "*1 Sege mit einem eisern Bogen*" (one saw with an iron bow).
J.B.

Leonhard Danner,
Nuremberg, circa 1554–70
Iron, etched, blackened ground
Haft: ebony, turned on the lathe
L. 16 in. (40.5 cm)
First mentioned in the Kunstkammer inventory, 1587, fol. 118 or 122, 130
Armory, inv. no. P 259
Lit.: Hager 1916, no. II 86, plate 219; Bernt 1939, p. 100f., ill. 98

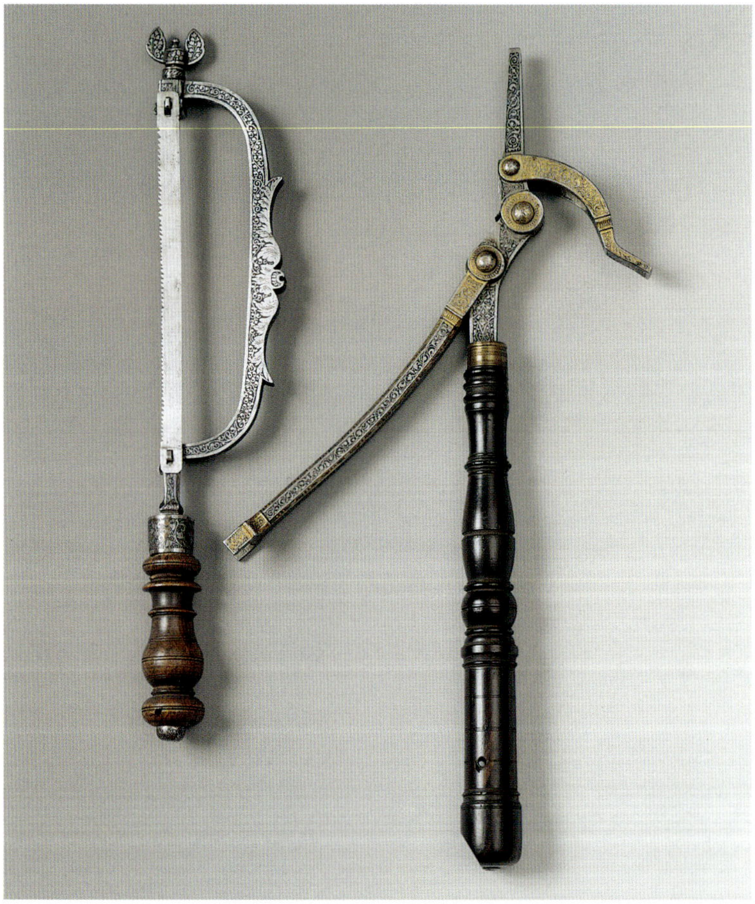

66 Jack

The jack is adorned with etched tendril ornament. In the 1587 inventory of the Kunstkammer, it is listed with the famous wire-drawing bench that Elector August bought from Leonhard Danner (ill. p. 57) in 1565: "*Zu dieser ziehebanck gehöret vnd ist beihunden* [...] *1 Eisern geetzte Hebestange mit einen schwarzen hefft*" (also belonging to this wire-drawing bench [...] one iron lifting tool with a black handle).
J.B.

Leonhard Danner, Nuremberg, circa 1565
Iron, etched, blackened ground, partly gilt; Haft: ebony, turned on the lathe, L. 22 in. (56 cm)
First mentioned in the Kunstkammer inventory, 1587, fol. 216
Armory, inv. no. P 226
Lit.: Hager 1916, no. II b 3, plate 149

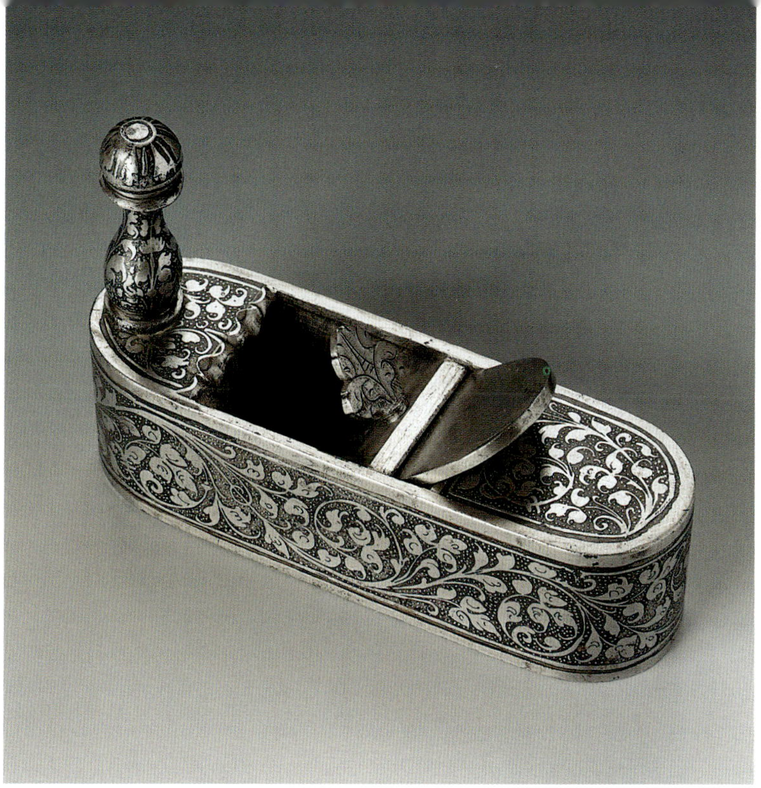

67 Block Plane

The entire surface of this plane is covered with hunting scenes and tendrils. The cutting blade is fixed with a winged nut instead of the more customary wedge. The 1587 Kunstkammer inventory lists similar planes under the category of tools for cabinetmakers, gunmakers, and locksmiths: "*5 Eisernn zihn hufell*" (five iron planes).
J.B.

Nuremberg, circa 1570
Iron, etched, blackened ground
L. 5 in. (12.7 cm)
First mentioned in the Kunstkammer inventory, 1587, fol. 100

Armory, inv. no. P 247
Lit.: Hager 1916, no. VII 166, plate 219; Bernt 1939, p. 114f., ill. 114; Washington 1978, cat. no. 78

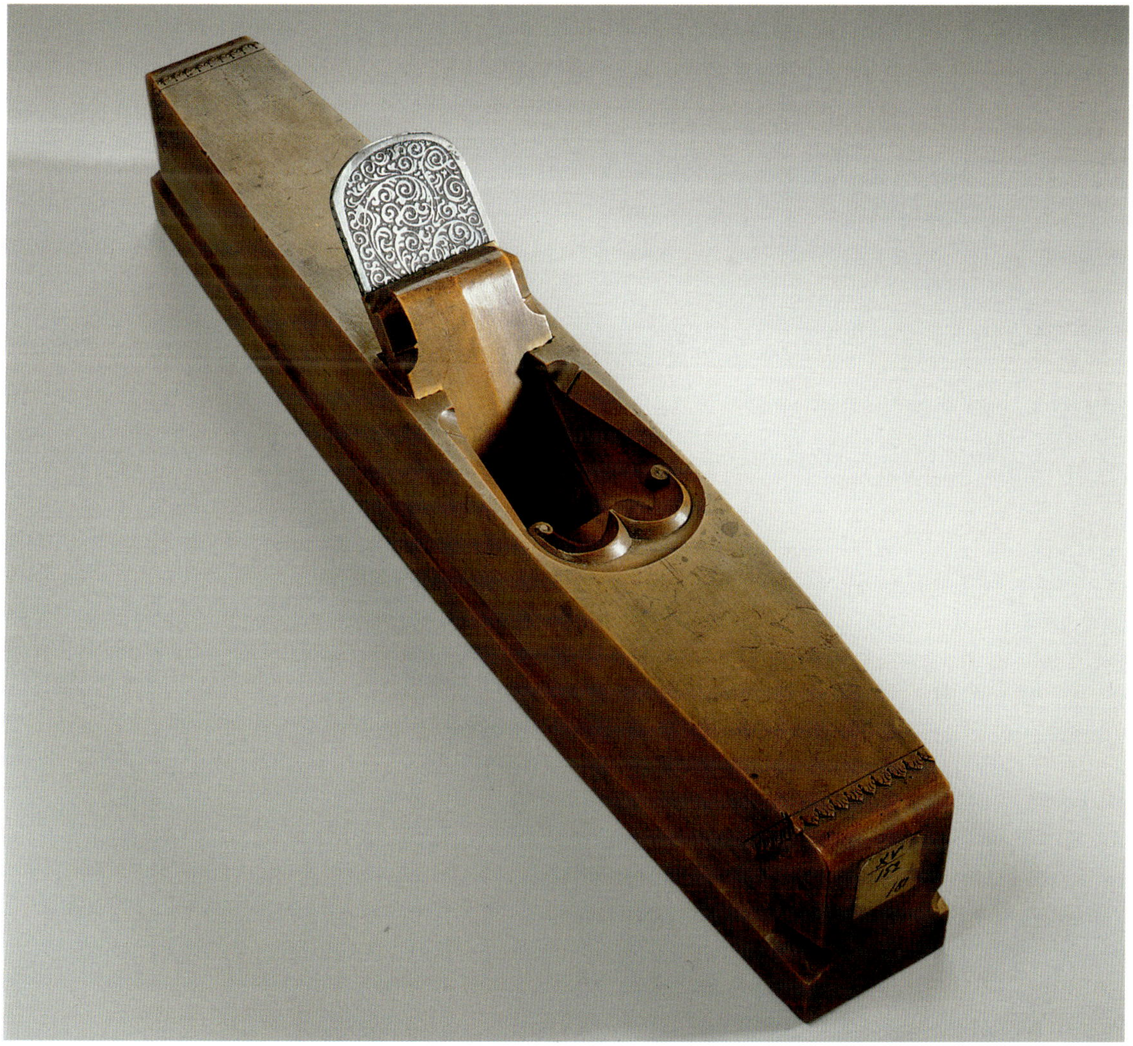

68 Jack Plane

In the Kunstkammer inventory of 1587, this beautifully rendered plane is listed among the tools for cabinetmakers: "*3 Lange Buxbeumene Höbell*" (three long boxwood planes).
J.B.

German, circa 1560–70
Boxwood, carved,
Cutting blade: iron, etched, blackened ground
L. 12⅝ in. (32.2 cm)
First mentioned in the Kunstkammer inventory, 1587, fol. 228
Armory, inv. no. P 249
Lit.: Hager 1916, no. II 2, plate 105; Washington 1978, cat. no. 77

69 Screw Box

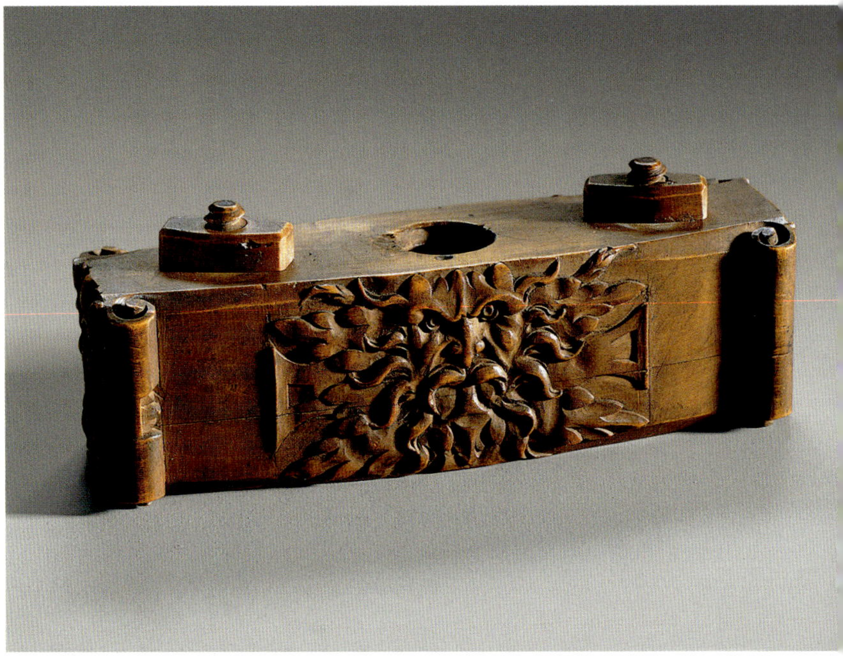

The 1587 Kunstkammer inventory mentions cutting tools for screws numerous times. With its carved foliage masks, this tool belonged to a group housed in a little desk: "*7 Buxbaumen geschnittene Schraub zeugleinn sambt ihren zugehörigen Löhern, zu iedem ein Nöber vnd Schrauben böhrer*" (seven boxwood tools [for making screws] with their matching templates, each one having a tap). In the holdings of the Armory, two decoratively carved cutting tools have survived, albeit without the attendant gadgets. The high quality suggests that this object was made in the workshop of Leonhard Danner. He employed a woodworker for such items–as he also did in connection with the wire-drawing bench (ill. p. 57)–who signed his works "AM."
J.B.

Nuremberg, circa 1570
Leonhard Danner, workshop
Boxwood, partly carved with figures
L. 5 in. (12.7 cm)
First mentioned in the Kunstkammer inventory, 1587, fol. 105
Armory, inv. no. P 243
Lit.: Hager 1916, no. I a 3; Welker 2002, p. 122

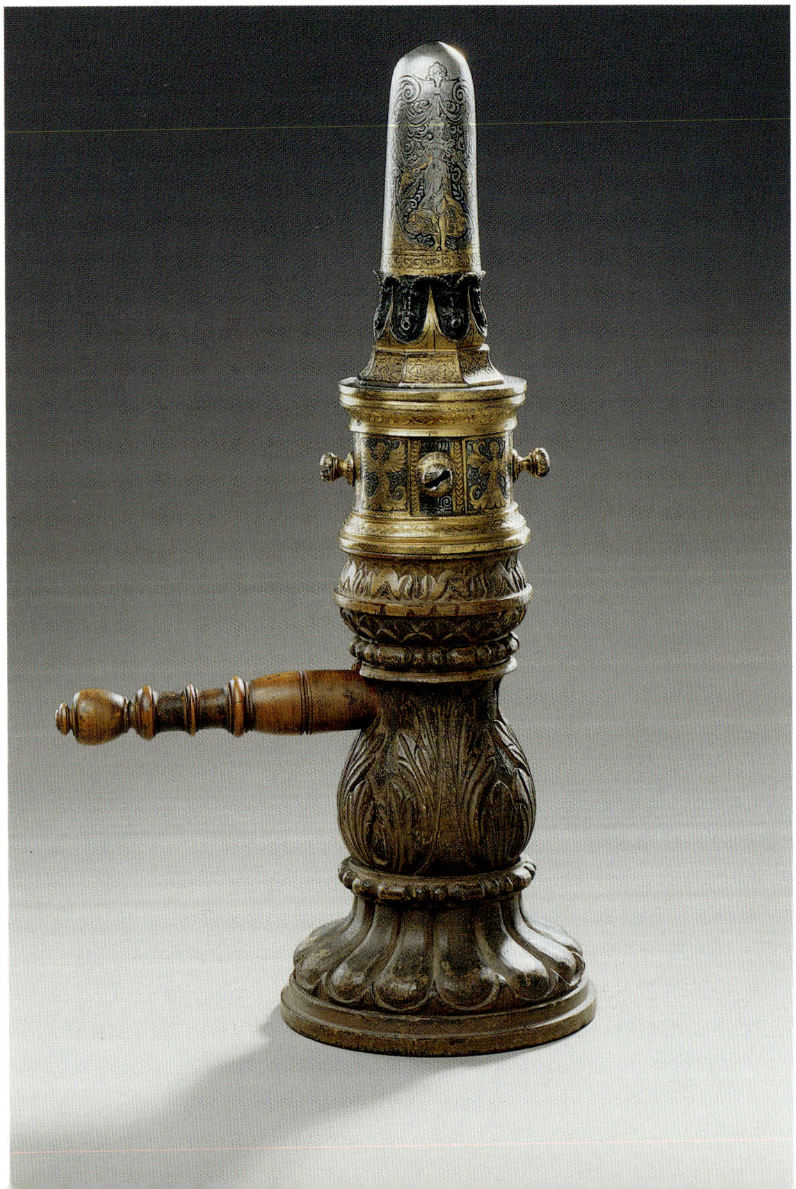

70 Auger for Making Bungholes

Like the following object (cat. no. 71), this exquisitely decorated tool is a masterpiece from Nuremberg. August obtained various admission pieces for Nuremberg metalworker's trades. The etched decoration applied to the cover for the bit shows Judith with the head of Holofernes. The tool served to produce bungholes in barrels. The bit of the auger was fixed by screws. It could be exchanged for a bit of a different size.
J.B.

Nuremberg, circa 1560–70
Iron, etched, partly blackened, partly gilt
Mount: boxwood, turned on the lathe and carved, wood of the handle turned on the lathe (lost on one side)
H. 14⅝ in. (37 cm)
Marked: toothed wreath
First mentioned in the Kunstkammer inventory, 1587, fol. 231
Armory, inv. no. P 235
Lit.: Hager 1916, no. II 90, plate 105; Bernt 1939, p. 130f., ill. 133

71 Auger for Making Bungholes

In the Kunstkammer inventory of 1587, the auger, abundantly decorated on its handle with sumptuous masks, foliage, and heads of satyrs, is listed among the cabinetmaker's tools, together with another one (cat. no. 70): "*2 Geetzte vnd vorgüldte Böhrer mit Birnholzen hefften als zappenbohrer oder winder, seindt Meisterstücke*" (two etched and gilt drills with pear wood handles for drilling peg holes are masterpieces). Thanks to alternating gilt and plain fields on the drill staff, the depth of the auger can be established. Among other applications, the long and narrow auger served to cut wooden pipes for water. A similar type of auger is depicted on the tomb of a Nuremberg drillmaker and smith (*Neberschmied*), dated 1566.
J.B.

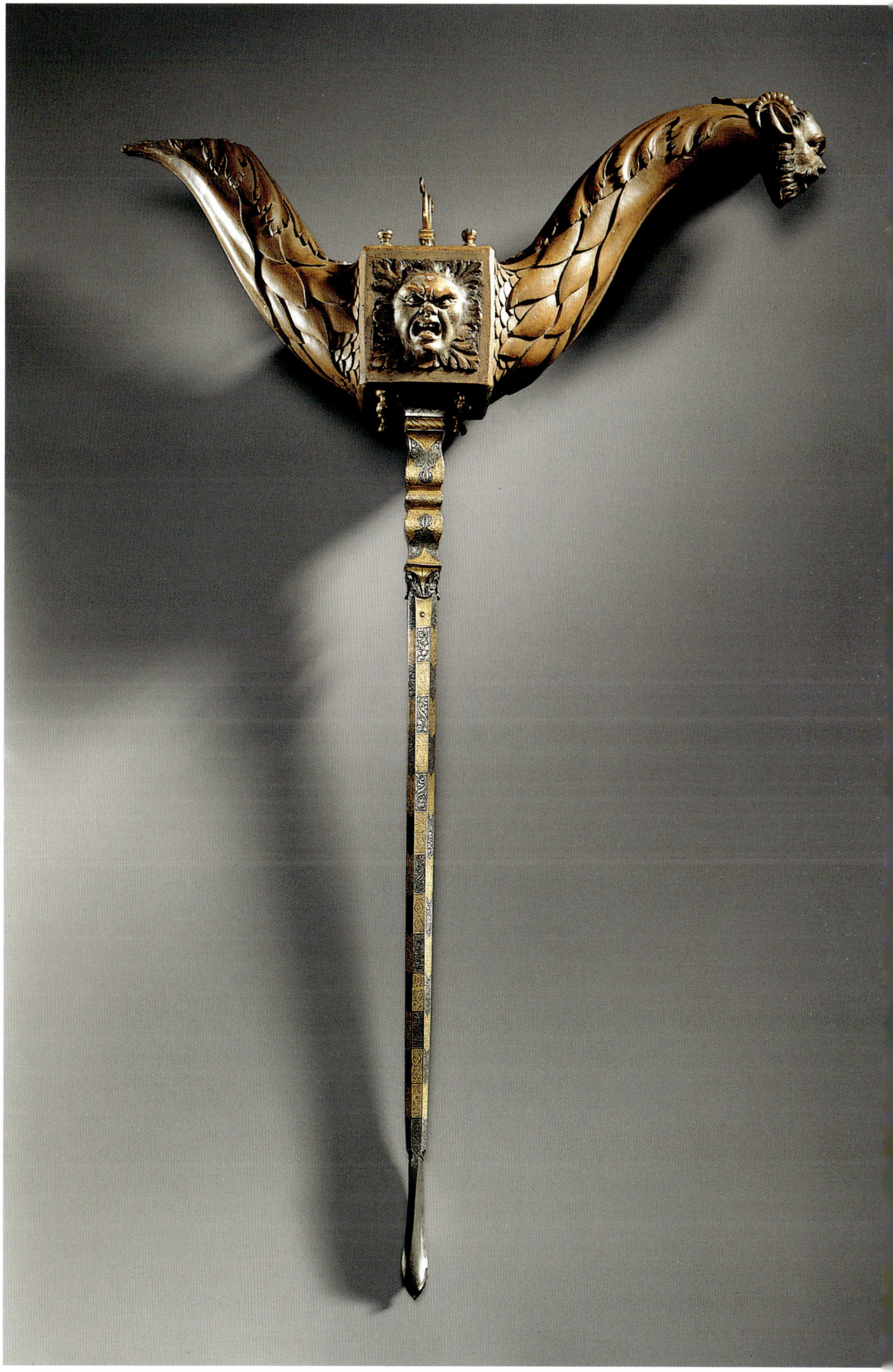

Nuremberg, circa 1560–70
Iron, etched, partly blackened, partly gilt
Mount: pear wood, carved, partly painted, one of the handle ends lost
H. circa 35⅜ in. (90 cm)
Marked: toothed wreath, lily, bird, and undetermined
First mentioned in the Kunstkammer inventory, 1587, fol. 231
Armory, inv. no. P 234
Lit.: Hager 1916, no. II 91;
Bernt 1939, pp. 132–35, ill. 136/137

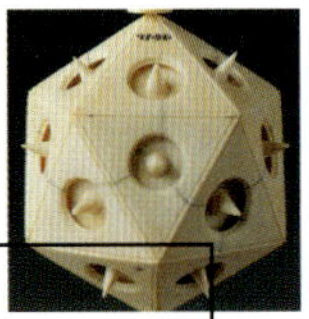

Turned Ivory Works

Jutta Kappel

Elector August of Saxony, one of the most important rulers of his time, pursued an exceedingly courtly activity in his scarce leisure time: he worked the lathe.

In Dresden's Residential Palace as well as in the country estates of Annaburg, Augustusburg, and Lichtenburg, there were rooms that could accommodate a lathe.[1] Such an instrument was fascinating because it involved both a predictable work process and the elimination of unpredictable results—if one had sufficient knowledge and the ability to master all the mechanical aspects. While working the lathe was a princely pastime, it also required skill and practice. Knowledge of mathematics, geometry, mechanics, and perspective were required, as were experienced specialists to instruct the *souverain ouvrier* in handling the lathe.

Elector August managed to secure experts for his court. They were instrumental in the further development of his lathes, and they qualified as "master instructors" in the art of turning. A document dated May 17, 1559, records that the Nuremberg turner Christof Koller was appointed to the Dresden court. In March 1561 Elector August commissioned the Nuremberg toolmaker Leonhard Danner, whom he held in high esteem, to manufacture numerous instruments that could be used in connection with a lathe. By 1570 Hans Seher is mentioned as court turner in Dresden. Hieronymus Steinbeisser came from Prague. As his employment documents of July 9, 1575, reveal, he was commissioned to execute several unique turned objects for the elector and to keep their creation a secret (*"in geheimb haltenn"*).[2] Georg Ha[i]n, also employed as court turner in 1575, built a small lathe (*"klein Drehebäncklein"*)—still listed in the Lathe Chamber inventory of 1622[3]—for Duke Christian.

Christian was the only surviving male descendant of the electoral couple, and their high expectations rested on him. After a rigorous curriculum based on Lutheran principles, he was instructed in all court customs; he learned Latin and Italian and was instructed in nature studies, history, art, geometry, and mathematics.[4] His teachers ranked among the best imaginable. At Electress Anna's request, the Nuremberg goldsmith Hans Lencker had already spent time in Dresden in 1572.[5] He had presented a deluxe edition of his *Perspectiva literaria* (1567) and *Perspectiva corporum* (1571) to the electoral couple. These treatises recommended him as an excellent authority in the field of modern perspective. A volume subsidized by Christian containing his perspectival sketches and drawings was begun on the last day of February 1576. Executed under Hans Lencker's guidance, it was bound in parchment in 1577.[6] It appears that the duke, a youth of sixteen, pursued his work with both ambition and talent. One of his drawings (ill. p. 177) indicates that Lencker must have included in his drawing curriculum the *Perspectiva corporum regularium* (1568) of the Nuremberg goldsmith Wenzel Jamnitzer. This work, at the time also owned by the elector, could have been used as a textbook.[7] The drawing lessons were intended to enable Duke Christian to do what his father already diligently pursued and what his mother enthusiastically encouraged:[8] he was to learn to work the lathe.

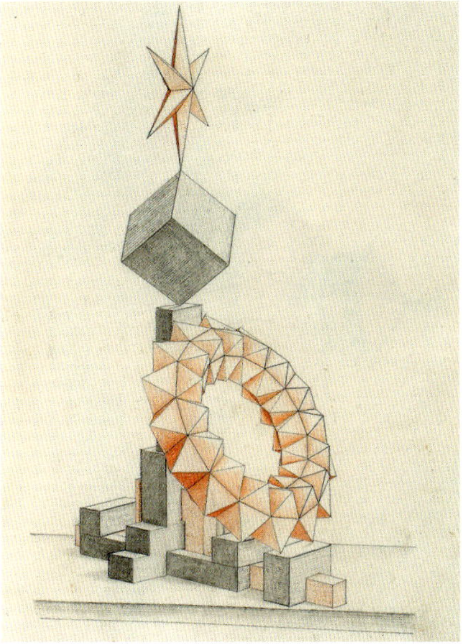

"Perspectif Buch"
(Book of Perspectives) with drawings
by Duke Christian
Pen and ink, colored
16¾ × 11⅜ in. (41.7 × 29 cm)
Kupferstich-Kabinett, Staatliche
Kunstsammlungen Dresden,
inv. no. Ca 61, fol. 27

Apparently, the combined abilities of Koller, Steinbeisser, and Ha[i]n in this field were deemed insufficient, so Elector August exploited his relationship with the Wittelsbachs of Bavaria to find the most qualified court turner. The Wittelsbachs were also devoted turners. In December 1575[9] August requested their recommendation of a capable turner who would instruct him and, more importantly, Duke Christian in the art of turning.

The person selected was Georg Wecker. Through his father, Hans Wecker, court turner under the ruling Duke Albrecht V of Bavaria, he received a superb reference. Georg Wecker may have studied with the Milanese ivory turner Giovanni Ambrogio Maggiore, who was about his age and who had first traveled to Bavaria in 1574 upon the recommendation of the art agent Prospero Visconti. Maggiore went to Bavaria various times between 1574 and 1593. There he taught Duke Wilhelm of Bavaria a newly invented art, which at first only he could do. He was able to manufacture oval shapes and so-called *contrefait* spheres in ivory on the lathe (cf. cat. no. 91).[10] Even though Munich and the court of Landshut had, at least periodically, a virtuoso turner-artist in Maggiore, the Wittelsbachs were reluctant to allow Georg Wecker to move to Dresden. Duke Ferdinand, the son of Albrecht V, negotiated an agreement in early 1576, initially "lending" the turner to Dresden for two years. Munich also left open the option to recall the young Wecker in the event that his father died. Georg Wecker, described as rather skillful, made his first brief visit to Dresden and Annaburg Castle in late January 1576. At the end of June of the same year, a lathe arrived in Dresden as a gift of Duke Wilhelm of Bavaria. It was suggested to Elector August that he should wait for Georg Wecker's arrival to use this machine because Wecker knew better than anyone else. When Wecker came, Elector August asked the court in Munich to let him keep the turner indefinitely, not just for two years. Toward the end of October 1577 (at the latest) Wecker moved to Dresden permanently. Persistence and diplomacy had resulted in success, and the Saxon elector felt himself lucky: he obtained not only the gift of a modern lathe but also one of the leading experts from Munich. As early as January 13, 1578, Georg Wecker was made court turner "for life" and was paid the respectable annual sum of 200 fl.[11] Might he have brought with him, as preliminary sketches, six pen-and-ink drawings inscribed 1578 of turned vessels (ill. p. 178 below) listed in the inventory of the Dresden Turning Chamber of 1684?

It is unclear why there are no works by Wecker, a successful artist, from before 1581. The objects that can be dated to 1581 are three small ivory polyhedrons, all signed. Most likely, he spent the first three years of his tenure in Dresden instructing the elector and Duke Christian in the use of the lathe. The 165 ivories turned by August himself and transferred to the Kunstkammer upon his death on October 12, 1586,[12] were probably made under the guidance of this master. Elector Christian I arranged 134 of the turned works inherited from his father on a five-stepped structure. Based on the descriptions in the 1587 and 1595 Kunstkammer inventories, it must have been an impressive display. This princely collection, however, mysteriously vanished. In 1605, Electress Hedwig, married to Christian II of Saxony in 1602, removed them from the Kunstkammer, and their whereabouts remain unknown.[13] In the Green Vault are twenty-eight minute ivories mounted on wood (ill. p. 178 top), which might have been part of the collection of sixty-seven small objects identified as "Pößlein" or "*Piramides, Columnen und andere sorten.*"[14] Georg Wecker donated a plain beaker vessel, turned by the elector himself, to the Kunstkammer in 1587; it is preserved in the Green Vault (inv. no. II 65).

It was only after Elector August's death that Wecker's independent artistic work at the lathe began. This is indicated by the fact that all of his signed and dated ivories—in their scope and diversity quite unique—originate from between 1586 and 1589. His works (cat. nos. 72–79) are distinguished by their elegance. The goblets and bowls are purely decorative vessels, precluding use for drinking or pouring liquids because of the medium and the design. Only the writing tools (Schreibzeuge, see cat. no. 79) could actually have been used; but they, too, show no sign of use and thus retain their status as precious objects in the collection of the Kunstkammer. Wecker used a wide variety of turning techniques. He relied on the beauty of shapes that could be produced on the lathe, refraining almost completely from carved figural embellishments. Only one of his signed ivory counterfeit spheres, dated 1594, was crowned with a figure of Neptune and embellished at its foot with numerous carved animals.

1. Syndram 1995, p. 8.
2. SächsHStA Dresden, Copial 300, fol. 343r, Copial 345, fol. 387v–388r, Rep. LII. Gen. 1924, Loc. 33341, fol. 9r-v, 196v; cf. Gurlitt 1888, p. 9f.; Kappel 1995a, p. 14 with footnotes 1, 3.
3. Inventar der Drechselkammer (Lathe Chamber inventory) 1622, fol. 2r.
4. Richter 1913, p. 59–70.
5. Cf. Weber 1865, p. 338 (letter from Electress Anna to Paul Buchner); cf. also: SächsHStA Dresden, Rentkammer invoices, no. 183 (=Crucis 1571-Crucis 1572), fol. 228r (payment to Lencker on June 8, 1572).
6. Cf. Spitzer 1990, p. 246 and cat. no. 386. For more information pertaining to this book of perspective studies in Dresden's Collection of Prints, Drawings, and Photographs, inv. no. Ca 61, see also: Schade 1969, cat. no. 6.
7. Cf. Nuremberg, 1985, cat. no. 756; Hauschke 2002, p. 376, cat. no. 142.
8. Cf. Richter 1913, p. 71 with footnotes 1, 2, and 3.
9. Cf. Diemer 1985, p. 308 with document 5 (Munich, Geheimes Hausarchiv, Korr. Akt. 606/VIIa).
10. Cf. Diemer 1985, p. 301–03, 305, 308f.; Syndram 1995, p. 7f.
11. Cf. some correspondence concerning Georg Wecker: SächsHStA Dresden, Loc. 8506/2, fol. 102r–v, 116r–v, 159r–160v, SächsHStA Dresden, Rep. LII. Gen 1925, Loc. 33342, fol. 506r–507v (draft of Wecker's employment contract); Gurlitt 1888, p. 79; Diemer 1985, p. 308 with document no. 7.
12. Distel 1887, p. 149f.; SächsHStA Dresden, Loc. 9835/15, fol. 7r.
13. Hantzsch 1902, p. 246.
14. Inventory of the Kunstkammer 1587, fol. 146f.

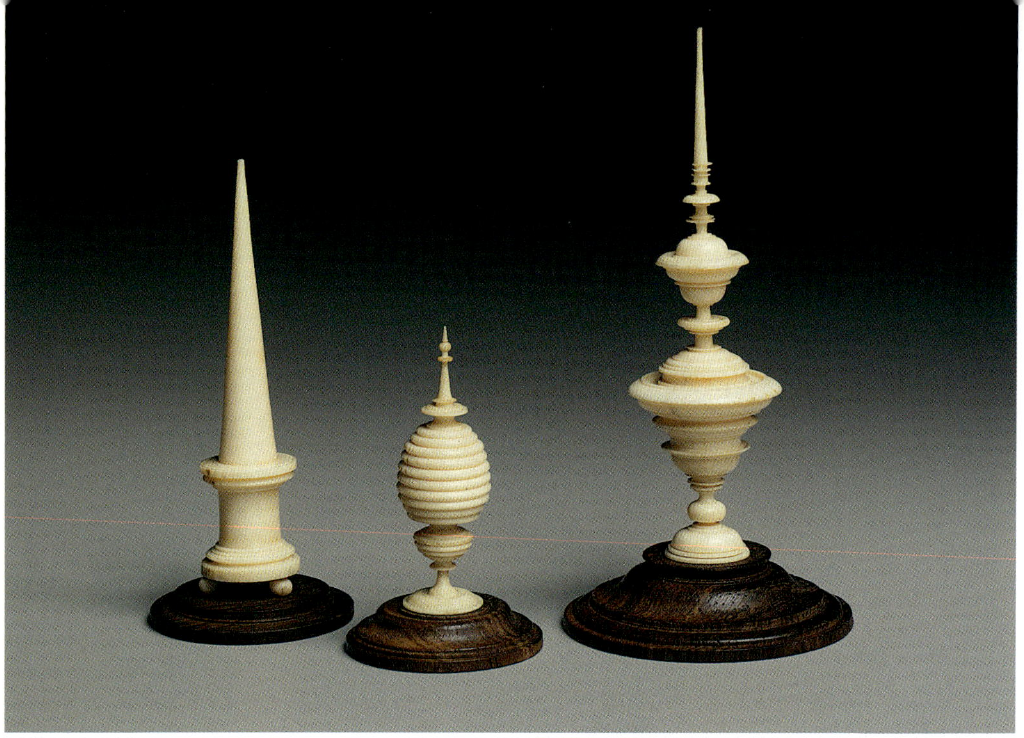

Three small turned ivories
Almost certainly turned on the lathe by Elector August himself
Ivory, wood
H. 2⅞ (7.4 cm), 2 in. (5 cm)
3¾ in. (9.6 cm, from left to right)
Staatliche Kunstsammlungen Dresden, Grünes Gewölbe, inv. no. II 453–455 (Nachträge)

below
Pen and ink drawing of a turned ivory vessel
Possibly by Georg Wecker, dated 1578
Pen and gray-blue wash
12 × 7⅝ in. (30.5 × 19.5 cm)
Drechselkammer inventory of 1684

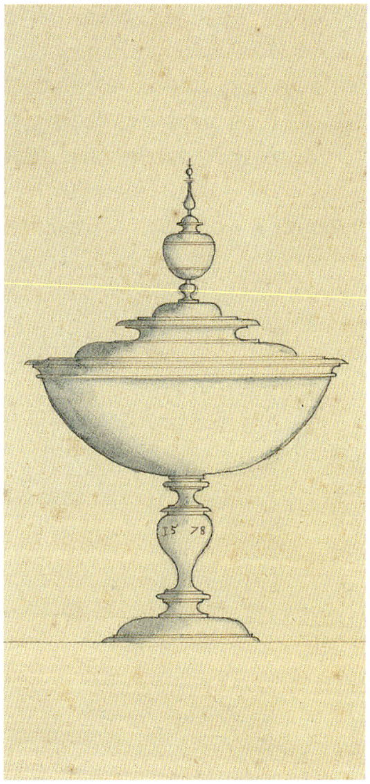

opposite
Medallion in *verre églomisé* with the stamp of Egidius Lobenigk on the underside of the wood foot of the ivory counterfeit sphere
Staatliche Kunstsammlungen Dresden, Grünes Gewölbe, inv. no. II 286

Once kept in Emperor Rudolph II's Kunstkammer in Prague, it was one of seven turned works by Georg Wecker owned by the appreciative emperor.[15]

Egidius Lobenigk from Cologne was appointed the second court turner on November 20, 1584. Like Georg Wecker, he was responsible for the continuing education of Duke Christian.[16] Lobenigk's workshop was located in the attic of the Dresden Residential Palace's west wing, in immediate proximity to the Kunstkammer.[17] The first dated and signed work to come from that shop, a delicate ivory polyhedron, was made during his first year in Dresden. In the surviving archival documents the name of this court turner varies; sometimes he is referred to as "Meister Egidius" or "Egidien Löbenigk"; other times, "Egidius Lobenigk." In the stamp on a colorful medallion in *verre eglomisé* attached to the bottom of the wood foot of his large counterfeit sphere his name reads "Gilius Lebenich" and the date is 1586 (ill. p. 179). The reason Lobenigk affixed such a lavish medallion, with its inscription and the Lutheran creed "All Glory to God" ("ALLEIN GOTT DIE EHRE"), to the sphere was that, aside from Giovanni Ambrogio Maggiore, who first produced such a sphere on a lathe in 1582 "*non si sà come,*"[18] he was the only artist who mastered this form, and it was he who introduced it to Dresden. Many of Lobenigk's cups were turned in oval forms; he preferred sudden changes in shapes, and with his imposing ivory columns he created unique works of art (cat. nos. 87, 88). The combination of turned vessel with figural carving appears first in his work, albeit in a somewhat restrained way (cf. cat. nos. 85, 86). His carvings are rather undistinguished due to a lack of sophistication in the designs. As a turner, however, he was a true virtuoso and extremely prolific.

Together with Georg Wecker, Lobenigk made the turner's workshop in the Dresden Residential Palace truly productive. Over the next ten years these two created a collection of unparalleled scope and quality that became one of the highlights of the electoral Kunstkammer, already full of countless precious objects. Christian I died in 1591 at the age of thirty-one. Despite his extensive training, there is not a single documented work produced by him on the lathe. After his death, new acquisitions of turned ivory pieces came to an abrupt end, as indicated by the Kunstkammer inventory of 1595. This clearly indicates that the elector's demise brought the production of turned ivory objects in Dresden to an end. Lobenigk, who had not become wealthy, died in early 1595. The court gave financial aid to his children, still under age, only once; the sum amounted to one half of Lobenigk's annual salary.[19] Wecker, however, remained active. In 1599 he installed a lathe for Emperor Rudolf II on Prague's Hradschin. In 1601 he delivered ivories to the emperor; they were gifts from Christian II, now the ruling elector of Saxony.[20]

According to family tradition, Christian II added some turned ivory objects to the holdings of the Kunstkammer, but his interest in this art was far less passionate and informed than that of his father or his grandfather.[21] A visit by the Ratisbone-born ivory turner Jakob

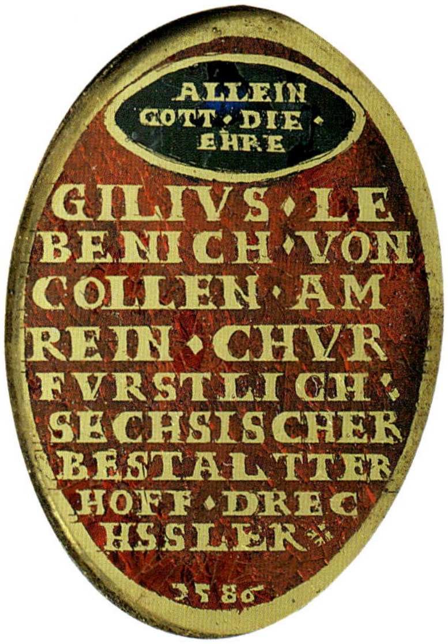

Zeller, who arrived from Prague with two servants on August 22, 1610,[22] seems to have deeply impressed Christian; shortly thereafter he appointed Zeller electoral Saxon court turner. Zeller, primarily active on behalf of Elector Johann Georg I of Saxony, became a specialist, mastering the most innovative techniques on the lathe. He was also an excellent ivory carver, and he was able to combine the techniques in astonishing ways, leaving a legacy of inspired and innovative style. His four key works—three in the collections of the Green Vault and one in Stockholm—are testimony to the highly satisfactory way that turned shapes could be exceptionally rendered ivory pieces. Unusual combinations were the result. The high goblet of 1610, for example, is crowned by an ivory group of Perseus and Andromeda. The turned ivory counterfeit sphere (1611) rests on the shoulders of a Hercules figure. The depiction of Saint George and the Dragon adorns the lid of another cup (1613), and the impressive ivory frigate of 1620 is supported by Neptune and his sea horses.[23] These signed and dated pieces enable us to define reliably Zeller's oeuvre.

The inventory of the Dresden Kunstkammer of 1619 mentions a total of thirty ivory works under Zeller's name. Recent research has shown that not all of them were by his hand as had previously been thought.[24] Detailed comparisons of inventory descriptions with the actual turned objects in the Green Vault revealed that Georg Friedel[25] was the author of numerous works. There are at least nine imaginatively constructed ivory columns, two goblets with lids, and four counterfeit spheres. Friedel marked his works with his initials GF and/or the engraved image of a heron with a fish in its beak (cf. cat. nos. 89–91). One can deduce from this that Georg Friedel—about whose origins nothing is known and who does not appear on the court's payroll—was a collaborator in Jakob Zeller's workshop between 1610 and 1619. He also may have received his training there or been one of the journeymen ("Geselle") whom the renowned court artist had taught ("*die er gelernet*").[26] The accomplished ivory artist and master turner Marcus Heiden likely also trained in Zeller's workshop.[27] Heiden's fascinating approach was to adapt the shapes of goldsmiths' vessels to turned and carved ivory.

After many years of service (1601–19) for the emperors Rudolf II and Matthias in Prague, Hans (Johann) Wecker, son of Georg Wecker, went to Dresden, where he was employed as court turner starting at the latest in mid-1622.[28] Although his father, who had served under four consecutive Saxon electors, is not mentioned in the court payrolls after the last quarter of 1620, a drawing dated 1626 and initialed "GW" shows that he was still actively working on designs for turned objects when he was an old man.[29]

During the period 1581–1620, an opulent, multifaceted, and unique collection of turned ivory objects was formed in Dresden. Originating as a princely pastime, the art of turning ivory developed into a highly respected court art about 1600 and emerged as a special field for collectors beyond Dresden's Kunstkammer. Connoisseurs marveled at the wonders of mechanically produced art by the court turners and admired the precision with which a precious natural material like ivory was worked in a seemingly effortless manner. Fascination with this virtuosity remains unchanged to this day.[30]

15. Bauer/Haupt 1976, nos. 880, 895, 915, 959, 960, 961, 962; cf. also Kappel 1995a, p. 14f.
16. SächsHStA Dresden, A. Rep. XXVIII NR. 4a, Loc. 32437 (Hofbuch 1582), fol.58v.; cf. also Kappel 1995a, p. 16f.
17. Hantzsch 1902, p. 234.
18. Morigi 1595, p. 297, in English: "one never knows how. Today, this piece is kept in the Museo degli Argenti in Florence.
19. SächsHStA Dresden, Special Rescripte 1595, vol. I, fol. 150r and vol. II, fol. 142r.
20. See Scheicher 1993/94, p. 347.
21. Christian II purchased numerous turned ivory pieces from Georg Wecker and his son, Hans Wecker, in 1601 and 1602 (SächsHStA Dresden, Rentkammer invoices, no. 184, fol. 107v, and no. 185, fol. 297v, 408r).
22. SächsHStA Dresden, Rentkammer invoices, no. 186, fol. 114v.
23. Chronology of the objects as cited: 1610: Stockholm (Kungl. Husgeradskammaren, inv. no. SS 141); Green Vault: 1611 (inv. no. II 296); 1613 (inv. no. II 154), 1620 (inv. no. II 107); cf. also: Haag 1996, p. 50 with ill. 3.
24. Maurice 1985, p. 56 lists 23 works by Zeller.
25. Friedel is mentioned in the 1640 Kunstkammer inventory by name as former court turner of the Palatinate and as the one who delivered a hunter's horn made of ivory, fol. 453r. Erbstein 1884, p. 29 is the first who mentions him in the Green Vault Guide; see also Sponsel/Haenel 1932, p. 48 with plate 4.
26. Quoted from the 1640 Kunstkammer inventory, fol. 455r. The supposition that Friedel might have been a journeyman of Georg Wecker's was proven incorrect (cf. Kappel 1995a, p. 16).
27. The Green Vault owns the earliest dated work by Heiden, an ivory goblet of 1623 (inv. no. II 354); additional objects by him may be found in Florence, Vienna, Weimar, and Los Angeles. Cf. also: Aschengreen-Piacenti 1964, p. 84f., Haag 1996, p. 49f. with footnotes 16–19, Ulferts 1999, p. 144f.
28. Essen 1988, cat. no. 411 (Rudolf Distelberger); Maurice 2004, p. 13; Hantzsch 1902, p. 257. Apparently in 1624 Johann Georg I purchased a collection of turned ivory works with a Wecker provenance. Crafted by court turner Hans (Johann) Wecker and his father Georg, they replaced the turned pieces by Elector August that Electress Hedwig had removed in 1605.
29. SächsHStA Dresden, Rentkammer invoices, no. 187, fol. 125v, 199r–239r; cf. also: Kappel 1995a, p. 15f. and p. 25, ill. 8. The drawing for the design is inserted as a loose sheet in the inventory of the Turning Chamber of 1684 (no. 33). The last dated work by Wecker in the Green Vault is a small hollow sphere dated 1611 (inv. no. II 355).
30. It was not until after the completion of extensive conservation by Helmut Jäger (Brombachtal bei Erbach im Odenwald) between 1992 and 2002 that the holdings regained their former splendor. Nearly the entire collection will be exhibited in the Green Vault's Ivory Room (*Elfenbeinzimmer*) in the Dresden Residential Palace once the final construction and renovation are complete. The anticipated opening date is the end of 2006.

72 Cup and Cover

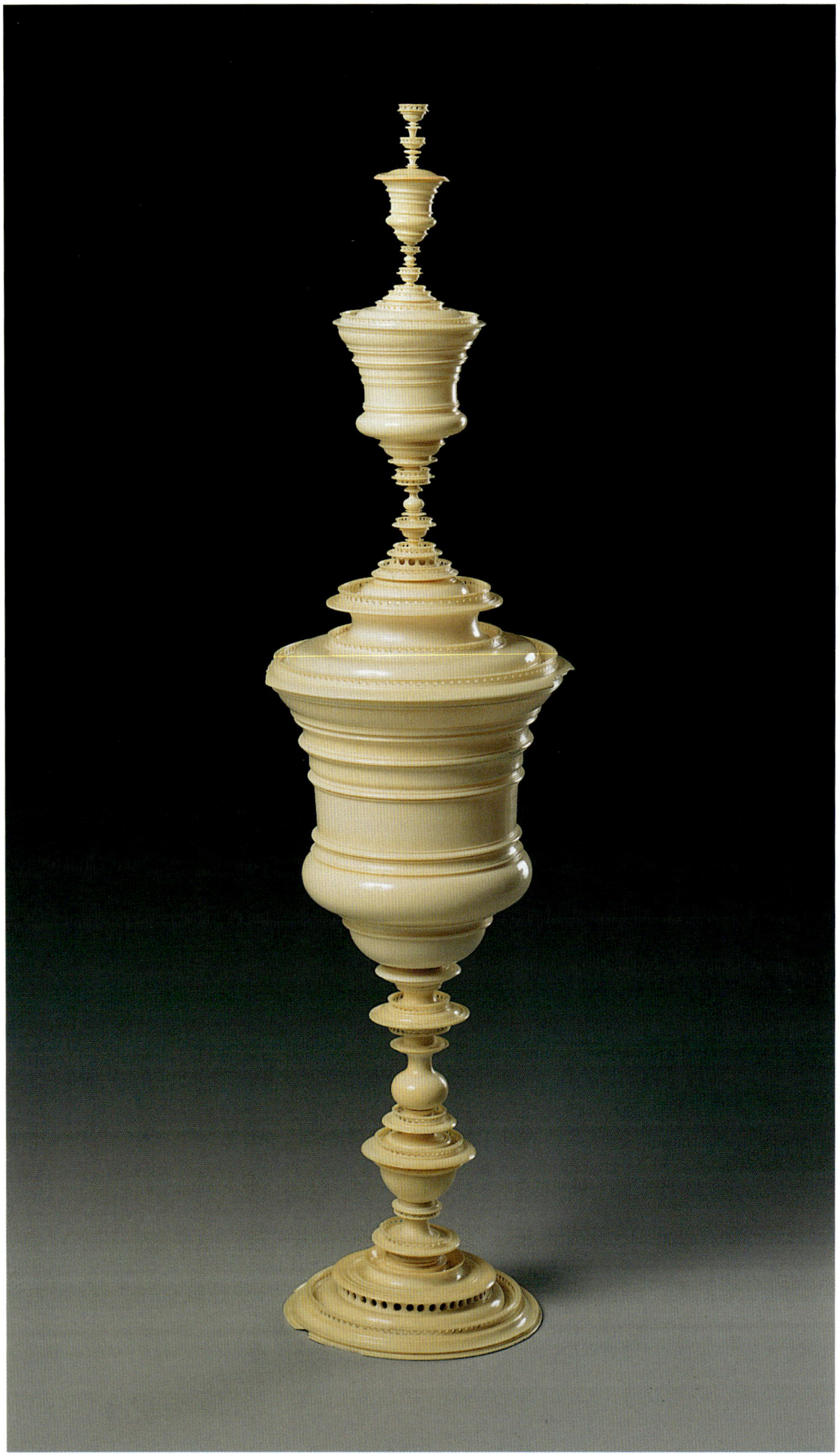

In early 1578 Georg Wecker accepted the appointment as Dresden court turner for life. Elector August of Saxony, occasionally working the lathe himself as the "turning sovereign" ("*drechselnder Souverän*"), soon became a passionate collector of this talented Munich artist's turned works. The first inventory of Dresden's Kunstkammer, compiled in 1587, a year after the elector's death, lists sixteen ivories by Wecker. Nine of Wecker's turned works dating to 1586 are preserved in the Green Vault. The cup shown here, not delivered to the Kunstkammer until 1589, belongs to this group. Two smaller vessels seem to emerge from its cover. Despite its imposing size, it appears delicate and graceful. Conservation treatment in 1992 revealed the interesting method of construction that Wecker used repeatedly. Instead of the object's being worked from a single piece of ivory, it is made up of individual parts that were joined by means of so-called bayonet mounts.
J.K.

Georg Wecker, Dresden, 1586
Ivory
H. 20⅞ in. (53 cm)
Signed and dated on the wall of the vessel: GW 1586
Since 1589 Kunstkammer
First mentioned in Kunstkammer inventory 1595, fol. 182
Staatliche Kunstsammlungen Dresden,
Grünes Gewölbe, inv. no. II 76
Lit.: Erbach 1995, cat. no. 75 (without text);
cf. also: Kappel 1995a, p. 14f.;
Syndram 1995, p. 9f.

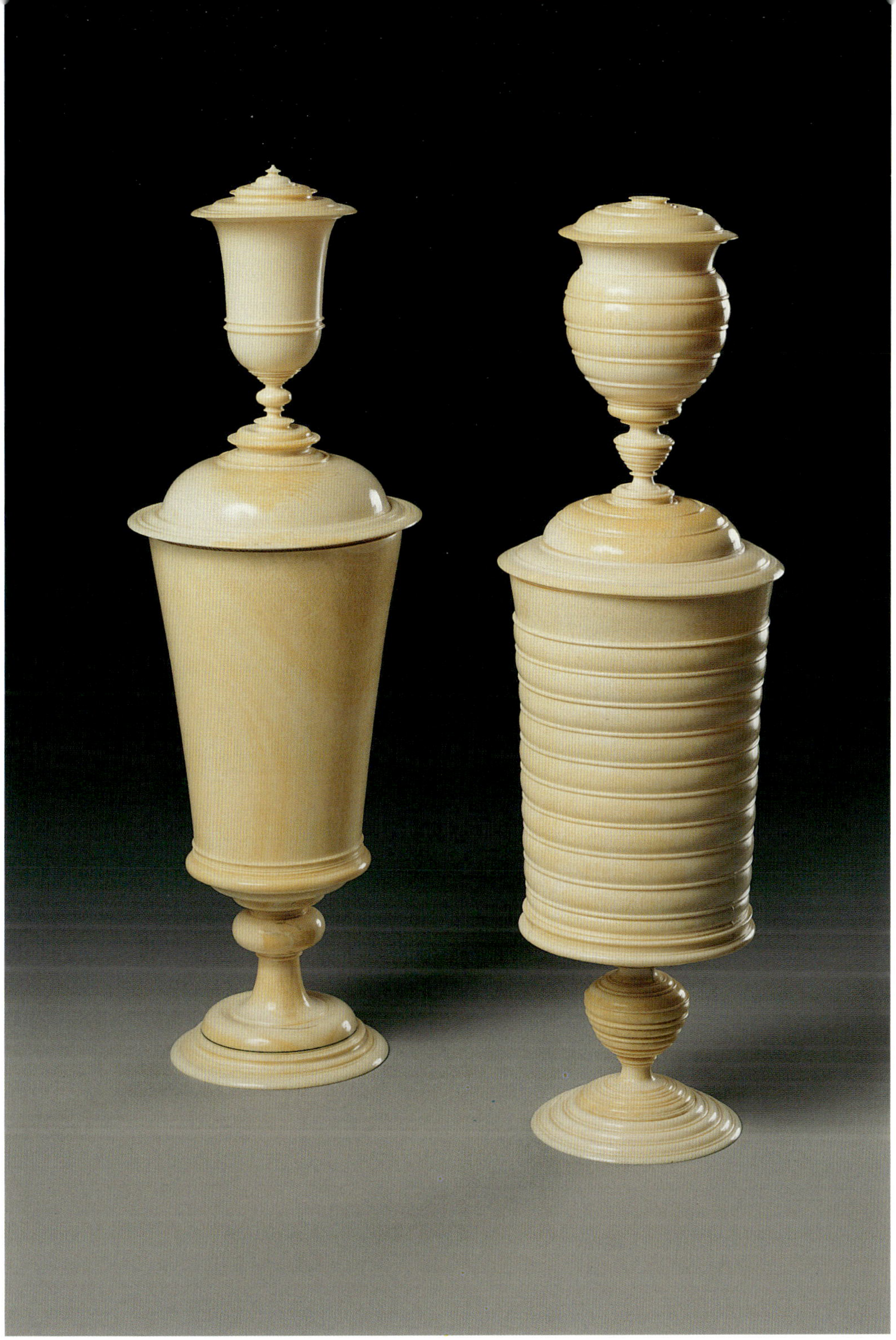

73 Cup and Cover

Georg Wecker, Dresden, 1586
Ivory, H. 17¾ in. (45 cm)
Signed and dated on the lid: GW 1586
Signed on the lid of the small vessel: GW
First mentioned in Kunstkammer inventory 1587, fol. 148v
Staatliche Kunstsammlungen Dresden, Grünes Gewölbe, inv. no. II 373 (left)
Lit.: Erbach 1995, cat. no. 31 (without text) and ill. 20, 21

74 Cup and Cover

Georg Wecker, Dresden, 1588
Ivory, H. 17⅜ in. (44 cm)
Signed and dated on the edge of the lid: GW 1588
Since 1590 Kunstkammer
First mentioned in Kunstkammer inventory 1595, fol. 183v
Staatliche Kunstsammlungen Dresden, Grünes Gewölbe, inv. no. II 89 (right)
Lit.: Erbach 1995, cat. no. 19 (without text) and ill. 20, 21

Whereas the viewer is fascinated by the matte finish of one cup's smooth surface (cat. no. 73), the second cup has a flat molding formed in the turning by even bulges. This decorative device was much favored and was used in various ways by Georg Wecker (cf. cat. nos. 72, 78). The two cups are quite similar in their construction: over a circular, turned disk foot with stout shaft rises a striking form. The same shape, slightly altered and much smaller, reappears as the cover's finial. These aesthetically pleasing repetitions of forms were intentional; they are found in the oeuvre of both Georg Wecker and Egidius Lobenigk. They can be explained as a testament to the efficiency of the court turners: once the metal disks of the lathe were made with different shapes and profiles, the material was mechanically sized during the turning process, making it relatively uncomplicated to produce multiple versions of a shape in the same or different sizes that could then be combined or mounted vertically.
J.K.

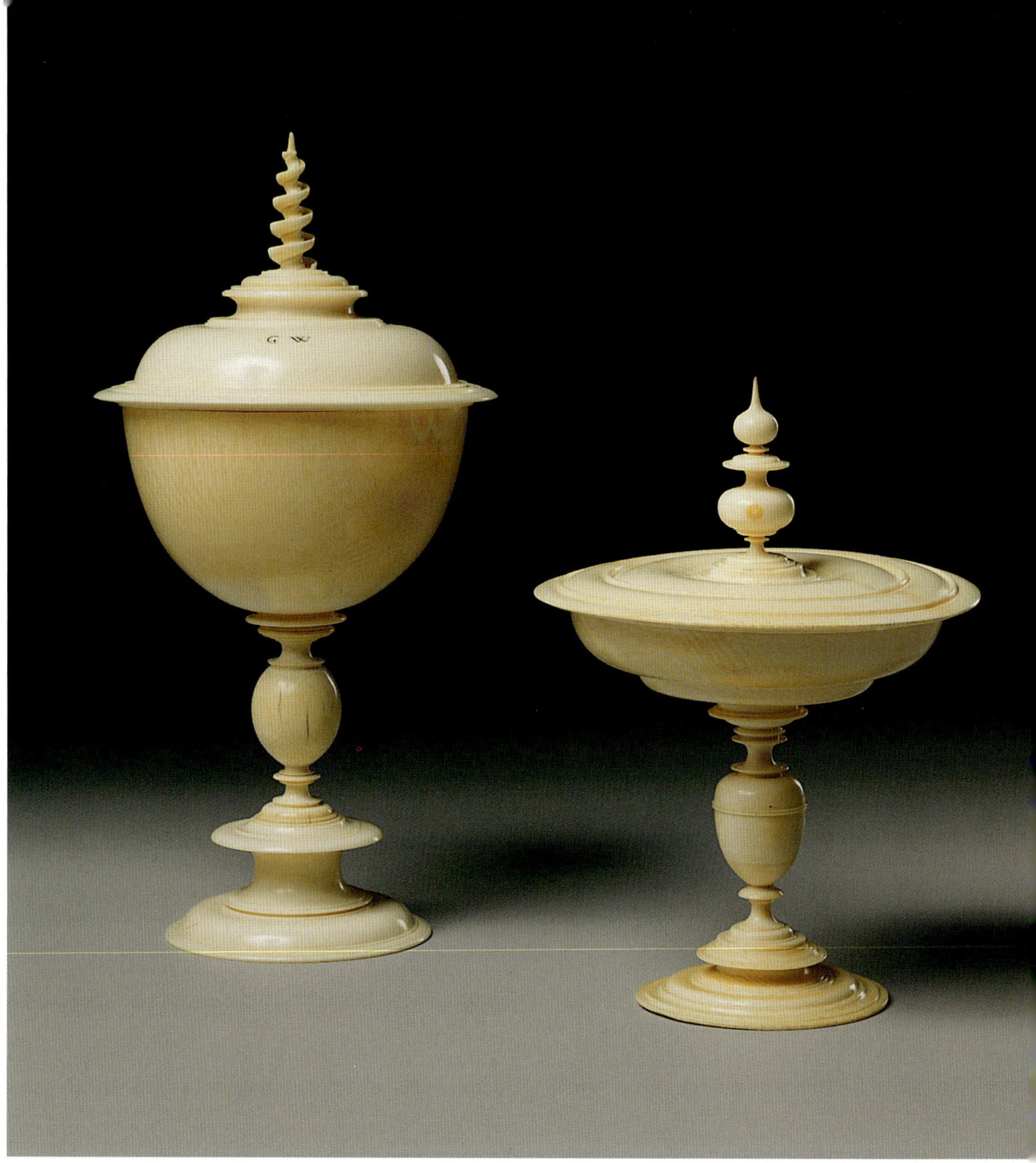

75 Footed Bowl with Cover

Georg Wecker, Dresden, 1588
Ivory, H. 8¾ in. (22.3 cm)
Signed and dated on the lid:
GW 1588
Since 1590 Kunstkammer
First mentioned in
Kunstkammer inventory
1595, fol. 184r
Staatliche Kunstsammlungen
Dresden, Grünes Gewölbe,
inv. no. II 260 (left)
Lit.: Erbach 1995, cat. no. 26
(without text)

76 Footed Bowl with Cover

Georg Wecker, Dresden, presumably between
1588 and 1590
Ivory, H. 6⅜ in. (16.2 cm)
Signed on the inside of the lid: GW
Since 1590 Kunstkammer
First mentioned in Kunstkammer
inventory 1595, fol. 184r
Staatliche Kunstsammlungen Dresden, Grünes
Gewölbe, inv. no. II 162 (right)
Lit.: Erbach 1995, cat. no. 37
(without text)
Cf. also: Gruber 1977, p. 18
and cat. nos. 183–216;
Essen 1986, cat. no. 533 (Gerd Spitzer);
Erbach 1995, cat. no. 32 (without text)
and ill. 12; Kappel 1995a, p. 14

Both lidded bowls, signed by Georg Wecker, entered the Dresden Kunstkammer in 1590. While one is marked 1588, the other (cat. no. 76) is undated. We do not know why Wecker signed but did not date many of his turned ivories. A total of eleven undated pieces have survived, but they can be relatively accurately dated based on the year they entered the Kunstkammer.

The simple elegance of these objects epitomizes the restrained, well-proportioned style that distinguishes Wecker's lathe-turned work. One of the prototypical sources of inspiration was apparently the tazza, a type of vessel that was popular and widespread since the last third of the sixteenth century, ultimately deriving from the art of the goldsmith. The clearly structured shapes, with wide bowls, torus profiles, grooves, and smooth baluster shafts, are, however, even more closely tied to the turner's art. Similarities in technique inevitably led to correspondence with other early-seventeenth-century turned objects of wood, serpentine, and alabaster. The unmistakable ingenuity displayed in many of the elegant turned ivories, which are understandably referred to as "art pieces" ("*Kunststücke*"), has never been achieved or even attempted in serpentine worked on the lathe.
J.K.

77 Beaker in Goblet Form on Stand

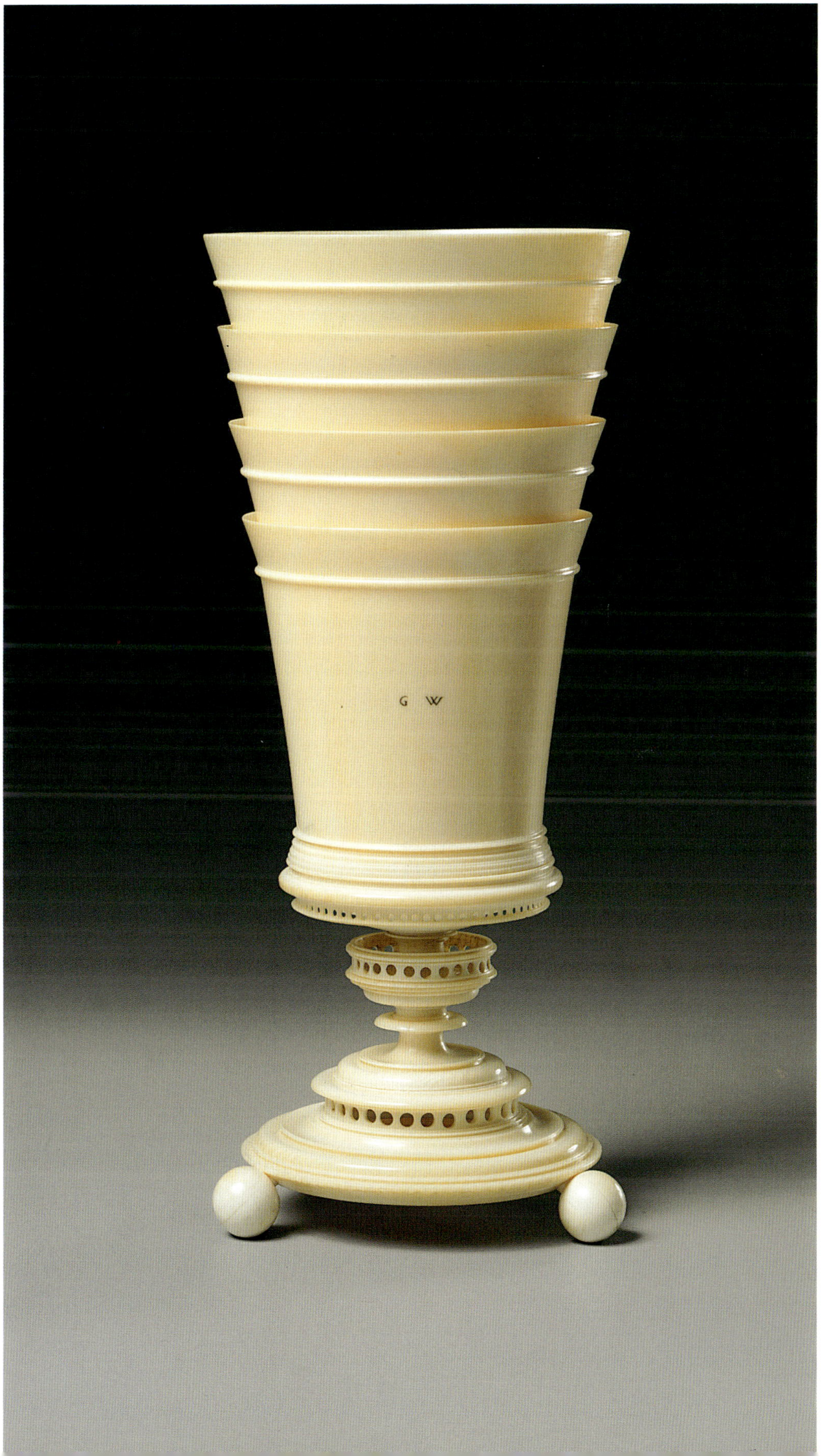

In this vessel, which originally had a cover, Georg Wecker achieved a striking optical illusion. Fabricated on the lathe from a single piece of ivory, the work looks like four individual tumblers stacked one inside the other. Wecker repeated this invention in another vessel in the Green Vault (inv. no. II 167), also completed by 1587.

Comparison of Wecker's work from between 1586 and 1589 reveals an astonishing stylistic continuity on the highest artistic level. His vessels are always clearly structured and well proportioned, yet they appear sturdier than they really are. The horizontal line is invariably emphasized and diagonals are avoided. Wecker's beakers and cups look functional, but they could not be put to practical use. Only a few of his pieces, such as the writing tools he made (cf. cat. no. 79), could actually be used.
J.K.

Georg Wecker, Dresden, 1587
Ivory, H. 8⅝ in. (22 cm)
Signed and dated on the wall of the vessel: GW 1587
Since 1588 Kunstkammer
First mentioned in Kunstkammer inventory 1595, fol. 180r
Staatliche Kunstsammlungen Dresden, Grünes Gewölbe, inv. no. II 34
Lit.: Menzhausen 1977, p. 101–04 and ill. 54; Erbach 1995, cat. no. 22 (without text); Prague 1997, cat. no. II.156 (Jutta Kappel)

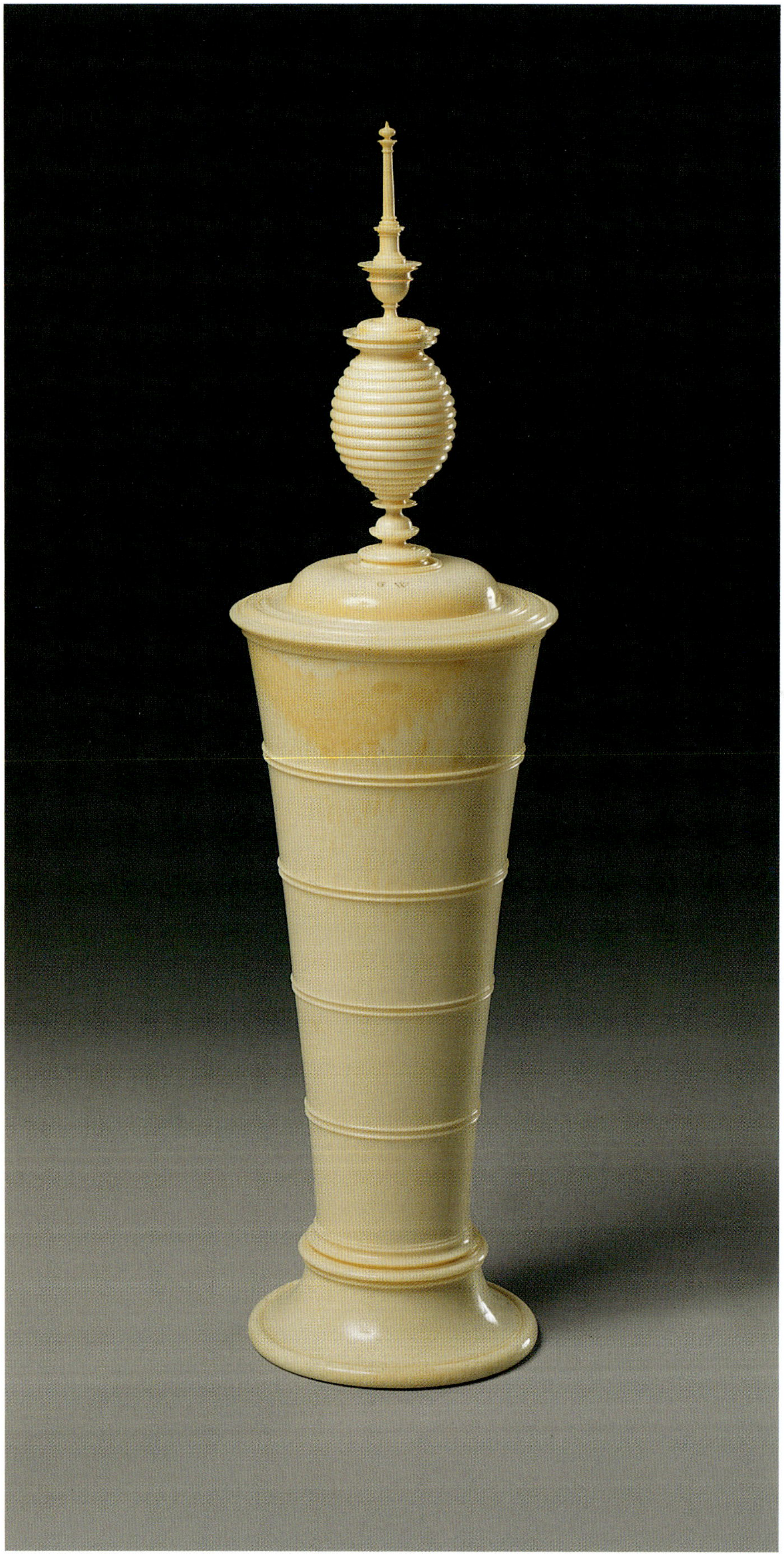

78 Tall Beaker with Cover

This slender, conical beaker follows a vessel type popular in goldsmiths' work since the mid-sixteenth century. The lid is crowned with a smaller turned vesssel with stripes; its lid in turn is decorated with a minuscule column.

A number of examples provide evidence that Georg Wecker did not deliver most of his pieces to the Kunstkammer in the same year they were completed. This piece, for instance, belongs among the turned objects that are signed and dated 1587. However, it was not received in the Kunstkammer until the following year, 1588. Another item by Wecker, described in almost identical terms but impossible to trace from the beginning of the seventeenth century, was deposited in 1589. Perhaps this vessel was intended as a duplicate and was later given away. The inventory of Emperor Rudolf II's Kunstkammer lists turned works by Georg Wecker and records that in 1601 further lathe-shaped ivories were given as presents by Elector Christian II of Saxony and dispatched to the imperial court in Prague.
J.K.

Georg Wecker, Dresden, 1587
Ivory, H. 11⅞ in. (30.3 cm)
Signed and dated on the lid: GW 1587
Since 1588 Kunstkammer
First mentioned in Kunstkammer inventory 1595, fol. 180v
Staatliche Kunstsammlungen Dresden, Grünes Gewölbe, inv. no. II 163
Lit.: Erbach 1995, cat. no. 23 (without text); cf. also: Bauer/Haupt 1976, pp. 48–53; Kappel 1995a, p. 15 with notes 8, 9

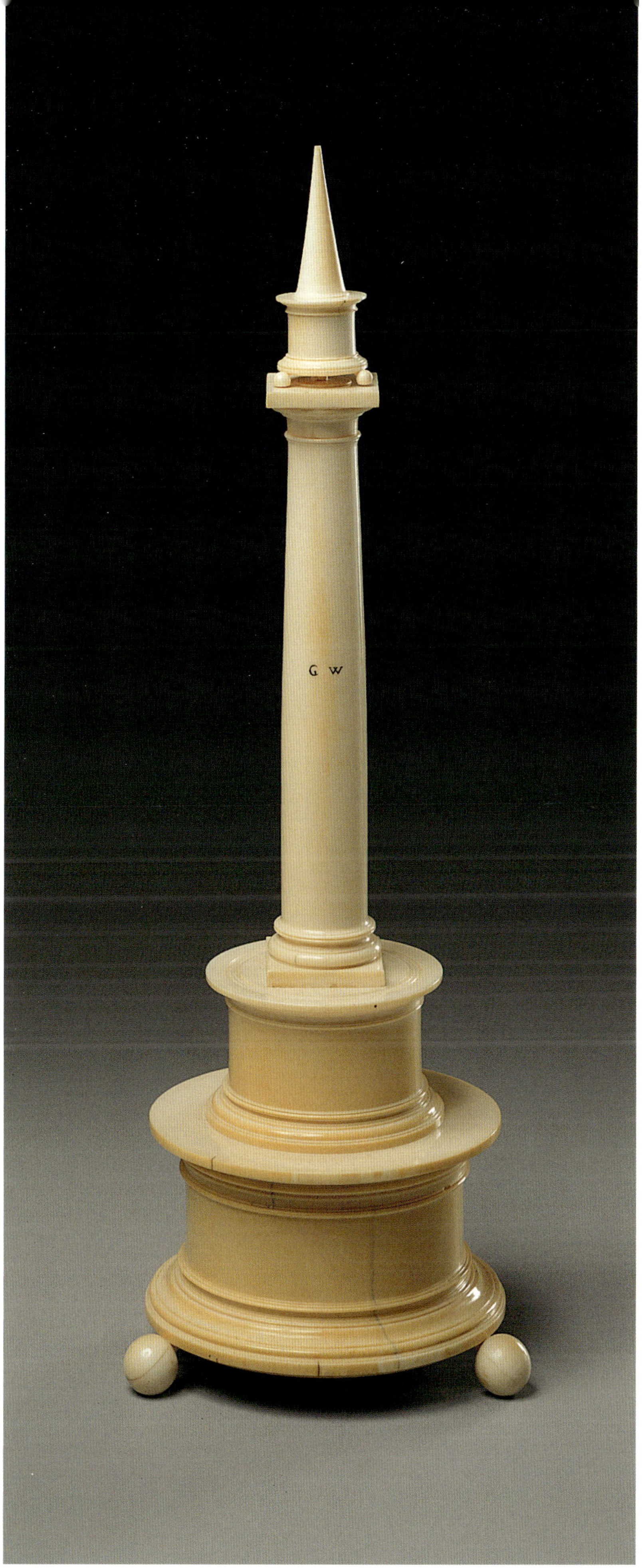

79 Writing Set on Ball Feet

Only after it was dismantled did this artwork of turned ivory reveal its intended purpose to its princely user. For convenient operation, Georg Wecker used bayonet mounts to attach the individual parts of his works to each other. Still functional, these locks can be opened by gently turning them. Inside the stout base was a thick-walled lead inkwell, which was not replaced after conservation (carried out in 1992). Over the inkwell is an ivory sieve for sprinkling fine sand over a completed document before folding and sealing it with wax. Reed pens, since lost, were stored in the shaft of the column. On top of this, Wecker put a much smaller yet equally practical and decorative column, with a base that can be unscrewed. According to the Dresden Kunstkammer inventory of 1595, this held the sealing wax. Another pen-and-ink set in a column by Wecker dates to 1588. Also in the Green Vault (inv. no. II 360), it follows similar principles of construction. Neither set shows any signs of wear, so it may be deduced that they were never actually put to use.
J.K.

Georg Wecker, Dresden, 1588
Ivory, H. 15 in. (38 cm)
Signed and dated on the column: GW 1588
Since 1588 Kunstkammer
First mentioned in Kunstkammer inventory 1595, fol. 180v
Staatliche Kunstsammlungen Dresden, Grünes Gewölbe, inv. no. II 63
Lit.: Erbach 1995, cat. no. 74 (without text);
cf. also: Menzhausen 1977, pp. 101–04 and ill. 54;
Erbach 1995, cat. no. 29 (without text) and ill. 15, 22;
Prague 1997, cat. no. II.162 (Sabine Haag)

80 Ointment Jar

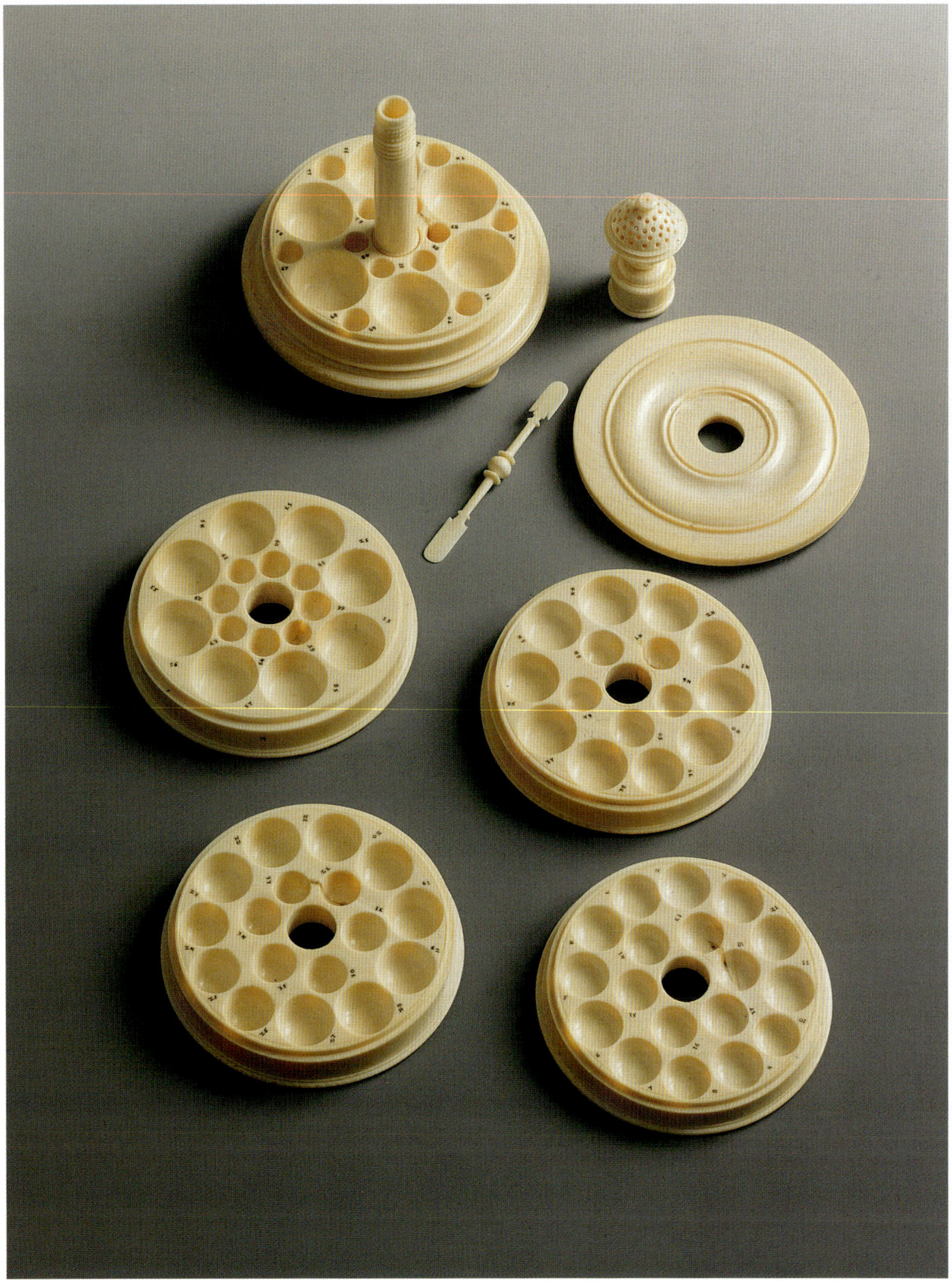

Workshop of Jakob Zeller
Dresden, between 1619 and 1620
Ivory
H. 4⅞ in. (12.3 cm)
First mentioned in Kunstkammer inventory 1640, fol. 456v, among the pieces delivered by Jakob Zeller and his journeymen to the Kunstkammer

Staatliche Kunstsammlungen Dresden, Grünes Gewölbe, inv. no. II 79
Lit.: unpublished; cf.: Essen 1988, cat. no. 411 (Rudolf Distelberger); Prague 1997, cat. no. II. 153 (Sabine Haag); Brunswick 2000, cat. no. 80 (Susanne König-Lein)

Referred to as an "ointment jar" ("Balsambüchse") in the 1640 inventory of the Dresden Kunstkammer, this object was listed among the pieces manufactured by the Dresden court turner Jakob Zeller and his journeymen. This exquisite work was not included in the Dresden Kunstkammer's inventory of 1619, so it must have been made in the short time between that date and 1620, the year of Zeller's death.

The jar is not hollow as might be assumed: it consists of five turned disks, each with a drilled hole in the center. The disks have a total of eighty-four numbered half spheres of different sizes. Attached to the center of the bottom section is a cylinder in which a tiny spatula is stored. The disks are stacked one above the other, with a flat lid on top. Atop the lid, the terminal is a two-part perforated sphere, which screws onto the central cylinder and thus holds the jar together.

The purpose of the vessel, rather plain and simple from the outside, can be discerned only after it is dismantled, which would have astonished its user. Although there is no trace of its ever having been used, the container could have served to preserve aromatic balms. Beginning in the sixteenth century, ointments were produced and sold in pharmacies, usually as mixtures of cold-pressed nutmeg butter and essential oils. The vessels for storing these precious salves were made of different materials. They were most often little jars with tops and bottoms threaded so they could be screwed to each other. One such example is in the Herzog Anton Ulrich-Museum, Brunswick. It is comparable to the piece shown here: the ivory components can be stacked (*Stapeldose*), and the object was intended to hold ointment. Another container of this type is in Vienna (Kunsthistorisches Museum, Kunstkammer). Originally in the collection of Emperor Rudolf II, it was produced in 1610 in Prague by the imperial court turner Hans (Johann) Wecker, a son of the Dresden-based Georg Wecker.
J.K.

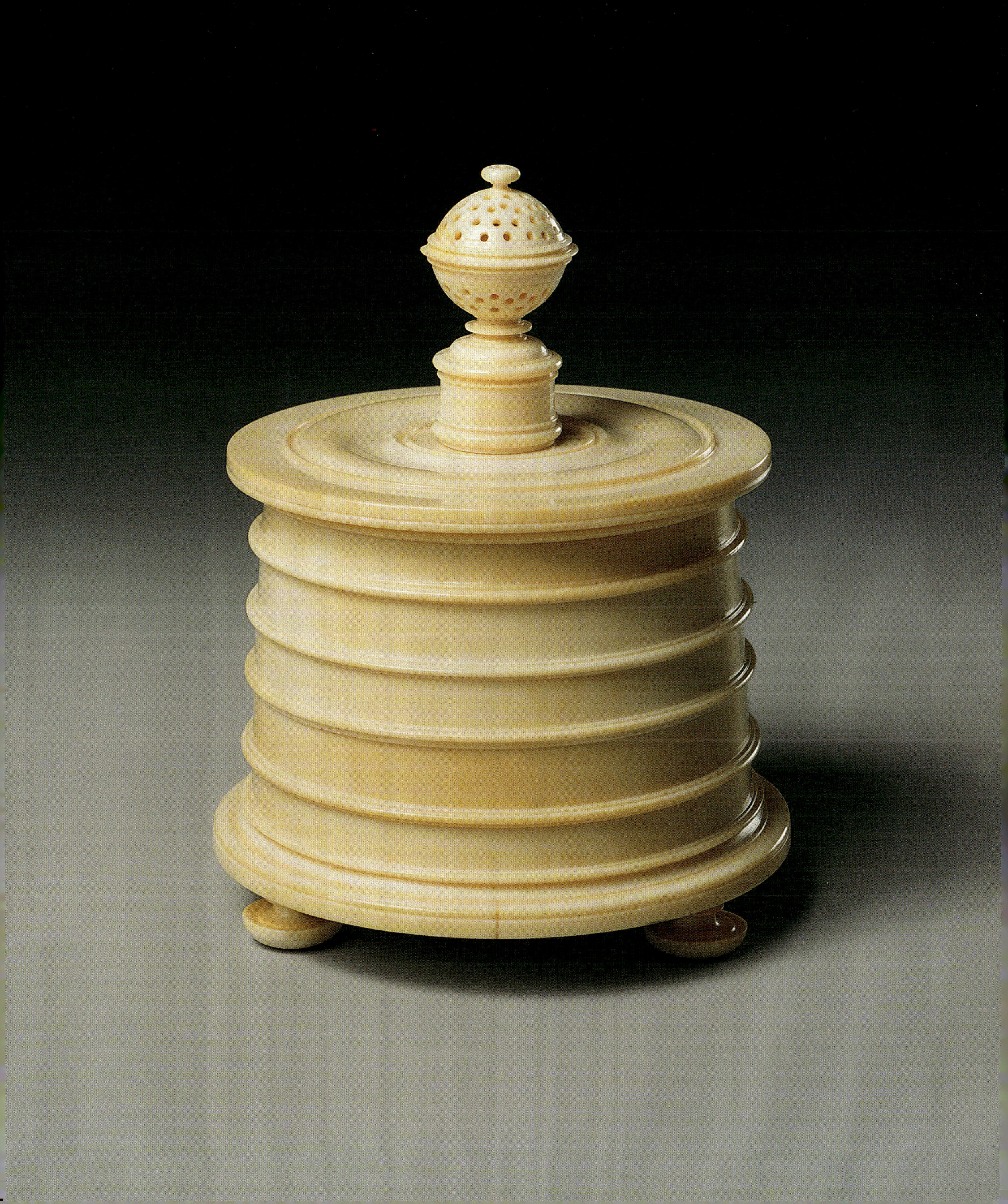

81 Oval Cup and Cover

Egidius Lobenigk, Dresden, 1586
Ivory, H. 13⅛ in. (33.5 cm)
In the lid a *verre églomisé* medallion
in gold, red, and blue; displaying the
electoral Saxon coat of arms;
inscribed in black: V·G·G·CHRISTIA: C·F·Z·S
Signed and dated on the lid: E.L 1586
Since 1588 Kunstkammer
First mentioned in Kunstkammer
inventory 1595, fol. 178r
Staatliche Kunstsammlungen Dresden,
Grünes Gewölbe, inv. no. II 147 (left)
Lit.: Erbach 1995, cat. no. 2 (without text);
cf. also: Diemer 1985, p. 307
with footnotes 93 and 94

82 Oval Cup and Cover

Egidius Lobenigk, Dresden, 1587
Ivory, H. 7 in. (17.8 cm)
Dated on the edge of the foot: *1587*;
signed on the lid: *E*L*;
on the finial cup: E.L
Since 1591 Kunstkammer
First mentioned in Kunstkammer
inventory 1595, fol. 179v
Staatliche Kunstsammlungen Dresden,
Grünes Gewölbe, inv. no. II 93 (right)
Lit.: Erbach 1995, cat. no. 4 (without text)
and ill. 17

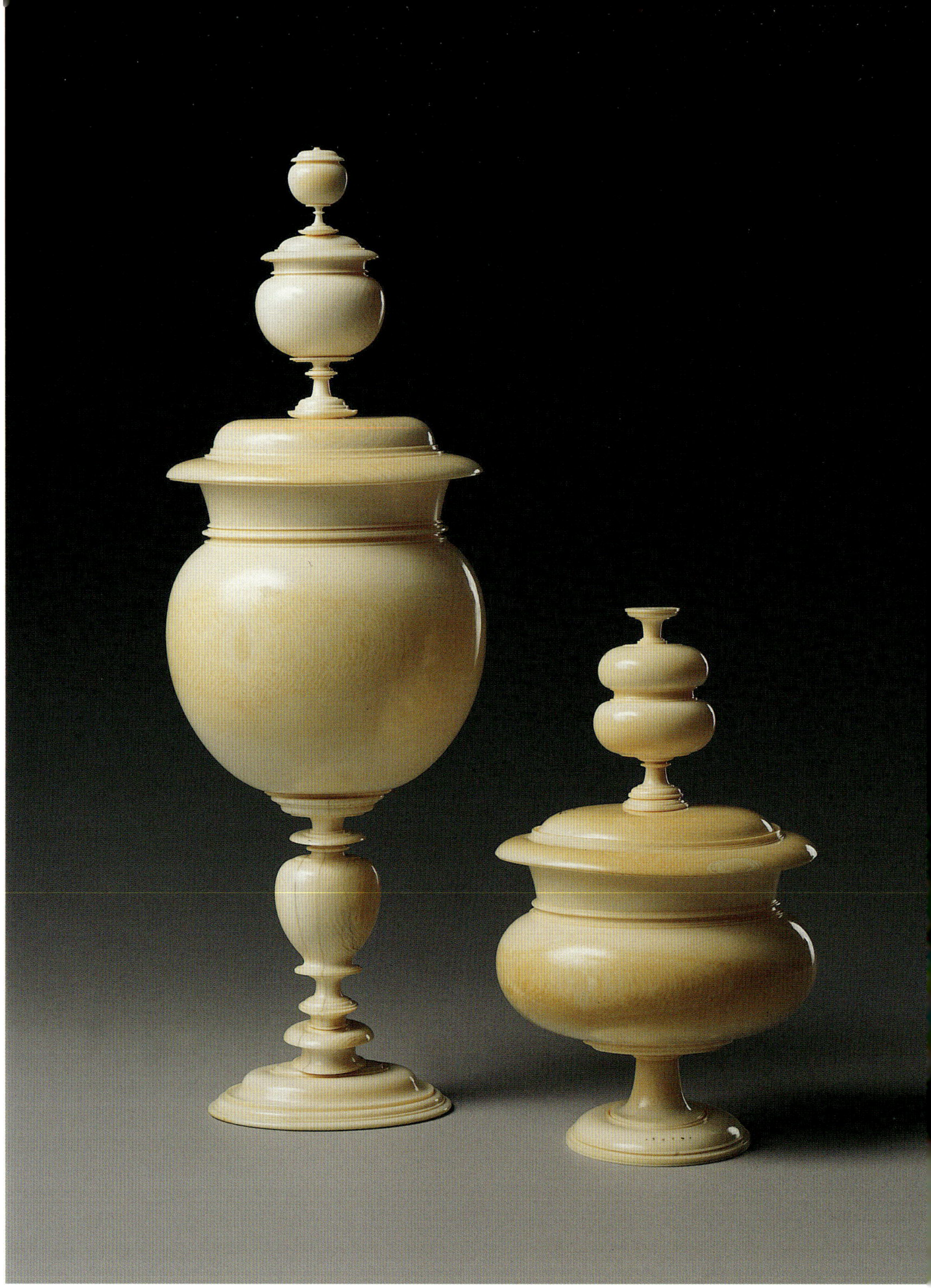

In 1584 Egidius Lobenigk from Cologne began his tenure as electoral court turner under Elector August of Saxony. Although his stylistic emphasis was different from Georg Wecker's and he tended to express himself with more daring shapes, he and Wecker worked as equals for more than a decade and were highly productive artists in Dresden.

Like Wecker, Lobenigk mastered the complicated technique of producing oval shapes on the lathe, a method practiced, not just understood in theory, with remarkable results as early as 1570 by the Milanese ivory turner Giovanni Ambrogio Maggiore. The two vessels shown here represent typical examples of Lobenigk's capabilities in this area. They were made during the early years of Elector Christian I of Saxony's reign. Hidden in the lid of the tall cup, dated 1586, is a *verre églomisé* medallion with the electoral Saxon coat of arms and the inscription V·G·G· (*Von Gottes Gnaden,* i.e., Through God's Grace) CHRISTIA: C·F·Z·S (*Christian Churfürst zu Sachsen*).

A special feature of both pieces is the replication in miniature of both vessel shapes on their lids (cf. also cat. nos. 83, 85, 86). This stylistic idiosyncrasy, typical of artworks turned in Dresden, may also be seen in the oeuvre of Georg Wecker (cat. nos. 72, 73, 74).
J.K.

83 Oval Cup and Cover

Inside the cover of the cup is a *verre églomisé* medallion with the electoral Saxon coat of arms and the inscription V·G·G· (*Von Gottes Gnaden*, i.e., Through God's Grace) CHRISTIA: C·F·Z·S (*Christian Churfürst zu Sachsen*). It belongs to the group of six turned ivory pieces extant that Lobenigk signed in 1587 (cf. cat. no. 82). They are all closely related in style: the objects are ovoid, and their lids are embellished with miniaturized vessels (cups or double cups, so-called Doppelscheuern). In comparison with other cups from 1587, the one shown here is noteworthy for its distinctive shape. The oval body appears to consist of two parts with the upper half overhanging the lower one at a ninety-degree angle. But this is a pure illusion. The body of the cup was carefully manufactured on the lathe from a single piece of ivory based on calculations determined by the shape it was meant to take. This shape is unique within Lobenigk's oeuvre, which may indicate that the cup's singular complexity was the objective in its creation.
J.K.

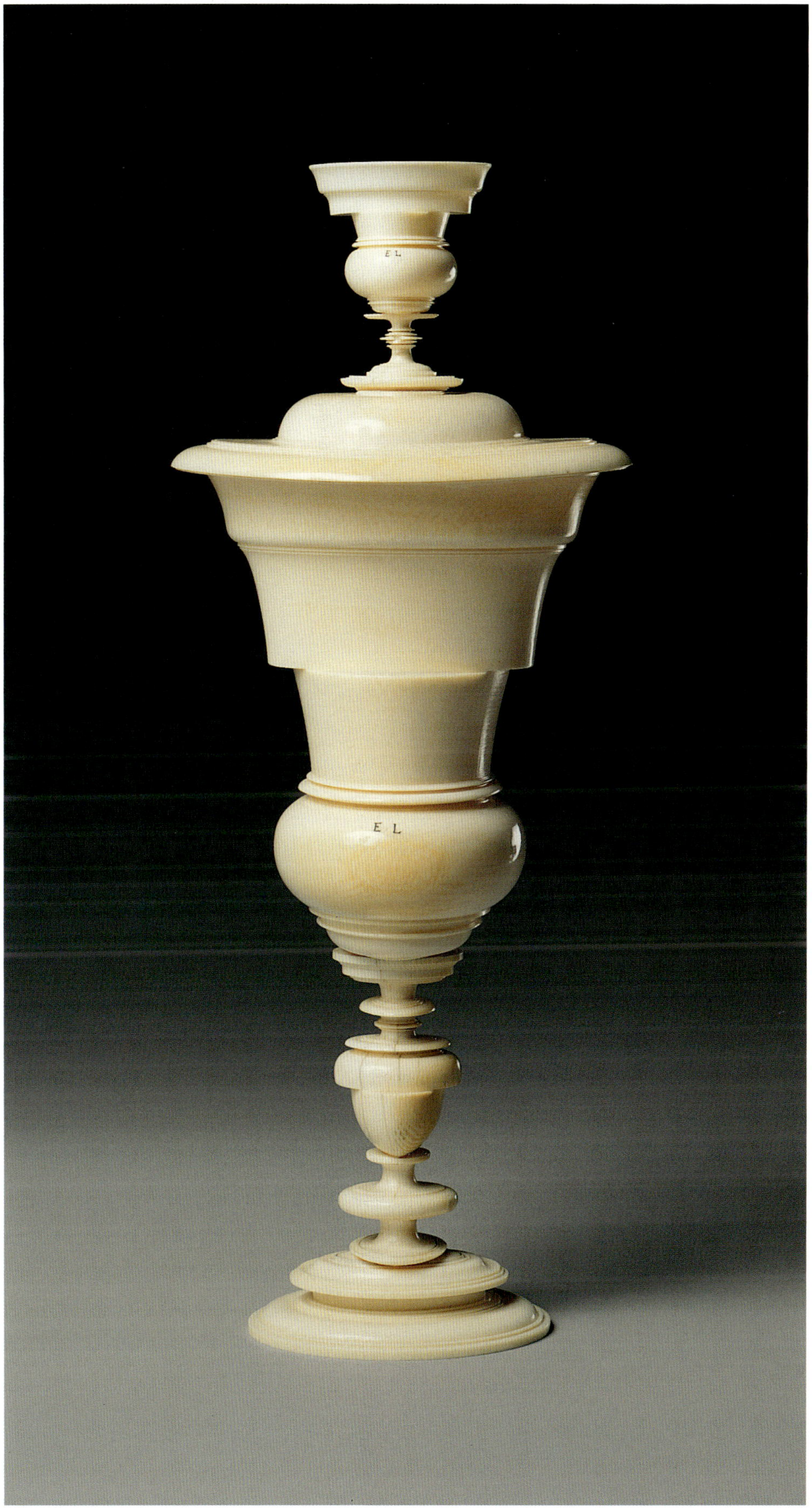

Egidius Lobenigk, Dresden, 1587
Ivory, H. $12\frac{1}{8}$ in. (30.9 cm)
In the lid a *verre églomisé* medallion in gold, red, and blue; displaying the electoral Saxon coat of arms; inscribed in black: V·G·G· CHRISTIA: C·F·Z·S
Signed and dated on the lid: EL 1587
Signed on the vessel's wall: EL
First mentioned in Kunstkammer inventory 1587, fol. 147r,
Staatliche Kunstsammlungen Dresden, Grünes Gewölbe, inv. no. II 80
Lit.: Erbach 1995, cat. no. 67 (without text)

84 Two Oval Bowls in the Form of a Double Cup

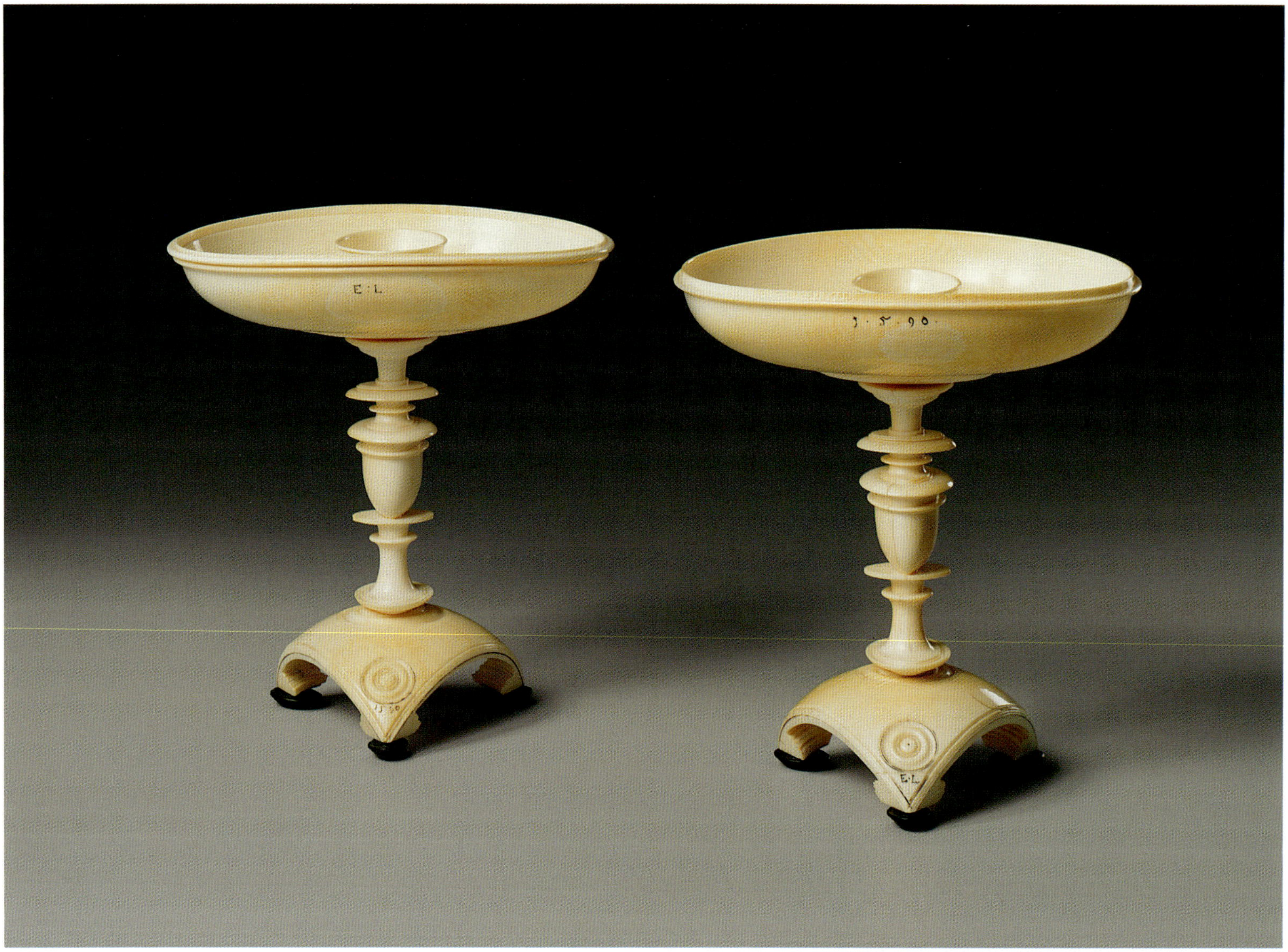

Egidius Lobenigk, Dresden, 1590
Ivory, ebony, H. 5⅞ and 5⅝ in. (14.5 and 15 cm)
Signed under the edge of the bowl:
E:L and dated 1590 on the foot (II 184)
Signed on the foot: E·L and dated 1·5·90·
beneath the edge of the bowl (II 332)
Since 1590 Kunstkammer
First mentioned in Kunstkammer
inventory 1595, fol. 179r
Staatliche Kunstsammlungen Dresden, Grünes
Gewölbe, inv. no. II 184 (left) and II 332 (right)
Lit.: Menzhausen 1977, p. 102 and ill. 52;
Erbach 1995, cat. nos. 8, 9 (without text) and ill. 16;
cf. also: Gruber 1977, p. 16 and cat. nos. 52–65,
p. 18 and cat. nos. 183–216

The two identically turned bowls are particularly ravishing in their subtle, seemingly functional design and the precision of their execution. The contours of the arched feet are outlined with black, as are the concentric circles decorating the feet. The vessels rest on tiny pieces of ebony, adding an accent that is both physically and aesthetically pleasing.

The appearance of the bowls is reminiscent of the tazza, a shape with origins in goldsmiths' work and increasingly popular from the last third of the sixteenth century (cf. cat. nos. 75, 76). As mentioned in the 1595 Kunstkammer inventory, the pieces could originally be joined to make into a so-called double cup (Doppelscheuer), a vessel type that became particularly popular in the late Middle Ages, especially in metalwork, but also in cut stone (see cat. no. 96).

Over the centuries the edges of the bowls became slightly distorted, marring the precise fit and precluding their display on top of each other. Their original appearance as a double cup can thus only be imagined.
J.K.

85 Cup and Cover Crowned with a Figure of Minerva

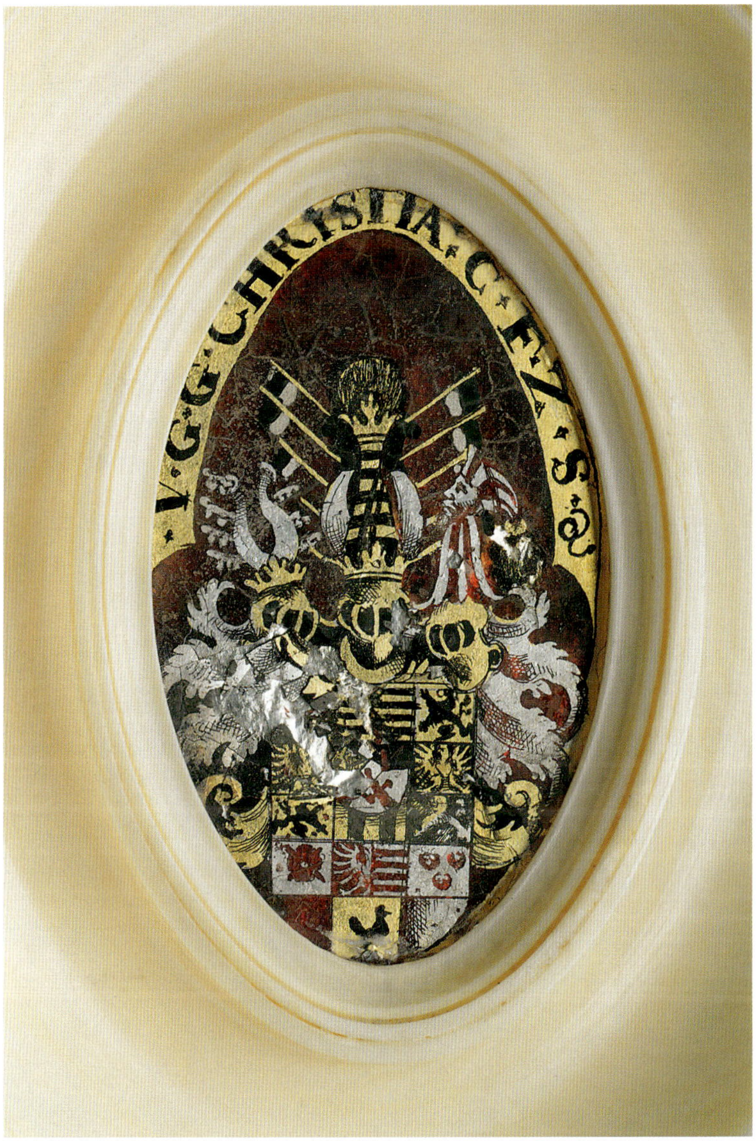

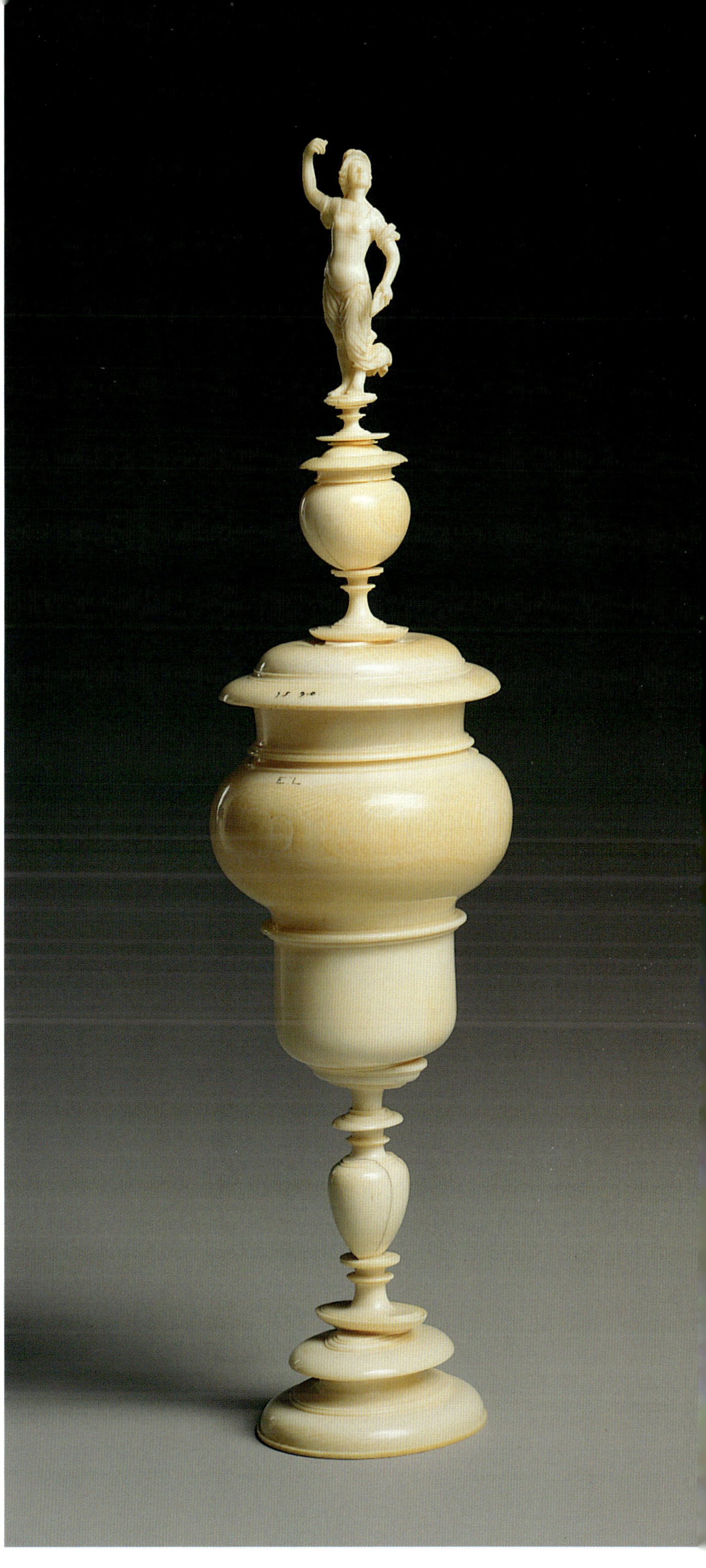

Egidius Lobenigk, Dresden, 1590
Ivory
H. 19⅝ in. (50 cm)
In the lid a *verre églomisé* medallion
in gold, red, and blue; displaying the
electoral Saxon coat of arms;
inscribed in black: V·G·G·CHRISTIA: C·F·Z·S
Signed on the wall of the vessel: E:L
Dated on the edge of the lid: 15.9.0.
Since 1591 Kunstkammer
First mentioned in Kunstkammer
inventory 1595, fol. 179v
Staatliche Kunstsammlungen Dresden,
Grünes Gewölbe, inv. no. II 9
Lit.: Erbach 1995, cat. no. 6 (without text);
cf. also: Haag 1996, p. 50

86 Cup and Cover Crowned with a Figure of a Roman Warrior

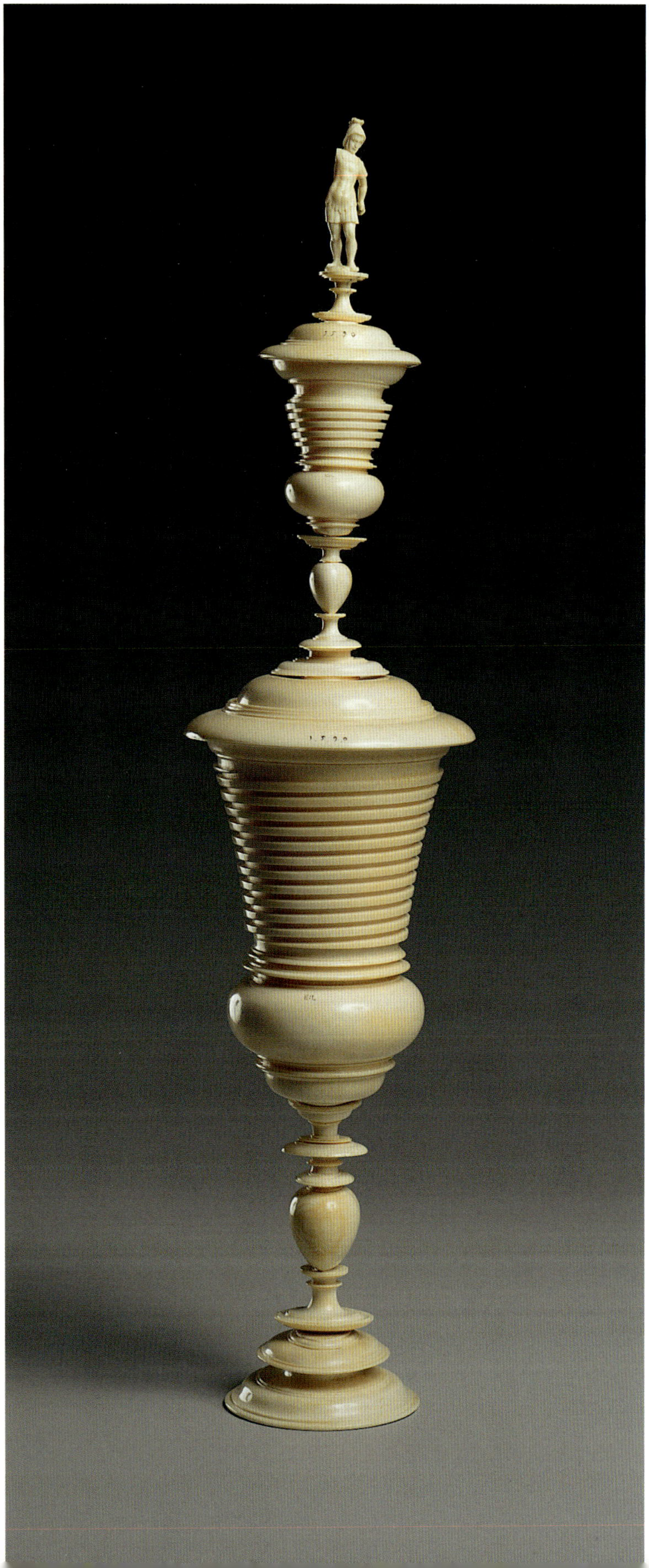

These two cups belong to a group from 1590 that are signed and dated by Egidius Lobenigk. One cup is turned in a bulbous shape with a smoothly polished surface that is articulated by slender torus molding. The other displays a sharply cut spiral around the cup and the smaller cup surmounting it. Inside the lids of both cups are *verre églomisé* medallions displaying the electoral Saxon coat of arms with the inscription V·G·G· (*Von Gottes Gnaden*, i.e., Through God's Grace) CHRISTIA: C·F·Z·S (*Christian Churfürst zu Sachsen*), referring to Elector Christian I, who was both the commissioner and the recipient of these pieces.

The vessels were not worked entirely on the lathe. The crowning figures–Minerva (cat. no. 85), originally carrying a spear and shield, and a Roman warrior (cat. no. 86), missing his right arm and the halberd–are carved, not lathe-turned. In the years 1590 and 1591 Lobenigk introduced in two more ivories this new element of carving, which is completely absent in the surviving oeuvre of Georg Wecker. On a cup lid (1590) he placed a small female figure with a fruit basket, possibly an allegory of summer, and on a high column over a counterfeit sphere (1591) he put the figures of Mercury and Sol.

Another noteworthy piece is the figure of the Roman hero Marcus Curtius mounted on a cylindrical base (ca. 1590). In these works Lobenigk realized the first stylistic innovations of the late sixteenth century in the art of working ivory on the lathe, a critical aspect of which was a move away from purely mechanical production to a combination of turning and carving. This was typical of Jakob Zeller's creative process later in Dresden and in yet later work by Marcus Heiden, still active in Weimar in 1664.
J.K.

Egidius Lobenigk, Dresden, 1590
Ivory
H. 21 in. (53.5 cm)
In the lid a *verre églomisé* medallion in gold, red, and blue; displaying the electoral Saxon coat of arms; inscribed in black: V·G·G·CHRISTIA: C·F·Z·S
Signed on the walls of each goblet: E:L
Dated on the lids of each goblet: 1.5.9.0.
Since 1590 Kunstkammer
First mentioned in Kunstkammer inventory 1595, fol. 179r,
Staatliche Kunstsammlungen Dresden, Grünes Gewölbe, inv. no. II 282
Lit.: Menzhausen 1977, p. 102 and ill. 51; Erbach 1995, cat. no. 12 (without text) and ill. 14; cf. also: Haag 1996, p. 50; Ulferts 1999, pp. 143, 145

87 Column with Icosahedron

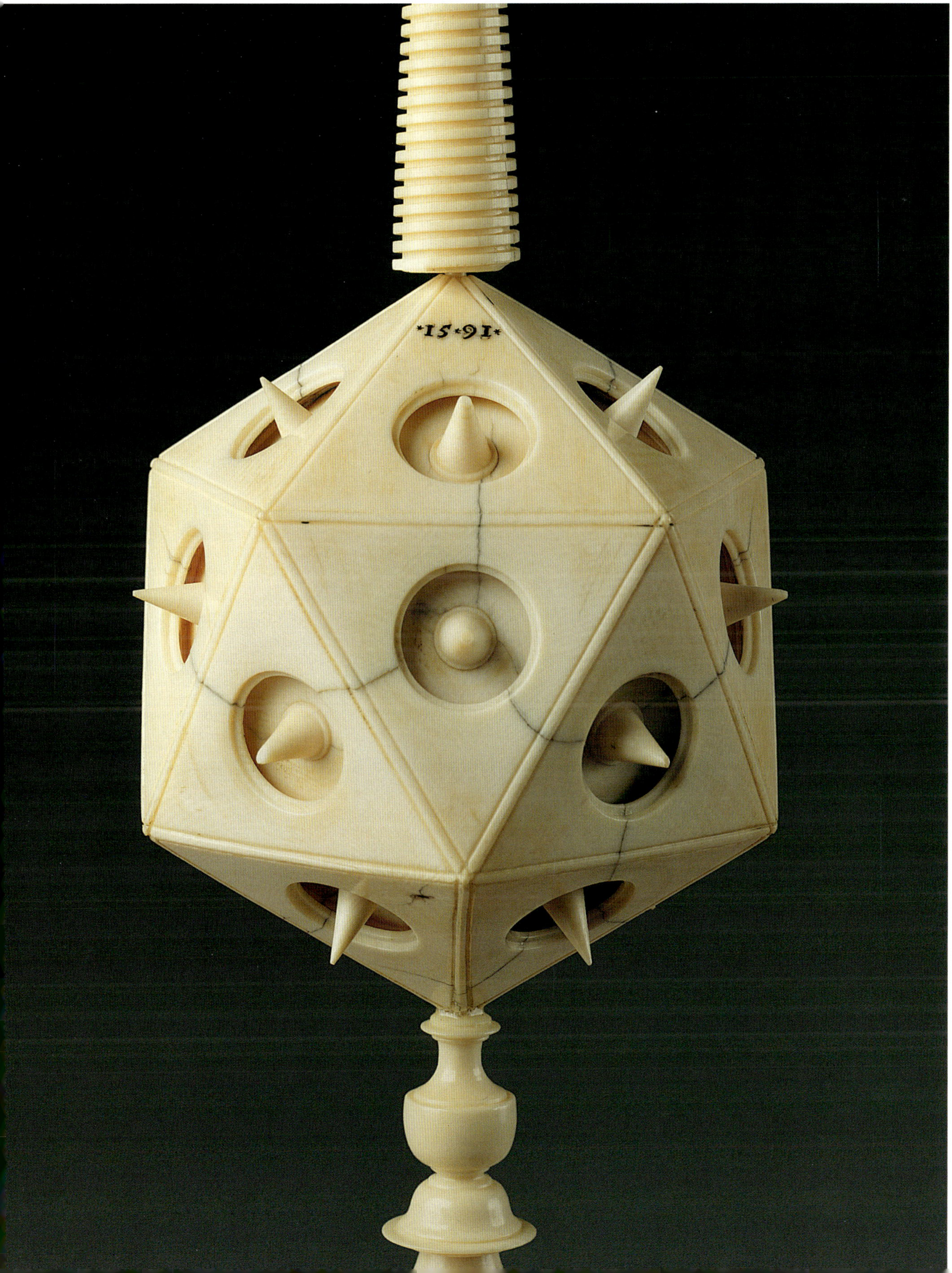

Egidius Lobenigk,
Dresden, 1591
Ivory
H. 27¾ in.
(70.6 cm)
Signed and dated
on the upper edge
of the foot and
on the icosahedron:
*E*L* and *15*91*
Signed on the
upper edge of the
column: *E*L*
Presented by Egidius
Lobenigk on April 13,
1591
First mentioned
in Kunstkammer
inventory 1595, fol. 118v
Staatliche Kunstsamm-
lungen Dresden, Grünes
Gewölbe, inv. no. II 99
Lit.: Menzhausen 1968,
p. 95 and ill. 76;
cf. also: Menzhausen
1977, p. 101–02
and ill. 50;
Nuremberg 1985, cat.
nos. 755, 756;
Maurice 1985, p. 117,
ill. 128.

88 Column with Tetrahedron

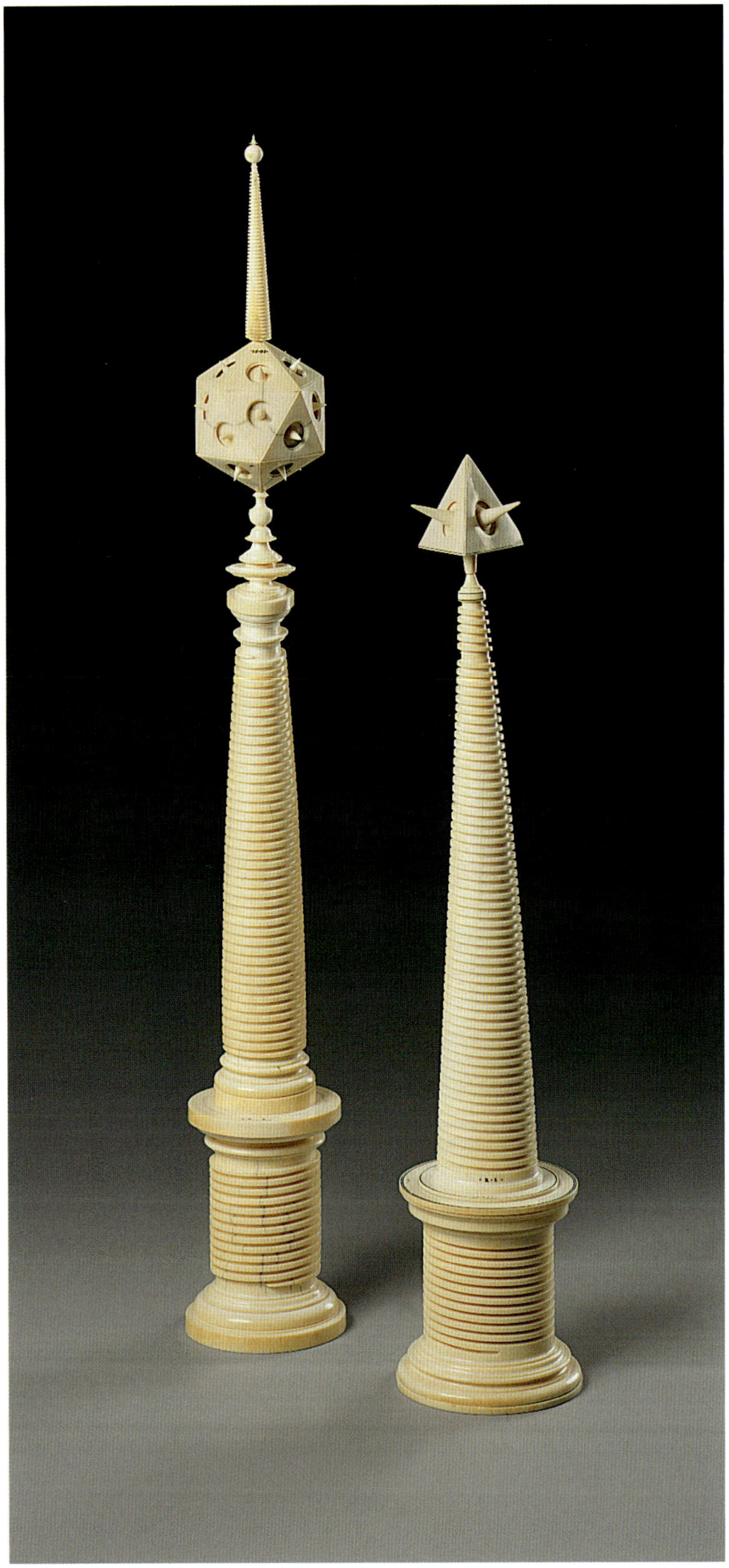

Egidius Lobenigk, Dresden, 1588
Ivory
H. 20⅝ in. (52.5 cm)
Signed and dated on the upper edge of the foot
and on the triangular pyramid: *E*L* and *1588*
Signed on the column's base: *E*L*
First mentioned in Kunstkammer inventory 1595, fol. 118v–119r
Staatliche Kunstsammlungen Dresden, Grünes Gewölbe, inv. no. II 7
Lit.: unpublished; cf.: Menzhausen 1977,
pp. 101–2 and ill. 50; Nuremberg 1985, cat. nos. 755, 756;
Maurice 1985, p. 117, ill. 128

Between 1588/89 and 1591, Lobenigk made eight of these large ivory columns. They are all preserved in the Green Vault. The two examples here illustrate the principles of design and construction of such columns. The turned cylindrical bases are hollow and form a stable stand; the shafts were turned from separate pieces of ivory. The columns are ovoid in cross section and taper toward the top. Their decoration consists of a continuous ivory spiral around their full length. The production of the basic shape required a tremendous amount of the precious raw material. The ivory spirals are so meticulously executed in their breadth and their regularity that the use of a special lathe may be assumed. Lobenigk himself must have invented the modification of the lathe specifically for creating this type of embellishment, because such precision can be seen only in works bearing his signature.

Lobenigk seems to have wanted to demonstrate the entire range of his abilities on the lathe in his ivory columns. The terminals of these impressive three-dimensional works are, yet again, absolute masterpieces of the art of lathe working. One is a pyramidal tetrahedron (cat. no. 88), and the other is an icosahedron made up of twenty equilateral triangles (cat. no. 87). The points that stick through round openings from within these complicated shapes are not added but are instead integral parts of the single piece of ivory from which the whole was made. Thus no joints can be found.

This penetration of geometric elements was not, however, an invention of artists working the lathe. Rather, it was a component of the design and of ideas about perspective that emerged during the second half of the sixteenth century. In 1568, Wenzel Jamnitzer published his *Perspectiva corporum regularium*. In 1571, the goldsmith Hans Lencker, who also worked in Nuremberg, printed his *Perspectiva corporum*. Both books were available in Dresden in various editions. Mentioned in the 1587 inventory of Dresden's Kunstkammer, they must have served as pattern books or sources of inspiration to the court turners.
J.K.

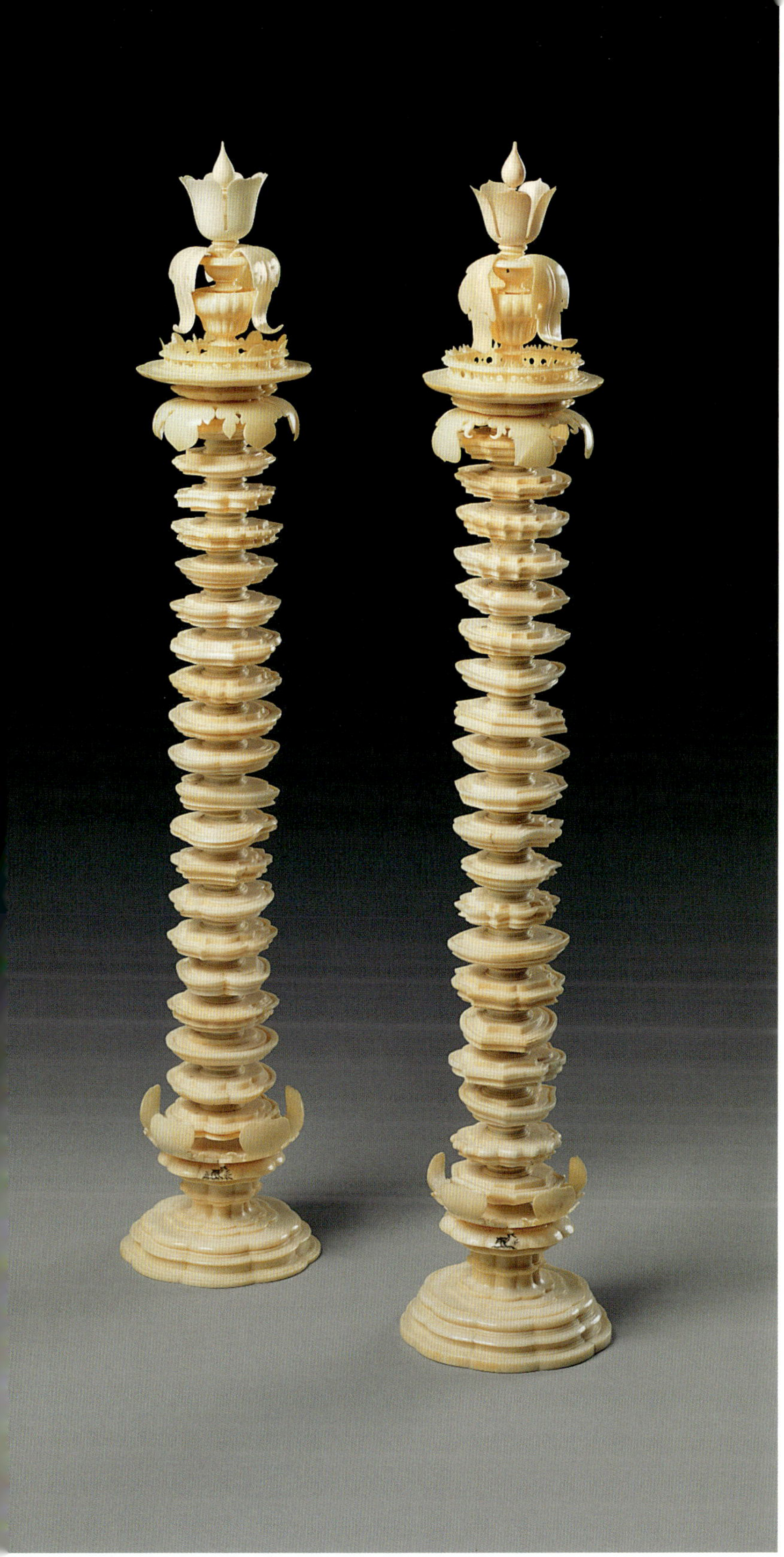

89 Two Tall Columns

These two columns and six other identically constructed examples are mentioned in the 1619 inventory of Dresden's Kunstkammer among the works delivered by court turner Jakob Zeller. The objects were neither designed nor made by him, for the tiny heron with a fish in its beak engraved on the columns' feet and blackened with sepia ink indicates that the maker was Georg Friedel (cf. cat. nos. 90, 91). Apparently Friedel was only temporarily active in Dresden, between about 1610 and 1620; later, he presumably worked as a turner at the electoral Palatine court. It is not known why he is not named in the Kunstkammer inventory.

Had there been a patent for the aesthetically pleasing and perfectly rendered columns, it would have been Friedel's. His columns remain unmatched. Conservation done in 1993 brought to light the method of their construction. At the core, a wood stick stands on a turned foot. Twenty differently shaped disks with holes drilled through their centers are mounted vertically on the stick, and nineteen tiny ivory rings ensure the necessary distance between them. The terminus of each column is a vase embellished with a stylized tulip above flat turned disks with foliate wreath decoration that is screwed to the wood staff.

Each column consists of a complete set of decorative disks. The disks on the left column are marked with the number 2, and those on the right column with a 6. These labels assured that the disks were attached to the appropriate column. As for their vertical arrangement within the column, the disks were interchangeable and their order was not specified, thus allowing many variations. Hypothetically the appearance of such a work could be altered ad infinitum. It is conceivable that this easygoing approach was intended, for on close scrutiny Friedel's decorative disks for his eight turned columns in the Green Vault show that they were not made singly. Instead they were produced in editions of two or three—i.e., miniseries. This execution on the lathe of one form multiple times underscores the ivory turner's highly efficient working methods.
J.K.

Georg Friedel, Dresden, 1616–19
Ivory, around a staff of plum wood
H. 19¾ and 20⅛ in. (50.3 cm and 51.2 cm)
Each piece marked on the foot: heron with a fish in its beak
First mentioned in Kunstkammer inventory 1619, fol. 218v, among the objects delivered to the Kunstkammer by Jakob Zeller
Staatliche Kunstsammlungen Dresden, Grünes Gewölbe, inv. no. II 382 (left) and II 189 (right)
Lit.: Erbach 1995, cat. nos. 100, 103 (without texts)

90 Cup and Cover

The oval vessel rests on a square foot and a shaft decorated with foliate wreaths. Its cross section is described in the 1619 inventory of the Dresden Kunstkammer as shaped "like a rose." Thus the form of a flower as found in nature was adapted for this mechanically produced masterpiece, a major artistic and technical challenge that could be met only by a first-rate ivory turner. As is evident from the two skillfully constructed columns (cat. no. 89), the dazzlingly turned sphere (cat. no. 91), and this cup, Georg Friedel particularly liked to invent original and complicated shapes on his lathe.

Oval forms could be made only on the most advanced lathes. One lathe was illustrated by Jacques Besson in his *Theatrum instrumentorum et machinarum* (Lyon, 1578). Lathes such as those employed in the workshops of Wecker, Lobenigk, and Zeller in Dresden's Residential Palace and also accessible to Georg Friedel rotated constantly and were equipped with a range of steel cutting tools that could be used in various combinations. Steel disks with different profiles (so-called stencils) facilitated multiple variations of diagonal and oblong volumetric forms when the ivory was turned in the round or the oval.
J.K.

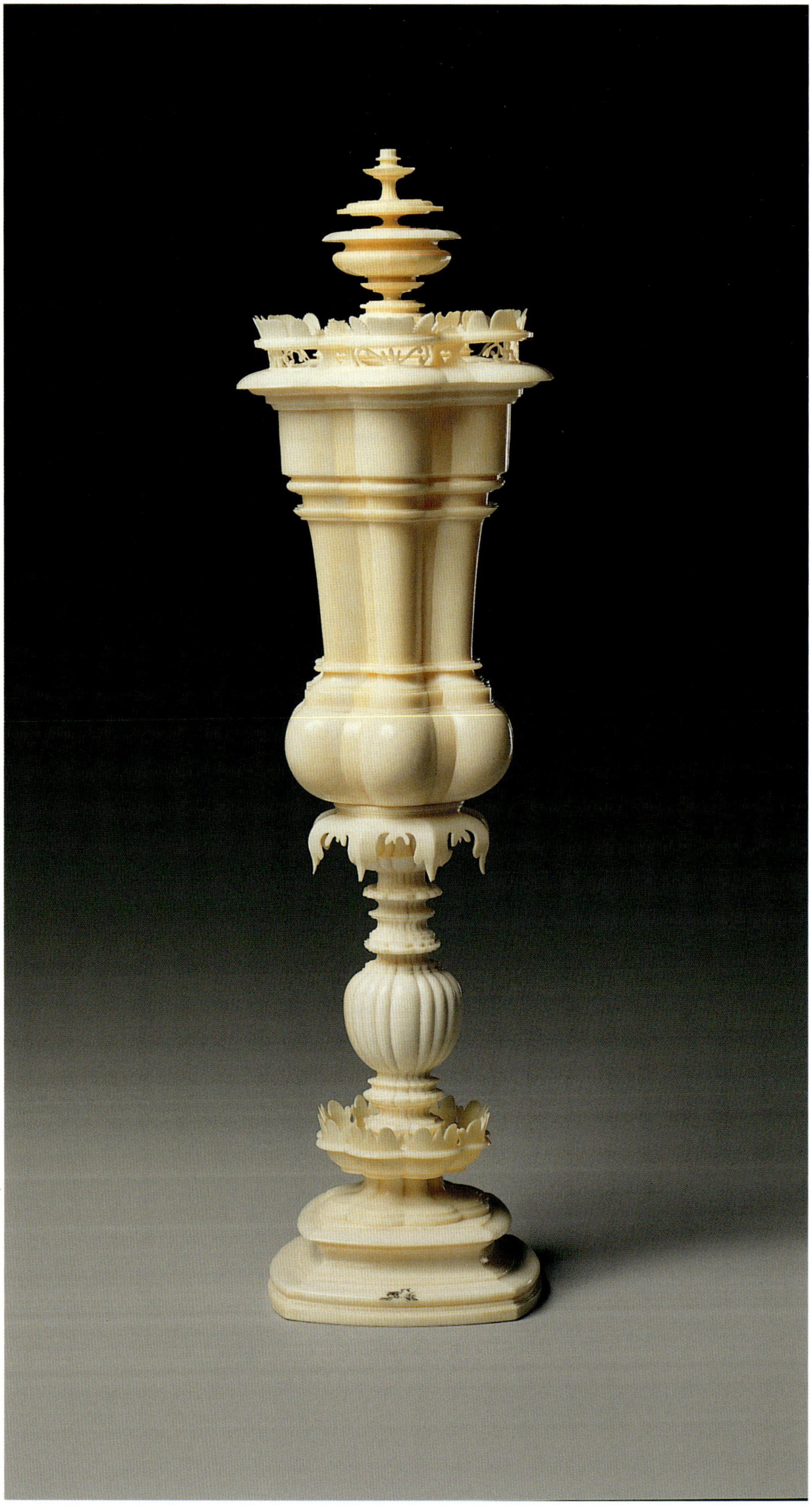

Georg Friedel, Dresden, between 1611 and 1619
Ivory
H. 14 in. (35.5 cm)
Marked on the foot: heron with a fish in its beak
First mentioned in Kunstkammer inventory 1619, fol. 217v, no. 13, among the objects delivered to the Kunstkammer by Jakob Zeller
Staatliche Kunstsammlungen Dresden, Grünes Gewölbe, inv. no. II 283
Lit.: unpublished, cf.: Maurice 1985, p. 68, ill. 63, p. 104 and ill. 7 and 8, Diemer 1985, p. 307 with footnote 90

91 Sphere on a Tall Shaft

The production of so-called counterfeit spheres—a term introduced in the late sixteenth century derived from the carvings inside the spheres—required great technical brilliance and knowledge of geometry and mechanics, as well as a superbly functioning lathe. Counterfeit spheres consist of multiple hollow spheres of diminishing size, similar to the layers of an onion, which can, however, be moved independently of each other. Pierced with round holes, the spheres contain tiny images in minuscule, oval, turned capsules that can be opened and closed from the outside with cords. Astonishingly, each sphere was turned, or rather worked, from a single solid ball of ivory, which makes them rare and much sought after collectors' items. The earliest counterfeit sphere, dated 1582 (Florence, Museo degli Argenti), was made by the Milan-based ivory turner Giovanni Ambrogio Maggiore. In Dresden, it was court turner Egidius Lobenigk who manufactured the first sphere. Later, Georg Friedel executed even more refined variations of this type. Four of Friedel's signed spheres, masterpieces in the art of turning, are preserved in the Green Vault. Only one of them is a counterfeit sphere. This little group of ivories is listed in the Dresden Kunstkammer inventory of 1619 among those donated by court turner Jakob Zeller but without mention of Friedel's name (cf. also cat. no. 89). J.K.

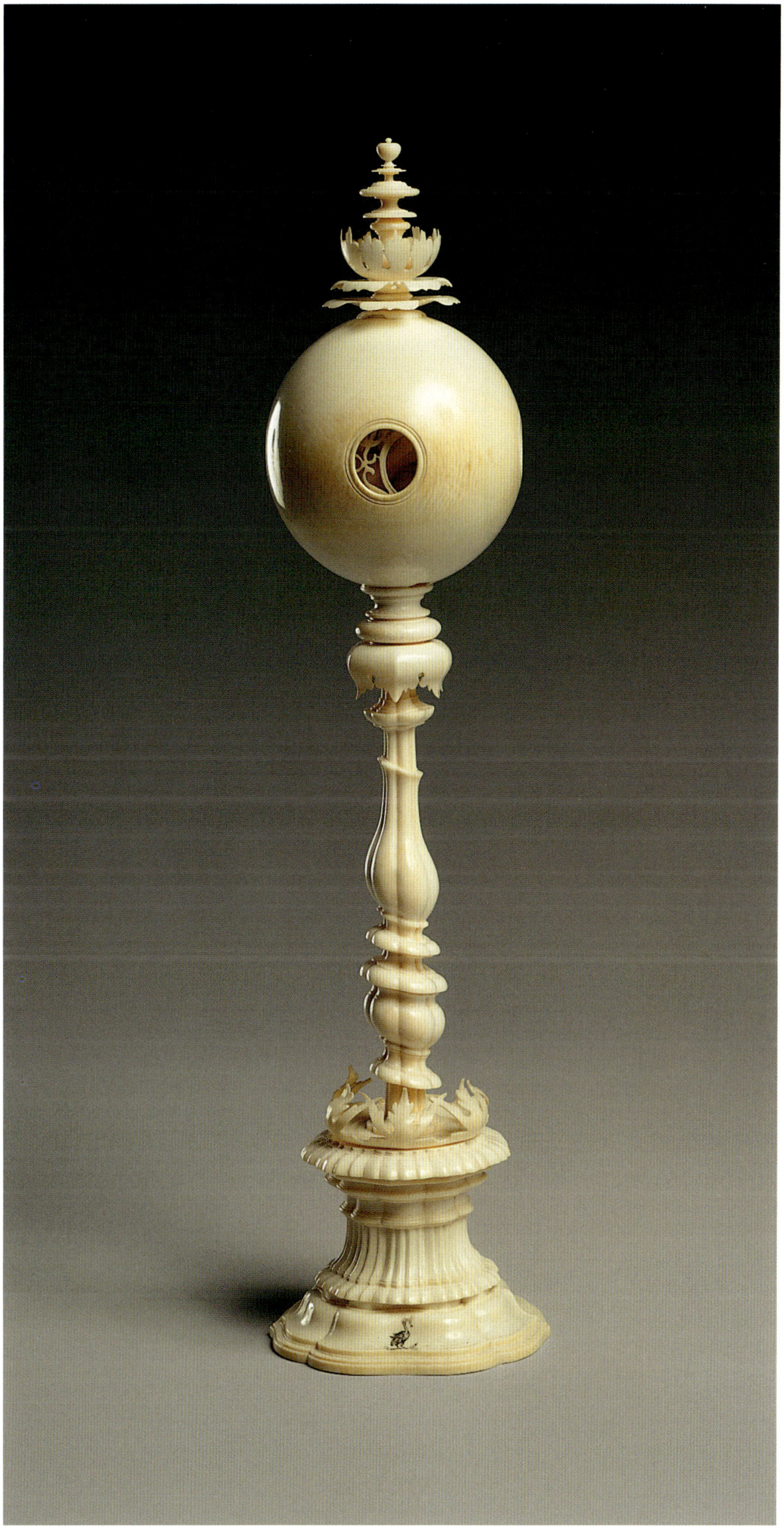

Georg Friedel, Dresden, between 1611 and 1619
Ivory, H. 13½ in. (39.5 cm)
Marked on the foot: heron with a fish in its beak
First mentioned in Kunstkammer inventory 1619, fol. 218r, no. 17, among the objects delivered by to the Kunstkammer by Jakob Zeller
Staatliche Kunstsammlungen Dresden, Grünes Gewölbe, inv. no. II 285
Lit.: Erbach 1995, cat. no. 96 (without text); cf. also: Maurice 1985, p. 138; Diemer 1985, pp. 296–301; Brunswick 2000, cat. nos. 232, 375
(Susanne König-Lein)

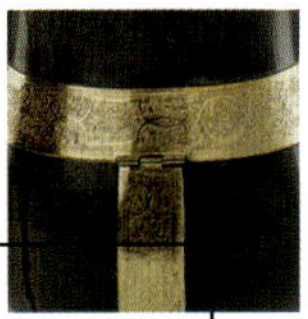

Turned Serpentine Works

Jutta Kappel

With the appointment of the Italian Giovanni Maria Nosseni by Elector August of Saxony to his court in 1575, he summoned a multitalented artist to Dresden.[1] Nosseni was not only a sculptor, an architect, and a painter, but he also had considerable mineralogical knowledge, enabling him to explore new domestic deposits of prized stone on the elector's orders.[2] Nosseni focused his attention on the deposits of alabaster, marble, and serpentine. By 1587, after numerous geological expeditions through the mountainous area of the Saxon Erzgebirge, thirty-six samples of different precious stones were in the Dresden Kunstkammer.[3] Their source location was precisely recorded, and this helps re-create the Italian's travel routes through electoral Saxony. Nosseni's knowledge regarding scope, size, and utility of the particular deposits was especially useful to the elector. David Uslaub, the art chamberlain, recorded this information meticulously in his Kunstkammer inventory. Five samples of serpentine from Zöblitz near Marienberg in Saxony are listed in the inventory with the notation that diverse serpentine in variant colors might be found.

To this collection of Saxon stone samples were added seven pieces of Italian marble. They may be the specimens Grand Duke Cosimo I of Tuscany[4] presented to Elector August in June 1572. The fact that polished marble morsels came to Dresden from Florence as diplomatic gifts illustrates the importance for the centuries-old ruling houses of Europe of mineral resources as a medium for state presentations and as economic wealth. It is no surprise, therefore, that in his privilege (*Privileg*) of May 5, 1585, Elector August commanded Nosseni to advertise the precious domestic resources to interested parties. Nosseni was to "dispatch to many fashionable places abroad" examples of Saxon stone "in order to further our country's glory and to increase the demand" (*an viel ausslendische fürnehme ortte zu vorschicken, und uns und unsern landes zu sonderlichen ruhm* [...] *und nachfrage zubringen*).[5] Thus Saxon stone samples were sent to the Medici and to the imperial court of Prague. In 1601 and 1605, Nosseni, in accordance with Rudolf II's request, sent him pieces of marble and other domestic stones. Saxon serpentine vessels made their way both to the Tuscan grand ducal Guardaroba and to the emperor's Kunstkammer.[6]

Serpentine, or more mineralogically correctly serpentinite, is a relatively soft hydrous magnesium silicate. Found in different colors, its traditional term is "serpent stone." Inclusions of garnet lend Saxon serpentine a particularly appealing composition. Red and transparent green serpentine are especially rare and precious; for a long time, red serpentine was restricted exclusively to use for the Saxon electors.[7]

Beginning in the mid-fifteenth century, serpentine was quarried in Zöblitz in many small mines, of which about twenty-five existed around 1600. Immediately after quarrying, the raw material is in its "mountain moist" state and is most pliable; as is the case with wood and ivory, serpentine can be easily cut and turned. After drying, it hardens and can be easily polished. Serpentine vessels were produced on simply constructed lathes, termed *Fitschel* because of the back-and-forth movement of the object spinning on its axis.[8] The inventors

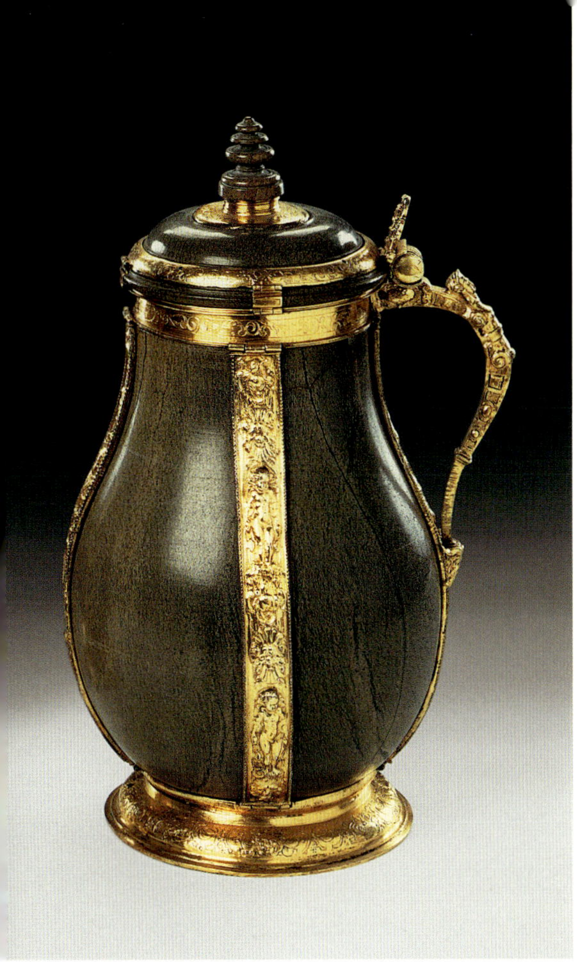

Tall Covered Flagon
with a medallion with the Danish
coat of arms inside the lid,
a heraldic device of Anna,
Danish wife of Elector August
of Saxony
Turned on the lathe
and polished: Zöblitz
near Marienberg in Saxony
Mount: Urban Schneeweiß,
Dresden, before 1585
Serpentine, silver-gilt
H. 11 in. (28 cm)
Staatliche Kunstsammlungen Dresden,
Grünes Gewölbe, inv. no. V 398

of this fabrication technique were presumably the Saxon serpentine turners Matthias Brändel and Mich(a)el Beßler.[9]

The theory that Nosseni, since his employment at the Dresden court in July 1575 as "designer," had direct influence on the form of the vessels of Zöblitz serpentine is well-founded.[10] However, no drawings or archival documents to support this are known, in contrast to such examples as those by Bernardo Buontalenti.[11] Even before 1590, when Nosseni was given the responsibility of supervising all electoral Saxon mines of precious stones and marble,[12] he was undoubtedly qualified to oversee the production of serpentine works turned by the Zöblitz masters and to influence their style with his own suggestions. This was most likely true for pieces expressly destined for the Dresden court.

Among the objects produced from Zöblitz serpentine in the late sixteenth century are pouring basins with ewers, tankards, other storage vessels, plates, bowls, lidded jars, and chandeliers, as well as knife handles. The technique used to shape the pieces left only a narrow margin for decoration. Although goldsmiths' works, tin tools, and ceramics served as models, most serpentine vessels have smooth walls, are of bulbous or cylindrical shape, and, according to type, are constructed with torus, grooved, or concave moldings. The majority of the pieces were adorned with silver-gilt mounts to lend them an especially stately appearance and to facilitate handling. For tankards, handles and lids were required. Ewers also needed handles and spouts. Bulbous vessels were preferably embellished with band and clip mounts because serpentine objects were generally sold as semifinished products, although with their grooves and moldings they were ready to be fitted with the goldsmiths' adornments. This presumed a detailed and well thought out design.

Unlike the plainer tin mounts, such as the ones made in Annaberg or Marienberg,[13] precious-metal mounts were produced by renowned goldsmiths in nearby Dresden (Urban Schneeweiß, Georg Mond), Leipzig (Elias Geyer), or Freiberg (David Winckler), but also in various South German workshops, especially in Augsburg and Nuremberg.[14] Some of the most beautiful serpentine vessels preserved in the Green Vault include mounts by court goldsmith Urban Schneeweiß (ill. above),[15] head of a large family of goldsmiths and one of the most important artists to work at the electoral court during the late sixteenth century. The silver-gilt mounts for ten precious serpentine vessels in the Green Vault, of which seven were made especially for Elector August and his wife,[16] illustrate this artist's extremely elegant style (see cat. nos. 92–94). Leipzig-based goldsmith Elias Geyer's main source of inspiration for his bizarre figure inventions was the matte shimmer of mother-of-pearl; he turned ostrich eggs and coconuts into splendid drinking vessels and designed cups as well as a tankard from finely polished nephrite (see cat. no. 120).[17] Geyer also manufactured the silver-gilt mount for a ewer made of Zöblitz serpentine (ca. 1590), a work presumably intended for the Dresden court that is now in The Hague (Gemeentemuseum).[18] The mount for the ewer of Zöblitz serpentine (early seventeenth century) in the Herzog Anton Ulrich-Museum, Brunswick, was

1. SächsHStA Dresden, Rep. LII. Gen. 1924, Loc. 33341 (= Bestallungen 1575), fol. 5r–6v (Letter of Nosseni's appointment of July 10, 1575, copy).
2. Menzhausen 1990, p. 234; Kappel 1998a, p. 59f.
3. Kunstkammer inventory 1587, fol. 298r–301v; Quellmalz 1990, p. 29f.
4. Marx 2000b, p. 240, the connection with the Kunstkammer marble samples of 1587 was not made; see also: Dombrowski 2000, p. 78 with footnote 94.
5. Quote after: Mackowsky 1904, p. 23.
6. Dombrowski 2000, p. 78 with footnotes 96, 97 and p. 79 with footnotes 105, 106.
7. See Syndram 1991b, p. 80f.; Hoyer 1995, pp. 11–15; Ulferts 2000, p. 17–19.
8. See Kiontke 1974, p. 25; Syndram 1991b, p. 81; Hoyer 1995, p. 24 with illustration of such a lathe; Idar-Oberstein 1998, cat. nos. 2, 3. "*Fitscheln*" is old Saxon dialect meaning to pull or spin something back and forth indefinitely.
9. Schmidt 1868, p. 10. Beßler died in 1614 at the age of seventy.
10. See e.g..: Schmidt 1868, p. 11; Syndram 1991b, p. 81.
11. Kris 1929, vol. I, p. 131ff., p. 187, nos. 574–76, and vol. II, p. 168, 171, 173.
12. See Mackowsky 1904, p. 24; see also Dombrowski 2000, p. 78 with footnote 99, where the reference to the renowned Milanese stonecutter Ottavio Miseroni, who, soon after his arrival in Prague, was given a similar mandate by Rudolf II to explore quarries in Bohemia.
13. See Ulferts 2000, p. 25.
14. For more information regarding the specifics of precious-metal mounts for Saxon serpentine vessels: Hoyer 1995, p. 27 (also with the reference to numerous Netherlandish mounts).
15. See Essen 1986, cat. nos. 527, 528; Dresden 1990, cat. nos. 374–378, Hoyer 1995, cat. nos. 5, 6.
16. Six balloon vessels belonged to the Saxon elector (inv. nos. V 380, V 386, V 389, V 390, V 397, V 399), as well as one ewer (inv. no. V 398); in 1725, two tankards were in the Pretiosen inventory (inv. nos. V 392, V 393). The 1587 Kunstkammer inventory counted a little box (inv. no. V 384) that shows the elecoral Saxon and Danish coats of arms on its lid, as well as the date 1572. The object is attributed to Urban Schneeweiß (see Hoyer 1995, cat. no. 108).
17. For the surviving oeuvre of Geyer in the Green Vault see: Menzhausen 1973.
18. Hoyer 1995, p. 102, and cat. no. 7.

Serpentine Jug
turned on the lathe/polished:
Zöblitz near Marienberg in Saxony,
presumably third quarter
of the 16th century
Serpentine, H. 7⅞ in. (20 cm)
Staatliche Kunstsammlungen Dresden,
Grünes Gewölbe, inv. no. V 612

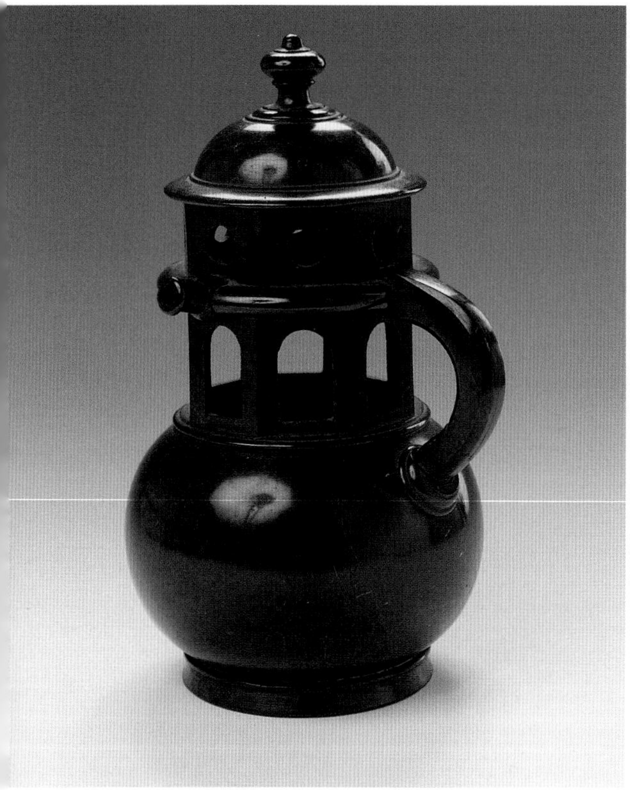

made by Georg Mond of Dresden. The serpentine body was transformed into a functional ewer only through the mount, the focal point of which is a cut pomegranate on its lid.[19] The Museum für Kunsthandwerk in Leipzig owns a serpentine tankard with a silver-gilt mount created between 1617 and 1620 by the Freiberg goldsmith David Winckler. This vessel must have been produced as a commission of the Dresden court since the silver taler on its lid shows Elector Johann Georg I of Saxony and his brother August (administrator of Naumburg, 1611–15) (see cat. no. 94).[20]

In 1617, during the reign of Johann Georg I, the "marble laboratories" began operations in the Lusthaus (Pleasure House) on the Jungfernbastei (known today as Brühlsche Terrasse), located near the Elbe and close to Residential Palace. Vast quantities of domestic marble, mostly destined to expand the Pleasure House designed by Nosseni, were refined and polished there. Its shops, which may have been modeled after the Florentine Galleria dei Lavori[21] but never achieved the level of its artistic quality or productivity, were where the masters of vessel cutting worked.

The best known of these masters was Barthel Börner, son of a Zöblitz serpentine turner. He was an apprentice of the renowned stonecutter Hans Kobenhaupt in Stuttgart and appears to have been extraordinarily talented. This is illustrated by the fact that when the Augsburg patrician and connoisseur Philipp Hainhofer sojourned in Dresden in 1629, he visited Börner's workshop, where he saw numerous vessels made from jasper, agate, and rock crystal.[22] In addition to Börner, other turners and stonecutters must have worked there to be able to produce the impressive collection of vessels made of alabaster, serpentine, and other local precious stones intended for the ballroom of the Pleasure House.[23] The entire room was embellished with Saxon marble and with colored stone from diverse electoral Saxon depositories, and this space was thus intended to symbolize the sovereign's power. Masterworks of stonecutting produced in Saxony and elsewhere were deposited there permanently, making it in effect a branch of the Kunstkammer. Nearly three hundred alabaster and serpentine works, mostly conceived as tableware, were kept there.[24] In 1673 Johann Georg II ordered the stone vessels to be transferred to the Dresden Kunstkammer, as the state hall in the Pleasure House had never been completed. A curiously shaped little serpentine jug (ill. at left) was also part of this group.[25] Most of the abundant holdings of alabaster and serpentine table services, many of which had belonged to the Kunstkammer since 1587 or were added from the Pleasure House in 1673, were lost when the Dresden Kunstkammer was dissolved in 1832.[26]

Some of the Saxon serpentine objects in the Green Vault came from the Geheime Verwahrung, the treasury of the Dresden Residential Palace. Others, such as a sphere and two small gold-mounted bowls, were in the Kunstkammer. The 1725 Green Vault inventory of precious objects (*Pretioseninventar*) provides a complete list of the small but distinguished store of approximately twenty serpentine works. Whereas at first the state vessels—displayed on gilt wood consoles in front of the mirrored walls—were placed in the Hall of Precious Objects (*Pretiosensaal*) of the Green Vault, fourteen of them were later moved to the Chamber of the Coats of Arms of the Provinces (Provinzwappen-Zimmer), where they were inventoried in 1733. In this chamber they were interspersed with the Saxon territories' gilded coats of arms, coat of arms and initials of the electors of the House of Wettin, and the state coat of arms of the Polish-Lithuanian kingdom. Here, next to the priceless collection of ruby glasses, the serpentine objects held their own.

19. Hoyer 1995, cat. no. 45; Schütte 1997, cat. no. 110.
20. Hoyer 1995, cat. no. 27; see also the goblet of the *Saigerhütte Grünthal* by Winckler (dated 1625, inv. no. IV 17) in the Green Vault.
21. This interesting hypothesis was first proposed by Barbara Marx (2000b, p. 244f. with footnote 125).
22. See Kappel 1998a, pp. 62–64.
23. Eva Maria Hoyer connected a serpentine ewer (dated 1664; Kunsthistorisches Museum Vienna, Sammlungen Schloss Ambras) with the Dresden workshops in the *Lusthaus* (Pleasure House) (see Hoyer 1995, cat. no. 93).
24. Hoyer 1995, p. 73.
25. Although this little jug was not acquired for the Green Vault until 1890, it is identical with the one mentioned in the Pleasure House's inventory (see Hoyer 1995, cat. no. 62). The inventory of November 1673, signed by Wolf Caspar von Klengel and mentioning all stone vessels from the Pleasure House transferred to the *Kunstkammer* is preserved: SächsHStA. Dresden, Loc. 8693/20, fol. 1r–5v.
26. See Kappel 1998b, pp. 92–96

92 State Canister

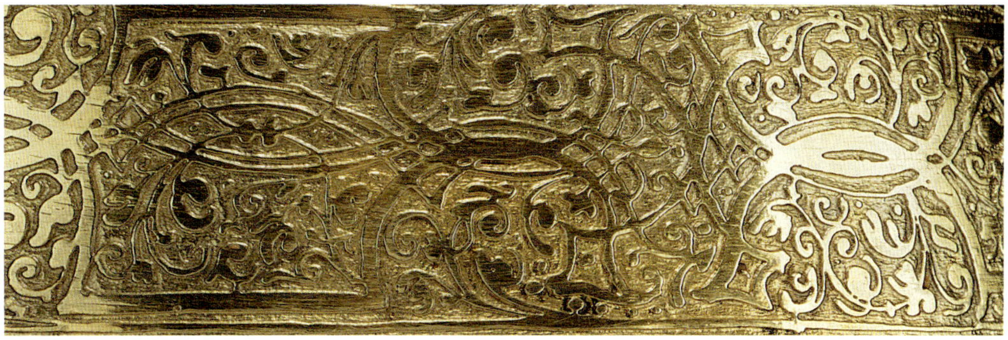

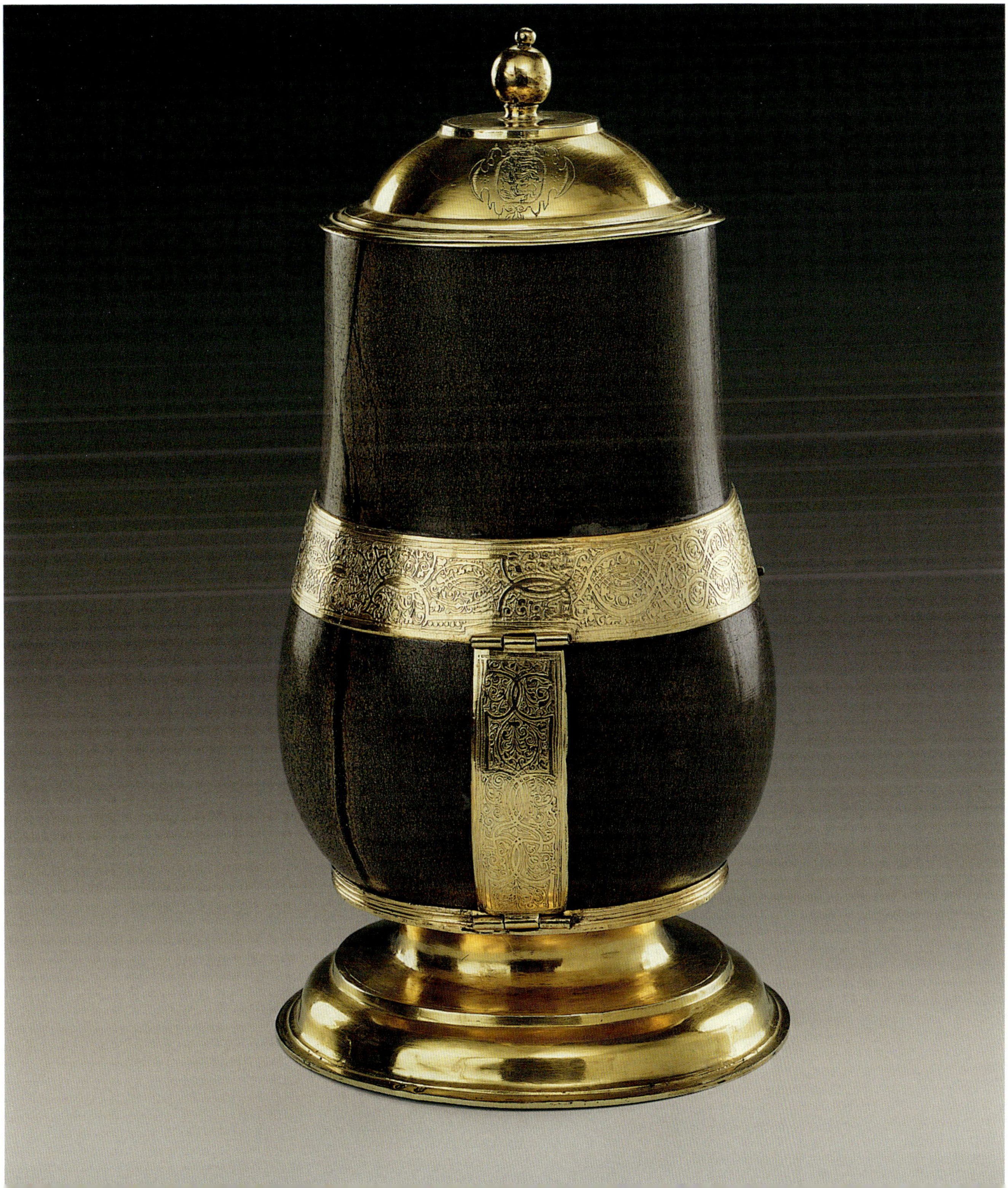

93 Five State Canisters

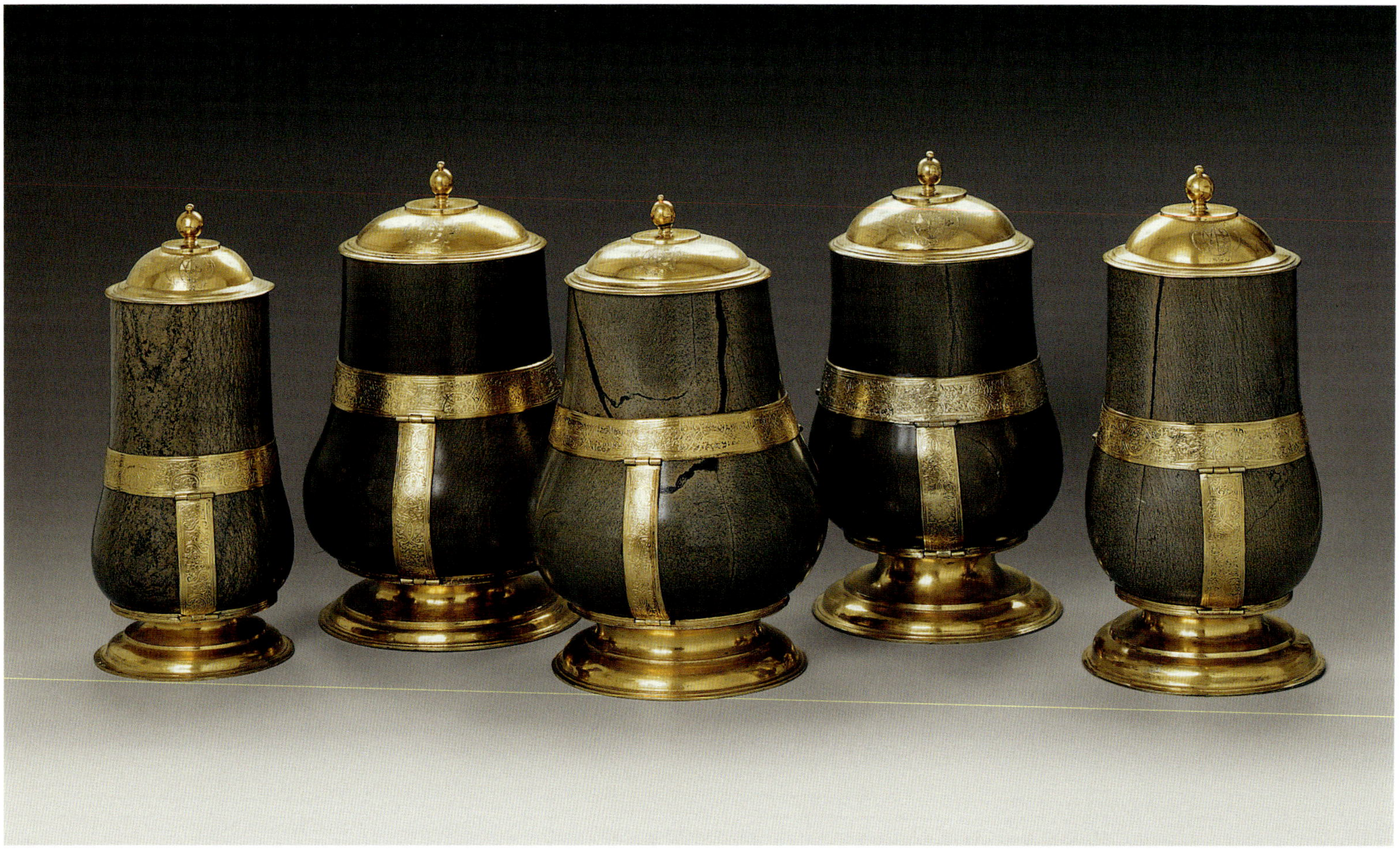

Lathe work / polishing: Zöblitz near Marienberg in Saxony, shortly before 1585
Design: presumably Giovanni Maria Nosseni, shortly before 1585
Mount: Urban Schneeweiß, Dresden, shortly before 1585
Gray-green serpentine, silver-gilt
H. between 11⅜ and 12¼ in. (29 and 31.3 cm)
Hallmark for Dresden and maker's mark "VS" (in ligature)
First mentioned in the Schatzkammer (Treasury) inventory 1586/87, fol. 89r
Staatliche Kunstsammlungen Dresden, Grünes Gewölbe, inv. no. V 380 (individual photo cat. no. 92 and detail p. 201), V 397, V 389, V 390, V 386, V 399 (group, from left to right)
Lit.: Rosenberg 1923, no. 1726; Essen 1986, cat. nos. 527, 528; Dresden 1990, cat. no. 375; Hoyer 1995, p. 27, 99 and cat. no. 5; Florence 1997, cat. no. 127 (Jutta Kappel); Idar-Oberstein 1998, cat. nos. 2, 3.

The electoral ruling house in Dresden ordered and purchased serpentine vessels from Zöblitz, placing them on the courtly table or displaying them in the Kunstkammer. The six lidded vessels here, however, were kept in the elector's own treasury, the so-called Geheime Verwahrung in Dresden's Residential Palace. They are listed in its inventory, compiled after Elector August's death, at the latest in the autumn of 1587.

The Dresden goldsmith Urban Schneeweiß embellished the impressive smooth-walled vessels having bulbous centers with uniformly crafted mounts and lids of silver-gilt. The vertical and horizontal bands are decorated with etched arabesques, and they are joined with hinges. The engraving on the domed lids shows the electoral Saxon coat of arms opposite the coat of arms of the Danish kingdom as heraldic attributes of Elector August of Saxony and his wife, Anna of Denmark. This group, intended for the couple, must have been completed before Anna's death in 1585. A serpentine ewer, also embellished with mounts by Urban Schneeweiß (ill. p. 199) and in the collection of the Green Vault, has a medallion with the Danish coat of arms on the inside of its lid. On the basis of stylistic and dynastic considerations, it is safe to say that the ewer is contemporary with the six vessels shown here.
J.K.

94 Two Tankards

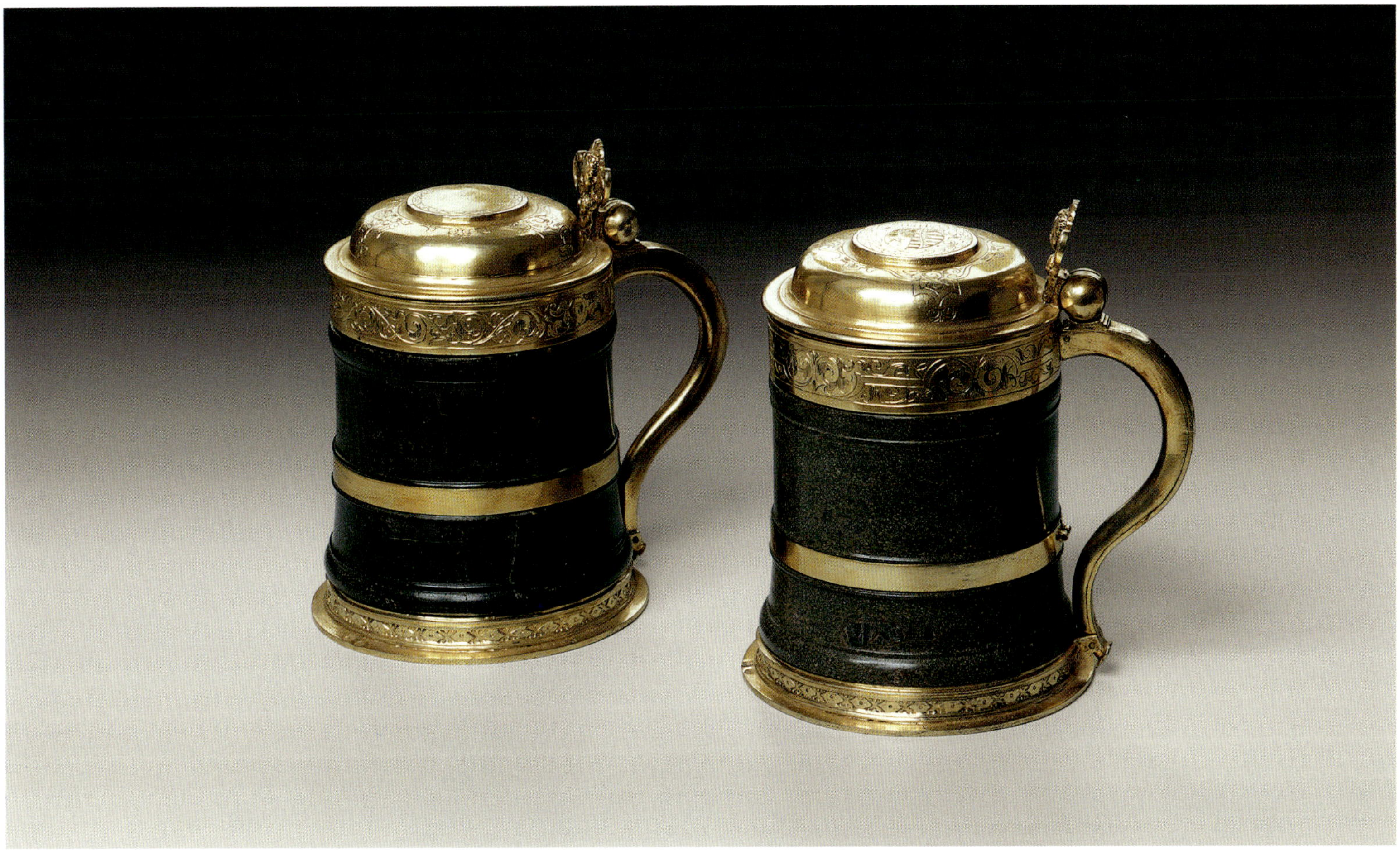

Lathe work / polishing: Zöblitz near Marienberg in Saxony, late 16th century
Mount: Urban Schneeweiß, Dresden, late 16th century
Dark green serpentine, silver-gilt
H. 5⅜ in. (13.9 cm)
Hallmark for Dresden and maker's mark "VS" (in ligature)
First mentioned in the Pretiosen inventory 1725, fol. 186r, no. 16, 17
Staatliche Kunstsammlungen Dresden, Grünes Gewölbe, inv. no. V 392 (left) and V 393 (right)
Lit.: Rosenberg 1923, no. 1726; Dresden 1990, cat. nos. 377, 378; Idar-Oberstein 1998, cat. nos. 4, 5; see also Hoyer 1995, pp. 99–104 and cat. no. 27

This pair of serpentine tankards represents the most popular vessel type among the diversely shaped group of turned Saxon serpentine works (see also cat. no. 95). Although the tankards do not show any significant signs of use, in form and fabrication they meet all criteria required of an elegant drinking vessel. A distinctive characteristic of serpentine vessels is their permeability to liquid; as a consequence they develop a film of evaporation on their outer surface and slightly alter their color.

The tankards are shaped in a characteristically late-sixteenth-century manner, with turned concave bands and grooves on otherwise smooth walls. The simple and robust mounts of silver-gilt were made by the Dresden goldsmith Urban Schneeweiß (see cat. nos. 92, 93). The electoral Saxon coat of arms and the monogram "HGHZS" are engraved onto the domed lid of the right tankard. When deciphered, the letters reveal the name "Hans Georg Herzog [Duke] zu [of] Sachsen [Saxony]," the son of Christian I, the future Elector Johann Georg I of Saxony. The pair of tankards may thus be dated with some certainty since Johann Georg was born in 1585, and the goldsmith Schneeweiß died in 1600. The abbreviation of the name of Johann as Hans could indicate that these vessels were produced on the occasion of Johann Georg's birth or one of his early name days.

J.K.

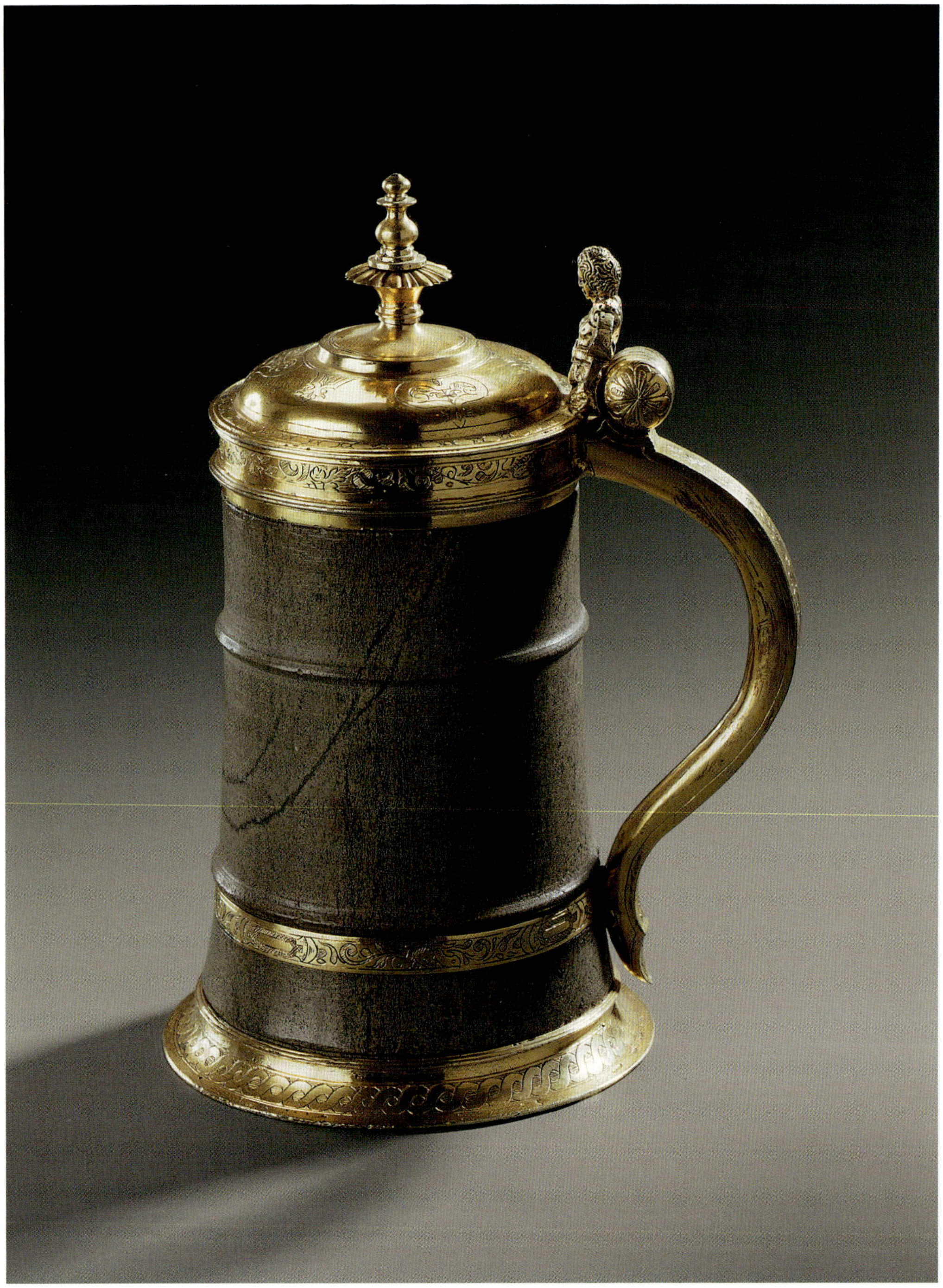

95 Tankard

Among the serpentine objects from Zöblitz, there were some without mounts (cat. no. 96). Others required tin or silver mounts to make them functional (cat. nos. 92–94). A talented goldsmith could transform a vessel with a simple serpentine body into an exquisite object. But the opportunity for fanciful design was quite limited, as the Saxon serpentine vessels characteristically had horizontal bands or grooves on the otherwise smooth surface. In other words, the vessels were already prepared to receive their mounts, as shown in this tankard. Its cylindrical shape, slightly flaring toward the bottom, rests on a ring-shaped base engraved with an interlacing design. The body is encircled by a ring with foliate decoration that fits in the space meant to receive it and supports the slightly curved handle. The thumb rest in the shape of a male half-figure is mounted above the hinge that enables the lid to open and close.

In the details of its design, the tankard follows a vessel type popular in the late sixteenth century that seems to have been particularly practical for drinking beer. Surviving examples and variations in silver or with carved-ivory ornamentation prove that tankards, apart from their everyday utilitarian function, fulfilled a particularly noble role as objects for collecting and display.

J.K.

Lathe work / polishing:
Zöblitz near Marienberg in Saxony,
late 16th century
Mount: Saxony or Dresden, late 16th century
Gray-green serpentine, silver-gilt
H. 6⅝ in. (16.9 cm)
First mentioned in the Pretiosen inventory 1725,
fol. 186r, no. 15

Staatliche Kunstsammlungen Dresden,
Grünes Gewölbe, inv. no. V 388
Lit.: Hoyer 1995, p. 27, 103 and cat. no. 12;
see also Gruber 1977, p. 18 and
cat. nos. 223–241; Hernmarck 1978,
pp. 114–16 and ill. 207; Hoyer 1995,
cat. no. 14, 16; Heller 2003, cat. nos. 2, 71

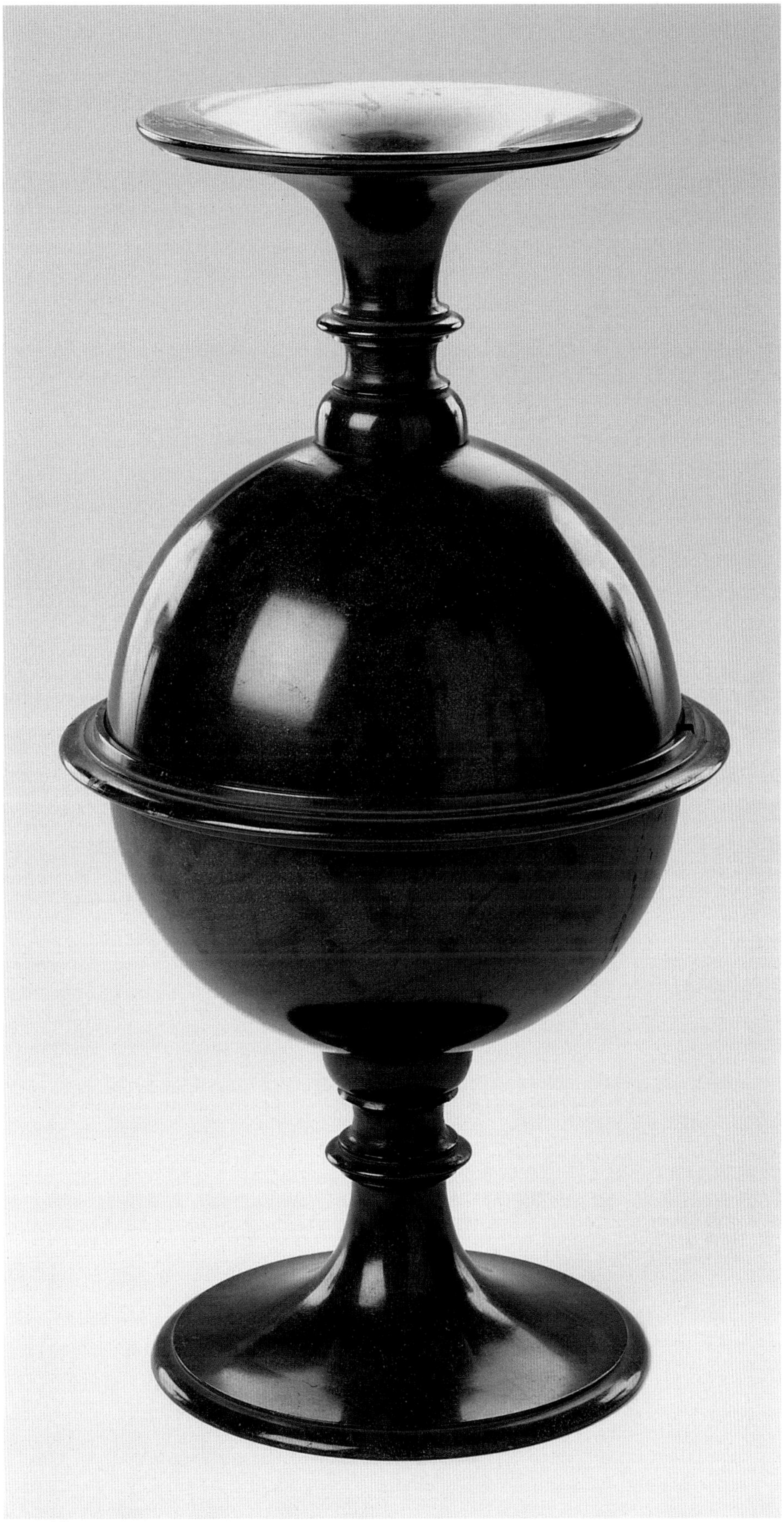

96 Double Cup

This tall double cup of dark green, matte polished serpentine testifies to the degree of perfection and stylistic sensibility of the objects produced by the masters of turned Saxon serpentine from Zöblitz. Evidence of their mastery of this complicated craft is seen in the precisely turned hemispheres that constitute the cups with conical feet and tall shafts. Between the cups is a round, smooth serpentine plate with a circular lip into which the edges of the cups fit exactly, resulting in a perfect sphere. While the plate guarantees stability for the cups when mounted one on top of the other, it could also have been used separately as a tazza-like bowl. This composition, equally practical and imposing, would have been the epitome of the Kunstkammer piece but for the fact that about 1600 it did not yet belong to the electoral collection in Dresden.

The art of producing spherical serpentine vessels was likely known at the beginning of the seventeenth century. Yet such a double cup, demonstrating as it does a turner's proficiency and skill, was not required of masters by the Zöblitz serpentine turners guild until 1665, when it became a prominent mark of the order of this strict guild. Evidently, until the end of the eighteenth century, several similar pieces must have been created each year, but this one in the Green Vault is the only known example to have survived. Its origins are uncertain. Although it was conceivably a gift of the Zöblitz guild of turners to the Dresden court, no archival documents that support this suggestion have yet come to light. The double cup certainly came to the Kunstkammer in 1673. Might it have been part of the complete collection of stone vessels that was transferred in November or December 1673 from the Pleasure House on Dresden's Jungfernbastei to the Kunstkammer?
J.K.

Lathe work / polishing: Zöblitz near Marienberg
in Saxony, presumably between 1665 and 1673
Dark green serpentine, H. 12⅞ in. (32.8 cm)
1673 (presumably from the Lusthaus [Pleasure House]
on Dresden's Jungfernbastei) to the Kunstkammer
First mentioned in the 1741 Kunstkammer inventory,
fol. 77v, no. 14
Staatliche Kunstsammlungen Dresden,
Grünes Gewölbe, inv. no. V 613
Lit.: Menzhausen 1977, p. 187f. and ill. 119; Hoyer 1995,
pp. 25, 123, 172 and cat. no. 76; Kappel 1998b, pp. 94f.;
see also Schmidt 1868, p. 19 (article 19)

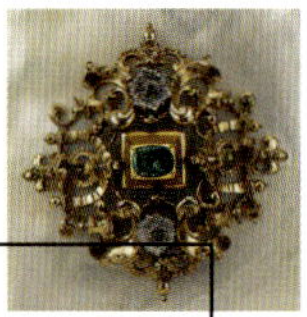

Goldwork

Ulrike Weinhold

On April 23, 1477, near the little Saxon town of Schneeberg in the Erzgebirge mountain range, Duke Albrecht the Brave entered Georg's Mine and dined there on a table formed of a gigantic silver matrix. Subsequently, more than two thousand pounds of silver was extracted from this mine. The duke's visit celebrated one of the largest silver-ore finds ever recorded; a piece from the find weighing more than one and a quarter pounds has been preserved.[1] According to tradition, the duke remarked that, rich as the emperor was, he almost certainly did not own an equally impressive table. Duke Albrecht was apparently well aware of the potential mineral wealth hidden beneath the surface of his lands, as it helped the margravate of Meissen, which was part of the duke's realm, to become one of the most prosperous territories in the entire empire. The earliest mining records for the Erzgebirge region date to 1168. Beginning in the late fifteenth and early sixteenth century, mining developed as one of the fundamental sources of the wealth and the political power of the Wettins, who secured sovereign authority over this industry.

This history establishes the crucial importance of goldwork as a medium for courtly representation in electoral Saxony, as reflected, for instance, in the formation of the Silver Chamber (Silberkammer)—documented as early as 1443—where dining services and drinking vessels used by the princely entourage were kept. Inventories, the earliest preserved dating to 1586, indicate a noticeable increase in such holdings and document a steady rise in courtly life. Lists specifying the contents of the eight cabinets of the Silver Chamber suggest the enormous number of objects. The (predominantly gilt) tableware comprised 24 basins, 20 ewers, 215 tureens and bowls, 819 plates of different sizes, 231 spoons and forks, 78 saltcellars, 59 candelabra, and a total of 145 gilt drinking vessels and so-called Scheuern, cup-shaped vessels, often of great size. Another category lists vessels and flatware distinguished by the use of precious stones or exotic materials such as coral, mother-of-pearl, or coconut.[2] Finally, the inventory also names "*1 Silberne taffel / Die grosse Stuff Erzs*" (one silver slab / the great ore matrix), which can only be the one that served as a table when Duke Albrecht dined in Georg's Mine. As documented in the respective inventories, specific sets of flatware were taken along when the court traveled, as indications of princely rank even beyond Dresden. In addition, there were Silver Chambers, either permanent or temporary, in all the other places where court stayed.

That the Silver Chamber in the Schössereiturm of the Dresden Residenzschloss was not the only place where precious silver tableware was kept is revealed by the Schatzkammerinventar (Inventory of the Treasury) probably started by command of Elector Christian I in the early autumn of 1587. It appears that this register was begun when the so-called Geheime Verwahrung in the palace's west wing was furnished. Apart from ore matrixes, vessels made of gold and precious stones, splendid boxes, mother-of-pearl objects, and gems, the Schatzkammerinventar also lists a large quantity of gilded tableware.[3] As for the Silver Chamber, initially it also contained ecclesiastical objects, jewelry, precious stones, ore matrixes, and an

1. Dresden 1990, p. 19, no. 1, ill. p. 73; cf. also O'Byrn 1880, p. 21.
2. SächsHStA Dresden, Loc. 32449, Dresden no. 88 (not paged).
3. For this compare the essay by Dirk Syndram in this volume.
4. Cf. here extensively O'Byrn 1880, p. 21, which mentions numerous inventories lost today, citing some of them verbatim.
5. Numerous goldsmiths' work from the Green Vault from circa 1600 can be documented only in eighteenth-century archival documents. It seems that these objects were kept in the Geheime Verwahrung, whose seventeenth-century inventories have not survived.
6. O'Byrn 1880, p. 63.
7. Green Vault, inv. no. VI 4 and VI 6.
8. For more information pertaining to the Stable Court (Stallhof) cf. the essays by Jürgen Müller, Dirk Syndram, and Heinz-Werner Lewerken.
9. Münzberg, 2002.
10. Vermisste Kunstwerke 1990, p. 96, no. 275.
11. Green Vault, inv. no. IV 187.

abundance of diverse curiosities. It was not until the beginning of the reign of Elector Johann Georg I, in February 1612, that the silver intended for daily use was separated from the *Antiquitäten* (antiquities) and *Curiositäten* (curiosities). From then on, the latter group was housed in the Geheime Verwahrung, or the Kunstkammer. Strictly speaking, this is also the inauguration of the court's *Hofsilberkammer* (Silver Chamber).[4] Silver works of outstanding artistic merit were henceforth kept in the Kunstkammer, along with vessels that were embellished with precious stones or made from exotic materials.[5] Kunstkammer objects had a greater chance for survival over the centuries than utilitarian silver, particularly because tableware always tended to follow the latest fashion. Consequently, older objects were usually melted down to create new ones. The silver holdings were considered to be a financial reserve, and therefore they could be sold in times of need. For this reason, silver tableware from those times has survived in very small quantities.

Tiered Buffet in the Form of a Mountainside, formerly in the Electoral Chambers of the New Stable (lost during World War II)

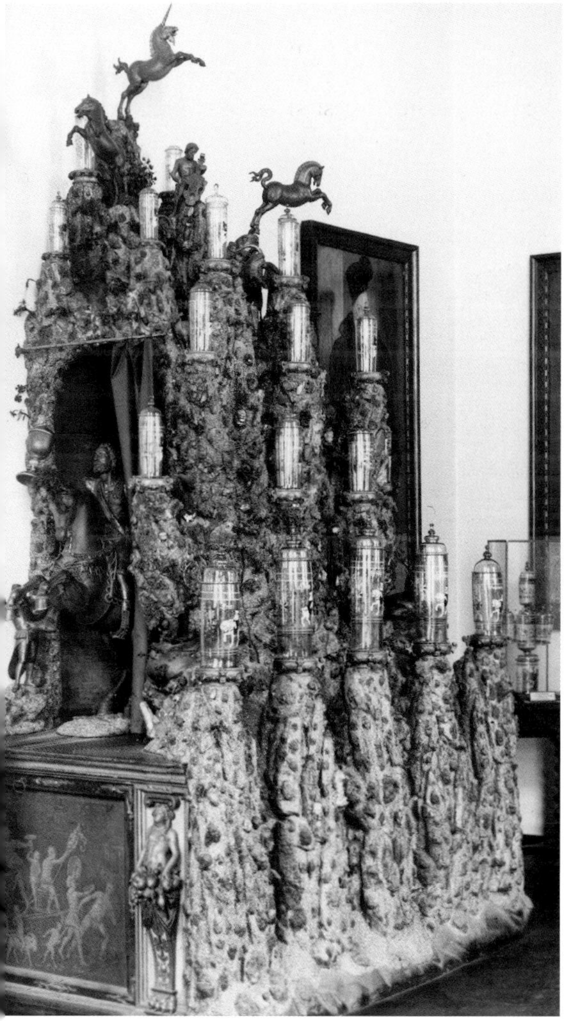

One of the most noble tasks for any goldsmith was to create the so-called *Willkomm* (Welcome) cups, from which guests were served their welcome drink. These luxurious vessels, crafted in a variety of fantastical forms, played a central role in courtly ceremonies. The vivid imagination of their creators led to ever new and original pieces, many one of a kind and most having a direct connection with the place for which they were intended. As the inventories reveal, even palaces that served only as temporary residences were equipped with one or more Welcome goblets. In the Moritzburg Hunting Castle, for instance, the goblets were formed in animal shapes—a stag, a deer, and a horse.[6] In Augustusburg Castle, which also served as the stage for courtly hunts, the shaft of the *Willkomm* consisted of a vintner holding a bowl in the shape of a cluster of grapes. Additional figural elements alluded to the hunt: the lid held a hunter with his dog, the pedestal a bear. The theme of winemaking was personified by the vintner and his wife: it was from their cask that the festive libation was drunk when visiting the winery of Hoflössnitz.[7] The greatest example of the *Willkomm* goblet, by the Dresden goldsmith Georg Mond, incorporates the location for which it was destined by taking the shape of the Pirna Palace itself (cat. no. 128). The detailed rendering even refers to the coats of arms of the sovereign, Elector Christian II, and the aldermen of Pirna Castle.

Possibly the most impressive *Willkomm* ceremony was that offered in the Neuer Stall (New Stable), erected under Elector Christian I between 1586 and 1591. The building, connected with the Residential Palace by a wing measuring about 350 feet in length, contained the stables and the armory and surrounded the Stallhof (Stable Court), which served as a field for tournaments.[8] The electoral apartments, a suite serving ceremonial functions, were located near the Jüdenhof.[9] Kept in these rooms were, among other items, two-tiered buffets whose wood frameworks were entirely covered with ore matrixes (ill. left).[10] Mounted on the protrusions of these artificial mountains were twenty silver-gilt drinking vessels. The two most prominent, commissions of the elector, were expressly created for the Stable Court by the Dresden goldsmith Valentin Geitner. These are the monumental coconut goblet (cat. no. 122), whose cast equine heads were a reference to the tournaments that occurred there, and the precious goblet with fourteen smaller vessels inside its bowl—a joke vessel affectionately referred to as "*die Alte mit den 14 Jungen*" (the old one with fourteen cubs) (ill. p. 208).[11] In his travel accounts, the Augsburg patrician Philipp Hainhofer remarks that this *Willkomm* was meant to embarrass the drinker who selected it, as its total of fifteen vessels could hold much more wine than expected. The other drinking vessels assembled on the sideboard were predominantly cups with figures of warriors on their lids and *Doppelscheuern* (also called *Dupplets*) (see cat. no. 123). The true attraction of the two remarkable sideboards was, however, located within. Through the opening on the narrow side of the artificial mountain range (watched over by a miner), a rider would emerge on a set of tracks; dressed in an ancient Roman suit of armor, he would offer the stupefied individual participating in the feast a *Willkomm* goblet. This dramatic figure was intended to add a special message to the buffet, one deeply rooted in the symbolism of princely magnificence. The horseman not only underscored the country's abundance of mineral wealth but also demonstrated its artistic achievements and the superiority of its craftspeople, who were capable of turning raw materials into incomparably precious artifacts.

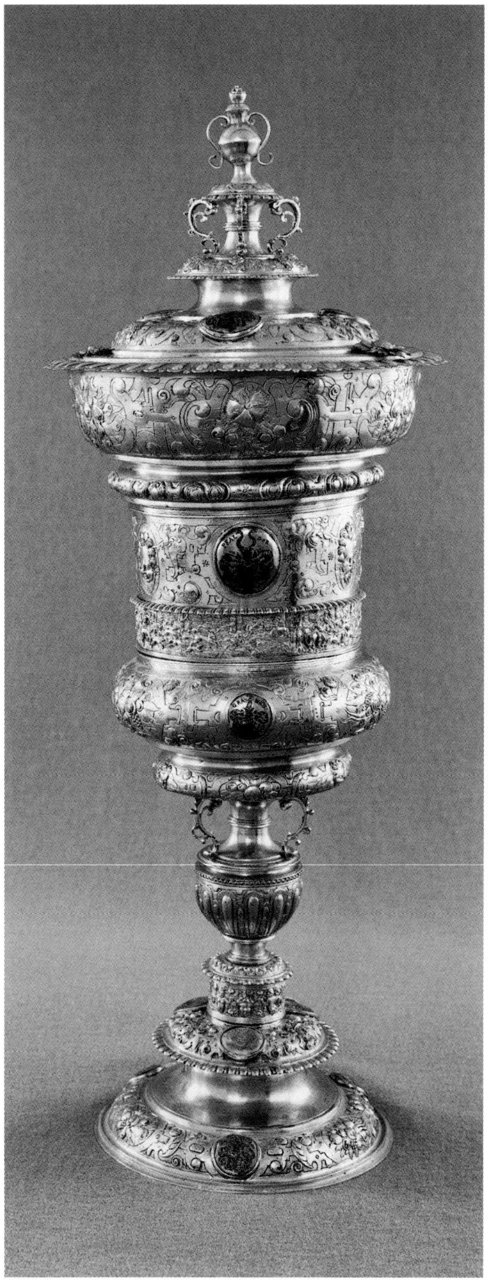

"The Mother with Fourteen Cubs"
so-called *Willkomm* (Welcome)
goblet, Valentin Geitner, Dresden, 1590
Silver-gilt, enamel
H. 21¼ in. (54 cm)
Staatliche Sammlungen Dresden,
Grünes Gewölbe, inv. no. IV 187

The Erzgebirge's rich supply of silver was clearly a factor in the development of the Saxon goldsmith's art. Time and again, from the second half of the sixteenth century, it made possible the emergence of artists whose works compared favorably with those produced in other artistic centers in the empire. The reasons why the electors procured vast numbers of objects outside the borders of their territories are many. For one thing, it was impossible to satisfy the court's tremendous need with domestic products alone. Larger commissions inevitably required a resort to considerably more efficient centers of production. In this context, it must be noted that, following the Peace of Augsburg in 1555, Nuremberg eventually lost its dominance in the market to that city. Both places were imperial cities whose wealth was primarily based on flourishing trade connections. They both housed many workshops and had very well organized retail systems. In the first decade of the seventeenth century, for instance, 130 workshops are documented in Nuremberg;[12] in Augsburg, there were 200 masters in 1594,[13] while, roughly at the same time, in Dresden and Leipzig there were only approximately twenty workshops active.[14]

These capitals were not only efficient but prestigious as well. Artworks of the highest standard could be obtained nowhere else. The large number of workshops, particularly in Augsburg, led to a division of labor that proved to be an enormous advantage. The fabrication of complex works of art required the cooperation of specialized workshops, each capable of producing a desired result. Thus, Augsburg was considered the leader in the production of table automatons, which are also represented in the electoral-Saxon Kunstkammer, for example, by the drinking game "Saint George Slaying the Dragon" (cat. no. 132). In order to create such works, the goldsmith required the support of a modelmaker, for the cast figures; a watchmaker, for the running gear and/or clockwork; and a casemaker, in the event that the pedestal was made of wood. Also among the Augsburg specialties was the production of cabinets and writing caskets made of ebony with silver mounts, most notably those originating from Matthäus Wallbaum's workshop. The use of prefabricated cast parts enabled the serial production of such smaller items of furniture, which princely collectors held in high esteem (cat. nos. 158, 159).

Nuremberg,[15] on the other hand, was famous for the high quality of its lobed cups. Originating in the Late Gothic era, this vessel type represented an old tradition in Nuremberg, but the skillful chasing during this period resulted in objects of an unsurpassed refinement and virtuosity. Wenzel Jamnitzer, active in Nuremberg between 1534 and 1585, particularly attracted the attention of princely collectors, including the emperor. Jamnitzer, a highly creative and also scientifically minded goldsmith, won the support of the leading specialists in realizing his ingenious designs. For more than half a century, he was instrumental in defining the character of Nuremberg goldwork. He brought casts from nature to a state of perfection, and they became the epitome of Nuremberg's arts and craft production. This is convincingly demonstrated by the lizards on the pedestal of his elephant figure (cat. no. 104) or the naturalistic legs of his rooster and hen (cat. no. 113). Jamnitzer's splendid caskets, incorporating artistic accomplishment, technical bravado, and intellectual rigor, were crucial components of any princely Kunstkammer and were also highly valued by the Saxon electors.

Goldsmiths rarely sold their works themselves. Instead, purchases were made mostly through art agents and dealers who had close contacts to princely courts and other wealthy individuals. Jewelers also played a substantial role: as predominantly specialized silver dealers, they could competently supervise commissions. At fairs in Leipzig, Frankfurt, and elsewhere, they offered merchandise from their inventories and took special orders from princely clients. Naturally, the Saxon electors preferred the fairs in nearby Leipzig, where they were able to meet their requirements for jewels and gems, silver objects, precious stones, and pearls three times a year. One particularly close connection was with the Leipzig jeweler Veit Böttiger, who negotiated the acquisition of the Leipzig goldsmith Elias Geyer's eccentric drinking vessels. Böttiger's particular specialty was the acquisition of Oriental mother-of-pearl objects, which appear to have been collected in Dresden with special urgency. As a result, the Green Vault collection now owns the largest and most beautiful collection of Indian mother-of-pearl objects—and their European adaptations—in the world. These holdings comprise garnitures of ewers and basins, caskets and boxes, and drinking vessels. For the most part, they came to Dresden through acquisitions negotiated by Böttiger between 1589 and 1602.[16] The majority of the imported works purchased from him are embellished with silver-gilt mounts, which increased their value and were intended to adapt these foreign works to Western European taste. It is not known whether Böttiger obtained the pieces in this condition or whether he had the mounts added by goldsmiths in Nuremberg, Torgau, or Leipzig.

In addition to self-employed jewelers, there were also dealers who acted under the direct order of the court. One of them, Hieronymus Kramer, worked as an art agent for Dresden's electors. Apparently, he, too, was instructed to make a special attempt to purchase precious objects from the Far East. As can be deduced from Kramer's employment document, dated March 15, 1575, Elector August commissioned him expressly to visit Spain, England, Portugal, and other faroff places in order to procure "*Cleinodien Hals vnnd arm bande Ringe, Edelgestein perlen, silber geschir, specerey vnd anderes*" (jewels and gems, necklaces and bracelets, precious stones, pearls, silver dishes, spices, and other things).[17] In fact, Kramer undertook two trips to Lisbon, yet nothing is known about what he obtained. It can be assumed that his major interest was the Indian mother-of-pearl products so loved by the Dresden court, for Lisbon was the main harbor through which these were imported into Western Europe. Some years later, Kramer delivered a *Doppelscheuer* (double cup), made of mother-of-pearl bowls, which Christian I then gave to his wife as a Maundy Thursday present (cat. no. 105). He may have acquired the bowls on one of his travels and had them reworked into a cup in Nuremberg. This elector–ambitious, art-minded, and filled with a young sovereign's urge to assert his power–employed Kramer more extensively than his father had, ordering him to secure luxury items on a grand scale. On the occasion of the Danish king's visit, for example, the dealer was to obtain "*ahnsehnliche wahren, zu Ihrer Kön: Mayt: hoheit zugebrauchen*" (estimable merchandise for the use of His Royal Majesty / Highness). For this Christian advanced the extravagant sum of 60,000 florins.[18] In 1590 Kramer spent 16,000 florins for precious stones on the elector's behalf.

Even if, for the reasons stated above, the Saxon goldsmiths could not compete with those in Augsburg and Nuremberg, they regularly achieved a high level of success.[19] The lead was taken by Dresden, where the court's proximity assured numerous commissions. The high craftsmanship of Dresden artisans is exemplified in the undisputed quality and originality of Georg Mond's and Valentin Geitner's work (cat. no. 122). Unique pieces were also created in other media: Hans Kellerthaler's monumental Kunstkammer cabinet, for instance, is an independent artistic achievement, comparing favorably with furniture by such Augsburg masters as Philipp Hainhofer.[20] Kellerthaler's complex iconographic program, expressed in silver sculpture and reliefs, suggests the participation of a consultant conversant in humanist ideas, possibly the artist-theoretician Giovanni Maria Nosseni.[21] Also warranting a mention as major goldwork of the time–and executed under the Prague court's influence–are the ewer and basin garnitures of Daniel Kellerthaler, another member of this well-known Dresden goldsmith family.[22]

Apart from these exquisite works, a plethora of objects seemingly survive only in archival references. Since these sources frequently provide insufficient descriptions, the objects named cannot be identified with surviving pieces. Other works were given away as presents. Among the goldsmiths particularly active for the Dresden court are Abraham Schwedler, Valentin Geitner, Urban Schneeweiss, Georg Mond, Michael Botza, and Hans Dürr the Younger. Account books reveal that they were commissioned to work on the manufacture of silver dishes and jewelry embellished with precious stones and enamel. The resulting production of *Hofbecher* (silver drinking vessels) and *Schenck-Ketten* (Honor Necklaces) with the elector's image (*Kontrafekte*), as well as so-called *Gesellschaften* (Societies), jewels and gems intended for people connected by a common interest, was so lavish that it bordered on the wasteful. All these objects were tokens of princely favor, presented on occasions such as marriages, baptisms, birthdays, or holidays; they also served as tournament prizes and as awards in recognition of special achievements. The generosity with which priceless gifts were dispensed was a reflection of the continual flowering of courtly splendor, most notably during the reign of Elector Christian II. His gifts were particularly lavish with regard to Emperor Rudolf II. In anticipation of his 1607 journey to Prague, the elector visited the Leipzig New Year's and Easter fairs, spending more than 55,000 florins on presents that included silver dishes, jewels, gems, and necklaces. Such an expenditure exceeded the customary budget several times over.

12. Cf. Schürer 2002, p. 175.
13. Cf. Schürer 1994, p. 60.
14. Between 1573 and 1593 the number of workshops in Dresden fluctuated between seventeen and twenty-one (cf. Holzhausen/Kesting 1966, p. XIX). In Leipzig, an average number of nineteen masters were active (Schröder 1935, p. 10).
15. Dates and attributions of the Nuremberg goldsmiths' works in this catalogue are based on the conclusions of the *Forschungsprojekt zur Nürnberger Goldsmithekunst 1541–1868* am Germanischen Nationalmuseum. I would like to thank Frau Dr. Karin Tebbe and Mr. Ralf Schürer for the materials they supplied.
16. Holzhausen 1935, pp. 234–39.
17. SächsHStA Dresden, Rep.LII. Gen. 1925 Loc. 33342 Registratura Über das Bestallungs Buch, Anno 1576. 1577. 1578. 1579. and 1581., fol. 503r–504r.
18. This can be deduced from a petition by Hieronymus Kramer, dated September 12, 1592 (SächsHStA Dresden, Special-Rescripte 1592, Vol. II, fol. 125r–127r, quote: fol. 125v). This quote reveals his massive financial difficulties. Because of the cancellation of the Danish king's visit and the untimely death of Christian I, Kramer was unable to sell his inventory.
19. Cf. extensively Holzhausen/Kesting 1966.
20. Green Vault, inv. no. I 20, Holzhausen/Kesing 1966, p. XIX.
21. Cf. the essay of Jürgen Müller in this volume.
22. Marsyas basin and Midas ewer (inv. no. IV 9 and 57) and baptismal basin of the Wettins (lost in World War II); cf. Holzhausen/Kesting 1966, pl. 44–46.

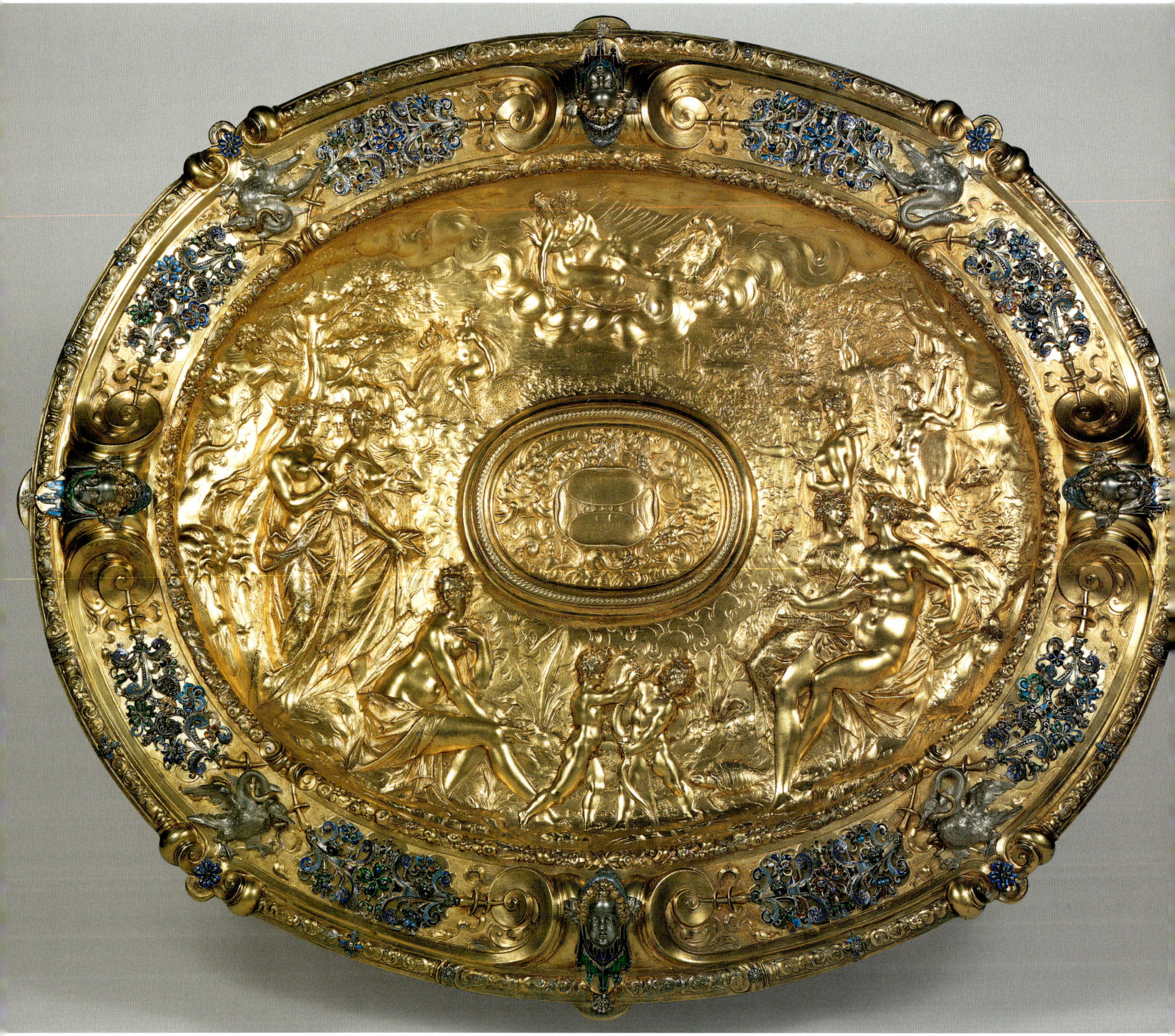

Display Basin with the History of Europe
Christoph Lencker
Augsburg, circa 1600
Silver, mostly gilded, enamel, emeralds
W. 27 in. (68.5 cm), D. 22⅜ in. (57 cm)
Kunsthistorisches Museum Vienna,
Kunstkammer, inv. no. KK 1110

In Dresden foreign masters were often hired in order to invigorate local crafts. On July 4, 1587, Christian I inquired of Nuremberg's city council whether he could employ the goldworker Matthäus Karl for one year. After his request was approved, he commissioned the master, who "*fur einen Goldschmid und Contrafectern sonderlich gerühmet worden*"[23] (was particularly praised as an artistic goldsmith and craftsman), to fabricate jewels embellished with precious stones. The two industrious Nuremberg goldsmiths Hans Dürr the Elder and Gabriel Gipfel also came to the Dresden court.

Although its goldsmiths' guild was among the oldest in Germany, neighboring Leipzig was not a significant supplier of silver to the Saxon electors. The one exception was Elias Geyer, one of the most innovative masters of his time, who appears to have worked exclusively for Dresden's court. Approximately thirty of his works—by far the majority of those surviving—are preserved to this day in the collections of the Green Vault.[24] It can be assumed that many of them were direct court commissions, which would explain the lack of hallmarks, otherwise obligatory as controls for the prescribed silver content. Once again, Veit Böttiger was the agent, having previously negotiated for Christian II the purchase of numerous Geyer works between 1601 and 1605. The goldsmith most likely bought ostrich eggs, sea-snail shells, coconuts, and nephrite from the Leipzig dealer, who, as mentioned above, also supplied the court with pearls and Oriental mother-of-pearl objects. Geyer's numerous ostrich-egg cups, sea horses, and other sea monsters comprise a curious group, singular for any princely Kunstkammer of the time. Gabriel Kaltemarckt was the first to define them as a specific subspecialty within a Kunstkammer, terming them "*was durch Natur und Kunst von solchen Gewechsen*[25] *zu trinck und anderen Geschirren formirt und gemacht*"[26] (those products which nature created and art transformed into drinking vessels and other dishes). Geyer's works exemplify this category: while they unite *naturalia* and *artificialia*, they also embody the contest between nature and the human reaction to it, expressed in the artistic spirit and the ability to invent. Even if documents refer to them as drinking vessels, the functional aspect of these and other related objects was almost certainly insignificant—a fact further evidenced by the details of their manufacture. In his late basin with hunting scenes, made around 1611–13 (cat. no. 98), Geyer left the traditional themes of figural goldwork and dared to compete with one of the leading masters of his time. The basin's close resemblance to Augsburg goldsmith Christoph Lencker's "Europe Basin" in Rudolf II's Kunstkammer (Kunsthistorisches Museum, Vienna, ill. p. 210) leads to the assumption that the work was commissioned by Christian II. It is possible that the elector may have seen the famous basin during one of his visits to Prague and subsequently ordered a work from Geyer that would correspond to the new type while also representing an independent Saxon artistic achievement.

23. SächsHStA Dresden, Copial no. 543, fol. 171v.
24. About Elias Geyer cf. Menzhausen 1973.
25. By this, Kaltemarckt meant "*in und auslendische Gewechse. von Metallen, Stein, Holcz, Kreutern so uff der Erden, in der Erden in Wassern und Meer, gefunden wirdt,*" (about domestic and foreign plants, about metals, stones, wood, and herbs which are found on the ground, in the ground, in [fresh] water, and in [salt water] oceans) cited in Gutfleisch/Menzhausen 1989, p. 11.
26. Gutfleisch/Menzhausen 1989, p. 1.

97 Ewer

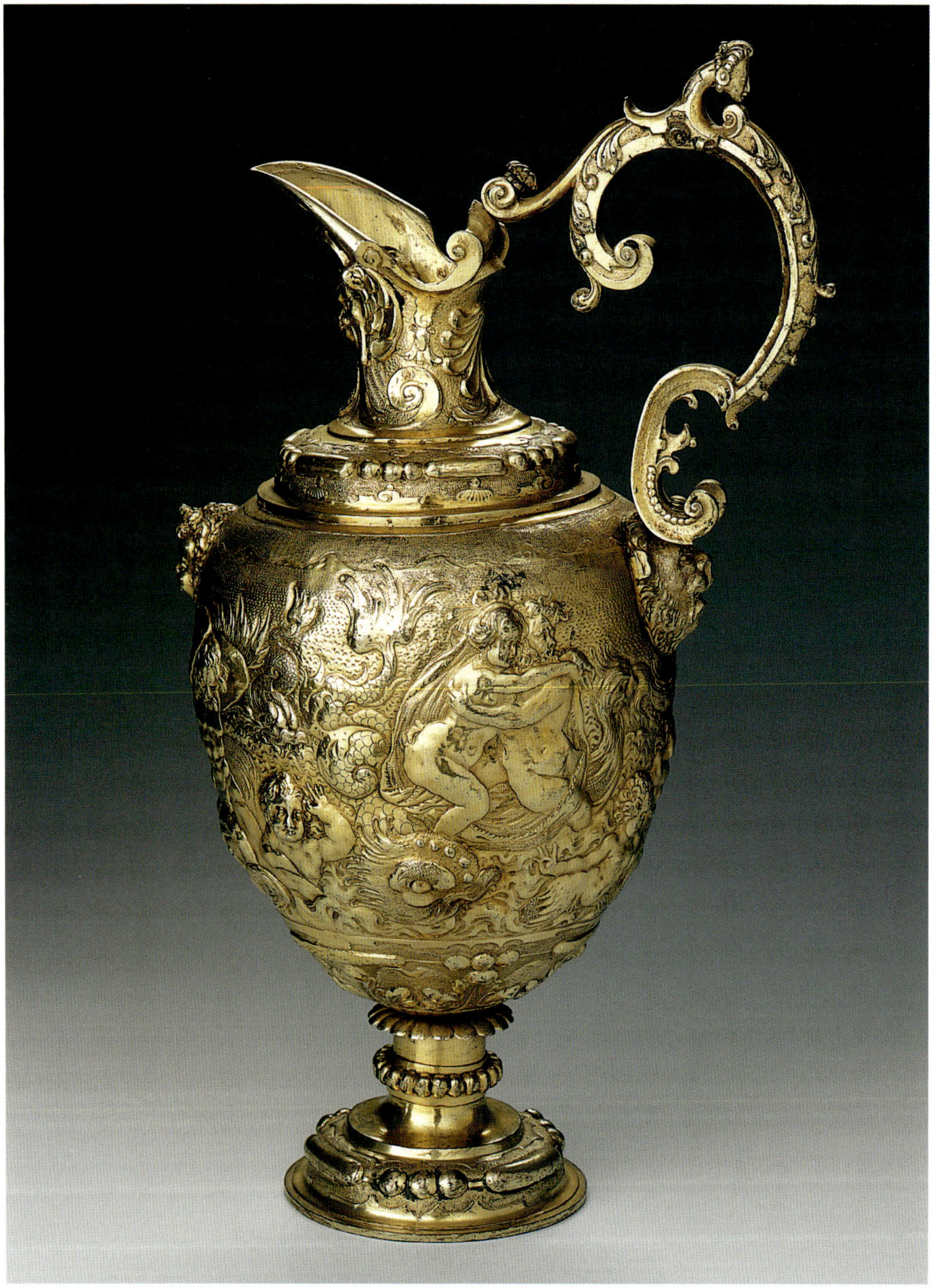

This work, made by Balthasar Grill in Augsburg about 1613–15, is first mentioned in the silver inventory of 1723, where it appears with the hunting basin by the Leipzig goldsmith Elias Geyer (cat. no. 98). At this time, the original counterparts of the garnitures were lost; hence this ewer and Geyer's basin were combined.

The ewer's body is embellished with fantastic sea creatures resembling those on innumerable drinking and pouring vessels of the time. Amid the bustle of diverse composite creatures, dolphins, and putti, a couple, most likely Neptune and Amphitrite, may be seen in an intimate embrace. On the opposite side is an abduction scene. As is seen often in other pieces, Grill has freely combined a number of different models from engravings, thereby deemphazising the meanings of the individual scenes. The idea was to symbolize the element of water in general and to thus make reference to the container's intended use. What distinguishes this particularly heavy cast piece is the abundant use of precious material and the virtuosic surface treatment. In its powerful plasticity, this ewer is fundamentally different from Geyer's basin and ewer (cat. no. 100). Although both were inspired by the same type of Italian goldsmith's work, this object is distinguished by its refined decoration, which is subtly welded to the surface.
U.W.

Balthasar Grill, Augsburg, circa 1613–15
Silver-gilt
H. 15½ in. (39.5 cm)
Hallmark for Augsburg and
maker's mark of a stork (to the left in a circle)
First mentioned in the silver inventory 1723,
p. 77, no. 4
Staatliche Kunstsammlungen Dresden, Grünes
Gewölbe, inv. no. IV 291
Lit.: Sponsel 1928, pp. 117f. and plate 52;
Seling 1980, vol. II, ill. 82, vol. III,
p. 19, no. 36 (Hallmark) and no. 1091b;
Guide Green Vault 1997, p. 55,
no. 95b; Warsaw 1997, p. 164,
no. V 38

98 Oval Basin with Hunting Scenes

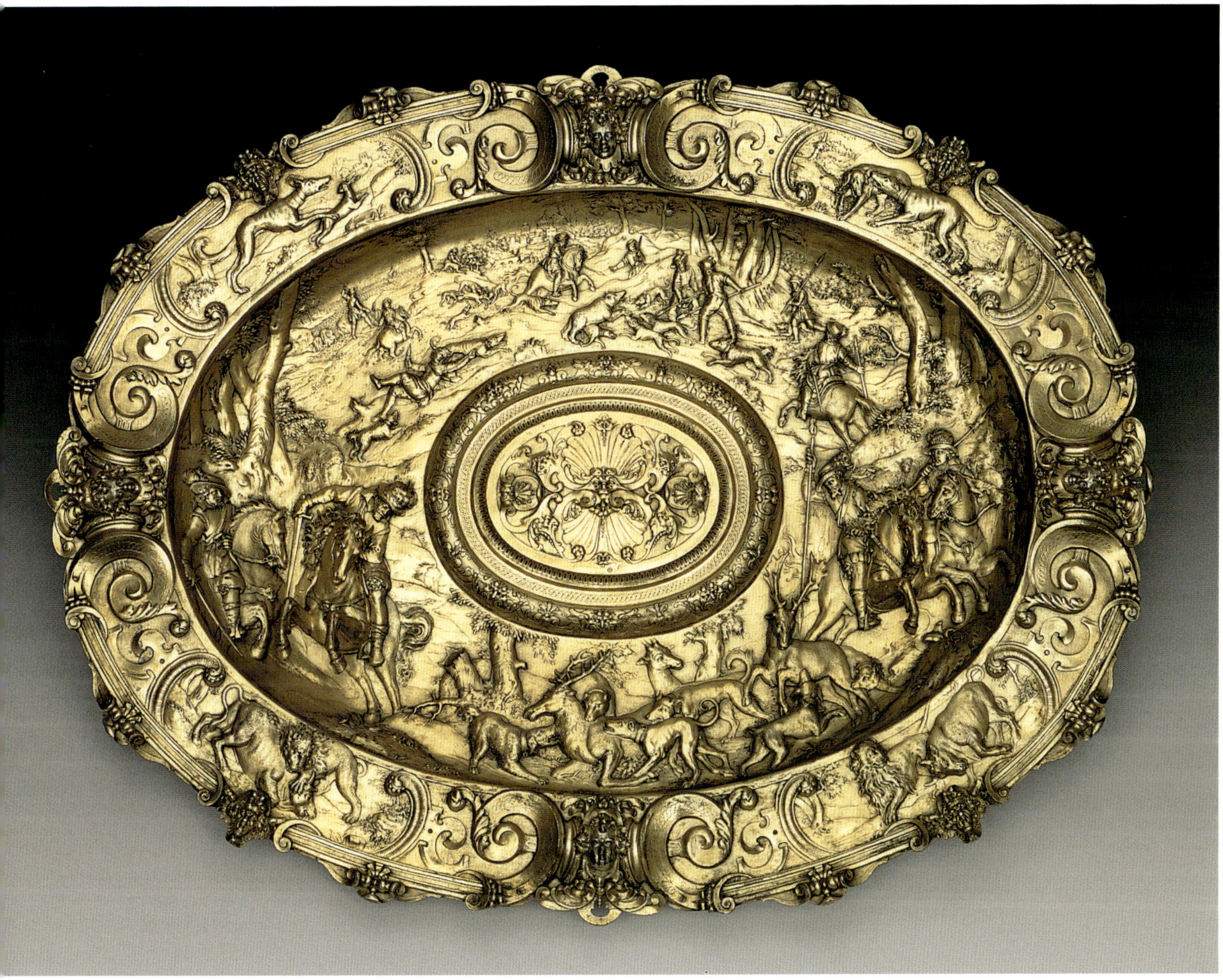

Elias Geyer,
Leipzig, circa 1611–13
Silver-gilt
L. 29½ in. (75 cm),
W. 22⅜ in. (57 cm)
Hallmark for Leipzig
date letter "F"
(in mirror image) and
maker's mark "EG"
(in ligature in circle)
First mentioned in
the silver inventory 1723,
p. 77, no. 4
Staatliche Kunstsammlungen Dresden, Grünes Gewölbe,
inv. no. IV 250
Lit.: Graul 1910,
plate XXIV;
Sponsel 1928,
pp. 119–21, plate 53;
Schröder 1935, p. 83;
Menzhausen 1973,
pp. 51f., ill. 13–14;
Guide Green Vault 1997,
p. 51, no. 69b;
cf. also The Illustrated
Bartsch 1983,
pp. 178f., nos. 933–35;
The Illustrated Bartsch
1984, p. 68, no. 1170

Elias Geyer's beautiful hunting basin first appears in the 1723 silver inventory, where it is mentioned alongside the ewer of Balthasar Grill (cat. no. 97). However, the two works do not belong together. As revealed by a comparison with Christoph Lencker's famous "Europe Basin" (Kunsthistorisches Museum, Vienna, ill. p. 210), already mentioned in the 1607/11 Kunstkammer inventory of Emperor Rudolf II, the Geyer basin presents a new type that was substantially influenced by Augsburg goldsmiths. Although it lacks the Mannerist elongation of Lencker's figures, which no longer show the influence of the Rudolfian art circle, its composition is still closely related to that of the Augsburg work. The two basins no longer display the typical sixteenth-century radial frieze, which can be viewed only by turning the piece. Instead they feature a single grand representation—interrupted only by the oval-shaped reserve for the ewer—that is to be looked at from one side only. This is a clear indication that they were for display in an upright position on the silver buffet, a particularly fitting feature during times in which narrative composition was highly valued. In addition, each basin exhibits a similar treatment of the rim, which is organized into four cartouches flanked by sturdy volutes of scrollwork. Parts of the hunting scenes here follow a 1590 print of Antonio Tempesta, an engraver active in Rome. Geyer modified the model, adjusting the format to the pictorial composition and adding further motifs. A suite of copperplate engravings published in Rome in 1600 by the same artist served as prototypes for the cartouches with fighting animals on the rim.

Despite some perspectival weaknesses, Geyer's basin has considerable spatial depth, achieved in part by virtue of the reliefs' subtle gradations, which range from highly raised elements to minute transitions. Geyer even violates the boundaries of the chased relief worked in repoussé: he attaches two independently cast, three-dimensional horses to the foreground. By accentuating the four noble riders on the left and right sides, the basin deliberately emphasizes the hunt as a princely privilege and courtly divertissement.
U.W.

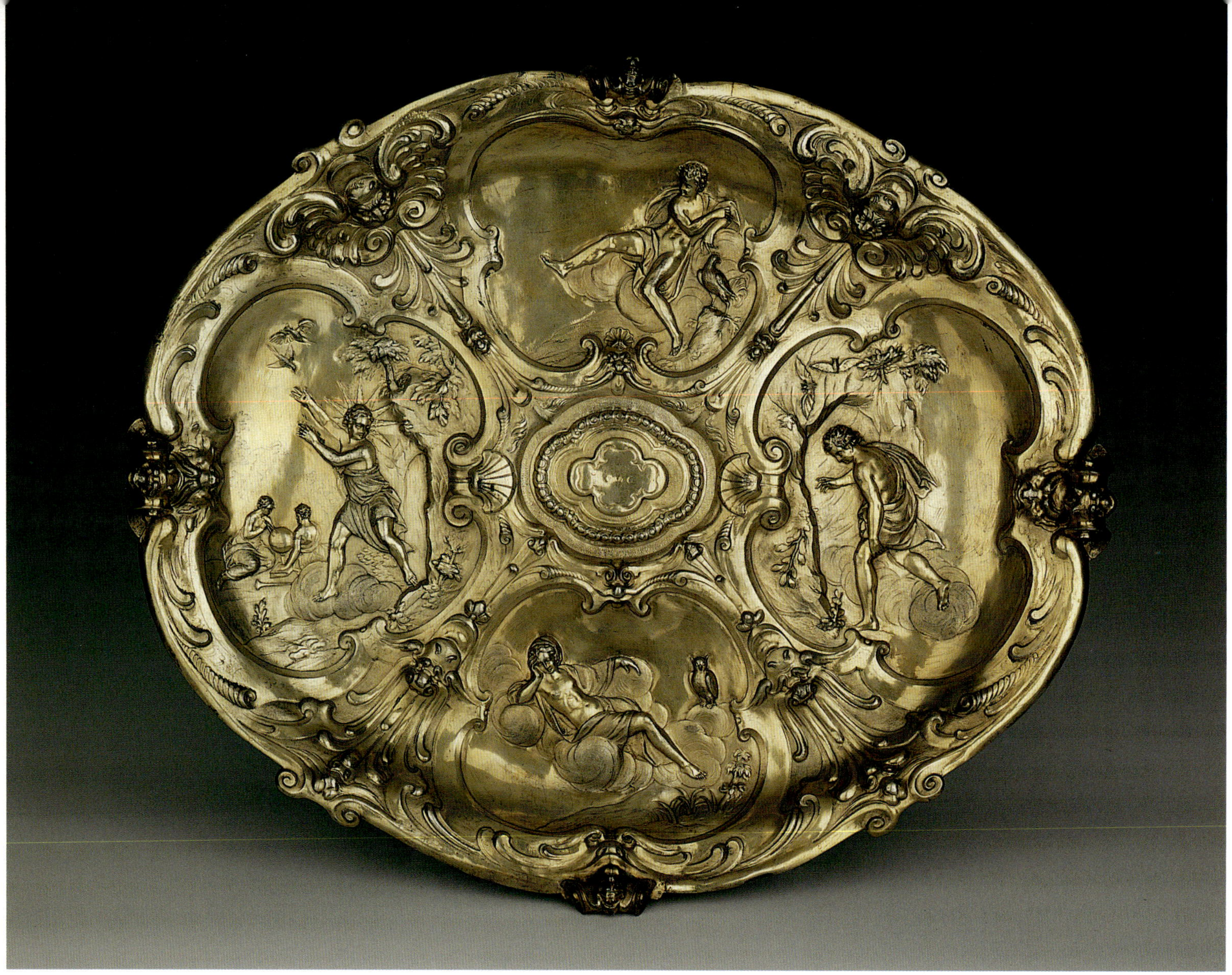

99 Basin with the Four Times of Day

In of four large reliefs, the basin shows allegories of the four times of day. The personification of Morning reclines on a cloud and is accompanied by a rooster (top). Day, stepping out of a cave, his head surrounded by rays of light, is accompanied by two female figures with globe, compass, and book which refer to art and science, the fruit of the day's work (left). The figure of Evening, disappearing into a cave as bats hover above (right), is shown near the personification of Night (below), resting on a bed of clouds and accompanied by an owl. The remaining smooth surfaces display traces of finely embossed figural representations, barely visible today owing to abrasion. A quatrefoil at the center indicates the spot for the placement of the matching ewer, which was melted down in 1772 along with numerous other pieces of plate. Inventories describe the ewer's lid, which was crowned by a Chronos figure with a scythe, a personification of Time. The ornamented borders of the cartouches are decorated with grotesques and masks whose powerful plasticity contrasts with the finely punched scrollwork (the latter also severely abraded). Like the reliefs in the cartouches, the ornamental frame is intended to be viewed from one side only. The flowing contours linking the grotesques with the scrollwork and the symmetrical, gnarled shapes are reminiscent of the work of the Nuremberg goldsmith Christoph Jamnitzer, who in 1610 published a pattern book of ingenious inventions, *Neüw: Grottessken Buch.*
U.W.

Hans IV Pfleger, Augsburg, circa 1613–15
Silver-gilt
L. 31⅜ in. (79.8 cm), W. 26½ in. (67.3 cm)
Hallmark for Augsburg and
maker's mark with "HP" (in circle)
First mentioned in the silver inventory
1723, pp. 77–78, no. 5
Staatliche Kunstsammlungen Dresden,
Grünes Gewölbe, inv. no. IV 183
Lit.: Sponsel 1928, p. 121 and plate 54;
Seling 1980, vol. III, p. 19, no. 37
(Hallmark) and p. 106, no. 1028i;
Seling 1994, p. 25, no. 1028*i;
Guide Green Vault 1997, p. 55, no. 95a;
Warsaw 1997, p. 164, no. V 37

100 Basin and Ewer with Mother-of-Pearl

This precious ewer and basin garniture belongs to the Green Vault's rich holdings of Oriental mother-of-pearl objects that were embellished with silver-gilt mounts by European goldsmiths in Leipzig, Nuremberg, and Torgau. All these objects were first kept in the Dresden Kunstkammer and were transferred to the Green Vault when the Kunstkammer was dissolved in 1832. It can be assumed that this garniture, first mentioned in the 1610 Kunstkammer inventory, was among the mother-of-pearl items purchased in 1602 from Veit Böttiger. Elector Christian II's acquisitions from the Leipzig dealer included three little boxes, one game board, five drinking services, as well as "*zwey begkenn vnd kannen von Perlmutter in vergültt Silver eingefast*" (two basins and ewers of mother-of-pearl and in silver-gilt; Dresden, SächsHStA, Rentkammer-Rechnungen no. 185, fol. 323r).

The mosaic work is typical of the Gujarat region and can also be found on two caskets kept in the Green Vault (inv. nos. III 245 and III. 247, the latter also with mounts by Elias Geyer). Inlay work of this type is an arduous process: Small mother-of-pearl tesserae, arranged in stylized floral motifs, are adhered to a wooden support, and the interstices are filled with dark varnish or mastic. Here, foliate tendrils are skillfully and generously dispersed across the basin's surface, encircling regularly spaced reserves adorned with geometric patterns.

The Leipzig goldsmith Elias Geyer completed the iridescent mosaic work with thin, concentrically arranged silver-gilt bands with scrollwork and bunches of fruit. In an attempt to structure the surface, the floral ornament that originally covered the basin was modified. To facilitate framing the bands with narrow strips of mother-of-pearl, innumerable tiny, leaf-shaped tesserae had to be removed. Geyer further emphasized the centers of the reserves with small silver-gilt frogs and lizards. Depicted on the back of the basin—originally lacquered red but overpainted by Geyer during the process of attaching the mounts—are four concentrically arranged sea deities, positioned either on shells or fantastic sea creatures. These images are framed by a green border ornament populated with animals—a homage to water as creator of the fascinating mother-of-pearl.

The heavy, cast ewer was presumably made during the modification of the mother-of-pearl basins. In this case, Geyer refrained from any adaptation or imitation of the Far Eastern style. Instead, he juxtaposed the Indian basin with a ewer having the balanced proportions and lucid shapes of the European Renaissance. The vessel's elements—the small foot, the egg-shaped body with its flattened top, the narrow neck, and the vertically extended spout—create a contrast and dominate the ornamentation. By inserting six oval cabochons of mother-of-pearl, into both the wall and shoulder, Geyer also took the basin's hexagonal structure into account. By emphasizing the opposition between the inlaid Oriental works and the natural form of the precious material, Geyer apparently intended to highlight the mastery of the Far Eastern artist. Riding on a dolphin over the winged herm on the handle is the sea god Neptune (his trident is lost); he can also be seen on the painting affixed to the underside of the base.

U.W.

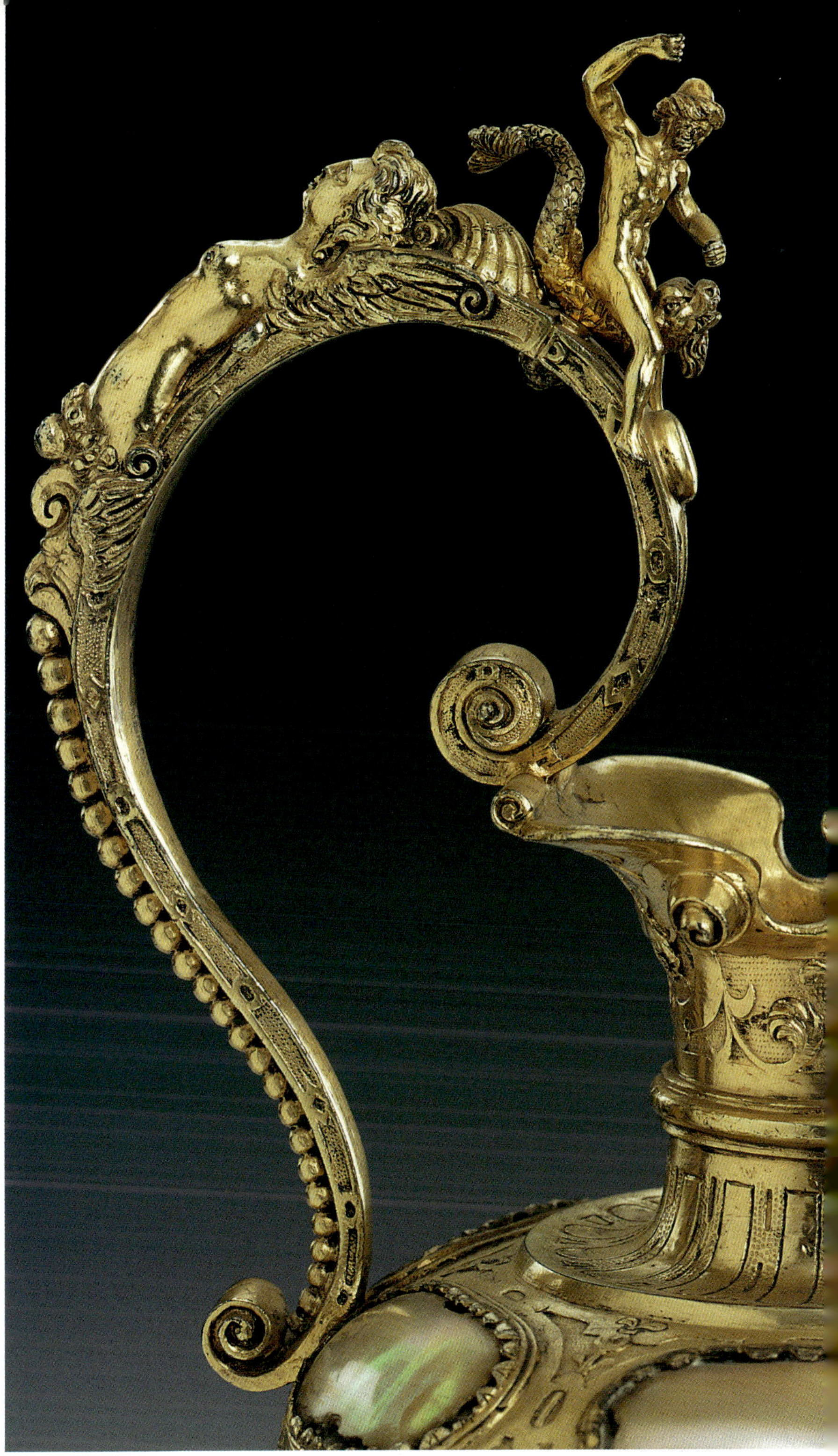

Basin mosaic: mother-of-pearl
Gujarat (India), late 16th century
Mounts: Elias Geyer, Leipzig
circa 1600
Basin: wood, bitumen varnish, mother-of-pearl cut from turban-snail shells, silver-gilt, oil paint
Diam. 23⅝ in. (60.1 cm)
Ewer: Silver-gilt, turbo-snail mother-of-pearl, H. 13⅞ in. (35.2 cm)
Hallmark for Leipzig, date letter "F" (mirror image) and maker's mark "EG" (in ligature, in circle)
First mentioned in the Kunstkammer inventory 1610, fol. 191v
Staatliche Kunstsammlungen Dresden, Grünes Gewölbe, inv. no. IV 287 (basin) and IV 189 (ewer)
Lit.: Graul 1910, plate XX and XXI; Sponsel 1925, p. 51 and plate 29 and 30; Schröder 1935, p. 83; Menzhausen 1973, p. 45, ill. 1 and p. 46, ill. 3; Hayward 1976, p. 265 and ill. 561; Guide Green Vault 1997, p. 53, no. 82; Sangl 2001, p. 271, with ill. 11, p. 275

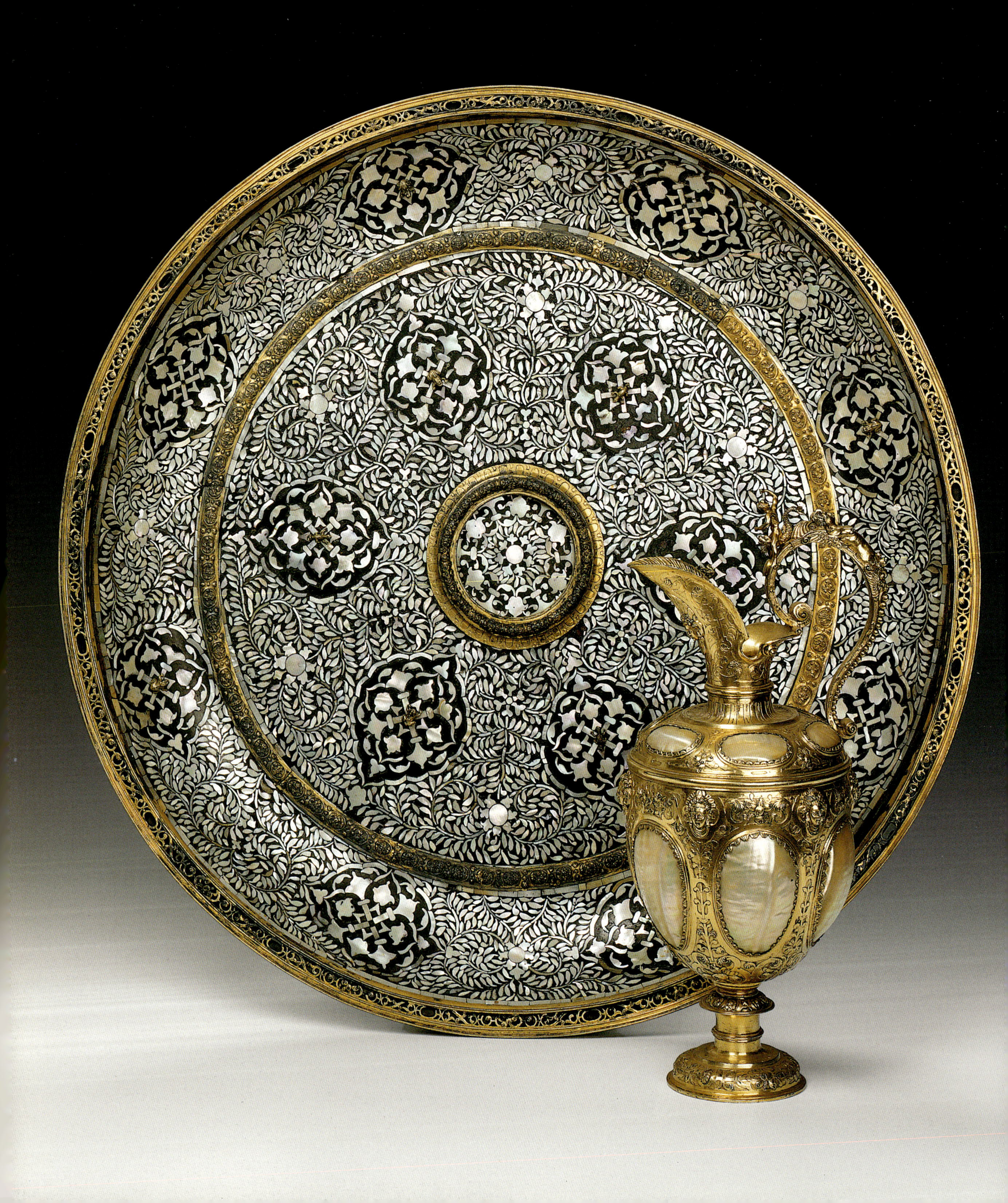

101 Bottle in the Form of a Pilgrim's Flask

The works created by Joerg Ruel characterize him as a versatile goldsmith whose prolific workshop specialized in figural drinking vessels that frequently included exotic shells or ostrich eggs. Unusual for its type, this chain bottle testifies to Ruel's artistry and technical virtuosity. It is distinguished by the use of unusually large disks of mother-of-pearl embellishing the front and back of the vessel. The exotic natural materials, subtly enclosed by finely pierced borders, are accentuated by a handsome applied trim at the center. "*Durchbrochene[n] Rosenn wie kleinoth*" (pierced roses that appear like gems; Kunstkammer inventory 1640) garnished with precious stones also decorate the bottle's narrow sides; these are common decorative elements of the period (see cat. nos. 102, 103). In its present form, this type of bottle epitomizes a Kunstkammer *par excellence*. It transforms the pilgrim's flask into a virtuosic item of princely display. It could be filled with a libation, taken along when traveling, and cooled by immersion in water. The present work embodies the artistic accomplishment of a great master.
U.W.

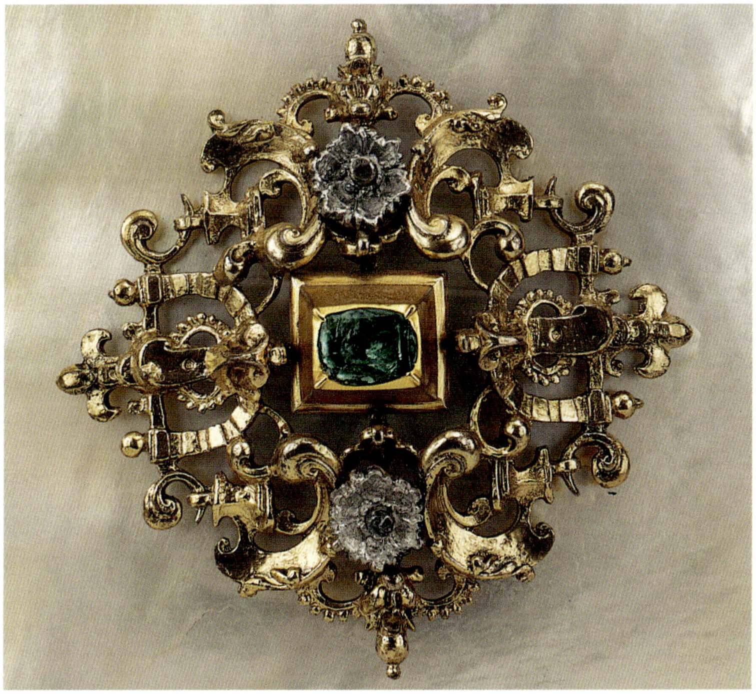

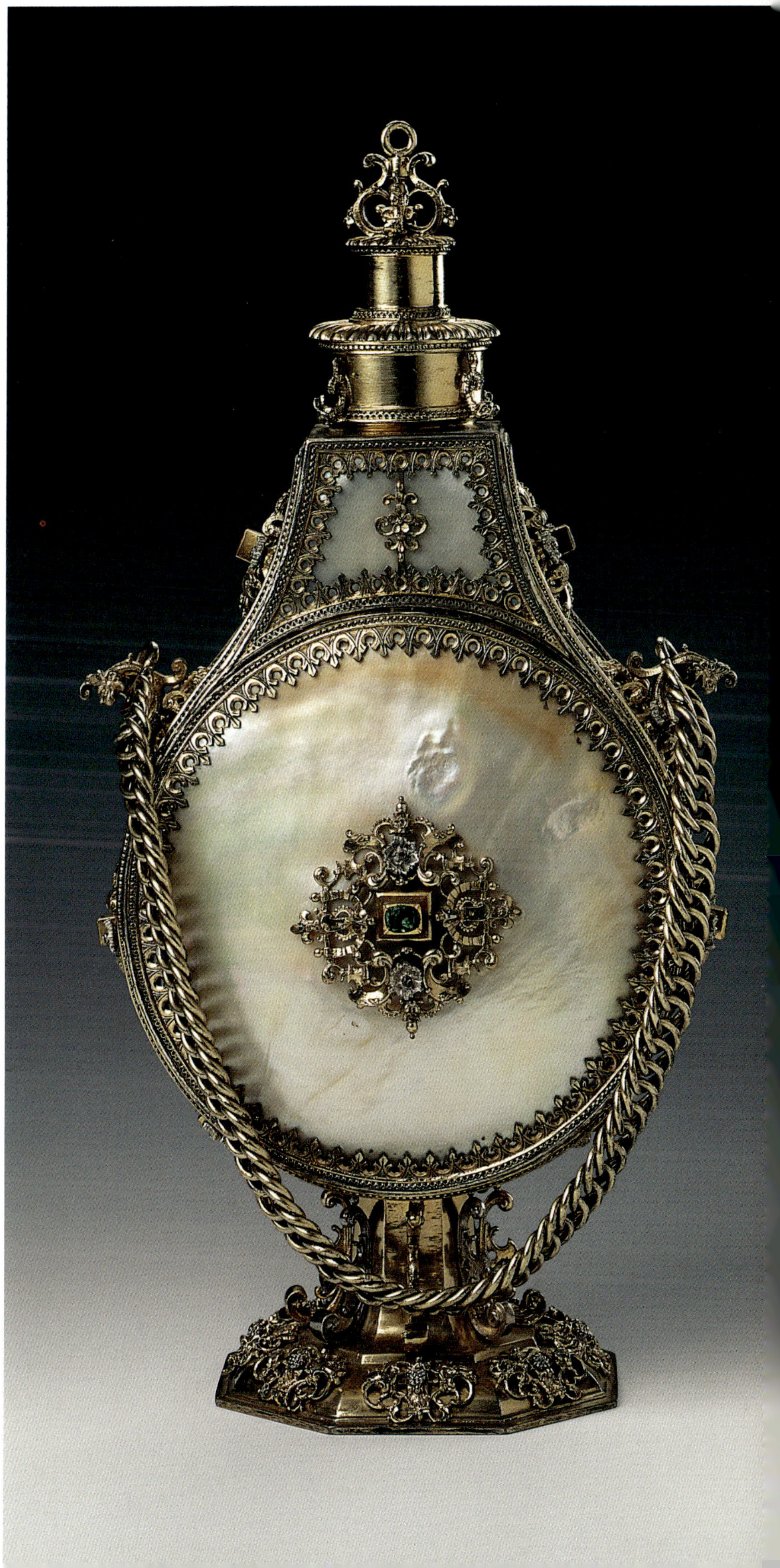

Joerg Ruel
Nuremberg, circa 1598–1602
Silver-gilt, mother-of-pearl, emeralds
H. 10¾ in. (27.4 cm)
Hallmark for Nuremberg
and maker's mark "IR"
(in leaf-shaped field)
First mentioned in the Kunstkammer
inventory 1640, fol. 111v–112r
Staatliche Kunstsammlungen Dresden,
Grünes Gewölbe, inv. no. III 192
Lit.: Sponsel 1925, p. 59
and plate 50; Rosenberg 1925, p. 161,
no. 4086p; Washington 1978, p. 152,
no. 252; Menzhausen 1977, pp. 142f.
and ill. 89; Essen 1986, pp. 372f.,
no. 514 and p. 378 (Ill.);
Koeppe 1989, p. 41, ill. 18;
Guide Green Vault 1997, p. 66, no. 9

102 Cup in the Form of a Partridge

Friedrich Hillebrand, Nuremberg, circa 1593–1602
Silver-gilt, mother-of-pearl, emeralds, garnets
H. 10¾ in. (27.2 cm)
Hallmark for Nuremberg and maker's mark "FH" (in a rectangle)
First mentioned in the Kunstkammer inventory 1640, fol. 141r
Staatliche Kunstsammlungen Dresden, Grünes Gewölbe, inv. no. III 150
Lit.: Sponsel 1925, pp. 52f. and plate 33; Rosenberg 1925, p. 132, no. 4017l; Menzhausen 1977, pp. 142f. and ill. 92; Guide Green Vault 1997, p. 46, no. 42; Tebbe 2003, pp. 2f.

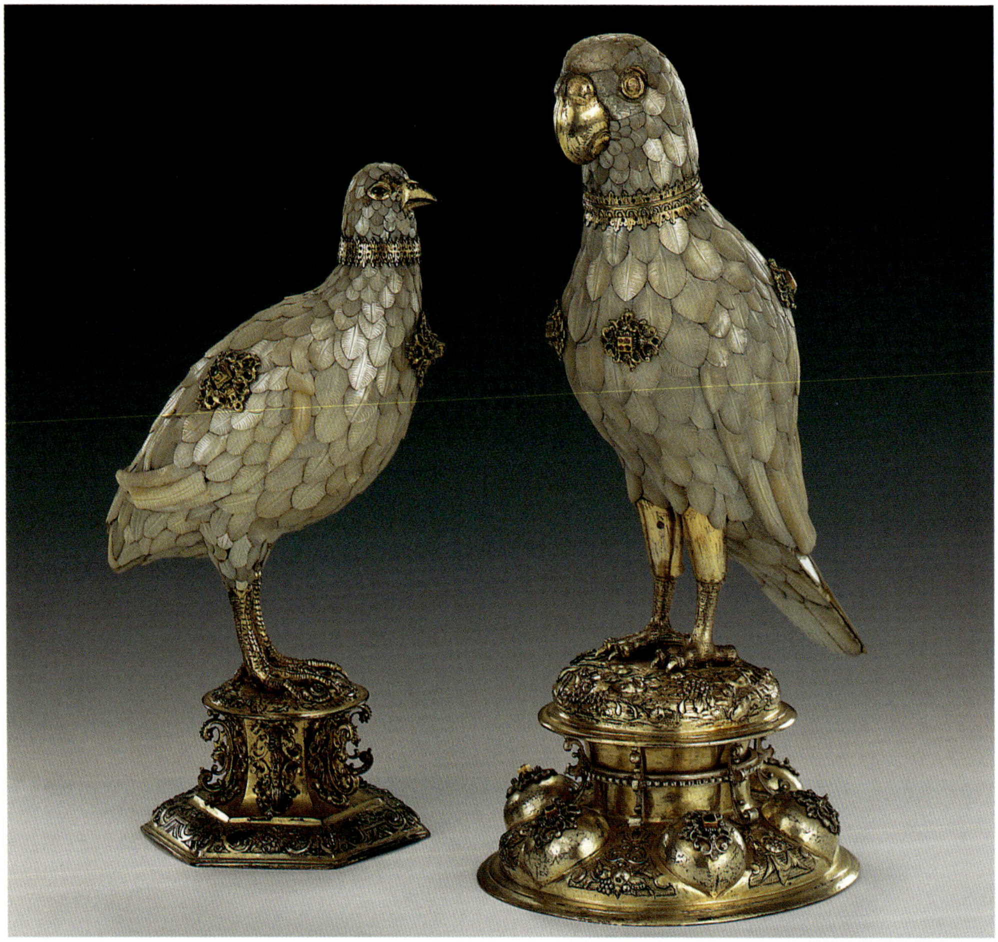

103 Cup in the Form of a Parrot

Hans I Rappolt, Nuremberg, circa 1593–1602
Silver-gilt, mother-of-pearl, emeralds, rubies, enamel, traces of colored mounts, H. 12⅞ in. (32.6 cm)
Hallmark for Nuremberg and maker's mark with leaf and caterpillar
First mentioned in the Kunstkammer inventory 1640, fol. 140v–141r
Staatliche Kunstsammlungen Dresden, Grünes Gewölbe, inv. no. III 151
Lit.: Sponsel 1925, pp. 52f. and plate 33; Rosenberg 1925, no. 4005; Menzhausen 1977, pp. 142f. and ill. 92; Guide Green Vault 1997, p. 50, no. 64

In Nuremberg, cups in the shape of birds with feathers made of small pieces of mother-of-pearl were produced under the influence of imported Indian works. During this time, the goldsmiths Friedrich Hillebrand, Joerg Ruel, and Hans I Rappolt were the most notable contributors to this popular category.

In contrast to exotic inlay work, here the emphasis was not on abstract decoration but on the reproduction of nature. Arranged like roof tiles on the receptacle's silver body, the tiny disks are delicately engraved with striations indicating the texture of the feathers. Both parrot and partridge bear rosettes embellished with precious stones on their sparkling plumage, an incongruous ornament in the ordinarily faithful rendering of nature attempted in these animal sculptures and a feature that underscores their artificial character. As may be deduced from the 1640 inventory entry pertaining to the partridge, the "*Rößlein*" (little roses) were formerly colored, which would have made the objects even more striking.

The use of exotic materials and precious stones combined with their skillful execution transform these cups into stately goldsmith's sculptures. Nearly identical partridges have survived in the National Museum of Copenhagen (Hillebrand) and in the Gilbert Collection, London (Ruel). In 1683, another example, a so-called *Willkomm* goblet by Hillebrand, now in Saint Petersburg's State Hermitage, was given to Schloss Tenneberg, Waltershausen, by Duke Friedrich I.
U.W.

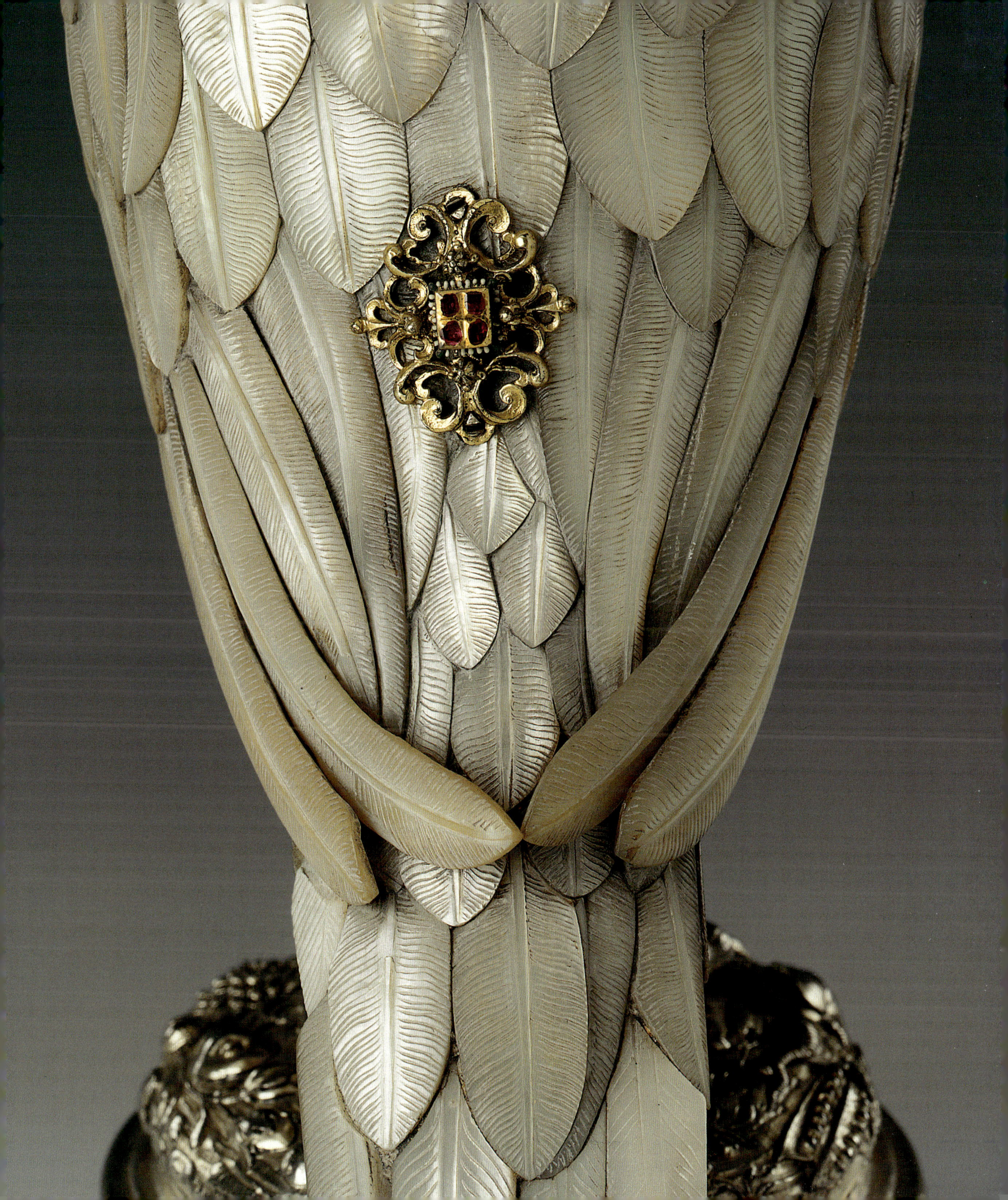

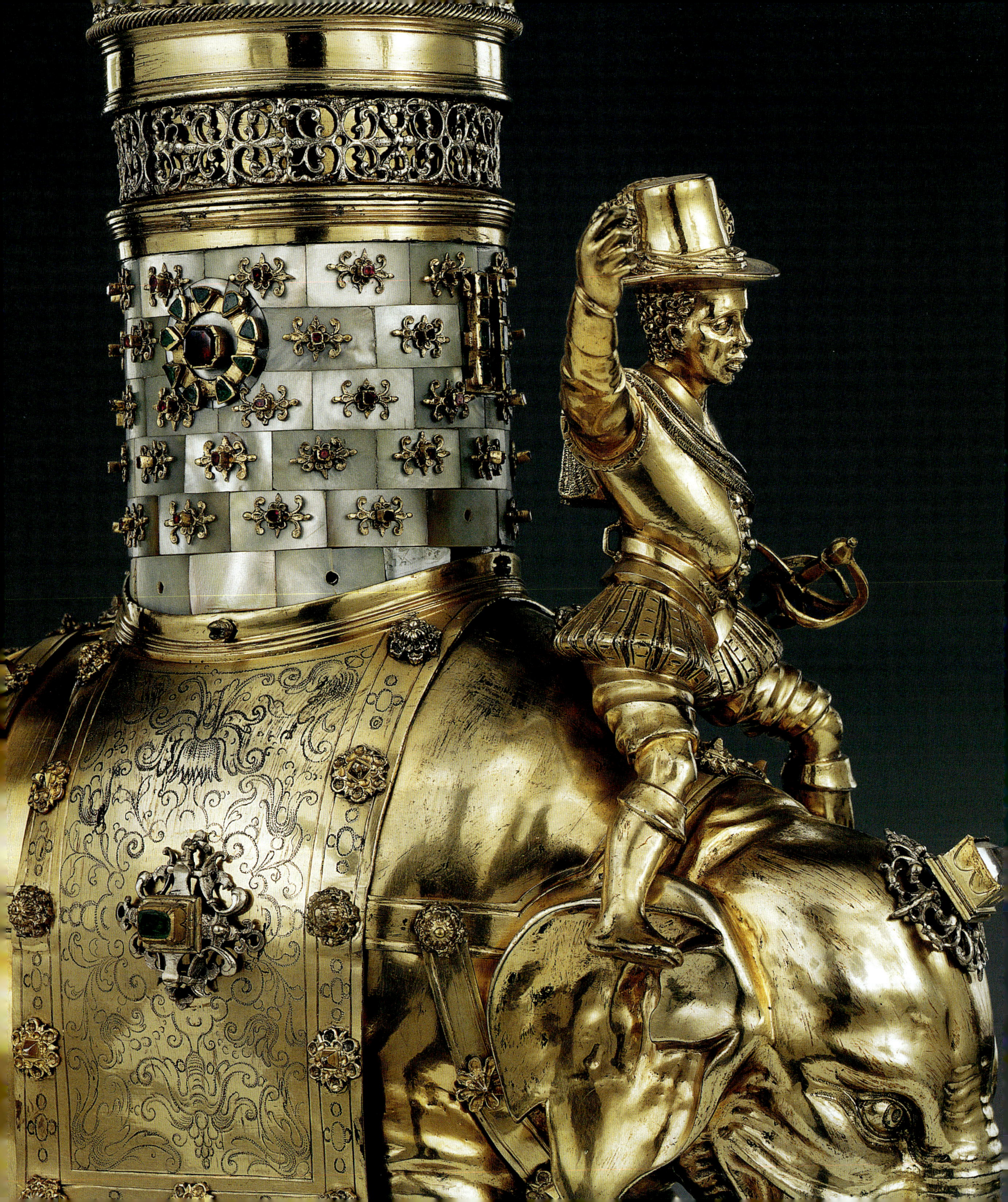

104 Drinking Vessel: Elephant with Tower

The elephant appears in numerous guises in sixteenth-century princely Kunstkammers. Admired as a natural wonder, it was also thought to personify the virtues of strength and wisdom; hence the animal was elevated to a symbol of the ruler himself. As early as 1587, the Dresden Kunstkammer included an elephant tusk that was suspended from an iron chain. It also preserved a mechanical elephant equipped with a Moor shooting a bow and arrow from a tower, a clock, and various other movements (formerly Dresden, Mathematisch-Physikalischer Salon, destroyed in 1945). Like this technical miracle, Urban Wolff's drinking vessel also alludes to the legendary war elephants that Hannibal used to cross the Alps.

Urban Wolff, also the maker of the *Doppelscheuer* constructed from Indian drinking bowls (cat. no. 105), was inspired by Oriental works to incorporate the mother-of-pearl technique into his own artistic repertoire. He covered the tower's wall here with rectangular mother-of-pearl plates, and following the contemporary Western European style of goldwork, he then embellished them with appliqués.
U.W.

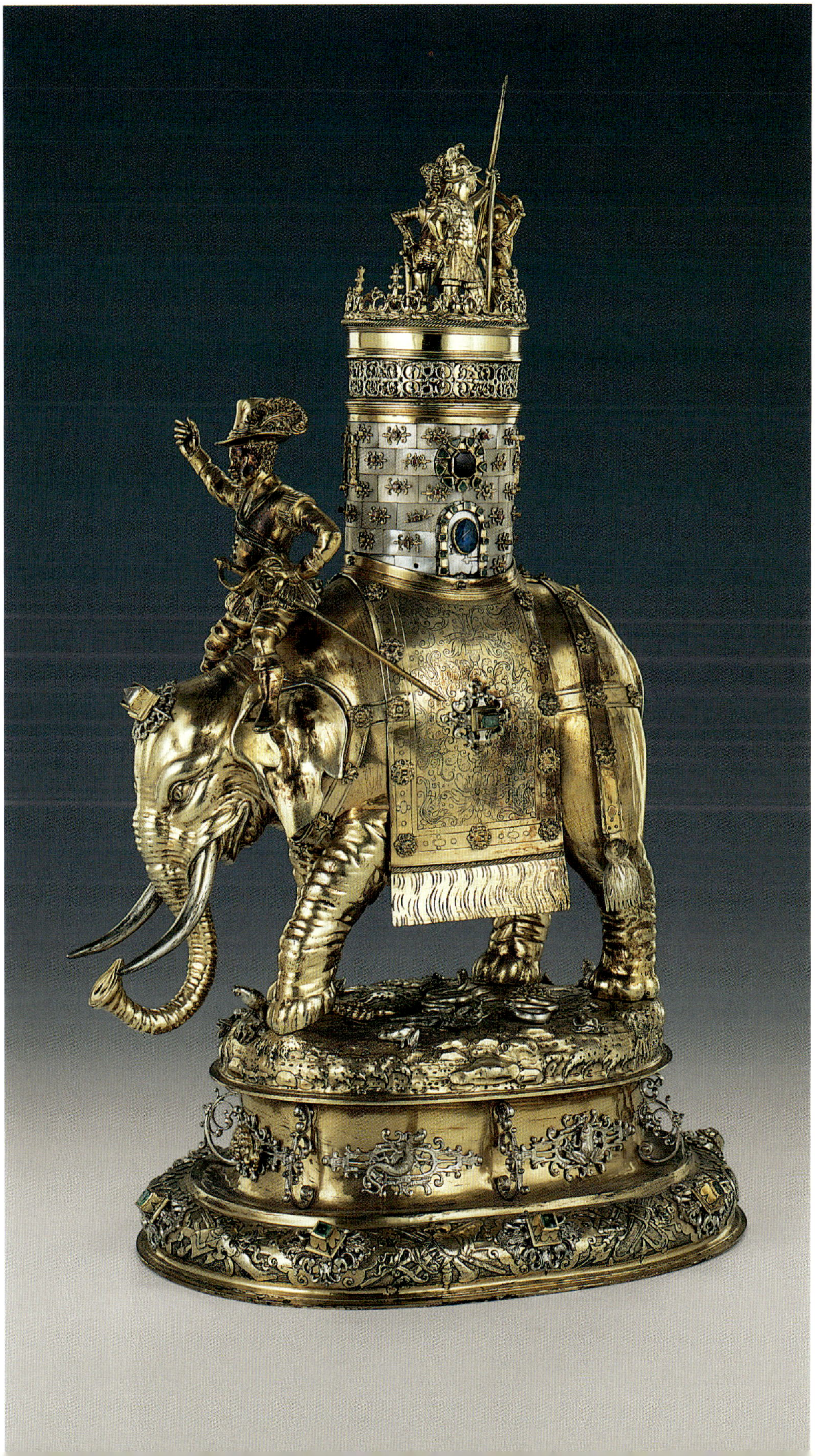

Urban Wolff, Nuremberg
circa 1593–98
Silver-gilt, mother-of-pearl, colored stones
H. 20½ in. (52 cm)
Hallmark for Nuremberg and maker's mark "VW" (in ligature, in trapezoidal field)
First mentioned in the Kunstkammer inventory 1640, fol. 145v–146r
Staatliche Kunstsammlungen Dresden, Grünes Gewölbe, inv. no. IV 120
Lit.: Rosenberg 1925, p. 143, no. 4044c; Sponsel 1928, p. 73 and plate 35; Menzhausen 1977, pp. 142f. and plate 81; Washington 1978, p. 153, no. 256; Guide Green Vault 1997, p. 41, no. 19

105 Small Double Cup with Mother-of-Pearl

Urban Wolff is represented in this exhibition with all three of his works owned by the Green Vault (see cat. nos. 104, 130). The Nuremberg goldsmith reworked two differently shaped Indian drinking bowls to create this typical German drinking vessel, a so-called double cup or *Doppelscheuer.* Its silver-gilt feet and broadly lipped borders are both attached to the bowls by clasps, while hinges allow mobility. The 1640 entry in the Kunstkammer inventory reveals that the mount was originally not only decorated with finely engraved and elegantly embossed ornaments but was also "*mit Lasurfarben eingelassen*" (painted with transparent colors). Traces of such painted decoration, in this case presumably intended to imitate champlevé enamel, are found on numerous goldworks owned by the Green Vault.

The manufacture of such Indian drinking vessels required sophisticated craftsmanship. The small mother-of-pearl plates are actually not mounted onto the wooden support but assembled in two layers, one atop the other; their natural curvature conforms to that of the vessel. Apparently, the Saxon court valued such objects from the Far East even without European mounts of precious metals. The 1586 electoral inventory of the Silberkammer, compiled immediately following the death of Elector August, cites, among other items, "*Trinkgetässe von Perlmutter*" (drinking vessels made of mother-of-pearl; O'Byrn 1880, p. 32). In 1590, the double cup exhibited here, acquired by Christian I from the Dresden dealer Hieronymus Kramer, served as a Maundy Thursday present for the elector's wife (SächsHstA Dresden, Loc. 8694/10, fol. 198v). The previous year, Christian had given her an herb jar, likewise decorated with mother-of-pearl, which he obtained directly from Urban Wolff.

U.W.

Mother-of-pearl work:
India
16th century
Mount: Urban Wolff
Nuremberg, circa
1585–90
Silver-gilt,
mother-of-pearl
H. (assembled)
14⅞ in. (37.7 cm)
Hallmark for Nuremberg
and maker's mark "VW"
(in ligature, in
trapezoidal field)
First mentioned in the
Kunstkammer inventory
1640, fol. 119r
Staatliche Kunstsammlungen Dresden, Grünes
Gewölbe,
inv. no. III 154
and III 155
Lit.: Rosenberg 1925,
p. 143, no. 4044f.;
Sponsel 1928, p. 33
and plate 15;
Menzhausen 1977,
p. 142 and plate 90;
Guide Green Vault 1997,
p. 56, no. 99;
Sangl 2001, p. 279, ill. 19

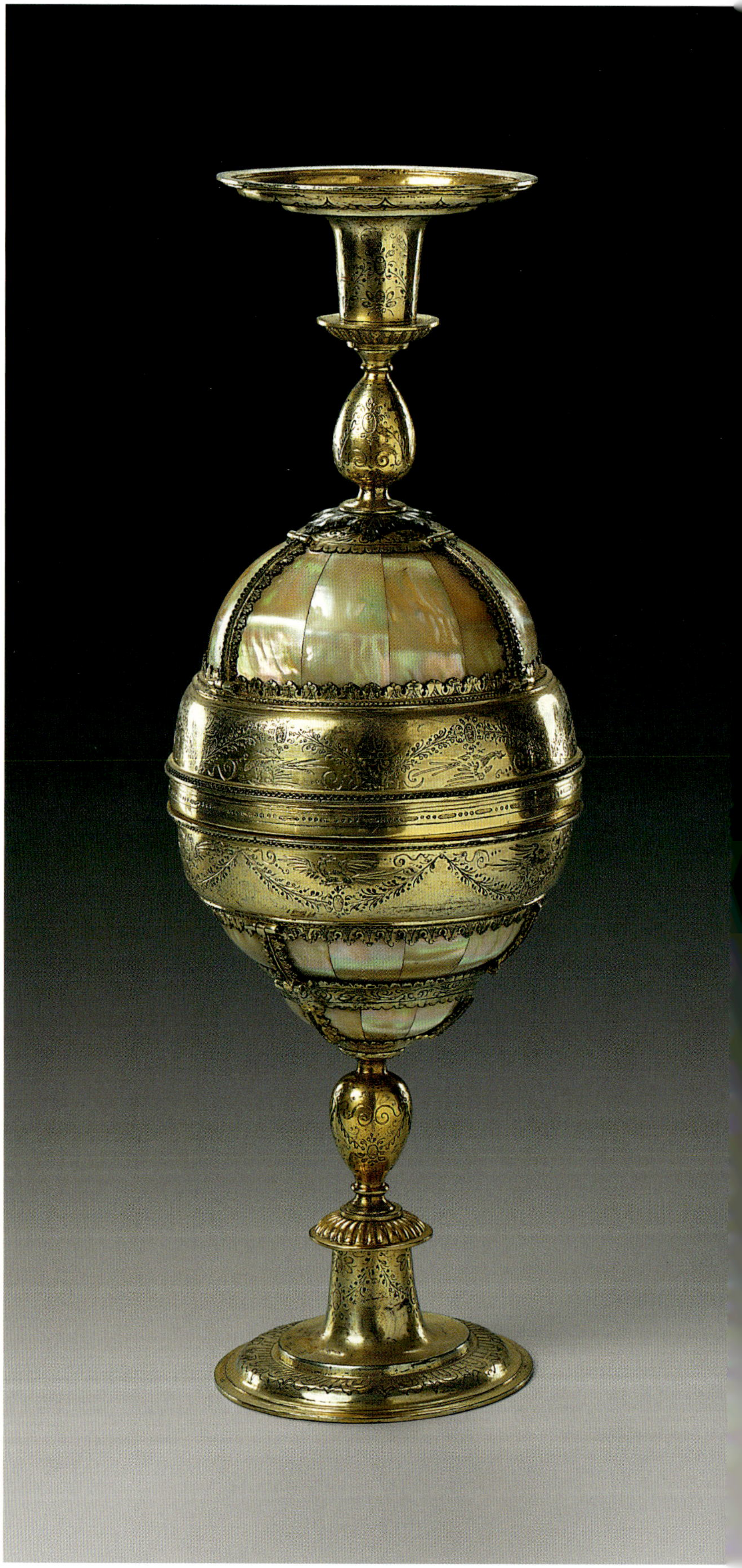

106 Drinking Vessel: Bacchus on a Barrel

In a time partial to banquets and drinking vessels in every conceivable form, Bacchic themes were appropriate artistic associations. The composition of the chubby wine god sitting astride a barrel as he prepares to drink from his cup can already be found in early-sixteenth-century prints. Later, Bacchus was developed into a frequently used motif for drinking and pouring containers, centerpieces, and table automatons. Here, his body is affixed to the barrel's top through a quatrefoil-shaped protrusion and serves as a receptacle for the alcoholic beverage. The detachable head acts as this peculiar drinking vessel's lid.

Apart from the present Green Vault artifact, Marc Rosenberg (1925) cites two additional versions of the Bacchus by Meinrad Bauch: one very similar to the Dresden piece in the British Museum (Waddesdon Bequest), as well as one formerly in a private collection in Stuttgart (whereabouts unknown). Another, more complex rendering of the same theme was created in Augsburg, the capital of goldsmiths, for Emperor Rudolf II's Prague Kunstkammer (today Vienna, Kunsthistorisches Museum). This automaton in the shape of a triumphal chariot showing Bacchus accompanied by his entourage was particularly fascinating because the figures' movements were accompanied by music played by a organ concealed in the mechanical object.
U.W.

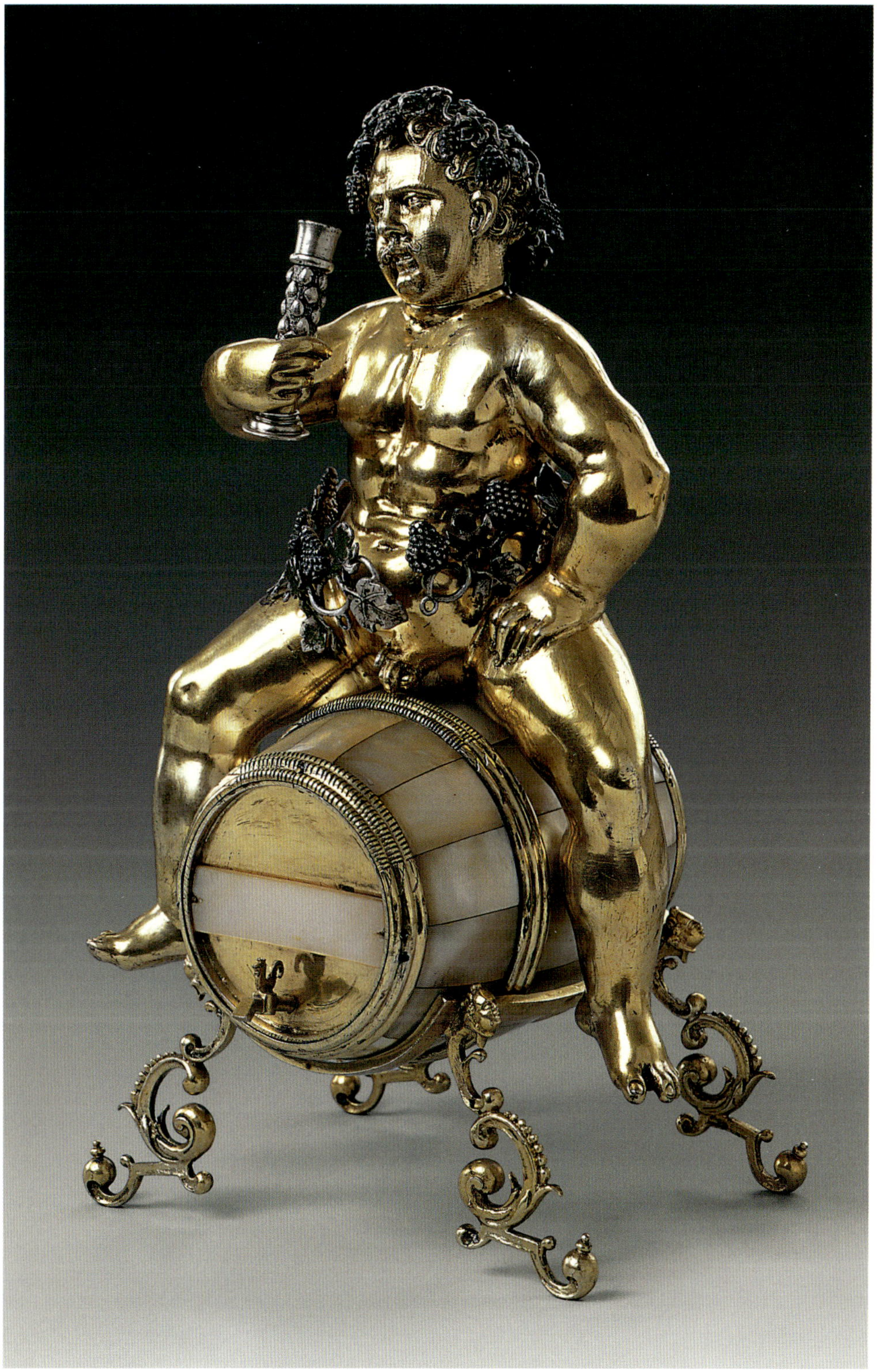

Meinrad Bauch the Elder, Nuremberg
1593–1602
Silver-gilt, mother-of-pearl, cold enamel
H. 10⅜ in. (26.5 cm)
Hallmark for Nuremberg and maker's mark "MB" (in ligature, in circle)
First mentioned in the Kunstkammer inventory 1640, fol. 111v

Staatliche Kunstsammlungen Dresden, Grünes Gewölbe, inv. no. IV 265
Lit.: Rosenberg 1925, p. 119, no. 3993a; Menzhausen 1977, pp. 140f. and plate 96; Warsaw 1997, p. 159, no. V 25; cf. also Tait 1988, pp. 214–18, no. 41; Munich 1994, pp. 160–63, no. 12 (about the Viennese automaton)

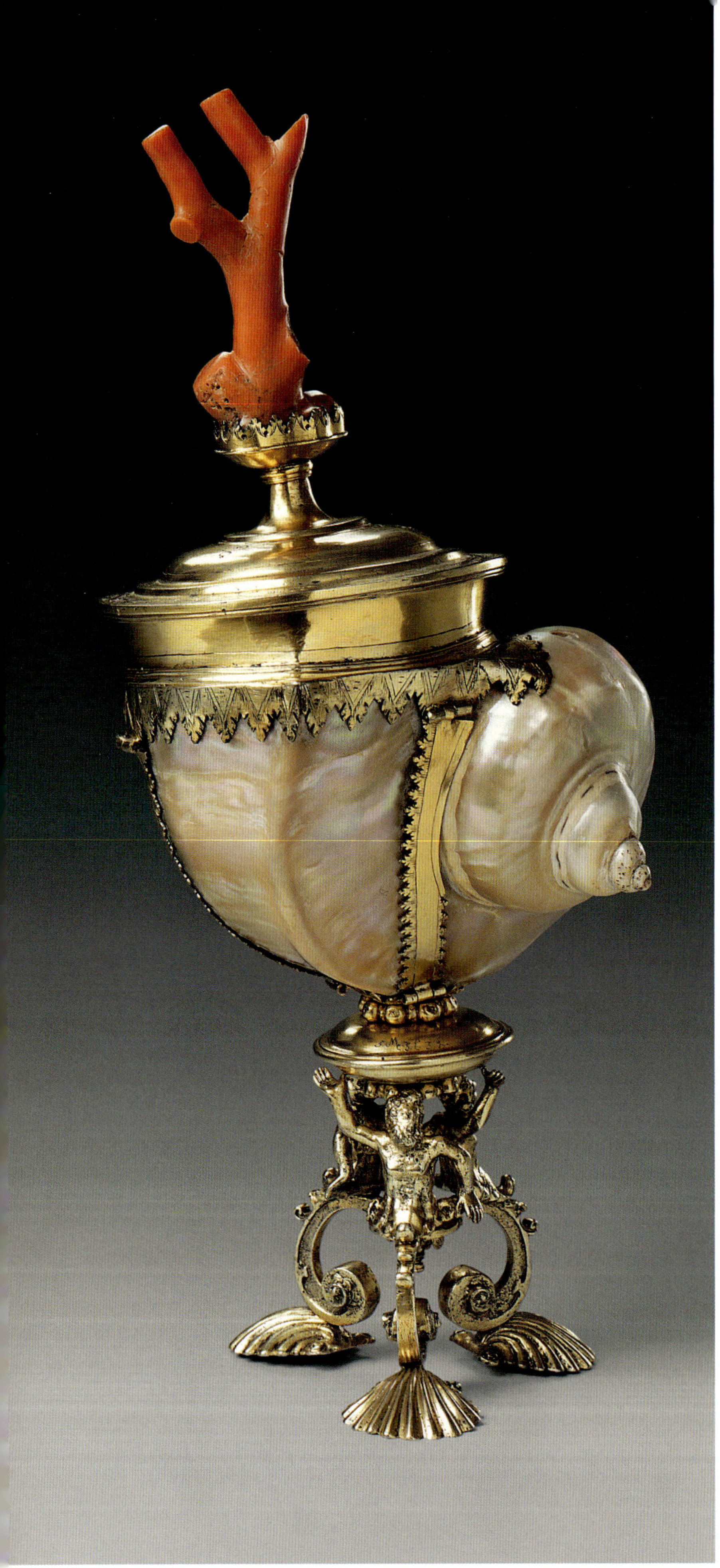

107 Turban-Snail Cup and Cover

Germany (Saxony?)
early 17th
century
Silver-gilt, turbo snail shell, coral branches
H. 13¾ in. (34.9 cm)
No marks
First mentioned in the Kunstkammer inventory 1640, fol. 109r
Staatliche Kunstsammlungen Dresden, Grünes Gewölbe,
inv. no. III 205
Lit.: Menzhausen 1977, p. 144 and plate 86; Berlin 1985, p. 317, no. 302; Essen 1986, p. 376, no. 521

This cup is most likely the one cited in the list of diplomatic gifts and presents covering 1611 to 1628 and mentioning "*Perlmutterschnecken, in Silber vergült gefasst vndt vfn Deckel mit gewachsenen Corallen gezieret*" (silver-gilt mounted mother-of-pearl snails, with coral embellished lid; SächsHStA, Loc. 8685, vol. I, fol. 242). According to the source, the vessel was presented to the Saxon elector on June 24, 1626, by the landgrave of Hesse. Both princely houses were probably busy preparing a wedding scheduled for the spring of 1627: The eldest daughter of the Saxon Elector Johann Georg, Sophia Eleonora, was to marry Georg II of Hesse-Darmstadt. The sovereign of Hesse apparently took the object, at the time approximately twenty years old, from his own silver collection, which comprised numerous turban-snail cups originating in Augsburg, Nuremberg, and Torgau.

The mounts of the unusual cup have parallels in examples from South Germany and Saxony, such as the items made by the Leipzig goldsmith Elias Geyer. The oddly shaped three-part foot—shell forms with superimposed herm volutes—corresponds to those of the cups with nephrite plates (cat. no. 120), whose bowls rest on three volutes. Similarly, the crocket mount on the lip's border is directly comparable to the mounts on Geyer's fabulous creatures (cat. nos. 108–110).

Conversely, another detail connects this cup with the art of Nuremberg goldsmiths: nearly identical herms decorate the shafts of goblets by Christoph Jamnitzer and Andreas Rosa (see cat. no. 124). In these examples, however, the supporting motif is somewhat more convincingly worked into the vessel's overall structure. This does not preclude a Saxon origin for the present object, especially since prefabricated cast elements were sold beyond the borders of Nuremberg.
U.W.

108 Cups in the Form of Triton and a Nereid

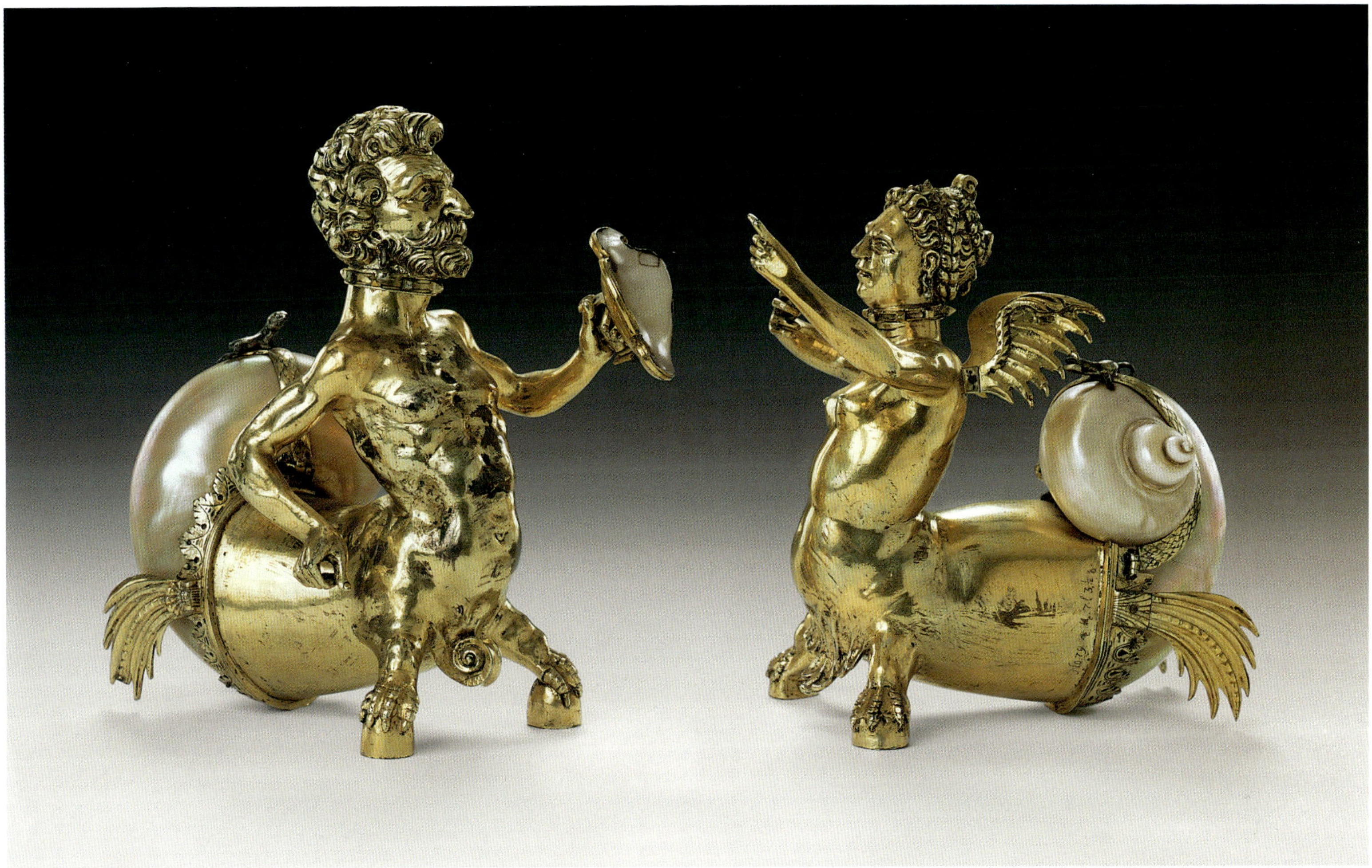

Elias Geyer, Leipzig, circa 1600
Silver, mostly gilded, traces of cold enamel, turban-snail shell
H. 8 in. (20.3 cm) (Triton)
H. 7⅛ in. (18.1 cm) (Nereid)
No marks
First mentioned in the Kunstkammer inventory 1610, fol. 192r
Staatliche Kunstsammlungen Dresden, Grünes Gewölbe, inv. no. IV 118 (Triton), IV 116 (Nereid)
Lit.: Graul 1910, p. VIII and plate XIX; Sponsel 1925, p. 54, plate 38; Schröder 1935, p. 84; Menzhausen 1973, p. 54, no. 17, p. 57, no. 22 and ill. 17, 22; Guide Green Vault 1997, p. 47, no. 48, p. 50, no. 63; s'Hertogenbosch 2003, p. 79 and p. 81, ill. 31

It is highly probable that these two silver sea creatures were acquired by Elector Christian II in 1602 from the Leipzig dealer Veit Böttiger. Although they are cited among the newly obtained mother-of-pearl objects in only a general way, as "*fünff allerley dergleichen Tringkgeschirr*" (five similar drinking vessels), the 1610 and 1619 Kunstkammer inventories describe them in more detail, identifying them as Geyer's creations. The other objects belonging to the group are a basilisk (inv. no. IV 158), unicorn (cat. no. 109), and sea horse with Neptune.

Their postures and the specific description in the Kunstkammer inventories indicate that each figure was originally equipped with a weapon: Nereid was bending a bow, while Triton held a dagger in his right hand. Similarly armed fantastic creatures originate from depictions of mythological sea battles such as the ones shown in relief on the surfaces of ewers or basins. The noble and graceful posture of each personage, further enhanced by such details as the Nereid's earrings, her necklaces of precious stones, and her elaborate coiffure, forms an odd contrast to their militant stance. Both appear to be derived less from the realm of mythology than from court circles, although Triton's physiognomy—with heavy eyebrows and crooked nose—corresponds more to the coarse features typically portrayed on more grotesque creatures.
U.W.

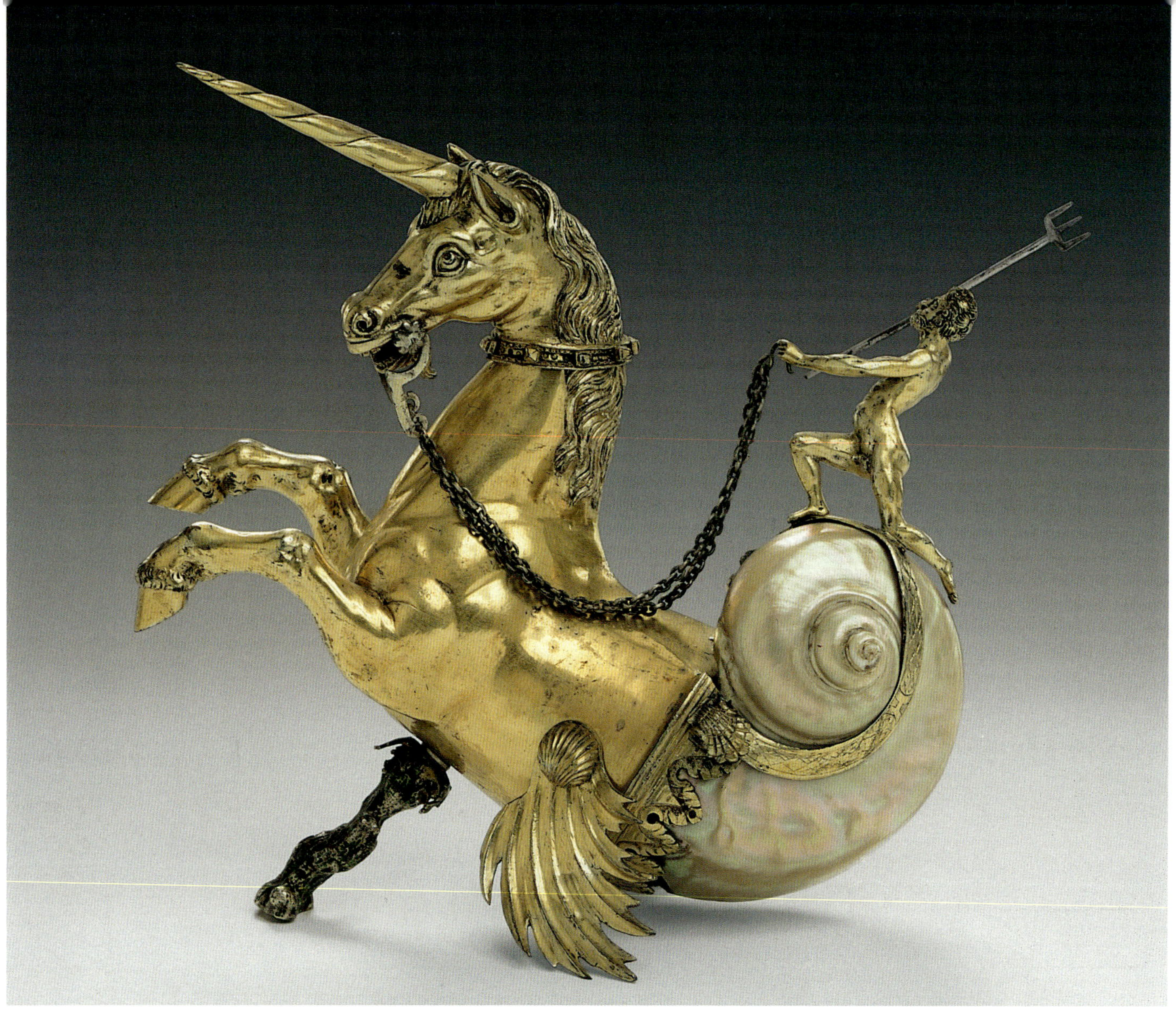

109 Cup in the Form of a Sea Unicorn

Elias Geyer, Leipzig, circa 1600
Silver, mostly gilded, traces of cold enamel, turban-snail shell,
H. 7⅞ in. (20 cm)
No marks
First mentioned in Kunstkammer inventory 1610, fol. 191v
Staatliche Kunstsammlungen Dresden, Grünes Gewölbe, inv. no. IV 133
Lit.: Sponsel 1925, p. 54, plate 38; Menzhausen 1973, p. 55, no. 18 and ill. 18; Menzhausen 1977, p. 144 and plate 97; Guide Green Vault 1997, p. 50, no. 62; Syndram 1999, p. 24

Composite sea creatures surrounding the triumphal procession of Neptune and Amphitrite have been depicted in art since the fourth century B.C. and underwent a renaissance during the course of the sixteenth century. Their fantastic, supernatural character made them suitable for the plethora of grotesques popular in all the arts, albeit mostly as decorative components. While numerous prototypes were thus available to the Leipzig goldsmith Elias Geyer, he modified and varied them in innovative ways, giving the creatures lives of their own by removing them from their ornamental contexts and transforming them into three-dimensional works.

Like other comparable works by Geyer, this sea unicorn that Elector Christian II purchased in 1602 from the Leipzig dealer Veit Böttiger (see cat. no. 108) is equipped with a detachable head. Although this points to its possible use as a drinking vessel, close examination reveals this to be impossible, as the liquid would run out between the snail bowl and the silver mount. Even though the Kunstkammer inventories refer to these fabled beasts as drinking vessels, it is highly unlikely that they were ever used for this purpose. Instead, by pointing out the close connection between nature and art, these subtle sculptures go far beyond any utilitarian function. U.W.

110 Two Cups in the Form of Sea Horses

Elias Geyer, Leipzig, before 1609
Silver, mostly gilded, traces of cold enamel, turban-snail shell, H. 7⅛ in. (18.1 cm) (IV 4), H. 8⅝ in. (21.9 cm) (IV 295); no marks
The sea horse (IV 295) is first mentioned in the Kunstkammer inventory 1610, fol. 195v; the Kunstkammer inventory of 1610 mentions two, the inventory of 1640 four, of today's five sea horses
Staatliche Kunstsammlungen Dresden, Grünes Gewölbe, inv. no. IV 4 (left) and IV 295 (right)
Lit.: Graul 1910, plate XXVI; Sponsel 1925, p. 55 and plate 39; Menzhausen 1973, p. 57, no. 21a and d, ill. 21; Warsaw 1997, p. 155, no. V 15; Guide Green Vault 1997, p. 57, no. 106 and 107; Antwerp 1999, p. 40 (ill.) and p. 194, no. 119 (IV 4)

The larger of these two sea horses was given by Elector Christian II to Duke Johann Georg in 1609. Included in the generous Christmas and New Year's presents to his brother were also a griffin with halberd (inv. no. IV 132) and a now-lost sea lion; both objects also originated from the workshop of Elias Geyer.

The 1610 Kunstkammer inventory already lists all these pieces, with special mention of their provenance from Johann Georg, who apparently derived great pleasure from eccentric drinking utensils equipped with sea snails. By 1640 the group of fantastic composite creatures assembled in the Kunstkammer had increased from eight to thirteen examples. Only one of them, a Nereid playing the trombone, was not made by Geyer; it bears the marks of the Nuremberg goldsmith Hans Rappolt (inv. no. IV 149).

The larger, less meticulously mounted turban snail of the second sea horse and its slightly disproportional, elongated body indicate a later modification. Very likely, the original shell broke and needed to be replaced. Mounting the new, larger piece necessitated the elongation and extension of the horse's body. U.W.

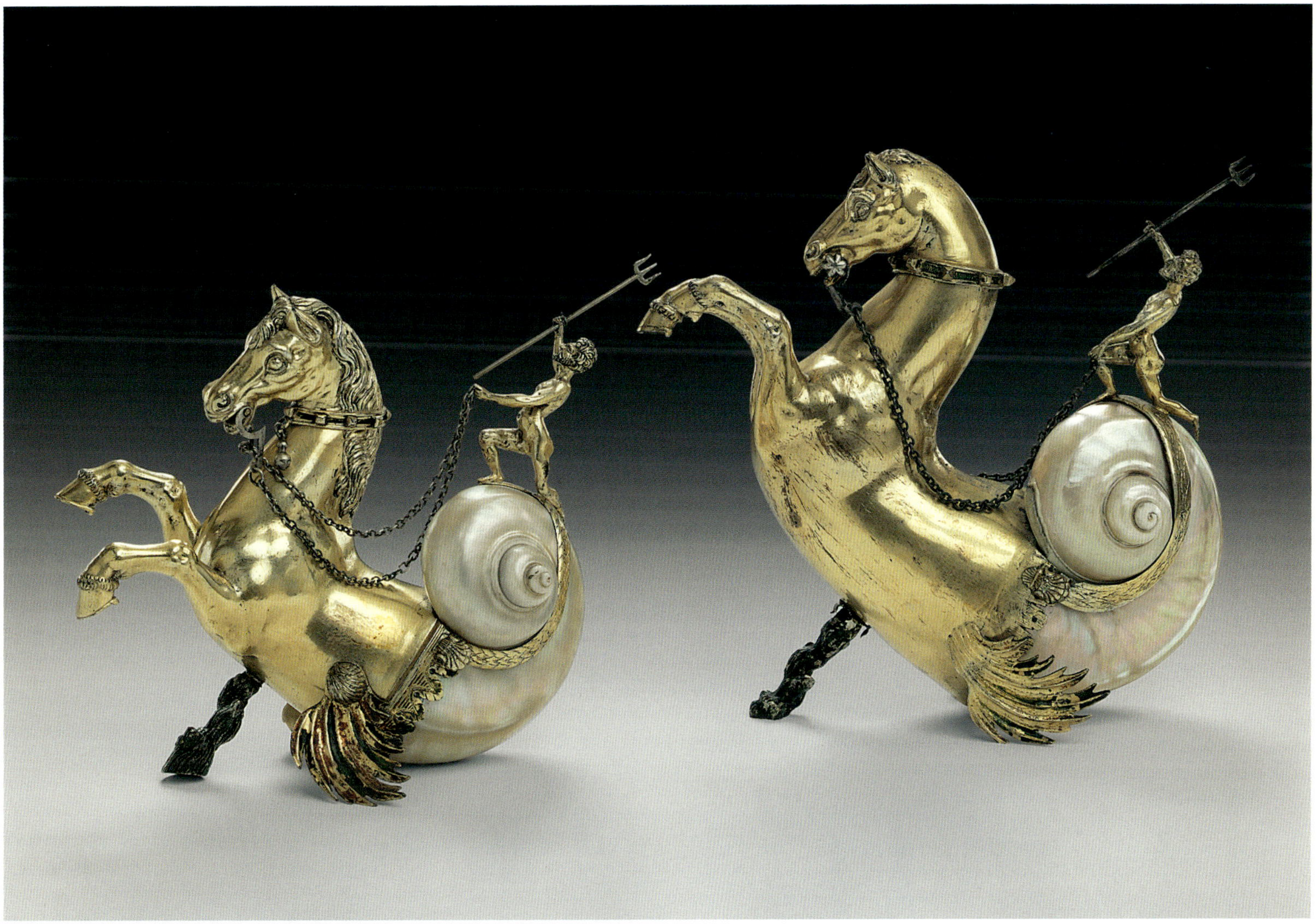

111 Maiden Goblet

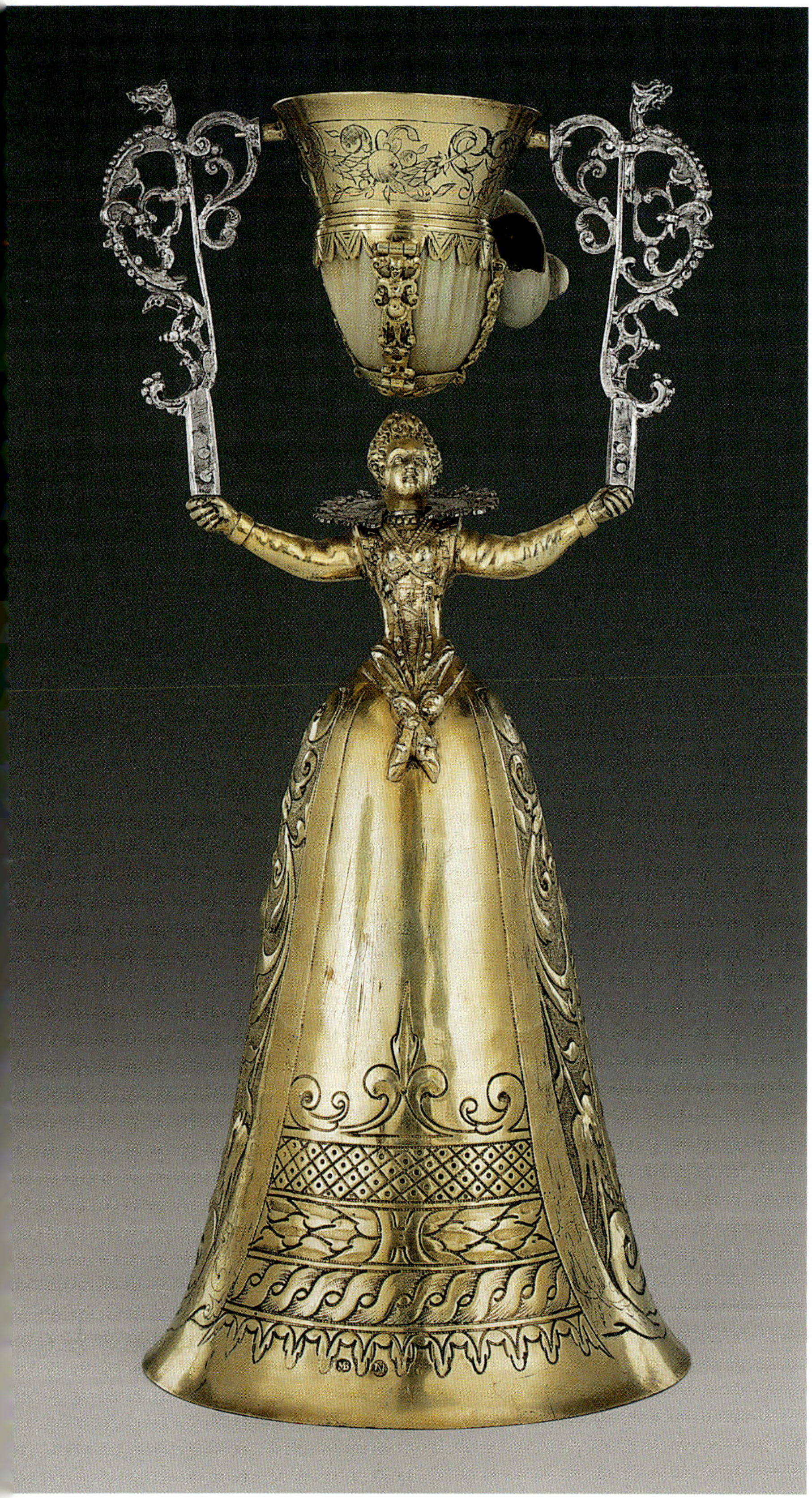

Meinrad Bauch the Elder
Nuremberg, circa 1603–9
Silver, partly gilded, turban-snail shell
H. 10⅞ in. (27.5 cm)
Hallmark for Nuremberg and maker's mark "MB" (in ligature, in circle)
First mentioned in the Kunstkammer inventory 1640, fol. 113v
Staatliche Kunstsammlungen Dresden, Grünes Gewölbe, inv. no. III 190
Lit.: Rosenberg 1925, p. 119, no. 3993e; Menzhausen 1968, p. 86, no. 53; Menzhausen 1977, pp. 144f. and plate 99; Hernmarck 1978, p. 82 and ill. 52; Guide Green Vault 1997, p. 50, no. 65

The first so-called maiden cups (Jungfrauenbecker) appear to have been made around 1550 in the goldsmiths' capital of Nuremberg; later they were also fabricated in such cities as Augsburg and Breslau. It is assumed that the popular drinking game that employed them was generally played in connection with wedding ceremonies. According to custom, the groom drank from the large beaker, which resembles a bell-shaped skirt, while the bride was expected to empty the smaller vessel, suspended over the figure's head by two hinged, ornamental clasps. However, a note in the silver inventories of Duke Moritz of Saxony, dated 1543–46, states that "*2 Junnckfrawen becher [...] Im tegelichen brauchs des Kellers*" (two maiden cups [were] used daily in the basement). This is a clear indication that such vessels were not exclusively used during weddings.

A typical feature of these amusing vessels is the female's elegant dress, complete with lace collar, solid bodice, cinched-in waist, and conical crinoline, all of which are derived from sixteenth-century Spanish court fashion, then also obligatory at other European courts. The goldsmiths used contemporary prints of court fashion as prototypes for such vessels.

The two cups preserved in the Green Vault were manufactured by the Nuremberg masters Friedrich Hillebrand and Meinrad Bauch, famous, among other things, for their drinking vessels with mother-of-pearl decoration (cat. nos. 102, 106). In this instance, goldwork was combined with *naturalia* by replacing the smaller beaker, customarily made of silver, with a silver-gilt mounted turban-snail shell. This resulted in an increased value, which likely caused the cups' transfer to the Kunstkammer, where they were particularly valued, along with the other "*sachen aus Berlenmutter in Silver and vergüld gefast*" (objects made of mother-of-pearl with silver and silver-gilt mounts).
U.W.

112 Turban Cup: Hercules Bearing the Globe

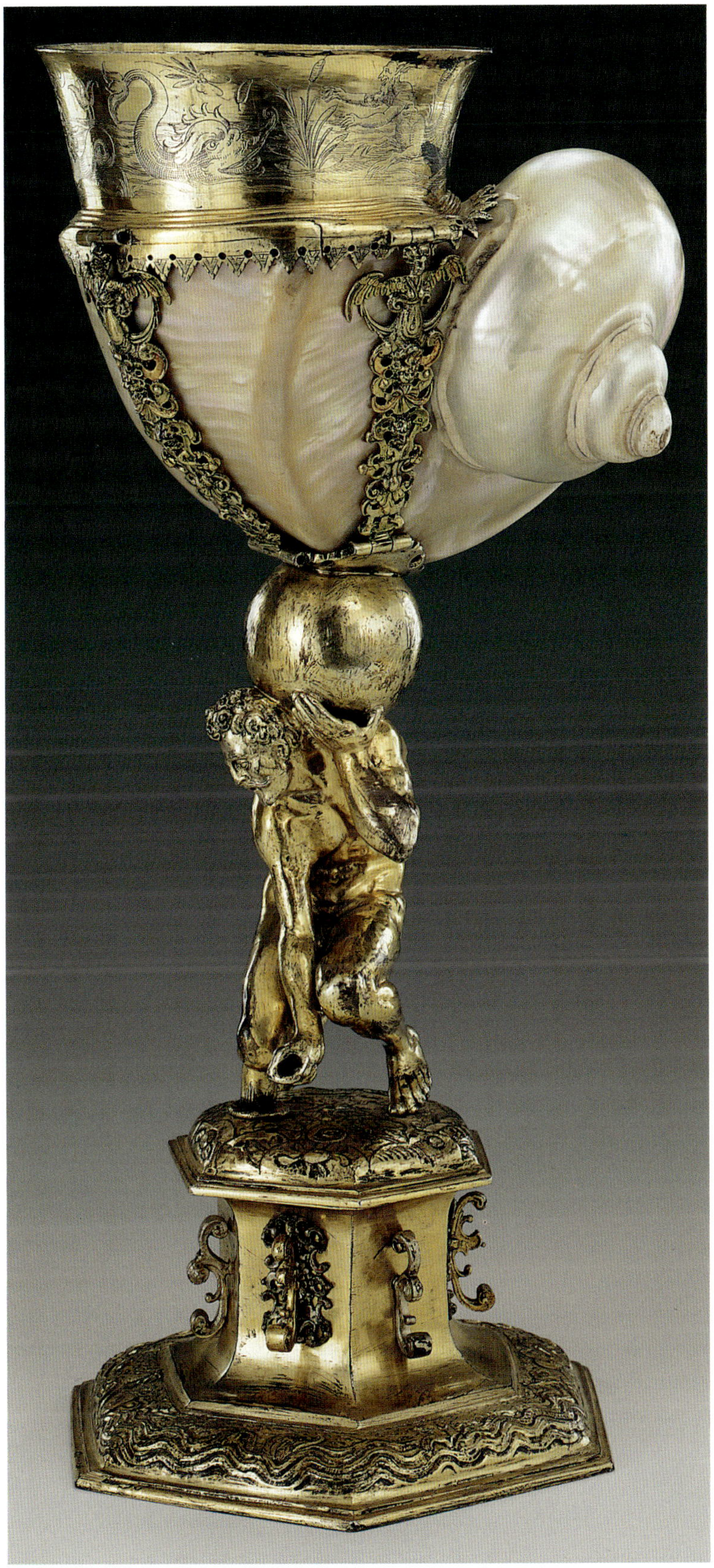

The present state of this cup, incorporating a turban-snail shell, does not reflect its original shape. As stated in the 1640 Kunstkammer inventory, one lizard, two serpents, two crabs, a fly, and a frog were placed at the figure's feet. Initially, the figure held a club in his right hand, thereby distinguishing him beyond doubt as Hercules. Formed as a figural shaft, the hero supports the globe with his left hand and shoulder, which is a rather unusual feature for a turban-snail cup. There is no obvious connection between him and the remainder of the precious mount, which relates to the sea snail as a maritime creature. A chased convex molding with fish and grotesque creatures decorates the foot, while the border of the lip is adorned with finely engraved scenes of sea battles.
U.W.

Friedrich Hillebrand,
Nuremberg, circa 1603–8
Silver-gilt, turban-snail shell, traces of cold enamel
H. 13⅞ in. (35.3 cm)
Hallmark for Nuremberg and maker's mark "FH" (in a rectangle)
First mentioned in the Kunstkammer inventory 1640, fol. 119v–120r
Staatliche Kunstsammlungen Dresden, Grünes Gewölbe, inv. no. III 147
Lit.: Rosenberg 1925, p. 132, no. 4017c; Sponsel 1925, p. 58 and plate 47; Menzhausen 1968, p. 85, no. 50; Guide Green Vault 1997, p. 42, no. 24

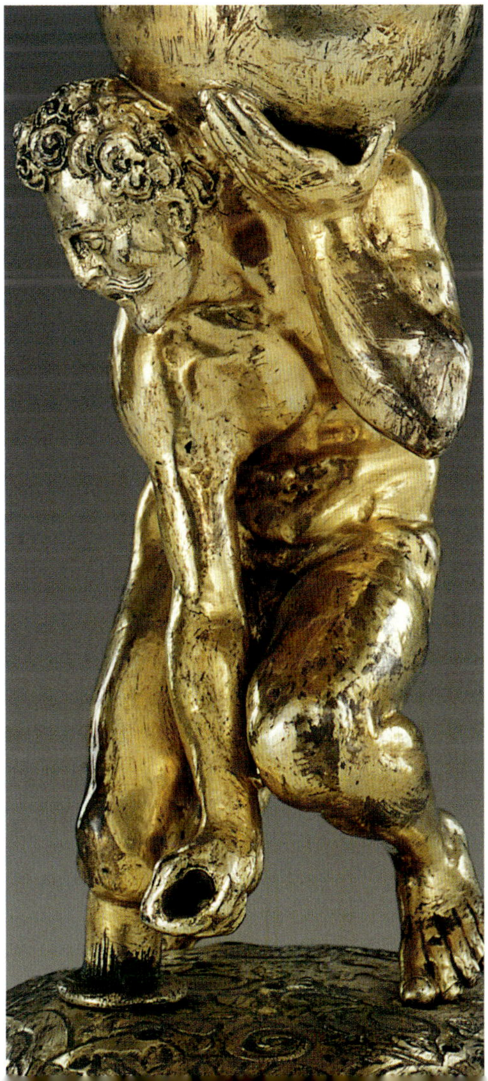

113 Two Nautilus Cups in the Form of a Hen and a Rooster

Friedrich Hillebrand,
Nuremberg, circa 1593–1602
Silver-gilt, nautilus shells
H. 12⅛ in. (30.9 cm) (rooster),
11¾ in. (29.8 cm) (hen)
Hallmark for Nuremberg and
maker's mark "FH" (in a rectangle)
First mentioned in the Kunstkammer
inventory 1640, fol. 143v
Staatliche Kunstsammlungen Dresden,
Grünes Gewölbe, inv. no. III 193 (hen)
and III 156 (rooster)
Lit.: Sponsel 1925, p. 53
and plate 34; Rosenberg 1925,
p. 132, no. 4017n and p;
Menzhausen 1977, pp. 144f.
and ill. 95; Mette 1995,
p. 188, no. 19 and 20;
Guide Green Vault 1997,
p. 38, no. 1 and 2

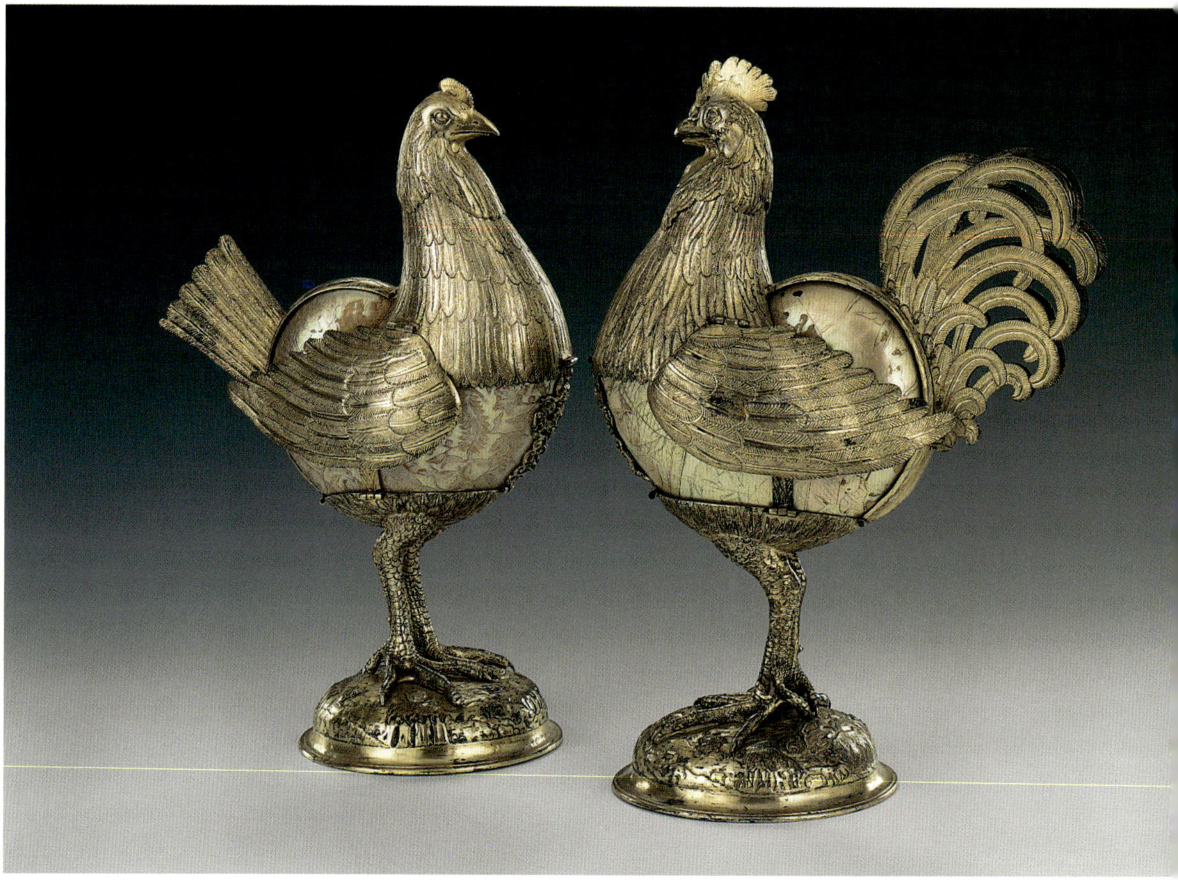

Containers in the shape of roosters with nautilus-shell bodies are documented from as early as the fourteenth century in secular and ecclesiastical inventories (so-called *Heiltümer* [collections of relics]). While originally serving as reliquaries, aquamanilia, or saltcellars, around 1600 they entered Western European princely Kunstkammers as bizarre vessels. The moveable wings were hinged and could fall into the face if the object was used for drinking, thereby irritating the user. It remains unclear whether the birds were employed in such drinking games or not. As in the case of the ostrich cups (cat. no. 116), it is highly unlikely that the containers were even completely sealed between the egg or the nautilus and the mount. For the ostrich, a connection between the bird and the egg is apparent, but the use of the nautilus for a rooster and hen appears to be motivated only by the analogous shapes of the mother-of-pearl shell and the bird's body. This illustrates the goldsmiths' primarily intuitive, playful approach to *naturalia.*

For the rendering of these birds, Friedrich Hillebrand applied numerous goldsmiths' techniques. The plumage is indicated by engraving, while the rooster's tail feathers are executed in openwork and sawn out of sheets of silver. The relatively stylized, barely three-dimensional rendering of the plumage is contrasted with the execution of the feet, which were fabricated as casts from nature and thus appear accordingly naturalistic. Although the embellishment of the nautilus shells with engraving and low relief is a slightly clumsy emulation of Chinese decoration, the objects appear to be of Western European manufacture. U.W.

114 Nautilus Cup: A Pelican with Its Young

Christof Kunad, Nuremberg
dated 1609
Silver-gilt, nautilus shell,
precious stones (emeralds, rubies)
H. 16⅛ in. (41 cm)
Hallmark for Nuremberg and
maker's mark with three acorns
on a branch (in circle)
First mentioned in the
Kunstkammer inventory 1640,
fol. 142v
Staatliche Kunstsammlungen Dresden, Grünes Gewölbe,
inv. no. III 145
Lit.: Sponsel 1925, p. 53 and plate 35;
Rosenberg 1925, p. 77, no. 3867f.;
Mette 1995, p. 191, no. 30;
Guide Green Vault 1997, p. 45, no. 39

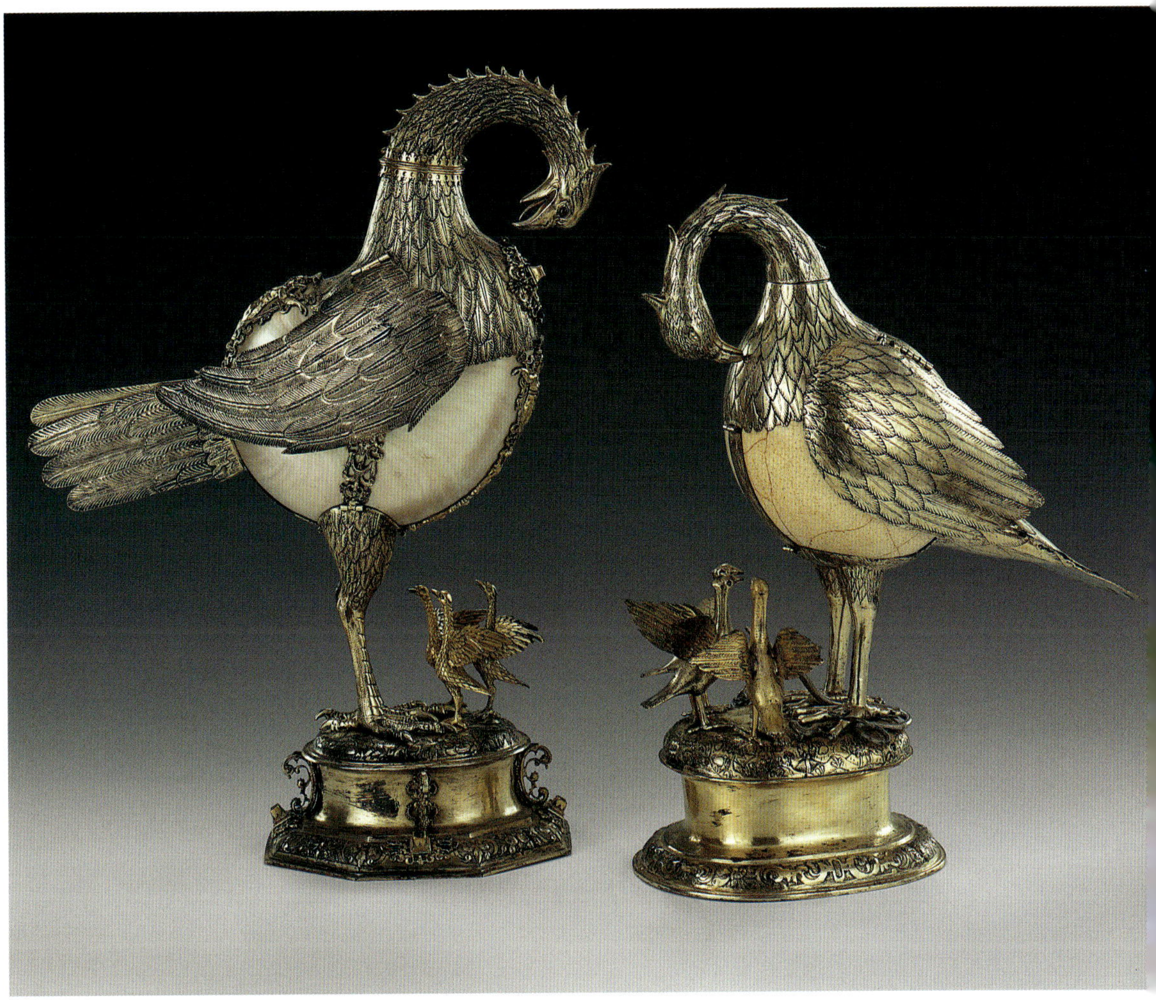

115 Ostrich-Egg Cup: A Pelican with Its Young

Torgau, early 17th century
Silver-gilt, ostrich egg
H. 13⅞ in. (35.1 cm)
Hallmark for Torgau
and maker's mark "AK"
(incomplete, in a rectangle)
First mentioned in the Pretiosen
inventory 1725, fol. 220r–220v,
no. 11. To the Green Vault
on September 20, 1724,
from the Kunstkammer
Staatliche Kunstsammlungen Dresden,
Grünes Gewölbe, inv. no. III 106
Lit.: Erbstein 1884, p. 47, no. 106;
Sponsel 1925, p. 53 and plate 35;
Rosenberg 1925, p. 331, no. 4675b;
Guide Green Vault 1997, p. 45, no. 40

From its inception, the image of the pelican piercing its breast with its beak in order to nourish its young with its blood was seen as symbolizing God's love for humankind and our salvation through Christ's sacrificial death. Similarly, this image was later applied to the prince's willingness to sacrifice himself for his subjects.

Nuremberg, famous for the manufacture of figural drinking vessels, is the place where the piece with a nautilus-shell body was produced (cat. no. 114). The year 1609 and the city of Zwickau's coat of arms engraved under the base might indicate that the object came to the Dresden court as a gift from this city. This piece is clearly superior to the one of a pelican with ostrich egg from the hand of a Torgau goldsmith who remains unidentified (cat. no. 115). Its engraved plumage is differentiated and less schematic, and its head and feet are depicted in a much livelier manner. The more elaborate execution is clearly demonstrated by the pierced, herm-shaped clasps, as well as by the decorative appliqués adorned with precious stones. Since models such as these were mass-produced in Nuremberg and could be ordered by other workshops, identical mounts often appeared on works by different masters. For the Torgau goldsmith it would have been more difficult to obtain prefabricated articles, which explains his less abundantly decorated cup. Yet it appears certain that he was familiar with similar objects. U.W.

116 Three Ostrich-Egg Cups in the Form of Ostriches

Elias Geyer
Leipzig, circa 1589–95
Ostrich eggs, silver (III 115); silver-gilt (III 227 and III 228),
H. 18¾ in. (47.6 cm) (III 228),
18¼ in. (46.3 cm) (III 115), 18⅛ in. (46.2 cm) (III 227)
No marks
First mentioned in the Kunstkammer inventory 1595, fol. 306v
Staatliche Kunstsammlungen Dresden, Grünes Gewölbe, inv. no. III 228, III 115, III 227 (from left to right)
Lit.: Sponsel 1925, p. 68 and plate 67; Menzhausen 1973, p. 53, no. 15a, c and d; Menzhausen 1977, pp. 143f. and plate 79; Essen 1986, pp. 372–73, no. 515; Dresden 1990, p. 359, no. 566; Guide Green Vault 1997, pp. 40f., no. 13–15

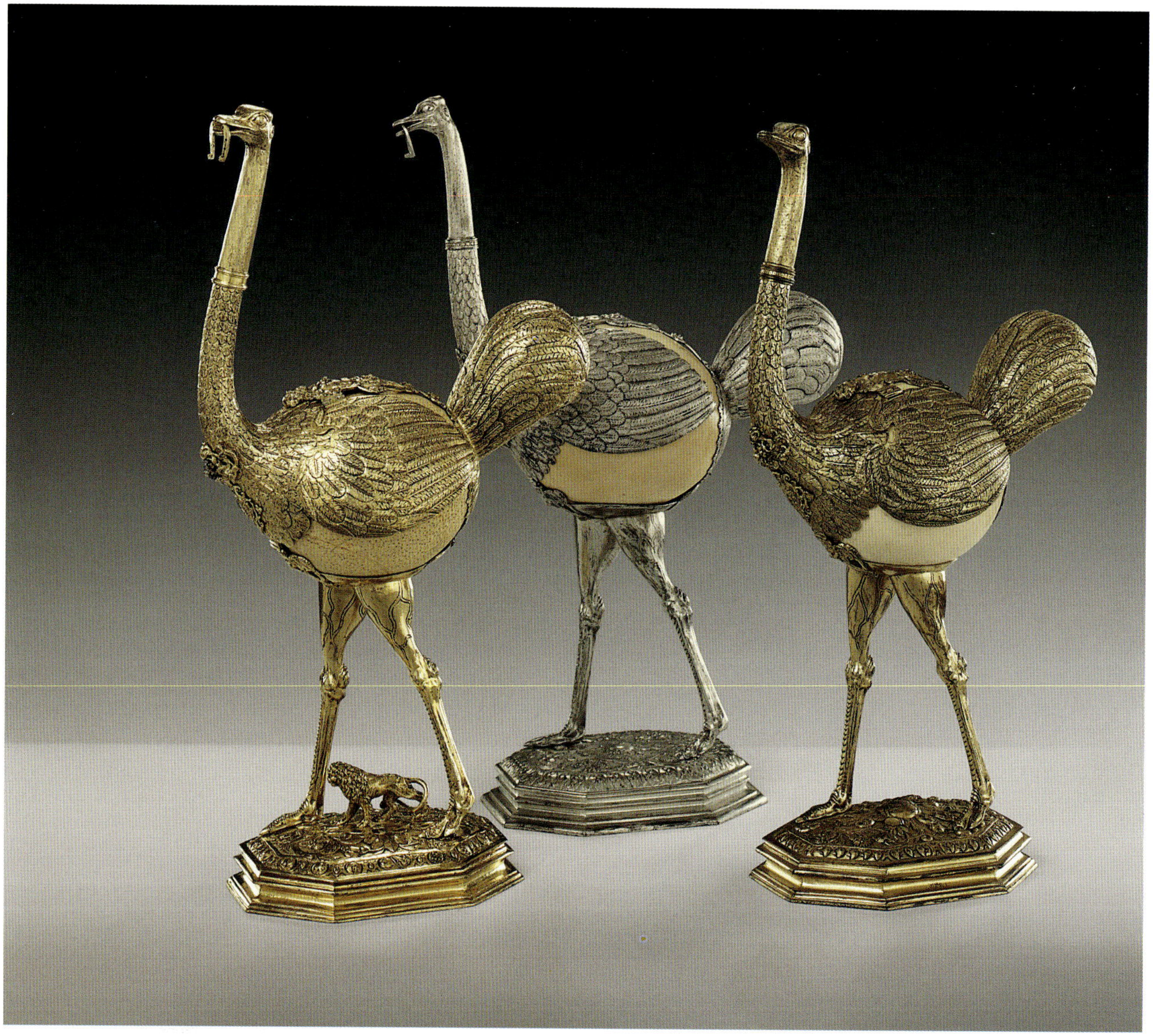

Seven ostrich-egg cups were itemized in the Kunstkammer inventory as early as 1595. They were probably the first of Elias Geyer's works to enter the Dresden Kunstkammer; five of them still belong to the Green Vault. Although they bear no goldsmiths' marks, stylistic similarities confirm that they were made by the Leipzig goldsmith. This is especially evident in the cast parts such as the herm-shaped clasps on the ostrich's back and the miniature lion on the pedestal (III 228), which may be found again on a small, engraved travel box in the Green Vault (inv. no. III 247).

Even though their detachable heads and moveable wings are reminiscent of rare drinking-game cups, it appears that none of these works was ever actually used (see cat. nos. 109, 113). Despite their similarities, the animals reveal slight variations in their pedestal design, gilding, and other details. Arranged as a group, they represent a most lively ensemble, evidently so pleasing that the count was determined to acquire additional objects by the Leipzig master. The educated viewer of the time was most likely aware of the ostrich's multilayered symbolism. For example, the image of the bird devouring iron—indicated by the horseshoe in its beak—signifies its ability to derive good things even from bad, a meaning based in antiquity. Christian iconography, on the other hand, interpreted the ostrich as symbolic of the Virgin Birth, because the ostrich buries its eggs in the sand, leaving them to be hatched by the sun.
U.W.

117 Cup: Rampant Stag

Andreas Rosa, Nuremberg
circa 1603–9
Silver, for the most part gilded, coral
H. 17¼ in. (43.7 cm)
Hallmark for Nuremberg and maker's mark with "AR" over a flower. First mentioned in the Kunstkammer inventory 1640, fol. 108v

Staatliche Kunstsammlungen Dresden, Grünes Gewölbe, inv. no. IV 119
Lit.: Rosenberg 1925, p. 165, no. 4099a; Sponsel 1928, pp. 14f. and plate 8; Menzhausen 1968, p. 86, no. 55; Menzhausen 1977, p. 146 and plate 91; Washington 1978, p. 156, no. 266; Guide Green Vault 1997, p. 47, no. 46

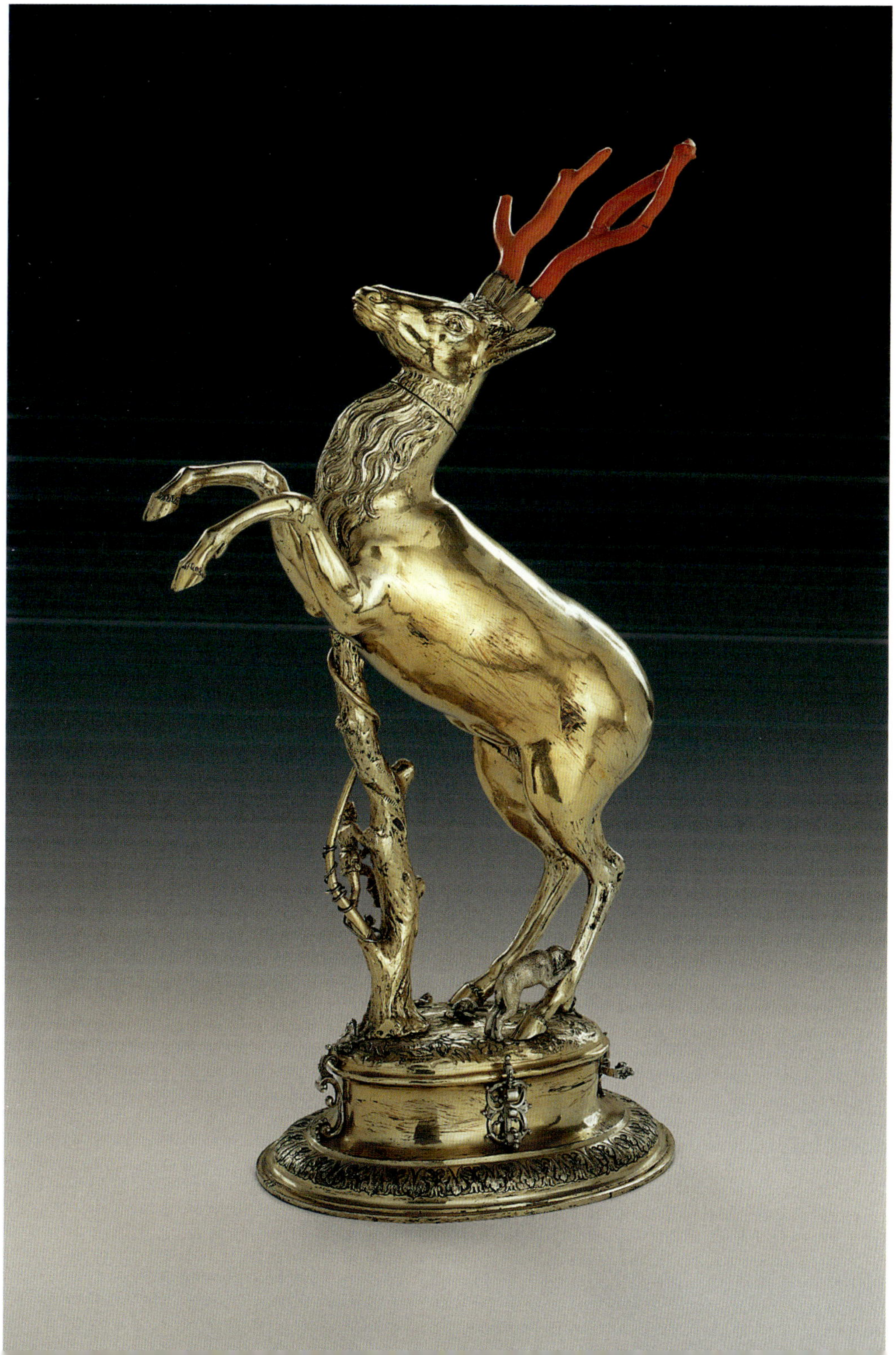

This sculpture by Andreas Rosa came to the Dresden Kunstkammer between 1619 and 1640 along with three more cups of the same shape. The inventories record that similar pieces had long been owned by the Saxon electors: While one stag was preserved in the Silberkammer, five others, also bearing coral branches, were kept in the Schatzkammer (Treasury).

Drinking utensils of this type were preferred for use as princely hunting Welcome goblets, as the stag hunt—together with heron hawking—was an aristocratic privilege and considered the most noble type of hunt. While the stag cups were customarily displayed on the silver buffet, they also served as popular gift items on special occasions. The examples with coral branches as antlers represented a particularly precious variant, combining artistic dexterity with a rare product of the sea. This explains the gift to Elector Johann Georg I by his chamber squires on the occasion of his name day in 1634, of "*ein Hirsch oben mit geweihe von Corallen*" (a stag adorned, at its top, with antlers of coral).

In contrast to the other Dresden stag vessels, this animal rears up at a particularly steep angle and is supported by a tree trunk. The proportions of the minuscule male figure who chops away at the trunk with a hatchet form a sharp contrast with those of the beast and the dog that attacks the stag's hind legs.

It is likely that Rosa added the tree trunk for stability. Such supports are frequently encountered in sculptures as well. The workshop of Ludwig Krug was presumably responsible for introducing this feature into Nuremberg goldwork, where it can often be seen from the early sixteenth century as cup shafts.
U.W.

118 Cup: Actaeon

In his *Metamorphoses* (3: 138–253), Ovid describes how the princely hunter Actaeon, upon catching a glance of Diana at her bath, was punished by the goddess, who transformed him into a stag that was torn to pieces by his own dogs. In former times, this tragic story was widely known and depicted in all the arts. The theme may be encountered, in multiple variations, as early as the 1595 Kunstkammer inventory: on copper plates, in watercolors and paintings, and as three-dimensional objects made of ivory and wax.

The work of the Nuremberg goldsmith Jeremias Ritter comprises lobed cups and other vessels as well as innumerable figural pieces. He is likely to have taken a bronze model as his point of departure for the creation of this drinking vessel. Its posture and antique armor connect this silver figure with a bronze statue of the same subject made in South Germany that originally served as a fountain figure and is dated to the last quarter of the sixteenth century (Bayerisches Nationalmuseum, Munich).

The 1640 entry in the inventory mentions a colored mount and presumably refers to the two ungilded dogs, whose bodies have received different surface treatments. The similarity in form appears to have inspired Ritter to use a coral branch as the stag's antlers. The result was a work that intelligently combines *naturalia* and *artificialia*, the two traditional collecting areas of the Kunstkammer.
U.W.

Jeremias Ritter, Nuremberg, circa 1609–29
Silver, partly gilded, coral
H. 19⅜ in. (49.2 cm)
Hallmark for Nuremberg and maker's mark with arm and sword between three stars
First mentioned in the Kunstkammer inventory 1640, fol. 108r–108v
Staatliche Kunstsammlungen Dresden, Grünes Gewölbe, inv. no. IV 261
Lit.: Rosenberg 1925, p. 84, no. 3882d; Menzhausen 1977, p. 144 and plate 82; Washington 1978, p. 155, no. 263; Guide Green Vault 1997, p. 41, no. 16; cf. also Weihrauch 1956, pp. 52–54, no. 74 (bronze statue)

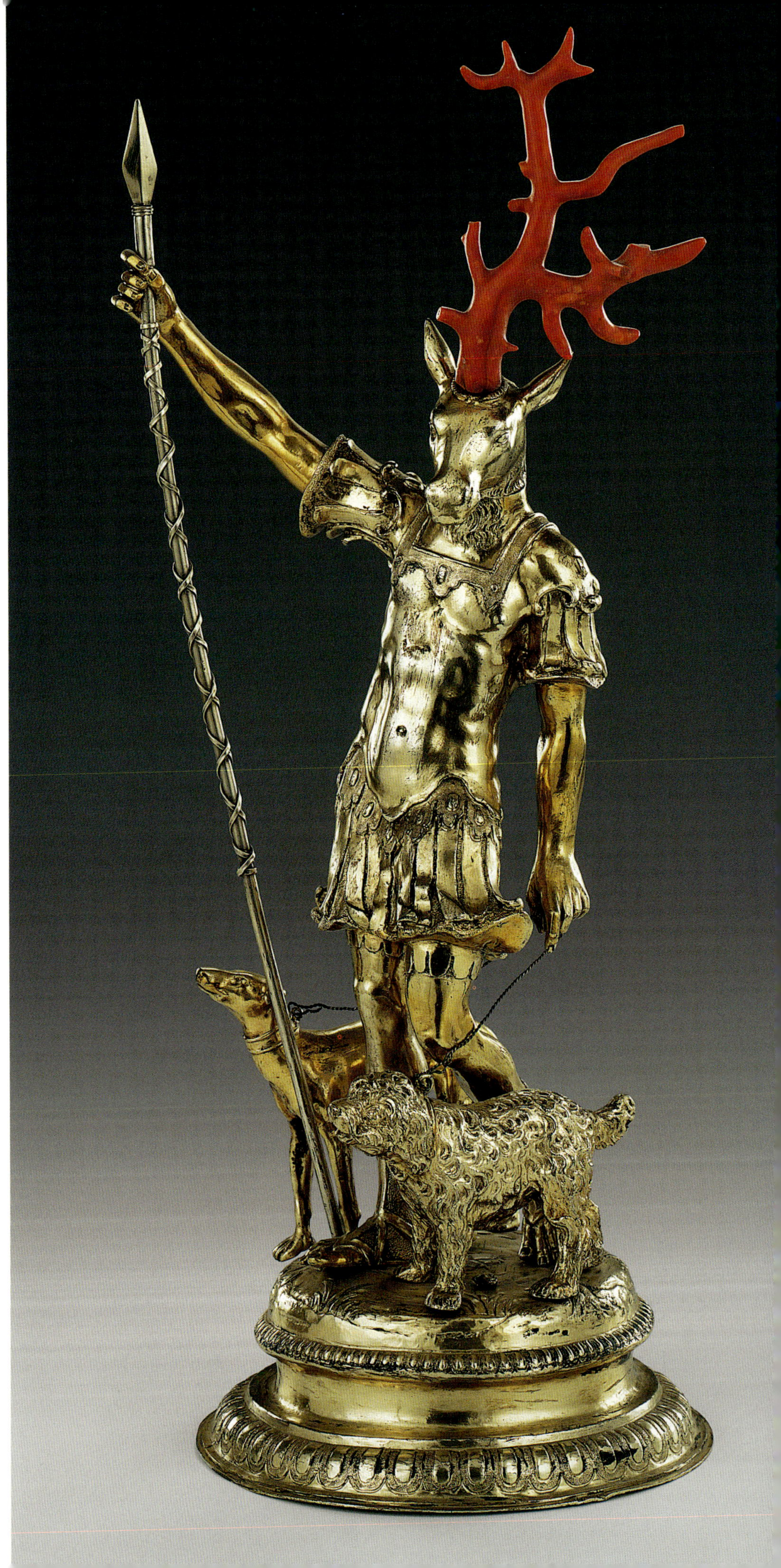

119 Two Cups in the Form of a Courtly Couple

Along with the lidded cup in the shape of a small castle (cat. no. 128), these two vessels are among the most bizarre drinking items of their time. While the majority of the figural Welcome vessels either bear reference to hunters' game or to heraldic animals, or hint at mythological or Christian themes, these are made in the guise of the courtly drinkers themselves. The costumes reflect their high rank: The gentleman wears a ruff and a doublet, as well as a Spanish coat, customary in the 1580s; the lady is bedecked with necklaces made of pearls and precious stones, and her artfully arranged coiffure is decorated with costly jewels.

The lower portion of each seat takes the shape of a foot and the handle of a vessel. Worked in two parts, the upper bodies can be detached, serving as lids. In the cups in the form of a stag (cat. no. 117) and of Actaeon (cat. no. 118), the shape of the coral branches has determined their use as the antlers, but there is no such concrete connection here.

It is thanks to Julius Erbstein that the maker's mark is related to the otherwise unknown Torgau goldsmith Eberhard Lindemann.
U.W.

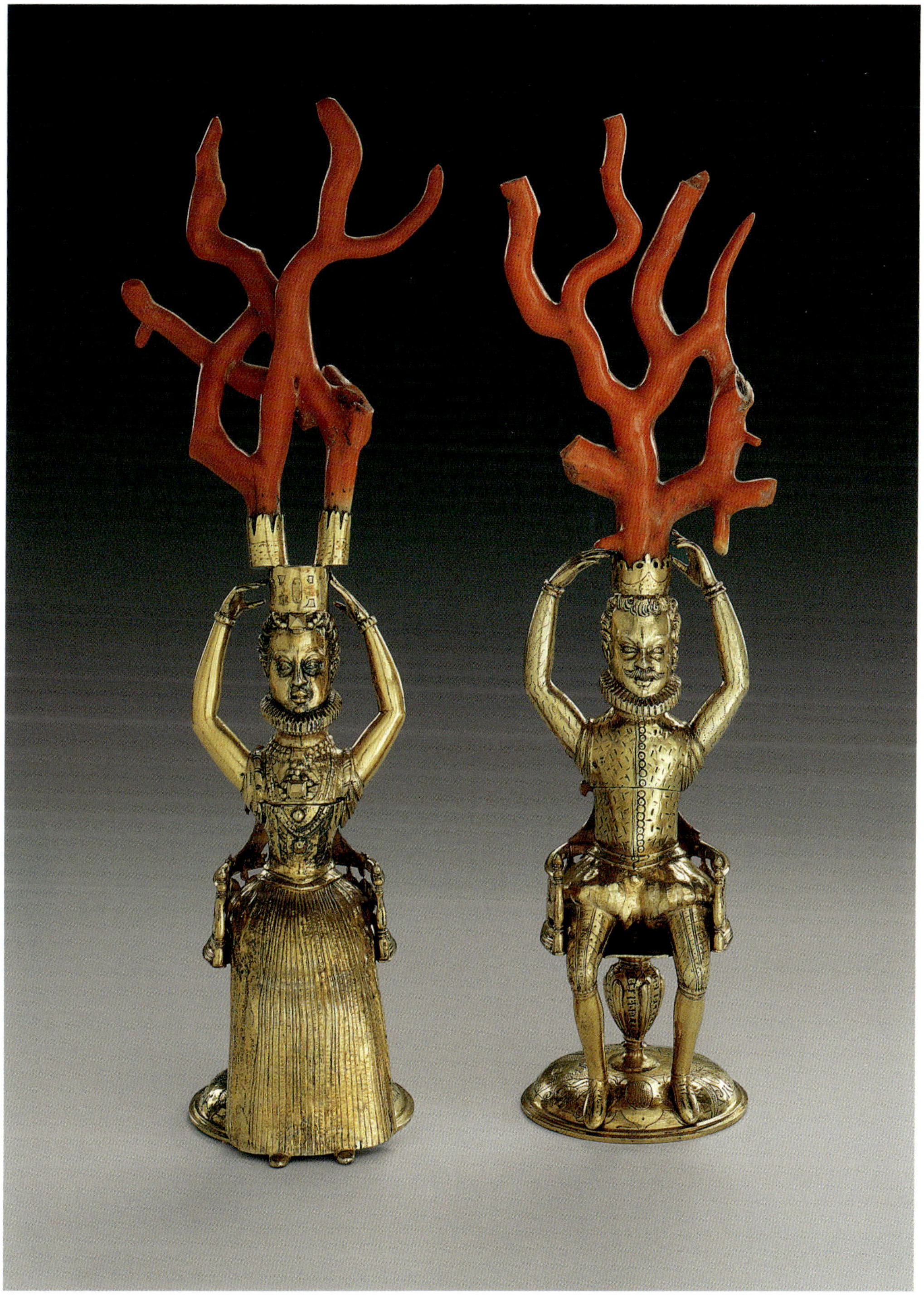

Eberhard Lindemann, Torgau, circa 1600
Silver-gilt, coral, H. 13 in. (33.1 cm) (lady) and H. 12⅞ in. (32.7 cm) (gentleman)
Hallmark for Torgau and maker's mark "EL" (in rectangle). First mentioned in the Kunstkammer inventory 1640, fol. 109v

Staatliche Kunstsammlungen Dresden, Grünes Gewölbe, inv. no. IV 204 (lady) and IV 267 (gentleman)
Lit.: Erbstein 1892, p. 20, no. 116 and 117; Rosenberg 1925, p. 332, no. 4678a/b;
Menzhausen 1977, pp. 145f. and plate 84;
Essen 1986, p. 373, no. 518

120 Two Triangular Nephrite Cups and Covers

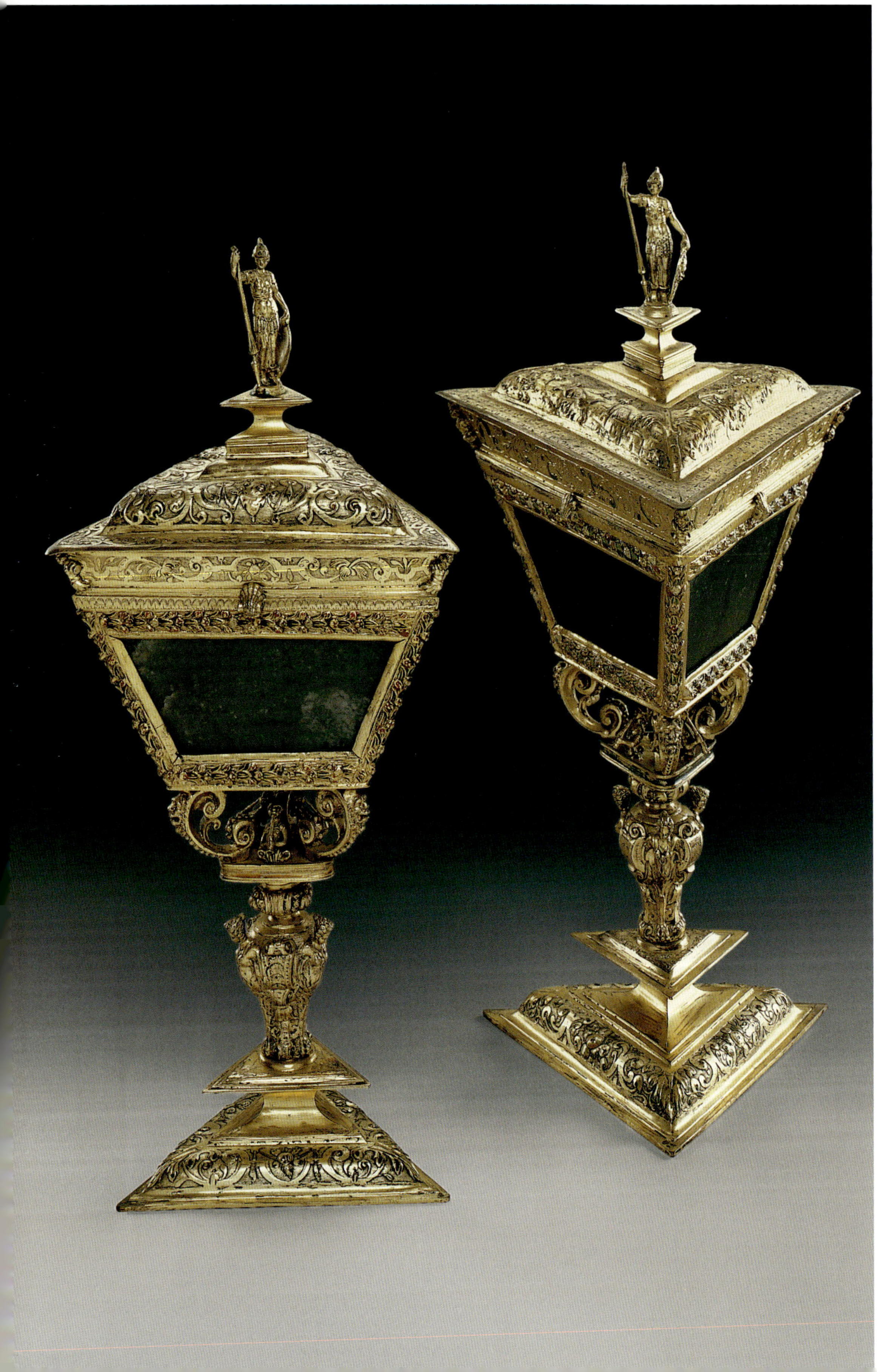

Their triangular shape makes these cups highly unusual. Elector Christian II acquired them on December 4, 1605, from Veit Böttiger. The purchase from the Leipzig dealer comprised a total of five similar "*Tringkgeschirre als Triangel von Lapide Nefritico in vorguldt Silver gefast*" (drinking utensils in triangular shape, made of nephrite stone and mounted in silver-gilt), of which four have survived in the Green Vault (SächsHStA Dresden, Loc. 7340/1, fol. 281r). In 1932 the fifth cup was donated to the House of Wettin's Familienverein. Elias Geyer shows his creative abilities once again with the nephrite cups, which are developed from the simple geometric shape of the triangle. The objects consist of individual stone pieces: for the wall, they are trapezoidal; for the floor, they are cut triangularly. Joined by strips of canvas, the pieces are glued with a putty that also seals the vessels. The edges are covered with silver-gilt; these formerly painted frames create a decorative setting for the precious stone slabs. Other details demonstrate Geyer's search for unusual solutions, including the three volutes (located between shaft and cup) separated by musicians playing their instruments. This device imparts a weightlessness to the vessels, and the translucence of the thinly cut stone is beautifully revealed. The two other similar nephrite cups owned by the Green Vault replace the musicians with a pyramid, which reemphasizes the triangular design.
U.W.

Elias Geyer, Leipzig, circa 1604–5
Silver-gilt, traces of cold enamel, nephrite
H. 16⅝ in. (42.5 cm) (IV 196)
16¾ in. (41 cm) (IV 262)
Hallmark for Leipzig, date letters "Y" (IV 262) and "Z" (IV 196), as well as maker's mark "EG" (in ligature in circle)
First mentioned in the Kunstkammer inventory 1640, fol. 367r (one of the two goblets)
Staatliche Kunstsammlungen Dresden, Grünes Gewölbe, inv. no. IV 196, IV 262
Lit.: Graul 1910, plate XII; Sponsel 1925, p. 63, plate 58; Schröder 1935, p. 82; Menzhausen 1973, pp. 48f., no. 7 and 8, Guide Green Vault 1997, p. 52, no. 74 and 75

121 Coconut Cup and Cover

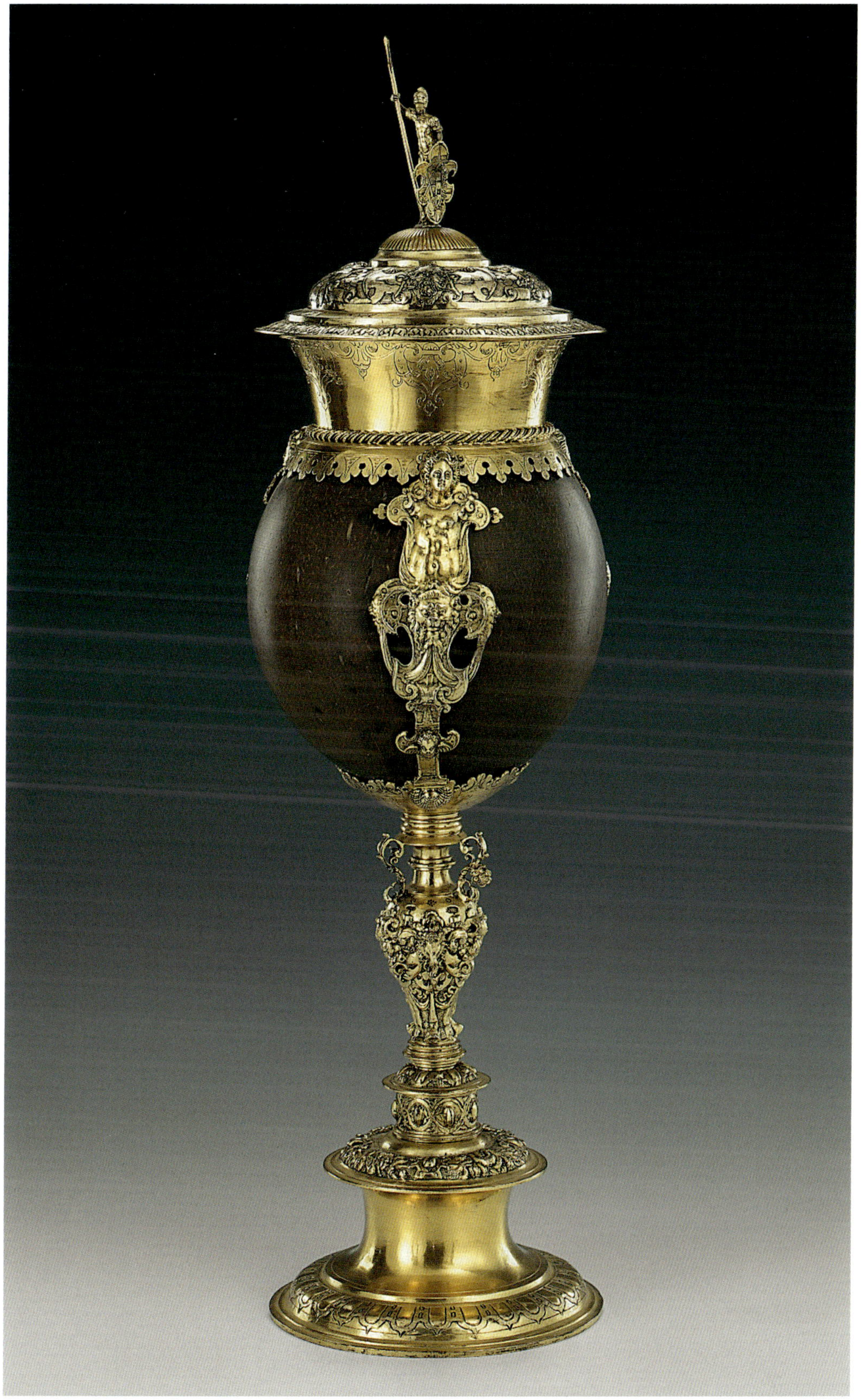

Vessels with a *cuppa* made of coconut are mentioned in inventories dating as far back as the thirteenth century, when they were primarily used as reliquaries; very few of these early examples have survived. The precious nuts were imported from Alexandria, through Venice, or from Lisbon, where African coconuts and, later, ones from Portuguese colonies in India and the Seychelles were sold. Owing to imports from Central and South America, their distribution in Central Europe increased during the second half of the sixteenth century. The mysterious "Indian nuts," said to be an antidote for poison, reached the princely Kunstkammers as highly desirable *naturalia*. Beautifully carved or enriched by precious mounts, these curiosities were frequently transformed into objets d'art.

In 1640, a large group of fourteen coconut cups was listed in the Dresden Kunstkammer for the first time. However, this object cannot be identified as one of them. Like other works by Elias Geyer in the Green Vault, it is unmarked. Its attribution to Geyer is based on stylistic similarities with other marked pieces, including the herm-shaped clasps seen on catalogue number 116.
U.W.

Elias Geyer (?)
Leipzig, early 17th century
Silver-gilt, coconut
H. 17⅛ in. (43.5 cm)
No marks
First mentioned in the Kunstkammer inventory after 1732, fol. 35r, no. 2
Staatliche Kunstsammlungen Dresden, Grünes Gewölbe, inv. no. IV 326
Lit.: Sponsel 1925, p. 70 and plate 69,1;
Schröder 1935, p. 84;
Menzhausen 1973, p. 59, no. 24;
Fritz 1983, p. 120, no. 199 and plate 105a;
Guide Green Vault 1997, p. 43, no. 26

122 Coconut Cup and Cover: The Welcome Goblet of the New Stable

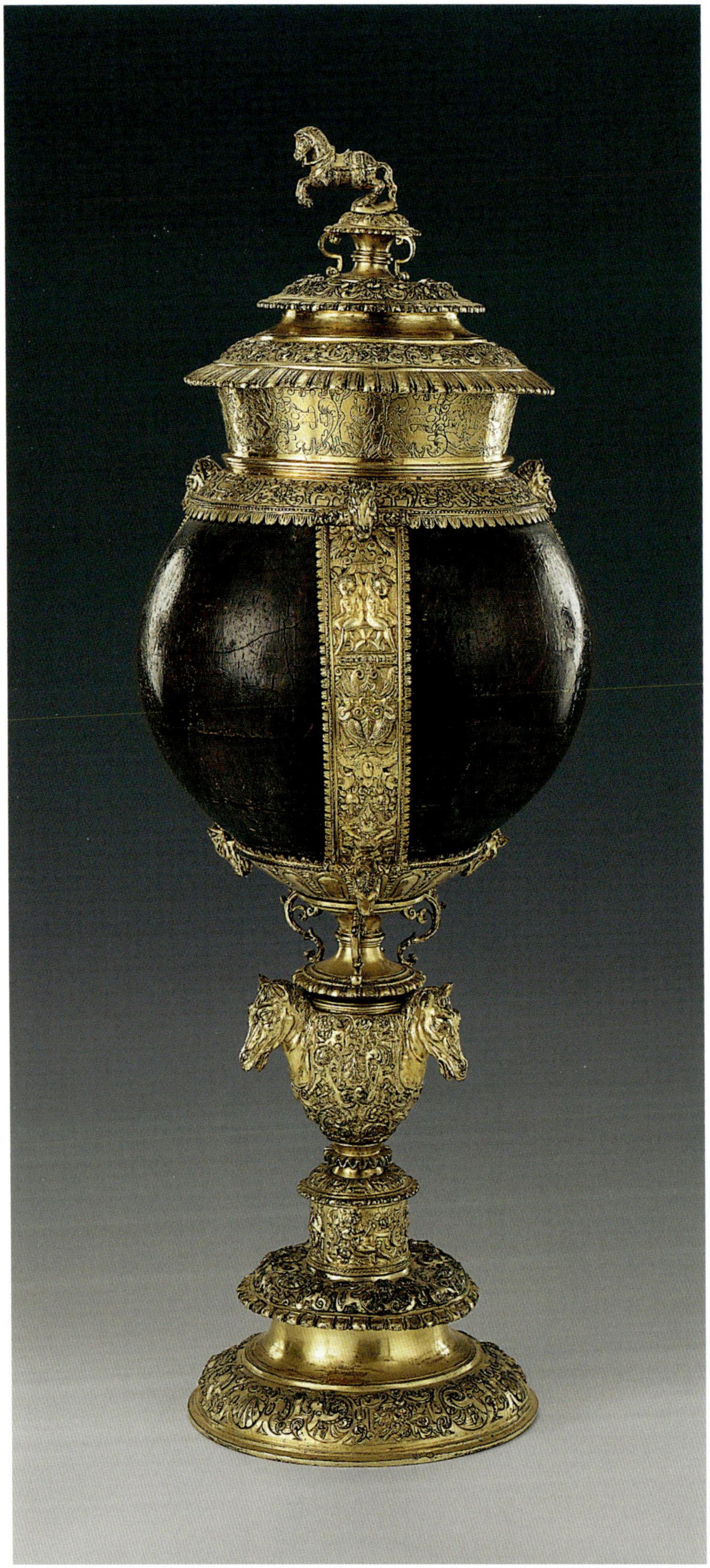

Elector Christian I commissioned this imposing coconut cup from Valentin Geitner. The Dresden goldsmith produced not only the silver-gilt mount of the almost perfectly round nut but also Christian I's coat of arms in *verre églomisé,* fitted in the lid. The surviving receipt, dated May 21, 1588, reveals that the precious drinking vessel was intended as a Welcome cup to be used in the New Stable, a structure finished the same year (SächsHStA Dresden, Loc. 8694/10, fol. 152v–153r). This building, begun by Christian immediately after his accession in 1586, served as more than just accommodation for the electoral horses and the armory. In addition, it was to be used for the steadily expanding festivities undertaken by the Dresden court, and its inner courtyard could be employed as a racetrack. Further references to the tournaments, which were held there beginning in 1589, are worked into the cup and include the cover's jumping horse as well as the equine heads embellishing the cup's knop and mounts. Until 1718, the cup was housed in one of the two electoral chambers located in the New Stable. A tiered buffet in each chamber held at least twenty silver-gilt drinking vessels (ill. p. 207). Inside each structure was a rider who emerged on tracks and then proceeded to offer the guests either Geitner's coconut cup or another, similar one, as a Welcome.
U.W.

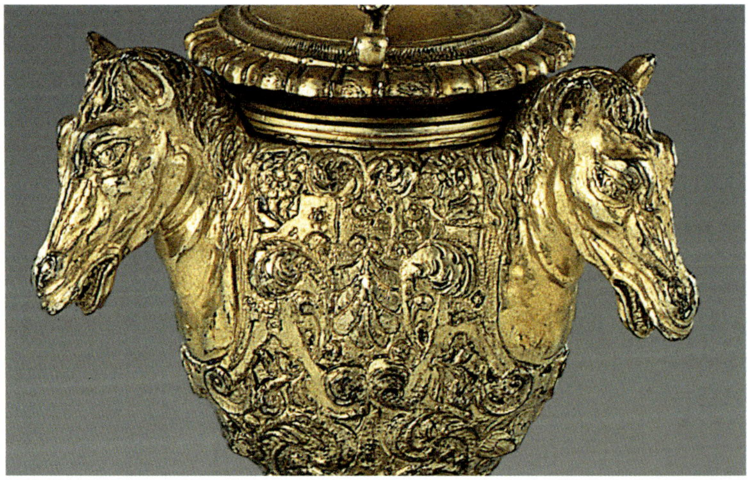

Valentin Geitner
Dresden, circa 1586–88
Silver-gilt, coconut, *verre églomisé*
H. 18⅞ in. (48.1 cm)
Hallmark for Dresden and maker's mark "VG" (in ligature, in the shield)
First mentioned in the inventory of the Electoral Chambers 1591, fol. 4r

Staatliche Kunstsammlungen Dresden, Grünes Gewölbe, inv. no. III 257
Lit.: Rosenberg 1923, p. 28, no. 1731b; Sponsel 1925, p. 69 and plate 69,2; Weinholz 1961, pp. 128f.; Fritz 1983, pp. 112f., no. 148 and color plate 13; Guide Green Vault 1997, p. 44, no. 30; Münzberg 2002, p. 137, no. A0

123 Two Double Goblets

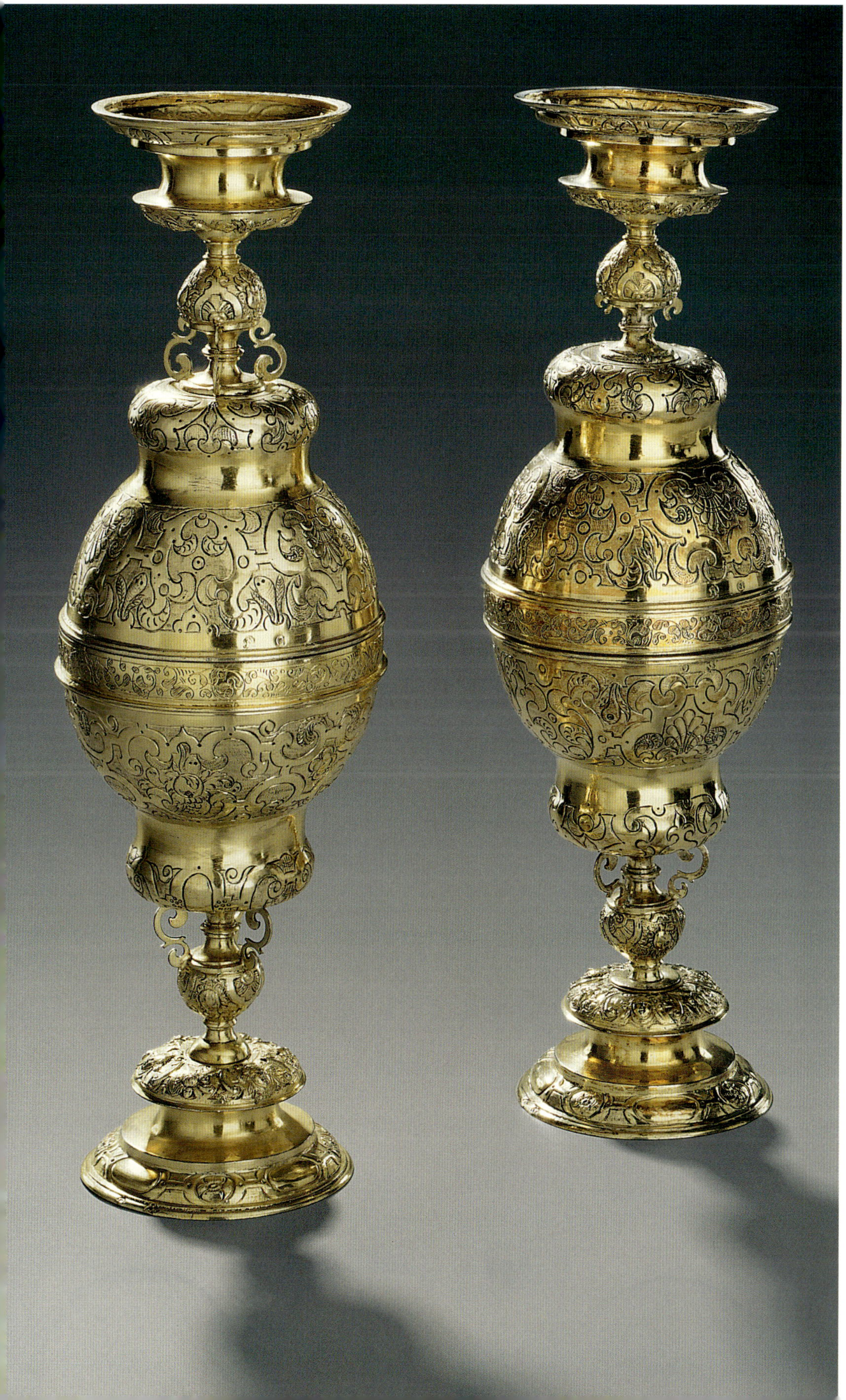

Each of these vessels is constructed by pinning together two pear-shaped cups so that the upper bowl serves as lid to the lower one; both bowls make an almost round shape. The double goblet, also known as a *Doppelscheuer*, is a type particularly popular during the sixteenth century. The inventory of the electoral Saxon Silberkammer, compiled between 1575 and 1586, lists a total of thirty such drinking vessels. The examples exhibited here were manufactured by Urban Schneeweiß, a goldsmith very often employed by the Dresden court. Called *Dupplet* upon their first mention in the inventories of 1591, they were also exhibited—along with the coconut cup by Valentin Geitner (cat. no. 122)—from 1591 until 1718 on the tiered state buffet that was shaped like a mountainside and located in the New Stable.

Decorated with heavy scrollwork whose interstices are filled with shells and bundles of fruit, the bowls are decorated as if they were more planar in shape. The Dresden goldsmith was quite skillful in executing the ornaments, which were influenced by the vessel designs (1579) of Georg I Wechter from Nuremberg. The surface treatment is particularly striking for its variety of minute and less minute punchwork and hatching.
U.W.

Urban Schneeweiß,
Dresden, circa 1590
Silver-gilt
H. assembled 11⅜ in. (28.8 cm - IV 164/IV 304)
and 11 in. (28.1 cm - IV 68/IV 303)
Hallmark for Dresden and maker's mark "VS"
(in ligature, in the shield)
First mentioned in the inventory of the
Electoral Chambers 1591, fol. 5r
Staatliche Kunstsammlungen Dresden,
Grünes Gewölbe, inv. no. IV 164, IV 304 (left)
and IV 68, IV 303 (right)
Lit.: Sponsel 1928, pp. 32f. and plate 13;
Holzhausen/Kesting 1966, p. XIX
and plate 26 and 27; Menzhausen 1968, p. 83
and plate 39; Münzberg 2002, pp. 130f.,
nos. A19 and A 24, 168, ill. 35

124 Double Cup

Andrea Rosa's *Doppelscheuer,* richly covered with ornaments, is a variation on a type developed during the Late Gothic period. Called a lobed cup (*Buckelpokal*), it experienced renewed popularity starting in Nuremberg in the early seventeenth century. Among its distinguishing marks are the bulbous, nearly hemispherical bosses, the luxurious decoration, and the broad lip of the border, engraved with sumptuous sculptural ornamentation, scrolls, and hunting motifs. Interestingly, various lobed cups that are approximately one hundred years older are similarly decorated. These features—but most strikingly the figurally conceived shaft—connect this vessel with the embossed cup by Christoph Jamnitzer that is preserved in Copenhagen (Danske Kunstindustrimuseum, inv. no. B 56/1933). The three half-figures—a female, a bearded man, and a male youth—emerging from a foliated cuff reappear, in almost identical form, in the other object (see also cat. no. 107). The same applies to the lower, hexagonal shaft segment, which is alternately covered with strings of pearls and clasps and terminates in sturdy volutes and mascarons.

In his *Doppelscheuer,* Rosa emphasizes such contrasts even more than the Nuremberg goldsmiths Hans Pezolt and Peter Wiber do in their contemporaneous embossed cups. This double goblet is distinguished by a particularly exciting structure, characterized by the opposition between convexity and concavity and by the play between smooth bosses and vital sculptural decoration.
U.W.

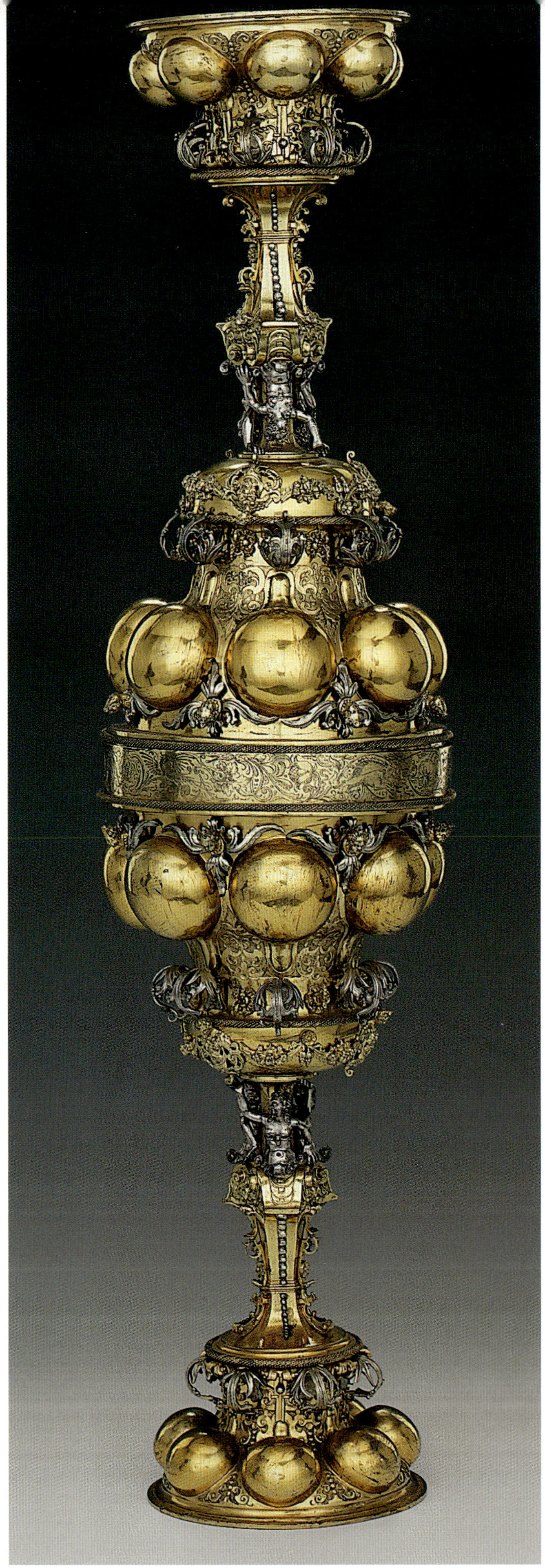

Andreas Rosa
Nuremberg,
1599–1602
Silver, partly gilt
H. 13¾ and 14 in.
(35 and 35.7 cm),
assembled 26⅜ in.
(67 cm)
Hallmark for Nuremberg and maker's mark with "AR" over a flower
First mentioned in the silver inventory of 1723, pp. 44–45
Staatliche Kunstsammlungen Dresden, Grünes Gewölbe, inv. no.
IV 296 and IV 301
Lit.: Rosenberg 1925, p. 165, no. 4099b; Menzhausen 1968, p. 81, no. 29; Washington 1978, p. 155, no. 264; Guide Green Vault 1997, p. 40, no. 9

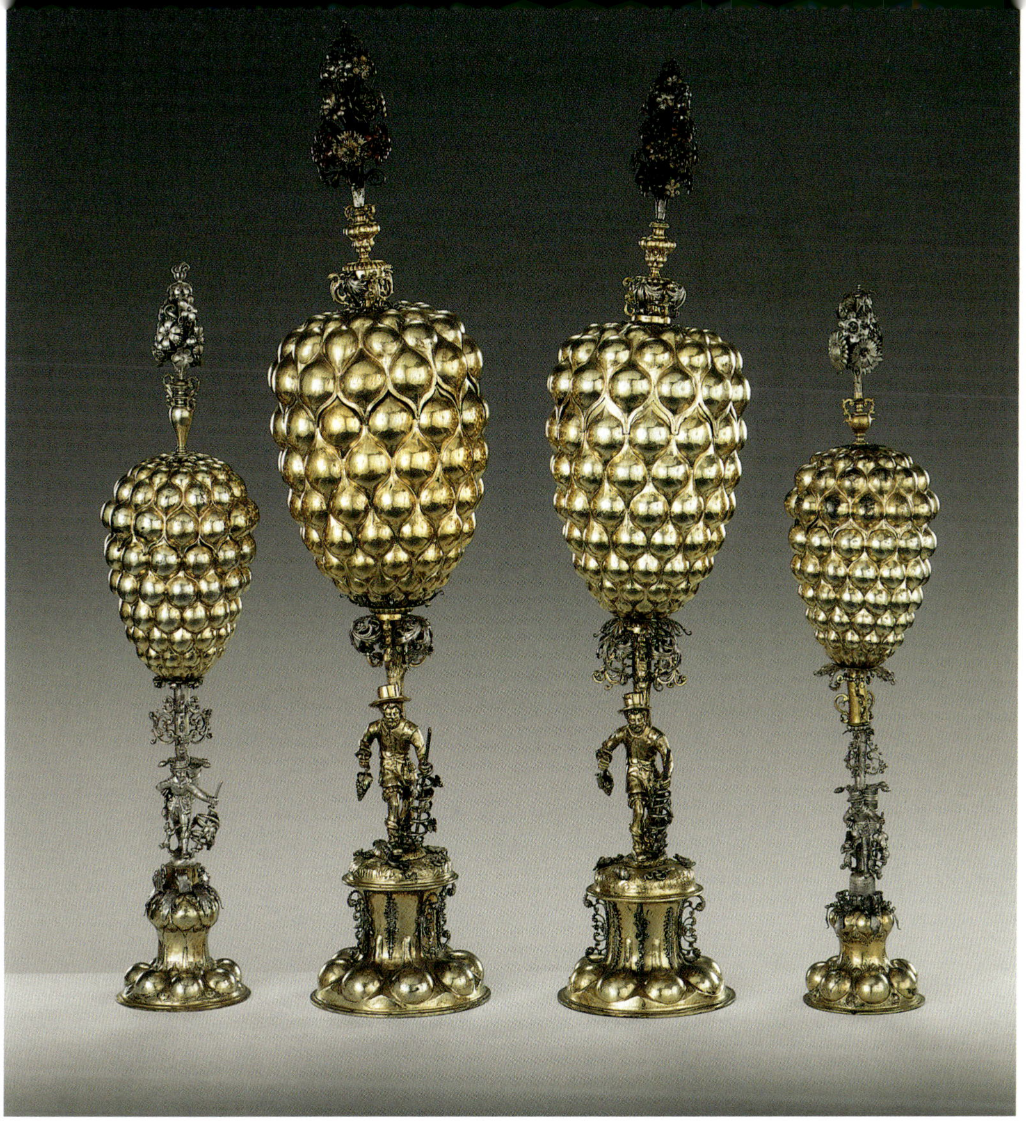

125 Two Grape Cups and Covers

Hans Beutmüller
Nuremberg, 1603–9
Silver-gilt, cold enamel
H. 31 3/4 in. (80.8 cm) (IV 8)
and 30⅜ in. (77.2 cm) (IV 12)
Hallmark for Nuremberg and maker's mark
with a mill wheel (in the shield)
First mentioned in the silver inventory 1723, p. 34,
no. 1 and 2
Staatliche Kunstsammlungen Dresden, Grünes
Gewölbe, inv. no. IV 8 and IV 12 (center)
Lit.: Rosenberg 1925, p. 150, no. 4054/4055 n-o;
Sponsel 1928, p. 36 and plate 16 (IV 12); Menzhausen
1968, p. 81, no. 29 (IV 12); Guide Green Vault 1997,
p. 54, no. 86 and 87; Syndram 1999, p. 188

126 Two Grape Cups and Covers

Paulus Baier
Nuremberg, 1613–29
Silver, partly gilded, H. 24 in. (61.1 cm) (IV 18)
and 23 in. (58.4 cm) (IV 21)
Hallmark for Nuremberg and maker's mark
with a bear's head in a circle
First mentioned in the silver inventory
1723, p. 37, no. 8 and 9
Staatliche Kunstsammlungen Dresden, Grünes
Gewölbe, inv. no. IV 18 and IV 21 (left and right)
Lit.: Rosenberg 1925, p. 196,
no. 4159 h-i; Sponsel 1928, p. 36 and plate 16;
Guide Green Vault 1997, p. 54, no. 88 and 89

All four drinking vessels belong to a type known as the lobed cup. Especially popular in Nuremberg, they can be traced back to the middle of the fifteenth century, when these "*knorreten*" (knobby) drinking utensils were frequently given as official or personal presents. This long tradition also explains the high esteem in which Late Gothic forms were held: this shape that survived in various revivals until the second half of the seventeenth century. The advantages of these refined cups, which were also extraordinary *repoussé* creations, were well known: Their bosses not only guaranteed greater stability but also produced fascinating reflections under candlelight.

One type was the columbine cup, a prerequisite for a journeyman's becoming a guild master in Nuremberg since the late fifteenth century; another variant, the grape goblet (*Traubenpokal*), took natural forms as a model emerged. Intended for drinking wine on festive occasions, the bowls of these vessels bear a direct resemblance to the fruit from which that beverage was made. The winemaking process is referred to in a direct manner: a vintner, sporting his cask and holding his vine-covered staff, serves as the shaft figure. The motif of the "cask man" or "cask woman" can be traced back to the late fifteenth century and was extremely popular during the sixteenth and seventeenth centuries, when it was turned into small wooden or silver sculptures or grape cups.

Two of the four Dresden pieces (IV 8 and IV 12) show remains of cold enamel, which suggest that they were originally quite colorful objects. At the time of their fabrication, the coloring was certainly stronger, emphasizing the figural components' naturalistic traits; this is particularly true for the bouquet serving as the cover's finial, for the vintner, and presumably also for the animals gathered on the platform.

Originally, the two cups by Paulus Baier (IV 18 and IV 21) were clearly distinguished from each other. Obviously, the piece with the smaller bowl (IV 21) was adapted to look more like its larger counterpart: an extra shaft element was added sometime later.
U.W

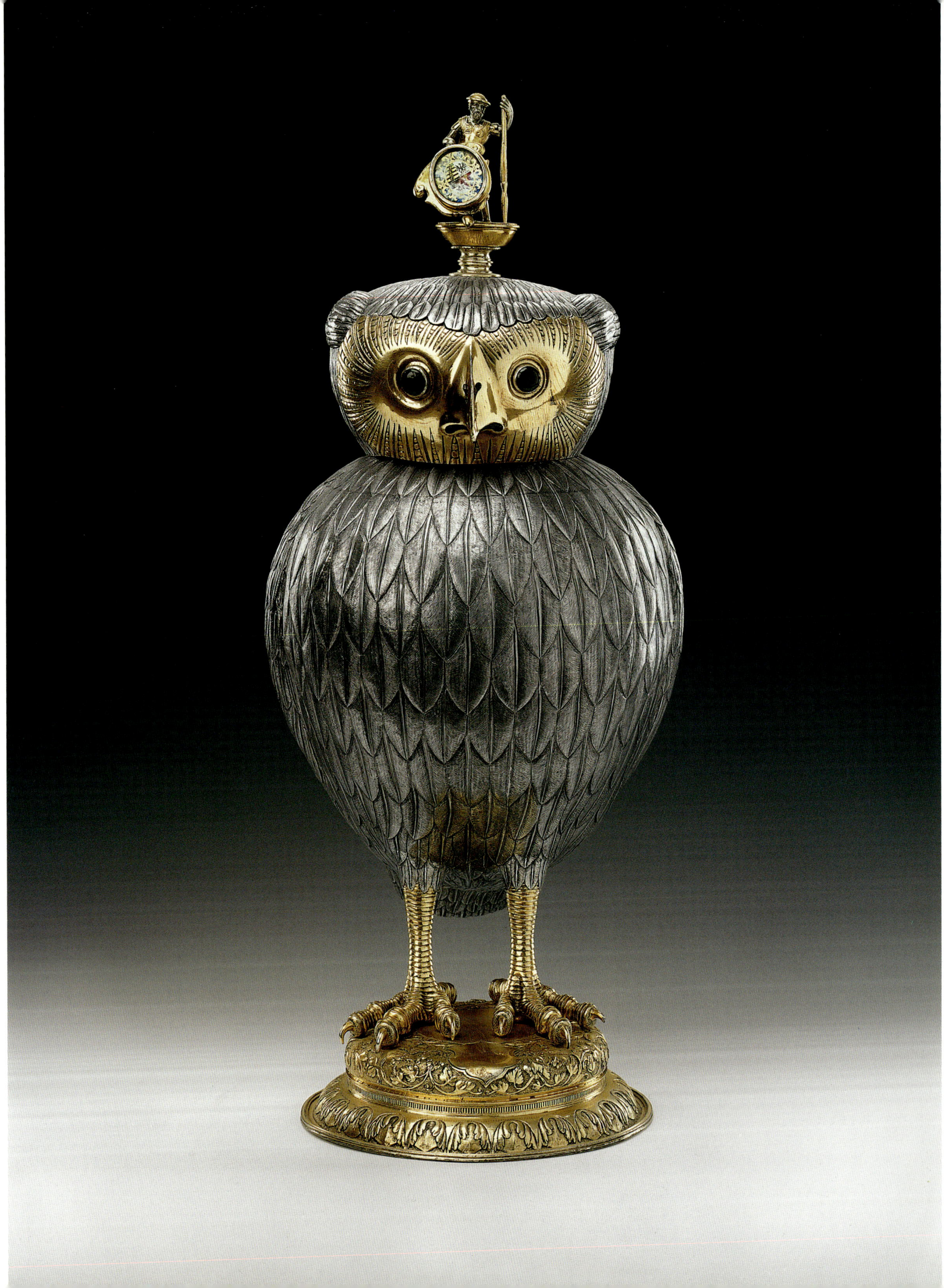

127 Cup in the Form of an Owl

This owl cup entered the Green Vault only in the early nineteenth century. The fact that it was transferred by the Geheimes Finanz-Collegio (Secret Finance College) might indicate that it had been kept in one of the numerous sovereigns' palaces, as this institution was then in charge of estate inventories. The 1587 inventory, a compilation of jewelry and plate, also lists "*1 Silberne Eul mit einem kopf*" (one silver owl with a head), which could be identified with this cup.

Among drinking utensils in the form of animals—a category in which German goldsmiths of the sixteenth and seventeenth centuries were prodigiously inventive—the owl cups represent one of the largest groups. The example kept in the Green Vault has not received much scholarly attention, although it is a rare and precious object of princely rank. Not only is it one of the earliest examples of its kind, but its height also exceeds that of most other owl vessels, which average between six and nine inches. The chased plumage is extraordinary, as is the design of the stand with its sublimely modeled foliage over an embossed ground. Such ornaments were popularized during the 1530s through the prints of Heinrich Aldegrever and Gilg Kilian Proger, the latter a Nuremberg goldsmith and ornament engraver originally from Dresden.

The smooth, round surface visible on the top of the base indicates that it was initially intended for a different context. The cartouches on the front of the base and in the hand of the figure crowning the lid, reserved for engraved coats of arms, remained blank and hence cannot provide information concerning the original owner. The medallion with *verre églomisé* was attached later; displaying the electoral Saxon and Brandenburgian coats of arms as allies, it was likely added under Christian I.

Because of the animal's numerous symbolic meanings, it is difficult to identify specific sixteenth-century associations with owl cups. The bells frequently attached to the owls' legs refer to their use as decoys and thus to their status as a symbol of temptation (in this case, to drink alcohol). Inscriptions on some pieces indicate that owls also served as the attribute of the goddess Minerva and as a symbol of wisdom. Consequently, it appears that multiple layers of meaning and even contradictory allegorical interpretations were intentional in depictions of these creatures.

U.W.

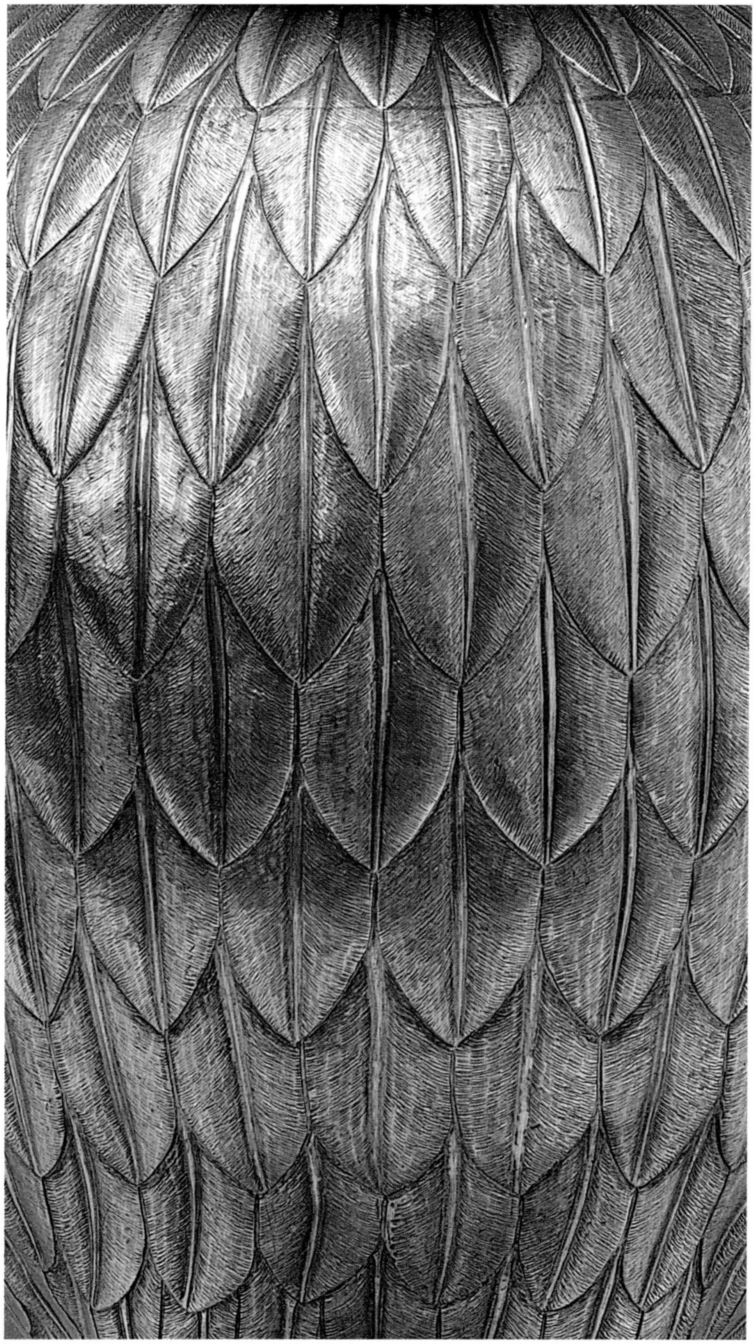

Presumably South Germany
circa 1540
Silver, partly gilded, *verre églomisé*, enamel
H. 17⅝ in. (44.9 cm)
No marks
First mentioned in the Silbervergoldetes Zimmer inventory 1817, p. 68, no. 97
Staatliche Kunstsammlungen Dresden, Grünes Gewölbe, inv. no. IV 302
Lit.: Guide Green Vault 1997, p. 55, no. 92; see also Wirth 1968; Wirth 1973; König-Baudouin-Stiftung 2003

128 Cup and Cover in the Form of a Small Castle

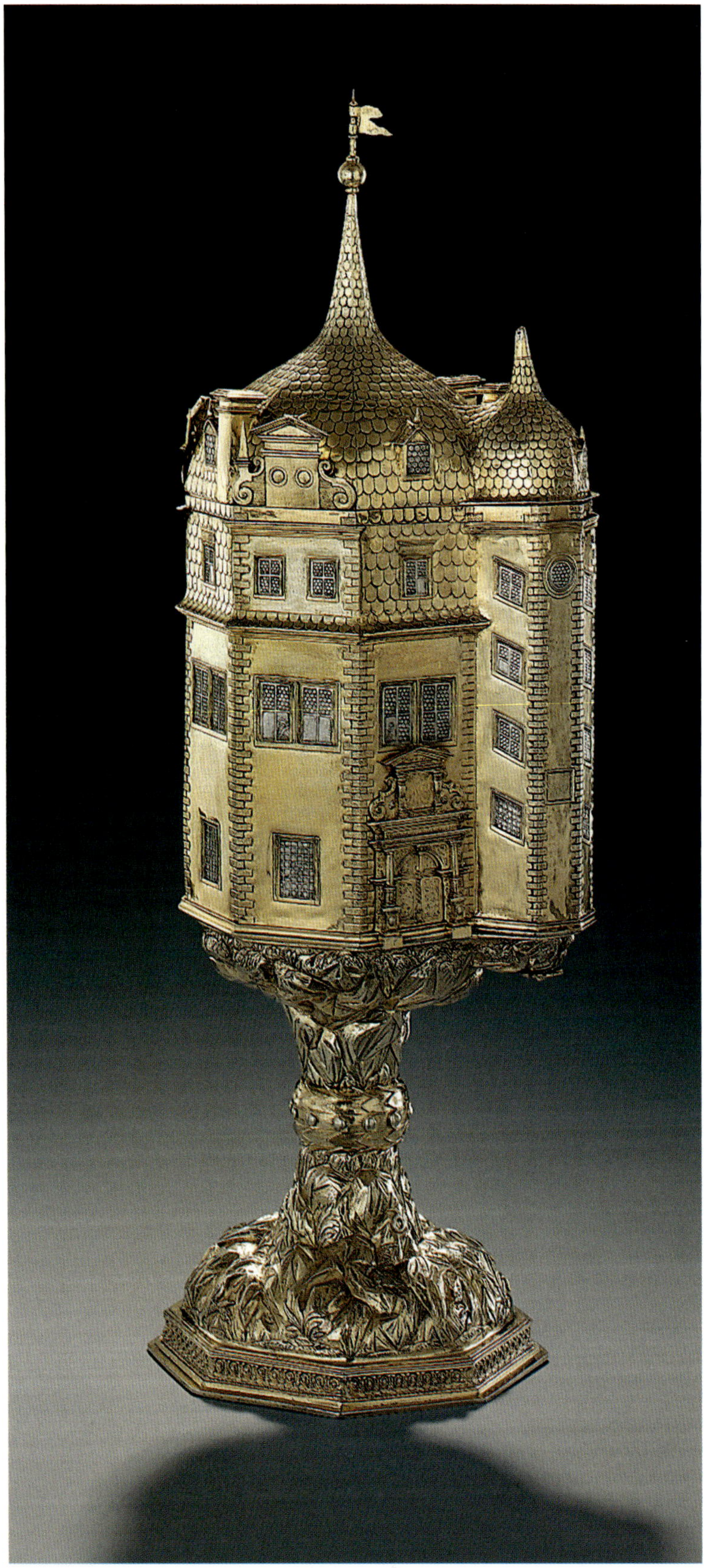

A surviving receipt dated January 24, 1606 (SächsHStA Dresden, Loc. 7340/1, fol. 124), indicates that this unusual cup was commissioned by Elector Christian II from the Dresden goldsmith Georg Mond. It served as a vessel from which guests were offered their festive initial drink. Although a device hidden on the inside of this gigantic vessel reduces its volume by approximately one third, the capacity of the vessel is almost three-quarters of a gallon.

The shape of this stately container mirrors that of the dynastic building for which it was intended. Its body is a detailed reproduction of the small pleasure castle commissioned by Elector Christian II in 1604 to be erected on the Sonnenstein Fortification in Pirna. The castle's architectural peculiarities were faithfully copied, and even its location on top of the rock was indicated. Over the portal, the Saxon coat of arms, as well as the name and title of the building's owner, may be seen; near the stair turret is the coat of arms of Rudolf von Bünau, Sonnenstein's alderman from 1586 until 1615. Numerous details give life to the edifice: the inhabitants can be spotted behind the windows' bull's-eye glass, and on the rocky, overgrown ground, hares, squirrels, and other animals bustle about.

The castle was available to the Saxons for hunting parties and other courtly pleasures for only about thirty-five years. During the Thirty Years War it was destroyed by fire while the Swedish army was entrenched there.

The cup itself survived the fire and was moved to the Königstein Fortification, where it was displayed along with other famous drinking vessels on the large wine barrel. When the barrel was taken down in 1819, the cup was transferred to the Kunstkammer; after the latter was dissolved in 1832, it went to the Armory. Not until 1890 did this unusual welcome cup find its way to the Green Vault.
U.W.

Georg Mond, Dresden, 1606
Silver-gilt
H. 25¾ in. (65.5 cm)
Hallmark for Dresden and maker's mark "GM" (in ligature, in the oval)
First mentioned as postscript in the Kunstkammer inventory 1741, fol. 766, no. 5: transferred in August 1819 from the Königstein Fortification to the Kunstkammer
Staatliche Kunstsammlungen Dresden, Grünes Gewölbe, inv. no. IV 345
Lit.: Rosenberg 1923, p. 29, no. 1739a; Holzhausen/Kesting 1966, p. LII, no. 28; Zurich 1971, p. 162, no. 114; Washington 1978, p. 154, no. 261; Dresden 1990, p. 358, no. 564 (Ulli Arnold); Guide Green Vault 1997, p. 51, no. 72

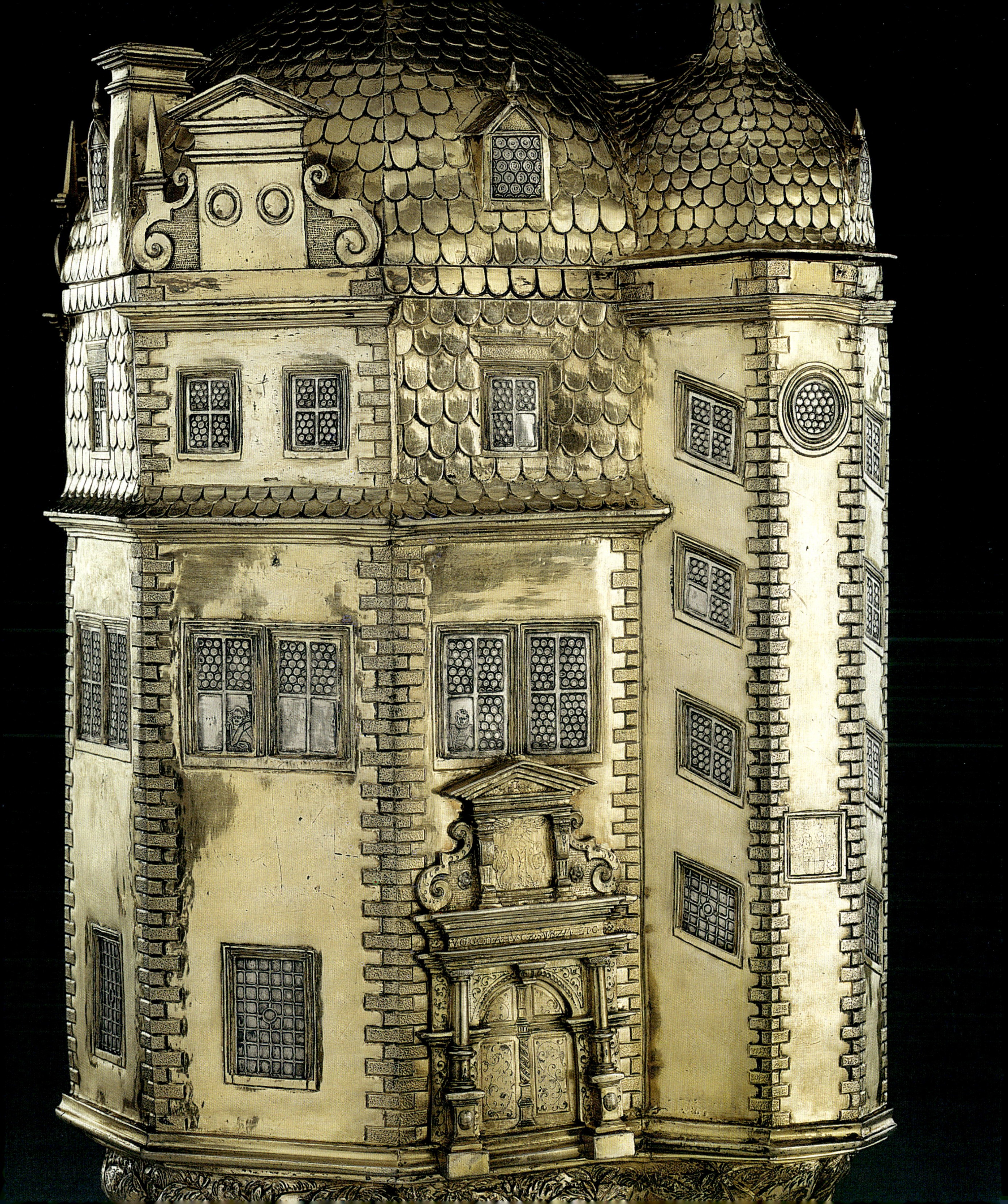

129 Cup and Cover: Hercules Supporting the Celestial Sphere

The motif of Hercules carrying the celestial sphere on his shoulders has its origin in classical mythology. According to legend, the hero briefly relieved Atlas from the heavy weight of the heavens, while the Titan, in return for the favor, went to fetch the apples of the Hesperides.

This artistically remarkable object was also functional. The upper portion of the large celestial sphere could be removed and used as a cup. Unlike the other two globe goblets kept in the Green Vault, which were created between 1625 and 1629 by the Augsburg goldsmith Elias Lencker, the Nuremberg piece has no movement built into its pedestal. Instead, it contains a rectangular drawer at the bottom—a highly unusual detail whose original purpose remains unclear.

Heinrich Mack left the execution of the engraved zodiacal images to the etcher Johann Hauer, because a Nuremberg guild law required all etching and engraving to be done exclusively by specialists. Hauer employed as his model a globe published in 1601 by the Amsterdam cartographer and engraver Jodocus Hondius. He transferred its designs to the silver sphere segment by segment in order to attain the most exact rendering possible. The minutely executed engraving here is the first of a number of similar works by Hauer. In 1632, two additional globe cups, now in Stockholm's Historiska Museet, served as diplomatic gifts from the imperial city of Nuremberg to King Gustav Adolf of Sweden, underscoring the high prestige of such objects. Monumental goldsmiths' sculptures as well as drinking vessels, they also reflect the most advanced contemporary accomplishments in the field of astronomy.
U.W.

Goldwork:
Heinrich Mack;
engraving:
Johann Hauer
Nuremberg, 1617
Silver-gilt, traces of cold enamel
H. 29½ in. (75 cm)
Hallmark for Nuremberg and maker's mark "HM" (in ligature, in the shield)
Signed on the sphere "*Ioh: Hauer fecit Norimb: Anno 1617*"
First mentioned in the silver inventory 1723, fol. 58, no. 8
Staatliche Kunstsammlungen Dresden, Grünes Gewölbe, inv. no. IV 292
Lit.: Sponsel 1928, p. 69 and plate 33; Rosenberg 1925, p. 188, no. 4145b; Guide Green Vault, p. 45, no. 34; Tacke 2001, p. 67, ill. 17 and pp. 70f.

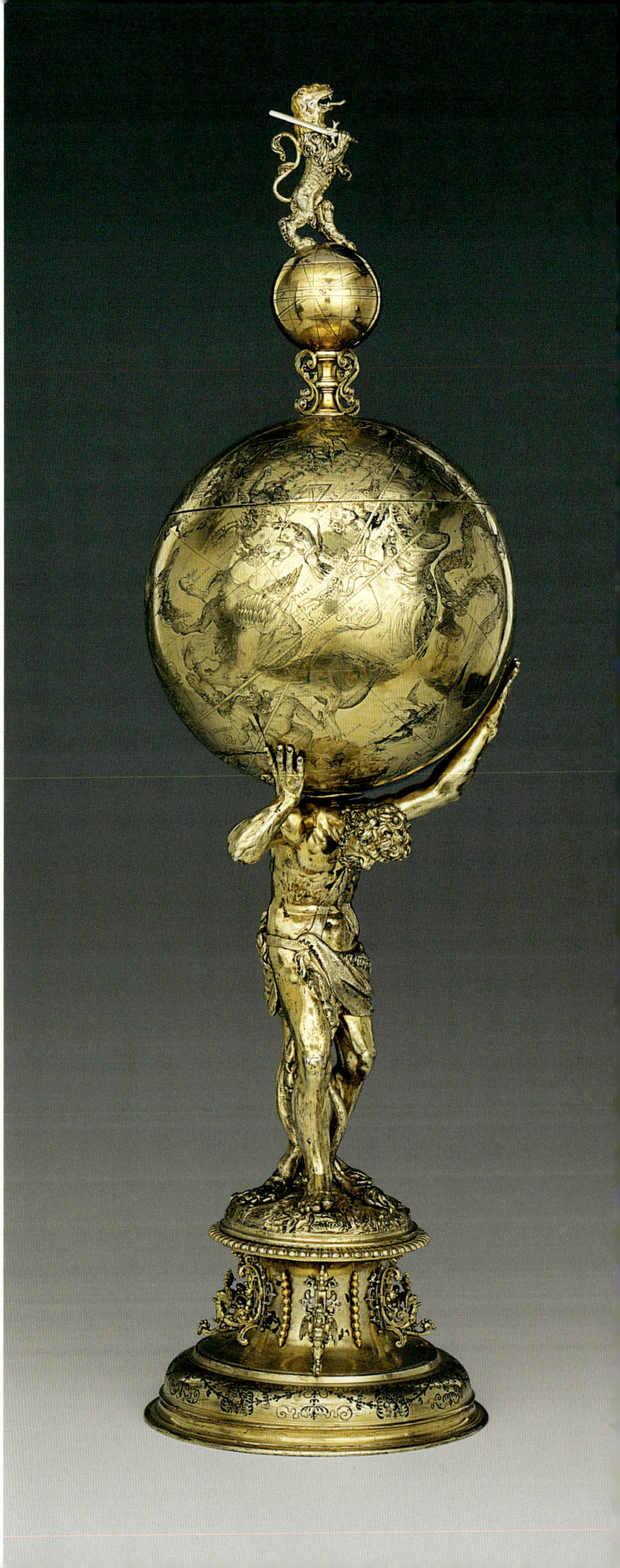

130 Standing Lion with Crown

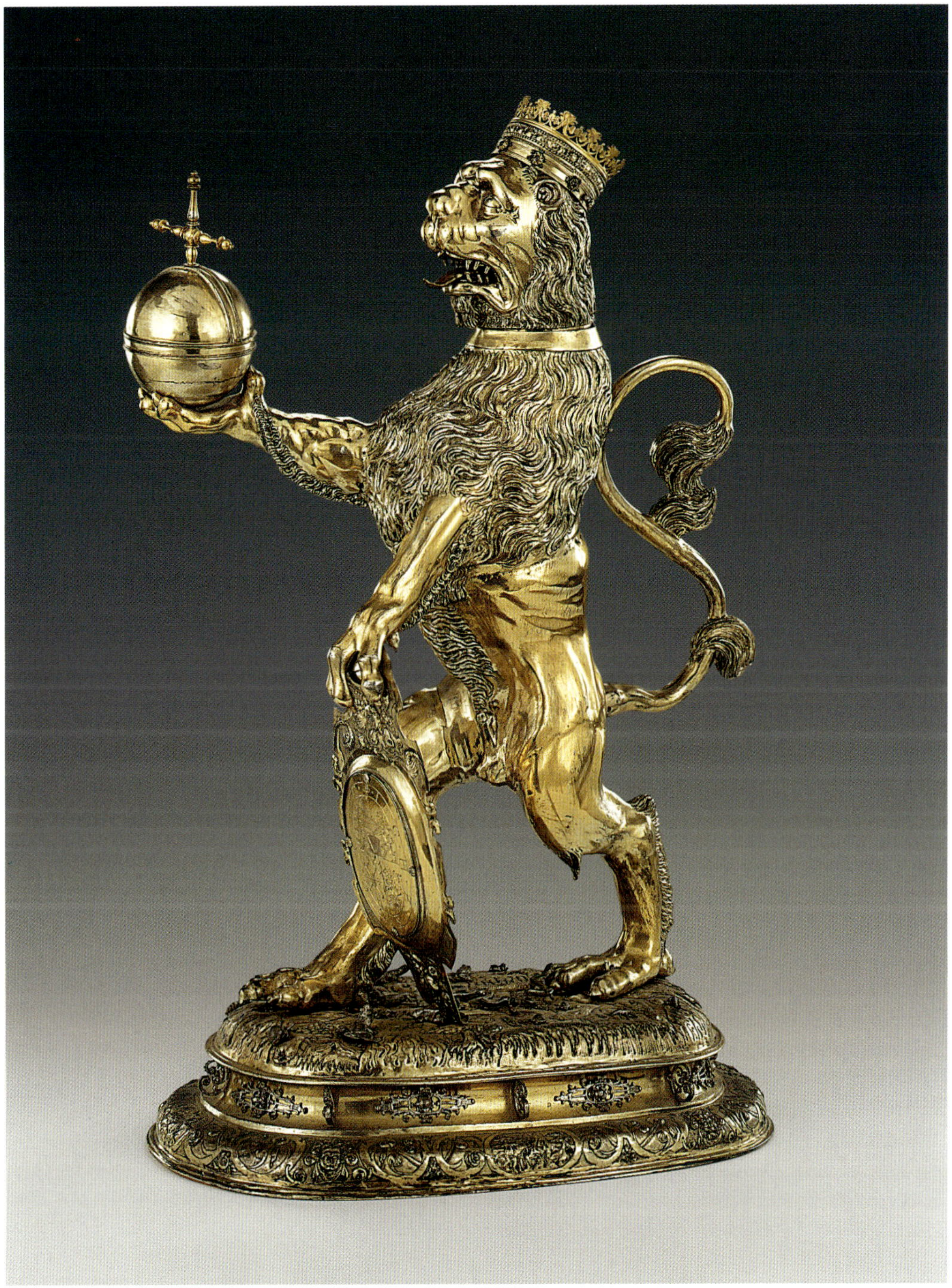

This unusually large silver sculpture is conceived as a representation of princely power. Even though the lion's removable head suggests that the object could be used as a ewer, this appears to be impossible. Employing the thin, S-curve tail as a handle for a vessel weighing almost twenty pounds would clearly be impractical. The details of how and when this extraordinary display object came to Dresden have not been known until now. However, the heraldic aspect of the lion itself supplies important clues as to its original meaning.

The standing crowned lion presenting the imperial orb in its right paw closely resembles motifs appearing on the coat of arms of the Palsgraves near the Rhine and the electors of the Holy Roman Empire of the German Nation. And indeed, there are ties between the two dynasties that might account for how the silver sculpture came into electoral Saxon possession. Christian I, striving for a moderate Saxon position toward Calvinism, found an ally in the Palsgrave Johann Casimir, with whom he tried to advance the unification of the empire's Protestant territories. A total of three meetings during 1590 were intended to establish the planned defense alliance. However, its ratification never materialized, owing to Christian's sudden death in September 1591 and the demise of Johann Casimir a few months later. Nevertheless, the hypothesis that the lion may have been created in this context is contradicted by the preliminary dating of the hallmark to about 1593–98.

The Saxon coat of arms with the initials of Johann Georg I on the lion's shield is a later addition.
U.W.

Urban Wolff, Nuremberg, circa 1585–91 or circa 1593–98
Silver-gilt, colored stones, traces of cold enamel
H. 26⅜ in. (67 cm)
Hallmark for Nuremberg and maker's mark "VW" (in ligature, in trapezoidal field)

First mentioned in the silver inventory 1723, fol. 55
Staatliche Kunstsammlungen Dresden, Grünes Gewölbe, inv. no. IV 10
Lit.: Sponsel 1928, pp. 73f. and plate 36; Rosenberg 1925, p. 143, no. 4044b; Syndram 1998/1999, p. 13, ill. 8; Syndram 1999, p. 187

131 Saint George Slaying the Dragon

Saint George, epitome of the virtuous Christian knight, attained great importance after being made patron saint of the Order of the Garter, founded in 1348 by Edward III of England. As a military saint, George was a figure that both Catholics and Protestants could identify with, and ultimately he came to play an important role in the art of goldsmiths. In addition to the especially fashionable "Saint George jewels," countless gold and silver statues were produced until the sixteenth century, most serving as reliquaries. With the growing importance of courtly table etiquette, the saint's image was eventually introduced into the secular realm of drinking utensils and drinking games. As in other art forms, his role as dragon slayer was particularly significant. The story of George rescuing the Libyan princess, as related in the *Legenda Aurea,* a thirteenth-century compilation of saints' legends, soon became an allegory for victory over the religious enemy.

Close examination reveals the utilitarian aspect of this monumental work, for the heads of the rider, horse, and dragon can be removed and used as drinking vessels. According to the 1610 entry in the Kunstkammer inventories, this opulent piece was given by Duke Johann Georg to his brother Elector Christian II, whom he succeeded in the following year. The Saxon-Merseburgian coat of arms, originally visible on the dragon-slayer's shield, may be connected to the gift-giver. Starting in 1592, Johann Georg was the administrator of the Stift Merseburg (a secularized former monastery with a large amount of land, then under Saxon supervision), and, of course, his name linked him with the equestrian saint. The engraved monogram visible today, "FAC" (Friedrich August Churfürst), must have been placed there on the order of Elector Friedrich August I (better known as Augustus the Strong) between 1694 and 1697. This act implied that Augustus the Strong also saw the virtues of the military saint in himself.
U.W.

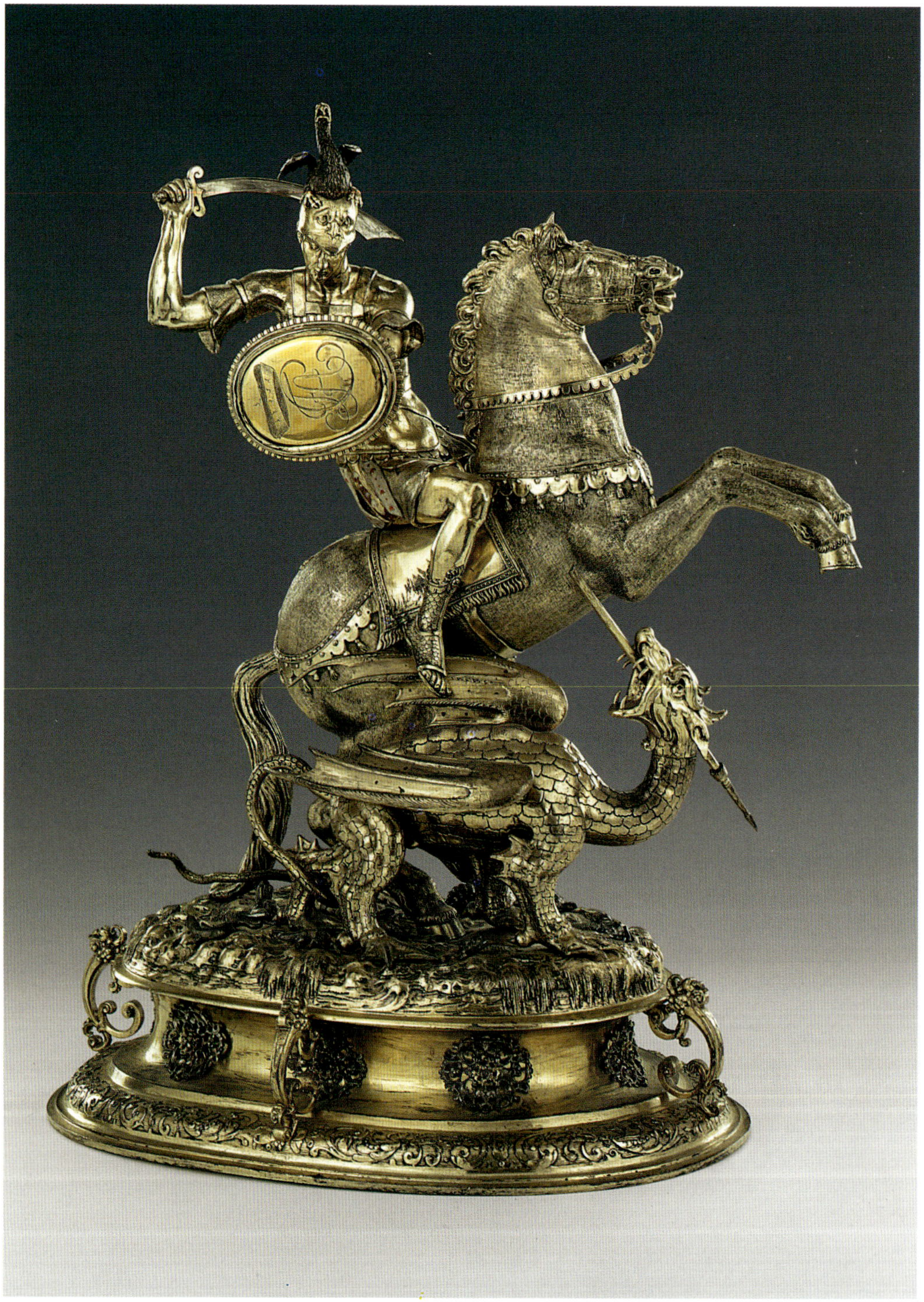

Hans Kellner, Nuremberg, circa 1603–9
Silver-gilt, traces of cold enamel, H. 20½ in. (52 cm)
Hallmark for Nuremberg and maker's mark with scepter in the shield; first mentioned in the Kunstkammer inventory 1610, fol. 195v–196r
Staatliche Kunstsammlungen Dresden, Grünes Gewölbe, inv. no. IV 124

Lit.: Sponsel 1928, p. 68 and plate 31; Rosenberg 1925, p. 138, no. 4031/4032e; Hernmarck 1978, p. 109 and ill. 178; Seelig 1987, pp. 53–59 and ill. 41; Guide Green Vault 1997, p. 39, no. 5; Syndram 1999, pp. 44f.

132 Automaton: Saint George Slaying the Dragon

In contrast to the Saint George group by Hans Kellner of Nuremberg (cat. no. 131), this sculpture by Joachim Fries contains a mechanism in its base that enabled it to move across the table. Once it came to a standstill, the person closest to it was to remove the horse's head and drink the contents of the body, which was filled with wine. The monopoly for the manufacture of such courtly drinking amusements lay in Augsburg, capital of goldsmiths. There, in the workshop of Jakob I Miller, another two closely related Saint George groups were executed (today in the Bayerisches Nationalmuseum, Munich, and the Hessisches Landesmuseum, Darmstadt). All automata are based on the same prototypes and deviate from each other only in the arrangement of their figures, their embellishment, and their surface treatment. Augsburg examples tend to be more formulaic and stylized, especially when compared with those from Nuremberg, which are distinguished by careful sculptural modeling and a dramatic rendering of the equestrian combat.

Although Dresden documents mention two such automata, a definite connection with this piece cannot be established. In 1612, "*ein Silvern trinckgeschirr, wie der Ritter S. Georg, vnten mit einem vhrwergk*" (a silver drinking utensil in the shape of Saint George, with a clockwork movement at the bottom) came to the Kunstkammer. However, the 1619 inventory reported this piece as stolen (only the movement could be found). In 1630, the documents once again mention a Saint George automaton given to Elector Johann Georg I as a birthday present (no longer listed in the Kunstkammer inventory of 1640). Initially, this object may have been stored in the Geheime Verwahrung, where particularly valuable objects were kept for display on the silver buffet on festive occasions. When, in 1693, the Order of the Garter was bestowed upon Elector Johann Georg IV of Saxony, a "Riding Saint George" was displayed on the specially erected silver buffet, taking advantage of an appropriate opportunity to remember the patron saint of this English order.
U.W.

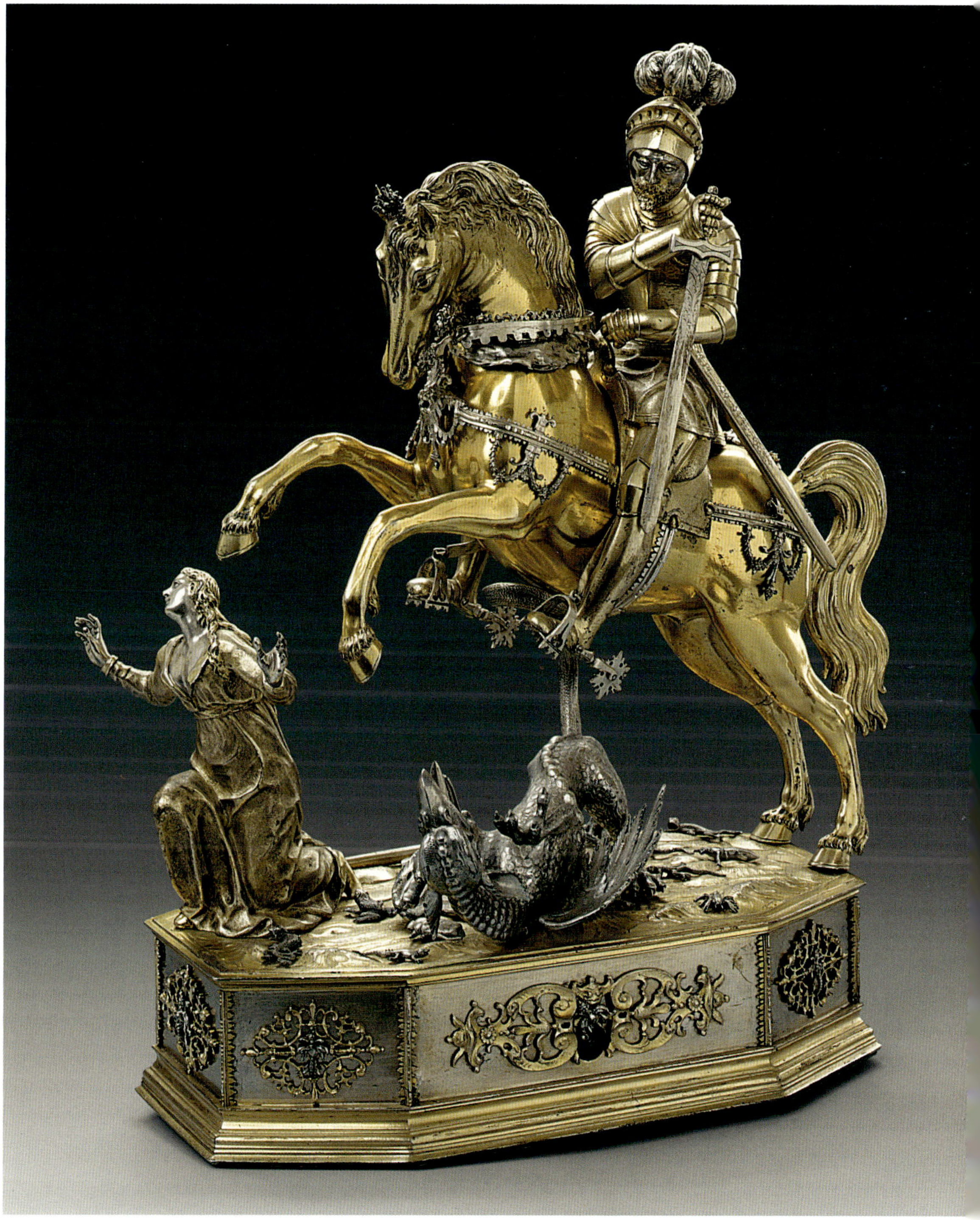

Joachim Fries, Augsburg, circa 1620
Silver-gilt, iron, H. 14¼ in. (36.2 cm)
Hallmark for Augsburg and maker's mark "IF" (in a square)
First mentioned in the Kunstkammer inventory after 1732, fol. 190r

Staatliche Kunstsammlungen Dresden, Grünes Gewölbe, inv. no. IV 154
Lit.: Seling 1980, vol. II, ill. 178, vol. III, p. 19, no. 46 (Hallmark) and p. 143, no. 1248f; Essen 1986, pp. 375f., no. 520; Seelig 1987, pp. 23–27 and ill. 21; Warsaw 1997, p. 160, no. V 27

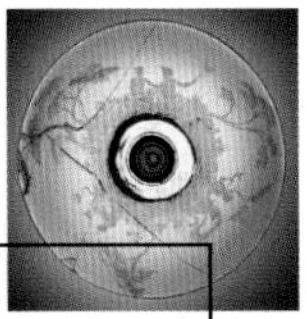

Rock-Crystal Works

Jutta Kappel

The large and heavy sphere of clear rock crystal kept by Elector August in the Geheime Verwahrung (Treasury) of the Dresden palace felt ice cold.[1] When the princely collector held the globe in his hands, he perceived everything he saw in it as "upside down." Amazement at this heretofore unexplained phenomenon must have been overwhelming. The miraculous sphere came to Dresden between 1574 and 1578 as a present from Duke Emmanuel Philibert of Savoy. This item was apparently the subject of a now-lost description in the 1587 Kunstkammer inventory concerning the "*Effecten und wirckungen des Cristals, welchen der Herzogk v. Sophoye dem Churfürsten, Herzogen Augusten zu Sachßen seliger zugeschickett*" (purposes and effects of the crystal the deceased Saxon elector Duke August received from the duke of Savoy).[2]

The word "crystal" derives from the Greek "to freeze" or "to congeal with frost." In fact, the ancient Greeks believed that clear rock crystal was water that had solidified and turned into eternal ice.[3] To rock crystal was accorded the power to work miracles and to heal. In the Christian liturgy of the Middle Ages, this precious mineral was considered a symbol of divine purity and strong faith.[4] Beyond all mythical interpretations and traditional symbolism, rock crystal is still considered a wonder of nature. But its mineralogical origins have long since been demystified. It belongs to the quartz group of minerals. Under ideal conditions a hexagonal prism is formed that terminates in pointed, pyramidal ends.[5] Large crystals of outstanding purity were to be found in the central massifs of the Alps. This hard quartz was as sought after as the superb decorative vessels that were created from it in the stonecutting workshops of the Miseroni and the Saracchi in Milan. It was only the stonecutter's virtuosity and command of many varied techniques that elevated the valuable raw material to the rank of artwork. The Milanese workshops produced exquisite vessels in the shape of fantastic beasts and sailing vessels, as well as jugs, bowls, and vases. All objects were fitted with locally made precious mounts. Figural scenes and plant forms, often only the barest fractions of an inch in depth and having a matte gray look, were engraved into the bodies of the vessels. These engraved designs were considered masterful accomplishments in the *arte minuta*. They followed the Mannerist desire for designs rich in contrasts.[6]

Such vessels were enormously expensive. During the second half of the sixteenth century it was considered a sign of the most distinguished taste to own Milan-made vessels of rock crystal, and they were a conspicuous mark of princely power.

For storing his collection of rock-crystal objects, which consisted of forty-two vessels plus the aforementioned sphere, Elector August of Saxony selected a very special place. It was kept, along with other precious objects, not in the Kunstkammer but in the Treasury of the Dresden palace. An almost complete reconstruction of the rock-crystal holdings can be made on the basis of the inventory of this vault.[7] Many of the entries in the inventory are very brief, however, and thus preclude comparison with the objects preserved in the Green Vault. Others entries are precise and permit identification of objects, although in some cases with

1. Treasury inventory 1586/87, fol. 76v. The sphere (inv. no. V 174; Diam. 6¾ in. [17 cm], weight 16½ lbs [7.5 kg]) is different from the substantially smaller "Kühlkugeln." See also Darmstadt 1992, cat. nos. 17, 19, 20.
2. Kunstkammer inventory 1587, fol. 198r–v, no. 211.
3. Darmstadt 1992, pp. 131–33.
4. Hahnloser/Brugger-Koch 1985, p. 10.
5. Darmstadt 1992, p. 132f.; Kandutsch 2003, p. 35.
6. See also Kris 1929, vol. 1, p. 6.
7. The most recent comparison of inventories revealed that the undated Treasury inventory was compiled in 1586/87 and not, as previously thought, in 1588; this means that it predates the first Kunstkammer inventory.

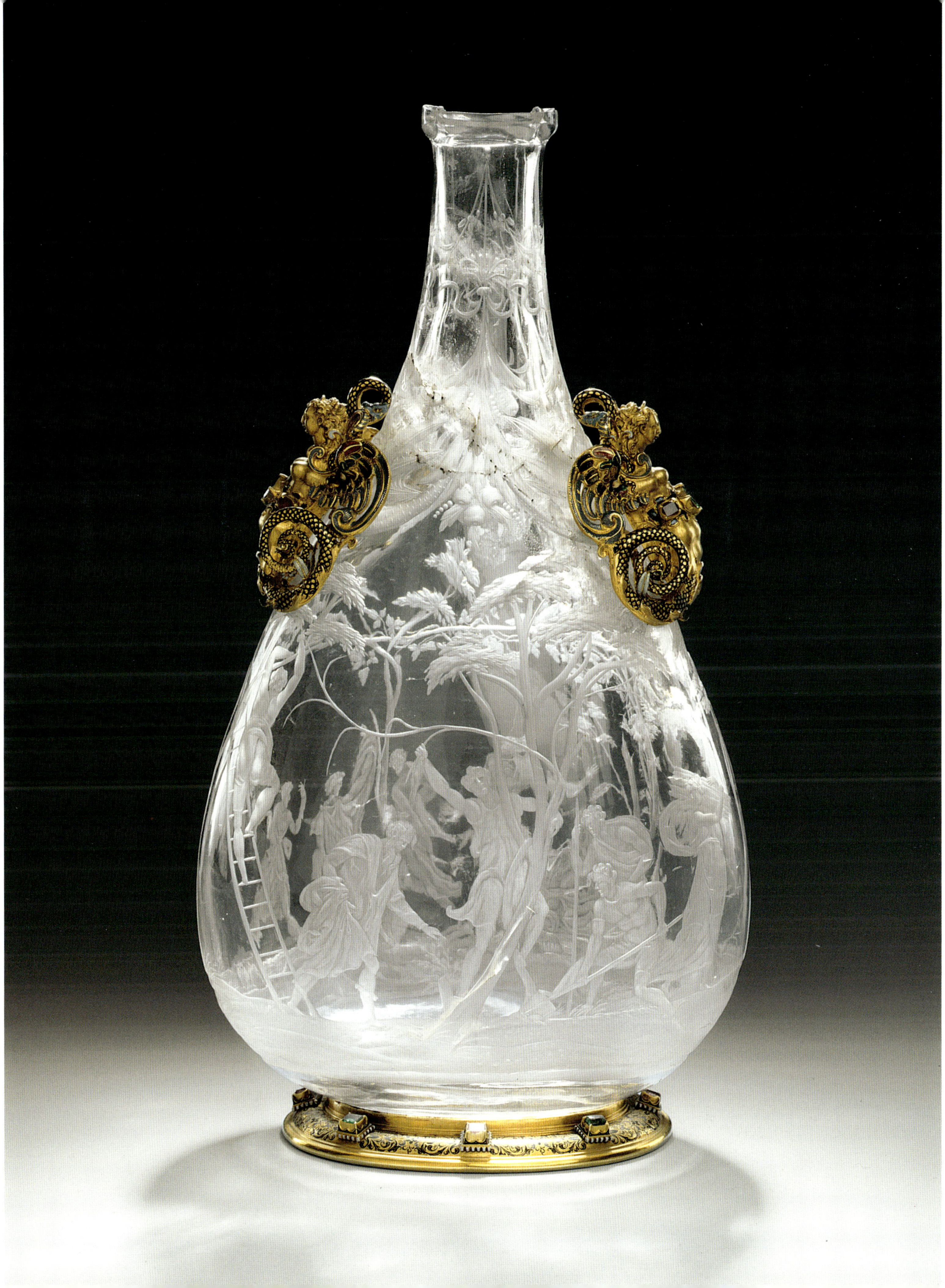

previous page
Flask with Scenes
from the Story of Noah
Design: Annibale Fontana
Saracchi workshop, Milan, after 1572
Rock crystal, gold, enamel,
rubies, emeralds
H. 12⅜ in. (31.5 cm)
Staatliche Kunstsammlungen Dresden,
Grünes Gewölbe, inv. no. V 186

qualifications (i.e., cat. nos. 133, 134). Included in the works that can be identified without doubt are examples of the medieval art of cut rock crystal.[8] Among the works from the Saracchi workshop in Milan[9] are a decorative vessel in the shape of an owl, a lidded vessel with garnet decoration, and a flask with scenes from the story of Noah (ill. p. 251) inspired by a drawing by Annibale Fontana (Biblioteca Ambrosiana, Milan).[10]

While information pertaining to gifts or purchases of rock-crystal vessels is scarce, it invariably leads to Turin, Mantua, Milan, and Prague. Until recently, the hypothesis was that most Milanese rock-crystal vessels assembled in Dresden's electoral Treasury until shortly before 1580 were gifts from Turin from Duke Emmanuel Philibert of Savoy.[11] This suggestion

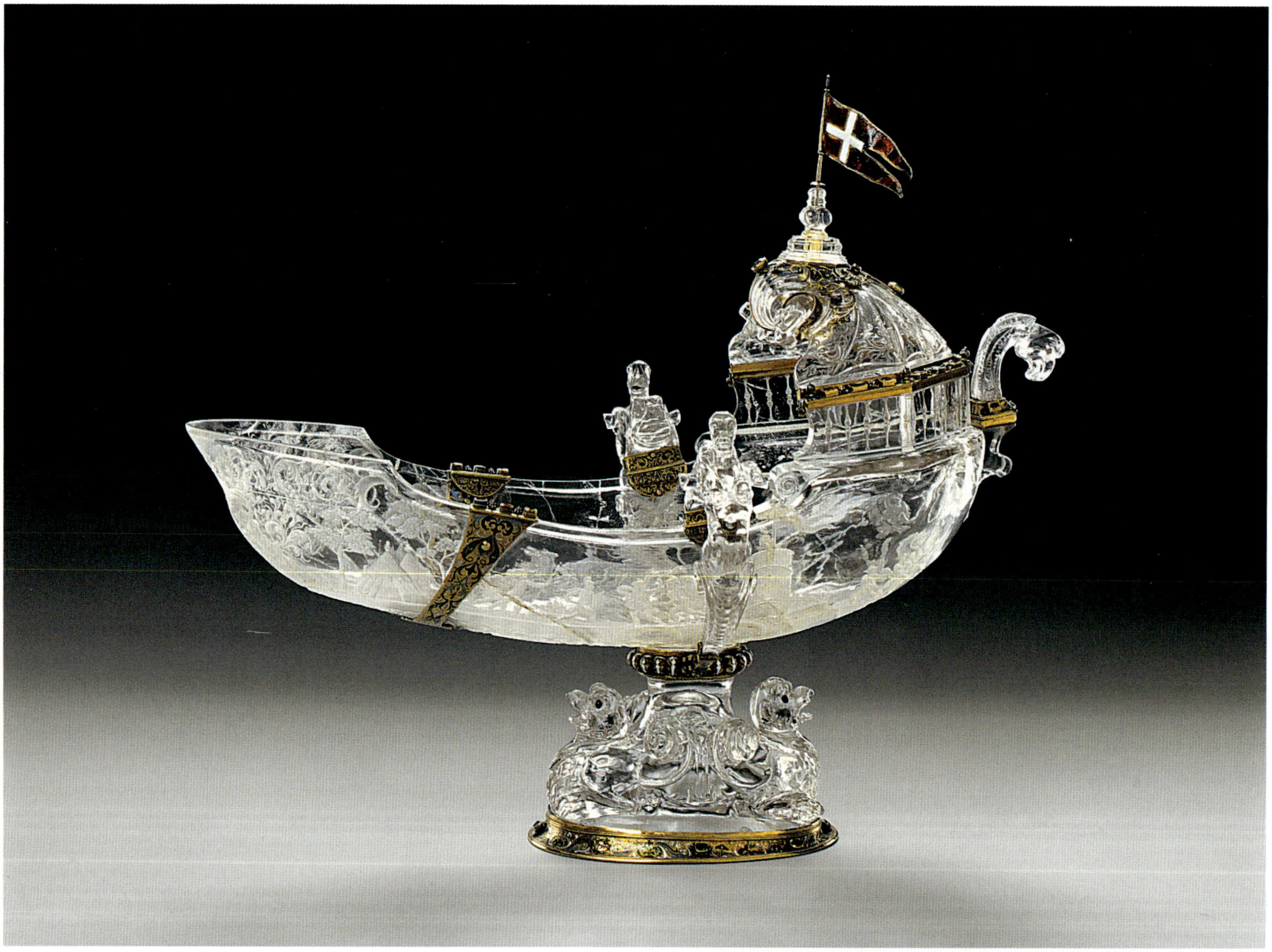

Galley with Scenes from Ancient Mythology
Saracchi workshop, Milan, end of the 16th century
Addition to the mount: Dresden, before 1709
Rock crystal, gold, enamel, precious stones
H. 14⅝ (37 cm), L. 17⅜ in. (44 cm)
Staatliche Kunstsammlungen Dresden,
Grünes Gewölbe, inv. no. V 185

can be neither confirmed nor ruled out, as archival material has not yet been fully assessed.[12] We do have documents dated 1581 providing evidence that the diplomat and electoral councillor Andreas Paul took six crystal vessels to Dresden from Mantua as gifts from Duke Guglielmo Gonzaga for Elector August of Saxony.[13] These presents went immediately to the Treasury, but their identity can no longer be established.

In 1601, upon the order of Christian II, Giovanni Maria Nosseni acquired three crystal vessels from Giovanni Ambrogio Saracco in Milan.[14] Giovanni Ambrogio and his brother Steffano were masters of the *arte grossa*, whereas their brother Simone oversaw the much more highly valued *arte minuta*; he was considered a skilled carver of intaglio decoration.[15] The exhibition includes a bowl from this famous Milanese workshop that collaborated closely with Annibale Fontana (cat. no. 135).

Exquisite decorative vessels from the Milanese studios of the Miseroni also came to Dresden.[16] The reputation of this family of superb master stonecutters was stellar. Three of Girolamo Miseroni's sons moved from Milan to the court of Emperor Rudolf II in 1588. Ottavio Miseroni became head of this workshop and was largely responsible for the unmistakable style of the Prague vessels.[17] Elector Christian II of Saxony, who had excellent diplomatic contacts with the nearby imperial court,[18] purchased three crystal vessels by Ottavio Miseroni that were paid for on July 14, 1610, in Prague.[19] Two of them may have been the delicate bowls that clearly display his "soft style" (cat. nos. 144, 145).

In contrast to the diversity of other groups of objects in the Green Vault, vessels of rock crystal were not documented in the five inventories of the Kunstkammer, compiled between 1587 and 1640, nor were new acquisitions added to these inventories because they remained in the Treasury. After the compilation of the 1586/87 Treasury inventory, significant time passed before the next one was made. We therefore have little data to rely on in documenting when and how rock-crystal objects were added until the 1725 inventory of precious objects of the Green Vault.[20]

On February 24, 1668, vessels made of topaz and rock crystal and decorated with gold and precious stones went to the Kunstkammer. Their estimated value was 20,140 taler.[21] This must have been a large portion of the material heretofore kept in the Treasury. The reason for this transfer was likely the visit of Cosimo III, grand duke of Tuscany, for whom they were displayed most effectively.[22] In 1674 the learned traveler Charles Patin saw the impressive collection of rock crystal and described it as "*une infinité de vaisseaux de crystal de roche.*"[23] In 1683 art chamberlain Tobias Beutel mentioned "*Edelgestein Geschirre, die seynd aus Crytsall, Topaß und Achat*" (vessels of precious stones are [made] of crystal, topaz, and agate) as well as two "*herrliche Geschirre aus Crystall*" (wonderful services made of crystal) that came to Dresden as presents of Emperors Ferdinand III and Leopold I.[24] One of the two gifts is preserved in the Green Vault.[25] Finally, in 1691 Elector Johann Georg IV initiated the transfer of numerous works within the collection, including the rock-crystal vessels; they were moved from the Kunstkammer to the Treasury of the Dresden palace.[26]

It is a miracle that these extremely fragile objects survived the turmoil of the centuries almost unblemished. They were precious collector's items and so were practically never used. Only on major festive occasions were they publicly displayed. Elector Friedrich August I of Saxony, famous as August the Strong, had particular respect for the objects he inherited from his ancestors. In addition to a selection of masterly goldsmith's works, he ordered an exquisite array of seventeen rock-crystal vessels to be taken to Krakow in 1697 for the festive banquet on the occasion of his coronation as Polish king. These included the priceless crystal galley (ill. p. 252) and the flask (ill. p. 251) from the Saracchi workshop.[27]

After the death of the king, who with a connoisseur's determination had purchased fine vessels by the Milanese Giovanni Battista Metellino, the collection of rock crystal in the Green Vault's Hall of Precious Objects was not substantially enlarged. In 1746 five more rock-crystal vessels were added to the holdings of the Green Vault (cat. no. 138). They were a bequest from the estate of Duke Johann Adolf II of Saxony-Weißenfels.[28] The duke was an art lover who acquired Meissen figures and started a collection of arms. It is not well known that he also had a small yet extremely sophisticated collection of cut-stone works, some of which he had inherited, possibly from the Dresden property of Johann Georg I. Undoubtedly the most outstanding item in this group was the heliotrope bowl by Ottavio Miseroni from Prague.[29]

8. See also Kappel 2000.
9. In the order of their mention in the Treasury inventory 1586/87, fols. 74r, 75r–v (inv. nos. V 295, V 217, V 186).
10. See also Lugano 1998, cat. no. 66 (Paola Venturelli).
11. Apart from the sphere, the only other presents that can be documented are those referenced in the Kunstkammer inventory 1587, fols. 6v–7v.
12. See also Marx 2000b, p. 248 with footnote 137.
13. Marx 2000b, p. 248 with footnote 137; see also Sogliani 2002, p. 338 (under the year 1582).
14. Sponsel 1929, p. 58; Kris 1929, vol. 1, p. 118 with footnote 7. The price of 275 taler is too low for the purchase of an item such as the large rock-crystal galley (inv. no. V 185).
15. Distelberger 2002, p. 85. For the terms *arte grossa* and *arte minuta*, see also cat. no. 136.
16. This catalogue is the first to publish an extensive discussion of this material and bring it to the attention of the public.
17. See Distelberger 1997, pp. 190f.; see also Distelberger 2002, pp. 81, 245.
18. See also Kappel 1995b; Kappel 1998c.
19. Holzhausen 1934, pp. 99, 117 with Regest 73. This purchase from Ottavio Miseroni was possibly negotiated by the glass- and stonecutter Caspar Lehmann, who was also active in Prague from 1588.
20. This is why almost all of the rock-crystal works are mentioned for the first time in the 1725 Pretiosen inventory. Although they were acquired long before this date, they were not mentioned in writing after the holdings of the Treasury had been compiled in 1586/87.
21. Hantzsch 1902, p. 273.
22. Cosimo III visited the Dresden Kunstkammer on March 14, 1668: see also SächsHStA Dresden, Loc. 8792/6, fol. 67r.
23. "An infinite array of rock-crystal vessels." Patin 1674, p. 112f. With this mention it is clear that the rock-crystal vessels were never part of the furnishings of the Dresden Lusthaus. At any rate, they were not noted in its 1673 inventory.
24. Beutel 1683, p. 48; see also Syndram 1999, p. 31.
25. This is the large rock-crystal barrel (inv. no. V 281) given by Emperor Ferdinand III to Johann Georg I; see Holzhausen 1934, pp. 101f., p. 116 with Regest 66; SächsHStA Dresden, Loc. 8693/21, fol. 207v.
26. The relevant Specifikation no longer exists; see also Hantzsch 1902, p. 284 with footnote 287; Syndram 1999, pp. 33, 72, 223.
27. Bäumel 1997, pp. 68, 72, 223; Syndram 1999, pp. 46f. The rock-crystal vessels for the coronation ceremonies were taken from the Bethstübchen, a highly private place of devotion, located in the king's personal chambers.
28. See also Kappel 1998b, pp. 89f. (with further bibliography); Vötsch 2000, pp. 182f.
29. See also Guide Green Vault 1997, p. 132 (inv. no. V 19).

133 Two-Handled Bowl

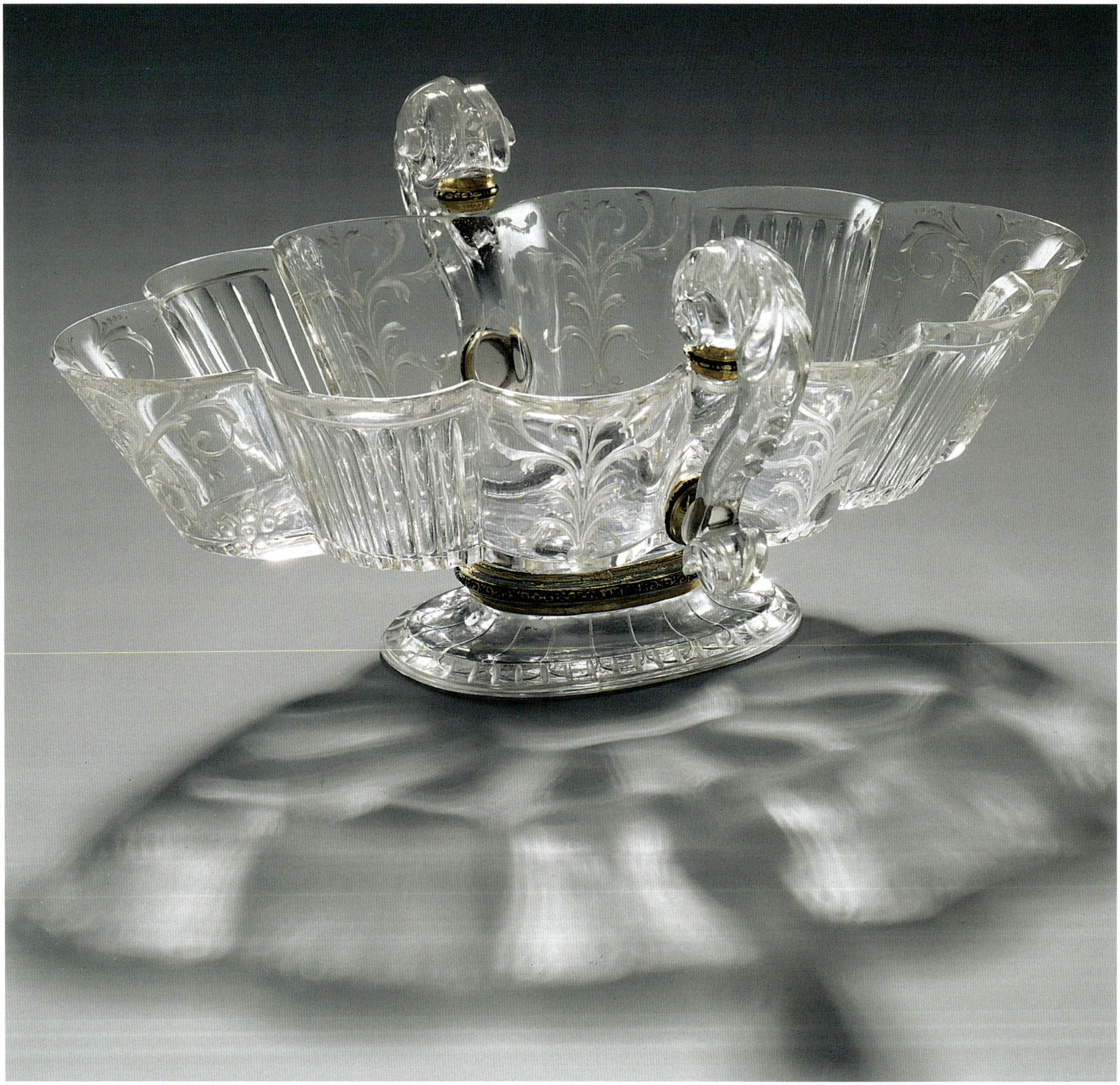

Workshop of Gasparo Miseroni, Milan, ca. 1550
Rock crystal, gold, enamel
H. 3½ in. (8.9 cm)
Case (not ill.): wood, leather with gold stamping, dark-red velvet lining, small brass hooks
H. 4¼ in. (10.8 cm), L. 8⅞ in. (22.5 cm)

First mentioned (without leather case) in Pretiosen inventory 1725, fol. 248v; possibly also identical with the briefly described long bowl "*mit Schnurckeln*" (with scrolls) in the Treasury inventory 1586/87, fol. 75v
Staatliche Kunstsammlungen Dresden, Grünes Gewölbe, inv. no. V 345
Lit.: Unpublished; but see Distelberger 1978, pp. 98f. with ill. 71–73; Alcouffe 2001, cat. no. 98; Arbeteta Mira 2001, cat. no. 64 (with similarly shaped leather case); Distelberger 2002, cat. nos. 35, 59–61

The decafoil body of this vessel is embellished with convex carved Pfeifen (the result of a special lapidary cutting technique) and extremely thinly ground walls that widen toward the top. Four foils are decorated with vertical grooves, and the others have finely executed tendril intaglios. The narrow ends display additional miniscule fruit garlands as decoration. The elegant handles are made up of double volutes.

Characteristics pointing to Milan as the place of manufacture include the combination of precisely cut Pfeifen decoration and tendrils with suspended bundles of fruit (see cat. no. 140), as well as the exactitude and shallowness of the intaglio work. A precious rock-crystal tazza in Vienna (Kunsthistorisches Museum, Kunstkammer), identified by Rudolf Distelberger (2002) as coming from the workshop of Gasparo Miseroni, is the critical reference point regarding the date of this decafoil vessel and its maker. The mount further affirms the attribution of our bowl to this workshop. Gold mounts ringed with black-enamel tendrils are similarly rendered on the exquisite, largely unknown shell-shaped bowl made of rock crystal that is preserved in the Green Vault (inv. no. V 206). They appear again on a rock-crystal vessel in Paris (Musée du Louvre, Département des Objets d'Art) and on a small, shell-shaped chalcedony bowl in Vienna (Kunsthistorisches Museum, Kunstkammer). All these mounts were made by the same goldsmith, who must have worked in or for the workshop of Gasparo Miseroni in the mid-sixteenth century. This argument is amplified by the fact that from 1541 to 1542, and again in 1546, a jeweler by the name of Camillo de Vignono is mentioned as working in the studios of both Gasparo and Girolamo Miseroni.
J.K.

134 Decorative Vessel with Cover

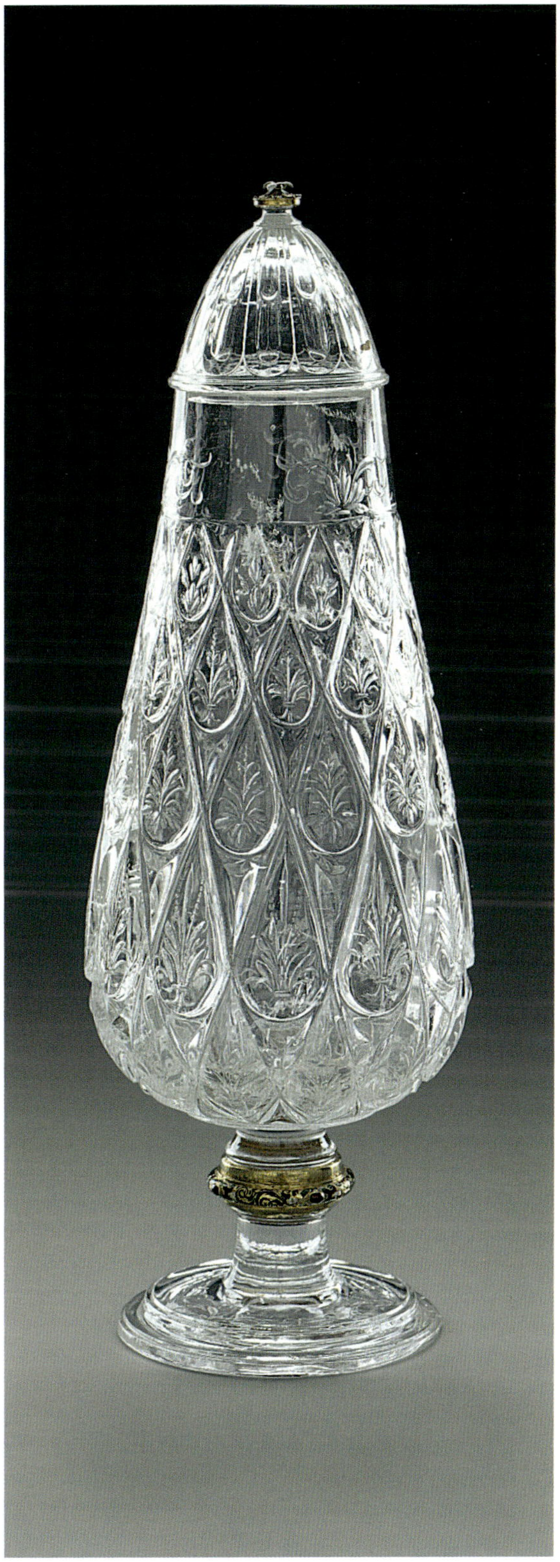

Milan, ca. 1580–85
Rock crystal, gold, enamel
H. 10⅜ in. (26.3 cm)
Presumably first mentioned in the Treasury inventory 1586/87, fol. 75r
Staatliche Kunstsammlungen Dresden, Grünes Gewölbe, inv. no. V 197
Lit.: Guide Green Vault 1997, p. 154, no. 6; see also Alcouffe 2001, cat. nos. 113–116 (with special reference to Milanese mounts)

Among the priceless holdings of the electoral Treasury in the Dresden palace was a collection of forty-two rock-crystal vessels. The descriptions in the inventory of 1586/87 are mostly too brief to identify any of the items still preserved in the Green Vault with absolute certainty. Thus it remains unresolved whether this vessel, decorated with a white enameled flower and Pfeifen on its lid, was originally part of the group of five "*Christalin glaß oben spizig zu, mit kleinen deckeln, darauf gulden knopfichen mit Laubwerck*" (crystal glasses with pointed tops and with small lids on which small gold buttons with foliage may be seen). If one accepts this, it establishes a terminus ante quem for dating the rock-crystal vessel.

Its unusual decoration, consisting of a multitude of tightly arranged droplets that remained higher than the surface after the cutting process, is stylistically unique. It cannot be compared with any rock-crystal works reliably ascribed to the Saracchi or the Miseroni in Milan. Yet the goldsmith's work, with the gold mount ring, the black enameled ornament, and the ovoid fields of red enamel in imitation of rubies, displays typical Milanese features (see cat. no. 135).
J.K.

135 Circular Bowl

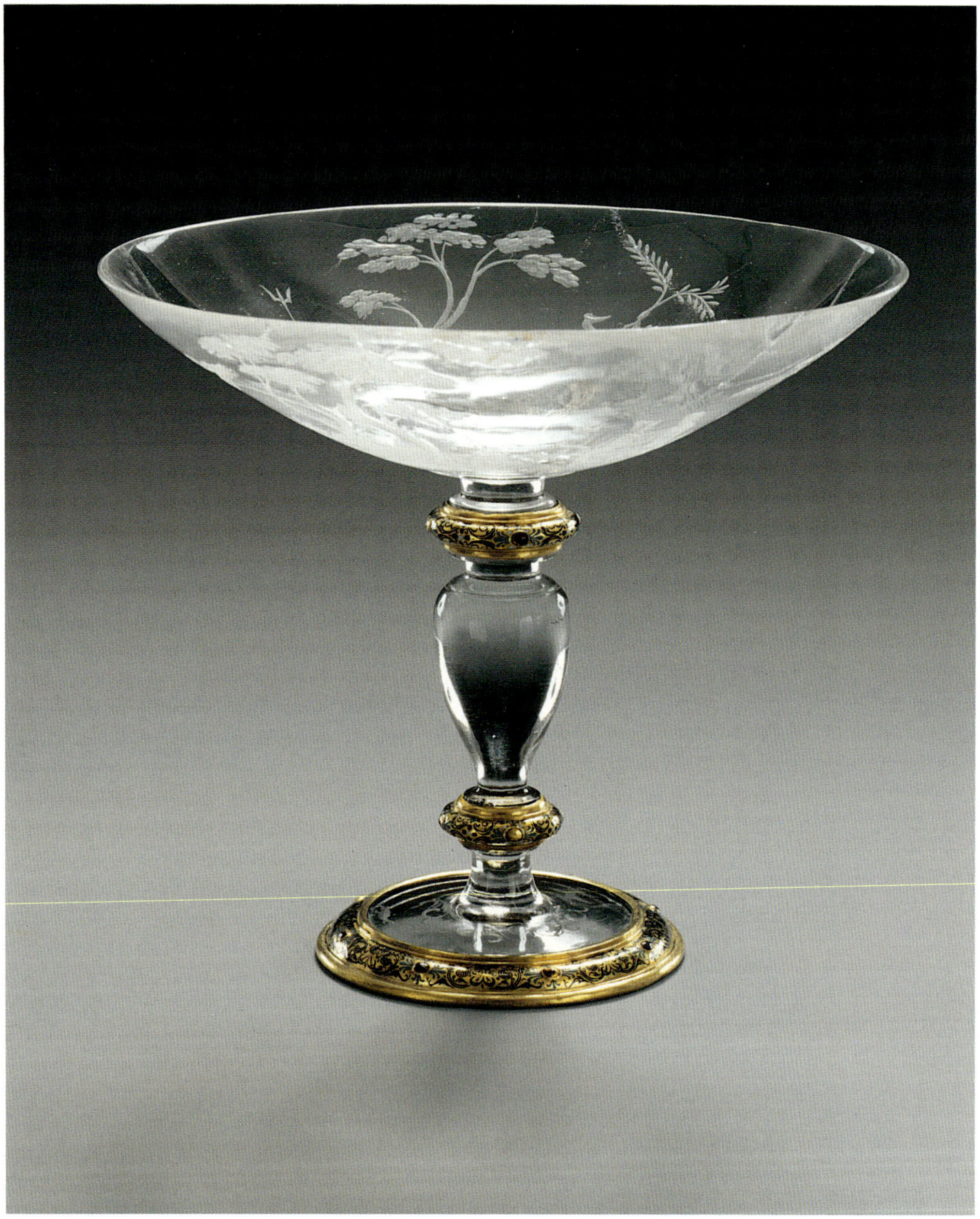

Workshop of the Saracchi,
possibly based on a design by Annibale Fontana
Milan, ca. 1575–80
Rock crystal, gold, enamel
H. 6⅛ in. (15.5 cm)
First mentioned in the Pretiosen inventory 1725, fols. 245v–246r
Staatliche Kunstsammlungen Dresden, Grünes Gewölbe, inv. no. V 344
Lit.: Kris 1929, vol. I, p. 186, no. 557 and vol. II, p. 82 (ill. 557); see also Kris 1929, vol. I, p. 172, no. 337, and vol. II, p. 82 (ill. 337); Distelberger 1978, pp. 98f. with ill. 72; Venturelli 1998, pp. 59 and 61; Alcouffe 2001, cat. nos. 113–116 (here with special reference to Milanese mounts); Arbeteta Mira 2001, cat. nos. 10, 90, 93; Distelberger 2002, cat. no. 40 (signed bowl by Tortorino), cat. no. 47 (bowl in the Prado Museum by A. Fontana, before 1569)

The bottom of this smooth and extremely thinly ground bowl is occupied by a circular aquatic zone. Around the edge are three water nymphs facing water deities with fish tails. The scene is divided into three areas by trees with spreading branches and foliage. In the far distance, beyond the water and behind the trees, cityscapes can be seen. This typical Milanese rock-crystal vessel dates to about 1570–80. Its distinguishing features include the gold mounts with black-enamel ornamentation and red-enamel imitations of rubies around the bowl's foot and shaft. A particularly apt comparison is preserved in the Louvre (Département des Objets d'Art).

The first scholar to take note of this bowl, mentioned in the Green Vault's 1725 Pretiosen inventory was Ernst Kris, in his 1929 publication on the lapidary art of the Italian Renaissance. He illustrated the bowl together with another one, dated to about 1569 and signed by Francesco Tortorino, that is in Vienna (Kunsthistorisches Museum, Kunstkammer). Kris based his attribution on the fact that the intaglio on the ground of both bowls follows a common idea and is similar to that on a crystal bowl in the form of a ship in the Prado (dated before 1569), cut by Annibale Fontana. The same basic motif may be observed in the shell-shaped bowl (dated between 1560 and 1570) in the Green Vault (inv. no. V 206). Rudolf Distelberger (1978) attributed the last cited example to Gasparo Miseroni: legendary inhabitants of the water sit or ride on waves. The contours of their minuscule bodies are raised above the surface of the smooth vessel walls, an aspect of these typical Milanese marine scenes of cut rock crystal.

Kris surmised that the present bowl in the Green Vault is a work from the Saracchi workshop in Milan. He proposed a date in the second half of the sixteenth century and saw stylistic analogies with the intaglios on the rock-crystal bowl in Madrid (Museo Nacional del Prado). While Paola Venturelli (1998) attributed the Dresden bowl to Gabriello Saracco, Letizia Arbeteta Mira (2001) evaluated it as an earlier work from the Saracchi workshop; her suggested date is 1570–80.
J.K.

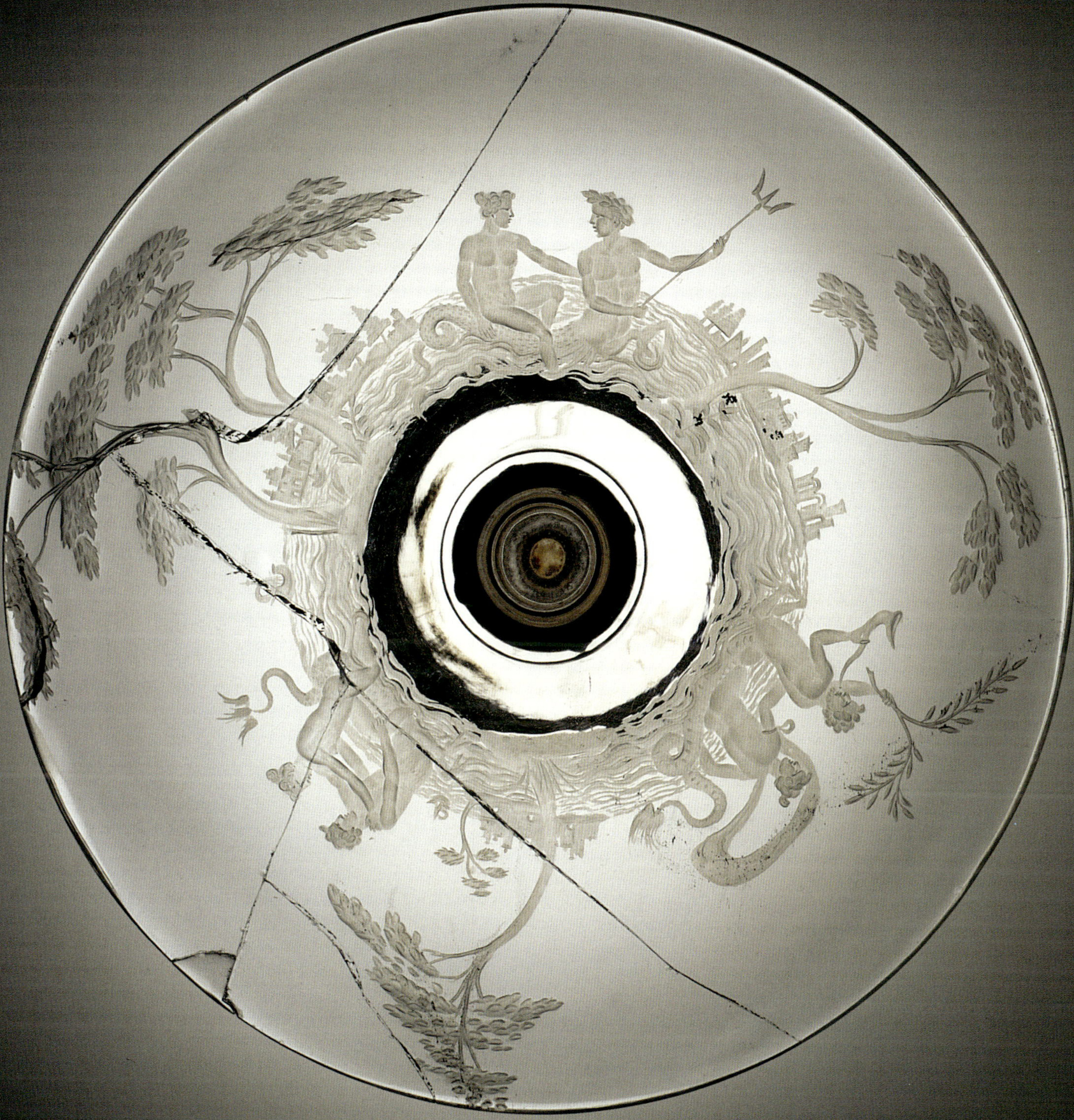

136 Ewer with a Handle with a Dragon's Head

Workshop of Girolamo Miseroni
Milan, ca. 1580–90
Rock crystal, gold, enamel
H. 8½ in. (21.5 cm, with handle)
First mentioned in the Pretiosen inventory 1725, fols. 274v–275r
Staatliche Kunstsammlungen Dresden, Grünes Gewölbe, inv. no. V 292
Lit.: Unpublished; but see Distelberger 1975, pp. 103f.; Arbeteta Mira 2001, cat. no. 69; Distelberger 2002, pp. 82, 85, 96, and cat. nos. 52–56, 75, 95, 99, 100

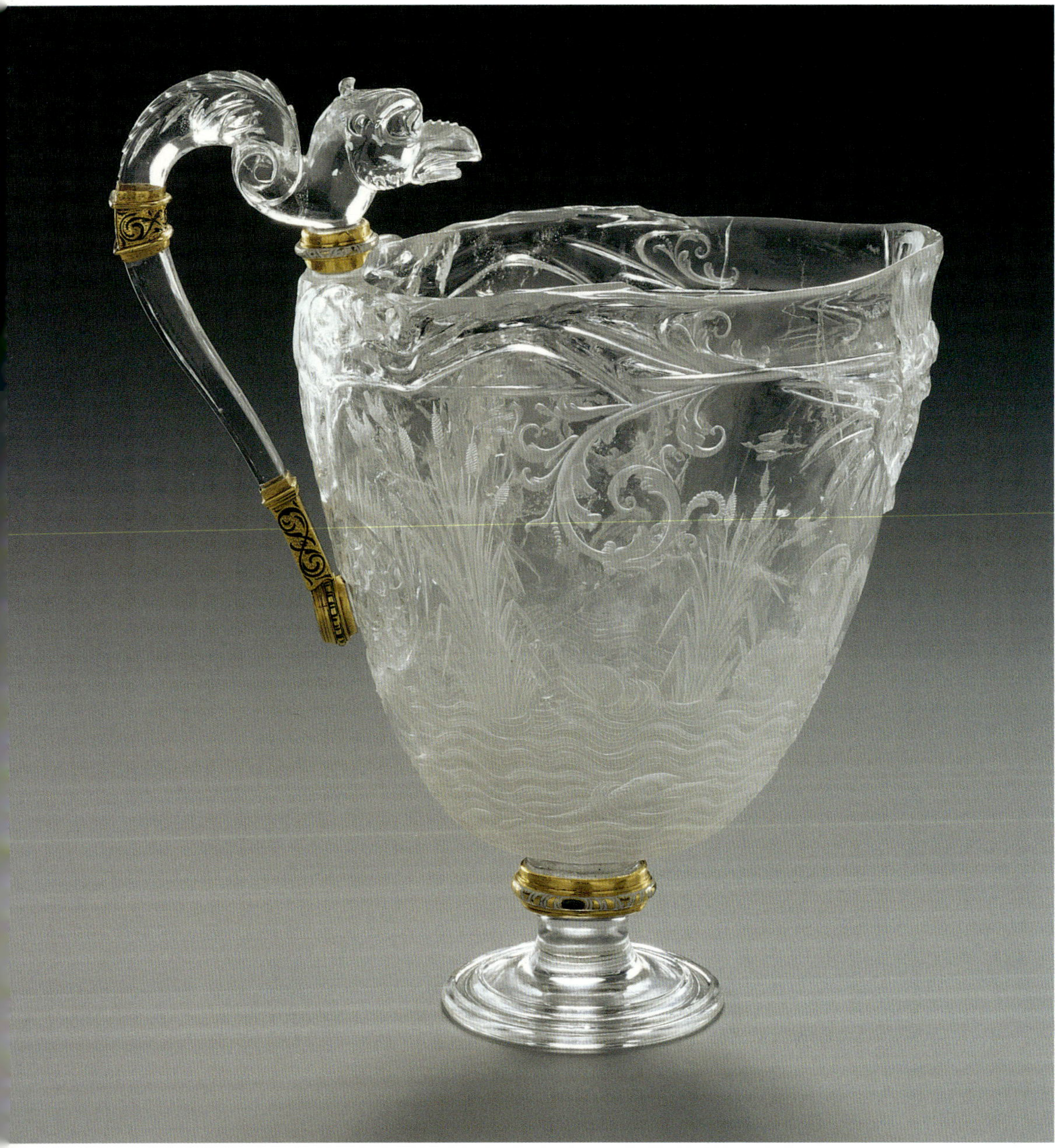

As was the custom in the leading Milanese lapidary workshops, this rock-crystal vessel was created in two separate but concordant work processes. The *arte grossa* master was responsible for grinding the vessel and for its subtly raised figural decoration. The back of a headless nude sea monster covers the body of the ewer below the handle. The legs of this fantastic creature take the shape of fish tails, and his muscular arms, terminating in elongated, pointed fins, embrace the top edge of the ewer and reach almost to the spout, which is adorned with a winged mask of a woman cut in relief.

The execution of the intaglio was reserved for the *arte minuta* master, whose abilities were more highly prized. He decorated the ewer's ground with a broad area of water that includes lively fish, a putto on a sea horse, and a winged water nymph. Tall marsh grasses and small birds create a natural setting and hide minute irregularities in the rock crystal. In contrast, the intaglio tendrils at the top of the ewer seem slightly alien to this maritime ambience. On the whole, the intaglio and the vessel shape are harmonious, a further manifestation of the Milanese origins of this ewer. Marine scenes were favored in the workshops of the Saracchi and the Miseroni (see cat. nos. 135, 137). The sea monster squatting on the back of the ewer is a variation of the so-called *mostro marino* type invented by Gasparo Miseroni (see also the shell-shaped lapis lazuli bowl in the Museo di Mineralogia in Florence). This attractive *arte grossa* motif was used by the younger generation of the Milanese Miseroni until the late sixteenth century.

The gold mounts of this ewer, some enameled with black tendrils and some enameled in white and blue, are equally typical of Milan. They may, for example, be observed on a ewer in Madrid (Museo Nacional del Prado) and on vessels from the workshop of Girolamo Miseroni preserved in Vienna (Kunsthistorisches Museum, Kunstkammer).
J.K.

137 Bowl in the Shape of a Galley

Workshop of the Miseroni (?)
Milan, ca. 1580–90
Rock crystal, silver-gilt, gold, enamel, rubies
H. 7½ in. (19.2 cm), L. 13¾ in. (35 cm)
First mentioned in the Pretiosen inventory 1725, fols. 241r–241v
Staatliche Kunstsammlungen Dresden, Grünes Gewölbe, inv. no. V 264
Lit.: Sponsel 1929, pp. 70f., 208 and plate 21; see also: Alcouffe 2001, cat. nos. 139–141, 143, 145–147 (refers to the mounts with enameled tendrils); Distelberger 2002, pp. 84f. with ill. 19 and cat. no. 47, cat. nos. 95–97, 108 (refers to the mounts with enameled tendrils and offers more comparisons)

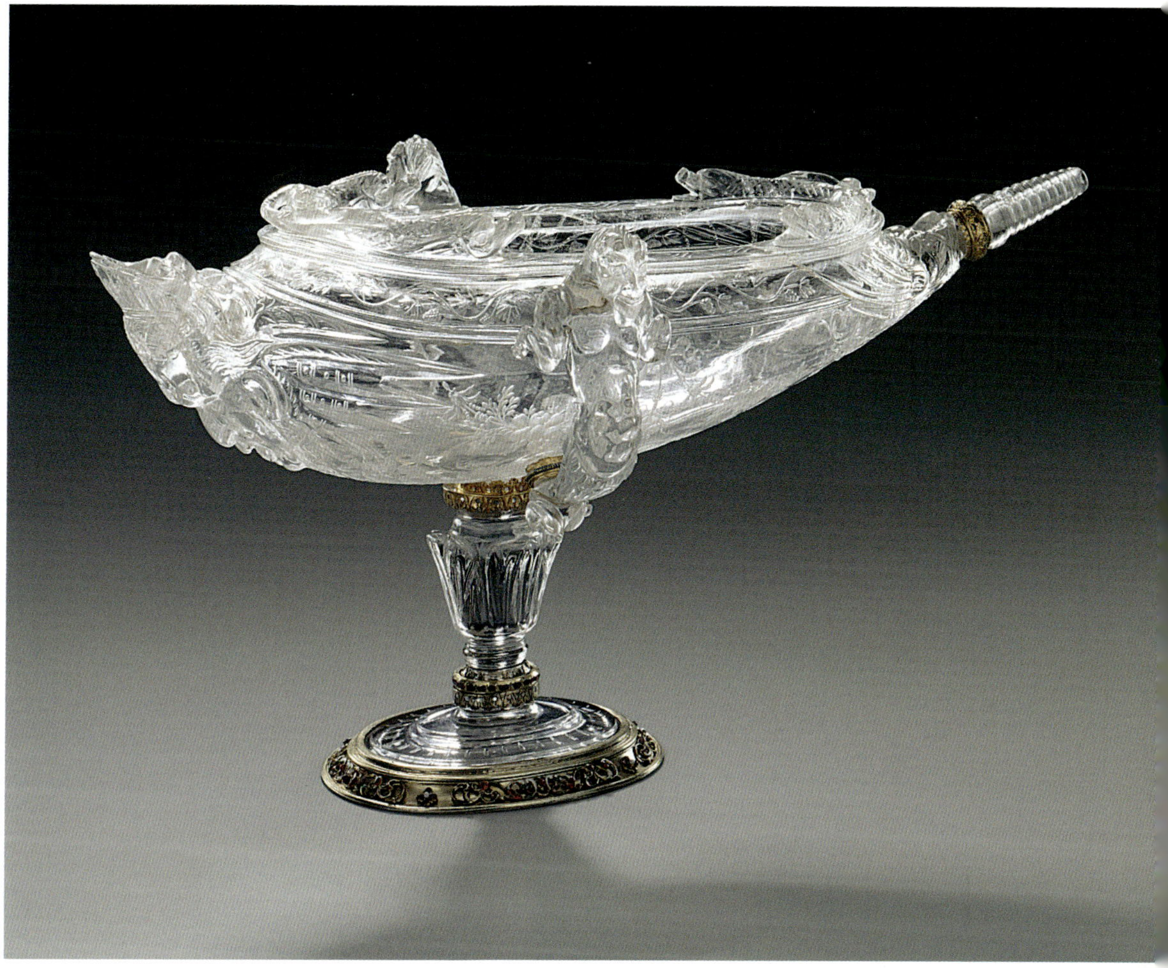

This display vessel originally belonged to a group of seven large "*Cristallene Galeeren*" (crystal galleys) mentioned in the Green Vault's Pretiosen inventory of 1725. Fantastic *arte grossa* motifs define its appearance. At the bow a pierced spine projects from the mouth of a winged fish head. The body of the fish is shaped like an acanthus leaf in relief raised and reaching almost to the bottom of the bowl. A female mask with wavy hair and, above it, another winged fish head, intended as the spout, are at the stern of the galley. The two handles, of solid rock crystal, are in the shape of monsters. Two pairs of dolphins, their tails intertwined, rest on the top edge of the bowl.

The ground of the keel is decorated with a water scene, including tritons and dolphins. The exquisite quality of the figural intaglios suggests the hand of Annibale Fontana, and the galley might just as plausibly have been made in the Saracchi workshop. The maritime scene on a crystal galley (private collection), illustrated by Rudolf Distelberger (2002) and evaluated as a late-sixteenth-century work from the Miseroni workshop, can also serve as a comparison.

The smooth mount of the foot with its applied gold and enameled tendrils is another reason for a Milanese place of origin for this piece and for its dating. The tendrils consist of numerous individual pieces, attached to the mount by very thin gold wires threaded through tiny holes drilled in the mount and soldered to it. This versatile type of mount was utilized in the late-sixteenth century for vessels from the workshop of Girolamo Miseroni; these mounts were sometimes augmented with rubies or pearls. Examples are three nephrite bowls, one in Stuttgart (Württembergisches Landesmuseum) and two in Vienna (Kunsthistorisches Museum, Kunstkammer). The same type of mount was still being used about 1610–15 in the workshop of Giovanni Ambrogio Miseroni. Applied enameled tendrils, mounted like the ones on our piece, may also be found on numerous late-sixteenth- and early-seventeenth-century foot mounts on rock crystal vessels, as, for example, on one in the Louvre (Département des Objets d'Art), and also on a rock-crystal ewer and basin garniture in Kassel (Sammlung Kunsthandwerk und Plastik im Hessischen Landesmuseum).
J.K.

138 Bowl with Mascaron

Motifs carved in relief and delicate intaglios create a perfect harmony in this rock crystal vessel. It came to Dresden's Green Vault on August 6, 1746, from the bequest of Duke Johann Adolf II of Saxony-Weißenfels. The opening of the bowl is the wide-open mouth of a sculpted mask. Monstrous wings spread evenly over both sides from a jagged central ridge covering the end of the bowl. The centers of this fantastic creature's eyes were originally adorned with garnets (now lost), which provided an attractive accent of color. In the Green Vault's Pretiosen inventory of 1819 the garnets are no longer mentioned.

Over the surface of the bowl are symmetrically incised tendrils enlivened with birds, dolphins, a cherub's head, two cornucopias with fruit, a graceful mask, and a delicate fruit garland. The type and the abundance of motifs, derived from both *arte grossa* and *arte minuta*, suggest that this bowl was almost certainly created in Milan. The mask with its wide-open mouth follows one of the four variants of the so-called *mostro marino* type invented by Gasparo Miseroni (see cat. nos. 136, 139). The incised tendrils with ethereal birds that seem to balance weightlessly are also typical of the Milanese decorative style for cut rock crystal, especially around 1580–1600.

Although this little bowl with a smooth shaft cannot be assigned to the spectacular creations produced by the Miseroni or the Saracchi, it represents a vessel type that was produced in Milan. A comparable object from the last quarter of the sixteenth century, published by Daniel Alcouffe (2001), may be found in the Louvre (Département des Objets d'Art).
J.K.

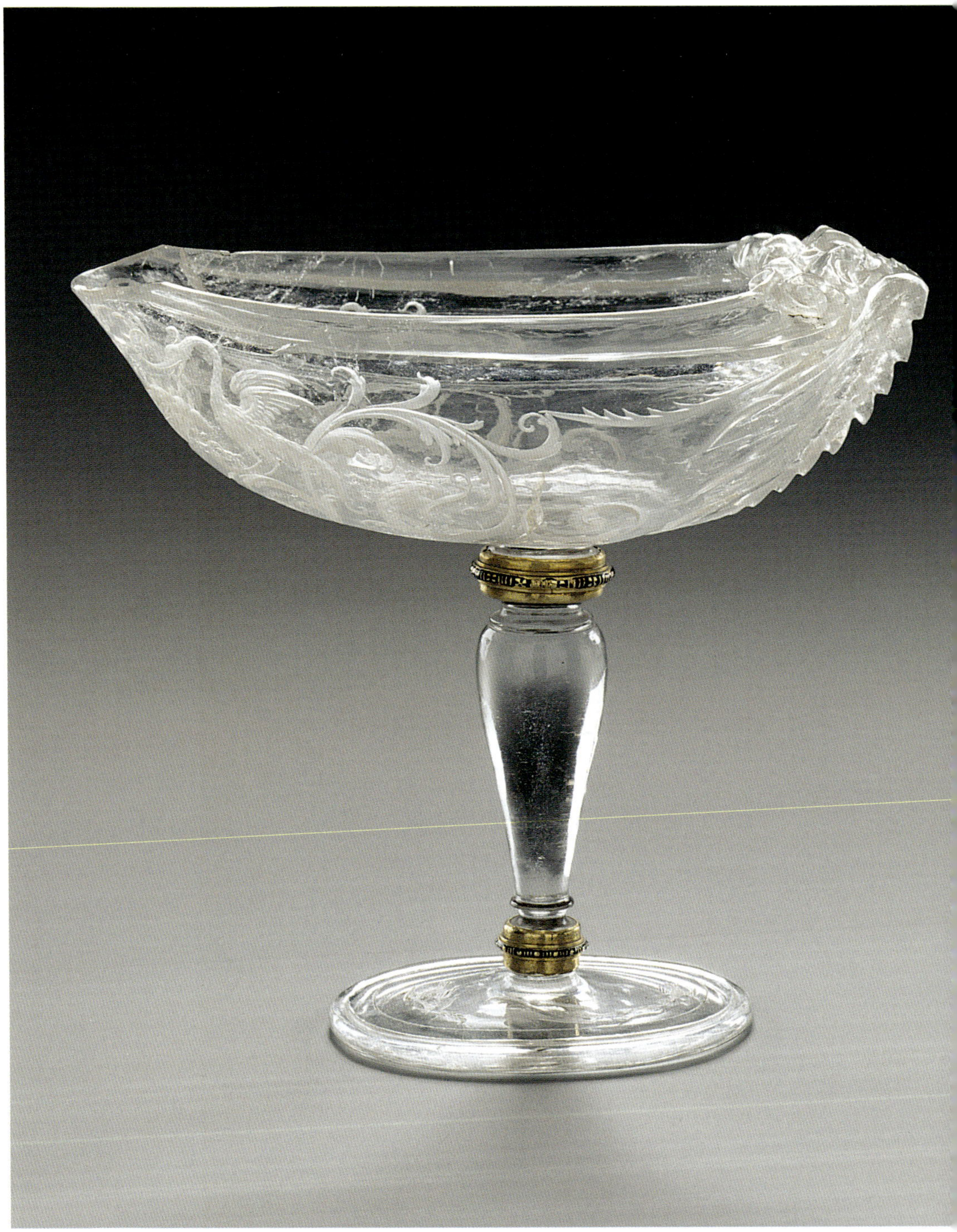

Milan, ca. 1590–1600
Rock crystal, gold, enamel, H. 5⅝ in. (14.3 cm)
Moved to the Green Vault, August 6, 1746, from the bequest of Duke Johann Adolf II of Saxony-Weißenfels
First mentioned in the Inventory of the Pretiosen Chamber in 1733, p. 281, no. 271 (addendum)
Staatliche Kunstsammlungen Dresden, Grünes Gewölbe, inv. no. V 283
Lit.: Unpublished; but see Alcouffe 2001, cat. no. 137; Distelberger 2002, p. 82 and cat. nos. 57, 96, 97, 102

139 Bowl in the Shape of a Mask

Smoky quartz vessels, which show their appealing coloration through fluctuating light and shadow, were precious rarities of the lapidary art. Emperor Rudolf II owned a venerable collection of fourteen pieces. Four of the bowls were taken to Prague "*von Mayland*" (from Milan) by a cousin of Ottavio Miseroni, active there as court artist since 1588. The principal of these pieces was the large mask bowl in the Wallace Collection (London). The three other bowls received their mounts later; these are preserved in Vienna (Kunsthistorisches Museum, Kunstkammer). Rudolf Distelberger (2002) ascribed the entire group to the workshop of Giovanni Ambrogio Miseroni, dating the vessels about 1610, and he hoped that similar works from the Miseroni workshop dated about 1600 might be found.

The Green Vault's massive smoky quartz bowl, whose top edge is in the shape of the wide-open mouth of a grotesque face, might possibly be such a discovery. At a single glance, the surface of the bowl reveals the brilliance of the soft, three-dimensional modeling and points to a comparable work in Vienna (Kunsthistorisches Museum/Kunstkammer). Although the smoky quartz bowl preserved there was not part of the shipment from Milan mentioned above, it is also listed in the Rudolfian Kunstkammer inventory, and it has recently been evaluated by Distelberger (2002) as a work from the workshop of Girolamo Miseroni. Like the Dresden bowl, the Vienna bowl follows the particular kind of *mostro marino* (see cat. no. 138) that Gasparo Miseroni invented. In contrast to the smoky quartz bowl in Vienna, with its sculpturally conceived design, the decoration on the Dresden bowl consists of four flat reliefs of bands of volutes cut with sharp contours. In between these, four equally spaced, frosted indentations can be seen, which were intended for the mount. The bowl never made it to a goldsmith and remained unfinished. This may explain why it is listed neither in the inventories of the Kunstkammer nor in the 1725 and 1733 Pretiosen inventories of the Green Vault. It can be assumed that this object was put aside and placed in the so-called "reserve," where damaged artworks were normally stored. Although the bowl was inventoried in 1819, this is the first time it has been published, and it is hoped that it will give rise to further discussions.

J.K.

In the style of the workshop
of Girolamo Miseroni
Milan, ca. 1600
Smoky quartz, H. 3⅝ in. (9.2 cm)
First mentioned in the Inventory of the Pretiosen Chamber in 1819, p. 185, no. 78
Staatliche Kunstsammlungen Dresden, Grünes Gewölbe, inv. no. V 300 ooo
Lit.: Unpublished; but see Bauer/Haupt 1976, p. 72 (nos. 1322–35, especially nos. 1328, 1331–34); Distelberger 1978, pp. 102–6; Hein 1985, p. 40 with ill. 8, Distelberger 2002 p. 82, 84, 245 with ill. 18, and cat. nos. 102, 105–107 (with further bibliography)

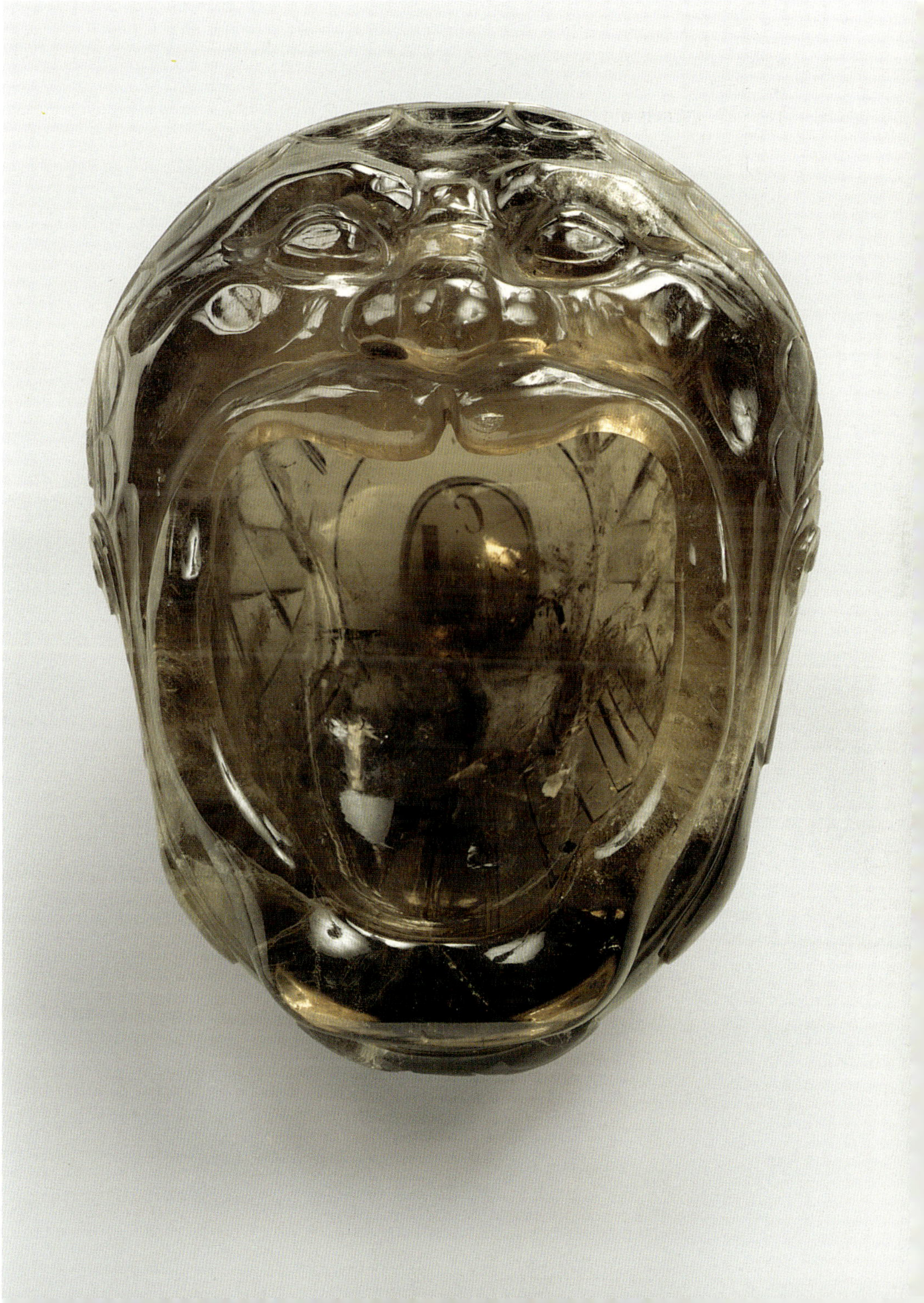

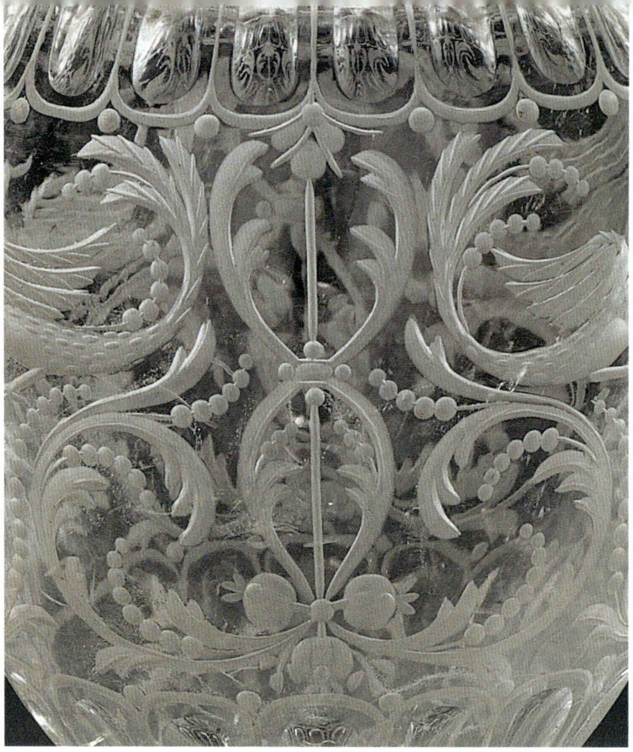

Milan, late 16th century
Rock crystal, silver-gilt, enamel
H. 7½ in. (19 cm)
First mentioned in the Pretiosen inventory 1725, fol. 282r
Staatliche Kunstsammlungen Dresden, Grünes Gewölbe, inv. no. V 286
Lit.: Guide Green Vault 1997, p. 100, no. 12; see also Alcouffe 2001, cat. nos. 133–136; Arbeteta Mira 2001, cat. nos. 53, 92; Distelberger 2002, cat. nos. 93, 99

140 Vase with Two Volute Handles

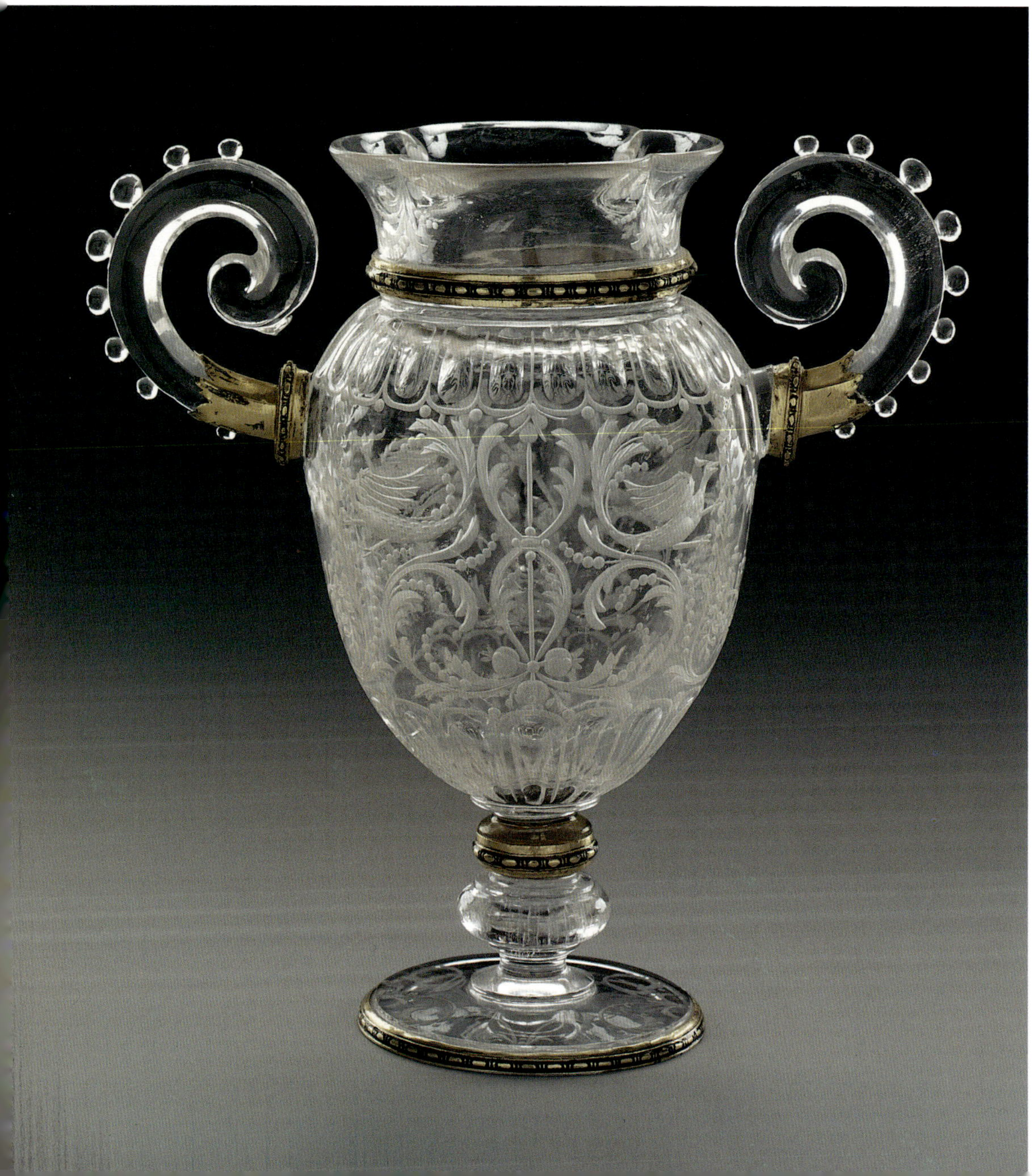

The shoulder and lower body of this slender, egg-shaped vase are decorated with fluting. A dense network of symmetrically arranged leafy tendrils with birds and miniature fruit garlands is incised over the central area of the body. The smooth, slightly concave neck of the vessel widens toward its quatrefoil, lipped edge; it is embellished with delicate fruit festoons. The volute-shaped handles, attached low on the shoulder, were each cut from a single piece of rock crystal together with the beads along their outer edge.

Several characteristics help ascribe this little-known piece to Milan. With its precisely cut tendril intaglios and the zones of fluting on shoulder and lower body, one of its closest relatives is a crystal vase in Vienna (Kunsthistorisches Museum, Kunstkammer), from the workshop of Girolamo Miseroni, dated to the late sixteenth century. Whereas the beaded handles are not usual features in works known to come from the Miseroni workshop, stylistically they connect this vessel to two flat Milanese rock-crystal bowls from the last quarter of the sixteenth century at the Louvre (Département des Objets d'Art). The black-enameled gold mounts further indicate a Milanese origin for our vase. While they are not among the most skillfully made enameled gold mounts, they are frequently observed in Milanese rock-crystal vessels dated to the second half of the sixteenth century, as is aptly illustrated by examples in the Louvre and the Prado.
J.K.

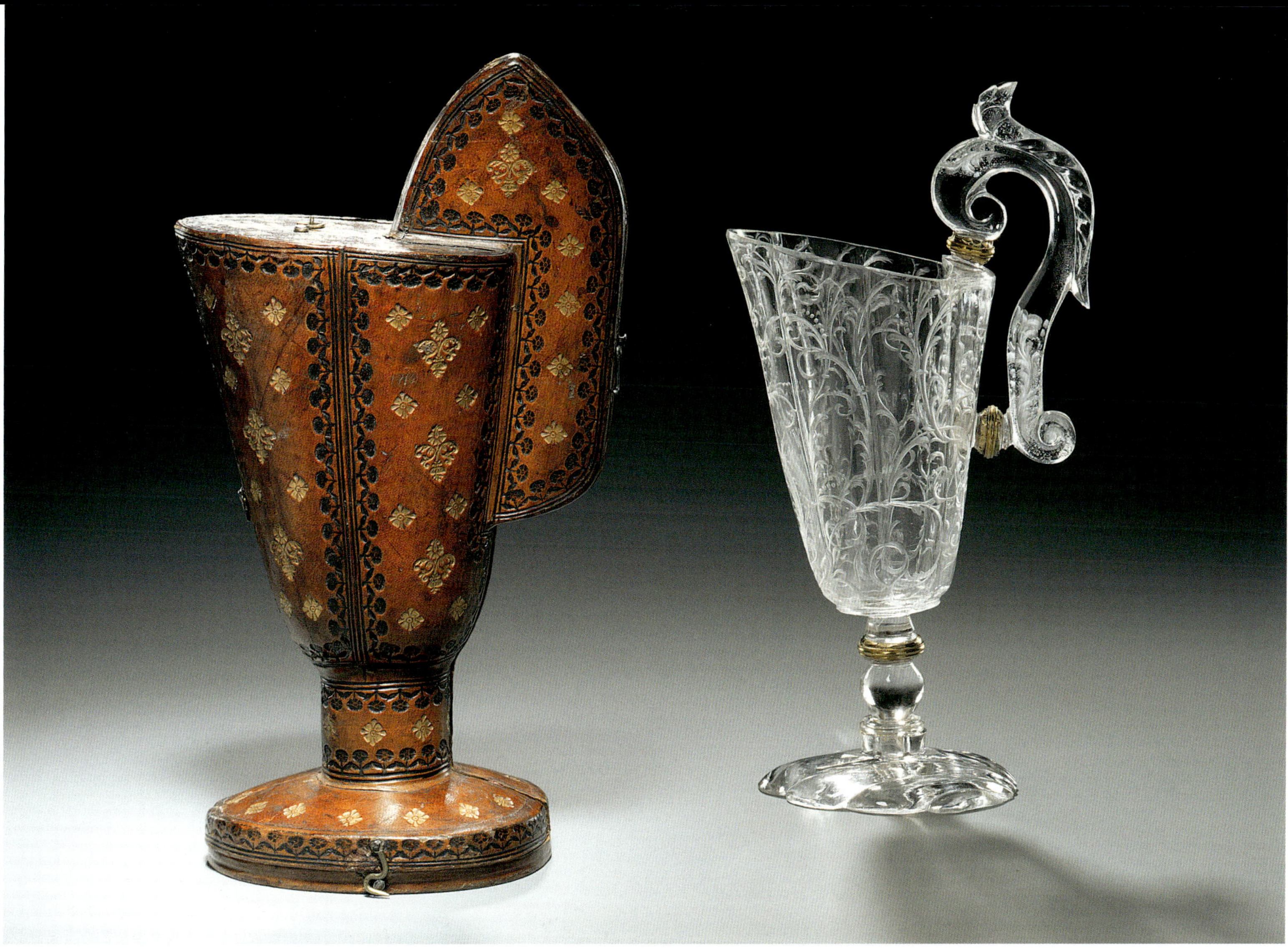

141 Ewer with Handle and Case

Milan, early 17th century
Rock crystal, silver-gilt
H. 10 in. (25.4 cm, with handle)
Case: wood, leather with gold and black stamping, lining of thin, bright red suede, brass hooks
H. 10¾ in. (27.3 cm)
First mentioned (without leather case) in Pretiosen inventory 1725, fol. 273v
Staatliche Kunstsammlungen Dresden, Grünes Gewölbe, inv. no. V 278
Lit.: Unpublished; but see Angulo Iñiguez 1989, cat. nos. 98, 99;
Lugano 1998, cat. no. 76
(Paola Venturelli with reference to the Milanese provenance of the leather case); Arbeteta Mira 2001, cat. nos. 96, 112 (with more leather cases); Alcouffe 2001, cat. no. 151; SächsHStA Dresden, Loc. 898, vol. II, fol. 20–23

Precisely executed incised tendrils symmetrically arranged over the thinly cut hexafoil body of this ewer result in a dense and particularly lively decorative rhythm. The handle is a sturdy volute, and the foot is cut in the shape of a shell.

There is no doubt as to the Milanese origin of this vessel. The question of its date is more difficult because this particular type of delicate tendril intaglio embellishment was widely and variously used on Milanese rock-crystal vessels until the first quarter of the eighteenth century. Two ewers in the Prado can be compared to our vessel, and they illustrate the challenges posed by the dating issues. While initially they were dated about 1600 (Angulo Iñiguez 1989), they have most recently been attributed (Arbeteta Mira 2001) to the Milanese workshop of Giovanni Battista Metellino and dated to the last quarter of the seventeenth century.

The case consists of a wood core in the shape of the ewer covered with leather. Gold-stamped ornamentation gives it a luxurious appearance. The inside is lined with soft suede dyed bright red. More than two hundred ivories, small precious objects, and almost all of the Italian rock-crystal works in the Green Vault have such custom-made cases. Presumably, numbers of the rock-crystal vessels reached their princely patron in Dresden with appropriate cases, while for other vessels, cases may have been made in Dresden. Documentary evidence shows that in 1699 and 1700, Christian Schneider delivered different leather cases "*zu vielen Sachen aus dem Grünen Gewölbe u. Kunst Cammer*" (to store many items from the Green Vault and the Kunstkammer) that Elector Friedrich August I of Saxony (since 1697, king of Poland) temporarily took with him to his royal residence in Warsaw. Leather cases were indispensable for storing the Treasury pieces and for their safe travel.
J.K.

142 Bowl with Lid and Two Spouts

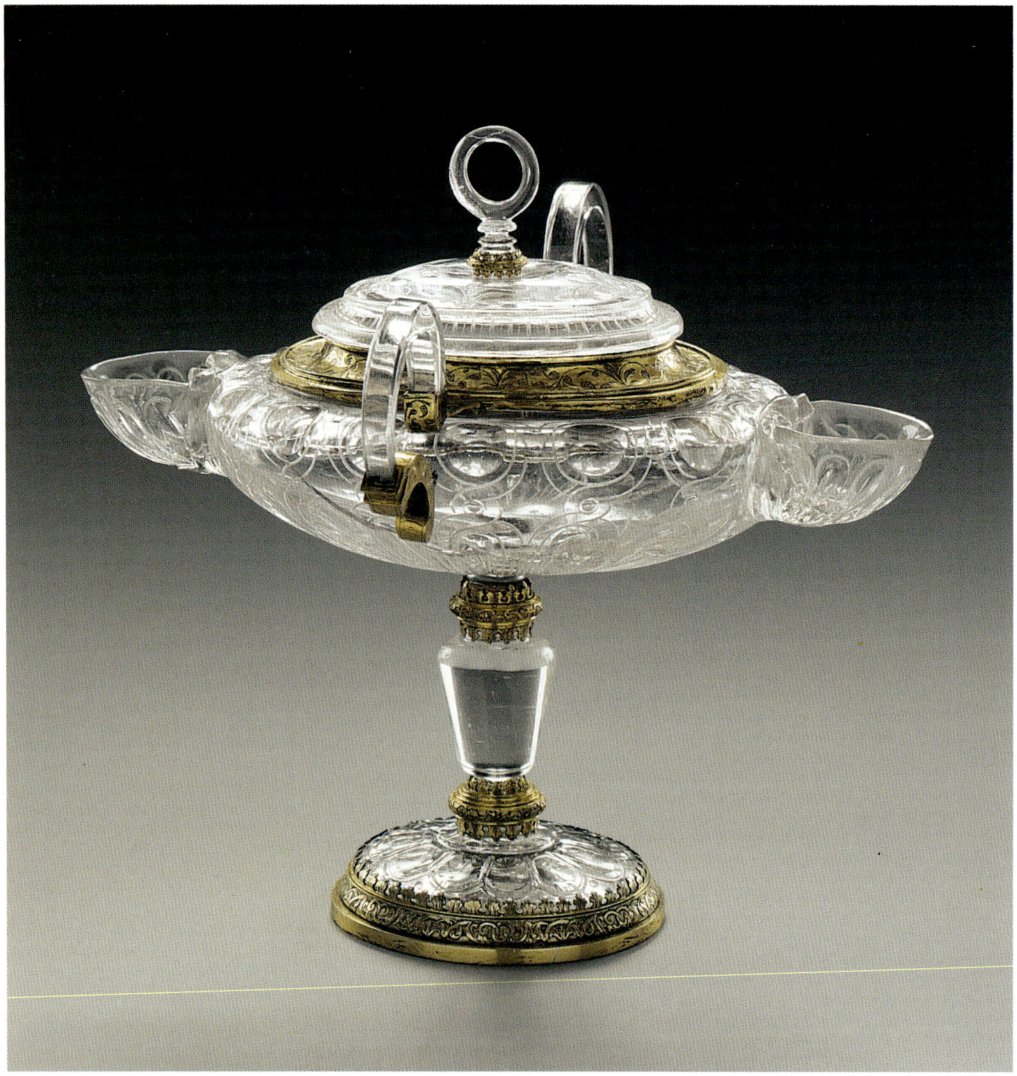

Bowl: workshop of the Miseroni (?)
Milan, ca. 1570
Foot, shaft, handle and mount:
Freiburg im Breisgau, ca. 1570
Rock crystal, silver-gilt
H. 8⅜ in. (21.4 cm, with lid)
First mentioned in the Pretiosen inventory 1725, fols. 254v–255r
Staatliche Kunstsammlungen Dresden,
Grünes Gewölbe, inv. no. V 368
Lit.: Unpublished; for information pertaining to the vessel type see: Lugano 1998, cat. no. 76 (Paola Venturelli); Distelberger 2002, cat. no. 62; Parma 2003, cat. no. 3.5.10 (Rudolf Distelberger); for information pertaining to the special stone cutting decoration entitled *Pfeifen* see: Distelberger 2002, cat. nos. 41, 62, 93, 99, 100; for information pertaining to the Freiburg mounts see: Irmscher 1997, especially cat. nos. 1, 35; for information pertaining to the models for the ornaments see: Berliner / Egger 1981, vol. I, p. 64, no. 564, vol. 2, ill. 564

right
South German (Freiburg?),
first quarter of the 17th century
Rock crystal, silver-gilt
H. 2⅞ in. (7.2 cm)
First mentioned in the Pretiosen inventory 1725, fol. 247v
Staatliche Kunstsammlungen Dresden,
Grünes Gewölbe, inv. no. V 256
Lit.: Unpublished; but see: Schwarzacher 1984, pp. 126–29, 142; Irmscher 1997, p. 54 and cat. no. 14, Idar-Oberstein 1998, cat. nos. 29–32; Ebner 2002, cat. nos. 21, 33 (Salzburg rock crystal from the last quarter of the 17th century)

As revealed in the 1725 Pretiosen inventory of the Green Vault, this bowl owes its appearance to several workshops. The body with two spouts, made of flawless rock crystal, relates to a form invented by Gasparo Miseroni. The spouts protruding from the narrow sides are not just decorative: they cover circular holes drilled into the wall of the vessel, and so could have served a practical purpose. The precisely cut fluting on the bowl and the spouts also points to Milan. Although frequently used, this usually occurs in combination with incised tendril figural decoration, for instance in works by Francesco Tortorino and on vessels from the workshops of Gasparo and Girolamo Miseroni.

The rest of the bowl's rock-crystal parts (foot, smooth shaft, handle, and lid) are additions, possibly made in Freiburg im Breisgau. Stylistic characteristics of the silver-gilt mounts, which are certainly not of Milanese origin, argue in favor of this tentative attribution. The mount around the lip and the fittings for the crystal handle were decorated with finely engraved, once blackened foliate motifs. Such engraving derives directly from examples by the copperplate engraver Franz Brun, datable to about 1560. Such models, plentiful and widely distributed, were also used in Freiburg, as demonstrated by the mount on a rock-crystal goblet by the "Master with the Half Moon" in Munich (Bayerisches Nationalmuseum), and by another very similar rock-crystal goblet, dating about 1560/70, in New York (The Metropolitan Museum of Art). The mounts of the delicate foliate wreaths that embellish shaft and foot—although an odd contrast to the engraved mount of the lip—also indicate a Freiburg im Breisgau manufacture in the third quarter of the sixteenth century.
J.K.

143 Flat Bowl in Milanese Style

This quatrefoil bowl is based on Milanese prototypes. The symmetrical tendril decoration points toward this place of origin, where it frequently appears in conjunction with motifs of birds with long plumage (see cat. nos. 138, 140). Certain elements of the intaglios are direct imitations of nature, but while faithful copies were intended, the results are not overly successful. They are altogether different from the delicate and highly synthetic fruit garlands executed on Milanese vessels.

An emblematic motif was cut into the bottom of the ovoid bowl. It depicts two winged blindfolded cupids facing each other. Each holds an arrow in the left hand and a heart in the right. The oval crystal foot is adorned with stylized flowers with leaves around them. The plain silver-gilt ring mount is rather coarsely worked.

Despite the bowl's pleasing appearance overall, details of the cutting technique do not show the level of precision known in Milanese vessels. Freiburg im Breisgau took up the enormous artistic challenge of imitating Milanese-style crystal vessels even though facet cutting was the city's specialty. This was primarily an attempt to satisfy the taste of the times and the requests of patrons. Despite the efforts of scholars (Schwarzacher 1984, Irmscher 1997), it has so far not been possible to determine with any certainty to what extent Freiburg produced intaglio embellishment on rock-crystal vessels based on Milanese models.
J.K.

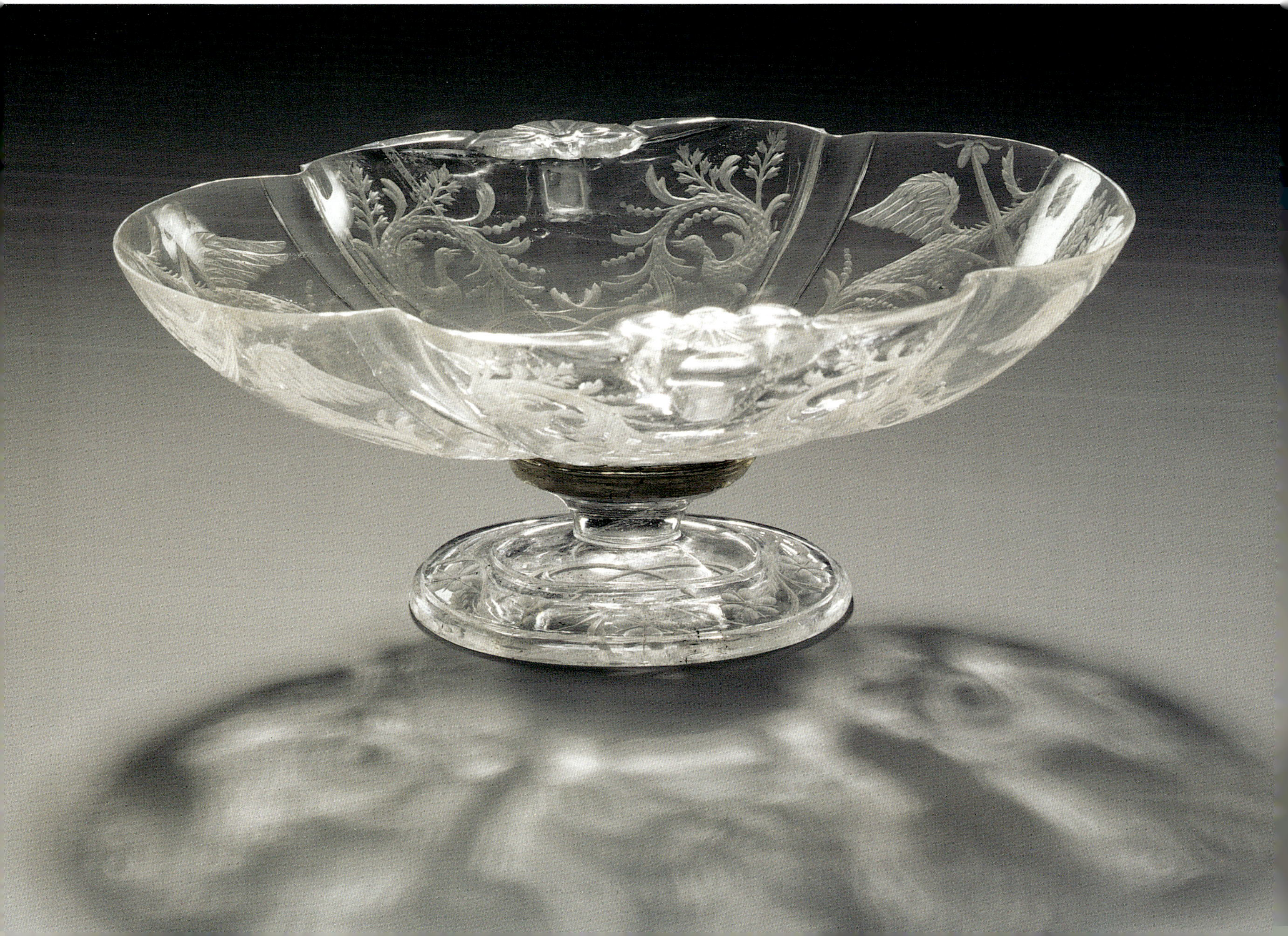

144 Bowl on a Dolphin

Ottavio Miseroni, Prague, ca. 1605–10
Rock crystal, gold, enamel
H. 5⅛ in. (13 cm)
First mentioned in the Pretiosen inventory 1725, fols. 245r–245v
Staatliche Kunstsammlungen Dresden, Grünes Gewölbe, inv. no. V 310

Lit.: Sponsel 1929, p. 224 and plate 29; Guide Green Vault 1997, p. 139, no. 4; see also Distelberger 1978, pp. 134, 145 with ill. 126, 127; Distelberger 2002, p. 246 (for information about the "soft style" of Ottavio Miseroni), p. 248 with footnote 12 and cat. nos. 151, 153, 165, 167, 168

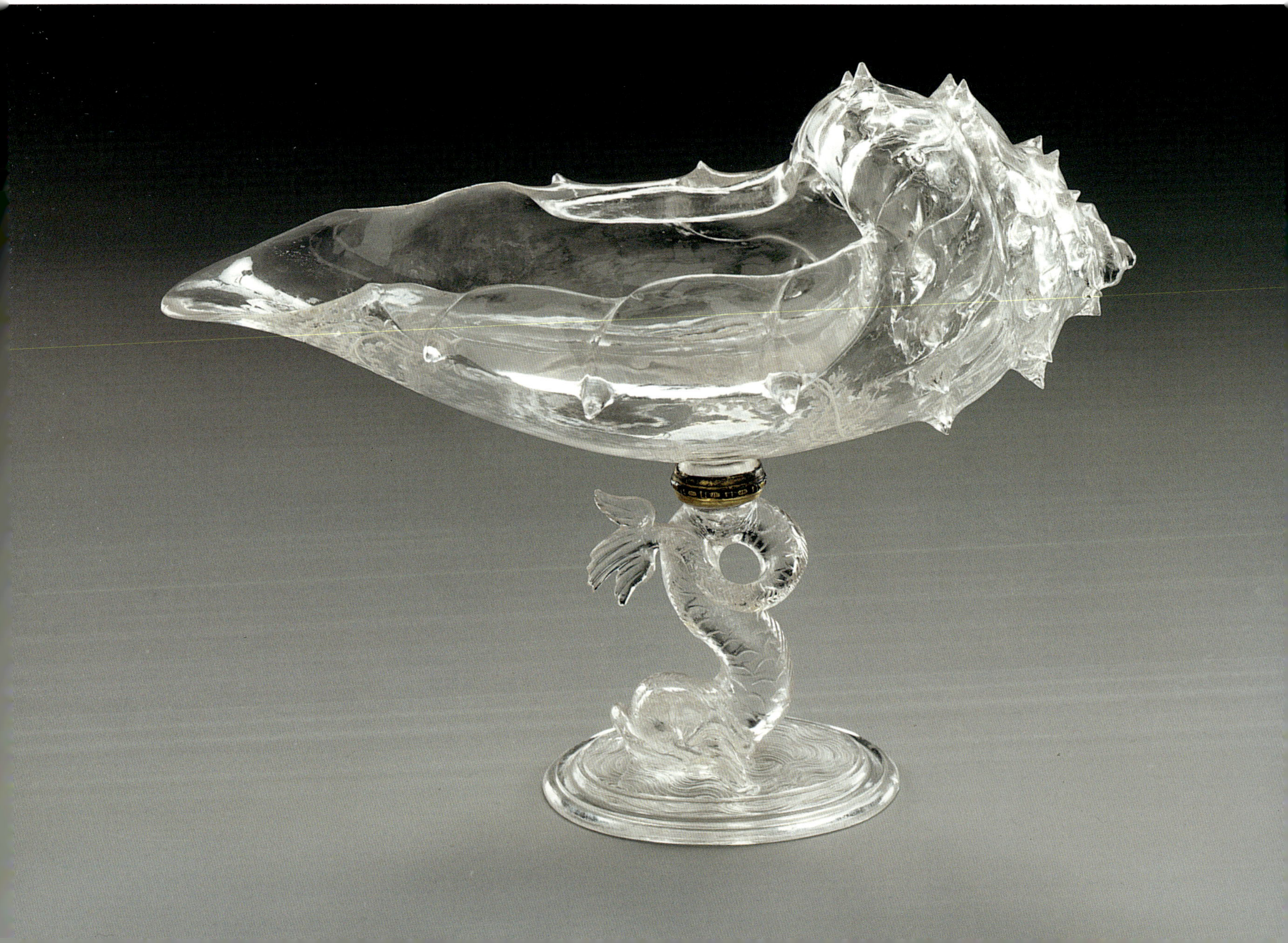

145 Bowl

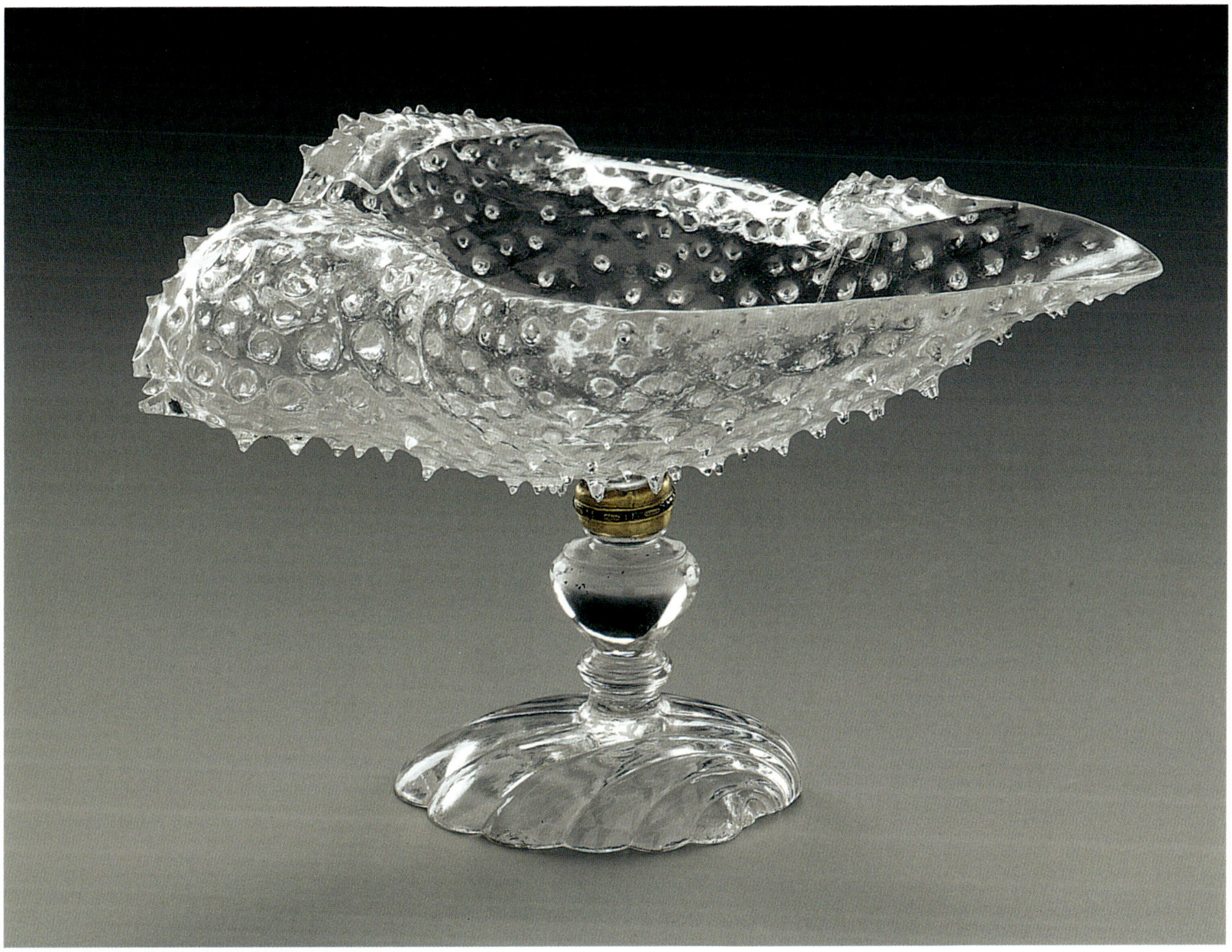

Ottavio Miseroni
Prague, ca. 1605–10
Rock crystal, gold, enamel
H. 4⅛ in. (10.5 cm)
First mentioned in the Pretiosen inventory 1725, fol. 245v
Staatliche Kunstsammlungen Dresden, Grünes Gewölbe, inv. no. V 319
Lit.: Guide Green Vault 1997, p. 139, no. 7; see also Distelberger 1978, pp. 134, 145 with ill. 126, 127

Snail shells and seashells served as the models for these two exotic decorative bowls. The abstract imitation of these natural maritime wonders presupposed virtuosic abilities in the precise realm of cutting rock crystal. After the basic shape was cut, the walls of the vessel were still rather thick. In subsequent steps, minute bits were cut from the surface until the bowls reached their final form. While this laborious technique entailed substantial losses of the precious raw material, it led to fascinating results. The bowls have extraordinarily thin walls, and they are consequently very light. Apart from some delicate ivy tendrils on the ground of one bowl (cat. no. 144) there is no intaglio decoration. These objects, which required intricate grinding work, give the impression of having been easily formed as though from wax and the hardness of the rock crystal overcome effortlessly.

These *arte grossa* masterworks from the Green Vault have no comparable vessels in the sizable collections of rock crystal preserved in Paris, Madrid, and Munich. Since their attribution by Jean Louis Sponsel (1929), they have been considered Milanese. However, their attributes point to the "soft style" that characterized the lapidary work of Ottavio Miseroni in the years 1600–12. From 1588, he was active in Prague at the imperial court of Emperor Rudolf II, where he produced mostly vessels from colored, opaque stones such as jasper, agate, nephrite, or heliotrope. Since that was his strength and since his rock-crystal production was not nearly as extensive as that of the Miseroni working in Milan (Ottavio temporarily employed young crystal cutters from Milan in his Prague workshop), knowledge of his rock-crystal oeuvre is not yet sufficiently researched. Rudolf Distelberger (1978) suggested Ottavio Miseroni as the author of two delicate little rock crystal bowls in Vienna (Kunsthistorisches Museum, Kunstkammer). Their walls are equally as thin and their modeling equally as soft as the two bowls from the Green Vault shown here. In their appearance, they, too, cannot be confused with Milanese pieces.
J.K.

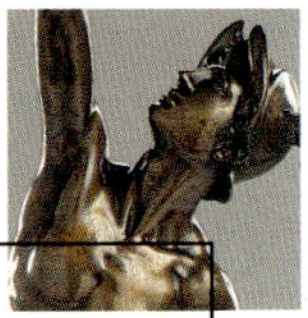

Bronze Sculpture

Antje Scherner

In the summer of 1587, the Dresden art scholar Gabriel Kaltemarckt dedicated a treatise to the then-twenty-seven-year-old Elector Christian I of Saxony. Addressing the question of "*wie eine Kunst-Cammer aufzurichten seyn möchteo*"[1] (how a Kunstkammer might be established) and obviously impressed by princely galleries in Italy, he suggested that the collection should be divided into three sections: sculptures, paintings, and curiosities. As an aid in acquiring sculptures and paintings, Kaltemarckt furnished his princely reader with extensive lists of important artists, arranged by period and nationality. The sculpture section of the Kunstkammer might, for instance, contain works by such artists as Donatello, Bandinelli, Michelangelo, and Giambologna in addition to ancient examples and plaster casts. Kaltemarckt emphasized that works of this kind were to be found not only in Italy but also in Germany, especially in Austria and Bavaria, as well as in the Augsburg-based Fugger collections.[2] Although he offered specific proposals concerning how the selected pieces were to be acquired and transported over the Alps, his treatise had no noticeable effect on the electoral collection.

Kaltemarckt's discourse might therefore seem negligible, if it were not for the canon of an ideal collection that he presented therein. His text gives a fair idea of the works available to an ambitious art-lover in Renaissance Dresden. Both Kaltemarckt's recommendations and the private collection of the electoral Saxon art supervisor Giovanni Maria Nosseni (who died in 1620) illustrate that art collections comprising works of important masters were also feasible in Dresden. In addition to copies after Titian, Tintoretto, and others, Nosseni owned originals by Parmigianino and Salviati, as well as small bronzes, terracottas, and plaster casts of sculptures by Giambologna, Carlo di Cesare, and Adriaen de Vries; he also possessed replicas of ancient artworks.[3] The inventory of his estate suggests what an artist with collecting ambitions was capable of bringing to the city on the river Elbe. It reveals the particular preferences of the Saxon sovereigns, who unlike their counterparts in Munich or Prague, did not make special efforts to establish a collection of sculpture or works from antiquity.[4]

An inventory drawn up by art chamberlain David Uslaub in 1587, only months after the completion of Kaltemarckt's treatise, lists, among approximately 9,500 Kunstkammer objects, exactly eleven small sculptures or sculptural groups made of bronze, alabaster, or terracotta.[5] The most significant were not electoral purchases but came to Dresden as gifts from Italian princes. Among them are the alabaster replicas of Michelangelo's *Four Times of Day* from the Medici tombs in Florence that presumably came to Dresden before 1574 as gifts from Cosimo I de' Medici.[6] The three Giambologna bronzes—*Mercury* (cat. no. 146), *Nessus and Deianira* (cat. no. 147), and *Sleeping Nymph with Satyr* (cat. no. 148)—were given to the collection in 1587 by the grand duke of Tuscany.[7] Further presents to the elector included Antonio Filarete's equestrian statuette of Marcus Aurelius (see ill. opposite) given by Guglielmo Gonzaga, duke of Mantua, and Giambologna's bronze statuette of Mars (ill. p. 270), sent by the artist himself.[8] These works were exhibited in the *Reißgemach* (Drawing Room), the Kunstkammer's most important space, and the important donors are meticulously mentioned in all inventories—facts signifying that they were held in high regard. This is also underscored by the creative imagination of Nosseni, who had them replicated in edible materials for the 1607 wedding banquet of Johann Georg I and Magdalena Sibylla of Brandenburg.[9]

Yet, until 1619, the electors made few efforts to further the holdings of small sculpture listed in 1587 in any significant way. Subsequent acquisitions included the 1589 purchase of three bronze sculptures by the Augsburg artist Hans Reisinger,[10] some small terracotta figures that no longer exist, a crucifix and a Mercury of alabaster, as well as two epitaphs. Significant additions may be noted, however, in the category of wax miniatures, some of which were made by the Dresden-based wax modeler and medalist Nikolaus Schwabe.[11] Nevertheless, it appears that most acquisitions of small sculptures were incidental, unlike those of ivories turned on the lathe or goldworks, which the electors specifically commissioned from their own court artists or bought through art agents. Only with the purchase of Nosseni's collection in 1622 is it possible to speak of a substantial expansion of the sculpture collection. Key works such as the *Faun and Nymph* by Adriaen de Vries (cat. no. 150),

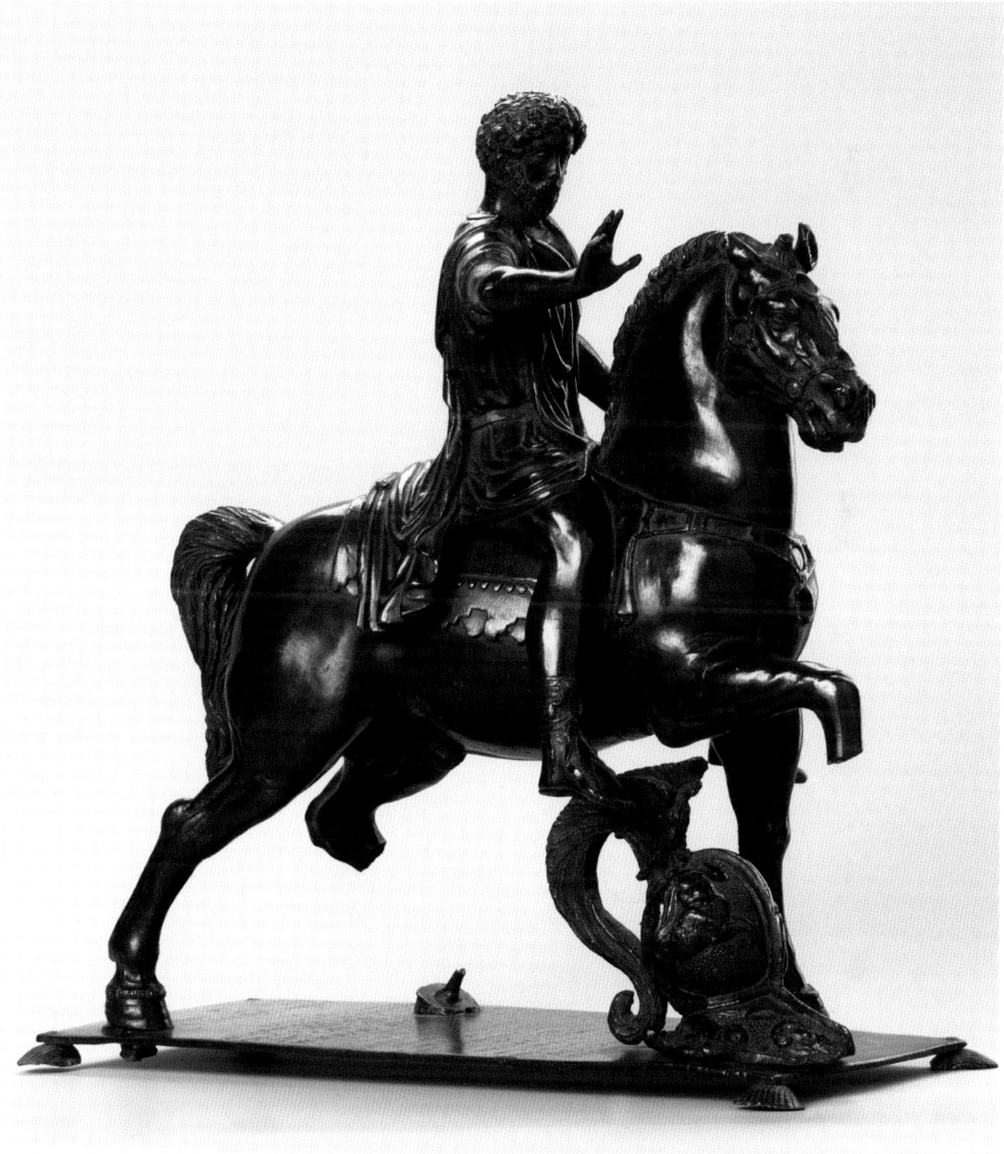

Marcus Aurelius
Antonio Averlino, called Filarete
circa 1440–45
Bronze
H. 14⅝ in. (37.1 cm),
Staatlichen Kunstsammlungen
Dresden,
inv. no. H^4 155/37

1. See also Holzhausen 1933, pp. 46–49, Gutfleisch/Menzhausen 1989.
2. Gutfleisch/Menzhausen 1989, p. 18. It is almost certain that Nosseni was largely responsible for Kaltemarckt's suggestions. As early as September 1586, he advised Elector Christian I to ask Francesco I de' Medici, grand duke of Tuscany, for works by the leading Florentine masters. See also Marx 2000b, pp. 261f., 268, 279f. appendix I, doc. 5.
3. Cf. the inventory of Nosseni's estate, SächsHStA Dresden, Loc. 8693/23 and Hantzsch 1903.
4. Emperor Rudolf II owned an extensive collection of small sculptures that included works by Giambologna and Adriaen de Vries (see also Bauer/Haupt 1976, pp. 95–104). The 1598 inventory of the ducal Munich Kunstkammer documents a large collection of sculptures and antiques that comprised originals, plaster replicas, and small bronzes (see also Fickler [Diemer 1598] among others position 2274 [2232]ff.). The Munich inventory calls into question the arguments put forward in Marx 2000b, pp. 269f., suggesting that Kaltemarckt's proposals were not successful because of the princely collectors' concentration on Principalstücke (originals). Even though Nosseni's collection contained few originals, as its cataloguers pointed out shortly after his death (Hantzsch 1903, p. 158), the vast majority of the material was purchased in 1622 for the Kunstkammer.
5. Inventory 1587, fol. 65v–66v. Beyond that, mention is made of ten "*Contrafect von Gibß in schwarzen runden Ringen*" (plaster objects mounted by black, round rings) and "*in Birnbaumen Ringen eingefast*" (mounted with pear wood rings) as well as five "*Figuren von Gibß*" (plaster figures) with identical mounts. These are likely plaster medallions. See also 1587 Kunstkammer inventory, fol. 70v–71r.
6. This provenance may be deduced thanks to a later pencil note in the 1640 Kunstkammer, fol. 514r: "*vier alabaster Bildlein* [...] *liegend* [...] *so von den Weltberühmten [?] Michael Angelo Buonarotta gefertigt [und] von Cosimo Grosherzog von Florenz S. Churffl.* [...]. *ubersandt worden*" (four small alabaster images [...] made by [...] the world-famous Michael Angelo Buonarotta [and] presented to Our Prince lectors by Cosimo, grand duke of Florence). Marx 2000b, p. 219, surmised that, with reference to SächsHStA Dresden, Loc. 8517/5 fol. 1r, this was a gift of the duke of Savoy, Emanuele Filiberto, of 1576. In the letter in question, the duke writes of "[...] *Tabulas quattuor lapideas, iunctis earundem–opportuni ornamentis construi feci,* [...]." The term "lapideas" (stone board) in itself rules out that they could be statuettes; in addition, no mention is made of either the artist or any theme.
7. For a conjectural valuation of these gifts see also Marx 2000b, p. 252, source material ibid. pp. 285–90 App. II, doc. 3 and 4.
8. Giambologna's *Mars* could have already come to Dresden in 1584; see also Dombrowski 2000, p. 90, footnote 63. Marx implicitly contradicts Dombrowski in her statements: Marx 2000b, p. 271.
9. Marx 2000a, p. 28. Among the ten bronzes reproduced were *Nessus and Dejanira*, *Sleeping Nymph with Satyr*, and a third unidentified piece from the Kunstkammer, as well as small bronzes from the Nosseni collection.
10. These served as models for wood objects exhibited on the two buffets erected in the New Stable (ill. p. 207). They may even have been acquired for this purpose; see also Holzhausen 1933, p. 83.
11. See also Holzhausen/Watzdorf, 1931, pp. 240–57 and the 1595 Kunstkammer inventory, fol. 92, and the 1619 Kunstkammer inventory, fol. 313r–317v.

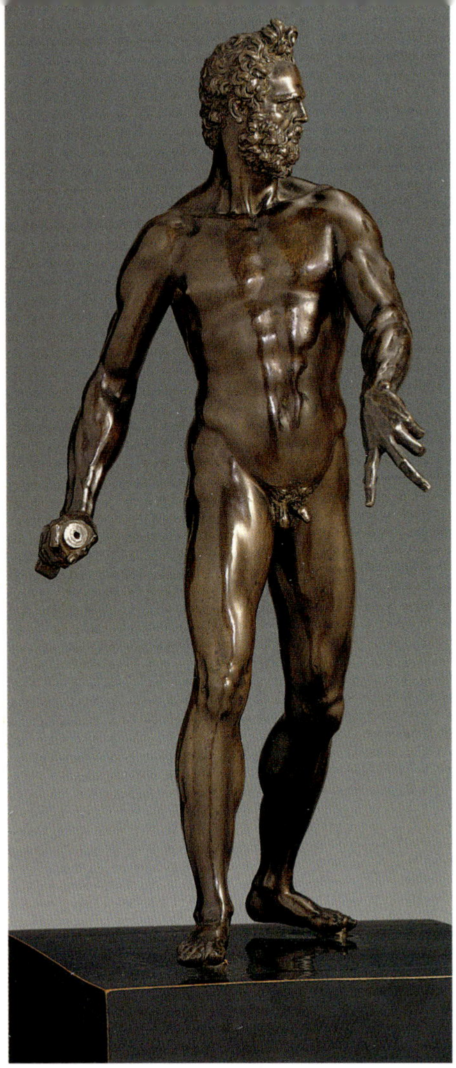

Mars
Giambologna, before 1587
Bronze, H. 15⅝ in. (39.6 cm)
Gift of the artist to Prince
Elector Christian I of Saxony,
Bayer AG Collection, Leverkusen

as well as examples by Carlo di Cesare and Giambologna, thus came to the electoral Kunstkammer.[12]

The electors' hesitance in collecting small bronzes should not be regarded as stemming from a lack of interest. Elector August, and especially his son Christian I, initiated numerous building projects in Dresden and Saxony, many of which entailed a great deal of sculptural ornamentation. In 1590 Christian I commissioned the Florentine Carlo di Cesare, a student of Giambologna who had previously worked with his master at the imperial court in Vienna and at the Munich court, as well as with the Fuggers and the grand duke of Florence, to work on the Wettin burial chapel in Freiberg Cathedral. Di Cesare, also made a bust of Christian I (cat. no. 2), specialized—like most of Giambologna students—in large-scale plaster, terracotta, and especially bronze sculpture. He was also capable of producing technically complex casts of large bronzes.[13] During the course of only three years, from his 1590 arrival in Dresden and his departure for Florence and Munich in 1593, the Italian created twenty monumental bronze sculptures and more than forty princely plaster portraits. But the elector's Kunstkammer did not contain a single small bronze firmly attributed to him.[14] This alone gives rise to the supposition that Christian I's priority was the commission of large, impressive stately sculptures rather than the creation of a sculpture collection based on Kaltemarckt's theorems.[15]

Nevertheless, from today's vantage point, Dresden's collection of Renaissance bronzes is important primarily because of the acquisitions made under Christian I. That works by Giambologna, employed as the grand duke of Tuscany's court sculptor, were presented to Dresden during the artist's lifetime by his princely employer and the sculptor himself suggests that they were either by his own hand or at least authorized by him, distinguishing them from the plethora of extant replicas. The situation is comparable with regard to the works by Adriaen de Vries. Nosseni, who collected these, appears to have obtained pieces during a personal meeting with the artist, for unchased casts—the term applied to the *Faun and Nymph* (cat. no. 150) when it entered the electoral collections from Nosseni's estate—were not regular trade items.[16] Nosseni could have met de Vries at least twice: on his 1588 trip to Italy—when the young sculptor first worked in the Milan studio of Pompeo Leoni and then at the duke of Savoy's court in Turin—and in 1608, when Nosseni collaborated with de Vries on the mausoleum in Stadthagen.

Although the acquisition of the remaining Renaissance bronzes in this exhibition cannot be verified prior to the year 1640, the works are mentioned, at the very latest, in the collection inventories by 1726. Therefore, they can still be dated to the seventeenth and early eighteenth centuries. These objects are thus firmly tied to the œuvre of Giambologna, probably the most important sculptor of the time around 1600. Antonio Susini, thought to be responsible for the cast of Giambologna's *Striding Horse* (cat. no. 153), was a close associate of the master. Hans Reichle, until now considered the author of *Allegory of Spring* (cat. no. 151), appears to have come to Florence at the recommendation of the Munich court, and he worked in Giambologna's studio until 1595.

The exhibited group of Renaissance bronzes therefore shows not only Giambologna's masterful accomplishments but also the influence of his work on North Alpine art. This great Italian was pivotal in forming the artistic sensibilities of an entire generation of sculptors and left a lasting imprint on the leading courts of Europe, including that of Dresden.

12. For Nosseni's estate see also Hantzsch 1903.
13. The attempts of Emperor Rudolf II to lure away students of Giambologna from other contracts illustrate how much Italian bronze sculptures were prized in German courts at the end of the sixteenth century. In 1591, Rudolf approached Christian I, without success, for a two-week "loan" of di Cesare. In 1601, he called Adriaen de Vries to Prague. For Carlo di Cesare del Palago see most recently Diemer 2004 (forthcoming). I thank Dorothea Diemer for letting me use the relevant passages of her manuscript, as well as for her critical review of this essay.
14. Nosseni, in contrast, owned numerous small sculptures by di Cesare; see also Hantzsch 1903 and most recently Diemer 2004 (forthcoming).
15. This suggestion is further supported by the fact that Christian I ignored Nosseni's 1586 proposal to ask the grand duke of Tuscany for works of famous sculptors. Instead, the elector inquired about obtaining sculpting tools for those working on decorating Saxon churches (Marx 2000b, pp. 261–62, 279–81, App. I, doc. 5 and 6).
16. Augsburg 2000, p. 195, cat. no. 6.

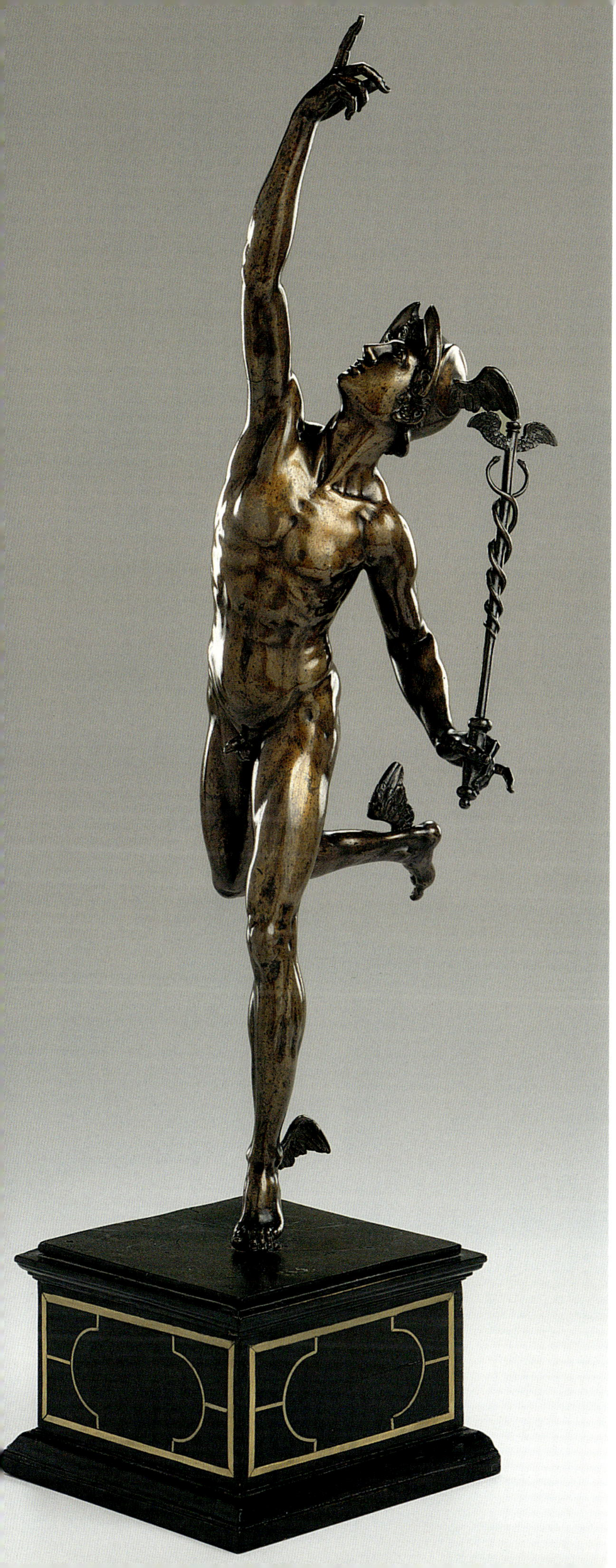

146 Mercury

In early 1587, *Mercury* came to the collection of Christian I as a gift from the grand duke of Tuscany, Francesco I de' Medici. The elector, who had begun his rule the previous year, would have considered this present a token of high esteem, as Florence bestowed the winged *Mercury* only upon valued recipients. Almost twenty years before, Francesco I had presented a *Mercury* to Emperor Maximilian II on behalf of his father, Cosimo I, to advance his courtship of Johanna of Austria. Florence also presented this statuette to princely courts at Parma (1579), Rome (1580), Prague (1588), and Paris (1598).

As an allegorical figure, Mercury was closely tied to the Medici family. Since the time of Lorenzo il Magnifico, but especially under Cosimo I and Francesco I, the god of trade and eloquence had gained increasing popularity in fresco programs and festival decorations not only in Florence but elsewhere as well, including Dresden. As an embodiment of princely virtues and a symbol of *industria* (industry) and *felicitas* (in this context, glory, success), *Mercury* could be interpreted, both by giver and recipient, as a wish for a "good reign." Since the deity was also favored by the Hapsburgs, he could be viewed as an indication of Saxon and Florentine fidelity to the Catholic imperial house, despite religious differences.

One of Giambologna's most popular compositions, the extraordinary *Mercury* exemplifies the artist's virtuoso transgression of the design and material confines posed by sculpting bronze. The messenger god rushes off hastily, with only the tip of his foot touching the ground. The raised arm, elongated index finger, and gaze directed toward heaven all point to the realm into which he will momentarily disappear. Despite the heavy bronze material, the figure has an air of carefree ease, nearly making the viewer forget just how artistically daring and challenging a compositional solution this is.

Today, four versions of *Mercury* in varying sizes are known. On formal grounds, the Dresden *Mercury*'s closest relative is the small bronze in Vienna, assumed to be the artist's gift to Emperor Rudolf II. Both statuettes would then be contemporaneous, dating to before 1587; they were possibly cast from the same form.

A.S.

Giambologna, before 1587
Bronze, H. 27⅞ in.
(73.4 cm, with base)
Gift of the grand duke of Tuscany, Francesco I de' Medici, to Elector Christian I of Saxony
First mentioned in the 1587 Kunstkammer inventory, fol. 65v–66r
Staatliche Kunstsammlungen Dresden, Grünes Gewölbe, inv. no. IX 94

Lit: Holzhausen 1933, pp. 58f.; Berlin 1995, pp. 365–67, cat. no. 113; Florence 1997, p. 151, cat. no. 114; Syndram 1999, p. 28; Augsburg 2000, pp. 309–11, cat. no. 37 (with additional bibliography); Dombrowski 2000, pp. 73f. and footnote 64; Marx 2000b, pp. 252f., 265f., 286; see also Vienna 1978, pp. 112–19; Brink 1987

147 Nessus and Deianira

This bronze group depicts an event from book 9 of Ovid's *Metamorphoses*. The centaur Nessus, who carried travelers across the Euenos River, encountered Deianira, the wife of Hercules. Infatuated by her beauty, Nessus tried to abduct her in the middle of the river, whereupon Hercules shot him with a poisoned arrow. As he lay dying, Nessus handed Deianira his blood-soaked garment and promised it would ensure that her husband would remain faithful to her. The garment, which was poisoned, eventually led to the painful death of Hercules.

The sculpture derives its appeal from the unequal battle between animal/human and woman. The centaur's ferocious spirit, captured in his bushy beard, wild hair, and intricate, lashing tail, distinguishes him as an impulsive creature from nature. He is in sharp contrast to the horrified, helpless Deianira, who stretches out her arms in vain as she struggles.

The small bronze came to the Kunstkammer in 1587 as a gift of the Florentine grand duke. One of two versions executed during Giambologna's lifetime, it is notable for its freshness and daring detailed work, particularly apparent around Nessus' head. The signature under the base and the princely rank of the donor make it highly likely that Giambologna himself finished the bronze.

Prevailing Late Renaissance theories of sculpture mandated that this group was to be seen from all sides, thus offering a charming view from almost any vantage point.
A.S.

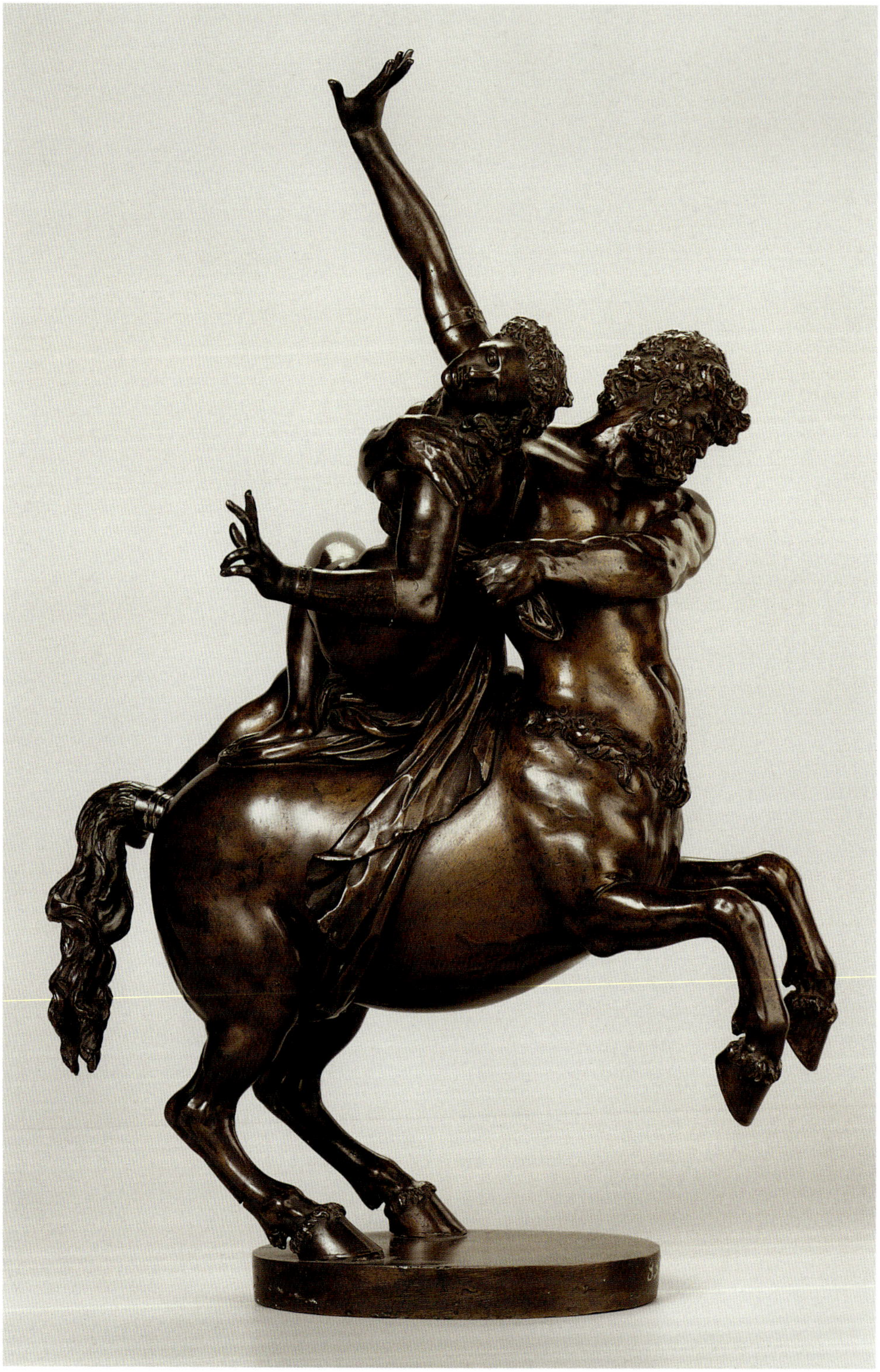

Giambologna, before 1587
Bronze, H. 16⅝ in. (42.2 cm)
Signed on the underside of the base I.B. (chased)
Gift of the grand duke of Tuscany, Francesco I de' Medici, to Elector Christian I
First mentioned in the 1587 Kunstkammer inventory, fol. 66r

Sculpture Collection, inv. no. H^2 23/95
Lit.: Holzhausen 1933, pp. 56f.; Weihrauch 1967, pp. 220ff.; Vienna 1978, p. 151, cat. no. 61 (with more bibliography); Essen 1986, no. 231; Berlin 1995, pp. 367f., cat. no. 118; Avery 2000a, p. 145, p. 264, cat. no. 92; see also Vienna 1978, pp. 147–61

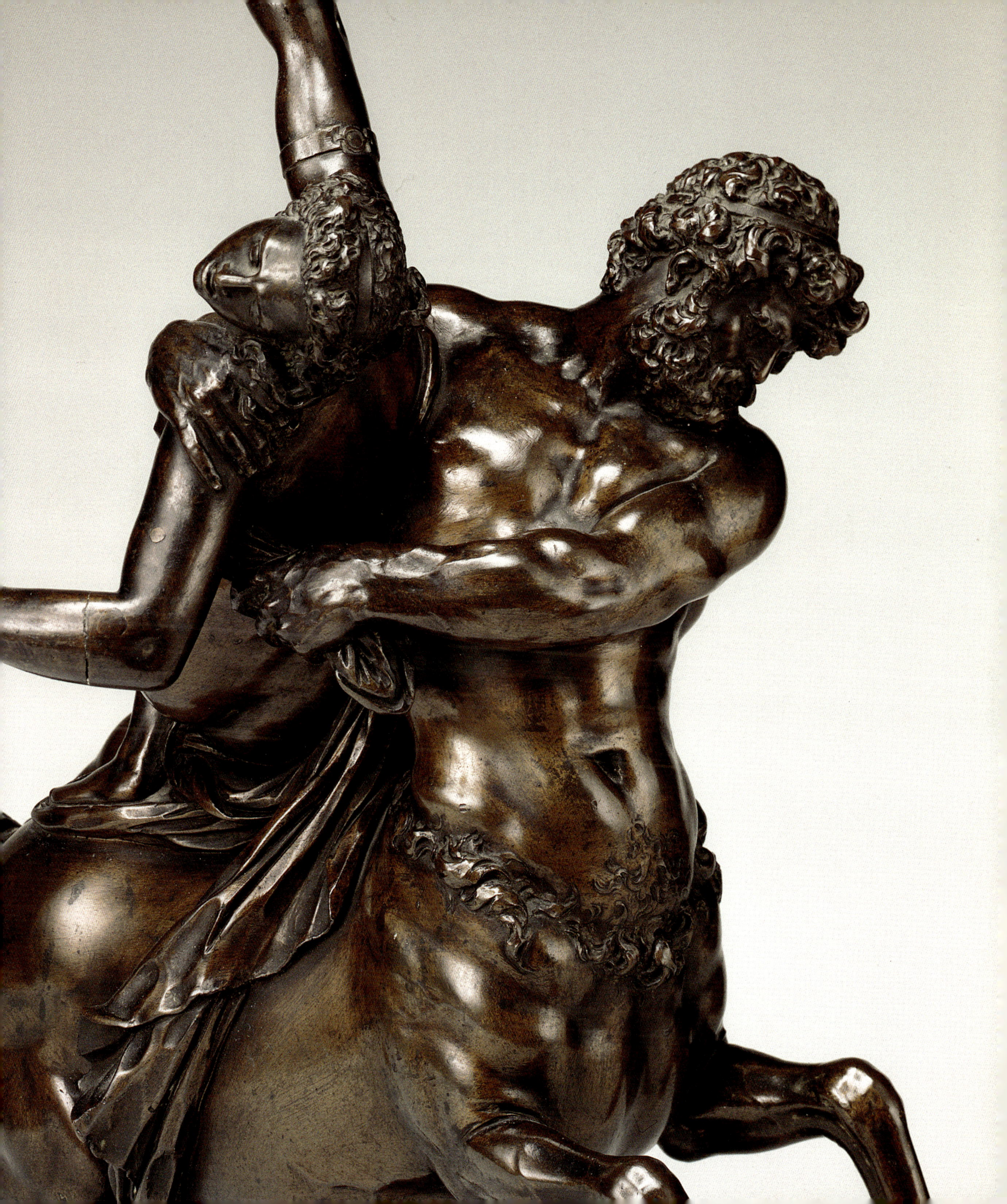

148 Sleeping Nymph with Satyr

The group, interpreted as a *Sleeping Venus* during the Baroque era, employs the popular motif of a barely clothed female beauty, spied upon by a satyr or shepherd while she sleeps. Despite the familiar subject, it appears that this group was not conceived as one piece, because nymph and satyr were separately cast and display substantial formal differences. The faun is smaller, shows a darker patina, and was affixed to the base at a later time.

The earliest mention of Giambologna's *Sleeping Nymph* is in a letter of 1584 by the grand duke of Tuscany, Francesco I de' Medici, to his brother Ferdinando, referring to a female "*nuda in atto di dormire*" (naked and asleep) that Ferdinando had received as a gift. About three years later, Francesco I presented another *Sleeping Nymph*, this time with satyr, to Elector Christian I.

As the bronze mentioned in 1584 has been lost, the one now in Dresden may be considered the oldest known version of this much-reproduced sculpture. That it was fabricated during Giambologna's lifetime and came to Dresden as a princely gift strongly implies that it was chased by the master himself.

Giambologna took the famous *Sleeping Ariadne* (Musei Vaticani, Rome), which he could have seen during his stay in Rome, as his model for the figure of the nymph. There are also striking similarities with paintings of the sleeping Venus by such artists as Titian and Giorgione.

The Faun, on the other hand, appears to be based on an original study by Adriaen de Vries (see also cat. no. 149). Giambologna obviously approved the figure, which was then cast by Antonio Susini and added to the *Sleeping Nymph*.
A.S.

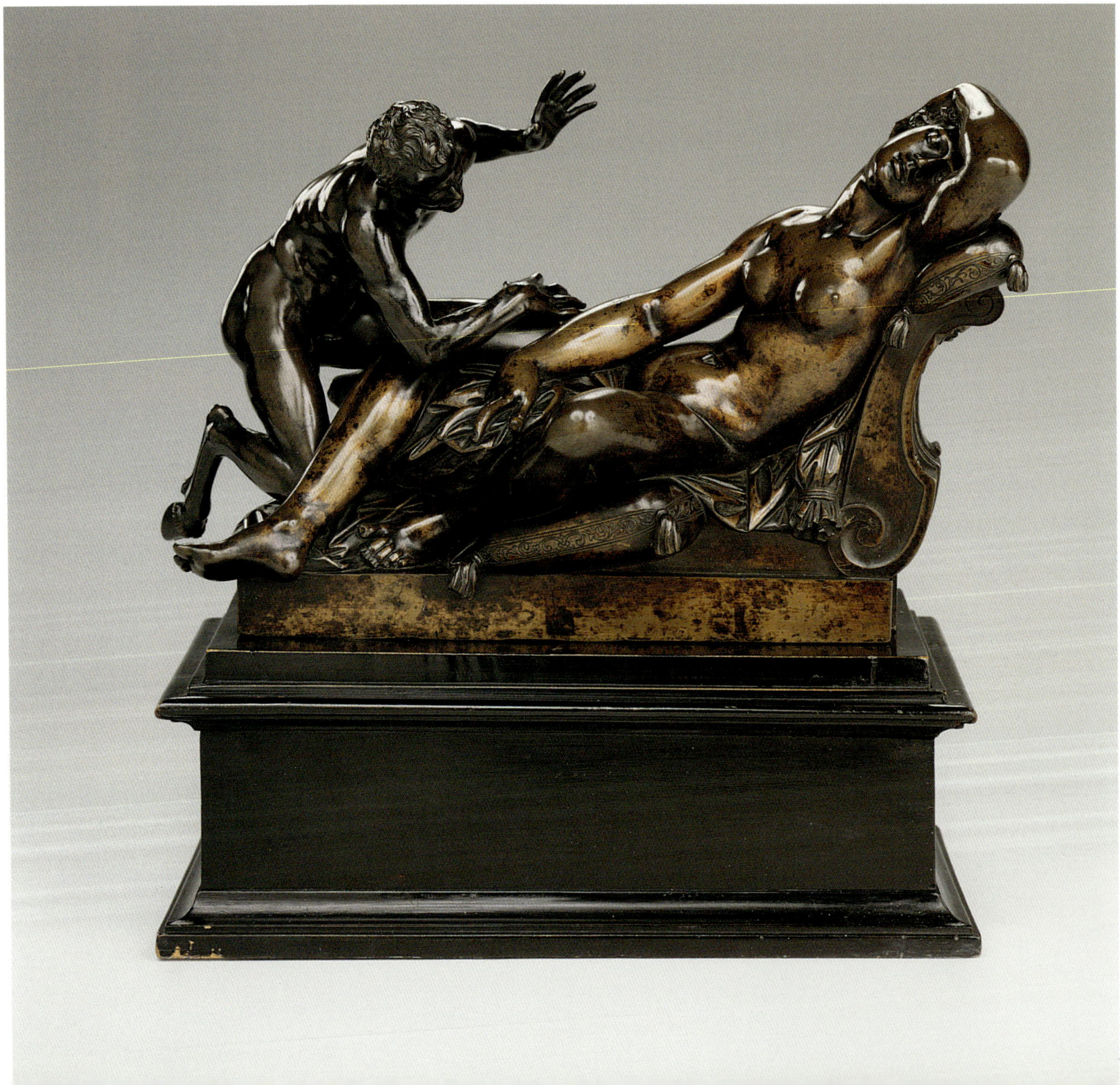

Giambologna (Nymph) and Antonio Susini, probably after a model by Adriaen de Vries (Satyr)
Bronze, H. 12⅜ in. (31.4 cm, with base), L. 13⅜ in. (34 cm)
Gift of the grand duke of Tuscany, Francesco I de' Medici, to Elector Christian I of Saxony
First mentioned in the 1587 Kunstkammer inventory, fol. 66
Staatliche Kunstsammlungen Dresden, Grünes Gewölbe, inv. no. IX 34
Lit.: Holzhausen 1933, pp. 60f; Vienna 1978, p. 161, cat. no. 69; Berlin 1995, pp. 370f, cat. no. 115; Marx 2000b, pp. 266, 287; Augsburg 2000, pp. 186–88, cat. no. 3; Avery 2000b, v. a. S. 16f., 36, cat. no. C.1 (with additional bibliography)

149 Crouching Satyr

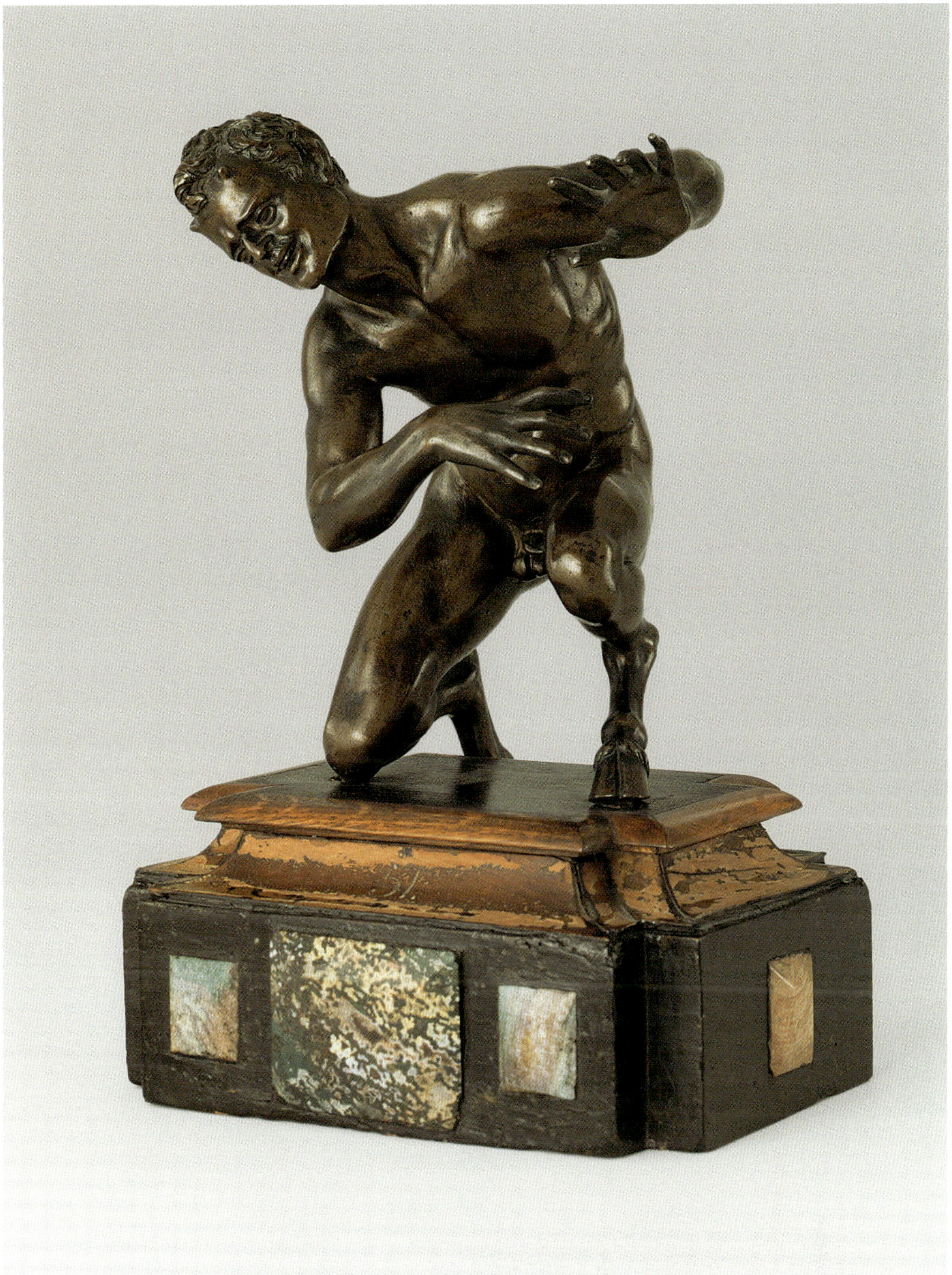

Early in his career, between 1581 and 1585, Adriaen de Vries worked in Giambologna's studio. The *Approaching Satyr*—convincingly attributed to de Vries by Raumschüssel (Berlin 1995)—could conceivably have been created during this time. In 1586/87, a cast of Giambologna's *Satyr* was combined with the *Sleeping Nymph* to form one group (cat. no. 148); thus, the model must have been created earlier.

The provenance of the bronze remains unclear. Raumschüssel argued that its prominent, stone-studded Renaissance pedestal, in the style of Nosseni, indicated that it must have been in Dresden about 1600. According to the inventories, however, the base was not added until the eighteenth or early nineteenth century, making this argument unconvincing. The most recent examination of Nosseni's estate inventory does not support the theory that this might be one of his "Satyrus" or "Adone," for all the relevant figures are expressly referred to as "standing."

Distinguished by its fine chasing, the statuette is skillfully executed, especially in the facial areas; and spontaneous movement of the forward-leaning, slightly turned body lends it a lively air. It has therefore been suggested that the young artist created the figure as a virtuoso study of movement, possibly adopting as his model a North Italian bronze depicting a gladiator. De Vries may also have been inspired by the so-called Belvedere Torso. This ancient sculpture, missing its head, arms, and lower legs, was studied intensely by sixteenth-century sculptors and could have inspired the complicated posture of this small satyr.

A.S.

Adriaen de Vries (attributed)
Model circa 1581/85
Bronze; painted wood, precious stones (base)
H. 9⅜ in. (23.9 cm, with base)
First mentioned in the 1726 sculpture inventory, fol. 20, no. 165
Staatliche Kunstsammlungen Dresden, Grünes Gewölbe, inv. no. IX 14
Lit: Berlin 1995, pp. 372f., cat. no. 116; Avery 2000b, pp. 16f.

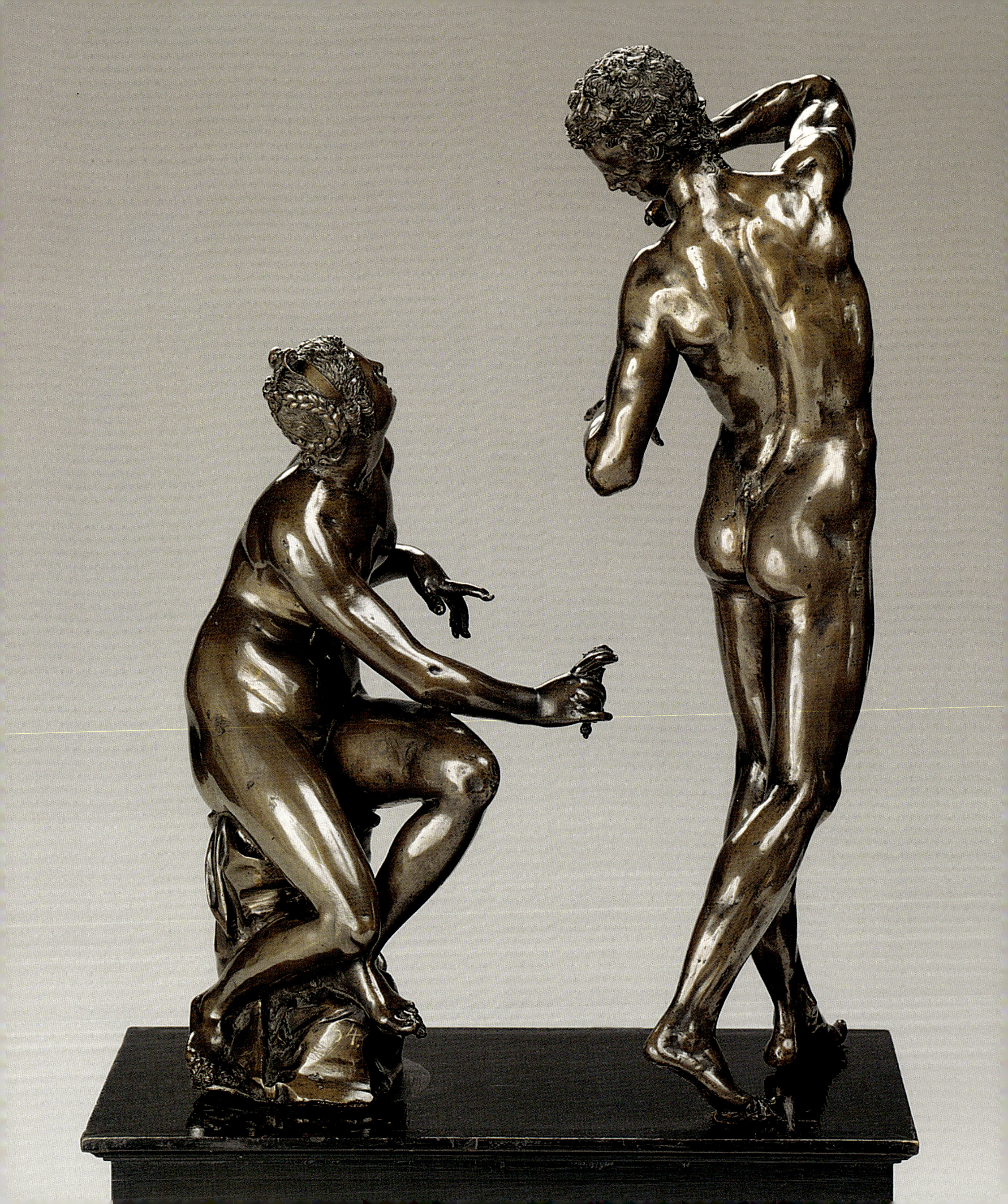

150 Faun and Nymph

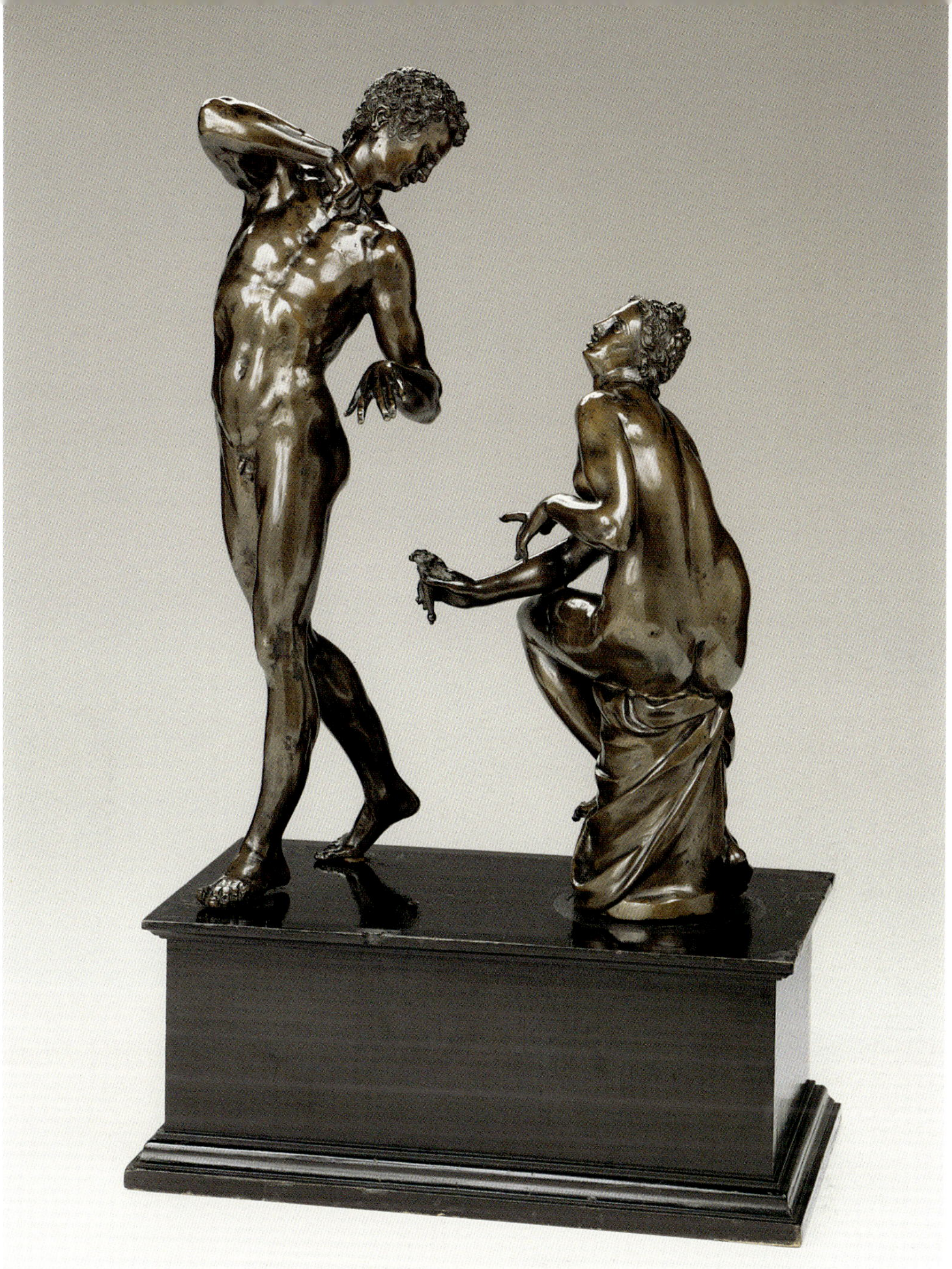

Adriaen de Vries, before 1621
Bronze, H. 25 in. (63.6 cm, faun), 19⅝ in. (49.9 cm, nymph) (with respective bases)
Acquired in 1622 from the estate of Nosseni
First mentioned in the 1640 Kunstkammer inventory, fol. 502v, 509r or 513r
Staatliche Kunstsammlungen Dresden, Grünes Gewölbe, inv. no. IX 36 (Faun) and IX 20 (Nymph)
Lit.: Holzhausen 1933, see especially pp. 77–79; Berlin 1995, pp. 440f., cat. no. 152; Augsburg 2000, pp. 195f., cat. no. 6 (with more bibliography); Krahn 2000; Scholten 2000, pp. 28f.

The youthful faun turns to the seated nymph beside him in an elegant twisting motion. With his right hand he makes an obscene gesture, directed at the beauty with neatly arranged hair, who looks at him while gesturing toward the broken mirror in her right hand. In Giovanni Maria Nosseni's estate lists, as well as in the early Kunstkammer inventories, this group was always thought to be *Venus and Adonis*, a portrayal of the amorous mythological couple whose happiness was terminated by Adonis' fatal hunting accident. Today the laurel-wreathed young man's tiny tail and his coarse gesture are taken as evidence that he is a faun approaching a nymph.

The present group is one of three versions that came to the electoral Kunstkammer in 1622 as part of Nosseni's estate. Two of the three were unchased, raw casts. In 1619, Nosseni had offered the elector a third version for purchase with the words: "cast by Adriano de Fries and chased by Gaurer[?]" (translated from SächsHStA Dresden, Loc. 8693/23, fol. [2r], no. 14). This note suggests that, contrary to common belief, de Vries did not in fact complete the group himself. It appears that the two raw casts were completed after coming to the Kunstkammer. This is supported by an order for payment dated 1631 and addressed to the goldsmith Enoch Bachmann (the Elder or the Younger), who was ordered to "chase cast metal works" (translated from SächsHStA Dresden, Loc. 9835/15, fol. 158r [104r]). The group exhibited here is generally considered to be one of the raw casts that were chased later. Raumschüssel (Berlin 1995) believed that Nosseni might have acquired the bronzes directly from Adriaen de Vries, who was working in Milan and Turin at the time of Nosseni's trip to Italy in 1588. The unchased, raw casts support this hypothesis, for de Vries presumably would not have given them to a collector but might have to an artist colleague. Nosseni could also have obtained the work in 1608, when he was in touch with de Vries about the sculptural decoration of the mausoleum in Stadthagen. Until 1924, both the Green Vault and the Skulpturensammlung of Dresden's Staatlichen Kunstsammlungen owned one complete group.
A.S.

151 Allegory of Spring

Seated on the stump of a pillar, a female nude calmly examines the flower bouquet in her left hand. The large rose bush she touches with her right hand, her floral head decoration, the little head of the Zephyr, the spring wind, at her feet, and the zodiacal signs (Aries, Taurus, Gemini) arranged on the quadrant in front of her all identify the young woman as an allegory of spring.

This statuette is similar in form to figures by Giambologna. Her seated posture with crossed leg and arm hanging down are mirror-image adaptations of features found in his *Allegory of Architecture*. However, the artist, very likely North Alpine, replaced the virtuosity and complexity of his prototype with a natural air. Thus, *Spring*'s pronounced turn of the head is a result of her gazing at the bouquet of flowers and not, as in Giambologna's *Architecture*, an artistic effect only.

Hans Reichle was the only German to work in the Florentine studio of Giambologna (in 1587–95 and again in 1601–2) and is considered one of the key mediators of the master's style north of the Alps. There is some discord among scholars regarding the attribution of *Spring* to Reichle, especially since no other small bronzes by him are known and his large pieces are all robed figures. The most recent, stylistically compelling attribution of the *Venus Kallipygos* (Ashmolean Museum, Oxford) to him (Diemer 2001) raises the question of whether the more elegantly proportioned *Spring*, this extraordinary female nude with finely executed details, could actually have been made by the same artist and produced in the early seventeenth century.
A.S.

Hans Reichle
(attributed)
circa 1601/2
Bronze
H. 13⅜ in. (33.9 cm)
First mentioned in the 1726 sculpture inventory, fol. 15, no. 127
Staatliche Kunstsammlungen Dresden, Grünes Gewölbe, inv. no. IX 99
Lit.: Kriegbaum 1931, pp. 237f.; Bruhn 1981, pp. 88, 178, no. 32, p. 260, ill. 86 (reversed); Duisburg 1994, pp. 164f., cat. no. 65; Berlin 1995, pp. 472f., cat. no. 168; Augsburg 2000, pp. 334–36, cat. no. 46 (with additional bibliography); see also Vienna 1978, p. 100, cat. no. 18; Diemer 2001, pp. 200f.

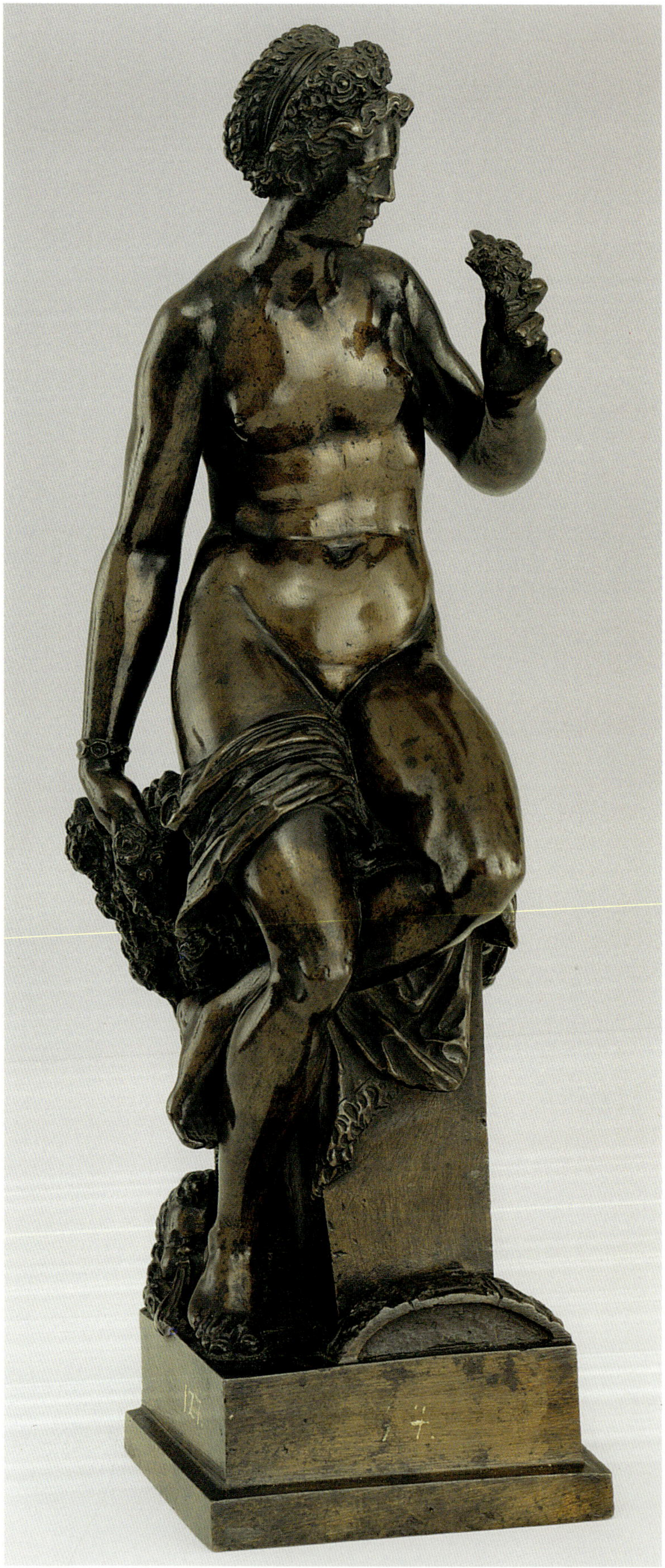

152 African Woman with Mirror, the so-called Black Venus

Because of its facial features, this beautiful figure with earrings, necklace, and bracelet was originally identified as a "nude female Moor" when it was first mentioned, in the inventory of 1726, which does not associate it with Venus. Its current appellation, the "Black Venus," stems from the twentieth century.

The subject of the piece, of which at least thirteen versions are known, remains uncertain. The hand mirror and the drape around the head have led scholars to consider the figure a depiction of Venus at her toilet. Although the stance and attributes are reminiscent of this theme there are no images predating 1600 in which black African women are shown in this role; instead they are predominantly rendered as slaves or servants. However, Bückling (1991) notes that there are Early Baroque love poems praising slaves as paramours and patronesses of courtly love. The contradiction between low social status and exotic beauty could also have conceivably shaped the Black Venus type; especially noteworthy in this regard is how the Dresden version's pearl-embellished nudity stresses the erotic aspect.

The statuette's authorship is also disputed, and the original has never been identified. It has been variously ascribed to the French sculptor Barthélemy Prieur and the Dutchman Johann Gregor van der Schardt. The most recent hypothesis surmises that the Dresden replica—because of its preserved mirror, one of the so-called complete versions—might have been cast in early-seventeenth-century France.
A.S.

France(?)
early 17th century
Bronze
H. 13⅞ (35.3 cm, with base)
First mentioned in the 1726 sculpture inventory, fol. 16, no. 135
Staatliche Kunstsammlungen Dresden, Grünes Gewölbe, inv. no. IX 59
Lit.: Stuttgart 1987, p. 310, cat. no. 1.37; Bückling 1991, p. 34; Krahn 1995, p. 108, E 15; Bonn 1999, pp. 194f. (Jutta Kappel, with more bibliography); Cologne 2000, pp. 485f., cat. no. P 2; see also Berlin 1995, pp. 324–27, cat. no. 98

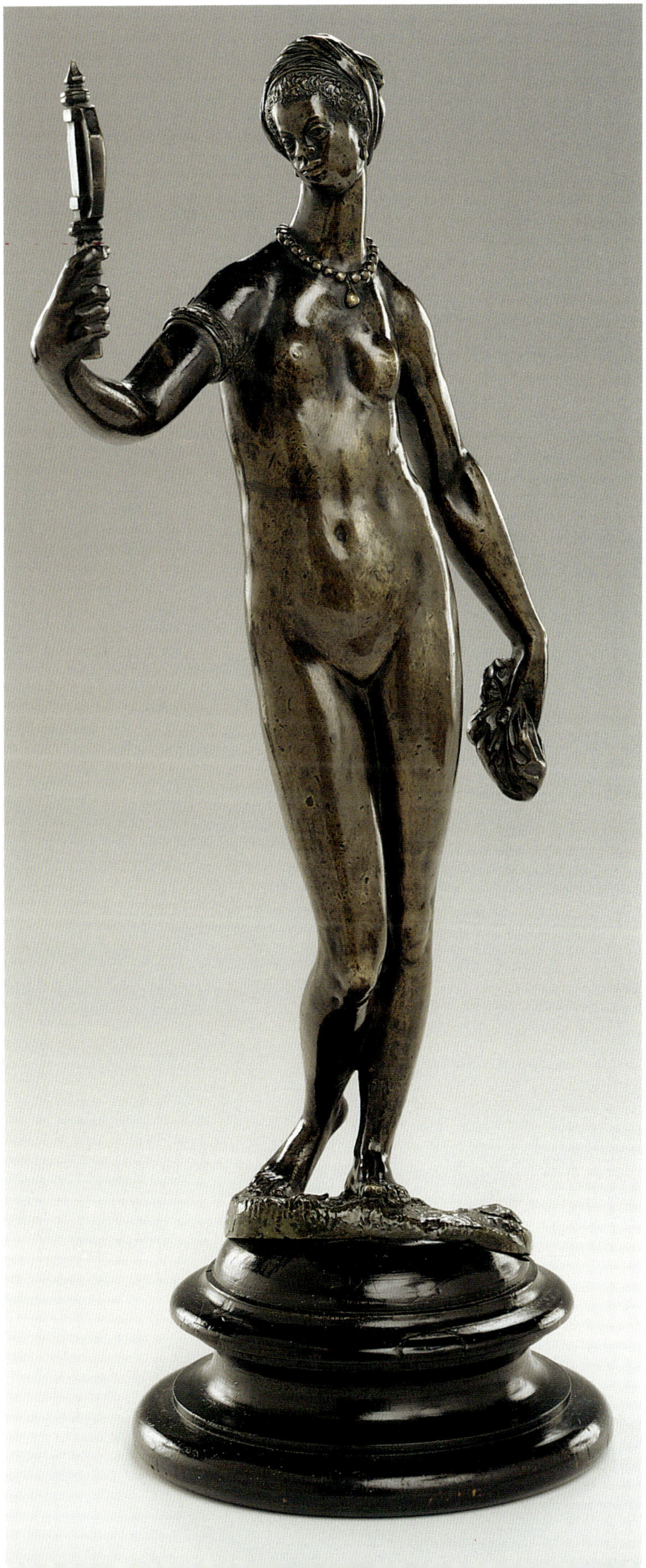

153 Striding Horse

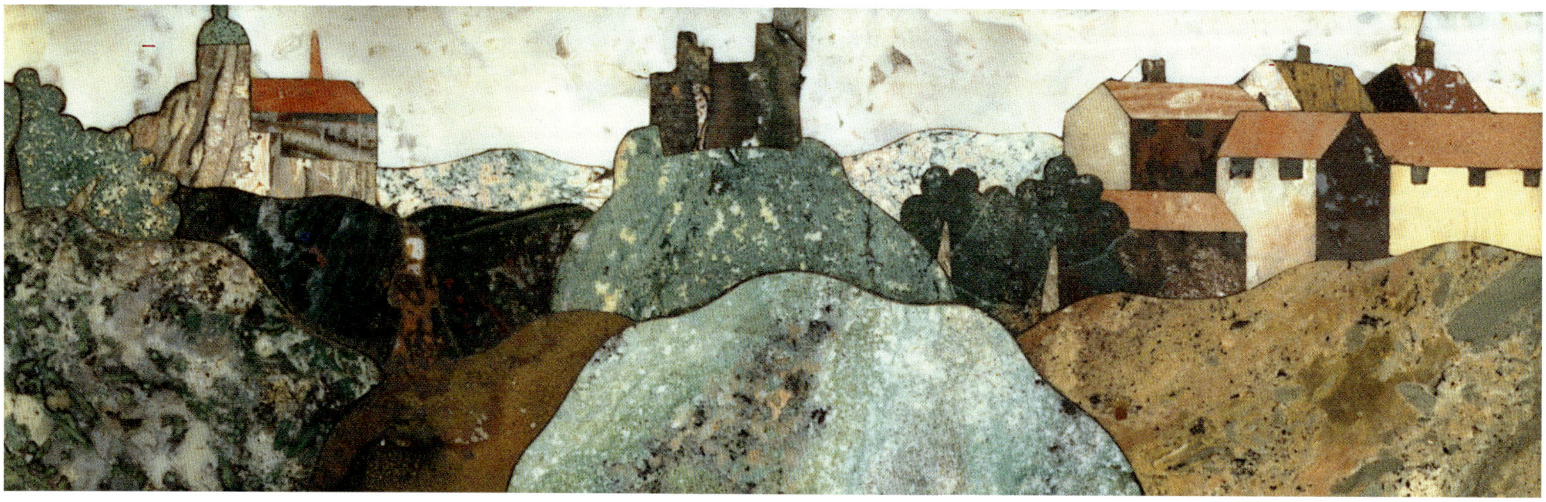

This exquisite stallion with elegantly lifted forelegs turns its head slightly to the side and bends downward as if led by the reins of an experienced rider. The bridle bit, visible at the side of the mouth, and the wrapped tail indicate that this bronze animal is modeled after those on equestrian monuments.

The prototype for this piece was derived by Giambologna, who began to study striding horses early on. In 1593, he completed his monumental equestrian statue of Cosimo I de' Medici in Florence, which was succeeded by numerous bronze reductions of striding horses with and without riders. It appears that the Dresden horse was produced after a model by Antonio Susini, a member of Giambologna's workshop, who probably also cast the piece. The *Striding Horse* has survived in numerous examples, of which this is one of the best. It appears to be contemporaneous with a version in the Victoria and Albert Museum, London, that has been firmly dated to 1605 through thermoluminescent testing.

A significant feature of this statuette is its precious pedestal with pietra dura inlays. Judging from its style, Kappel (1992) was able to assign it to the Prague workshop of Cosimo Castrucci and to propose a mounting of the bronze horse to its intarsia base in about 1610. Emperor Rudolf II considered the combination of small bronzes with pietra dura decoration particularly exuberant. Although the *Striding Horse* is not confirmed in Dresden's inventories until 1726, it is still conceivable that it could have come to the city as an imperial gift in the early seventeenth century.

A.S.

After Giambologna;
model/cast probably Antonio Susini
circa 1605
Pedestal: Castrucci workshop, circa 1610
Bronze, veneered wood base
with framed pietra dura plaques
H. 15¾ in. (38.9 cm, with pedestal)
First mentioned in the 1726 sculpture inventory, fol. 22, no. 181
Staatliche Kunstsammlungen Dresden,
Grünes Gewölbe, inv. IX 33
Lit.: Holzhausen 1933, pp. 65–68;
Kappel 1992; Berlin 1995, pp. 384–85, cat. no. 121,
Dombrowski 2000, p. 81 and color plate VII;
see also Weihrauch 1967, pp. 225–29; Vienna 1978, pp. 231–38, cat. nos. 149–158

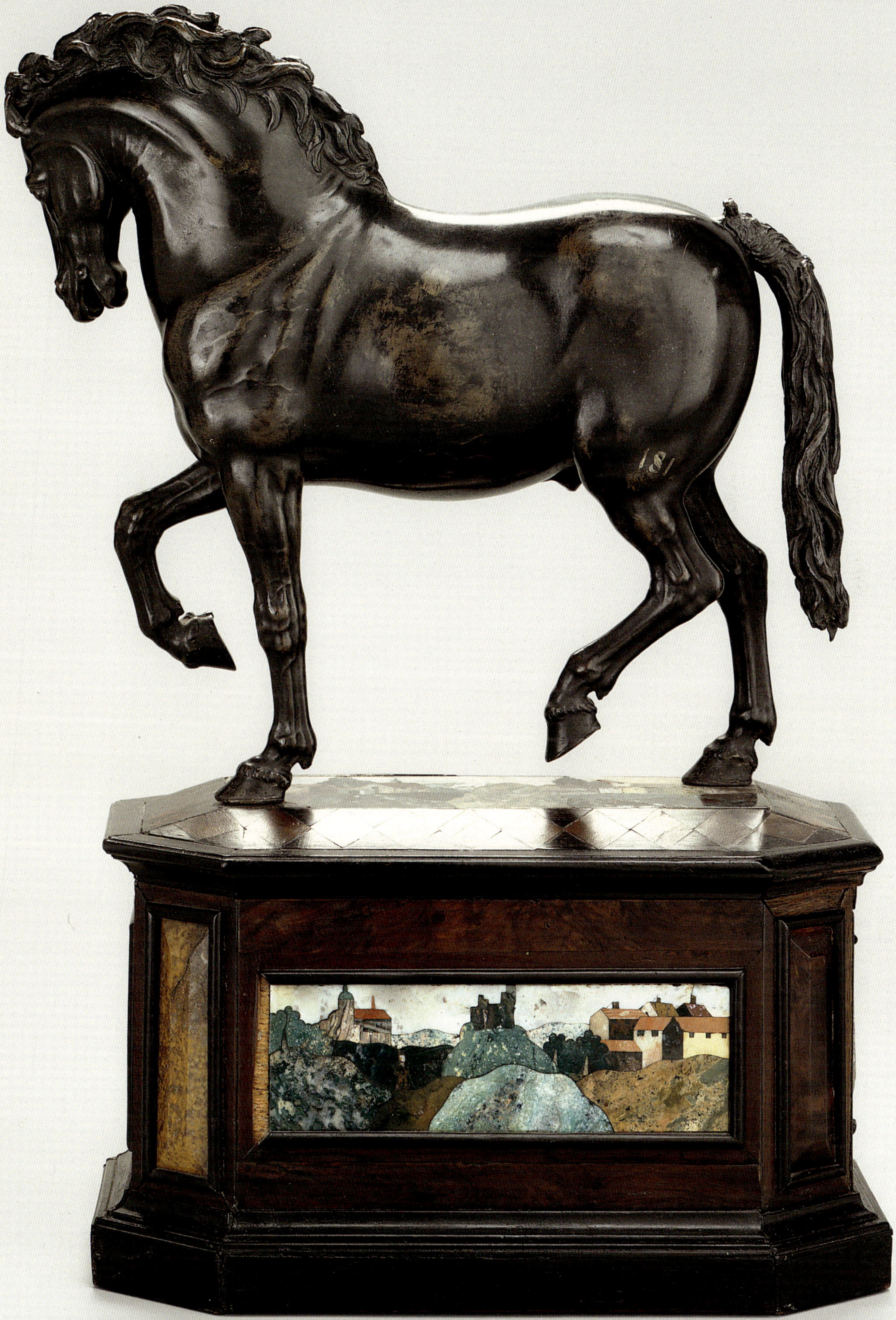

Stately Order

Dirk Syndram

In the macrocosm of the tangible world and in the microcosm of the princely collection the principal order was *politike techne*, referring to the art of governing as well as to the mastery of collecting. About 1600, the Saxon electors defined themselves as strictly Protestant. They believed that they were God's legitimate counselors and guarantors of a "judicious" order that they in turn granted their subjects. According to Luther's teachings, God elected the sovereign to maintain order and to punish evil. In keeping with this faith, the electors from August to Johann Georg I saw themselves as the fatherly rulers of their territories. This traditional image of the prince as father was elevated even further by the Reformation. To this day, popular historians ascribe the role of housefather to Elector August, characterizing him as "father August." With the rank of paterfamilias in his meticulously ordered realm, the Protestant prince saw himself as the father and thus as a unifying element of his state, of which he thus became a symbol. The prince was expected to create and to preserve the order of society and that was his primary goal.[1]

Although the Dresden Kunstkammer incorporated the most basic systematic order only during its first few decades of existence, there were always groups of objects particularly closely tied to a systematic order within the microcosm of the collection. Among these were astronomical table clocks, cabinets, and small boxes.

The perfecting of the clock movement was a brilliant technical and artistic achievement of the German Renaissance. Yet, as an horological device, it was neither practical nor useful because it was imprecise and had only one hand to indicate the hours. Not until 1658, when Christian Huygens invented the pendulum clock, could time be precisely measured to determine how minutes elapsed and thus determine the course of a prince's day. The owner did not expect his astronomical clock to tell him the exact time. He was much more interested in its more subtle functions such as signs regarding astrology and the calendar. The primary function of clocks was not so much their indication of terrestrial time but their ability to illustrate the movement of sun and moon through the planets' orbits. Astrolabes enabled the owners of astronomical clocks to project the changing sky of stars fixed on a single dial located in their secluded study. But this was not all: astronomical clocks assisted in drawing up horoscopes, showed the position of the sun and the phases of the moon, made possible the identification of the respective Golden Number corresponding to the Dominical Letters, and helped their owners calculate the date of Easter, necessitated for different denominations as a consequence of the Gregorian calendar's introduction.[2] Numerous other possibilities were added by the creators of these precision instruments; they united multiple functions in the very limited space offered within the case of the clock. Measuring time became secondary and assumed a largely symbolic function.

It is worth mentioning that, proportionate to their symbolic function, partly miniaturized and, especially, "unusually inventive" clocks were frequently incorporated into automatons and other precious objects in the Kunst- and Schatzkammer. The weight-driven works were used not only as clocks but also for the mechanical production of music, or they were attached to objects in order to animate them. In the early 1600s, clocks were regarded as miraculous creations not only

Planetary Clock
Eberhardt Baldewein,
Hermann Diepel, and Hans Bucher
Kassel, 1563–67
Case 23⅝ in. × 23⅝ in. (60 × 60 cm),
H. 47¼ in. (120 cm)
Staatliche Kunstsammlungen
Dresden, Mathematisch-
Physikalischer Salon, inv. no. D IV
d4

1. Bauer/Matis 1989, pp. 195f.
2. Maurice 1976, vol. 1, p. 53.

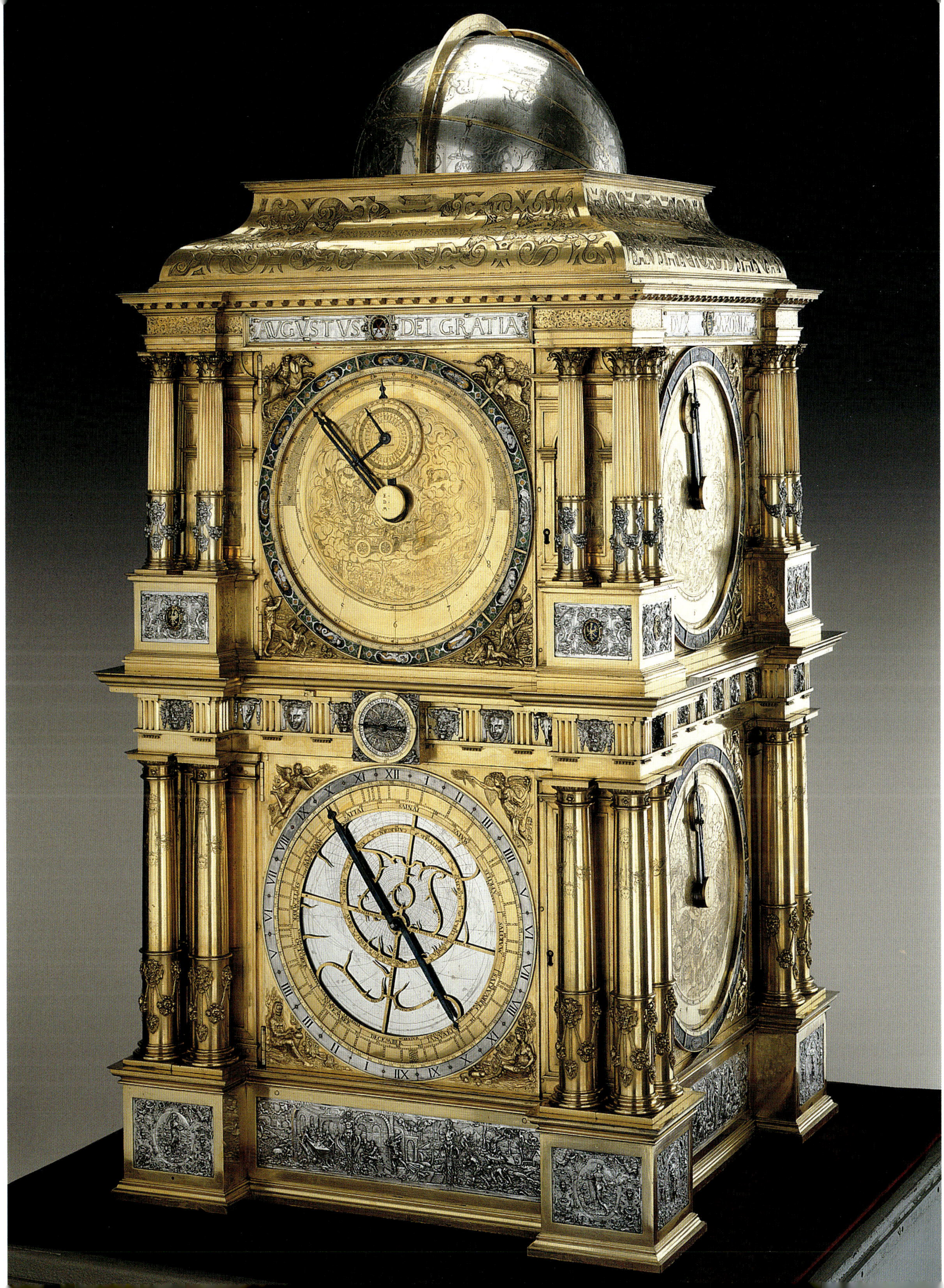
AVGVSTVS DEI GRATIA

by inventive geniuses, but also, as Maurice stated, by engineers as symbols of the avant-garde of European precise mechanics and industry.

Clocks had an even greater significance. They epitomized a centrally organized and unfailingly functional and rational order. Indeed, the mechanical clock had already become such a metaphor in the thirteenth century. The Late Renaissance worldview took the clockwork mechanism as its model. People were convinced that the macrocosm of the world and the microcosm of the human body were both organized by the divine "clockmaker." The world's harmony was analogous to the clockwork: as in the work of a clock, the world's course was initiated by an impulse from a central, divine spot, precisely predetermining the course of all events. From the point of view of space, construction, and intellect, God had created the world based on a strict order.

Around 1600, the clock metaphor also served as an intellectual model for states. Order, peace, and the equilibrium of society were thus determined by the prince's initiative and the virtues of his central guidance, plan, and judgment.[3] Consequently, the individual's role within the state was but that of a wheel within the larger machinery.

One of Elector August's most expensive acquisitions is indicative of the symbolic function attributed to astronomical clocks. Since 1562, Landgrave Wilhelm IV of Hesse had owned a planetary clock, constructed according to his specifications by Eberhardt Baldewein. In those days, this was a perfect instrument for illustrating astrological movement. The case was designed by Hermann Diepel and Hans Bucher. In 1563, shortly after the completion of the "Wilhelm Clock," today in Kassel's Astronomisch-Physikalisches Kabinett, Elector August persuaded his princely cousin to commission a second instrument of this type. Its history is revealed in the correspondence between the two Lutheran princes.[4] In 1568, after almost five years in production, the instrument was delivered to Saxony. The otherwise thrifty elector did not regret having spent sixteen thousand guilders on the impressive projection of the planets' course. August expressed his satisfaction in a letter to the landgrave: "*Haben uns auch ob Ersehung desselben Bewegung und Gebrauch nicht wenig erlustigt und ergötzt, bedarf auch des Verzuges wegen keine Entschuldigung, denn solch ein Werk darf nicht übereilet werden*" (We have derived plenty of pleasure and satisfaction from observing, moving, and utilizing said object. And it really does not matter so much that its delivery was delayed as [the creation of] such a work never ought to be hurried).[5]

The elector's planetary clock is technologically more advanced than the "Wilhelm Clock" and is embellished with a more elaborate case. With a height of almost four feet and the rigid architectural order of its body, this is a monumental object. It is based on the geocentric world order according to Ptolemy. On each of its four sides, two large dials indicate the course of the seven classical planets—Mercury, Venus, Mars, Jupiter, Saturn, plus the moon and the sun—through the twelve zodiacal signs of the ecliptic, as they revolve around the *centrum mundi*, the earth. The eighth disk is an astrolabe with sun and hour dial. A number of extra features are also included.[6] It is somewhat surprising that this symbolic masterpiece of scientific and artistic achievements, which also incorporates the elector's specific iconographic requirements, was not immediately integrated into the electoral Kunstkammer, then in the process of being established. The planetary clock was not exhibited there until 1592, i.e., twenty-four years after its completion.[7]

The acquisition of a parade casket has a more domestic spirit than the planetary clock in its aura of privacy. In 1588, Christian I gave his wife, Sophie of Brandenburg, this precious box as a Christmas gift. Its creator was the Nuremberg goldsmith Nikolaus Schmidt, presumably in collaboration with the elderly Wenzel Jamnitzer. On January 1, 1589, the so-called *Kestlein oder Nöhe Ledtlein* (literally, little box or sewing drawer), equipped with elaborate drawers as well as tools used by women, was delivered to the Kunstkammer (ill. p. 285). In 1590, Christian I received another decorative casket, also containing sewing tools (cat. no. 155), from Elisabeth, Electress of Brandenburg and stepmother of Electress Sophie. A New Year's gift from Christian's mother-in-law, this object was transferred to the electoral Kunstkammer, soon after it was received on February 28.

The Kunstkammer's stately order culminated in miniature cabinets, caskets, and boxes created specifically for collections of this type. The miniature cabinets, the smallest means identified for establishing order, were valuable collector's items whose elaborate designs ennobled their contents. It was not mandatory that these items have a storage function, however. Even without contents, as symbols of princely order, they were prestigious components of Kunstkammers.

3. Maurice 1976, vol. 1, p. IX.
4. See for this Maurice 1976, vol. 1, pp. 64ff.
5. Translated after Maurice 1976, vol. 1, p. 66.
6. Schillinger 1994, pp. 84, 94f.
7. Kunstkammer inventory 1595, fol. 297r, Mathematisch-Physikalischer Salon, State Art Collections Dresden, inv. no. D IV d 4.
8. It remains to be stated that apart from the art furniture in the strict sense of the word, Kunstkammers also contained functional cupboards built into the walls, shelves, almars, repositories, and chests, some of them in fact with decorative embellishments.
9. Alfter 1986, p. 30.

Parade Casket of Electress Sophie
Design: Wenzel Jamnitzer
Execution: Nikolaus Schmidt
Nuremberg, 1585
Silver, partly gilded, mother-of-pearl, velvet, silk, glass, precious stones,
H. 19⅝ in. (50 cm),
W. 22⅜ in. (57 cm),
D. 15⅜ in. (39 cm),
Staatliche Kunstsammlungen Dresden, Grünes Gewölbe, inv. no. IV 115

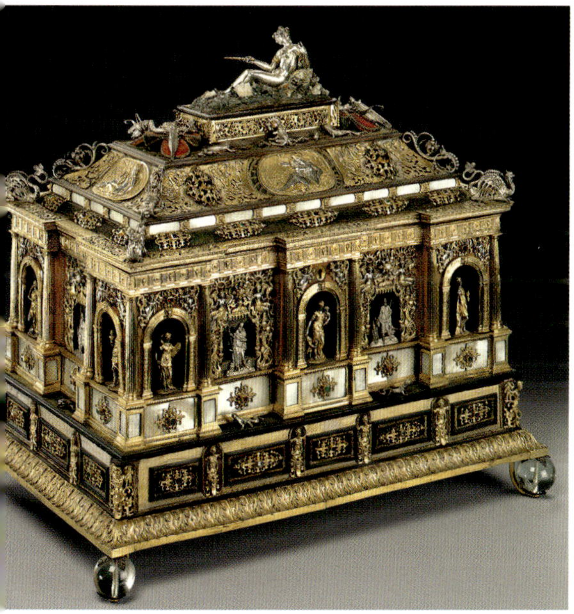

The apex of all Kunstkammer furniture was the cabinet (*Kabinettschrank*).[8] In the sixteenth and seventeenth centuries, this furniture was generally called *Schreibtisch* (writing desk) without further specification of its real function. As a piece of furniture to store things in, it was considered the epitome of any collection and was a particularly prized Kunstkammer piece.

Changes in the design, in general beginning in the late sixteenth century and affecting caskets and cabinets alike, are exemplified mostly in the medium-size objects represented in this exhibition. In the second half of the sixteenth century, works made from colorful contrasting materials by Nuremberg goldsmiths following Wenzel Jamnitzer's inventions dominated the market. The minutely conceived caskets and boxes were frequently decorated with silver or gold reliefs on colored grounds, as well as with exotic materials. Their decoration generally followed conventional humanist iconography.

In the last two decades of the sixteenth century, taste began to change in favor of ebony furniture with applied silver plaques and ornaments. Spanish fashion, with black robes adorned by lace trimmings and collars, obviously influenced styles in furniture.

Augsburg, eventually the leading city for luxury goods, became the center for the production of cabinets and caskets with ebony veneer. Ultimately, these commodities were among Augsburg's most important exports. The successful monopoly of the city's cabinetmakers and goldsmiths is due in part to the fact that, with specialized workshops and division of labor, they were able to fabricate extraordinarily complex furniture relatively quickly. Boas Ulrich and Matthäus Wallbaum specialized in high-quality small furniture that was much sought after in princely circles as collector's items and bridal gifts.[9]

The production of large cabinets reached its zenith in the masterworks of those Augsburg artisans who worked under the guidance of the learned traveler and successful art dealer Philipp Hainhofer, especially between 1610 and 1617, culminating in the almost legendary *Pommerscher Kunstschrank* (Pomeranian cabinet). A relatively late and particularly mature example of a Hainhofer piece of furniture is presented in this exhibition: the work desk of Johann Georg I (cat. no. 161) elucidates most impressively the uniqueness of Dresden's Kunstkammer as it had evolved over the decades. The focus of this piece is not so much facets of the princely life as it is the elector's active role as courtly craftsman. With this desk, its owner continued the tradition begun by his grandfather, Elector August, who founded the Kunstkammer about 1560 as a private place where he could pursue princely work as an analogy of the craft of ruling and in accordance with the Lutheran theology.

154 Two Astronomical Table Clocks

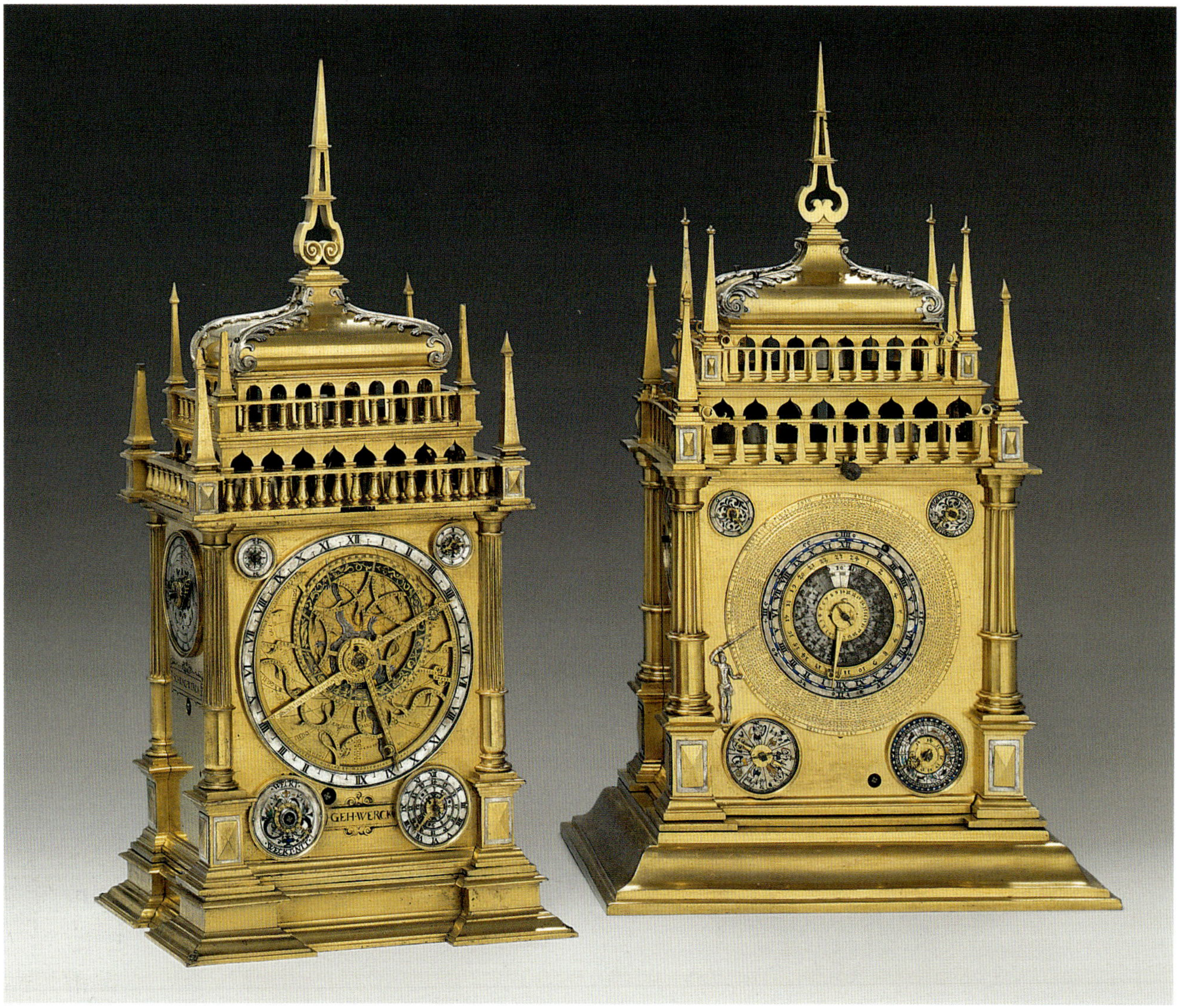

Unknown Master
Augsburg, end of 16th century
Gilt brass, steel, enamel, silver
H. 16⅛ in. (41 cm, base), W. 8 in. (20.2 cm), D. 1⅞ in. (4.8 cm) (IV 283) and
H. 16¼ in. (41.3 cm, base), W. 10 in. (25.4 cm), D. 7½ in. (19 cm) (IV 285)
First mentioned in the inventory of the *Wappenzimmer* 1733, p. 4
Grünes Gewölbe, inv. no. IV 283 (left) and IV 285 (right)
Lit.: Sponsel 1928, p. 192; Maurice 1976, vol. 2, p. 33, no. 183 and 185; see also: Maurice 1976, p. 108

Like other spring-driven astronomical clocks of this period, these two clocks measure terrestrial time as only one of their uses. During the Late Renaissance, such table clocks were considered extraordinary products of human ingenuity. By looking at their dials it was possible to read the position of the celestial bodies regarded as images of divine order and harmony.

These two clocks incorporate a type of mechanically driven astrolabe, which was a specialty of Augsburg clockmakers. Freestanding clocks with comparatively sober cases in the shape of towers adhering to strick architectural principles began to be produced there in the last quarter of the sixteenth century. Their cases house complicated movements that furnish information for a variety of dials on the exteriors of the cases. These two are nearly identically constructed: each has two broad sides and two narrow ones; in the center of one of the broad sides there is a mechanically driven astrolabe; on the second of the broad sides, the time in various systems for counting the hours, as well as calendrical information, is displayed. The two main dials are each framed by four smaller ones variously used for regulating the clock and for conveying further calendrical and astronomical information. Two other dials for indicating the hours and quarter hours struck by the movement on bells housed in the pierced dome of the clock are found on the narrow sides of the clock's case.

The electoral Saxon Kunstkammer's collection of elaborate instruments, to which these two objects also belong, was largely transferred to the Mathematisch-Physikalischer Salon when the art treasures were organized under Augustus the Strong. A number of particularly appealing horological devices were incorporated into the collection of treasury objects within the Green Vault as precious table decorations.
D.S.

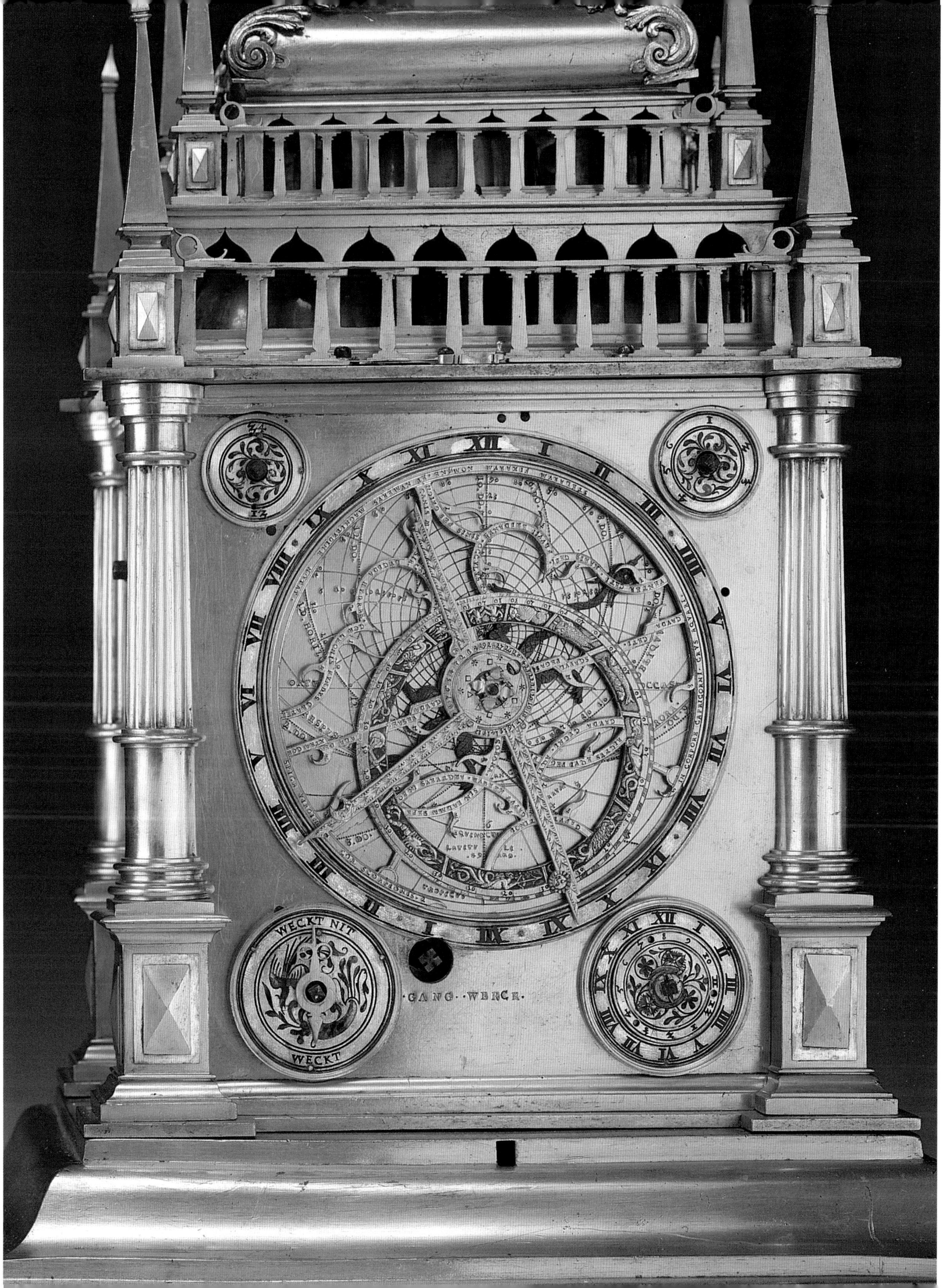
WECKT NIT
WECKT
·GANG·WERCK·

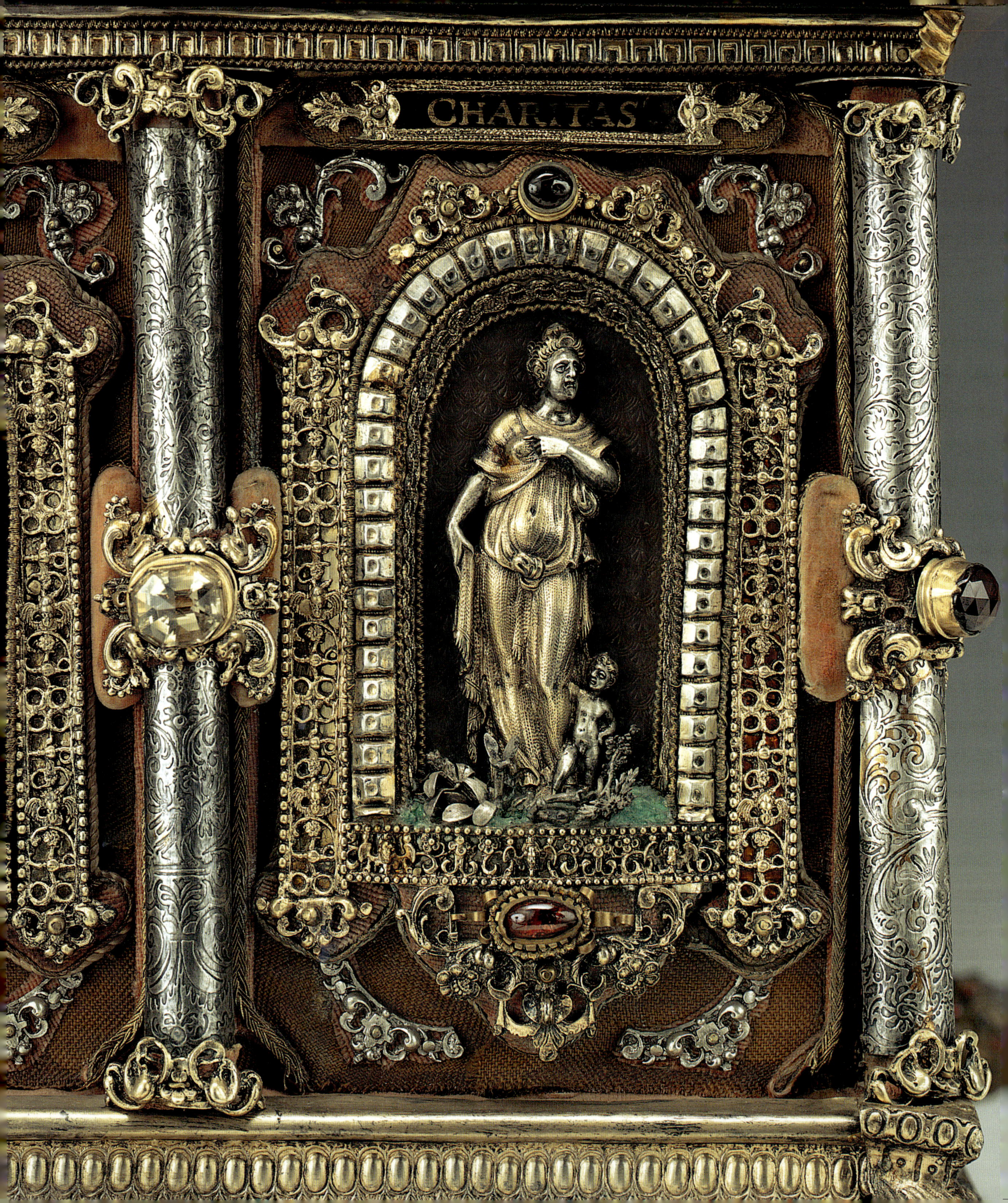
CHARITAS

155 Parade Casket of Elector Christian I of Saxony

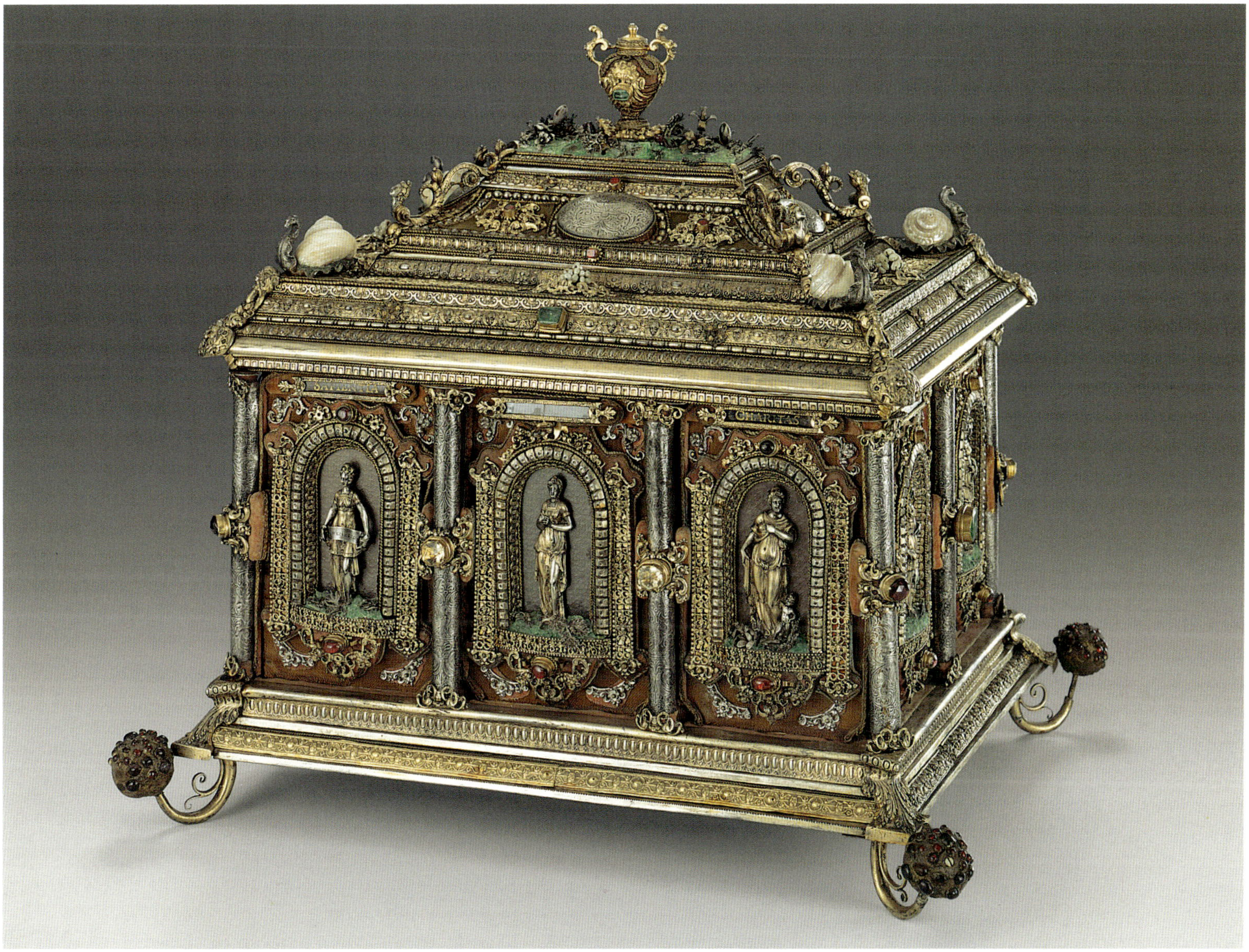

Nuremberg (?), before 1590
Wood, glass, silver, partly gilded, enamel, shells, pearls, precious stones, velvet, silk, braided gold trimmings, metal threads, cantils
H. 16½ in. (42 cm), W. 19¼ in. (49 cm), D. 14⅛ in. (36 cm)
First mentioned in the Kunstkammer inventory 1595, fol. 167v–168r
Staatliche Kunstsammlungen Dresden, Grünes Gewölbe, inv. no. IV 145
Lit.: Menzhausen 1977, p. 40, plate 13; see also: Steingräber 1956, ill. 217; Pechstein 1985, pp. 57–70; for the term "*höfisches Modemöbel*" see Alfter 1986, p. 30

According to the 1595 Kunstkammer inventory, Electress Elisabeth of Brandenburg, stepmother of Electress Sophie of Saxony, presented this so-called *Kestlein oder Nöhe Ledtlein* (literally, little box or sewing drawer) to her son-in-law, Christian I, on February 28, 1590, as a New Year's gift. A year before, Christian had given his wife a Christmas present of a precious box (inv. no. IV 115, ill. p. 285) acquired in Nuremberg. The Wettin family thus followed a fashion favored in numerous European princely houses during the course of the sixteenth century. Whereas in Italy and France most of the "*höfischen Modemöbel*" (fashionable court furniture) did not survive, Dresden's Green Vault competes with Munich's Treasury for the largest number and the highest quality of preserved objects. The creator of these unique Kunstkammer items in Germany was primarily the Nuremberg goldsmith Wenzel Jamnitzer, whose monopoly lasted until his death in 1585.

The undated casket of Christian I has neither hallmarks nor maker's marks. In its construction, iconographic program, and arcaded niches and columns, it follows the style of Jamnitzer. As in his Madrid casket in the Convent of the Descalzas Reales or in Nikolaus

Schmidt's parade casket for Electress Sophie, the ten cast figures of Virtues symbolize desirable characteristics of the princely owner. However, while on the architecturally structured caskets made by Jamnitzer the hand of the goldsmith can always be recognized in the invisibly linked mounted, cast, and chiseled friezes, columns, and capitals, the casket of Christian I reveals a different style. It is distinguished by the predominance of sumptuous embroidery, the use of isolated architectural elements, and a method of manufacture quite unlike that of a goldsmith. While use of precast decorative elements may be seen, there is an interplay with gold trimmings and stamped silver friezes. Form is achieved by cloth-covered wood substructures, and the pomegranate feet are made of a puttylike substance. Although such fabrication methods save metal, they result in diminished sturdiness. The 1764 inventory lists damage as a result of a "*Bombardement*." This would also explain the clearly visible alterations on the casket's exterior. Because of those alterations, the character and the quality of the splendid casket can be best seen in the largely undamaged interior of the lid and the elaborate system of drawers.

The lack of durability seems to be responsible for the rarity of comparable objects. A single woman's decorative headdress in the Germanisches Nationalmuseum Nuremberg (inv. no. T 3683, kind reference made by Ralf Schürer) shows a striking similarity with the rosettes in the four corners of the lid interior. Based on the repertoire of applied ornaments and this object's general construction—and with all due caution—the casket is tentatively located to the Nuremberg area.
A.V.

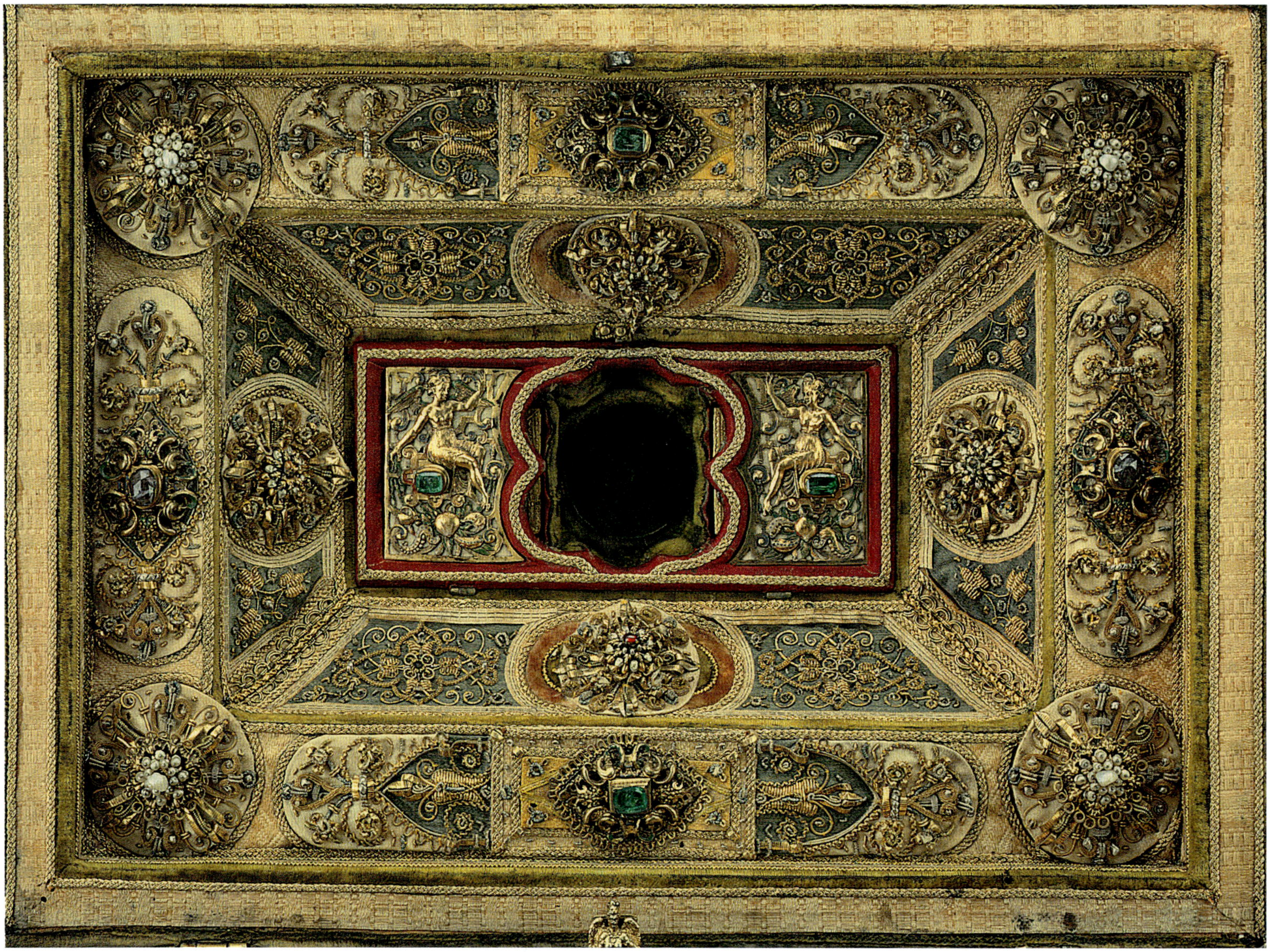

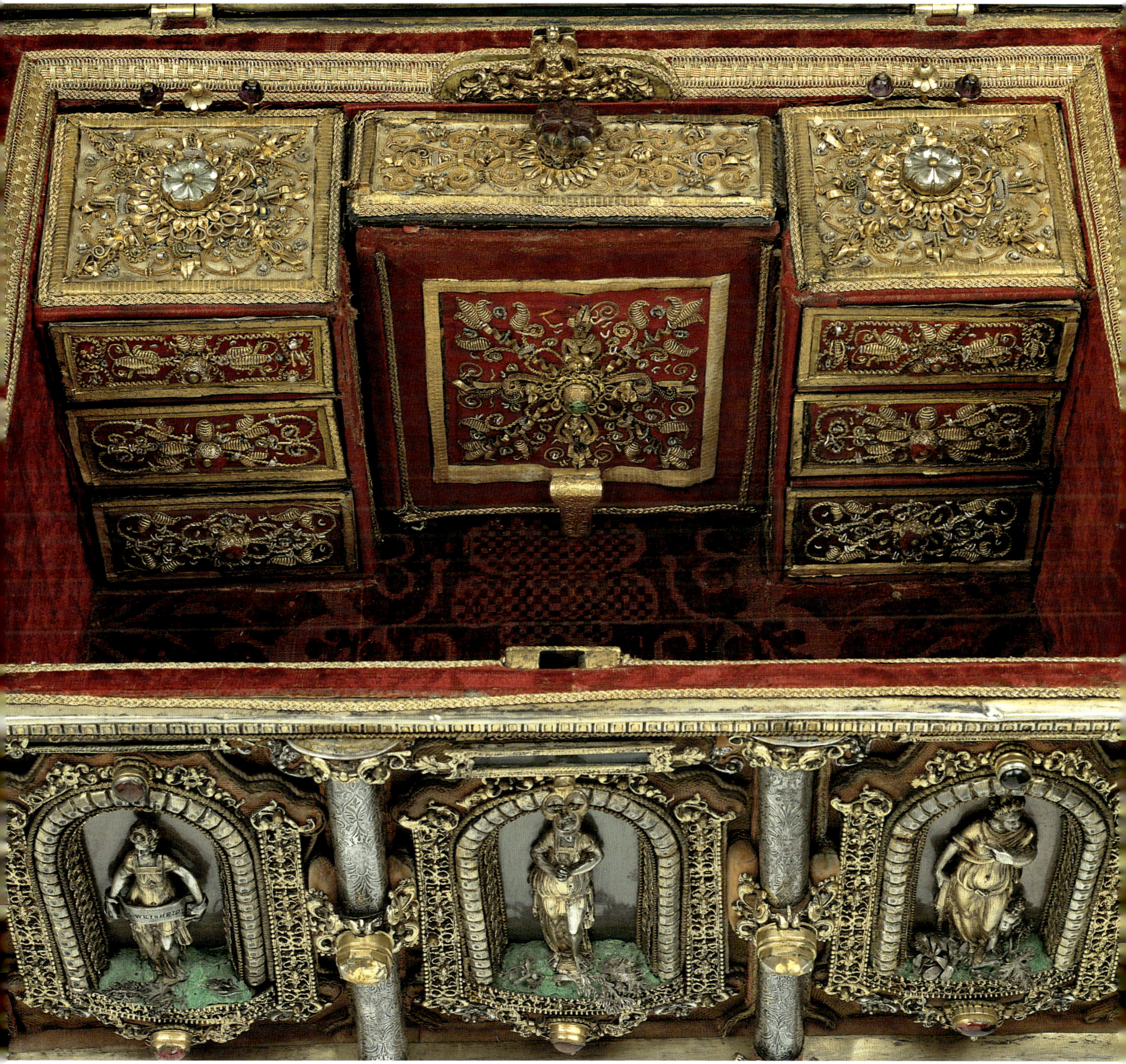

156 Mother-of-Pearl Box

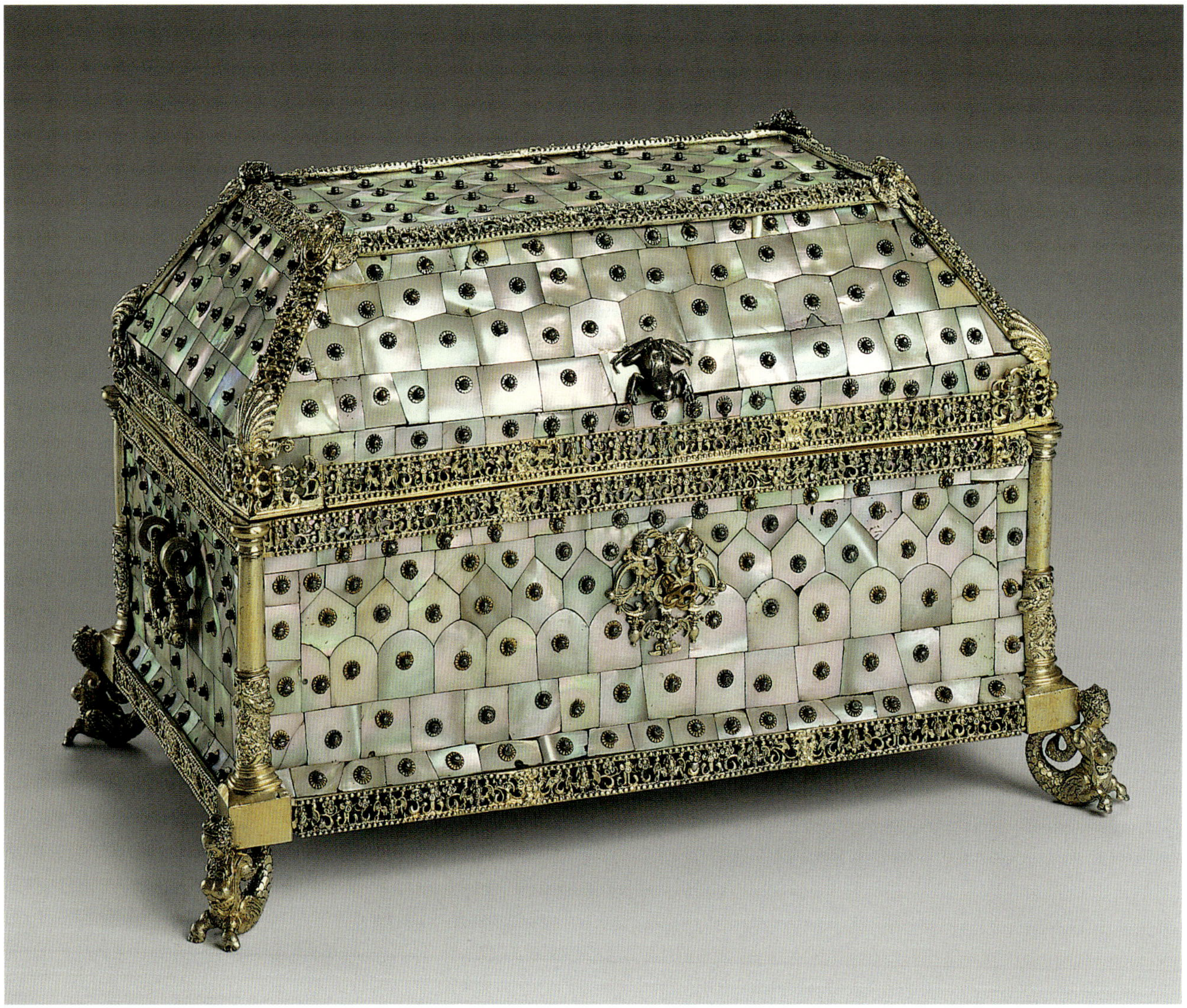

Box: Gujarat
End of the 16th century
Goldsmith's mount:
Nikolaus Schmidt
Nuremberg, circa 1600
Stained wood,
mother-of-pearl,
silver-gilt, velvet, silk,
gold-braided trimmings
H. 6¼ in. (16 cm),
W. 10⅞ in. (27.5 cm),
D. 8⅛ in. (18 cm)
Hallmark for Nuremberg
and maker's mark
"Hammer" in an oval
shape
First mentioned
in the Kunstkammer
inventory 1610,
fol. 194v–195r, no. 3
Staatliche Kunstsammlungen Dresden, Grünes
Gewölbe, inv. no. III 55
Lit.: Rosenberg 1925,
p. 137, no. 4030b;
Menzhausen 1968, p. 91,
ill. 69; Dresden 1990b,
pp. 61–63, cat. no. II.3
(Christine Wendt),
ill. p. 105; see also:
Holzhausen 1935,
pp. 234–44;
Sangl 2001, pp. 273-78;
London 2002,
cat. no. 195

Five of the initial seven valuable mother-of-pearl boxes acquired by the Saxon court in the late sixteenth and early seventeenth century still belong to the holdings of the Green Vault today. In 1924, two of the caskets were given to the House of Wettin as princely compensation (old inv. nos. III 221, III 246). One of them (III 246) has been part of the British royal collection since 1938.

For Christmas of 1589, the Leipzig dealer Veit Böttiger delivered a box for Electress Sophie that rests on lions that display shields (inv. no. III 245). This acquisition was followed in 1602 with payment for three further caskets from the Leipzig Easter Fair, among them the elaborately embellished so-called Torgau Pharmacy (inv. no. III 243) and a travel casket (inv. no. III 247). Between 1595 and 1609, two precious boxes by the Nuremberg goldsmith Nikolaus Schmidt arrived in Dresden (inv. no. III 55, III 244). Starting in 1610, these four boxes were kept in the Saxon Kunstkammer, whereas the remaining three caskets were added in 1623 from the bequest of Electress Sophie.

The casket rests on so-called "sea wonders"; according to the inventory description, it originally contained a chess game with twenty-six lacquered bone figures and thirty black and yellow game pieces made of stained horn. Compared to the casket on snail feet, the goldsmith's work Nikolaus Schmidt designed for the casket are somewhat more restrained. The four corners are embellished with columns, whereas all edges are decorated with perforated friezes and bead moldings. The handle is a nature cast in the form of a frog. Functional elements such as the keyhole, hinges, and handles are richly decorated accents.

Since the recent conservation treatment brought to light original Near Eastern paint layers below the textile cover, it may be deduced that the casket is definitely not a European imitation. Nevertheless, Schmidt substituted the mounts of the mother-of-pearl pieces by using gadrooned rosettes.
A.V.

157 Little Cabinet

In the last quarter of the sixteenth century, Nuremberg lost its lead as the goldsmiths' metropolis to Augsburg. During this time, ebony caskets embellished with multitudes of silver ornaments began to replace, little by little, the precious display boxes. This was stimulated by Wenzel Jamnitzer's small cabinets such as the example from the Martin D'Arcy Gallery of Art in Chicago or the lost example from Berlin's Kunstgewerbemuseum.

With its fall front, lateral handles, and complex system of drawers, this small cabinet by the Augsburg goldsmith Boas Ulrich is derived *en miniature* from the collector's cabinet. However, in this case, the practical function was replaced by its ostentatious character and a need for storage. None of the inventory entries lists any ancillary utensils.

In 1832, when transferred to the Green Vault after the dissolution of the Kunstkammer, this piece had already lost its crab-shaped feet. By 1879, the flower vases on the cabinet's four corners were also lost. Desite the decorative elements, the overall impression would be more modest than in Ulrich's cabinet in London's Victoria and Albert Museum, whose crowing figure, while identical to our example, still holds its original attribute, the mirror, in its hand.

A.V.

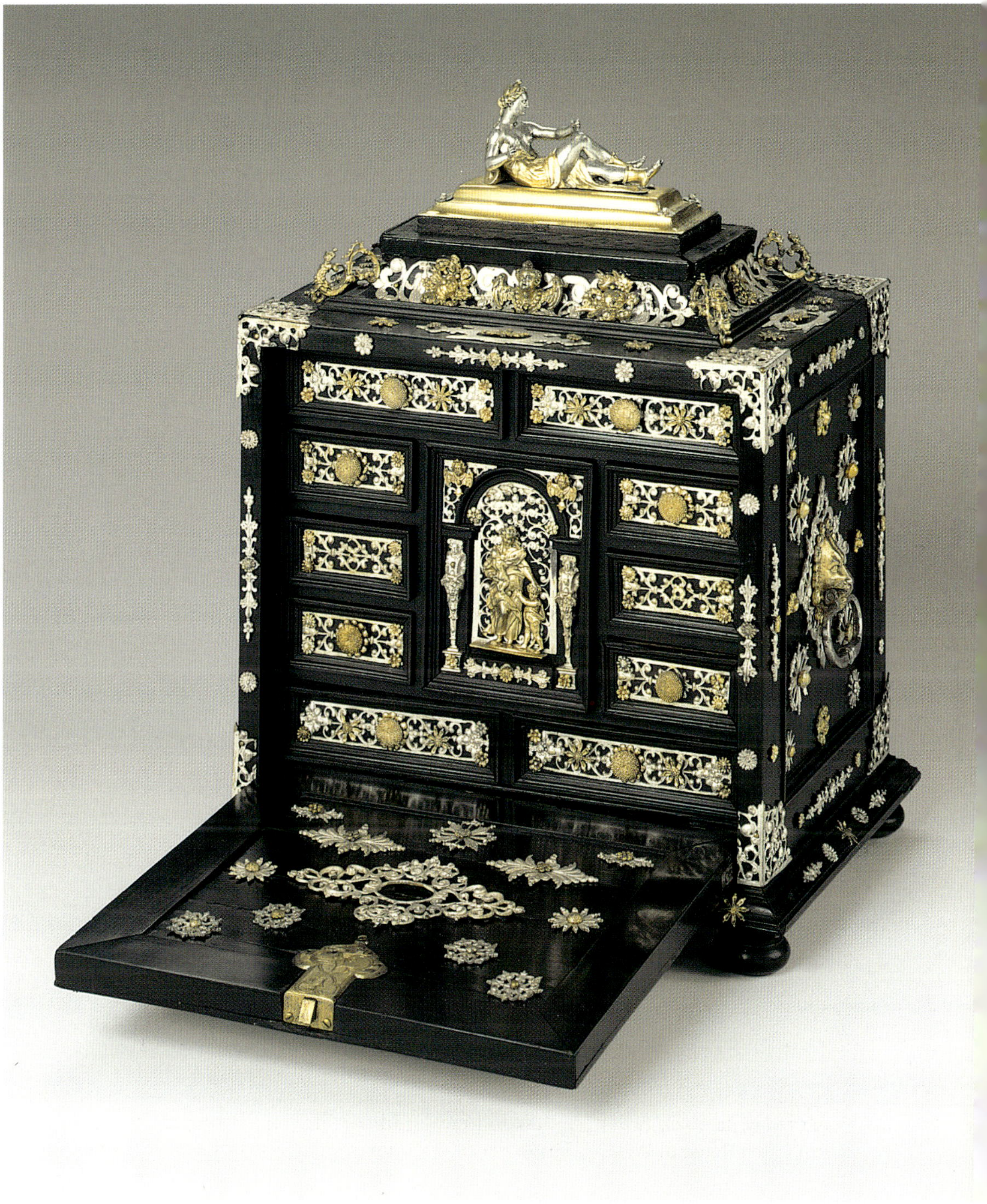

Boas Ulrich, Augsburg, circa 1600
Oak, ebony, silver, partly gilded, brass
H. 12 in. (30.5 cm), W. 10⅜ in. (24.6 cm),
D. 7¼ in. (18.4 cm) (opened 13⅛ in. / 33.5 cm)
Hallmark for Augsburg and maker's mark "BV" (in ligature in the shield)
First mentioned in the Kunstkammer inventory 1640, fol. 163r

Staatliche Kunstsammlungen Dresden, Grünes Gewölbe, inv. no. I 39
Lit.: Seling 1980, vol. III, no. 28, no. 906*c; Seling 1994, no. 906c; Munich 1994, vol. 2, cat. no. 59 (Ulli Arnold, with further bibliography); see also Seling 1980, vol. II, ill. 251; Pechstein 1985, pp. 57–70; Alfter 1986, p. 18

158 Pharmaceutical, Writing, and Toilet Casket

Documented in the Kunstkammer since 1640, this unmarked casket was transferred to the Armory on July 11, 1832 and passed on to the Green Vault in 1913.

Almost all the utensils listed in the inventory entries still exists today. They prove that this container is a casket incorporating writing, toilette, and apothecary devices. A mirror is mounted to the inside of the lid. Apart from a comb, the base drawer opening to the right contains a pair of scissors, a feather knife, as well as an ear cuvette whose handle terminates in a toothpick. A removable tray, located inside the casket, is divided into compartments. Its front row contains a little ebony box with a richly decorated, sliding lid. The box is flanked by a silver inkwell with screw-on lid, as well as a sandbox of identical size. Behind this, in two rows, four dice-shaped silver boxes with flat lids are arranged along with four glass bottles with silver caps to hold tinctures and ointments. When the tray is removed, a wooden device with four silver cupping-glasses can be seen. A little drawer at the end of the tray contains two silver venesection knives.

Accomplished proportions, well-balanced scrollwork ornaments, and the subjects of the plaques—an allegory of summer on the lid, as well as putti with marine creatures and illustrations of the zodiac—result in an harmonic overall impression and speak for Wallbaum's indisputable authorship of this work.
A.V.

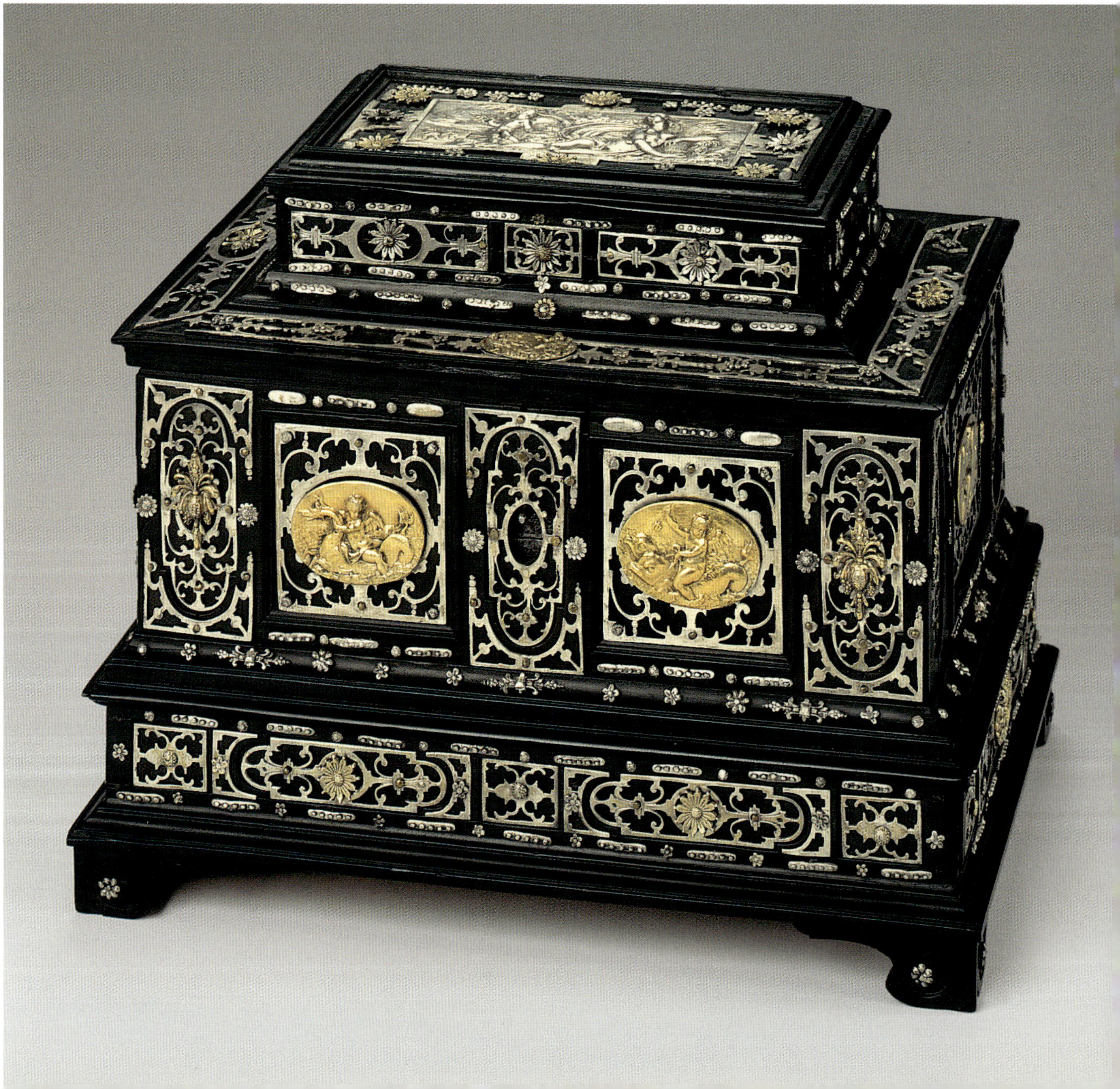

Ascribed to
Matthäus Wallbaum
Augsburg, circa 1600–20
Oak, ebony, silver, partly gilt, silk, mirrored glass, glass, iron
H. 7¼ in. (18.5 cm),
W. 9½ in. (24 cm),
D. 6⅞ in. (17.5 cm)
First mentioned in the Kunstkammer inventory 1640, fol. 163r–163v
Staatliche Kunstsammlungen Dresden, Grünes Gewölbe, inv. no. I 38
Lit.: Löwe 1975, cat. no. 56 (with further bibliography)

159 Two Writing and Toilet Boxes

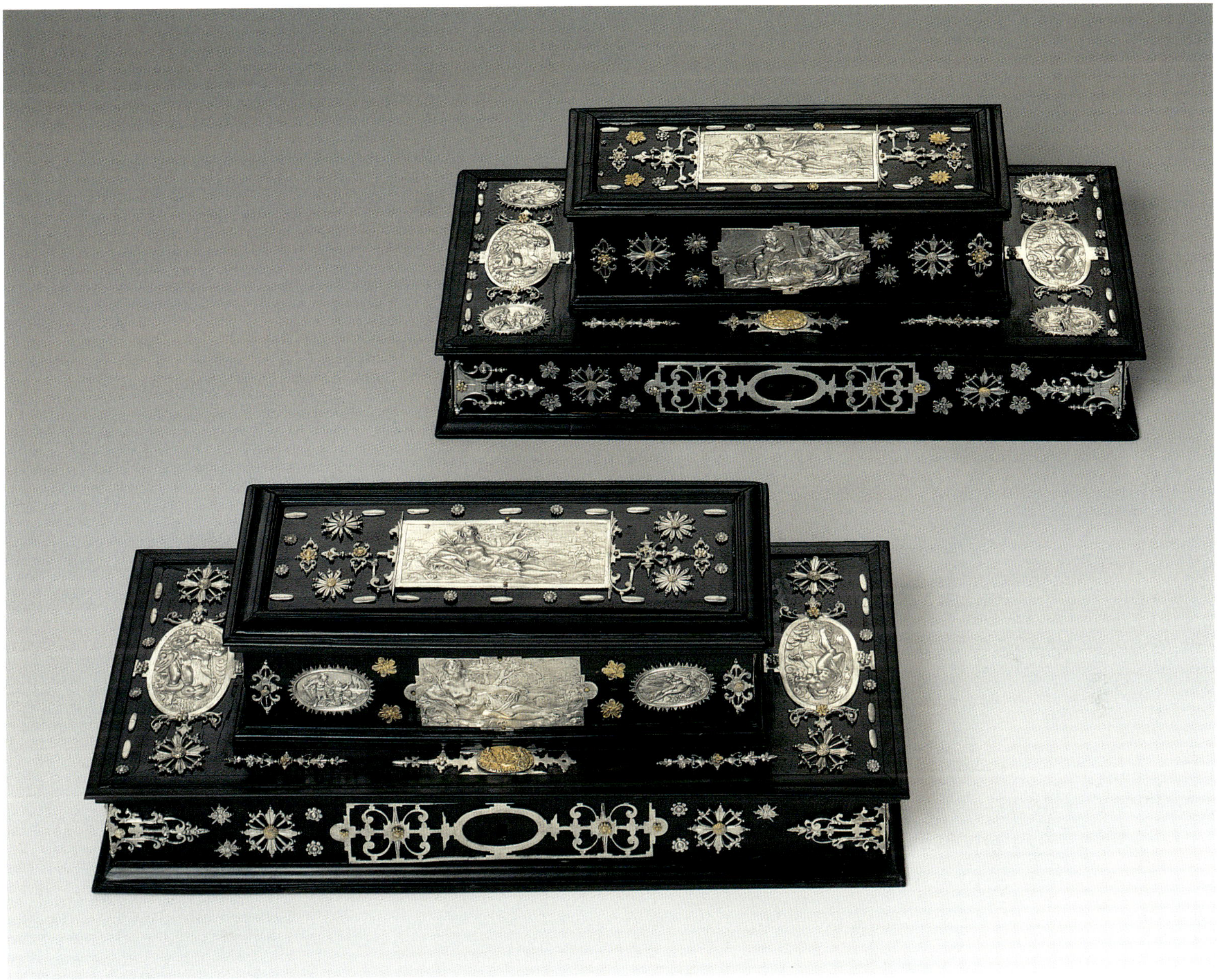

Between 1640 and 1832, these two boxes were documented without interruption in the inventories of the Kunstkammer. Although they came to the Armory after that, they were assigned to the Green Vault on December 20, 1913. Sadly, lost today are the combs, scissors, tongue scrapers, ear-picks, punches, feather knives, silver boxes, and inkwells listed in the inventories.

Apart from more ambitious commissions, the Wallbaum workshop also fabricated fair numbers of serially-produced caskets of this type. This is testified to by two almost identical examples kept in Augsburg's Maximilianmuseum and in the Historisches Museum Basel. The choice of plaques—consisting of the Four Seasons (with a repetition of the allegory of spring on the lid), symbols of the elements water and air, a small selection of zodiacal signs, as well as Old Testament scenes—further underscores a fabrication process comparable to a manufactory. A.V.

Matthäus Wallbaum, Augsburg, circa 1600
Oak, ebony, silver, partly gilded, mirrored glass
H. 4¾ in. (12.2 cm), W. 14⅜ in. (36.6 cm), D. 6⅛ in. (15.5 cm)
Hallmark for Augsburg with a maker's mark (tree in shield)
First mentioned in the Kunstkammer inventory 1640, fol. 164r–164v
Staatliche Kunstsammlungen Dresden, Grünes Gewölbe, inv. no. I 36 (foreground) and I 37 (background)
Lit.: Löwe 1975, cat. nos. 47 and 48 (with further bibliography); Seling 1980, vol. III, no. 22 (I 36), no. 1060d, see also no. 1060c; Seling 1994, no. 23* (I 37)

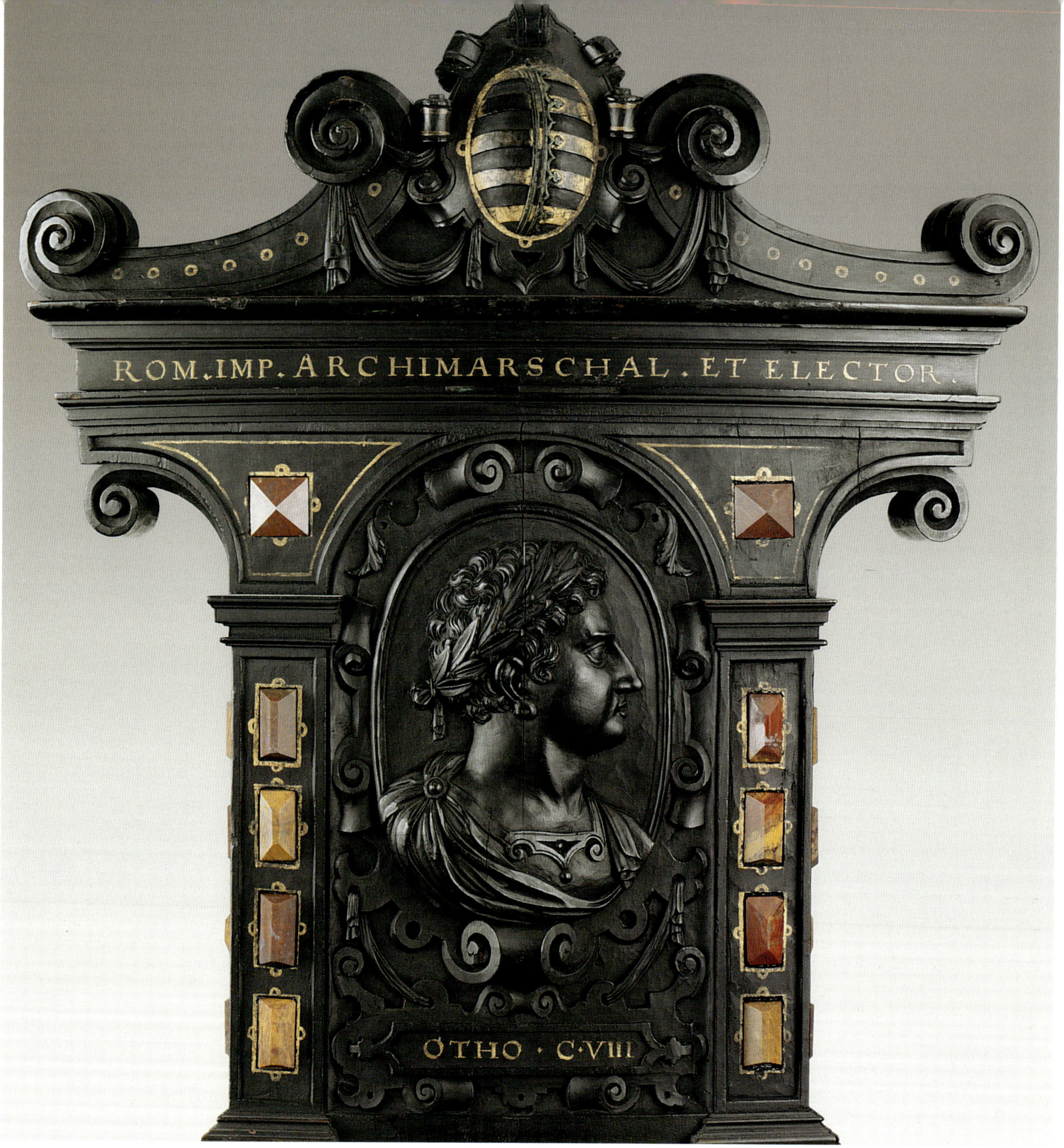

Giovanni Maria Nosseni
Torgau, circa 1579/80
Pear wood, ebonized, carved, partly painted and gilded, polished stone inlay of jasper, jaspagate, seats of serpentine from Zöblitz, black encrustation
H. 43¾ in. (111 cm), W. 19⅝ in. (49 cm), D. 18⅝ in. (48 cm)
Inscribed on the front of the backrest CHRISTIANVS· D· G · DUX SAXO· SAC., on the reverse of the backrest ROM. IMP. ARCHIMARSCHAL. ET ELECTOR., below this OTHO·C·VIII (inv. no. 47 719), CALLICVLA·C·IIII (inv. no. 47 720)
Conceived in 1576 as an ensemble of twelve chairs for Schloss Lichtenberg, transferred in 1579 from Torgau to Dresden; first mentioned in 1591 in the Dresden Residenzschloss.
Kunstgewerbemuseum, inv. no. 47 719 and 47 720
Lit.: Dresden 1960, p. 100; Kreisel 1968, vol. 1, p. 128; Washington 1978, cat. no. 95; Dresden 1981, cat. no. 23; Hoyer 1995, pp. 63–69, cat. nos. 253–255 (with reference to archival sources); Lemgo 2002, pp. 99, 260–62, cat. no. 95

160 Two Chairs

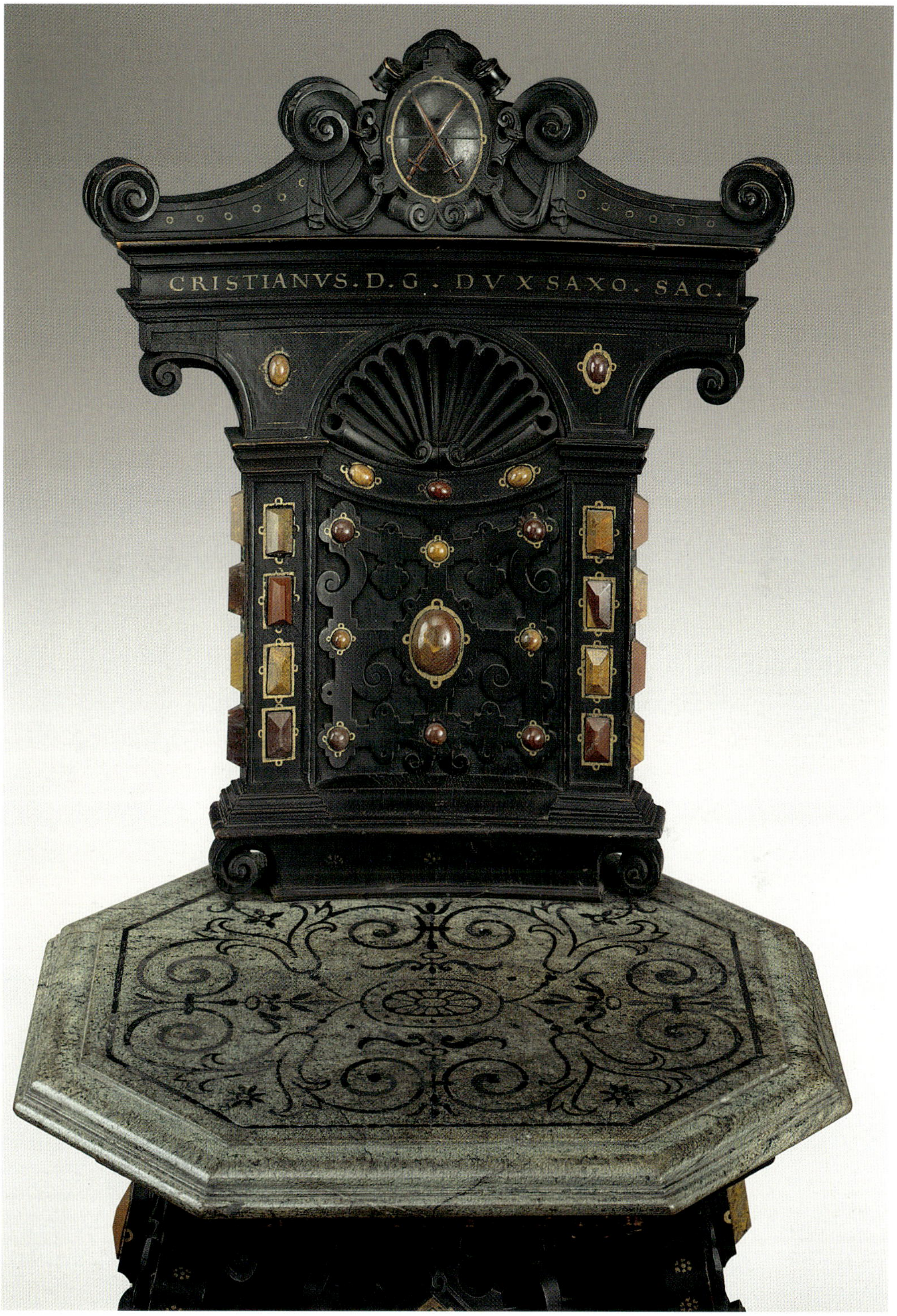

Starting in 1579, Nosseni began to design and produce a series of twelve chairs with portraits of Roman emperors as well as four stone tables for Elector August. These objects were not completed until the reign of his son and successor Elector Christian I. Christian installed the series of ceremonial chairs and one of the stone tables as an ensemble in one of the annexes of his Dresden Residenzschloss.

Based on the design of the first series, he ordered the production of another set of twelve chairs for one additional stone table. However, they were more modest and without portraits. A number of chairs from this latter series have equally survived and are today preserved in Dresden's Kunstgewerbemuseum.

The carvings of these unusual pieces of seating furniture—following the type of the Italian stool, the so-called *sgabello*—were direct adaptations of Hans Vredeman de Vries' style. De Vries came from the Northern part of the Low Countries and produced countless drawings of ornaments that greatly influenced northern Europe's Renaissance style. Models for the chairs' scrollwork and mounts were derived from de Vries' suite of engravings entitled *Dorica-Ionica*. For the creation of the "diamonds." Genuine semi-precious stones were applied instead of the customary wood or simple stones. Today some have been replaced by modern imitations. In their technical fabrication, the arabesques with paste encrustation on the stone seats resemble their Italian prototypes.

For the Saxon elector, the ambitious artistic design of these chairs also had a programmatic purpose: In 1548, Duke Moritz of Saxony had been officially appointed elector of Saxony by Emperor Charles V. Forty years thereafter, the still juvenile electoral dynasty created a worthy context and an historic continuity by taking this recourse to the well-known series of the twelve Roman emperors. The matching table also played a role within this symbolism. The chairs with the name of the elector and the Saxon coat of arms on their backrests, as well as the precious stones unearthed from Saxon soil thus emphasize the self-confidence of one of the most powerful territories within the Holy Roman Empire.
A.v.d.G.

161 Hunting and Work Desk of Elector Johann Georg I of Saxony

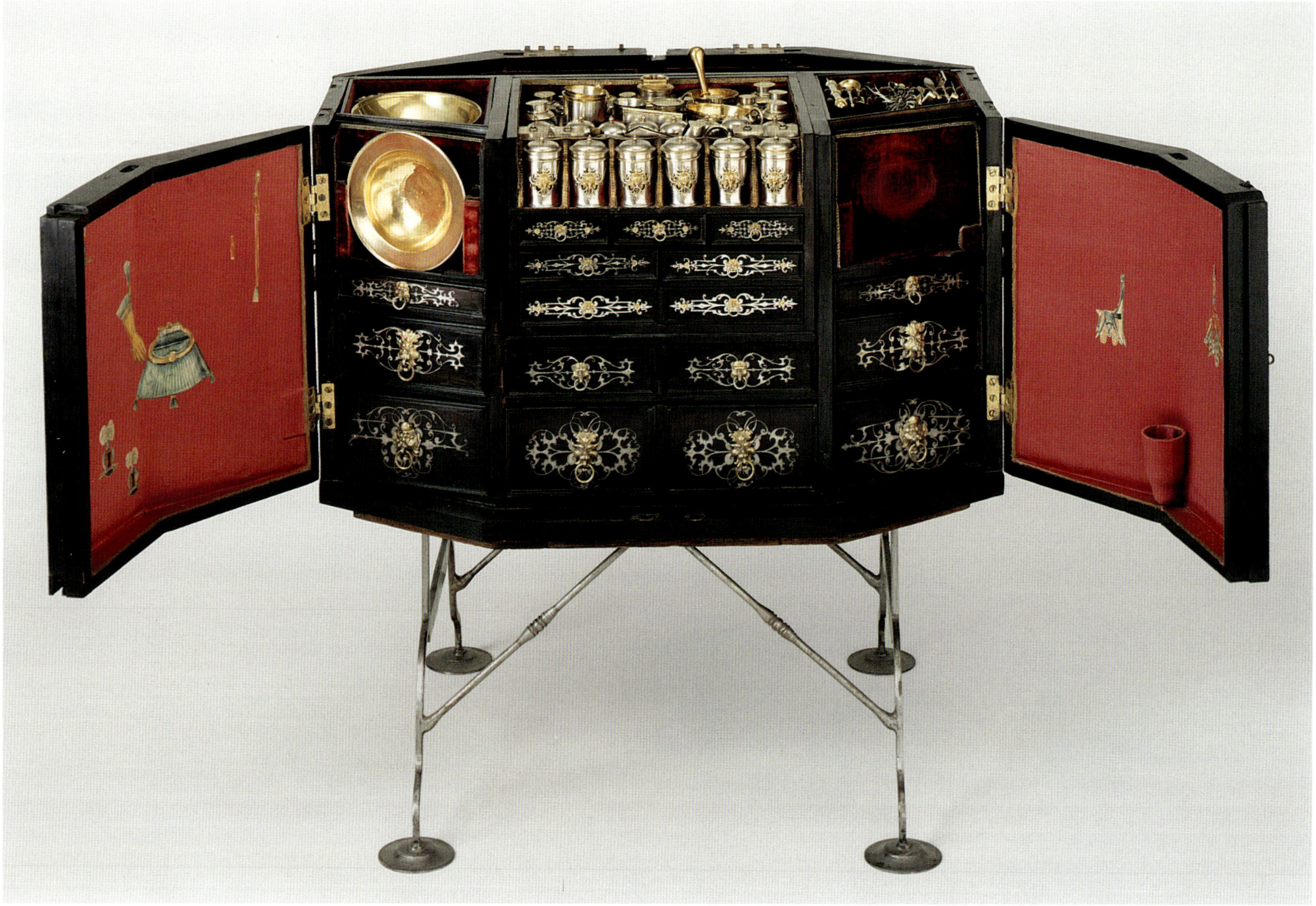

This kind of furniture is a mute servant who never abandons his master; it is a servant with a philosophical mind" (Heikamp).

The hunting and work desk of Elector Johann Georg I of Saxony consists of an octagonal case and a separate tabletop. The latter is composed of nine originally detachable parts of which the dimensions of the central part are approximately the same as those of the base of the case. The central section could thus be used as the case's cover. The remaining eight segments could be assembled into a larger tabletop. The case itself can be opened at its two long sides. Hidden behind the doors, whose insides were stocked with hunting and gardening tools (today in Dresden's Armory), are numerous drawers and boxes containing a total of about 250 items, among them toilet and pharmacy items, painting and turning tools, and craftsman's instruments. Their placements were precisely determined by small pen-and-ink drawings. Unfortunately, there is no information available about the original frame for the base.

Decorated with silver inlay, the tabletop is the most intricately adorned component. Its central image shows the ancient commander Coriolanus outside Rome, and the other eight segments display embellishments with trophies alternating with scenes of (clockwise from the front) the sacrifice of Marcus Curtius, Aeneas' arrival in Carthage and Queen Dido, Gaius Mucius Scaevola before the Etruscan king Lars Porsenna, and the flight of Aeneas and his father Anchises from Troy. The exterior of the case is decorated with narrow bands of inlaid silver; the drawer fronts are adorned with partly silver-gilt inlays.

The Kunstkammer furnishings that Philipp Hainhofer supplied to European princes during the first few decades of the seventeenth century are among the highlights of European art furniture. The most precious materials were used in the execution of these products, and yet they are more than simply beautiful cabinets and tables containing fascinating and valuable collections. Their contents of multitudes of the choicest objects mirror God's creation in a microcosmic manner. Through study and use of the items inside the furniture, the princely owner obtained singular insight into

Unknown Augsburg cabinetmaker,
Christoph Wild and Tobias Leucker, presumably based on the design and the specifications of Philipp Hainhofer
Augsburg, ca. 1620–25
Top: pine veneered with oak and ebony, with engraved silver inlays
W. 57⅛ in. (145 cm), D. 38½ in. (97.4 cm)
Chest: pine, walnut, ebony veneer;
drawers: oak, red velvet;
handles: iron; 1978 additions include the iron frame, the two middle drawers, parts of the velvet lining, and the gold-braid trimming
H. 17¼ in. (43.9 cm), W. 30⅞ in. (78.5 cm),
D. 21¼ in. (54 cm)
Silver inlay: hallmarked with a pinecone (*pyr*) for Augsburg and maker's mark of Christoph Wild
Tools and vessels: silver, partly gilt; brass; iron; glass; ivory, partly painted; ebony
Hallmarked with a pinecone (*pyr*) for Augsburg and maker's mark of Christoph Wild on two bottles with screw caps and scales
For Tobias Leucker: maker's mark TL and pinecone hallmark (*pyr*) for Augsburg on twenty-nine items: ten pharmacist's containers, scales, two soap boxes, six cupping glasses, one oil cruet, one strainer, two funnels, six boxes with lids
In the doors: implements for falconry and hunting weapons; instruments for military use: grappling hook, rope, and *Gitterspreizer* (device for spreading apart the iron grilles of a portcullis)
Trays and drawers: middle tray: traveling pharmacy and barber's instruments
In the drawers: engineering tools and instruments for both military and peaceful uses and farrier's tools, beautifully worked in wood, ivory, and other materials
Upper drawer left: (tray) sculptor's tools; (floor) files
Middle drawer left: (tray) metal tools and spatula; (floor) locksmith's tools
Bottom drawer left: farrier's tools
Upper drawer right: precision tools
Middle drawer right: (first tray) wood saw, plane blade, chisels, carving iron; (second tray) wood drill, shears; (floor) carpenter's tools: broad ax, saw, fretsaw
Bottom drawer right: (tray) sighting device, mathematical instruments; (floor) tinderbox, flintlock, powder horn, mortar (?)
Middle drawers bottom: (tray) turner's blades and shafts; (floor) machines and large tools: mill, turning lathe, and jack for raising doors off their hinges

First mentioned in the Kunstkammer inventory after 1732 with the notation that the table was delivered to the Kunstkammer in 1636; in 1741 listed in the Kunstkammer inventory with exact list of its contents and location
Staatliche Kunstsammlungen Dresden, Kunstgewerbemuseum, inv. no. 47 724
Lit.: Dresden 1960, cat. no. I 3; Heikamp 1966; Washington 1978, cat. no. 97; Seling 1980; Kreisel 1981, pp. 110, 171, ill. 367; Dresden 1981, pp. 48–53, cat. no. 30; Munich 1994, pp. 263–67, cat. no. 62 (Gisela Haase, with reference to archival material and further bibliography); Seling 1994; Seelig 1994

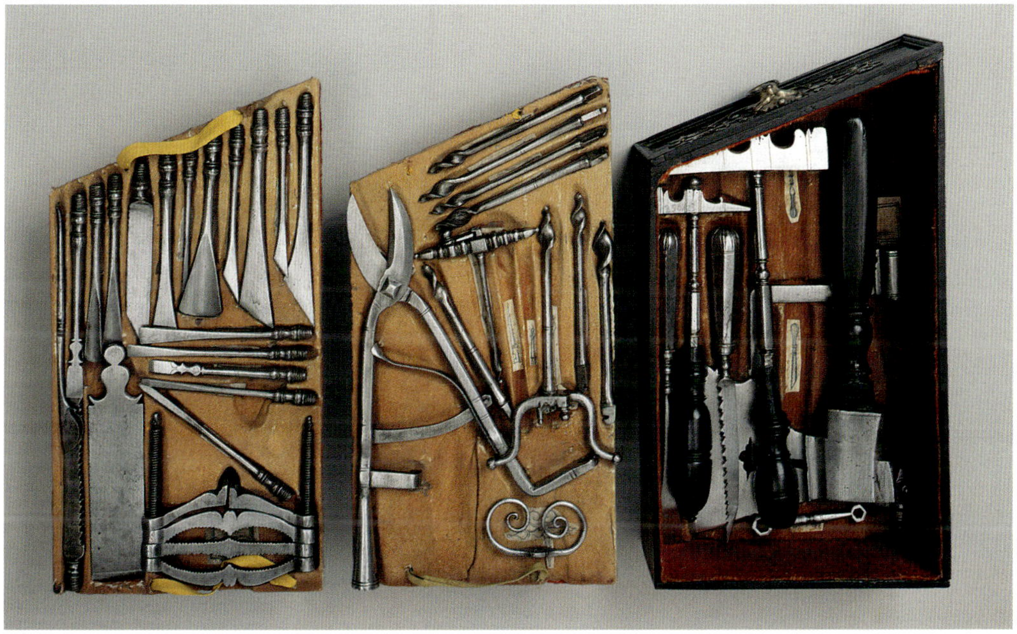

the laws of nature, as well as into the coherence and harmony of creation.

Philipp Hainhofer, an Augsburg patrician and merchant who also worked as art agent for numerous princes, initiated the production of art cabinets. These added another dimension to the collecting of *naturalia, artificialia, exotica,* and *mirabilia,* the types of objects Renaissance princes gathered in their Kunstkammers. Augsburg's best artists and artisans worked under Hainhofer's guidance, basing their work on his designs and producing the glorious and ingenious cabinets that were subsequently decorated and furnished with objects personally assembled by Hainhofer. As pieces of furniture, they are therefore *Gesamtkunstwerks.* The most significant art cabinets produced following Hainhofer's universal concept were either delivered by him to the duke of Pomerania (dated 1617, burned in World War II, its contents preserved in the Kunstgewerbemuseum of Berlin), or they came into the possession of Ferdinando II de' Medici, grand duke of Tuscany (dated 1628, today Florence, Museo degli Argenti) and King Gustav Adolf of Sweden (dated 1632, today Uppsala, Museum Gustavianum) as diplomatic gifts.

The development of a second variant of this kind of furniture, namely the princely work desk, occurred simultaneously with the evolution of universal art cabinets. In days when traveling was not yet a pleasant experience overall, the Augsburg furniture makers and silversmiths began to specialize in the production of thoroughly practical, ingenious travel furniture and *necessaires.* Apart from beds, chairs, and tables that could be folded up and put away in chests, it could include toilet garniture, travel pharmacies, flasks for fragrances, and boxes with writing implements. A table was developed that not only accommodated some of these elements but could also contain much more as well. Hainhofer created travel furniture that offered its owner all conceivable comforts while traveling. These works were equipped with additional instruments, tools, and devices organized in countless drawers. The prince was thus able to do practical work at any given moment, or he could demonstrate his universal collection and show off his related knowledge.

Starting in 1615, Hainhofer attempted, directly or through intermediaries, to draw attention to his travel tables at the princely courts of Bavaria, Pomerania, Florence, and Paris. It is uncertain, however, whether this campaign resulted in any orders.

There are only two known travel tables attributed beyond any doubt to the oeuvre of Hainhofer. Today, they belong to the collections of the Museum of Decorative Arts of the Staatliche Kunstsammlungen Dresden. They were once owned by Elector Johann Georg I of Saxony and his wife Magdalena Sibylla of Brandenburg. Although their exteriors are different from one another, they both follow the tradition of Hainhofer's furniture. The rectangular table for the electress is similar to the 1617 design of the Pomeranian Art Cupboard. Among other items, it contains a virginal, a folding chair, writing utensils, a toilet garniture, a sewing kit, a pharmacy, and game boards. The elector's hunting and work desk, on the other hand, is smaller and more compact. While its octagonal top was embellished with engraved silver inlays, the contents are of a more practical nature: it contains tools for the hunt and for falconry, pharmacist's implements, medical instruments, vintner's tools, as well as a multitude of other devices. This hunting and work desk did not contain any games. With respect to their execution, many of the items are similar to the ones in the table of the electress. Thus an attribution of the electress's table to Hainhofer is justified.

The outer shape of the work desk is relatively simple, and its contents are clearly distributed into numerous drawers and boxes. Thanks to its multiple toilet items, the princely owner of this travel table was able to take perfect care of himself. The well-stocked pharmacy and the surgical instruments guaranteed excellent medical care in the event of an emergency. The large variety of tools and devices enabled the prince to pursue diverse interests, from hunting to drawing and painting, or creating artworks with the lathe. The extensive tool assortment offered a talented individual unlimited opportunities to be creative. This is where the Humanist idea underlying Hainhofer's work tables becomes tangible: the belief that humans in general, but particularly princes, are capable, at least to a certain degree, of "creating" the world themselves. The prince could thus execute his tasks, entrusted directly to him by God. Consequently, he was the representative of God on earth and could fulfill the role attributed to him according to the divine plan. This "worldly Humanism," with a stress on the attribute "worldly," demanded from the prince a *vita activa* that would enable him to form society in a way comparable to his ability to produce tangible objects.

The top covering the table shows deeds of the ancient hero Aeneas and other Roman protagonists. It thus depicts the classical virtues that were supposed to be adopted by the prince and then would ennoble him. The table's owner intended that its contents would serve as a mirror of the divine mastermind and creator of the world. Thus, the hunting and work desk is directly connected to the encyclopedic program of the art cabinets.
A.v.d.G.

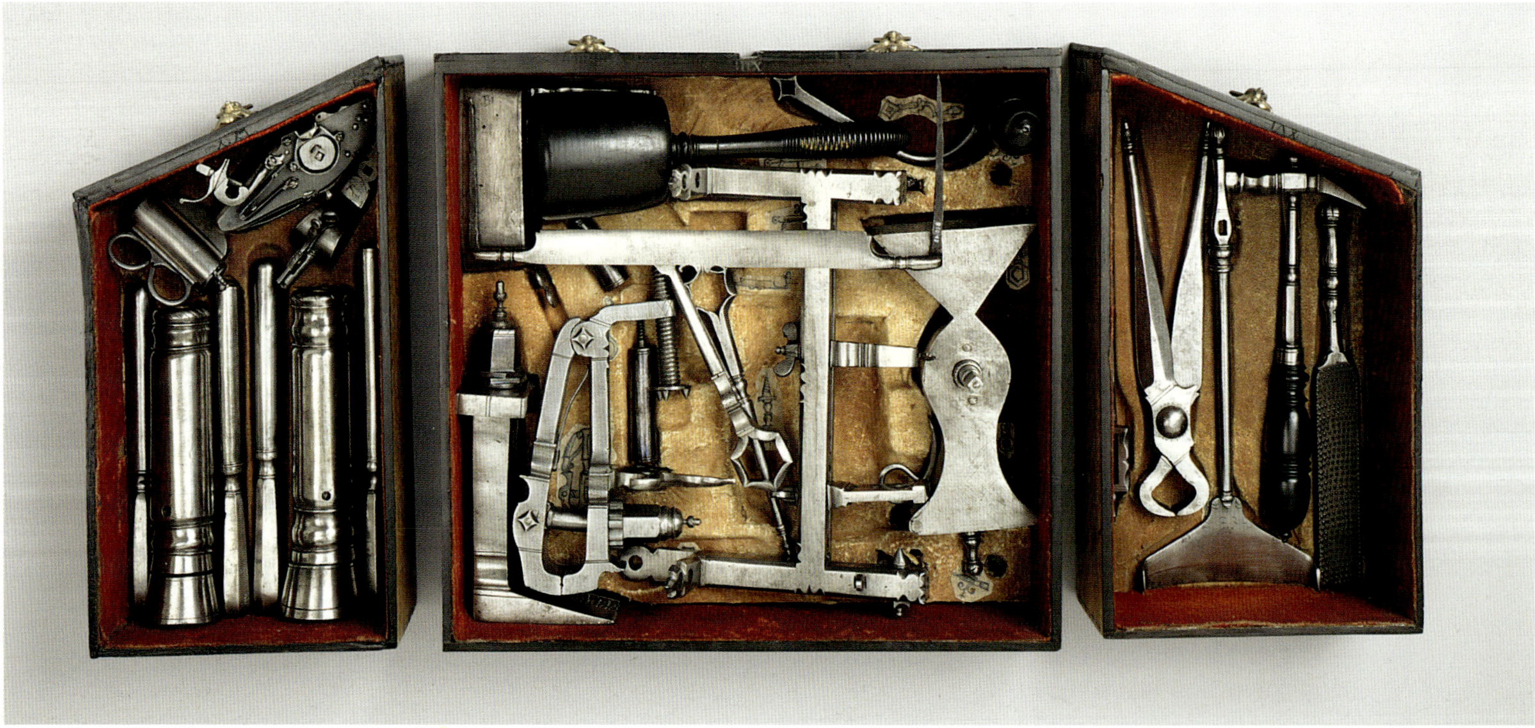

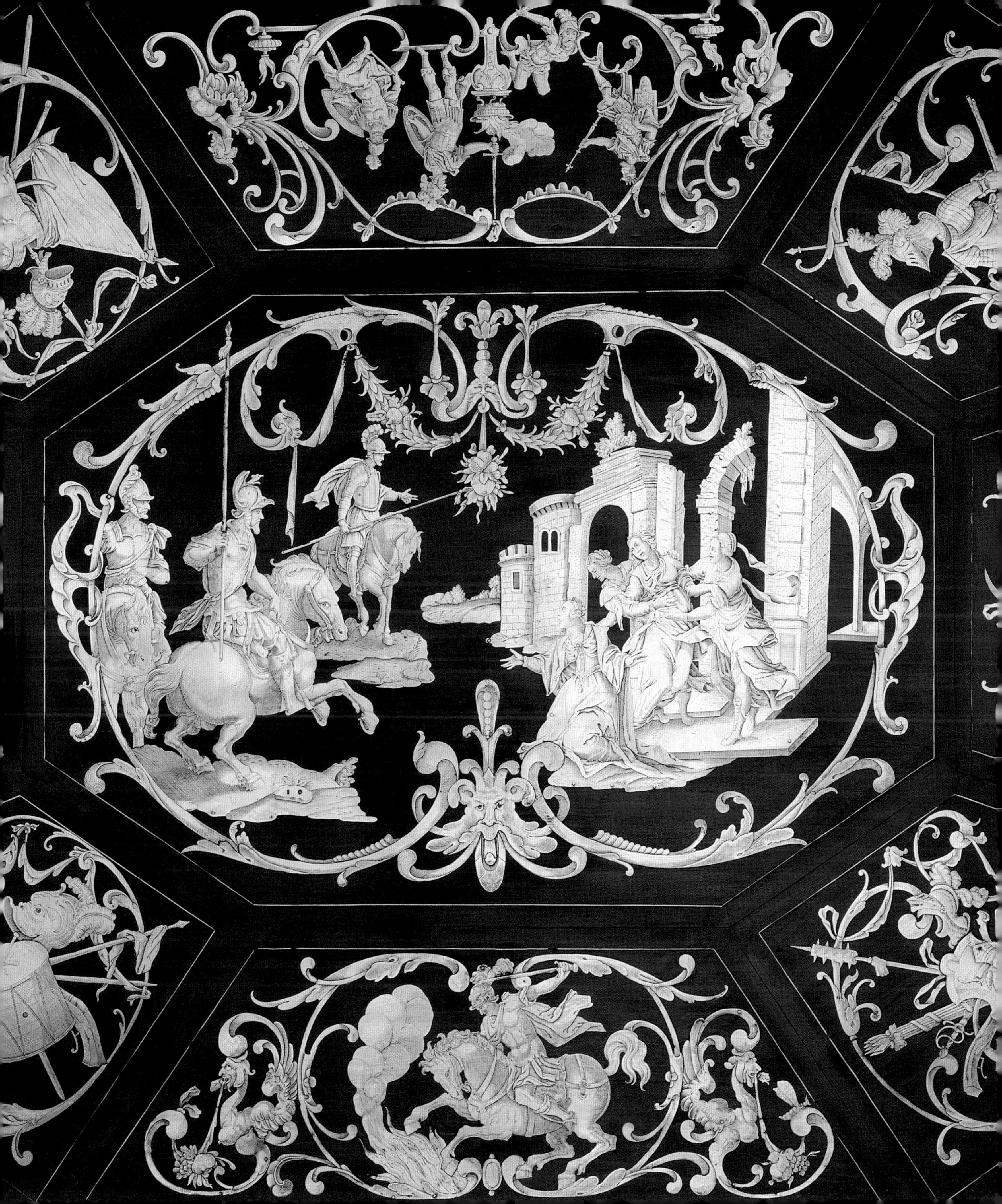

162 Emerald Cluster

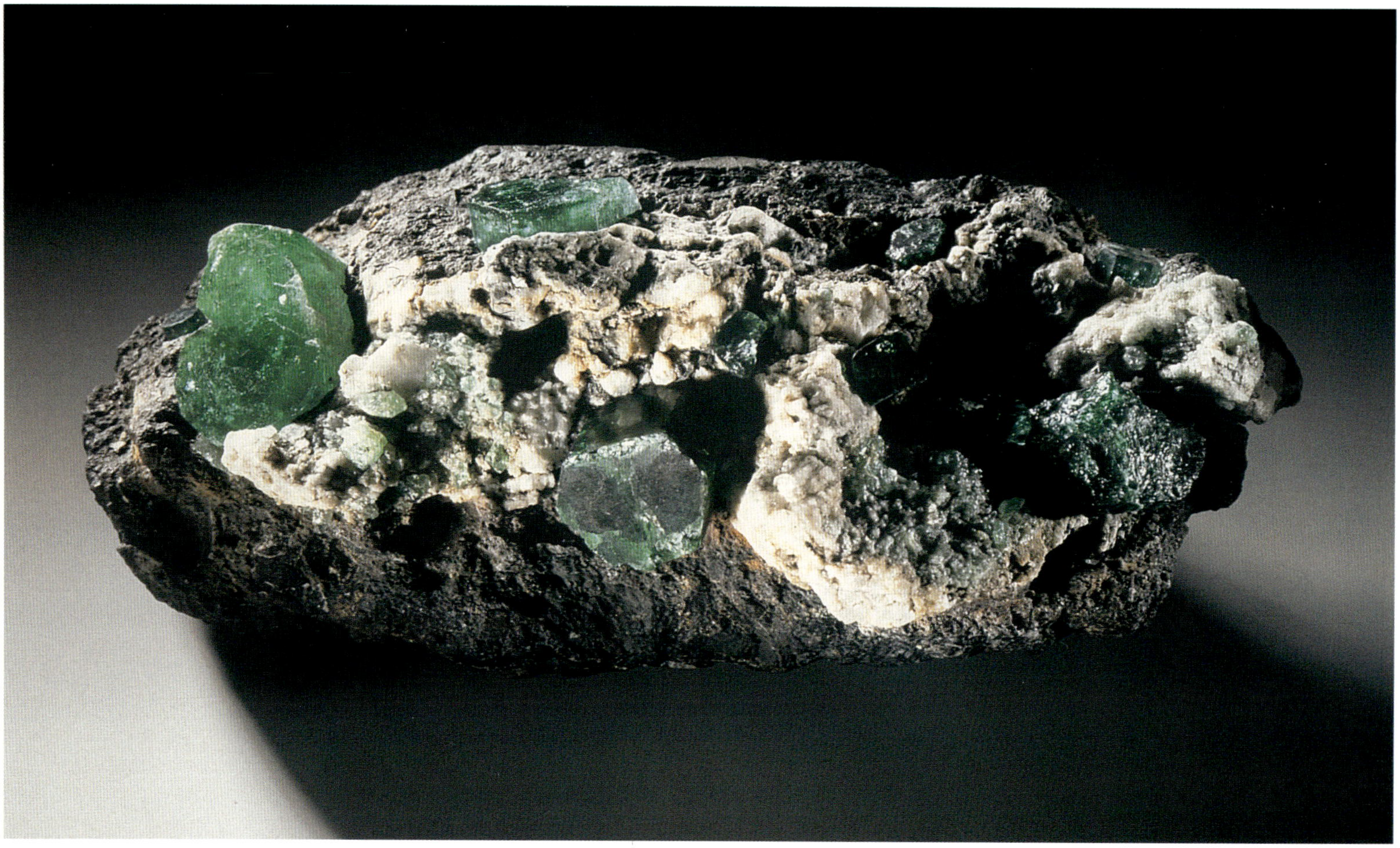

In 1581, on the occasion of his visit to Prague, Elector August of Saxony received this collection of precious emeralds as a present from Emperor Rudolf II. The stones were supposedly found in the mine of Chivor-Somondoco (Columbia), which had been made accessible only in 1580 on the order of the Spanish crown. Archduke Ferdinand II of Tyrol preserved a similar emerald cluster in his Schloss Ambras Kunstkammer near Innsbruck. It was given to Vienna's Museum of Natural History in 1881.

Both emerald clusters give the impression that they were naturally formed. In reality, they consist of emeralds of varying sizes that were placed into a limonitic compound (brown iron ore) and then cemented with pitch. The results of this trick are very effective re-creations of natural wonders that never cease to astonish their beholders.

Elector August attributed superior meaning to this gift of emeralds. Although he kept it in an unassuming box lined with red velvet in his Kunstkammer, he regarded it as a lasting symbol of the alliance with the Imperial House. He commanded that this present from Emperor Rudolf II remain forever with the Electoral House and its family. Elector Friedrich August I, after 1697 also king of Poland, remained faithful to this legacy. He commissioned a statuette from the Dresden court sculptor Balthasar Permoser to carry the cluster, which originally included sixteen emeralds. Intended as decoration for the Jewel Chamber in the Green Vault, it was installed there by 1729.

J.K.

Limonitic compound (brown iron ore), emeralds, L. 9 5/8 in. (24.5 cm)
Given as a present
by Emperor Rudolf II
to Elector August in 1581
First mentioned in the Kunstkammer inventory 1587, fol. 8r–v
Staatliche Kunstsammlungen Dresden, Grünes Gewölbe, inv. no. VIII 303
Lit.: Washington 1978, cat. no. 291; Nickel 1981; Syndram 1999, pp. 32, 149; Marx 2000b, pp. 247f.; Vötsch 2002, p. 209

Chronology 1553–1626

Compiled by Antje Scherner

Time Period	World History	History of the Holy Roman Empire of the German Nation	Saxony's History	Art–Culture–Science in Europe	Art–Culture–Science in Saxony
1553–59	1555 Cosimo de' Medici, duke of Florence, conquers Siena 1556 Philipp II crowned king of Spain (until 1598 †) 1557 First national bankruptcy of the House of Hapsburg 1558 Elizabeth I crowned queen of England (until 1603 †)	1555 Augsburg Peace of Religion (*Augsburger Religionsfriede*) 1556 Abdication of Emperor Charles V Ferdinand I becomes emperor (until 1564 †) 1558–59 Imperial Diet (*Reichstag*) in Augsburg, Formation of the Protestant estates	1553 Elector Moritz falls in the battle of Sievershausen August becomes elector of Saxony (until 1586 †)	1556 Ottheinrichsbau of Heidelberg Castle begun (until 1559) 1558 Gioseffo Zarlino publishes *Istitutioni harmoniche* (modern harmonics with definition of major and minor) 1558 First German stock exchange in Hamburg 1559 Gerhard Mercator's world map	1553 Lucas Cranach the Elder dies in Weimar 1555 Georgius Agricola dies in Chemnitz. His work on metallurgy and ironworks, *De re metallica libri XII*, is published in 1556 1556 Completion of Dresden's Residential Palace as a four-wing structure 1556 Electoral library established 1559 Death of Adam Ries(e) in Annaberg 1559 Arsenal established (until 1563, now Albertinum)
1560–64	1560 Charles IX crowned King of France (until 1574 †), until 1563 rule of Catharine de' Medici 1562 Start of the Huguenot wars in France (until 1598 with interruption) 1563 Conclusion of the Council of Trent	1564 Maximilian becomes Roman-German emperor until 1576 (†)	1562 Decree of an order against luxury	1560 Building of the Uffizi in Florence (Giorgio Vasari) begins 1560 Orlando di Lasso first concert master in Munich 1561 Giambologna comes to the Medici court in Florence 1564 Death of Michelangelo, birth of William Shakespeare	1560 Founding of the electoral Saxon *Kunstkammer* 1560 Philipp Melanchthon dies in Wittenberg
1565–69	1565 Start of the Netherlandish uprising against the Spanish rule 1567 Duke of Alba governor in the Netherlands 1568 Execution of Counts Egmont and Hoorn by the duke of Alba; open revolt of the Netherlands against Spain 1569 Cosimo I de' Medici becomes grand duke of Tuscany	1566 Imperial Diet of Augsburg; emperor and Catholic estates officially accept decrees of Council of Trent. Since the mid 1560s, Counter Reformation in the Empire; Palatinate turns to Calvinism	1565 Independence of Naumburg and Merseburg dioceses factually revoked 1566 On the Imperial Diet of Augsburg, the electoral office and the office of imperial grand marshal [*Reichserzmarschall*] are bestowed upon August of Saxony by Emperor Maximilian II 1566–67 *Grumbacher Händel*, Victory of Prince Elector August over the Ernestine Johann Friedrich the Middle through siege of Gotha 1566–67 Gain of Thuringian districts Weida, Ziegenrück, and Arnshaug 1569 Gain of Voigtsberg and Plauen districts	1567 English trade agency in Hamburg 1568 Building of Il Gesù, Rome, begins (Giacomo Vignola) 1568 Invention of the *Camera obscura* with lens 1568 Building of the Antiquarium in Munich's *Residenz* (until 1571), for Albrecht V of Bavaria's Collection of Antiques begins (Jacopo Strada)	1565 Building of Dresden's Chancellery (*Kanzleigebäude*) begins, one of the empire's first administrative structures 1568 Stephan Bretschneider sent to Italy as one of the first Saxon artists 1568 Antonio Scandello becomes first Saxon court conductor 1568 Building of Augustusburg begins (until 1573) 1569 Rocco di Linar becomes master builder of fortifications (until 1577)

Time Period	World History	History of the Holy Roman Empire of the German Nation	Saxony's History	Art–Culture–Science in Europe	Art–Culture–Science in Saxony
1570–74	1571 Naval battle near Lepano (Gulf of Corinth). Don Juan d'Austria, with a fleet of the Holy Alliance, defeats the Ottomans 1572 "St. Bartholomew's Night" ("Parisian Blood Wedding"): 3,000–4,000 Huguenots murdered in Paris 1574 Francesco I de' Medici becomes grand duke of Tuscany (until 1587 †) 1574 Henry III crowned king of France (until 1589 †)	1570 Imperial Diet in Speyer; due to the territorial interests of the imperial estates, the reform of the imperial war system fails	1570–73 The dukedom of Mansfeld, rich in copper deposits, is put under partial sequestration 1572 *Constitutiones* (uniform law code for Saxony) decreed 1574 Founding of the Secret Council (*Geheimer Rat*) as the country's highest authority 1574 Fight against "crypto Calvinism"	1570 North Sea flood said to kill 100,000 1572 Maximilian's tomb erected in Innsbruck's Court Church 1574 Façade of Il Gesù completed (Giacomo della Porta) 1574 Astronomical clock in Strasbourg completed	1572 David Uslaub appointed Art Chamberlain since 1574 Exploitation of Saxon alabaster deposits begins
1575–79	1579 Union of Arras (Southern provinces of Holland) signs separate peace treaty with Spain, Utrecht Union founded by the Northern provinces as counter treaty	1576 Rudolf II elected Roman-German emperor (until 1612 †) 1576 Imperial Diet of Ratisbone; religious clashes within the empire intensify, end of all efforts to reform the imperial constitution 1579 Wilhelm V becomes duke of Bavaria	1575 Emperor Maximilian II visits Dresden 1577 "*Konkordienformel*" (decision for the Lutheran creed)	ca. 1575 invention of turning lathe moved with weights (Jacques Besson) 1577 Accademia di San Luca, Rome, founded	1575 Arcimboldo's *Four Seasons* (Paris, Louvre) come to the *Kunstkammer* as gift of Emperor Maximilian II 1575 Giovanni Maria Nosseni appointed in Dresden 1576 Georg Wecker comes from Munich to Dresden, and is appointed court turner in 1578
1580–84	1581 Independence of the Dutch Northern provinces (The Netherlands founded; not recognized until 1648) 1582 Gregorian calender reform 1583 Newfoundland becomes English colony	1580 *Konkordienbuch* (standardized book of Lutheran faith) 1583 Prague becomes emperor's residence	1581 Duke Christian (I) chairs Secret Council 1584 Co-rule of Duke Christian (I)	1580 Completion of Palazzo Farnese, Rome 1583 Building of St. Michael in Munich begins (until 1597, Friedrich Sustris et al.) 1583 Galilei starts first experiments with pendulum 1584 Completion of the *Tribuna* in the Uffizi	1581 Dresden court pharmacy founded due to electoral couple's initiative 1584 Egidius Lobenigk from Cologne appointed court turner in Dresden 1584 Carlo Theti from Naples appointed master builder of fortifications
1585–89	1585 Sixtus V becomes pope (until 1590 †) 1587 Mary Stuart executed 1587 Ferdinando I de' Medici becomes grand duke of Tuscany 1588 England's victory over the Spanish Armada 1588 Christian IV crowned king of Denmark 1589 Henry III murdered; Henry of Navarre crowned French king as Henry IV (until 1610 †)	1586 Meeting of Protestant princes in Küstrin gather support Henry of Navarre 1587 Catholic princes boycott Imperial Law Court (*Reichskammergericht*), dominated by Protestants 1589 End of the Cologne War (started 1583) The Wittelsbach Ernst of Bavaria confirmed as archbishop of Cologne	1586 Death of Elector August, Christian I becomes elector (until 1591 †) since 1586 "Second Reformation" in Saxony (Calvinism introduced); new appointments of Calvinists to key offices 1586 Nikolaus Krell Secret Counsel (*Geheimer Rat*) 1586 Independent office for finance administration founded 1588 New order of Leipzig and Wittenberg universities 1589 Nikolaus Krell made chancellor since 1589 development of Königstein into an important fortification	1585 Death of Wenzel Jamnitzer 1586 Obelisk in front of St. Peter erected (Domenico Fontana) 1588 Ottavio Miseroni founds workshop for stone cutting in Prague 1588 Potato planted in Botanical Garden of Frankfurt/Main as botanical rarity 1588 Decision to unite the Florentine court workshops in the Uffizi 1589 General inventory of the *Tribuna* in the Uffizi	1586 Building of New Stable (*Neuer Stall*) begins 1586 Group of English comedians visit Dresden for the first time 1586–88 Giordano Bruno lectures in Wittenberg 1587 Gabriel Kaltemarckt completes *Bedenken wie eine Kunst-Cammer aufzurichten seyn möchte* 1587 Inventory of the *Kunstkammer* and the Treasury (1586/87) Dresden 1588 First vineyard order for electoral Saxony 1589 Building of the Pleasure House on the Jungfernbastei begins 1589 Building of the Wettins' tombs in Freiberg Cathedral begins

Time Period	World History	History of the Holy Roman Empire of the German Nation	Saxony's History	Art–Culture–Science in Europe	Art–Culture–Science in Saxony
1590–1594	1590 Gregor XIV becomes pope (until 1591 †) 1592 Clemens VIII becomes pope (until 1605 †) 1593 Henry IV of France (leader of the Huguenots since 1569) converts to Catholicism 1593 French sailors reach New France (Canada)	1591 Treaty of Torgau (defensive treaty of empire's Protestant princes) 1593 Long Turkish War begins (until 1606)	1591 Exorcism banned; "Krell-Bible" (Luther bible with commentary) issued 1591 Death of Elector Christian I, Duke Friedrich Wilhelm I of Saxony-Weimar-Altenburg administrates for the minor Christian II (until 1601) since 1592 Fight against Calvinism in Saxony 1593 "Run of Calvinists" in Leipzig	1590 Galilei conducts experiments concerning the downfall from the Tower of Pisa 1590–93 Dome of St. Peter's, Rome, completed (Giacomo della Porta)	1590 Ferdinando de' Medici's gift of Chinese porcelain transferred to *Kunstkammer* 1591 Potato planted as decorative plant at the Saxon court 1590–93 Carlo di Cesare del Palagio works in Freiberg and Dresden since ca. 1591 *Kunstkammer* publicly accessible
1595–1599	1598 Edict of Nantes confirms Catholicism as French state religion, tolerates Protestantism 1598 Peace of Vervins (between France and Spain)	1595 Second uprising of peasants in Upper and Lower Austria against Counter-Reformation measures (until 1597) 1597 Maximilian I becomes duke of Bavaria (until 1651 †)	1595 Beginning of the Saxon postal services	1595 Mercator's *Atlas*, his work on geography, published posthumously 1596–1602 Mercury and Hercules fountains in Augsburg (Adriaen de Vries) since 1597 Painting of Rome's Galleria Farnese (Annibale and Agostino Carracci), Caravaggio realizes the Contarelli Chapel paintings in S. Luigi dei Francesi, Rome	1595 Second *Kunstkammer* inventory since 1597 Nosseni cuts and polishes marble, crystals, and semi-precious stones in his own mill near the Wilsdruf Gate (*Poliermühle am Wilsdruffer Tor*) 1599 Georg Wecker installs lathe for emperor in Prague
1600–1604	1600 Giordano Bruno burned in Rome as heretic 1600 English East India trade company founded 1600 Henry IV marries Maria de' Medici 1602 Spain takes possession of California 1603 Death of Elizabeth I of England. James VI Stuart, king of Scotland, crowned king of England and Ireland as James I 1603 Tokyo becomes capital of Japan	1600 the imperial system of justice collapses 1603 Imperial Diet in Ratisbone; Palatinate opposes aid for the war against the Ottomans, granted during the Imperial Diet of 1594; the Imperial Diet increasingly ceases to function	1601 Accession of Elector Christian II (until 1611 †) 1601 Nikolaus Krell executed 1601 Grand Tour of Duke Johann Georg (I) to Italy 1602 Religious oath introduced (oath for Lutheran-orthodox creed by all civil servants)	1600 Inhabitants of Rome ca. 110,000; Hamburg ca. 40,000 1600 Telescope invented in Holland 1601 Adriaen de Vries appointed Imperial Sculptor, moves to Prague in 1602 1601 Johannes Kepler becomes court astrologer in Prague as Tycho Brahe's successor 1603 Façade of S. Susanna, Rome completed (Carlo Maderno)	since 1601 extensive acquisitions for the *Kunstkammer*, e.g. at Leipzig fair 1601 so-called *Lüneburg Mirror* to *Kunstkammer* 1601 Christian II sends turned ivories to Emperor Rudolf II 1602 Bartholomäus Spranger and Hans von Aachen visit Dresden
1605–1609	1605 Paul V becomes pope (until 1621 †) 1605 Willem Janszoon discovers Australia 1607 First English colony (Virginia) founded in North America 1608 France sets up colonial town of Quebec 1609 Cosimo II de' Medici becomes grand duke of Tuscany	1606 Emperor Rudolf II increasingly unable to rule; Archduke Matthias leader of House of Hapsburg and is authorized by Rudolf II to decide issues of war and peace 1608 Imperial Diet (*Reichstag*) in Ratisbone paralyzed due to religious struggles 1608 Protestant Union founded 1609 *Majestätsbrief* of Emperor Rudolf II assures Bohemian Protestants religious freedom	1607 Christian II travels to Prague	1605 Rudolf II acquires Ambras *Kunstkammer* ca. 1606 William Shakespeare publishes *King Lear* and *Macbeth* 1607 Monteverdi's *Orfeo* first opera in Italian style 1607 Building of nave and façade of St. Peter's, Rome, begins (Carlo Maderno) 1608 Privilege for telescope to Hans Lipperhey	1606 Complete Armory inventory 1607 Adriaen de Vries' bust of Christian II, made in 1603, presented to the elector as a gift by Emperor Rudolf II

Time Period	World History	History of the Holy Roman Empire of the German Nation	Saxony's History	Art–Culture–Science in Europe	Art–Culture–Science in Saxony
1605–09		**1609** Catholic League founded **1609** Conflict over heritage and succession of Jülich, Cleves and Berg (until 1614)		**1609** Johannes Kepler's *Astronomia nova* published	
1610–14	**1610** Henry IV murdered; Maria de' Medici rules for the minor Louis XIII **1611** Gustav Adolf II crowned king of Sweden (until 1632 †) **1614** General Estates summoned in France, Louis XIII declared of age	**1610** Rudolf II deposed as king of Bohemia **1612** Death of Emperor Rudolf II, Matthias becomes Roman-German emperor (until 1619 †) **1613** Elector Sigismund of Brandenburg converts to Calvinism to attain Cleves and Jülich **1614** Treaty of Xanten ends "*Jülich-Klevescher Erbfolgestreit*"	**1610** Christian II travels to Prague **1610** Enfeoffment of dukedoms Jülich, Cleves, and Berg to Christian II **1611** Death of Elector Christian II, Johann Georg I becomes Elector of Saxony **1612** Johann Georg I Imperial Curate (*Reichsvikar*) until Matthias is elected emperor	**1610** With the telescope, Galilei discovers Jupiter's moons, rings of Saturn, and moon craters, among others **1610** Hamburg lotto founded **1613** Galilei defends teachings of Copernicus (paper about the sun spots) **circa 1614** Guido Reni paints the fresco *Aurora* in the Palazzo Rospigliosi, Domenichino paints the *Communion of St. Jerome* for St. Peter in Rome	**1610** Third *Kunstkammer* inventory **1610** Jakob Zeller moves to Dresden, 1613 appointed court turner **1612** Court Silver Chamber established **1613** Two telescopes come to the *Kunstkammer* **1613** Ethnographic objects from America come to the *Kunstkammer*
1615–19	**1616** Netherlands strike trade agreement with Japan **1617** End of Russian-Swedish war **1619** First North American parliament (Virginia) **1619** Import of slaves from Africa to North America begins	**1615** Imperial postal services invested with Princes of Thurn and Taxis (until 1866) **1617** Archduke Ferdinand of Austria elected Bohemian king **1618** the "Prague Fenestration" initiates the Thirty-Year War **1619** Death of Emperor Matthias, Ferdinand II becomes emperor (until 1637 †) **1619** The Protestant opposition dethrones Ferdinand II and elects Friedrich V of the Palatinate king of Bohema (Winterkönig)	**1617** Visit of Emperor Matthias and King Ferdinand IV in Dresden **1617** One-hundredth anniversary of the Reformation **1619** Johann Georg I refuses royal Bohemian crown	**1615** Hamburg founds jail with forced labor for prisoners (textile manufactory) **1616** Death of Shakespeare and Miguel de Cervantes (author of *Don Quixote*) **1616** Copernican writings indexed, Galilei admonished **1618** Johannes Kepler's *Harmonice mundi* published **1619** Building of Banqueting House in London begins (until 1622, Inigo Jones) **1619** First transfer bank founded in Hamburg	**1616** Set up of Anatomy Chamber in the Palace **1617** Heinrich Schütz court music master in Dresden, with interruptions until 1672 (†) **since 1617** Creation of workshop for stone cutting in Jungfernbastei's Pleasure House, based on Florentine model of *Galleria dei Lavori* **1619** Lucas Brunn appointed Art Chamberlain **1619** Fourth *Kunstkammer* inventory **1619** Nosseni offers parts of his collection to the elector for purchase **starting in 1619** the mystic Jakob Böhme publishes his theosophical writings
1620–26	**1620** Foundation of New England by the pilgrims **1621** Gregory XV becomes pope (until 1623 †) **1622** James I dissolves English parliament **1623** Urban VIII becomes pope (until 1644) **1624** Cardinal Richelieu is leading French minister **1626** Netherlands founds colony New Amsterdam (since 1664 New York)	**1620** victory of the imperial troops under the lead of Tilly over the Protestants in the battle near the White Mountain near Prague **1621** Bloody judgment against Bohemian estates; 27 leaders executed in the *Altstädter Exekution* in Prague. Bohemia becomes Catholic again **1621** Tilly occupies the Palatinate with Heidelberg **1625** Wallenstein appointed field marshal of the imperial troops	**1620** Johann Georg I suppresses uprising in the Lausitz territories, Bautzen conquered With Bohemia's return to Catholicism, thousands of exiled individuals find a new home in Saxony **1621–23** Deterioration of the mint (climax of the so-called Kipper- and Wipperzeit)	**1623** Shakespeare's complete works published **1623** Velázquez appointed Spanish court painter **1624** Building of baldacchino in St. Peter's, Rome (Bernini) **1625** *Apollo and Daphne*, Villa Borghese, Rome (Bernini)	**1620** Ivory frigate by Zeller added to the *Kunstkammer* **1620** Death of Nosseni and Zeller **before 1622** Hans (Johann) Wecker appointed court turner **1622** Large portions of Nosseni's collection bought for the *Kunstkammer* **1623** Parts of the estate of Electress Sophie transferred to the *Kunstkammer*

General Bibliography and Inventories

Compiled by Eva Graßhoff and Christine Nagel

Inventories

Complete Armory Inventory 1719
Main inventory about the [...] Duke and Lord [...] Friedrich August, King of Poland, [...] Duke of Saxony [...] and Elector, [...] Armory of the Dresden Stables [...] AD 1719 [incomplete] (Lieber 1979, no. 76).

Inventory of the Rifle Chamber 1617
Inventory of the Rifle Chamber. Contains New Rifle Chamber, where items may be found belonging to the present Elector, Johann Georg of Saxony, pipes and other items. – The Other Rifle Chamber. – Rifle Chamber [ca. 1617], continued until 1638 (Lieber 1979, no. 161).

Inventory of the Turning Chamber 1667
Inventory about the [...] Duke and Lord [...] Johann Georg the Other, Duke of Saxony [...] and Elector, [...] the entire Armory contained in all the electoral stables. Begun June 13, 1667 (Lieber 1979, no. 162).

Inventory of the Turning Chamber 1622
(Inventory about the Lathe and the works supervised by the Court Turner Johann Wecker in the Turning Chamber and the chamber in the Electoral Palace located above the Kunstkammer. June 24, 1622 (Lieber 1979, no. 68).

Inventory of the Turning Chamber 1684
Inventory of the Turning Chamber in the Electoral Residential Palace in Dresden, in April 1684 (Lieber 1979, no. 69).

Inventory of the Good Saddle Chambers 1674
Inventory about the two Good Saddle Chambers facing the Race Track: the first Good Saddle Chamber. In the month of September 1674 (Lieber 1979, no. 217).

Inventory Old Armor Chamber 1688
Inventory concerning the Old Armor Chamber with plenty of rifles ... an Corsuletten, Panzerkragen, eisernen Hauben, Rundtartschen, Panzerhandschuhen, Lanzen, Trabharnischen, Panzerärmeln, Fausthämmern, Freiturnierschwertern, leichten, auch Paillenrüstungen, Beilen, Schefflinen, Knebelspießen, Pickelhauben, Rapieren und Dolchen, Handgewehren, Czákanen, Reiterdegen, Partisanen, Cordelassen, Band- und Seitengewehren, Haudegen, Leibgehängen und -gürteln, auch anderen befindlichen Dingen, and is the present inventory [...], later in different chambers all was changed and newly installed... In the months of July and August 1688, described by Christian Hader (Lieber 1979, no. 111).

Inventory of the Hunting Chamber 1620
Inventory about the Black Rider and Sleigh Chamber supervised by Nicol Körner, armory servant. It also contains the chamber behind the Race Track, where the hunting gear is kept. – Account statements from 1620 until 1692. Contained in same: *Inventar Jägerkammer* (inventory of the Hunting Chamber) (Lieber 1979, no. 123).

Inventory of the Hunting Chamber 1668
Inventory about the Hunting Chamber. Revised and approved in the month of September 1677. Also contains: Gardening Tools (Lieber 1979, no. [152]).

Inventory about the Electoral Chambers 1591
Inventory about the Electoral Chambers 1591 (Lieber 1979, no. 99).

Inventory of the Electoral Tailor Shop. List of Acquisitions 1612ff.
Inventory of the Electoral Tailor Shop and Tapestries, 1612ff., also contained: the inventory of the Electoral Tailor Shop. List of Acquisitions, SächsHStA Dresden, Loc. 423 448, 57b.

Inventory of the Electoral Tailor Shop 1612
Inventory of the Electoral Tailor Shop and Tapestries, 1612ff., also contained: Inventory of the Electoral Tailor Shop, 1612, SächsHStA Dresden, Loc. 423 448, 57b.

Inventory of the Electoral Tailor Shop 1660
Inventory of the Electoral Tailor Shop, 1660, SächsHStA Dresden, Loc. 8688.

Inventory of the Electoral Chamber 1671
Inventory of the Electoral Chamber. 1671. Revised in the month of May 1677 (Lieber 1979, no. 129).

Inventory of the Pistol Chamber 1683
Inventory of the Third or the Last Rifle Chamber beside the Pistol Chamber. Revised ... in the months of August and November 1683 also contained: Inventory of the Pistol Chamber (Lieber 1979, no. [163]).

Inventory of the Armory 1606
Inventory of the Armory and Invention Chambers in the ... New Stable. 1606 revised (Lieber 1979, no. 72).

Inventory of the Armory 614–1620
Inventory of the Armory, Part I [incomplete]. Also contained: Account statements from 1615 until 1675 (Lieber 1979, no. 73).

Armory of Johann Georg [I] 1608
Inventory of the Armory of Johann Georg, Duke of Saxony, in the Electoral House of Provisions in Dresden. Inventoried in the month of March in 1608 (Lieber 1979, no. 208).

Inventory of the Silver Chamber [after 1575–before 1586])
Inventory of the Silver Chamber with a total of eight Closets [after 1575-before 1586] SächsHStA Dresden, Loc. 32449, Dresden, no. 88.

Inventory of the Silver-Gilt Room 1817
Inventory of the Silver-Gilt Room in the Green Vault in Dresden. 1817. Continued until 1876 (Lieber 1979, no. 26).

"Geheime Verwahrung" Inventory of the Pike Servants Chamber 1677
Inventory of the Pike Servants Chamber wherein are contained Pistols, Powder Flasks ... Revised in the month of May 1677 (Lieber 1979, no. 143).

Inventory of the Turkish Chamber 1674
Inventory of the Turkish Chamber. In the month of July 1674 (Lieber 1979, no. 244)

Inventory of the Kunstkammer 1587
Inventory of the Kunstkammer of the Electors of Saxony and Princes of Magdeburg ... in the Palace and the Fortifications in Dresden, containing noble things, works of art, and provisions, especially sorted and put in order and kept in the following places. Inventoried and listed in 1587 by David Usslaub (Lieber 1979, no. 1).

Inventory of the Kunstkammer 1595
Inventory of the Electoral Saxon Kunstkammer in the Palaces and the Fortifications of Dresden. Renewed and listed in December 1595 (Lieber 1979, no. 3).

Inventory of the Kunstkammer 1610
Inventory of the Electoral Saxon Kunstkammer in the Palaces and the Fortifications of Dresden. Renewed and listed in August 1610 (Lieber 1979, no. 4).

Inventory of the Kunstkammer 1619
Inventory of the Electoral Saxon Kunstkammer in the Palaces and the Fortifications of Dresden. Renewed and listed on June 28, 1619 (Lieber 1979, no. 7).

Inventory of the Kunstkammer 1640
Inventory of the Electoral Saxon Kunstkammer in the Palaces and the Fortifications of Dresden. Renewed and listed on August 4, 1640 (Lieber 1979, no. 9).

Inventory of the Kunstkammer [after 1732]
Inventory of the Kunstkammer) [after 1732] (Lieber 1979, no. 10).

Inventory of the Kunstkammer 1741
Inventory of the Royal Dresden Kunstkammer, newly compiled in 1741, continued until 1827 (Lieber 1979, no. 11).

Pretiosen Inventory of 1725
Inventory of the Precious Objects contained in the Royal Green Vault. 1725 (Lieber 1979, no. 30).

Schatzkammer Inventory of 1586/1587
Inventory about Jewels and Silver Plate. Anno 1541. 1662. SächsHStA Dresden, Loc. 8694/10, also contained on fol. 62r-91r: inventory of the Treasury [1586/1587].

Silver Inventory 1723
Inventory about the gold, silver-gilt, and silver vessels contained in the Royal Green Vault. 1723, continued 1725 (Lieber 1979, no. 21).

Sculpture Inventory 1726
Inventory of the sculptures, portraits, groups, and other vessels, ancient and modern alike, ... compiled in 1723-1726 ... Dresden, December 5, 1726, author: Steinhäuser the Elder (Lieber 1979, no. 492).

Exhibition Catalogues

Amsterdam 1992
De wereld binnen handbereik: nederlandse kunst- en rariteitenverzamelingen, 1585–1735, Amsterdams Historisch Museum, Amsterdam 1992.
Amsterdam 2003
Hendrick Goltzius (1558–1617): drawings, prints and paintings, H. Leeflang (edited by), Rijksmuseum Amsterdam, Metropolitan Museum of Art New York, Toledo Museum of Art, Amsterdam, Toledo, Ohio, New York 2003.
Antwerp 1977
De Mode in Rubens' Tijd, Provenienze Antwerpen Tentoonstelling, Provincial Museum Sterckshof, Deurne 1977.
Antwerp 1999
Een vorstelijk Imago. Het Beeld van de Heerser sedert Antoon van Dyck, Antwerp 1999.
Augsburg 2000
Adriaen de Vries 1556–1626. Augsburgs Glanz – Europas Ruhm, B.R. Kommer (edited by), Städtische Kunstsammlungen Augsburg Maximilianmuseum, Heidelberg 2000.
Berlin 1985
Weltschätze der Kunst – der Menschheit bewahrt. Exhibition on the occasion of the 40th anniversary of the victory over Nazism and the liberation of the German people, Altes Museum Berlin, Berlin 1985.
Berlin 1995
Von allen Seiten schön. Bronzen der Renaissance und des Barock, V. Krahn (edited by), Skulpturensammlung Staatliche Museen Preußischer Kulturbesitz, Altes Museum Berlin, Heidelberg 1995.

Berlin 2003
Die öffentliche Tafel - Tafelzeremoniell in Europa 1300-1900, H. Ottomeyer, M. Völkel (edited by), Deutsches Historisches Museum, Berlin 2003.

Bochum 1994
Georgius Agricola. Bergwelten 1494-1994, Bernd Ernsting (edited by), Schlossberg-museum Chemnitz, Deutsches Bergbau-Museum Bochum, Essen 1994.

Bonn 1999
Zeitwenden - Rückblick, edited by F.G. Zehnder, Kunst- und Ausstellungshalle der Bundesrepublik Deutschland Bonn, Cologne 1999.

Brunswick 1998
Hofkunst der Spätrenaissance. Braunschweig-Wolfenbüttel und das kaiserliche Prag um 1600, Herzog Anton Ulrich-Museum Brunswick, Brunswick 1998.

Brunswick 2000
Weltenharmonie. Die Kunstkammer und die Ordnung des Wissens, Herzog Anton Ulrich-Museum Brunswick, Brunswick 2000.

Cologne 2000
Faszination Venus. Bilder einer Göttin von Cranach bis Cabanel, Ekkehard Mai, with Ursula Weber-Woelk (edited by), Wallraff-Richartz-Museum Köln, Alte Pinakothek Munich, Koninlijk Museum voor Schone Kunst Antwerpen, Cologne 2000.

Darmstadt 1992
Faszination Edelstein. Aus den Schatzkammern der Welt - Mythos, Kunst und Wissenschaft. Hanns Fenstel zum 65. Geburtstag, Hessisches Landesmuseum Darmstadt, Bern 1992.

Dresden 1960
400 Jahre Dresdener Kunstsammlungen, von der kurfürstlichen Kunstkammer zur sozialistischen Bildungsstätte des Volkes, Staatliche Kunstsammlungen Dresden, Dresden 1960.

Dresden 1981
Kunsthandwerk der Gotik und Renaissance. 13.-17. Jahrhundert, Staatliche Kunstsammlungen Dresden, Museum für Kunsthandwerk Schloss Pillnitz, Dresden 1981.

Dresden 1990
Der silberne Boden. Kunst und Bergbau in Sachsen, M. Bachmann, H. Marx, E. Wächtler (edited by), Staatliche Kunstsammlungen Dresden Albertinum 1989, Leipzig 1990.

Dresden 1990b
Restaurierte Kunstschätze aus Dresdner Museen, Staatliche Kunstsammlungen Dresden Albertinum, Dresden 1990.

Dresden 1991
Die Kurfürsten von Sachsen. Repräsentation in Bildnis und Rüstung, Staatliche Kunstsammlungen Dresden Historisches Museum, Dresden 1991.

Dresden 1992
Verborgene Schätze der Skulpturensammlung, Staatliche Kunstsammlungen Dresden Albertinum, Dresden 1992.

Dresden 1995
Im Lichte des Halbmonds. Das Abendland und der türkische Orient, Staatliche Kunstsammlungen Dresden Albertinum, Kunst- und Ausstellungshalle der Bundesrepublik Deutschland Bonn, Leipzig 1995.

Dresden 2001
Hauptsache Köpfe. Plastische Porträts von der Renaissance bis zur Gegenwart aus der Skulpturensammlung, B. Stephan, A. Scherner, A. Nielsen (edited by), Staatliche Kunstsammlungen Dresden Albertinum 2001.

Duisburg 1994
Die Beschwörung des Kosmos. Europäische Bronzen der Renaissance, C. Brockhaus (edited by), Wilhelm Lehmbruck Museum Duisburg, Duisburg 1994.

Erbach 1995
Wiedergewonnen. Elfenbeinkunststücke aus Dresden. Eine Sammlung des Grünen Gewölbes, Deutsches Elfenbeinmuseum Erbach, Erbach 1995.

Essen 1986
Barock in Dresden. Kunst und Kunstsammlungen unter der Regierung des Kurfürsten Friedrich August I. von Sachsen und Königs August II. von Polen, genannt August der Starke 1694-1733 und des Kurfürsten Friedrich August II. von Sachsen und Königs August III. von Polen 1733-1763, U. Arnold, W. Schmidt (edited by), Kulturstiftung Ruhr, Villa Hügel Essen, Leipzig 1986.

Essen 1988
Prag um 1600. Kunst und Kultur am Hofe Rudolfs II., Kulturstiftung Ruhr, Villa Hügel Essen, Freren 1988.

Florence 1997
Magnificenza alla Corte dei Medici. Arte a Firenze alla fine del Cinquecento, Firenze Museo degli Argenti Palazzo Pitti, Milan 1997.

Freiburg 1997
Der Breisgauer Bergkristallschliff der frühen Neuzeit. „Natur und Kunst beisamen haben", G. Irmscher (compiled by), Augustinermuseum der Universitätsbibliothek Freiburg i.Br., Munich 1997.

Geneva 2002
C'était en 1602. Genève et l'Escalade, Musée d'Art et d'Histoire Genève, Geneva 2002.

Hamburg 1986
Gold und Silber aus dem Moskauer Kreml. Meisterwerke Hamburger Goldschmiedekunst, Museum für Kunst und Gewerbe Hamburg, Hamburg 1986.

Hamburg 2002
Die Masken der Schönheit. Hendrick Goltzius und das Kunstideal um 1600, J. Müller et al. (edited by), Hamburger Kunsthalle, Hamburg 2002.

Hanover 1991
The Age of the Marvelous, edited by J. Kenseth, Hood Museum of Art Hannover, North Carolina Museum of Art Raleigh, Museum of Fine Arts Houston, High Museum of Art Atlanta, Hanover 1991

Heidelberg 1996
Liselotte von der Pfalz. Madame am Hofe des Sonnenkönigs, S. Paas (edited by), Heidelberger Schloss, Heidelberg 1996.

Idar-Oberstein 1998
Deutsche Steinschneidekunst aus dem Grünen Gewölbe zu Dresden, J. Kappel (edited by), Deutsches Edelsteinmuseum Idar-Oberstein, Kunstgewerbemuseum der Staatlichen Museen zu Berlin, Staatliche Kunstsammlungen Dresden Residenzschloss, Dresden 1998.

Lemgo 1997
„Moritz der Gelehrte. Ein Renaissancefürst in Europa", 1998, Lemgo, Weserrenaissance-Museum Schloss Brake und Kassel, Staatliche Museen Kassel, Orangerie, Eurasburg 1997.

Lemgo 2002
Hans Vredeman de Vries und die Renaissance im Norden, H. Borggreve, V. Lüpkes et al. (edited by), Weserrenaissance-Museum Schloss Brake Lemgo und Koninklijk Museum voor Schone Kunsten Antwerp, Munich 2002.

London 2002
Royal Treasures - A Golden Jubilee Celebrations, J. Roberts (edited by), The Queen's Gallery Buckingham Palace, London 2002.

Lugano 1998
G. Bora, M. Kahn-Rossi, F. Porzio, Rabisch, *Il grottesco nell'arte del Cinquecento*, Museo Cantonale d'Arte Lugano, Milan 1998.

Madrid 2001
El tesoro del Delfín. Alhajas de Felipe V recibidas por herencia de su padre Luis, gran delfín de Francia, L. Arbeteta Mira (edited by), Museo Nacional del Prado, Madrid 2001.

Mantua 2002
Gonzaga. La Celeste Galeria. L'esercizio del collezionismo, R. Morselli (edited by), Galleria Civica di Palazzo Te Mantua, Milan 2002.

Munich 1980
Um Glauben und Reich. Kurfürst Maximilian I., H. Glaser (edited by), Munich Residenz, Munich 1980.

Munich 1994
Silber und Gold: Augsburger Goldschmiedekunst für die Höfe Europas, R. Baumstark, L. Seelig (edited by), Bayerisches Nationalmuseum Munich, 2 Bde., Munich 1994.

Munich 2002
Der Mohrenkopfpokal von Christoph Jamnitzer, R. Eikelmann (edited by), Bayerisches Nationalmuseum Munich, Munich 2002.

Münster 1998
1648. Krieg und Frieden in Europa, edited by K. Bußmann und H. Schilling, Westfälisches Landesmuseum für Kunst und Kulturgeschichte Münster, Kulturgeschichtliches Museum Münster und Kunsthalle Dominikanerkirche Osnabrück, Munich 1998.

Nuremberg 1985
Wenzel Jamnitzer und die Nürnberger Goldschmiedekunst 1500-1700. Goldschmiedearbeiten - Entwürfe, Modelle, Medaillen, Ornamentstiche, Schmuck, Porträts, G. Bott (edited by), Germanisches Nationalmuseum Nuremberg, Munich 1985.

Nuremberg 2002
Quasi Centrum Europae. Europa kauft in Nürnberg 1400-1800, H. Maué, T. Eser, S. Hauschke, J. Stolzenberger (edited by), Germanisches Nationalmuseum Nuremberg, Nuremberg 2002.

Paderborn 2003
Wunderwerk. Göttliche Ordnung und vermessene Welt. Der Goldschmied Antonius Eisenhoit und die Hofkunst um 1600, C. Stiegemann (edited by), Diözesanmuseum Paderborn, Mainz 2003.

Parma 2003
Parmigianino e il manierismo europeo, L. Fornari Schianchi, S. Ferino-Pagden (edited by), Galleria Nazionale di Parma, Kunsthistorisches Museum Vienna, Milan 2003.

Prague 1997
Rudolf II. and Prague. The Court and the City, E. Fučíkovà et al. (edited by), Prague, London 1997.

s'-Hertogenbosch 2003
Monsters & Fabeldieren. 2500 jaar geschiedenis van randgevallen, Noordbrabants Museum s'-Hertogenbosch, Amsterdam, Ghent 2003.

Salzburg 2002
Salzburger Bergkristall - Die hochfürstliche Kristallmühle, compiled by H. Ebner, Dommuseum Salzburg, Salzburg 2002.

Stockholm 2002
Modelejon, Manligt Mode 1500-tal, 1600-tal, 1700-tal / Lions of Fashion, Male fashion of the 16th, 17th, 18th century, L. Rangström (edited by), Livrustkammaren Stockholm, Stockholm 2002.

Stuttgart 1987
Exotische Welten. Europäische Phantasien, eine Ausstellung des Instituts für Auslandsbeziehungen und des Württembergischen Kunstvereins, Kunstgebäude am Schlossplatz, Stuttgart 1987.

The Hague 2003
Meraviglie: Precious, Rare and Curious Objects from the Medici Treasure, M. Mosco (edited by), Haags Historisch Museum, Florenz 2003.

Warsaw 1997
Pod Jedna Korona. Królewskie zbiory sztuki w Dreźnie, Muzeum Narodowe w Warszawie, Warsaw 1997.

Washington 1978
The Splendor of Dresden. Five Centuries of Art Collecting, National Gallery of Art Washington, Metropolitan Museum of Art New York, The Fine Arts Museums of San Francisco, California Palace of The Legion of Honor, New York 1978.

Vienna 1978
Giambologna. Ein Wendepunkt in der europäischen Plastik, C. Avery, A. Radcliffe, M. Leithe-Jasper (edited by), Royal Scottish Museum Edinburgh, Victoria & Albert Museum London, Kunsthistorisches Museum Vienna, Vienna 1978.
Vienna 2000
Exotica. Portugals Entdeckungen im Spiegel fürstlicher Kunst- und Wunderkammern der Renaissance, W. Seipel (edited by), Kunsthistorisches Museum Vienna, Vienna 2000.
Vienna 2002
Die Kunst des Steinschnitts. Prunkgefäße, Kameen und Commessi aus der Kunstkammer, W. Seipel (edited by), Kunsthistorisches Museum Vienna, Milan 2002.
Vienna 2003
Kaiser Ferdinand I. 1503–1564. Das Werden der Habsburgermonarchie, J. Weitzer (edited by), Kunsthistorisches Museum Vienna, Vienna 2003.
Zittau 2002
Welt, Macht, Geist. Das Haus Habsburg und die Oberlausitz 1526–1635, J. Bahlke, V. Dudeck (edited by), Städtische Museen Zittau, Zittau 2002.
Zurich 1971
Kunstschätze aus Dresden, Kunsthaus Zurich, Zurich 1971.
Zurich 1985
Die Muschel in der Kunst: von der Renaissance bis zur Gegenwart, Museum Bellerive Zurich, Zurich 1985.

General Publications

Alcouffe 2001
D. Alcouffe, *Les Gemmes de la Couronne*, V. Leleu (edited by), exhibition catalogue, Musée du Louvre Département des Objets d'Art, Paris 2001.
Alfter 1986
D. Alfter, *Die Geschichte des Augsburger Kabinettschranks*, Augsburg 1986.
Angulo Iñiguez 1989
D. Angulo Iñiguez, *Catalogo de las Alhaja del Delfin*, 2nd edition, Madrid 1989.
Arbeteta Mira 2001
L. Arbeteta Mira (edited by), *El tesoro del Delfin. Alhajas de Felipe V recibidas por herencia de su padre Luis, gran delfin de Francia*, exhibition catalogue, Museo Nacional del Prado, Madrid 2001.
Arnold 1994
U. Arnold, *Dresdner Hofsilber des 18. Jahrhunderts*, Berlin 1994 (Kulturstiftung der Länder – Patrimonia 74).
Arnold 1995
P. Arnold, *Adolf III. Occo (1524–1606) und das Dresdener Münzkabinett im 16. Jahrhundert*, in: *Wissenschaftsgeschichte der Numismatik*, Proceedings from the Deutschen Numismatikertag 3.–5. März 1995 in Hannover, R. Albert, R. Cunz (edited by), Speyer 1995, S. 139–157.
Aschengreen-Piacenti 1964
K. Aschengreen-Piacenti, "'Beschreibung eines von Helfenbein gedrehten Kunststücks [...] beneben desselben geistliche Bedeutung' von Markus Heiden 1640," in: *Anzeiger des Germanischen Nationalmuseums* 1964, pp. 82–98.
Avenarius 1618
T. Avenarius, P. Caesarea, *Das ist Eigentliche Beschreibung der hochlöblichen prächtigen Ankunfft vnd Einzugs Des [...] Herrn MATTIAE, Erwählten Römischen Keysers [...] in die Chur Fürstliche Stadt Dreßden/[...] Anno 1617. den 14. Augusti*, Budissin [Bautzen] 1618.
Avery 2000a
C. Avery, Giambologna. *The Complete Sculpture*, reprint of the 1987 edition, London 2000.
Avery 2000b
C. Avery, Jean Bologne: *La Belle endormie*, exhibition catalogue of the Galerie Piltzer, Paris/Caudry 2000.
Basset 2002
J. Basset, *The J. Paul Getty Museum, Decorative Arts and Sculpture Conservation, Technical Examination: Bust of the Elector Christian II of Saxony, Adriaen de Vries*, Skulpturensammlung Staatliche Kunstsammlungen Dresden, Germany, Inventory # H^4 1/4, Bericht von J. Basset, Mai 2002 (unpublished manuscript, Library Sculpture Collection, State Art Collections Dresden).
Bauer/Haupt 1976
R. Bauer, H. Haupt, *Die Kunstkammer Kaiser Rudolfs II. in Prag. Ein Inventar aus den Jahren 1607–1611*, in: *Jahrbuch der Kunsthistorischen Sammlungen Wien*, 72 (1976).
Bauer/Matis 1989
L. Bauer, H. Matis, *Geburt der Neuzeit. Vom Feudalsystem zur Marktgesellschaft*, 2nd edition, Munich 1989.
Bäumel 1993
J. Bäumel, *Kleidung und Ausstattung zu den Hochzeiten des Herzogs Johann Georg (I.) von Sachsen 1604 und 1607 in Torgau*, in: *Jahrbuch der Staatlichen Kunstsammlungen Dresden*, 24 (1993), pp. 25–32.
Bäumel 1995a
J. Bäumel, "Ein festliches Jagdkleid, Kunstwerk des Monats in der Rüstkammer," in: *Dresdener Kunstblätter*, 39 (1995), issue 3, pp. 87–91.
Bäumel 1995b
J. Bäumel, "Fürstliche Bräutigamskleidung, Kunstwerk des Monats in der Rüstkammer," in: *Dresdener Kunstblätter*, 39 (1995),issue 6, pp. 186–89.
Bäumel 1995c
J. Bäumel, *Die Rüstkammer zu Dresden, Führer durch die Ausstellung im Semperbau*, Berlin/Munich 1995.
Bäumel 1997
J. Bäumel, *Auf dem Weg zum Thron. Die Krönungsreise Augusts des Starken*, Dresden 1997.
Bäumel 2002
J. Bäumel, "'Har burit en vit dräkt av silverty...' – om furstlinga brudgumsdräkter / 'Wore a white dress of silver cloth ...' – of princely bridegrooms' costumes," in: *Modelejon, Manligt Mode 1500-tal, 1600-tal, 1700-tal / Lions of Fashion, Male fashion of the 16th, 17th, 18th century*, L. Rangström (edited by), exhibition catalogue, Livrustkammaren Stockholm, Stockholm 2002, pp. 207–11.
Bäumel 2003
J. Bäumel, "Mit fliegenden Herzen. Das Bildnis des Kurfürsten August von 1561 als Botschaft an Erzherzog Ferdinand II. von Tirol," in: *Dresdener Kunstblätter*, 47 (2003), issue 2, pp. 81–91.
Bäumel/Blaut 1998
J. Bäumel, S. Blaut, "Jagdhörner des 16. bis 18. Jahrhunderts aus kurfürstlichem Besitz, Kunstwerk des Monats in der Rüstkammer," in: *Dresdener Kunstblätter*, 42 (1998) issue 4, pp. 144–55.
Berliner/Egger 1981
R. Berliner, G. Egger, *Ornamentale Vorlageblätter des 15. bis 19. Jahrhunderts*, 3 vols., 2nd much enlarged edition, Munich 1981.
Berling 1887
K. Berling, "Der kursächsische Hofmaler und Kupferstecher Heinrich Göding," in: *Neues Archiv für sächsische Geschichte*, 8 (1887), pp. 290–346.
Bernt 1939
W. Bernt, *Altes Werkzeug*, Munich 1939.
Beutel 1671
T. Beutel, *Chur-Fürstlicher Sächsischer stets grünender hoher Cedern-Wald, auf dem grünen Rauten-Grunde. Oder Kurtze Vorstellung Der Chur-Fürstl. Sächs. hohen Regal-Wercke, [...] der Fürtrefflichen Kunst-Kammer [...], allhier bey der Residentz Dresden / gantz kürtzlich in Lat. und Teutscher Sprache beschrieben [...] an das Arboretum mathematicum gebracht [...] von Tobias Beuteln*, Dresden 1671.
Beutel 1683
T. Beutel, *Chur-Fürstlicher Sächsischer stets grünender hoher Cedern-Wald, auf dem grünen Rauten-Grunde. Oder Kurtze Vorstellung Der Chur-Fürstl. Sächs. hohen Regal-Wercke, [...] der Fürtrefflichen Kunst-Kammer [...], allhier bey der Residentz Dresden / gantz kürtzlich in Lat. und Teutscher Sprache beschrieben [...] an das Arboretum mathematicum gebracht [...] von Tobias Beuteln*, 2nd edition, Dresden 1683.
Blaschke 1986
K. Blaschke, "Religion und Politik in Kursachsen 1586–1591," in: *Die reformierte Konfessionalisierung in Deutschland – Das Problem der ‚Zweiten Reformation*, H. Schilling (edited by), Gütersloh 1986, pp. 79–97 (Schriften des Vereins für Reformationsgeschichte, vol. 195).
Brink 1987
S. Brink, *Mercurius Medicus. Studien zur panegyrischen Verwendung der Merkurgestalt im Florenz des 16. Jahrhunderts*, Worms 1987 (Manuskripte zur Kunstwissenschaft in der Wernerschen Verlagsgesellschaft, edited by F. Werner, vol. 13).
Brodde/Schütz 1985
O. Brodde, H. Schütz, *Weg und Werk*, Berlin 1985.
Brückner 1866
G. Brückner, "Die zu Dresden im April 1575 zu Ehren des Kaisers Maximilian II. veranstalteten Festlichkeiten," in: *Archiv für die Sächsische Geschichte*, K. von Weber (edited by), vol. 4, Leipzig 1866, pp. 223–41.
Bruhn 1981
T. Paul Bruhn, *Hans Reichle (1565/70–1642): A Reassessment of his Sculpture*, PhD thesis, University of Pennsylvania 1981, Ann Arbor 1983.
Bruning 2002
J. Bruning, "Landesvater oder Reichspolitiker? Kurfürst August von Sachsen und sein Regiment in Dresden 1553–1586," in: *Figuren und Strukturen. Festschrift für Hartmut Zwahr*, M. Hettling, U. Schirmer, S. Schötz (edited by), Munich 2002, pp. 205–24.
Bückling 1991
M. Bückling, *Die Negervenus*, Frankfurt am Main 1991 (Liebieghaus Monographie, vol. 14).
Burkhardt 1998
J. Burkhardt, "Der Dreißigjährige Krieg – Einfluss der sächsischen Politik auf die deutsche Geschichte," in: *Dresdner Hefte*, 56 (1998), issue 4, pp. 3–12.
Butler 1884
A.J. Butler, *The Ancient Coptic Churches of Egypt*, Oxford 1884, pp. 77–79.
Campenhausen 1957
H. Freiherr von Campenhausen, "Zwingli und Luther zur Bilderfrage," in: *Das Gottesbild im Abendland*, Witten/Berlin 1957.
Castiglione/Baumgart 1986
B. Castiglione, *Das Buch vom Hofmann*, Fritz Baumgart (translated and commented by) Munich 1986.
Cherry 1997
J. Cherry (edited by), *Fabeltiere. Von Drachen, Einhörnern und anderen mythischen Wesen*, Stuttgart 1997.
Czok 1992
K. Czok, "Der sogenannte Calvinistensturm in Leipzig 1593," in: *Dresdner Hefte*, 29 (1992), issue 1, pp. 33–42.
DaCosta Kaufmann 1978
T. DaCosta Kaufmann, *Variations on the Imperial theme in the age of Maximilian II and Rudolf II*, New York/London 1978.
DaCosta Kaufmann 1978/1979
T. DaCosta Kaufmann, "Remarks on the Collections of Rudolf II: the Kunstkammer as a Form of Representatio," in: *Art Journal*, 38 (1978/1979), pp. 22–28.
DaCosta Kaufmann 1998
T. DaCosta Kaufmann, "Planeten im kaiserlichen Universum. Prag und die Kunst an den deutschen Fürstenhöfen zur Zeit Rudolfs II.," in: *Hofkunst der Spätrenaissance. Braunschweig-Wolfenbüttel und das kaiserliche Prag um 1600*, exhibition catalogue, Herzog Anton Ulrich-Museum Brunswick, Brunswick 1998, pp. 9–19.
De Jong/De Groot 1988
M. De Jong, I. De Groot, *Ornamentenprenten in het Rijksprentenkabinet*, Amsterdam 1988.
Delang 1992
S. Delang, *Das Renaissanceschloss*, in: *Das Dresdner Schloss. Monument sächsischer Geschichte und Kultur*, Dresden 1992, pp. 68–73.
Diemer 1985
D. Diemer, *Giovanni Ambrogio Maggiore und die Anfänge der Kunstdrechselei um 1570*, in: *Jahrbuch des Zentralinstituts für Kunstgeschichte München*, 1 (1985), pp. 295–342.
Diemer 2001
D. Diemer, "Small Bronzes by Hubert Gerhard: A Review of Recent Scholarship," in: *Small Bronzes in the Renaissance*, D. Pincus (edited by), New Haven 2001, pp. 195–209 (Studies in the History of Art, 62).
Diemer 2004
D. Diemer, *Hubert Gerhard und Carlo di Cesare. Bronzeplastiker der Spätrenaissance*, 2 vols., Berlin 2004 (at press).
Distel 1887
T. Distel, "Kunstgeschichtliche Notizen: Aus der Drehstube des Kurfürsten August," in: *Neues Archiv für Sächsische Geschichte und Alterthumskunde*, 8 (1887), pp. 148–50.
Distelberger 1975
R. Distelberger, "Die Sarachi – Werkstatt und Annibale Fontana," in: *Jahrbuch der Kunsthistorischen Sammlungen in Wien*, 71 (1975), pp. 95–164.
Distelberger 1978
R. Distelberger, "Beobachtungen zu den Steinschneidewerkstätten der Miseroni in Mailand und Prag," in: *Jahrbuch der Kunst-*

historischen Sammlungen in Wien, 74 (1978), special issue, no. 243, pp. 79–152.
Distelberger 1997
R. Distelberger, "*Versuch über das Rudolfinische in der Kunst der Prager 'Hofwerkstätten,'*" in: *Rudolf II. und Prag. Kaiserlicher Hof und Residenzstadt als kulturelles und geistiges Zentrum Mitteleuropas*, E. Fučíkovà, J.M. Bradburne, B. Bukovinská et al. (edited by), exhibition catalogue (German edition, Prager Burg, Wallenstein Palais Prague, Prague/London/Milan 1997, pp. 189–98.
Distelberger 2000
R. Distelberger, "'Quanta rariora tanta meliora.' Die Faszination des Fremden in Natur und Kunst," in: *Exotica. Portugals Entdeckungen im Spiegel fürstlicher Kunst- und Wunderkammern der Renaissance*, exhibition catalogue, Kunsthistorisches Museum Vienna, Vienna 2000, pp. 18–21.
Distelberger 2002
R. Distelberger, *Die Kunst des Steinschnitts. Prunkgefäße, Kameen und Commessi aus der Kunstkammer*, W. Seipel (edited by), exhibition catalogue, Kunsthistorisches Museum Vienna, Milan 2002.
Doering 1901
O. Doering, *Des Augsburger Patriciers Philipp Hainhofers Reisen nach Innsbruck und Dresden*, Vienna 1901 (Quellenschriften für Kunstgeschichte und Kunsttechnik des Mittelalters und der Neuzeit N.F. 10).
Dombrowski 1999
D. Dombrowski, "Das Reiterdenkmal am Pirnaischen Tor zu Dresden. Stadtplanung und Kunstpolitik unter Kurfürst Christian I. von Sachsen," in: *Münchner Jahrbuch der bildenden Kunst*, 3. Folge, 50 (1999), pp. 107–46.
Dombrowski 2000
D. Dombrowski, "Dresden–Prag: Italienische Achsen in der zwischenhöfischen Kommunikation," in: *Elbflorenz. Italienische Präsenz in Dresden 16.–19. Jahrhundert*, B. Marx (edited by), Dresden 2000, pp. 65–99.
Dombrowski 2001
D. Dombrowski, "Die Grablege der sächsischen Kurfürsten zu Freiberg: Ideelle Dimension eines internationalen Monuments, "in: *Zeitschrift für Kunstgeschichte*, 64 (2001), pp. 234–72.
Dresdner Geschichtsverein 2002
Dresden, *die Geschichte der Stadt von den Anfängen bis zur Gegenwart*, Dresdner Geschichtsverein e.V. (edited by), Dresden 2002.
Duchhardt 1977
H. Duchhardt, *Protestantisches Kaisertum und Altes Reich*, Wiesbaden 1977 (publication of the Institut für Europäische Geschichte Mainz, Abteilung Universalgeschichte, vol. 87).
Ebeling 1983
G. Ebeling, "Lehrer der Kirche, Erzieher des Volkes," in: Gerhard Ebeling, *Martin Luthers Weg und Wort*, Frankfurt am Main 1983.
Ebner 2002
H. Ebner (compiled by), *Salzburger Bergkristall – Die hochfürstliche Kristallmühle*, Dommuseum Salzburg, Salzburg 2002.
Ehrenthal 1899
M. von Ehrenthal, *Führer durch das Königliche Historische Museum zu Dresden*, 3rd edition, Dresden 1899.
Ehrenthal 1900
M. von Ehrenthal, *Führer durch die Königliche Gewehr-Galerie zu Dresden*, Dresden 1900.
Emerson/Feininger 1972
W.K. Emerson, A. Feininger, *Shells*, London 1972.
Engelmann 1914
M. Engelmann, "Mathematische Instrumente von Wenzel Jamnitzer," in: *Mitteilungen der sächsischen Kunstsammlungen*, 5 (1914), pp. 44–54.
Erbstein 1884
J. Erbstein, A. Erbstein, *Das königliche Grüne Gewölbe zu Dresden*, Dresden 1884.
Erbstein 1892
J. Erbstein, *Das königliche Grüne Gewölbe zu Dresden*, Dresden 1892.
Falke 1868
J. Falke, *Die Geschichte des Kurfürsten August von Sachsen in volkswirthschaftlicher Beziehung*, Leipzig 1868.
Fickler/Diemer
J.B. Fickler, *Das Inventar der Münchner herzoglichen Kunstkammer von 1598, Transkription der Inventarhandschrift cgm 2133 mit den wichtigeren abweichenden Lesarten der Handschrift cgm 2134*, edited in collaboration with E. Bujok and D. Diemer (unpublished manuscript, Munich).
Fischer 1939
W. Fischer, *Mineralogie in Sachsen von Agricola bis Werner. Die ältere Geschichte des Staatlichen Museums für Mineralogie und Geologie zu Dresden (1560–1820)*, Dresden 1939.
Fritz 1982
J.M. Fritz, *Goldschmiedekunst der Gotik in Mitteleuropa*, Munich 1982.
Fritz 1983
R. Fritz, *Die Gefäße aus Kokosnuss in Mitteleuropa 1250–1800*, Mainz 1983.
Führer Grünes Gewölbe 1997
Das Grüne Gewölbe zu Dresden. Führer durch seine Geschichte und seine Sammlungen, D. Syndram (edited by), 2nd edition, Munich, Berlin 1997.
Gabbi 2000
G. Gabbi, *Shells – Guise to the Jewels of the Sea*, New York 2000.
Gamber 1981
O. Gamber, *Erzherzog Ferdinand und die Ambraser Rüstkammern*, in: *Kunsthistorisches Museum. Sammlungen Schloss Ambras. Die Rüstkammern. Führer durch die Ausstellung*, Vienna 1981, pp. 24–32.
Gebhardt 2001
Handbuch der deutschen Geschichte, vols. 9 and 10, 10., new edition, W. Reinhard (edited by), Stuttgart 2001.
Gotthard 1993
A. Gotthard, "'Politice Seint Wir Bäpstisch.' Kursachsen und der deutsche Protestantismus im frühen 17. Jahrhundert," in: *Zeitschrift für Historische Forschung*, 20 (1993), pp. 275–319.
Gotthard 1999
A. Gotthard, *Säulen des Reiches. Die Kurfürsten im frühneuzeitlichen Reichsverband*, 2 vols., Husum 1999 (Historische Studien, vol. 457).
Gotthard 2000
A. Gotthard, "1591 – Zäsur der sächsischen und der deutschen Geschichte," in: *Neues Archiv für sächsische Geschichte*, 71 (2000), pp. 275–84.
Graul 1910
R. Graul, *Alte Leipziger Goldschmiede-Arbeiten und solche anderen Ursprungs aus Leipziger Besitz*, Leipzig 1910.
Gross 2001
R. Gross, *Geschichte Sachsens*, Leipzig 2001.
Gruber 1977
A. Gruber, *Weltliches Silber*, Catalogue of the collection of the Schweizerische Landesmuseum Zürich, Zurich 1977.
Gurlitt 1888
C. Gurlitt, "Aus den sächsischen Archiven – Drechsler am sächsischen Hofe," in: *Kunstgewerbeblatt*, 4 (1888), pp. 78–81.
Gurlitt 1901
C. Gurlitt, *Beschreibende Darstellung der älteren Bau- und Kunstdenkmäler des Königreichs Sachsen*, vol. 22: Stadt Dresden, Dresden 1901.
Gurlitt/Nerling 1888
C. Gurlitt, K.B. Nerling, "Aus den sächsischen Archiven. Dresdner Goldschmiede unter Christian I.," in: *Kunstgewerbeblatt*, 4 (1888), pp. 202–07.
Gutfleisch/Menzhausen 1989
B. Gutfleisch, J. Menzhausen, "'How a Kunstkammer should be formed.' Gabriel Kaltemarckt's Advice to Christian I of Saxony on the Formation of an Art Collection, 1587," in: *Journal of the History of Collections*, 1, no. 1 (1989), pp. 3–32.
Haag 1996
S. Haag, "A Signed and Dated Ivory Goblet by Marcus Heiden," in: *The J. Paul Getty Museum Journal*, 24 (1996), pp. 45–59.
Haase 1988
G. Haase, *Sächsisches Glas*, Leipzig 1988.
Hackenbroch 1979
Y. Hackenbroch, *Renaissance Jewellery*, London, Munich 1979.
Haenel 1911
E. Haenel, "Hofkleider Johann Georgs I. im Historischen Museum Dresden," in: *Mitteilungen aus den sächsischen Kunstsammlungen*, II (1911), Leipzig 1911, pp. 41–53.
Haenel 1914
E. Haenel, "Die Drahtziehbank des Kurfürsten August im Musée de Cluny in Paris," in: *Mitteilungen der sächsischen Kunstsammlungen*, V (1914), Leipzig 1914, pp. 31–43.
Haenel 1923
E. Haenel, *Kostbare Waffen aus der Dresdner Rüstkammer*, Leipzig 1923.
Hager 1916
J. Hager, *Die Handwerkszeuge des 16. Jahrhunderts im Historischen Museum Dresden bearbeitet nach Berufsarten und Kennzeichen (Werkzeugmarken)*, Dresden 1916 (unpublished manuscript, Library of the Armory, State Art Collecions Dresden).
Hahnloser/Brugger-Koch 1985
H.R. Hahnloser, S. Brugger-Koch, *Corpus der Hartsteinschliffe des 12.–15. Jahrhunderts*, Berlin 1985.
Hantzsch 1902
V. Hantzsch, "Beiträge zur älteren Geschichte der kurfürstlichen Kunstkammer in Dresden," in: *Neues Archiv für Sächsische Geschichte und Alterthumskunde*, 23 (1902), pp. 220–96.
Hantzsch 1903
V. Hantzsch, "Eine Dresdner Kunstsammlung vor 300 Jahren," in: *Dresdner Geschichtsblätter*, 12 (1903), issue 1, pp. 157–65.
Harff/Letts 1946
A. von Harff, *The Pilgrimage of Arnold von Harff, knight from Cologne, through Italy, Syria [...] accomplished in the years 1496 to 1499*, M. Letts (edited by), London 1946.
Hauschke 2002
S. Hauschke, *Globen und Wissenschaftliche Instrumente. Die europäischen Höfe als Kunden Nürnberger Mathematiker*, in: *Quasi Centrum Europae. Europa kauft in Nürnberg 1400–1800*, H. Maué, T. Eser, S. Hauschke, J. Stolzenberger (edited by), exhibition catalogue, Germanisches Nationalmuseum Nuremberg, Nuremberg 2002, pp. 364–89.
Hayward 1968
J.F. Hayward, *Die Kunst der alten Büchsenmacher: 1500–1830*, 2 vols., vol. 1, Hamburg/Berlin 1968.
Hayward 1976
J.F. Hayward, *Virtuoso Goldsmiths and the Triumph of Mannerism 1540–1620*, London 1976.
Heckner 1995
U. Heckner, *Im Dienst von Fürsten und Reformation: Fassadenmalerei an den Schlössern in Dresden und Neuburg an der Donau im 16. Jahrhundert*, Munich 1995.
Heer 1979
E. Heer, *Der Neue Støckel. Internationales Lexikon der Büchsenmacher, Feuerwaffenfabrikanten und Armbrustmacher von 1400–1900*, vol. 2 (1979), 3 vols., Schwäbisch Hall 1978–1982.
Heikamp 1966
D. Heikamp, "Reisemöbel aus dem Umkreis Philipp Hainhofers," in: *Anzeiger des Germanischen Nationalmuseums*, Nuremberg 1966, pp. 91–102.
Hein 1985
J. Hein, "Versteinertes Eis aus den Bergen der Götter. Gefäße aus Bergkristall und Halbedelsteinen des Grünen Kabinetts in Schloss Rosenborg," in: *Kunst & Antiquitäten*, 1985, issue 1, pp. 34–44.
Heitmann/Scholz et al. 1985
B. Heitmann, R. Scholz et al., *Die Goldschmiede Hamburgs*, E. Schliemann (edited by), 3 vols., vol. II, Hamburg 1985.
Heller 2003
I. Heller, *Europäische Goldschmiedearbeiten 1560–1860*, Munich 2003.
Henkel/Schöne 1996
A. Henkel, A. Schöne (edited by), *Emblemata. Handbuch zur Sinnbildkunst des XVI. und XVII. Jahrhunderts*, 2nd edition, Stuttgart 1996.
Hentschel 1966
W. Hentschel, *Dresdner Bildhauer des 16. und 17. Jahrhunderts*, Weimar 1966.
Hernmarck 1978
C. Hernmarck, *Die Kunst der europäischen Gold- und Silberschmiede 1450–1830*, Munich 1978.
Heyde 1986
H. Heyde, *Musikinstrumentenbau. 15.–19. Jahrhundert. Kunst-Handwerk-Entwurf*, 2nd edition, Leipzig 1986.
Historisches Museum 1985
Historisches Museum, 4th edition 1985, Dresden 1985.
Hofmann 1970
K. Hofmann, *Zwei Abhandlungen zur Weihnachtshistorie von Heinrich Schütz*, in: *Musik und Kirche*, Kassel, 40 (1970), pp. 80–87.
Holzhausen 1933
W. Holzhausen, *Die Bronzen der kurfürstlich sächsischen Kunstkammer zu Dresden*, in: *Jahrbuch der Preußischen Kunstsammlungen*, 54 (1933), pp. 45–88.
Holzhausen 1934
W. Holzhausen, "Dresden-Prager Glas- und

Steinschnitt um 1600 (Regesten aus Dresdner Archiven, gesammelt und erläutert)," in: *Neues Archiv für Sächsische Geschichte und Alterthumskunde*, 55 (1934), pp. 86–118.
Holzhausen 1935
W. Holzhausen, "Regesten über Leipziger Goldschmiede," in: *Albert Schröder, Leipziger Goldschmiede aus fünf Jahrhunderten (1350–1850)*, Leipzig 1935, pp. 234–56.
Holzhausen/Kesting 1966
W. Holzhausen (text), E. Kesting (images), *Prachtgefäße, Geschmeide, Kabinettstücke. Goldschmiedekunst in Dresden*, Tübingen 1966.
Holzhausen/Watzdorf 1931
W. Holzhausen, E. von Watzdorf, "Brandenburgisch-sächsische Wachsplastik des XVI. Jahrhunderts," in: *Jahrbuch der Preußischen Kunstsammlungen*, 52 (1931), vol. 4, pp. 235–57.
Houlihan 1996
P.F. Houlihan, *The Animal World of the Pharaohs*, London 1996.
Hoyer 1990
S. Hoyer, "Staat und Stände unter Christian I.," in: *Sachsen und die Wettiner. Chancen und Realitäten*, Dresden 1990, pp. 72–78 (Dresdner Hefte, special issue).
Hoyer 1992
S. Hoyer, "Die sächsischen Stände unter Christian I.," in: *Dresdner Hefte*, 29 (1992), issue 1, pp. 14–21.
Hoyer 1995
E.M. Hoyer, *Sächsischer Serpentin. Ein Stein und seine Verwendung*. Published on occasion of the exhibition "Marmor Zeblicius-Zöblitzer Serpentinstein. Ein unbekannter Schatz des Erzgebirges," Grassimuseum Leipzig, Leipzig 1995.
Iccander 1726
Iccander, d.i. Johann Christian Crell, *Das auf dem höchsten Gipfel der Vollkommenheit prangende Königliche Dresden*, 3rd edition, Leipzig 1726.
Illustrated Bartsch 1983
The Illustrated Bartsch. Italian Masters of the Sixteenth Century. Antonio Tempesta, vol. 36, New York 1983.
Illustrated Bartsch 1984
The Illustrated Bartsch. Italian Masters of the Sixteenth Century. Antonio Tempesta. vol. 37, New York 1984.
Irmscher 1997
G. Irmscher (compiled by), *Der Breisgauer Bergkristallschliff der frühen Neuzeit. „Natur und Kunst beisamen haben"*, exhibition catalogue, Augustinermuseum der Universitätsbibliothek Freiburg i.Br., Munich 1997.
Jahrbuch Wien 1887
"Inventar des Grazer Schatzes Kaiser Maximilian I. von 1525," in: *Jahrbuch der Kunsthistorischen Sammlungen des Allerhöchsten Kaiserhauses*, 5 (1887).
Jewish Encyclopedia
The Jewish Encyclopedia, 12 vols, New York, London 1901–06.
Kandutsch 2003
G. Kandutsch, "Bergkristalle als funkelnde Meisterwerke der Kunst," in: *Lapis (Mineralien Magazin)*, 28 (2003), issue 3, pp. 31–38.
Kappel 1990
J. Kappel, "Ein 'commesso in pietre dure' aus der Hofwerkstatt Kaiser Rudolfs II. zu Prag um 1600," in: *Dresdener Kunstblätter*, 34 (1990), issue 4, pp. 104–09.
Kappel 1992
J. Kappel, "Steinintarsien aus der kaiserlichen Hofwerkstatt zu Prag," in: *Dresdener Kunstblätter*, 36 (1992), issue 3, pp. 80–88.
Kappel 1995a
J. Kappel, "Die Elfenbeindrechsler am kurfürstlichen Hof zu Dresden," in: *Wiedergewonnen. Elfenbeinkunststücke aus Dresden. Eine Sammlung des Grünen Gewölbes*, exhibition catalogue, Deutsches Elfenbeinmuseum Erbach, Erbach 1995, pp. 14–19.
Kappel 1995b
J. Kappel, "Die Türkennot des Kaisers. Zu einigen Aspekten der Darstellung des Türkenkrieges (1593–1606) in der Hofkunst Rudolfs II.," in: *Im Lichte des Halbmonds. Das Abendland und der türkische Orient*, exhibition catalogue, Staatliche Kunstsammlungen Dresden Albertinum, Kunst- und Ausstellungshalle der Bundesrepublik Deutschland Bonn, Leipzig 1995, pp. 125–133.
Kappel 1998a
J. Kappel, "Einige Nachrichten über Steinschneider in Dresden von der Mitte des 16. bis zum Ende des 18. Jahrhunderts," in: *Deutsche Steinschneidekunst aus dem Grünen Gewölbe zu Dresden*, J. Kappel (edited by), exhibition catalogue, Deutsches Edelsteinmuseum Idar-Oberstein, Kunstgewerbemuseum der Staatlichen Museen zu Berlin, Staatliche Kunstsammlungen Dresden Residenzschloss, Dresden 1998, pp. 59–72.
Kappel 1998b
J. Kappel, "Gewinn und Verlust. Steinschneidekunst in der Sammlungsgeschichte des Grünen Gewölbes zwischen 1733 und 1877," in: *Deutsche Steinschneidekunst aus dem Grünen Gewölbe zu Dresden*, J. Kappel (edited by), exhibition catalogue, Deutsches Edelsteinmuseum Idar-Oberstein, Kunstgewerbemuseum der Staatlichen Museen zu Berlin, Staatliche Kunstsammlungen Dresden Residenzschloss, Dresden 1998, pp. 88–97.
Kappel 1998c
J. Kappel, "Der kaiserliche Glas- und Edelsteinschneider Caspar Lehmann: Betrachtungen zu seinen Werken für den kurfürstlichen Hof in Dresden," in: *Rudolf II, Prague and the World. Papers from the International Conference Prague*, L. Konecny (edited by), 2–4 September 1997, Prague 1998, pp. 254–61.
Kappel 2000
J. Kappel, "Das Bergkristallgefäß der Königin Jadwiga von Polen "in der Mitten mit einer Münchs Schrifft von schwarzen Buchstaben"," in: *Dresdener Kunstblätter*, 44 (2000), issue 3, pp. 76–84.
Kästner 1995
E. Kästner, *Als ich ein kleiner Junge war*, 25th edition, Hamburg 1995.
Keisch 1997
C. Keisch, *Das große Silberbuffet aus dem Rittersaal des Berliner Schlosses*, Berlin 1997.
Kiontke 1974
W. Kiontke, "Drei Serpentingefäße im Grünen Gewölbe," in: *Dresdener Kunstblätter*, 18 (1974), issue 1, pp. 22–28.
Klein 1962
T. Klein, *Der Kampf um die Zweite Reformation in Kursachsen (1586–1591)*, Cologne, Graz 1962 (Mitteldeutsche Forschungen, vol. 25).
Koch 1989
E. Koch, "Ausbau, Gefährdung und Festigung der lutherischen Landeskirche von 1553–1601," in: *Das Jahrhundert der Reformation in Sachsen*, H. Junghans (edited by), Berlin 1989, pp. 195–223.
Koeppe 1989
W. Koeppe, "...alles in vergüldt Silber gefasst". Über einen Nürnberger Turboschneckenpokal des späten Manierismus aus der Sammlung 'Europäische Wohnkultur aus Renaissance und Barock,' Dr. Irmgard Freiin von Lemmers-Danforth, Wetzlar," in: *Kunst & Antiquitäten*, issue I, 1989, pp. 34–43.
Koeppe 1992
W. Koeppe, *Die Lemmers-Danforth-Sammlung Wetzlar. Europäische Wohnkultur aus Renaissance und Barock*, Heidelberg 1992.
Koeppe 1997
W. Koeppe, "Chinese Shells, French Prints, and Russian Goldsmithing: A curious group of eighteenth-century Russian Tabel Snuffboxes," in: *Metropolitan Museum Journal*, 32 (1997), pp. 207–14.
Koeppe 2002
W. Koeppe, "An early Meissen Discovery: A Shield Bearer designed by Hans Daucher for the Ducal Chapel in the cathedral of Meissen," in: *Metropolitan Museum Journal* (Essays in Honor of Clare LeCorbeiller), 37 (2002), pp. 41–62.
Koeppe/Lupo 1991
W. Koeppe, M. Lupo, "Ori, argenti e reliquie della Chiesa tridentina nei documenti antichi," in: *Ori e argenti dei santi*, E. Castelnuovo (edited by), Trient 1991, pp. 239–80.
Koetschau 1905
K. Koetschau, "Ein Axthammer mit Schießvorrichtung," in: *Beiträge zur Geschichte der Handfeuerwaffen (Festschrift Thierbach)*, Dresden 1905, pp. 116–23.
Kohlhaussen 1968
H. Kohlhaussen, *Nürnberger Goldschmiedekunst des Mittelalters und der Dürerzeit 1240–1540*, Berlin 1968.
König-Baudouin-Stiftung 2003
König-Baudouin-Stiftung (edited by), *Der Antwerpener Eulenbecher*, Brussels 2003.
Kossol 1976
E. Kossol, *Die Reichspolitik des Pfalzgrafen Philipp Ludwig von Neuburg (1547–1614)*, Göttingen 1976 (Schriftenreihe der Historischen Kommission bei der Bayerischen Akademie der Wissenschaften, vol. 14)
Krahn 1995
V. Krahn, *Original – Reproduktion – Nachahmung – Metamorphose*, in: *Von allen Seiten schön. Bronzen der Renaissance und des Barock*, V. Krahn (edited by), exhibition catalogue, Skulpturensammlung Staatliche Museen Preußischer Kulturbesitz, Altes Museum Berlin, Heidelberg 1995, pp. 106–27.
Krahn 2000
V. Krahn, "Von der äußersten Drehung des Körpers. Die Gruppe Tanzender Faun und Nymphe des Adriaen de Vries," in: *Adriaen de Vries 1556–1626. Augsburgs Glanz – Europas Ruhm*, B.R. Kommer (edited by), exhibition catalogue, Städtische Kunstsammlungen Augsburg Maximilianmuseum, Augsburg 2000, pp. 59–65.
Kreisel 1968
H. Kreisel, *Die Kunst des deutschen Möbels*, vol. 1 (Von den Anfängen bis zum Hochbarock), Munich 1968.
Kreisel 1981
H. Kreisel, *Die Kunst des deutschen Möbels*, vol. 1 (Von den Anfängen bis zum Hochbarock), 3rd edition, compiled by Georg Himmelheber, Munich 1981.
Kriegbaum 1931
F. Kriegbaum, "Hans Reichle," in: *Jahrbuch der Kunsthistorischen Sammlungen Wien*, 42 (1931), pp. 189–266.
Kris 1929
E. Kris, *Meister und Meisterwerke der Steinschneidekunst in der italienischen Renaissance*, 2 vols., Vienna 1929.
Krusenstjern 1999
B. von Krusenstjern, "Prodigienglaube und Dreißigjähriger Krieg," in: *Im Zeichen der Krise. Religiosität im Europa des 17. Jahrhunderts*, Göttingen 1999, pp. 53–78 (publications of the Max-Planck-Instituts für Geschichte, vol. 152).
Krystof 1997
D. Krystof, *Werben für die Kunst. Bildliche Kunsttheorie und das Rhetorische in den Kupferstichen von Hendrick Goltzius*, Hildesheim 1997 (Studien zur Kunstgeschichte, vol. 107).
Kugler 2003
G. Kugler, "Kunst und Geschichte im Leben Ferdinands I.," in: *Kaiser Ferdinand I. 1503–1564. Das Werden der Habsburgermonarchie*, J. Weitzer (edited by), exhibition catalogue, Kunsthistorisches Museum Vienna, Vienna 2003, pp. 201–14.
Larsson 1967
Larsson, *Adriaen de Vries. Adrianvs Fries Hagiensis Batavvs 1545–1626*, Vienna, Munich 1967.
Lepie/Minkenberg 1995
H. Lepie, G. Minkenberg, *Die Schatzkammer des Aachener Domes*, Aachen 1995.
Lewerken 1989
H.-W. Lewerken, *Kombinationswaffen des 15.–19. Jahrhunderts*, Berlin 1989.
Lewerken 2002
A. Lewerken, *Die Ahnengalerie der Wettiner im Verbindungstrakt zwischen dem Dresdner Residenzschloss und dem kurfürstlichen Stallgebäude*, unpublished Master's Thesis, Leipzig University, Leipzig 2002.
Lexikon der Kunst
Lexikon der Kunst. Architektur, Bildende Kunst, Angewandte Kunst, Industrieformgestaltung, Kunsttheorie, L. Alscher (edited by), Leipzig 1968–78.
Lexikon des Mittelalters
Lexikon des Mittelalters, 10 vols., Munich 1980–99.
Lieber 1979
E. Lieber, *Verzeichnis der Inventare der Staatlichen Kunstsammlungen Dresden 1568–1945*, Dresden 1979.
Lietzmann 1977
H. Lietzmann, "Die Deutsch-Lutherische Dreifaltigkeits-, die spätere Ordenskirche St. Maria della Victoria auf der Kleinen Seite zu Prag," in: *Zeitschrift für Kunstgeschichte* 40 (1977), pp. 205–16.
Löffler 1987
F. Löffler, *Das alte Dresden, Geschichte seiner Bauten*, 8th edition, Leipzig 1987.
Löwe 1975
R. Löwe, *Die Augsburger Goldschmiedewerkstatt des Matthias Walbaum*, Munich 1975.
Mackowsky 1904
W. Mackowsky, *Giovanni Maria Nosseni und die Renaissance in Sachsen*, Berlin 1904 (Beiträge zur Bauwissenschaft, 4).
Marienlexikon
Marienlexikon, R. Bäumer (edited by), St. Ottilien 1994.
Marx 2000a
B. Marx, "Italianità und frühneuzeitliche Hofkultur: Dresden im Kontext," in: *Elbflorenz. Italienische Präsenz in Dresden*

16.–19. Jahrhundert, B. Marx (edited by), Dresden 2000, pp. 7–36.
Marx 2000b
B. Marx, "Künstlermigration und Kulturkonsum. Die Florentiner Kulturpolitik im 16. Jahrhundert und die Formierung Dresdens als Elbflorenz," in: *Deutschland und Italien in ihren wechselseitigen Beziehungen während der Renaissance*, B. Guthmüller (edited by), Wiesbaden 2000, pp. 211–97.
Marx 2004
"Die Italienreise Herzog Johann Georg von Sachsen (1601–1602) und der Besuch von Cosimo III. de' Medici in Dresden (1668). Zur Kausalität von Grand Tour und Kulturtransfert," in *Grand Tour. Adliges Reisen und europäische Kultur vom 14.–18. Jahrhundert*, Proceedings from the international meetings at the Villa Vigoni 1999 of the Deutsche Historische Institut Paris 2000, Ed. R. Babel – W. Paravicini, Stuttgart: Thorbecke, due to be pulished in October 2004 (supplement to the volume *Francia* vol. 60).
Matar 1996
N.I. Matar, "Renaissance England and the Turban," in: *Images of the Other, Cairo Papers in Social Science*, 19 (1996), pp. 38–56.
Maurice 1976
K. Maurice, *Die deutsche Räderuhr. Zur Kunst und Technik des mechanischen Zeitmessens im deutschen Sprachraum*, 2 vols., Munich 1976.
Maurice 1985
K. Maurice, *Der drechselnde Souverän*, Zurich 1985.
Maurice 2004
K. Maurice, "Fürstliche Drechselkunst. Zur ästhetischen Bedeutung von Naturwissenschaft und Technologie," in: *Gedrehte Kostbarkeiten*, Georg Laue (edited by), Munich 2004, pp. 8–15 (Kunstkammer Georg Laue, vol. IV).
Mauriès 2002
P. Mauriès, *Cabinets of Curiosities*, London 2002.
May 1992
W. May, "Die höfische Architektur unter Christian I.," in: *Dresdner Hefte*, 29 (1992), issue 1, pp. 63–71.
McCullouch 1960
F. McCullouch, *Mediaeval Latin and French Bestiaries*, Chapel Hill 1960.
Meine-Schawe 1989/1990
M. Meine-Schawe, "Giovanni Maria Nosseni. Ein Hofkünstler in Sachsen," in: *Jahrbuch des Zentralinstituts für Kunstgeschichte*, vol. V/VI. 1989/1990, Munich 1991, pp. 283–325.
Meine-Schawe 1992
M. Meine-Schawe, *Die Grablege der Wettiner im Dom zu Freiberg. Die Umgestaltung des Domchores durch Giovanni Maria Nosseni 1585–1594*, Munich 1992 (Reihe Kunstgeschichte, vol. 46).
Meiss 1976
M. Meiss, "Ovum Strutionis. Symbol and Illusion in Piero della Francesca Montefeltro Altarpiece," in: *The Painters Choice. Problems in the interpretation of Renaissance art*, New York (et al.) 1976, pp. 105–29.
Meisterwerke 1992
J. Bäumel, H-W. Lewerken, D. Schaal, W. Schmidt, H. Schuckelt, *Dresdner Rüstkammer. Meisterwerke aus vier Jahrhunderten*, Leipzig 1992.
Menzhausen 1968
J. Menzhausen, *Das Grüne Gewölbe*, Leipzig 1968.
Menzhausen 1973
J. Menzhausen, *Der Goldschmied Elias Geyer*, 4th edition, Dresden 1973 (Schriftenreihe der Staatlichen Kunstsammlungen Dresden).
Menzhausen 1977
J. Menzhausen, *Dresdener Kunstkammer und Grünes Gewölbe*, Leipzig 1977.
Menzhausen 1985
J. Menzhausen, "Kurfürst Augusts Kunstkammer. Eine Analyse des Inventars von 1587," in: *Jahrbuch der Dresdner Kunstsammlungen*, 17 (1985), pp. 21–29.
Menzhausen 1990
J. Menzhausen, "Sächsische Landedelsteine für Export und Staatsrepräsentation," in: *Der silberne Boden. Kunst und Bergbau in Sachsen*, M. Bachmann, H. Marx, E. Wächtler (edited by), Staatliche Kunstsammlungen Dresden Albertinum 1989, Leipzig 1990, pp. 234–40.
Mette 1995
H.-U. Mette, *Der Nautiluspokal: wie Kunst und Natur miteinander spielen*, Munich, Berlin (et al.) 1995.
Moran 1981
B.T. Moran, "German Prince-Practioners: Aspects in the Development of Courtly Science, Technology, and Procedures in the Renaissance," in: *Technology and Culture*, 22 (1981), pp. 260–261.
Morét 2003
S. Morét, *Der italienische Figurenbrunnen des Cinquecento*, Oberhausen 2003 (Artificium. Schriften zu Kunst, Kunstvermittlung und Denkmalpflege, 10).
Morigi 1595
P. Morigi, *La nobilità di Milano [...]*, Milan 1595.
Müller 1979
H. Müller, *Gewehre, Pistolen, Revolver*. Leipzig 1979.
Müller 1993
J. Müller, *Concordia Pragensis. Ein Beitrag zur Rhetorisierung von Kunst und Leben am Beispiel der rudolfinischen Hofkünstler*, Munich 1993 (Veröffentlichungen des Collegium Carolinum, vol. 77).
Müller 1997
F. Müller, *Kursachsen und der Böhmische Aufstand 1618–1622*, Münster 1997 (Schriftenreihe der Vereinigung zur Erforschung der Neueren Geschichte e.V., vol. 23).
Müller 2002
W. Müller, "Zur Entstehung städtischer Erinnerungskultur unter besonderer Berücksichtigung Sachsens," in: *Sachsen. Beiträge zur Landesgeschichte*, R. Wißuwa, G. Viertel, N. Krüger (edited by), Dresden 2002, pp. 1–19.
Müller/Kaschek 2001
J. Müller, B. Kaschek, "Adriaen de Vries: 'Bildnisbüste Rudolfs II.' von 1603," in: *Studia Rudolphina. Bulletin of the Research Center for Visual Arts and Culture in the Age of Rudolf II.*, 1 (2001), pp. 3–16.
Müller/Kaschek 2002
J. Müller, B. Kaschek, "'Diese Gottheiten sind den Gelehrten heilig.' – Hermes und Athena als Leitfiguren nachreformatorischer Kunsttheorie," in: *Die Masken der Schönheit. Hendrick Goltzius und das Kunstideal um 1600*, J. Müller et al. (edited by), exhibition catalogue, Hamburger Kunsthalle, Hamburg 2002, pp. 27–32.
Müller/Kölling 1981
H. Müller, H. Kölling, *Europäische Hieb- und Stichwaffen aus der Sammlung des Museums für Deutsche Geschichte*, Berlin 1981.
Münzberg 1999
E. Münzberg, "'Ein schwarz sammeter Sattell, ... mit schwarz eisenfarben getriebenen blech und allerley thieren und Römischen Historien Figuren ...': Kunstwerk des Monats in der Rüstkammer," in: *Dresdener Kunstblätter*, 43 (1999), issue 2, pp. 62–67.
Münzberg 2002
E. Münzberg, *Die kurfürstlichen Gemächer im Stallgebäude Dresden – ihre Rekonstruktion und Rolle im europäischen Kontext*, unpublished Master's Thesis for the TU Dresden, 2002.
Nicht 1960
J. Nicht, *Historische Prunkkleidung*, Dresden 1960 (Schriftenreihe der Staatlichen Kunstsammlungen Dresden).
Nickel 1974
H. Nickel, *Ullstein Waffenbuch*, Berlin, Frankfurt am Main, Vienna 1974.
Nickel 1981
H. Nickel, "Über die graphischen Vorlagen des 'Mohren mit der Smaragdstufe im Grünen Gewölbe zu Dresden'," in: *Dresdener Kunstblätter*, 1 (1981), pp. 10–19.
Nicklas 2002
T. Nicklas, *Macht oder Recht. Frühneuzeitliche Politik im Obersächsischen Reichskreis*, Stuttgart 2002.
Nienholdt 1961
E. Nienholdt, *Kostümkunde. Ein Handbuch für Sammler und Liebhaber*, Brunswick 1961.
O'Byrn 1880
F.A. Freiherr O'Byrn, *Die Hof-Silberkammer und die Hof-Kellerei zu Dresden*, Dresden 1880.
Patin 1674
C. Patin, *Relations historiques et curieuses de voyages, en Allemagne, Angleterre, Hollande, Bohème, Suisse etc.*, Lyon 1674.
Patry 1933
R. Patry, *Philippe du Plessis-Mornay. Un huguenot homme d'état, 1549–1623*, Paris 1933.
Patze/Schlesinger 1982
Geschichte Thüringens, vol. 5, 1 (Politische Geschichte in der Neuzeit, 1. Teilband), H. Patze, W. Schlesinger (edited by), Cologne, Vienna 1982 (Mitteldeutsche Forschungen, 48/V/1/1).
Pechstein 1985
K. Pechstein, "Der Goldschmied Wenzel Jamnitzer," in: *Wenzel Jamnitzer und die Nürnberger Goldschmiedekunst 1500–1700. Goldschmiedearbeiten – Entwürfe, Modelle, Medaillen, Ornamentstiche, Schmuck, Porträts*, G. Bott (edited by), exhibition catalogue, Germanisches Nationalmuseum Nuremberg, Munich 1985, pp. 57–70.
Perspectiva corporum 1571
H. Lencker, *Perspectiva: Hierinnen auffs kürtzte beschrieben [...] e. neuer besonder kurtzer doch gerechter u. sehr leichter weg wie allerley ding es seyen Corpora, Geben [...] verruckt oder unverruckt ferner in d. Perspectif gebracht werden mag [...]/ durch Hansen Lencker [...] publicirt*, Nuremberg 1571.
Perspectiva corporum regularium 1568
W. Jamnitzer, *Das ist Ein fleissige Fürweysung Wie die Fünff Regulirten Cörper [...] Durch einen sonderlichen newen und behänden und gerechten weg [...] inn die Perspectiva gebracht [...] werden mügen / Allen Liebhabern der freyen Kunst zu Ehrn durch Wentzeln Jamitzer burgern und goldschmid in Nürmberg [...] an tag geben*, Nuremberg 1568.
Perspectiva literaria 1567
H. Lencker, *Perspectiva literaria: Das ist ein clerliche fürreyssung/ Wie man alle Buchstaben des gantzen Alphabets/ Antiquitetischer oder Römischer Schrifften/ auff mancherley art vnd stellung/ durch sondere kunstliche behende weys vnd weg/ so bißhero nit ans liecht kommen/ in die Perspectif einer flachen ebnen bringen mag/ Durch Hansen Lencker [...]/ allen liebhabern guter Künsten zu ehren vnnd gefallen publicirt*, Nuremberg 1567.
Pezold 1615
G. Pezold, *Beschreibung Der Churfürstlichen Kindttauff vnnd Frewdenfestes zu Dreßden/ den 18. Septemb. des verlauffenen 1614. Jahres [...]*, Dresden 1615.
Philippovich 1966
E. von Philippovich, *Kuriositäten: Antiquitäten. Ein Handbuch für Sammler und Liebhaber*, 2nd edition, Brunswick 1966.
Pierius/Klein 1970
U. Pierius, *Geschichte der kursächsischen Kirchen- und Schulreformation*, T. Klein (edited by), Marburg 1970.
Posse 1897
O. Posse, *Die Wettiner: Genealogie des Gesamthauses Wettin Ernestinischer und Albertinischer Linie mit Einschluss der regierenden Häuser von Großbritanien, Belgien, Portugal und Bulgarien 1897*, reprint of the original edition of 1897, Leipzig 1994.
Prescher 1994
H. Prescher, *Georgius Agricola: Die historische Persönlichkeit*, in: *Georgius Agricola. Bergwelten 1494–1994*, B. Ernsting (edited by), exhibition catalogue, Schlossbergmuseum Chemnitz, Deutsches Bergbau-Museum Bochum, Essen 1994, pp. 55–59.
Press 1990
V. Press, "Wettiner und Wittelsbacher – die Verlierer im dynastischen Wettlauf des Alten Reiches: Ein Vergleich," in: *Sachsen und die Wettiner. Chancen und Realitäten*, Dresden 1990, pp. 63–71 (Dresdner Hefte, special issue).
Press 1991
V. Press, *Kriege und Krisen. Deutschland 1600–1715*, Munich 1991 (Neue Deutsche Geschichte, vol. 5).
Press 1994a
V. Press, *Außerhalb des Religionsfriedens? Das reformierte Bekenntnis im Reich bis 1648*, in: *Wegscheiden der Reformation. Alternatives Denken vom 16. bis zum 18. Jahrhundert*, G. Vogler (edited by), Weimar 1994, pp. 309–335.
Press 1994b
V. Press, "Böhmen und das Reich in der Frühen Neuzeit," in: *Bohemia*, 35 (1994), pp. 63–74.
Quellmalz 1990
W. Quellmalz, *Die edlen Steine Sachsens*, Leipzig 1990.
Rabe 1989
H. Rabe, *Reich und Glaubensspaltung. Deutschland 1500–1600*, Munich 1989 (Neue Deutsche Geschichte, vol. 4).
Rasmussen 1983
J. Rasmussen, "Mittelalterliche Nautilusgefäße," in: *Studien zum Europäischen Kunsthandwerk. Festschrift Yvonne Hackenbroch*, J. Rasmussen (edited by), Munich 1983, pp. 45–61.

Richter 1913
J. Richter, *Das Erziehungswesen der Wettiner Albertinischer (Haupt-) Linie*, Berlin 1913 (Monumenta Germaniae Paedagogica, vol. 52).
Risso 1995
P. Risso, *Mechants and Faith. Muslim Commerce and Culture in the Indian Ocean*, Oxford (et al.) 1995.
Robinson-Hammerstein 1992
H. Robinson-Hammerstein, "Sächsische Jubelfreude," in: *Die lutherische Konfessionalisierung in Deutschland*, H.-C. Rublack (edited by), Gütersloh 1992, pp. 460–94 (Schriften des Vereins für Reformationsgeschichte, vol. 197).
Röhricht/Weissner 1880
R. Röhricht, H. Weissner (edited by), *Deutsche Pilgerreisen nach dem heiligen Lande*, Berlin 1880.
Rosenberg 1923
M. Rosenberg, *Der Goldschmiede Merkzeichen*, vol. II, 3rd edition. Frankfurt am Main 1923.
Rosenberg 1925
M. Rosenberg, *Der Goldschmiede Merkzeichen*, vol. III, 3rd edition, Frankfurt am Main 1925.
Rudersdorf 1999
M. Rudersdorf, "Patriarchalisches Fürstenregiment und Reichsfriede. Zur Rolle des neuen lutherischen Regententyps im Zeitalter der Konfessionalisierung," in: *Reichsständische Libertät und habsburgisches Kaisertum*, H. Duchhardt, M. Schnettger (edited by), Mainz 1999, pp. 309–27 (publications of the Institut für Europäische Geschichte Mainz, Abteilung Universalgeschichte, supplemental issue 48).
Saldern 1965
A. von Saldern, *German Enameled Glass*, Corning, New York 1965.
Sangl 2001
S. Sangl, "Indische Perlmutt-Raritäten und ihre europäischen Adaptionen," in: *Jahrbuch des Kunsthistorischen Museums Wien*, 3 (2001), pp. 262–87.
Schaal 1975
D. Schaal, *Katalog Dresdener Büchsenmacher 16.–18. Jahrhundert*, Dresden 1975.
Schaal 1979
D. Schaal, *Katalog Suhler Feuerwaffen 17.–18. Jahrhundert*, Dresden 1979.
Schaal 1981
D. Schaal, *Suhler Feuerwaffen. Exponate aus dem Historischen Museum Dresden*, Berlin 1981.
Schaal 1991
D. Schaal, *Die Kurfürsten von Sachsen, Repräsentation in Bildnis und Rüstung*, exhibition catalogue, Historisches Museum, Staatliche Kunstsammlungen Dresden, Dresden 1991.
Schade 1969
W. Schade, *Dresdener Zeichnungen 1550–1650. Inventionen sächsischer Künstler in europäischen Sammlungen*, exhibition catalogue, Kupferstich-Kabinett der Staatlichen Kunstsammlungen Dresden, Dresden 1969.
Schade 1988
W. Schade, "Dresden und Prag um 1600," in: *Prag um 1600. Kunst und Kultur am Hofe Rudolfs II.*, exhibition catalogue, Kulturstiftung Ruhr, Villa Hügel Essen, Freren 1988.
Schedelmann 1972
H. Schedelmann, *Die Großen Büchsenmacher. Leben, Werke, Marken vom 15.–19. Jahrhundert*, Brunswick 1972.
Scheicher 1975
E. Scheicher, "Der Spanische Saal von Schloss Ambras," in: *Jahrbuch der Kunsthistorischen Sammlungen Wien*, 71 (1975), pp. 39–94.
Scheicher 1979
E. Scheicher, *Die Kunst- und Wunderkammern der Habsburger*, Vienna, Munich, Zurich 1979.
Scheicher 1993/1994
E. Scheicher, "Bemerkungen zu den gedrechselten Sachen Kaiser Rudolfs II. in Prag," in: *Jahrbuch der Kunsthistorischen Sammlungen Wien*, 89/90 (1993/1994), pp. 341–48.
Scheicher 1995
E. Scheicher, "Zur Ikonologie von Naturalien im Zusammenhang der enzyklopädischen Kunstkammer," in: *Anzeiger des Germanischen Nationalmuseums Nuremberg*, Nuremberg 1995, pp. 115–25.
Schiedlausky 1989
G. Schiedlausky, "Natterzungen. Ein Leitfossil in der Geschichte mittelalterlicher Giftfurcht," in: *Kunst & Antiquitäten*, 1989, issue 6, pp. 25–31.
Schilling 1986
Heinz Schilling (edited by), *Die reformierte Konfessionalisierung in Deutschland – Das Problem der „Zweiten Reformation"*, Gütersloh 1986 (Schriften des Vereins für Reformationsgeschichte, vol. 195).
Schilling 1988
H. Schilling, "Die Konfessionalisierung im Reich. Religiöser und gesellschaftlicher Wandel in Deutschland zwischen 1555 und 1620," in: *Historische Zeitschrift*, 246 (1988), pp. 1–45.
Schilling 1991
Heinz Schilling, "Nationale Identität und Konfession in der europäischen Neuzeit," in: *Nationale und kulturelle Identität. Studien zur Entwicklung des kollektiven Bewusstseins in der Neuzeit*, Frankfurt am Main 1991, pp. 192–252.
Schilling 1998
Heinz Schilling, "Die Konfessionalisierung Europas – ihre Ursachsen und die Folgen für Kirche, Staat, Gesellschaft und Kultur," in: *1648. Krieg und Frieden in Europa*, Textband I, Politik, Religion, Recht und Gesellschaft, K. Bußmann, H. Schilling (edited by), exhibition catalogue, Westfälisches Landesmuseum für Kunst und Kulturgeschichte Münster, Kulturgeschichtliches Museum Münster und Kunsthalle Dominikanerkirche Osnabrück, Munich 1998, pp. 219–28.
Schillinger 1994
K. Schillinger (edited by), *Kostbare Instrumente und Uhren aus dem Mathematisch-Physikalischen Salon Dresden*, Leipzig 1994.
Schindling 2001
A. Schindling, "Kurfürstenhöfe und Fürstenhöfe im Heiligen Römischen Reich," in: *Hofgesellschaft und Höflinge an europäischen Fürstenhöfen in der Frühen Neuzeit (15.–18. Jh.)*, K. Malettke, C. Grell (edited by), Münster 2001, pp. 245–55 (Forschungen zur Geschichte der Neuzeit. Marburger Beiträge, vol. 1).
Schlechte 1992
M. Schlechte, "Ein sächsischer Perseus? Die Hochzeit des Kurprinzen Christian im Jahr 1582," in: *Dresdner Hefte*, 29 (1992), issue 1, pp. 80–84.
Schmidt 1868
J. Schmidt, *Geschichte der Serpentin-Industrie zu Zöblitz im sächsischen Erzgebirge*, Dissertation for the University of Leipzig, Dresden 1868.
Schmidt 1999
G. Schmidt, *Geschichte des Alten Reiches. Staat und Nation in der Frühen Neuzeit 1495–1806*, Munich 1999
Schnitzer 1999
C. Schnitzer, *Höfische Maskeraden. Funktion und Ausstattung von Verkleidungsdivertissements an deutschen Höfen der Frühen Neuzeit*, Tübingen 1999.
Schöbel 1972
J. Schöbel, *Helme und Schilde*, Dresden 1972.
Schöbel 1973
J. Schöbel, *Prunkwaffen. Waffen und Rüstungen aus dem Historischen Museum Dresden*, Berlin 1973.
Schöbel 1976
J. Schöbel, *Jagdwaffen und Jagdgerät des Historischen Museums zu Dresden*, Berlin 1976.
Schöbel/Schaal 1981
J. Schöbel, D. Schaal, *Historisches Museum*, 2nd edition, Dresden 1981.
Scholten 2000
F. Scholten, "Adriaen de Vries, Kaiserlicher Bildhauer," in: *Adriaen de Vries 1556–1626. Augusburgs Glanz – Europas Ruhm*, B. Kommer (edited by), exhibition catalogue, Städtische Kunstsammlungen Augsburg Maximilianmuseum, Heidelberg 2000, pp. 19–45.
Schönberger 2001
O. Schönberger, (translated and edited by) *Physiologus: Greek/German*, Stuttgart 2001.
Schröder 1935
A. Schröder, *Leipziger Goldschmiede aus fünf Jahrhunderten (1350–1850)*, Leipzig 1935 (Schriften des Vereins für die Geschichte Leipzigs, 17. und 18. vol.).
Schuckelt 1998/1999
H. Schuckelt, *Die Dresdner Türkenkammer*, in: *Jahrbuch der Staatlichen Kunstsammlungen Dresden*, 27 (1998/1999), pp. 39–47.
Schuckelt 2002
H. Schuckelt, "Der Augsburger Plattner Anton Peffenhauser," in: *Dresdener Kunstblätter*, 46 (2002), issue 3, pp. 108–13.
Schürer 1994
R. Schürer, "ein erbar handwerckh von goldschmiden," in: *Silber und Gold: Augsburger Goldschmiedekunst für die Höfe Europas*, R. Baumstark, L. Seelig (edited by), Bayerisches Nationalmuseum Munich, 2 vols., Munich 1994, vol. 1, pp. 57–65.
Schürer 2002
R. Schürer, "Vom alten Ruhm der Goldschmiedekunst. Nürnberger Silber in Europa," in: *Quasi Centrum Europae. Europa kauft in Nürnberg 1400–1800*, H. Maué, T. Eser, S. Hauschke, J. Stolzenberger (edited by), exhibition catalogue, Germanisches Nationalmuseum Nuremberg, Nuremberg 2002, pp. 174–97.
Schütte 1997
R.-A. Schütte, *Die Kostbarkeiten der Renaissance und des Barock. „Pretiosa und allerley Kunstsachen" aus den Kunst- und Raritätenkammern der Herzöge von Braunschweig-Lüneburg aus dem Haus Wolfenbüttel*, Brunswick 1997 (Sammlungskataloge des Herzog Anton-Ulrich Museums Brunswick, vol. VI).
Schwarzacher 1984
S. Schwarzacher, *Studien zum barocken Gefäßschnitt in Süddeutschland und Österreich (Schwerpunkt Salzburg)*, Vienna 1984.
Seelig 1986
L. Seelig, *Die Münchner Kunstkammer. Geschichte, Anlage, Ausstattung*, in: *Jahrbuch der Bayrischen Denkmalpflege*, 40 (1986), pp. 101–38.
Seelig 1987
L. Seelig, *Der heilige Georg im Kampf mit dem Drachen. Ein Augsburger Trinkspiel der Spätrenaissance*, Munich 1987 (Bayerisches Nationalmuseum, Bildführer 12).
Seelig 1994
L. Seelig, "Die Kunstkammer als Mikrokosmos. Fürstliche Sammellust in Renaissance und Barock," in: *Silber und Gold: Augsburger Goldschmiedekunst für die Höfe Europas*, R. Baumstark, L. Seelig (edited by), Bayerisches Nationalmuseum Munich, 2 vols., Munich 1994, pp. 220–22.
Seelig 2002
L. Seelig, "Der Mohrenkopfpokal von Christoph Jamnitzer," in: *Der Mohrenkopfpokal von Christoph Jamnitzer*, R. Eikelmann (edited by), exhibition catalogue, Bayerisches Nationalmuseum Munich, Munich 2002, pp. 19–123.
Seifert 1964
S. Seifert, *Niedergang und Wiederaufstieg der katholischen Kirche in Sachsen 1517–1773*, Leipzig 1964 (Studien zur katholischen Bistums- und Klostergeschichte, vol. 6).
Seling 1980
H. Seling, *Die Kunst der Augsburger Goldschmiede 1529–1868*, 3 vols., Munich 1980.
Seling 1994
H. Seling, *Die Kunst der Augsburger Goldschmiede 1529–1868*, Supplement of vol. III, Munich 1994.
Shearman 1988
J. Shearman, *Manierismus. Das Künstliche in der Kunst*, translated from the English by M. Fienbork, Frankfurt 1988.
Smolinsky 1993
H. Smolinsky, "Albertinisches Sachsen," in: *Die Territorien des Reichs im Zeitalter der* Reformation und Konfessionalisierung. Land und Konfession 1500–1650", A. Schindling, W. Ziegler (edited by), vol. 2: Der Nordosten, 3rd edition, Münster 1993, pp. 8–32 (Katholisches Leben und Kirchenreform im Zeitalter der Glaubensspaltung, vol. 50).
Sogliani 2002
D. Sogliani, "Guglielmo Gonzaga fra gusto dell'antico e modernità: Rapporti artistici, acquisti e mercato (1563–1587)," in: *Gonzaga. La Celeste Galeria. L'esercizio del collezionismo*, R. Morselli (edited by), exhibition catalogue, Galleria Civica di Palazzo Te Mantua, Milan 2002, pp. 331–40.
Spitzer 1987
G. Spitzer, "Der Kunstkämmerer David Uslaub," in: *Dresdener Kunstblätter*, 31 (1987), issue 6, pp. 198–201.
Spitzer 1990
G. Spitzer, "Elfenbeinkunststücke," in: *Der silberne Boden. Kunst und Bergbau in Sachsen*, M. Bachmann, H. Marx, E. Wächtler (edited by), exhibition catalogue, Staatliche Kunstsammlungen Dresden Albertinum 1989, Leipzig 1990.
Sponsel 1906
J. L. Sponsel, *Fürsten-Bildnisse aus dem Hause Wettin*, Dresden 1906.
Sponsel 1924
J. L. Sponsel, *Der Zwinger, die Hoffeste und die Schlossbaupläne zu Dresden*, Dresden 1924.

Sponsel 1925
J. L. Sponsel, *Das Grüne Gewölbe*, vol. 1, Leipzig 1925.
Sponsel 1928
J. L. Sponsel, *Das Grüne Gewölbe*, vol. 2, Leipzig 1928.
Sponsel 1929
J. L. Sponsel, *Das Grüne Gewölbe*, vol. 3, Leipzig 1929.
Sponsel/Haenel 1932
J. L. Sponsel, E. Haenel, *Das Grüne Gewölbe zu Dresden*, vol. IV (vases and figurative works in ivory, horn and other materials such as stone, wood, bronze, iron), Leipzig 1932.
Stahl 2003
P. Stahl, "Im großen Saal des Römers ward gespeiset in höchstem Grade prächtig. Zur Geschichte der kaiserlichen Krönungsbankette in Frankfurt am Main," in: *Die öffentliche Tafel – Tafelzeremoniell in Europa 1300–1900*, H. Ottomeyer, M. Völkel (edited by), exhibition catalogue, Deutsches Historisches Museum, Berlin 2003, pp. 58–71.
Stark 2003/2004
M.P. Stark, "Mounted Bezoar Stones, Seychelles Nuts, and Rhinoceros Horns: Decorative Objects as Antidote in Early Modern Europe," in: *Studies in the Decorative Arts*, 11 (2003/2004), issue 1, pp. 69–94.
Steingräber 1956
E. Steingräber, *Alter Schmuck – Die Kunst des europäischen Schmuckes*, Munich 1956.
Stievermann 1994
D. Stievermann, "Reichsrechtliche und reichspolitische Rahmenbedingungen für die Konfessionen in der Frühen Neuzeit," in: *Rottenburger Jahrbuch für Kirchengeschichte*, 13 (1994), pp. 11–24.
Stievermann 1997
D. Stievermann, "Evangelische Territorien im Konfessionalisierungsprozess," in: *Die Territorien des Reichs im Zeitalter der Reformation und Konfessionalisierung. Land und Konfession 1500–1650*, A. Schindling, W. Ziegler (edited byr), vol. 7: *Bilanz – Forschungsperspektiven – Register*, Münster 1997, pp. 45–65 (Katholisches Leben und Kirchenreform im Zeitalter der Glaubensspaltung, vol. 57).
Stöcklein 1922
H. Stöcklein, *Meister des Eisenschnittes. Beiträge zur Kunst- und Waffengeschichte im 16. und 17. Jh.*, Esslingen 1922.
Syndram 1991a
D. Syndram (edited by), *Naturschätze – Kunstschätze. Vom organischen und mineralogischen Naturprodukt zum Kunstobjekt*, Bielefeld 1991.
Syndram 1991b
D. Syndram, "Serpentin – der drechselbare Schlangenstein," in: *Naturschätze – Kunstschätze. Vom organischen und mineralogischen Naturprodukt zum Kunstobjekt*, D. Syndram (edited by), Bielefeld 1991, pp. 80–83.
Syndram 1995
D. Syndram, "Die Elfenbeindrechseleien im Grünen Gewölbe – Von der Maschinenkunst zum fürstlichen Sammlungsgegenstand," in: *Wiedergewonnen. Elfenbeinkunststücke aus Dresden. Eine Sammlung des Grünen Gewölbes*, exhibition catalogue, Deutsches Elfenbeinmuseum Erbach, Erbach 1995, pp. 6–13.
Syndram 1998/1999
D. Syndram, "Der Pfälzer Löwe und Christian I. von Sachsen. Anmerkungen zu einem zurückerworbenen Kleinod," in: *Jahrbuch der Staatlichen Kunstsammlungen Dresden*, 27 (1998/1999), pp. 7–14.
Syndram 1999
D. Syndram, *Die Schatzkammer Augusts des Starken. Von der Pretiosensammlung zum Grünen Gewölbe*, Dresden, Leipzig 1999.
Syndram 2001
D. Syndram, *Das Schloss zu Dresden. Von der Residenz zum Museum*, Munich, Berlin 2001.
Tacke 2001
A. Tacke (edited by), *„Der Mahler Ordnung und Gebräuch in Nürnberg". Die Nürnberger Maler(zunft)bücher ergänzt durch weitere Quellen, Genealogien und Viten des 16., 17. und 18. Jahrhunderts*, Munich/Berlin 2001.
Tait 1988
H. Tait, *Catalogue of the Waddesdon Bequest in the British Museum*, 2, The Silver Plate, London 1988.
Tax 1995
C. Tax, "De Nautilus als Grondstof voor Edelsmeden en Parelmoerbewerkers," in: *Antiek*, March (1995), pp. 20–27.
Tebbe 2003
K. Tebbe, "Wertvolle Jagdbeute. Eine Nürnberger Goldschmiedearbeit in der Eremitage in St. Petersburg," in: *Monatsanzeiger. Museen und Ausstellungen in Nuremberg*, no. 270, September 2003, pp. 2–3.
Theumert 1963
J. Theumert, *Harnische*, Dresden 1963.
Thiel 1980
E. Thiel, *Geschichte des Kostüms. Die europäische Mode von den Anfängen bis zur Gegenwart*, 5th edition, Berlin 1980.
Thomas/Gamber/Schedelmann 1963
B. Thomas, O. Gamber, H. Schedelmann, *Die schönsten Waffen und Rüstungen aus europäischen und amerikanischen Sammlungen*, Heidelberg, Munich 1963.
Thomas/Oldknow 1991
N. Thomas, C. Oldknow (edited by), *Hans Cohn, By Judgement of the Eye. The Varya and Hans Cohn collection*, Los Angeles 1991.
Ulferts 1999
G.-D. Ulferts, "Artefacta Eburata. Elfenbeinarbeiten von Marcus Heiden und Jeremias Bezolt in der Kunstkammer der Herzöge von Sachsen-Weimar," in: *Niederdeutsche Beiträge zur Kunstgeschichte*, 38 (1999), pp. 141–52.
Ulferts 2000
G.-D. Ulferts, *Sächsischer Serpentin: Sammlung Jahn*, Berlin 2000.
Vehse 1854
E. Vehse, *Geschichte der Höfe des Hauses Sachsen*, part 3, Hamburg 1854.
Venturelli 1998
P. Venturelli, *Il* "'Piatto dei Dodici Cesari'. I Saracchi e Annibale Fontana," in: *Artes*, 6 (1998), pp. 58–69.
Vermisste Kunstwerke 1990
D. Schaal, J. Bäumel, H. Schuckelt, E. Lieber, *Vermisste Kunstwerke des Historischen Museums Dresden*, Dresden 1990.
Voragine/Granger Ryan 1993
J. de Voragine, *The Golden Legend. Reading by the Saints*, translated into English by W. Granger Ryan, Princeton 1993.
Vötsch 2000
J. Vötsch, "Um Einheit und Erhalt. Die kurfürstlichen Sammlungen als Hausfideikommiss 1737/1747," in: *Dresdener Kunstblätter*, 44 (2000), issue 6, pp. 181–85.
Vötsch 2001
J. Vötsch, "Eine Denkschrift Kurfürst Augusts von Sachsen im Vorfeld des Kölner Krieges (1582)," in: *Neues Archiv für sächsische Geschichte*, 72 (2001), pp. 275–282.
Vötsch 2002
J. Vötsch, "Kaiser, Reich und Religion im Spiegel des Kunstkammerinventars von 1595," in: *Dresdener Kunstblätter*, 6 (2002), pp. 208–14.
Vötsch 2003
J. Vötsch, *Kursachsen, das Reich und der mitteldeutsche Raum zu Beginn des 18. Jahrhunderts*, Frankfurt am Main (et al.) 2003.
Wagner 1985
F. Wagner, "Beschlagene Staussen-Ayer," in *Kunst & Antiquitäten*, 1985, issue II, pp. 32–42.
Walther 2003
H.-C. Walther, "Die Räume des Grünen Gewölbes im Westflügels des Dresdner Residenzschlosses von der Mitte des 16. Jahrhunderts bis zur Errichtung des barocken Museums (1723–1729)," in: *Denkmalpflege in Sachsen 2002*, Mitteilungen des Landesamts für Denkmalpflege, Dresden 2003, pp. 49–63.
Warnke 1985
M. Warnke, *Der Hofkünstler. Zur Vorgeschichte des modernen Künstlers*, Cologne 1985.
Watanabe-O'Kelly 2002
H. Watanabe-O'Kelly, *Court Culture in Dresden. From Renaissance to Baroque*, Brasingstoke (et al.) 2002.
Watzdorf 1935/1936
E. von Watzdorf, "Kursächsische Jagdwaffen von Gabriel Gipfel in der Dresdner Rüstkammer," in: *Zeitschrift für historische Waffen- und Kostümkunde*, vol. XIV, N.F. 5 (1935–1936), pp. 4–13.
Watzdorf o. J.
E. von Watzdorf, *Wachsbildwerke in der Dresdner Kunstkammer um 1600*, Typoskript o. J.
Weber 1865
K. von Weber, *Anna. Churfürstin zu Sachsen geboren aus Königlichem Stamm zu Dänemark. Ein Lebens- und Sittenbild aus dem sechzehnten Jahrhundert. Nach archivalischen Quellen*, Leipzig 1865.
Weber 1866
K. v. Weber, "Des Kurfürsten August „letzter Wille und väterliche Ermahnung" an seinen Sohn Christian," in: *Archiv für die sächsische Geschichte*, 4 (1866), pp. 396–403.
Weck 1680
A. Weck, *Der churfürstlich sächsischen weitberuffenen Residentz und Haupt-Vestung Dresden Beschreib[ung] und Vorstellung [...]*, Nuremberg 1680, pp. 53–61.
Weihrauch 1956
H.H. Weihrauch, *Die Bildwerke in Bronze und in anderen Metallen. Bayerisches Nationalmuseum München*, vol. XIII, 5, Munich 1956.
Weihrauch 1967
H.H. Weihrauch, *Europäische Bronzestatuetten 15.–18. Jahrhundert*, Brunswick 1967.
Weinholz 1961
G. Weinholz, "Trinkgefäße aus Kokosnuss," in: *Dresdener Kunstblätter*, 5 (1961), pp. 126–31.
Welker 2002
M. Welker, *Die Reichsstadt Nürnberg, ein Zentrum des Schmiedeeisen verarbeitenden Handwerks*, in: *Quasi Centrum Europae, Europa kauft in Nürnberg, 1400–1800*, H. Maué, T. Eser, S. Hauschke, J. Stolzenberger (edited by), exhibition catalogue, Germanisches Nationalmuseum Nuremberg 2002, pp. 116–137.
Winkler 1890
A. Winkler, *Die Handzeichnungen des Hamburger Goldschmiedes Jakob Mores in der Ornamentstichsammlung des königlichen Kunstgewerbe-Museums zu Berlin*, in: *Jahrbuch der Königl. Preußischen Kunstsammlungen*, 11 (1890), pp. 108–15.
Wirth 1968
K.-A. Wirth, "Von silbernen und silbermontierten Eulengefäßen," in: *Anzeiger des Germanischen Nationalmuseums Nuremberg*, Nuremberg 1968, pp. 42–82.
Wirth 1973
K.-A. Wirth, "Artikel 'Eulengefäß'," in: *Reallexikon zur deutschen Kunstgeschichte*, vol. VI, Munich 1973, Sp. 322–40.
Wozel 1979
H. Wozel, *Turniere. Exponate aus dem Historischen Museum zu Dresden*, Berlin 1979.
Wunderlich 1977
H. Wunderlich, *Kursächsische Feldmesskunst, artilleristische Richtverfahren und Ballistik im 16. und 17. Jahrhundert. Beitrag zur Geschichte der praktischen Mathematik, der Physik und des Artilleriewesens in der Renaissance unter Zugrundelegung von Instrumenten, Karten, Holz- und Druckschriften des Staatlich Mathematisch-Physikalischen Salons Dresden*, Berlin 1977.

Index of Names

Compiled by Eva Graßhoff and Maria Reichelt

Photograph Credits

Bayerische Verwaltung der staatlichen Schlösser, Gärten und Seen: pp. 85, 88
Agence Photographique de la Réunion des Musées Nationaux: p. 57 (photo by Mercator)
Atlas zur Geschichte (reproduced from), vol. 1, Leipzig 1973, p. 50, edited by Michael Wagner: p. 27
Electa-Archives, Milan: p. 81
Germanisches Nationalmuseum Nuremberg: pp. 33, 42
Gross 2001 (reproduced from), pp. 10f., edited by Antje Scherner: p. 24
Hentschel 1966, p. 80, ill. 8 (reproduced from): p. 41
Institute of Archaeology, Leeds University, U.K.: p. 89 (M.)
Kunsthistorisches Museum Vienna: pp. 39, 210
Michelangelo Lupo, Trent: p. 89 (bottom)
Museo degli Argenti, Florence: p. 82
Museum für Kunst und Gewerbe Hamburg: p. 93
Museum für Kunst und Gewerbe Hamburg and Armory of the Kremlin, Moscow: p. 95 (bottom), photo by Marion Höflinger
Reproduction: p. 58
Rheinisches Bildarchiv Cologne: p. 44
State Art Collections Dresden, photo by Elke Estel: p. 131
Staatliche Kunstsammlungen Dresden, photos by Jürgen Karpinski: pp. 22, 61–62, 65–67, 71, 74, 76–79, 86, 94 (left), 102–5, 108–12, 117–18, 123–30, 132–78 (top), 179–205, 212–67, 271–302; Hans-Peter Klut: pp. 16, 25, 30–31, 47, 50, 73, 100–101, 106–7, 113–16, 178 (bottom), 269–70
Sächsische Landesbibliothek Dresden (SLUB), Deutsche Fotothek: p. 28 (photo by Walter Möbius), 36 (photo by Regine Richter), 38 (left), 38 (right) (photo by Walter Möbius), 52 (top) (photo by Rous), 52 (bottom) (photo by Paetzold), 53 (top) (photo by Regine Richter), 53 (bottom) (photo by Reinecke), 59 (photo by Kramer), 72, 207
Staatliche Museen zu Berlin, Preußischer Kulturbesitz, Kunstbibliothek: pp. 92, 95 (top) (photos by Dietmar Katz)
Städtische Galerie Dresden, Kunstsammlung: p. 19
The Schroder Collection: p. 94 (right)
Ulrich Deiß, Wetzlar: p. 83
Westfälisches Landesmuseum für Kunst und Kulturgeschichte, no. 97.3.113: p. 23 (photo by Ahlbrand-Dornseif)
Württembergisches Landesmuseum, Stuttgart: p. 89 (top)

Section Frontispieces

p. 98 Residenzschloss Dresden, engraving from the Weck Chronicle, before 1680, Sächsische Landesbibliothek, Staats- und Universitätsbibliothek Dresden (SLUB), Deutsche Fotothek

p. 118 Parade Armor, Eliseus Libaerts, Antwerp, 1563–64, Staatliche Kunstsammlungen Dresden, Rüstkammer, inv. no. M 106, detail (cat. 13, p. 124, photo by Jürgen Karpinski)

p. 158 Ovoid Basin with Hunting Scenes, Elias Geyer, Leipzig, circa 1611–13, Staatliche Kunstsammlungen Dresden, Grünes Gewölbe, inv.-no. IV 250, detail (cat. 98, p. 213, photo by Jürgen Karpinski)

This book was printed by Mondadori Electa S.p.A.
at Martellago Mondadori Printing S.p.A.
Via Castellanza 98, Martellago (Venice) in 2004